WEBSTER'S
FRENCH-ENGLISH
ENGLISH-FRENCH
DICTIONARY

CONCISE EDITION
For school, home and office

STRATHEARN BOOKS LIMITED
Toronto, Canada

This edition published by
STRATHEARN BOOKS LIMITED
Toronto, Canada

© 1999 Geddes & Grosset, David Dale House, New Lanark
ML11 9DJ, Scotland

Reprinted 2000, 2001

This book is not published by the original publishers of Webster's
Dictionary or by their successors

ISBN 1 85534 931 0

Printed and bound in the UK

Abbreviations
Abréviations

abrev	abbreviation	abréviation
adj	adjective	adjectif
adv	adverb	adverbe
anat	anatomy	anatomie
art	article	article
auto	automobile	automobile
aux	auxiliary	auxiliaire
bot	botany	botanique
chem, chim	chemistry	chimie
cin	cinema	cinéma
col	colloquial term	expression familière
com	commerce	commerce
compd	compound	mot composé
comput	computers	informatique
conj	conjunction	conjonction
excl	exclamation	exclamation
f	feminine noun	substantif féminin
fam	colloquial term	expression familière
fig	figurative	figuré
geol	geology	géologie
gr	grammar	grammaire
imp	impersonal	impersonnel
inform	computers	informatique
interj	interjection	interjection
invar	invariable	invariable
irr	irregular	irrégulier
jur	law term	juridique
law	law term	droit
ling	linguistics	linguistique
m	masculine noun	substantif masculin
mar	marine term	vocabulaire marin
mat, math	mathematics	mathématiques
med	medicine	médecine
mil	military term	vocabulaire militaire
mus	music	musique
n	noun	substantif
orn	ornithology	ornithologie
o.s.	oneself	
pej	pejorative	péjoratif
pl	plural	pluriel
pn	pronoun	pronom

poet	poetical term	vocabulaire poétique
p.p.	past participle	participle passé
prep	preposition	préposition
qch		quelque chose
qn		quelqu'un
rad	radio	radio
rail	railway	chemin de fer
sb	somebody, someone	
sl	slang	argot
sth	something	
thea	theatre	théâtre
tec	technology	technologie
TV	television	télévision
vi	intransitive verb	verbe intransitif
vr	reflexive verb	verbe réfléchi
vt	transitive verb	verbe transitif
zool	zoology	zoologie

Français-Anglais
French-English

A

à *prép* (in) to; at; on; by, per; **aller ~ l'école** to go to school; **~ neuf heures** at nine o'clock; **c'est ~ toi** it's yours; it's your turn.

abaissement *m* fall, drop.

abaisser *vt* to lower; **s'~ à faire qch** to stoop to doing sth.

abandon *m* abandonment, desertion.

abandonné *adj* deserted.

abandonner *vt* to abandon, leave.

abasourdi *adj* stunned.

abasourdir *vt* to stun.

abats *mpl* giblets.

abat-jour *m* lampshade.

abattement *m* despondency; exhaustion.

abattoir *m* abattoir, slaughterhouse.

abattre *vt* to shoot; to slaughter.

abattu *adj* despondent; exhausted.

abbaye *f* abbey.

abbé *m* abbot.

abbesse *f* abbess.

abcès *m* abscess.

abdiquer *vt vi* to abdicate.

abdomen *m* abdomen.

abdominal *adj* abdominal.

abeille *f* bee.

aberrant *adj* aberrant; absurd.

aberration *f* aberration.

abêtissant *adj* mindless.

abêtissement *m* mindlessness.

abîme *m* chasm.

abîmer *vt* to spoil, damage; *** s'~** *vr* to get spoiled *ou* damaged.

abject *adj* abject.

abjection *f* abjectness.

abjurer *vt* to abjure.

ablatif *m* ablative.

ablation *f* (*med*) removal.

abnégation *f* abnegation.

aboiement *m* bark.

abolir *vt* to abolish.

abolition *f* abolition.

abominable *adj* abominable; **~ment** *adv* abominably.

abondamment *adv* abundantly.

abondance *f* abundance.

abondant *adj* abundant, plentiful.

abonder *vi* to be abundant *ou* plentiful.

abonné *m* **-ée** *f* subscriber.

abonnement *m* subscription.

abonner *vt* **~ qn** to subscribe, take out a subscription (*à* to); *** s'~** *vr* to subscribe, take out a subscription (*à* to).

abord *m*: **d'~** first (of all).

abordable *adj* affordable.

aborder *vt* to approach.

aborigène *mf* aborigine; ***** *adj* aboriginal.

aboutir *vi* to succeed.

aboutissement *m* outcome; success.

abrasif *adj* abrasive.

abrégé *m* summary; **en ~** briefly.

abréger *vt* to shorten; to abridge.

abreuver *vt* to water.

abreuvoir *m* drinking trough.

abréviation *f* abbreviation.

abri *m* shelter.

abricot *m* apricot.

abriter *vt* to shelter; *** s'~** *vr* to shelter.

abroger *vt* to repeal.

abrupt *adj* abrupt; **~ement** *adv* abruptly.

abruti *m* **-e** *f* idiot; ***** *adj* idiotic.

abrutir *vt* to make stupid.

abrutissant *adj* stunning; mind-numbing.

abscisse *f* (*math*) abscissa.

absence *f* absence.

absent *adj* absent.

absenter (s') *vr* to leave, go out.

abside *f* apse.

absolu *adj* absolute; **~ment** *adv* absolutely; ***** *m* absolute.

absolution *f* absolution.

absolutisme *m* absolutism.

absorbant *adj* absorbent.

absorber *vt* to absorb.

absorption *f* absorption.

absoudre *vt* to absolve.

abstenir (s') *vr* to abstain (from).

abstention *f* abstention.

abstentionniste *mf* abstainer.

abstinence *f* abstinence.

abstraction *f* abstraction.

abstrait *adj* abstract; ~**ement** *adv* in the abstract; * *m* abstract; abstract art.

absurde *adj* absurd; ~**ment** *adv* absurdly.

absurdité *f* absurdity.

abus *m* abuse.

abuser *vt* ~ **de** to exploit; to abuse.

abusif *adj* improper.

académicien *m* -**ne** *f* academician.

académie *f* academy; learned society.

académique *adj* academic.

acajou *m* mahogany.

acariâtre *adj* cantankerous.

accablant *adj* overwhelming.

accabler *vt* to overwhelm.

accalmie *f* lull, calm.

accéder *vi*: ~ **à** to reach.

accélérateur *m* accelerator.

accélération *f* acceleration.

accélérer *vi* to speed up, accelerate.

accent *m* accent.

accentuation *f* accentuation.

accentué *adj* pronounced.

accentuer *vt* to accentuate.

acceptable *adj* acceptable.

accepter *vt* to accept.

accès *m* access.

accessible *adj* accessible.

accessoire *adj* secondary; ~**ment** *adv* secondarily; if need be; * *m* accessory.

accident *m* accident.

accidentel *adj* accidental; ~**lement** *adv* accidentally.

acclamations *fpl* cheers; acclamation.

acclamer *vt* to acclaim, cheer.

acclimater *vt* to acclimatize; **s'~** *vr* to become acclimatized.

accolade *f* embrace.

accommodant *adj* accommodating.

accommoder *vt* to prepare; to adapt.

accompagnateur *m* -**trice** *f* (*mus*) accompanist; guide.

accompagnement *m* accompaniment.

accompagner *vt* to accompany.

accomplir *vt* to achieve, accomplish.

accomplissement *m* accomplishment.

accord *m* agreement; **d'~!** okay!, all right!; **être d'~** to agree.

accordéon *m* accordion.

accorder *vt* to grant; **s'~** *vr* to agree.

accoster *vt* to accost.

accouchement *m* (*med*) delivery.

accoucher *vi* to give birth.

accoudoir *m* armrest.

accouplement *m* coupling; joining.

accourir *vi* to run up (*à, vers* to).

accoutrement *m* (*pej*) outfit, dress.

accréditer *vt* to accredit.

accroc *m* tear, breach.

accrocher *vt* to hang up (*à* on).

accroissement *m* increase.

accroître *vt* to increase.

accroupir (s') *vr* to crouch.

accueil *m* welcome, reception.

accueillant *adj* welcoming.

accueillir *vt* to welcome.

accumulateur *m* battery.

accumulation *f* accumulation.

accumuler *vt* to accumulate.

accusateur *m* -**trice** *f* accuser; * *adj* accusing.

accusatif *m* accusative (case).

accusation *f* accusation.

accusé *m* -**e** *f* (*jur*) accused, defendant.

accuser *vt* to accuse.

acerbe *adj* harsh; acrid.

acétate *m* acetate.

acétone *f* acetone.

acharné *adj* bitter, fierce; unrelenting.

acharnement *m* relentlessness; determination.

acharner (s') *vr* ~ **à faire qch** to try desperately to do sth; ~ **contre qn** to hound sb.

achat *m* purchase.

acheminer *vt* to convey.

acheter *vt* to buy.

acheteur *m* -**euse** *f* buyer, purchaser.

achèvement *m* completion.

achever *vt* to finish, complete.
acide *adj* acid, sour; * *m* acid.
acidité *f* acidity.
acidulé *adj* acid, acidulous.
acier *m* steel.
aciérie *f* steelworks.
acné *f* acne.
acompte *m* deposit, downpayment.
à-côté *m* side issue.
à-coup *m* jolt.
acoustique *adj* acoustic; * *f* acoustics.
acquéreur *m* buyer, purchaser.
acquérir *vt* to buy, purchase.
acquiescer *vi* to agree, acquiesce.
acquis *adj* acquired; * *m* experience.
acquisition *f* acquisition; purchase.
acquittement *m* payment; (*jur*) acquittal.
acquitter *vt* to acquit; to pay.
acre *f* acre.
âcre *adj* acrid.
acrobate *mf* acrobat.
acrobatie *f* acrobatics.
acrobatique *adj* acrobatic.
acrylique *m*, *adj* acrylic.
acte *m* act; deed.
acteur *m*, **actrice** *f* actor.
actif *adj* active; * *m* (*ling*) active (voice).
action *f* act, action; share.
actionnaire *mf* shareholder.
actionner *vt* to activate; to drive.
activement *adv* actively.
activer *vt* to speed up; **s'~** *vr* to bustle about.
activité *f* activity; hustle and bustle.
actualité *f*: **l'actualité** current events.
actuel *adj* current, present; **~lement** *adv* currently, at present.
acuité *f* acuteness; shrillness.
acuponcture *f* acupuncture.
adaptable *adj* adaptable.
adaptateur *m* adaptor.
adaptation *f* adaptation.
adapter *vt* to adapt (*à* to); **s'~** *vr* to adapt o.s. (*à* to).
additif *m* additive.
addition *f* addition; bill.
additionnel *adj* additional.
additionner *vt* to add up.
adepte *mf* follower; enthusiast.

adéquat *adj* suitable, appropriate.
adhérence *f* adhesion.
adhérent *m* **-e** *f* member, adherent; * *adj* : **~ à** which adheres *ou* sticks to.
adhérer *vi* to adhere, stick.
adhésif *adj* adhesive.
adhésion *f* adherence; membership.
adjacent *adj* adjacent (*à* to).
adjectif *m* adjective.
adjoint *m* **-e** *f* assistant, deputy.
adjudant *m* warrant officer.
adjudication *f* sale by auction.
adjuger *vt* to auction.
admettre *vt* to admit; to accept; to assume.
administrateur *m* **-trice** *f* administrator.
administratif *adj* administrative.
administration *f* management; administration.
administrer *vt* to run, administer.
admirable *adj* admirable; **-ment** *adv* admirably, brilliantly.
admiratif *adj* admiring.
admiration *f* admiration.
admirativement *adv* admiringly.
admirer *vt* to admire.
admissible *adj* allowable.
admission *f* admission.
adolescence *f* adolescence.
adolescent *m* **-e** *f* adolescent.
adopter *vt* to adopt; to pass.
adoption *f* adoption; passing.
adorable *adj* adorable; **~ment** *adv* delightfully.
adorer *vt* to adore, worship.
adoucir *vt* to soften.
adrénaline *f* adrenalin.
adresse *f* address; skill.
adresser *vt* to address; to send; **s'~** *vr* **s'~ à** to apply to; to speak to.
adroit *adj* deft, skilful; **~ement** *adv* deftly, skilfully.
aduler *vt* to flatter.
adulte *mf* adult, grown-up; *adj* adult, full-grown.
adultère *m* adultery.
adverbe *m* adverb.
adverbial *adj*, *f* **-e** adverbial; **~ement** *adv* adverbially.
adversaire *mf* adversary, opponent.
adversité *f* adversity.

aération *f* ventilation.

aérer *vt* to air.

aérien *adj*, *f* **-ne** air, airy; aerial.

aérodrome *m* aerodrome, airfield.

aérodynamique *adj* aerodynamic; * *f* aerodynamics.

aérogare *f* (air) terminal.

aéroglisseur *m* hovercraft.

aéronautique *adj* aeronautic; * *f* aeronautics.

aéronaval *adj* air and sea.

aéroport *m* airport.

aérospatial *adj* aerospace.

affable *adj* affable.

affaiblir *vt* to weaken; **s'~** *vr* to weaken, grow weaker.

affaiblissement *m* weakening.

affaire *f* matter.

affaissement *m* subsidence.

affaisser *vt* to cause to subside *ou* cave in; **s'~** *vr* to subside; to cave in.

affamé *adj* starving.

affamer *vt* to starve.

affectation *f* allocation (*à* to); affectation.

affecté *adj* affected.

affecter *vt* to affect.

affectif *adj* emotional.

affection *f* affection.

affectueux *adj* affectionate.

affectueusement *adv* affectionately.

affermir *vt* to strengthen; to make firm.

affermissement *m* strengthening.

affichage *m* bill posting.

affiche *f* poster.

afficher *vt* to post *ou* put up.

affiner *vt* to refine.

affinité *f* affinity.

affirmatif *adj* affirmative.

affirmation *f* assertion.

affirmativement *adv* in the affirmative.

affirmer *vt* to assert.

affluent *m* tributary.

affluer *vi* to rush (*à* to).

afflux *m* influx, rush.

affolant *adj* alarming.

affolement *m* panic.

affoler *vt* to throw into a panic; **s'~** *vr* to get into a panic.

affranchir *vt* to frank, stamp; to free.

affranchissement *m* stamping, franking; freeing.

affréter *vt* to charter.

affreux *adj* horrible; awful.

affreusement *adv* horribly, dreadfully.

affrontement *m* confrontation.

affronter *vt* to confront; **s'~** *vr* to confront one another.

afin *prép*: **~ de** (in order) to; **~ que** in order that, so that.

africain *adj*, *mf* African.

Afrique *f* Africa.

agaçant *adj* annoying.

agacer *vt* to annoy, irritate.

âge *m* age; **quel ~ as-tu?** how old are you?

âgé *adj* old; **~ de 10 ans** 10 years old.

agence *f* agency; branch; offices.

agencement *m* organization, arrangement; equipment.

agencer *vt* to arrange; to equip.

agenda *m* diary.

agenouiller (s') *vr* to kneel (down).

agent *m* agent; policeman.

agglomération *f* town, urban area.

aggravant *adj* aggravating.

aggravation *f* worsening, aggravation; increase.

aggraver *vt* to make worse; to increase; **s'~** *vr* to get worse, worsen; to increase.

agile *adj* agile, nimble; **~ment** *adv* nimbly.

agilité *f* agility.

agir *vi* to act.

agitateur *m* **-trice** *f* agitator.

agitation *f* agitation.

agiter *vt* to shake; to wave; **s'~** *vr* to move about; to fidget.

agneau *m* lamb.

agonie *f* death throes.

agrafe *f* staple; hook.

agrafer *vt* to staple (together); to fasten up.

agrafeuse *f* stapler.

agraire *adj* agrarian; land.

agrandir *vt* to make bigger; to widen; to expand; **s'~** *vr* to get bigger; to widen; to expand.

agrandissement *m* enlargement.

agréable *adj* agreeable, pleasant; **~ment** *adv* agreeably, pleasantly.

agresser *vt* to attack.

agresseur *m* attacker.

agressif *adj* aggressive.

agression *f* attack.

agressivement *adv* aggressively.

agressivité *f* aggressiveness.

agricole *adj* agricultural.

agriculteur *m* farmer.

agriculture *f* agriculture, farming.

agripper *vt* to grab (hold of); **s'~** *à vr* to grab on to.

agronome *m* agronomist.

agronomie *f* agronomy.

agrumes *mpl* citrus fruits.

ahuri *adj* stunned; stupefied.

ahurissant *adj* staggering.

aide *f* help; aid.

aider *vt* to help.

aigle *m* eagle.

aigre *adj* sour, bitter; **~ment** *adv* sourly.

aigreur *f* sourness; acidity.

aigri *adj* bitter, embittered.

aigu *adj*, *f* **aiguë** shrill; acute; sharp.

aiguillage *m* shunting.

aiguille *f* needle.

aiguiller *vt* to direct; to shunt.

aiguiser *vt* to sharpen.

ail *m* garlic.

ailé *adj* winged.

aileron *m* fin; aileron.

ailleurs *adv* elsewhere; **partout ~** everywhere else; **nulle part ~** nowhere else; **d'~** moreover; by the way.

aimable *adj* kind; **~ment** *adv* kindly.

aimant *m* magnet.

aimanter *vt* to magnetize.

aimer *vt* to love.

aîné *m*, **aînée** *f* eldest *ou* oldest child; * *adj* elder, older; eldest, oldest.

ainsi *adv* so, thus; **puisque c'est ~** since this is the way it is *ou* things are.

air *m* air; **avoir l'~ content** to look happy; **d'un ~ moqueur** in a mocking fashion.

aire *f* area.

aise *f* ease, comfort.

aisé *adj* easy; well-off; **~ment** *adv* easily.

aisselle *f* armpit.

ajournement *m* adjournment; postponement.

ajourner *vt* to adjourn; to defer, postpone.

ajout *m* addition.

ajouter *vt* to add.

ajuster *vt* to adjust.

alarmant *adj* alarming.

alarme *f* alarm.

alarmer *vt* to alarm; **s'~** *vr* to get alarmed (*de* at, about).

albâtre *m* alabaster.

album *m* album.

albumine *f* albumen.

alcalin *adj* alkaline.

alcaloïde *m* alkaloid.

alchimie *f* alchemy.

alchimiste *m* alchemist.

alcool *m* alcohol.

alcoolique *adj* alcoholic; * *mf* drunkard.

alcoolisme *m* alcoholism.

aléatoire *adj* uncertain; risky.

alentours *mpl* surroundings, neighbourhood.

alerte *adj* alert; agile; * *f* alarm, alert.

alerter *vt* to alert; to notify; to warn.

algèbre *f* algebra.

algébrique *adj* algebraic; **~ment** *adv* algebraically.

algorithme *m* algorithm.

algue *f* seaweed.

alibi *m* alibi.

aliénation *f* alienation.

aliéner *vt* to alienate.

alignement *m* alignment; aligning.

aligner *vt* to align, line up.

aliment *m* food.

alimentaire *adj* alimentary, food.

alimentation *f* feeding; diet; food industry.

alimenter *vt* to feed; **s'~** *vr* to eat.

alinéa *m* paragraph.

allée *f* avenue; path.

alléger *vt* to make lighter; to alleviate.

allégorie *f* allegory.

allégresse *f* cheerfulness.

alléguer *vt* to allege, put forward.

aller *vi* to go; **comment allez-vous?** how are you?; **allons-y** let's go; **s'en aller** to go away, leave; * *m* outward journey; single ticket.

allergie *f* allergy.

allergique *adj* allergic (*à* to).

alliage *m* alloy.
alliance *f* alliance; marriage; wedding ring.
allié *m* **-e** *f* ally; * *adj* allied.
allier *vt* to combine.
allô *excl* hello!
allocation *f* allocation; allowance.
allongé *adj* **être allongé** to be lying (down).
allonger *vt* to lengthen; **s'~** *vr* to lengthen; to lie down.
allouer *vt* to allocate.
allumage *m* ignition.
allumer *vt* to light; to turn *ou* switch on.
allumette *f* match.
allure *f* speed; look.
allusion *f* allusion (*à* to).
alluvions *fpl* alluvium, alluvial deposits.
alors *adv* then; **~ que** while; whereas.
alouette *f* lark.
alourdir *vt* to make heavy; to increase.
alphabet *m* alphabet.
alphabétique *adj* alphabetical; **~ment** *adv* alphabetically.
alpinisme *m* mountaineering.
alpiniste *mf* mountaineer.
altération *f* alteration, change.
altercation *f* altercation.
altérer *vt* to change, alter.
alternance *f* alternation.
alternatif *adj* alternate.
alternative *f* alternative.
alternativement *adv* in turn, alternately.
alterner *vt vi* to alternate (*avec* with).
altitude *f* altitude, height.
altruisme *m* altruism.
aluminium *m* aluminium.
alvéole *f* cell.
amabilité *f* kindness.
amaigrir *vt* to make thin(ner).
amaigrissant *adj* slimming.
amalgame *m* mixture, amalgam.
amalgamer *vt* to combine.
amande *f* almond.
amant *m* lover.
amarrer *vt* to moor.
amas *m* pile, heap.
amasser *vt* to amass, pile up.
amateur *m* amateur; connoisseur.
ambassade *f* embassy.

ambassadeur *m* **-drice** *f* ambassador.
ambiance *f* atmosphere.
ambigu *adj*, *f* **ambigué** ambiguous.
ambiguïté *f* ambiguity.
ambitieux *adj* ambitious.
ambition *f* ambition.
ambivalence *f* ambivalence.
ambre *m* amber.
ambulance *f* ambulance.
ambulant *adj* travelling, mobile.
âme *f* soul.
amélioration *f* improvement.
améliorer *vt* to improve; **s'~** *vr* to improve.
aménagement *m* fitting out; adjustment; development.
aménager *vt* to fit out; to adjust; to develop.
amende *f* fine.
amendement *m* amendment.
amener *vt* to bring.
amer *adj* bitter.
amèrement *adv* bitterly.
Américain *m* **-e** *f* American.
américain *adj* American.
Amérique *f* America.
amertume *f* bitterness.
ameublement *m* furniture.
ami *m* **-e** *f* friend.
amiante *m* asbestos.
amibe *f* amoeba.
amical *adj* friendly; **~ement** *adv* in a friendly manner.
amincir *vt* to thin (down).
amiral *m* admiral.
amitié *f* friendship.
ammoniac *m* ammonia.
amnésie *f* amnesia.
amnistie *f* amnesty.
amnistier *vt* to grant an amnesty to.
amoindrir *vt* to weaken; to reduce.
amoindrissement *m* weakening; reduction.
amoncellement *m* pile; accumulation.
amorcer *vt* to bait; to begin.
amorphe *adj* apathetic.
amortir *vt* to soften; to deaden.
amortissement *m* paying off.
amour *m* love.
amoureux *adj* in love (*de* with).
amovible *adj* detachable.

ampère *m* ampere, amp.
amphibie *adj* amphibious.
amphithéâtre *m* amphitheatre.
ample *adj* roomy; wide; ~**ment** *adv* amply, fully.
ampleur *f* fullness; range.
amplifier *vt* to increase; to amplify.
amplitude *f* amplitude; magnitude.
ampoule *f* bulb; phial; blister.
amputation *f* amputation.
amputer *vt* to amputate.
amusant *adj* amusing.
amuser *vt* to amuse.
an *m* year; **avoir vingt ~s** to be 20 (years old).
anabolisant *m* anabolic steroid.
anachronisme *m* anachronism.
anagramme *m* anagram.
analgésique *adj* analgesic.
analogie *f* analogy.
analogique *adj* analogical.
analogue *adj* analogous (*à* to).
analphabète *adj* illiterate.
analyse *f* analysis; test.
analyser *vt* to analyse.
analyste *mf* analyst; psychoanalyst.
analytique *adj* analytical; ~**ment** *adv* analytically.
ananas *m* pineapple.
anarchie *f* anarchy.
anarchiste *mf* anarchist.
anathème *m* anathema.
anatomie *f* anatomy.
anatomique *adj* anatomical; ~**ment** *adv* anatomically.
ancestral *adj* ancestral.
ancêtre *m* ancestor.
anchois *m* anchovy.
ancien *adj* old; former; ~**nement** *adv* formerly.
ancienneté *f* (years of) service; seniority; age.
ancrage *m* anchorage.
ancre *f* anchor.
ancrer *vt* to anchor.
âne *m* ass, donkey.
anéantir *vt* to annihilate.
anéantissement *m* annihilation.
anecdote *f* anecdote.
anémie *f* anemia.

anémone *f* anemone.
anesthésie *f* anaesthetic; anaesthesia.
anesthésique *m* anaesthetic.
ange *m* angel.
angélique *adj* angelic; * *f* angelica.
angine *f* tonsillitis.
Anglais *m* **-e** *f* Englishman; Englishwoman.
anglais *adj* English; * *m* (*ling*) English.
angle *m* angle; corner.
Angleterre *f* England.
anglophone *adj* English-speaking; *mf* English speaker.
angoissant *adj* agonizing.
angoisse *f* anguish.
angoisser *vt* to cause anguish.
animal *m* animal.
animateur *m* **-trice** *f* host, compère; leader.
animation *f* animation; hustle and bustle.
animé *adj* busy; lively.
animer *vt* to lead; to host; to liven up; **s'~** *vr* to liven up.
animisme *m* animism.
animosité *f* animosity.
annales *fpl* annals.
anneau *m* ring.
année *f* year; **les ~s soixante** the Sixties.
annexe *f* annexe; * *adj* subsidiary.
annexer *vt* to annex; to append.
annihiler *vt* to annihilate.
anniversaire *m* birthday; **joyeux ~!** happy birthday!
annonce *f* advertisement; announcement.
annoncer *vt* to announce (*à* to).
annoter *vt* to annotate.
annuaire *m* telephone directory, phone book.
annuel *adj* annual; ~**lement** *adv* annually.
annulation *f* cancellation; nullification.
annuler *vt* to cancel; to nullify.
anode *f* anode.
anodin *adj* insignificant.
anomalie *f* anomaly.
anonyme *adj* anonymous; impersonal; ~**ment** *adv* anonymously.
anorexie *f* anorexia.
anorexique *adj*, *mf* anorexic.
anormal *adj* abnormal; ~**ement** *adv* abnormally.
anse *f* handle.

antagonisme *m* antagonism.

antagoniste *adj* antagonistic.

antécédent *m* antecedent.

antenne *f* (*rad*, *TV*) aerial; (*zool*) feeler.

antérieur *adj* earlier, previous; **~ement** *adv* earlier, previously.

anthologie *f* anthology.

anthracite *m* anthracite.

anthropologie *f* anthropology.

anthropologue *m* anthropologist.

antiaérien *adj* antiaircraft.

anticancéreux *adj* cancer.

antichambre *f* antechamber.

anticipation *f* anticipation.

anticonceptionnel *adj* contraceptive.

anticonformiste *adj*, *mf* nonconformist.

anticorps *m* antibody.

anticyclone *m* anticyclone.

antidater *vt* to backdate.

antidépresseur *adj*, *m* antidepressant.

antidote *m* antidote.

antigel *m* antifreeze.

antimilitariste *adj*, *mf* antimilitarist.

antinucléaire *adj*, *mf* antinuclear.

antipathie *f* antipathy.

antipathique *adj* unpleasant.

antipode *m* antipodes; **aux ~s de** the polar opposite of.

antiquaire *mf* antique dealer.

antique *adj* ancient.

antiquité *f* antiquity; antique.

antirouille *adj invar* rustproof.

antisémite *mf* antisemite; *adj* antisemitic.

antiseptique *adj* antiseptic.

antisocial *adj* antisocial.

antitétanique *adj* (anti-)tetanus.

antithèse *f* antithesis.

antitoxine *f* antitoxin.

antivol *m invar* anti-theft*ou* security device; lock; * *adj invar* anti-theft.

antonyme *m* antonym.

antre *m* den.

anus *m* anus.

anxiété *f* anxiety.

anxieux *adj* anxious.

aorte *f* aorta.

août *m* August.

apaisant *adj* soothing.

apaisement *m* calm(ing down); relief.

apaiser *vt* to calm (down); to relieve.

apathie *f* apathy.

apathique *adj* apathetic.

apercevoir *vt* to see; to catch a glimpse of.

aperçu *m* (overall *ou* general) idea.

apéritif *m* aperitif.

apesanteur *f* weightlessness.

apeuré *adj* frightened.

aphone *adj* voiceless, hoarse.

aphrodisiaque *adj*, *m* aphrodisiac.

apiculteur *m* beekeeper.

apitoyer *vt* to move to pity; **s'~** *vr* to feel pity (*sur* for).

aplanir *vt* to level (out); to smooth away.

aplati *adj* flat.

aplatir *vt* to flatten (out).

apocalypse *f* apocalypse.

apocalyptique *adj* apocalyptic.

apogée *m* apogee, peak.

apolitique *adj* apolitical; non-political.

apologie *f* apology.

apoplexie *f* apoplexy.

apostrophe *f* apostrophe.

apothéose *f* apotheosis.

apôtre *m* apostle.

apparaître *vi* to appear.

appareil*m* device; appliance; (tele)phone; **~ photo** camera.

appareillage *m* casting off; equipment.

appareiller *vi* (*mar*) to cast off.

apparemment *adv* apparently.

apparence *f* appearance.

apparent *adj* apparent.

apparition *f* appearance; apparition.

appartement *m* flat, apartment.

appartenance *f* membership.

appartenir *vi*: **~ à** to belong to.

appât *m* bait.

appâter *vt* to lure; to bait.

appauvrir *vt* to impoverish; **s'~** *vr* to grow poorer.

appauvrissement *m* impoverishment.

appel *m* call; appeal.

appeler *vt* to call; to call out; **s'~** *vr* **je m'appelle Léon** my name is Leon.

appellation *f* appellation; name.

appendicite *f* appendicitis.

appesantir *vt* to weigh down; to strengthen; **s'~** *vr* to grow heavier; to grow stronger.

appétissant *adj* appetizing.

appétit *m* appetite (*de* for).

applaudir *vt vi* to applaud.

applaudissements *mpl* applause.

applicable *adj* applicable (*à* to).

application *f* application; use.

appliqué *adj* thorough, industrious.

appliquer *vt* to apply (*à* to); **s'~** *vr* to apply o.s.

apport *m* supply.

apporter *vt* to bring.

apposer *vt* to append; to affix.

appréciable *adj* appreciable.

appréciatif *adj* evaluative; appreciative.

appréciation *f* estimation, assessment

apprécier *vt* to appreciate; to assess

appréhender *vt* to apprehend; to dread.

appréhension *f* apprehension.

apprendre *vt* to learn; **~ à lire** to learn to read; **~ à lire à un enfant** to teach a child to read.

apprenti *m* **-e** *f* apprentice.

apprentissage *m* apprenticeship.

apprêter *vt* to dress; to size; **s'~** *vr* to get ready.

apprivoiser *vt* to tame.

approbateur *adj*, *f* **-trice** approving.

approbation *f* approval.

approche *f* approach.

approcher *vt* to move near; to approach; **s'~** *vr* to approach.

approfondir *vt* to deepen.

approfondissement *m* deepening.

approprier (s') *vr* to appropriate.

approuver *vt* to approve of.

approvisionnement *m* supplying.

approvisionner *vt* to supply; **s'~** *vr* to stock up (*de*, *en* with).

approximatif *adj* approximate.

approximation *f* approximation.

approximativement *adv* approximately.

appui *m* support.

appuie-tête *m invar* headrest.

appuyer *vt* to press; to lean; to support; * *vi* to press; *vr* **s'~** to lean against; *vr* **s'~ sur** to lean on; to rely on.

âpre *adj* bitter, harsh; **~ment** *adv* bitterly.

après *prép* after; **après tout** after all; **d'~ elle** according to her; **collé ~ la vitre** stuck on the window; * *adv* after(wards); **tout de suite ~** immediately after *ou* afterwards.

après-demain *adv* the day after tomorrow.

après-midi *m/f invar* afternoon.

âpreté *f* bitterness.

a priori *m* apriorism; * *adv* a priori.

apte *adj* capable (*à* of).

aptitude *f* aptitude; ability.

aquarium *m* aquarium.

aquatique *adj* aquatic.

aqueduc *m* aqueduct.

aqueux *adj* aqueous, watery.

arabesque *f* arabesque.

arable *adj* arable.

arachide *f* peanut, groundnut.

araignée *f* spider.

arbalète *f* crossbow.

arbitrage *m* arbitration.

arbitraire *adj* arbitrary; **~ment** *adv* arbitrarily.

arbitre *m* arbiter; referee.

arbitrer *vt* to arbitrate; to referee.

arborer *vt* to wear; to bear.

arborescence *f* arborescence.

arboriculture *f* arboriculture, tree cultivation.

arbre *m* tree.

arbrisseau *m* shrub.

arbuste *m* bush.

arc *m* bow; arc; arch.

arcade *f* arcade.

arc-bouter (s') *vr* to lean.

arc-en-ciel *m*, *pl* **arcs-en-ciel** rainbow.

archaïque *adj* archaic.

archange *m* archangel.

arche *f* arch.

archéologie *f* archaeology.

archéologue *mf* archaeologist.

archétype *m* archetype.

archevêque *m* archbishop.

archipel *m* archipelago.

architecte *mf* architect.

architectonique *adj* architectonic

architectural *adj* architectural.

architecture *f* architecture.

archiver *vt* to file, archive.

archives *fpl* archives, records.

archiviste *mf* archivist.

ardemment *adv* ardently.

ardent *adj* ardent, burning.

ardeur *f* ardour.

ardoise *f* slate.

ardu *adj* difficult.

are *f* are, a hundred square metres.

arène *f* arena.

arête *f* (fish)bone.

argent *m* silver; money.

argenté *adj* silver; silver-plated.

argenterie *f* silverware.

argile *f* clay.

argot *m* slang.

argument *m* argument.

argumentation *f* argumentation.

argumenter *vi* to argue (*sur* about).

aride *adj* arid.

aridité *f* aridity.

aristocrate *mf* aristocrat.

aristocratie *f* aristocracy.

aristocratique *adj* aristocratic.

arithmétique *f* arithmetic; * *adj* arithmetical; ~**ment** *adv* arithmetically.

armature *f* (frame)work.

arme *f* arm, weapon.

armée *f* army.

armement *m* arms, weapons; armaments.

armer *vt* to arm; **s'~** *vr* to arm o.s.

armistice *m* armistice.

armoire *f* cupboard; wardrobe.

armure *f* armour.

aromate *m* herb; spice.

aromatique *adj* aromatic.

aromatiser *vt* to flavour.

arôme *m* aroma; flavour.

arpenteur *m* (land) surveyor.

arqué *adj* curved, arched.

arquebuse *f* arquebus.

arrachement *m* wrench; pulling *ou* tearing off.

arracher *vt* to pull (out); to tear off.

arrangeant *adj* obliging.

arrangement *m* arrangement.

arranger *vt* to arrange; to fix; **cela m'arrangerait** that would suit me; **s'~** *vr* to come to an arrangement; to manage; to get better.

arrestation *f* arrest.

arrêt *m* stopping; stop (button).

arrêté *m* order.

arrêter *vt* to stop; **s'~** *vr* to stop.

arrhes *fpl* deposit.

arrière *m invar* back; **en ~** back(wards); **à l'~** at the back; * *adj invar* back, rear.

arriéré *adj* backward.

arrière-goût *m* aftertaste.

arrière-grand-mère *f* great-grandmother.

arrière-grand-père *m* great-grandfather.

arrière-pays *m* hinterland.

arrière-pensée *f* ulterior motive.

arrière-petits-enfants *mpl* great grandchildren.

arrière-plan *m* background.

arrimer *vt* to stow.

arrivage *m* delivery.

arrivant *m* -**e** *f* newcomer.

arrivée *f* arrival, coming.

arriver *vi* to arrive, come.

arriviste *mf* careerist; social climber.

arrogance *f* arrogance.

arrogant *adj* arrogant.

arroger (s') *vr* to assume (without rights to).

arrondi *adj* round(ed).

arrondir *vt* to make round; to round off.

arrondissement *m* district.

arrosage *m* watering.

arroser *vt* to water.

arsenal *m* arsenal.

arsenic *m* arsenic.

art *m* art.

artère *f* artery; road.

artériel *adj* arterial.

arthrite *f* arthritis.

artichaut *m* artichoke.

article *m* article.

articulation *f* joint; knuckle.

articuler *vt* to articulate.

artifice *m* trick.

artificiel *adj* artificial; ~**lement** *adv* artificially.

artillerie *f* artillery.

artisan *m* artisan, craftsman.

artisanal *adj* craft.

artisanat *m* craft industry.

artiste *mf* artist.

artistique *adj* artistic; **~ment** *adv* artistically.

as *m* ace.

ascendance *f* ancestry.

ascendant *adj* upward, rising; * *m* (strong) influence, ascendancy (*sur* over).

ascenseur *m* lift, elevator.

ascension *f* ascent.

ascète *mf* ascetic.

ascétique *adj* ascetic.

aseptiser *vt* to sterilize; to disinfect.

asexué *adj* asexual.

asiatique *adj* Asian.

asile *m* refuge; asylum.

aspect *m* appearance, look.

asperge *f* asparagus.

asperger *vt* to splash (*de* with).

aspérité *f* bump.

asphalte *m* asphalt.

asphyxie *f* asphyxiation, suffocation.

asphyxier *vt* to asphyxiate, suffocate.

aspirateur *m* vacuum cleaner.

aspiration *f* inhalation.

aspirer *vt* to inhale.

aspirine *f* aspirin.

assagir *vt* to quieten (down); **s'~** *vr* to quieten (down).

assaillant *m* assailant.

assaillir *vt* to assail.

assainir *vt* to clean up; to purify.

assainissement *m* cleaning up.

assaisonnement *m* seasoning.

assaisonner *vt* to season.

assassin *m* murderer; assassin.

assassinat *m* murder; assassination.

assassiner *vt* to assassinate.

assaut *m* assault, attack (*de* on).

assécher *vt* to drain; **s'~** *vr* to dry (up *ou* out).

assemblage *m* assembly; assembling.

assemblée *f* meeting.

assembler *vt* to assemble; **s'~** *vr* to assemble.

assentiment *m* assent.

asseoir (s') *vr* to sit down.

assermenté *adj* on oath.

assertion *f* assertion.

asservissement *m* enslavement; slavery.

assez *adv* enough; quite, rather; **avoir ~ d'argent** to have enough money; **~ bien**

quite well; **j'en ai ~!** I've had enough!; I'm fed up.

assidu *adj* assiduous; regular.

assiduité *f* assiduity; regularity.

assiéger *vt* to besiege.

assiette *f* plate.

assigner *vt* to assign.

assimilation *f* assimilation; comparison; classification.

assimiler *vt* to assimilate.

assis *adj* seated, sitting (down).

assistance *f* audience; assistance.

assistant *m* **-e** *f* assistant.

assister *vt* to attend; to assist.

association *f* association.

associé *m* **-e** *f* associate, partner.

associer *vt* to associate (*à* with); **s'~** *vr* to join together.

assombrir *vt* to darken; **s'~** to darken.

assommer *vt* to stun.

Assomption *f* : **l'~** *the Assumption*.

assortiment *m* assortment.

assortir *vt* to match; **s'~** *vr* to go well together.

assoupir (s') *vr* to doze off.

assoupissement *m* doze.

assouplir *vt* to make supple; to relax.

assouplissement *m* softening; relaxing.

assourdir *vt* to deafen; to muffle.

assourdissant *adj* deafening.

assouvir *vt* to satisfy.

assouvissement *m* satisfying, satisfaction.

assujettir *vt* to subjugate.

assumer *vt* to assume.

assurance *f* (self-)assurance; assurance; insurance (policy).

assuré *m* **-e** *f* assured; * *adj* confident.

assurer *vt* to assure; **s'~** *vr* to insure o.s.

assureur *m* (insurance) agent; insurer(s), insurance company.

astérisque *m* asterisk.

asthmatique *adj*, *mf* asthmatic.

asthme *m* asthma.

asticot *m* maggot.

astigmate *adj* astigmatic.

astiquer *vt* to polish.

astre *m* star.

astreignant *adj* demanding.

astreindre *vt* to force, compel; **s'~** *vr* **s'~ à faire** to force *ou* compel o.s. to do.

astrologie *f* astrology.

astrologique *adj* astrological.

astrologue *m* astrologer.

astronaute *m* astronaut.

astronome *m* astronomer.

astronomie *f* astronomy.

astronomique *adj* astronomical.

astuce *f* shrewdness; (clever) trick; pun.

astucieux *adj* astute.

asymétrique *adj* asymmetric(al).

atelier *m* workshop; studio.

atermoyer *vi* to procrastinate.

athée *mf* atheist; *adj* atheistic.

athéisme *m* atheism.

athlète *mf* athlete.

athlétique *adj* athletic.

athlétisme *m* athletics.

atlas *m* atlas.

atmosphère *f* atmosphere.

atmosphérique *adj* atmospheric.

atome *m* atom.

atomique *adj* atomic.

atomiseur *m* spray; atomizer.

atout *m* trump; advantage, asset.

âtre *m* hearth.

atroce *adj* atrocious; dreadful; **~ment** *adv* atrociously; dreadfully.

atrocité *f* atrocity.

atrophié *adj* atrophied.

attachant *adj* endearing.

attache *f* fastener.

attaché *m* **-e** *f* attaché; assistant.

attachement *m* attachment (*à* to).

attacher *vt* to tie together; to tie up; to fasten; to attach (*à* to).

attaque *f* attack.

attaquer *vt* to attack; to tackle.

attarder (s') *vr* to linger.

atteindre *vt* to reach; to affect; to contact.

atteinte *f* attack (*à* on); **hors d'~** beyond *ou* out of reach.

attenant *adj* adjoining.

attendre *vt* to wait; **en attendant** meanwhile, in the meantime; **s'~** *vr* : **s'~ à qch** to expect sth.

attendrir *vt* to fill with pity, move; to soften;

to tenderize; **s'~** *vr* to be moved (*sur* by).

attendrissant *adj* touching, moving.

attendrissement *m* emotion.

attendu *adj* expected; long-awaited.

attentat *m* attack (*contre* on); murder attempt.

attente *f* wait; expectation.

attentif *adj* attentive; careful.

attention *f* attention; care.

attentionné *adj* considerate, thoughtful (*pour* towards).

attentivement *adv* attentively; carefully.

atténuation *f* alleviation; easing.

atténuer *vt* to alleviate, ease; to appease; to lighten.

atterrir *vi* to land, touch down.

atterrissage *m* landing, touchdown.

attester *vt* to testify to.

attirail *m* gear.

attirant *adj* attractive.

attirer *vt* to attract; **~ des ennuis à qn** to cause sb trouble.

attiser *vt* to stir up.

attitude *f* attitude; bearing.

attraction *f* attraction.

attrait *m* attraction, appeal.

attraper *vt* to catch.

attrayant *adj* attractive.

attribuer *vt* to attribute; to award.

attribut *m* attribute.

attribution *f* attribution.

attrister *vt* to sadden.

attroupement *m* crowd, gathering.

au = à le.

aube *f* dawn, daybreak.

auberge *f* inn; **~ de jeunesse** youth hostel.

aubergine *f* aubergine.

aucun *adj* no; not any; any; **sans ~ doute** without (any) doubt; **~ement** *adv* in no way; not in the least; * *pn* none; not any; any (one); **~ d'entre eux** none of them.

audace *f* audacity; daring.

audacieux *adj* audacious, bold; daring.

audience *f* audience; hearing.

audiovisuel *adj* audiovisual.

auditeur *m* **-trice** *f* listener; auditor.

auditoire *m* audience.

augmentation *f* increase, rise (*de* in); increasing, raising (*de* of).

augmenter *vt* to increase, raise.

augure *f* omen; oracle.

aujourd'hui *adv* today.

aumône *f* alms; **demander/faire l'~** to beg for/give alms.

auparavant *adv* before, previously; before, first.

auprès *prép*: **~ de** next to; (compared) with.

auquel = à lequel.

auréole *f* halo, aureole; ring (mark).

auriculaire *adj* auricular; * *m* little finger.

aurore *f* dawn, first light.

ausculter *vt* to auscultate.

aussi *adv* too, also; so; **nous ~** us too; **une ~ belle journée** such a beautiful day; **il est ~ petit qu'elle** he is as small as she is.

aussitôt *adv* immediately; **~ dit, ~ fait** no sooner said than done; **~ que** as soon as.

austère *adj* austere; **~ment** *adv* austerely.

austérité *f* austerity.

autant *adv* as much; as many; so much; such; so many; such a lot of; the same; **~ que je sache** as far as I know; **~ que possible** as much as possible; **elle n'est pas plus heureuse pour ~** she's not any happier for it *ou* for all that.

autel *m* altar.

auteur *m* author.

authenticité *f* authenticity.

authentifier *vt* to authenticate.

authentique *adj* authentic; **~ment** *adv* authentically.

autobiographie *f* autobiography.

autobiographique *adj* autobiographical.

autocar *m* coach.

autocollant *adj* self-adhesive.

autocuiseur *m* pressure cooker.

autodéfense *f* self-defence.

autodestruction *f* self-destruction.

autodidacte *adj* self-taught.

auto-école *f* driving school.

automate *m* automaton.

automatique *adj* automatic; **~ment** *adv* automatically.

automatiser *vt* to automate.

automatisme *m* automatism.

automne *m* autumn.

automobile *f* (motor) car.

automobiliste *mf* motorist.

autonome *adj* autonomous; self-governing.

autonomie *f* autonomy; self-government.

autoportrait *m* self-portrait.

autopsie *f* autopsy, post-mortem (examination).

autoradio *m* car radio.

autorisation *f* authorization, permission; permit.

autoriser *vt* to authorize, give permission for; to allow.

autoritaire *adj* authoritarian.

autorité *f* authority.

autoroute *f* motorway.

autosatisfaction *f* self-satisfaction.

auto-stop *m* hitch-hiking; **faire de l'~** to hitch-hike.

auto-stoppeur *m* **-euse** *f* hitch-hiker.

autour *prép* **~ de** (a)round; * *adv* (a)round; **il y en a tout ~** there is/are some all around.

autre *adj* other; **~ chose** something else *ou* different; **~ part** somewhere else; **d'~ part** on the other hand; moreover; * *pn* another (one); **j'en veux un ~** I'd like another (one); **encore deux ~s** another two; **les cinq ~s** the five others; the other five.

autrefois *adv* in the past, in days gone by.

autrement *adv* differently; otherwise; **je n'ai pas pu faire ~** I couldn't do differently *ou* otherwise.

autruche *f* ostrich.

autrui *pn* others.

aux = à les.

auxiliaire *adj* auxiliary; * *m* auxiliary; * *mf* assistant.

avachir (s') *vr* to become *ou* grow limp.

avalanche *f* avalanche.

avaler *vt* to swallow.

avance *f* advance; lead; **arriver en ~** to arrive early; **payer d'~** to pay in advance; **réserver à l'~** to book in advance; **avoir l'~ sur** to have the lead over.

avancement *m* promotion; progress; forward movement.

avancer *vt* to move forward; to bring forward; to put forward; **s'~** *vr* to advance, move forward; * *vi* to move forward, advance; to make progress; to project, stick out.

avant *prép* before; ~ **peu** shortly; ~ **tout** above all; * *adv* before; **en** ~ in front, ahead; * *m* front; (*mar*) bow; forward.

avantage *m* advantage.

avantager *vt* to favour; to flatter.

avantageux *adj* profitable, worthwhile; attractive; flattering.

avant-bras *m invar* forearm.

avant-coureur *adj* precursory.

avant-dernier *m* **-ière** *f, adj* next to last, second last, last but one.

avant-garde *f* avant-garde; vanguard.

avant-goût *m* foretaste.

avant-hier *adv* the day before yesterday.

avant-première *f* preview.

avare *mf* miser; *adj* miserly.

avarice *f* avarice, miserliness.

avarie *f* damage.

avarié *adj* rotting; damaged.

avec *prép* with; to.

avènement *m* accession (*à* to)*;* advent.

avenir *m* future.

aventure *f* adventure; venture; experience; affair.

aventurer (s') *vr* to venture.

aventurier *m* **-ière** *f* adventurer.

avenue *f* avenue.

avérer (s') *vr* to turn out, prove to be.

averse *f* shower (of rain).

aversion *f* aversion (*pour* to)*;* loathing (*pour* for).

avertir *vt* to warn; to inform (*de* of).

avertissement *m* warning.

aveu *m* admission, confession.

aveuglant *adj* blinding.

aveugle *adj* blind; * *mf* blind person.

aveuglement *m* blindness.

aveugler *vt* to blind.

aviateur *m* **-trice** *f* pilot, aviator.

aviation *f* flying; aviation.

avide *adj* greedy; eager; ~**ment** *adv* greedily; eagerly.

avidité *f* greed; eagerness.

avilir *vt* to degrade.

avilissant *adj* degrading.

avion *m* (air)plane, aircraft.

aviron *m* oar; rowing.

avis *m* opinion.

avisé *adj* wise, sensible.

aviser *vt* to advise, inform; to notice; **s'**~ *vr* **s'aviser de** to realize suddenly.

aviver *vt* to sharpen; to deepen; to arouse.

avocat *m* **-e** *f* lawyer, advocate; * *m* avocado (pear).

avoine *f* oats.

avoir *vt* to have; **il y a** there is/are; **il y a deux mois** two months ago; **qu'as-tu?** what's wrong (with you)?; **il n'avait qu'à le dire** he only had to say (the word); * *m* resources; credit.

avortement *m* abortion.

avorter *vi* to abort; to fail.

avoué *m* solicitor.

avouer *vt* to admit (to); to confess (to).

avril *m* April.

axe *m* axis; axle; main road.

axial *adj* axial.

azote *m* nitrogen.

B

babines *fpl* chops.

babiole *f* trinket, trifle.

bâbord *m* (*mar*) port.

babouin *m* baboon.

bac *m* ferry.

bâche *f* tarpaulin, cover.

bâcler *vt* to botch.

bactérie *f* bacterium.

badaud *m* idle onlooker.

badge *m* badge.

bafouer *vt* to scorn.

bafouiller *vi* to stammer; to babble.

bagage *m* luggage; stock of knowledge.

bagarre *f* fight, brawl.

bagarrer (se) *vr* to fight; to riot.

bagatelle *f* trinket; trifling sum.

bagne *m* penal servitude; (*fig*) grind.

bague *f* ring.

baguette *f* stick; loaf of French bread.

baie *f* (*geog*) bay.

baigner *vt vi* to bathe; * **se** ~ *vr* to have a bath, swim.

baignoire *f* bath(tub).

bâiller *vi* to yawn.

bâillon *m* gag.

bâillonner *vt* to gag.

bain *m* bath; bathe; swim.

baiser *m* kiss; * *vt* to kiss.

baisse *f* fall, drop.

baisser *vi* to fall, drop; * *vt* to lower.

bal *m* dance.

balade *f* (*fam*) walk; drive.

balader (se) *vr* (*fam*) to go for a walk; to go for a drive.

balai *m* broom, brush.

balance *f* scales; balance.

balancement *m* sway; rocking.

balancer *vt* to swing; to balance.

balançoire *f* swing; seesaw.

balayer *vt* to sweep, brush.

balbutiement *m* stammering, babbling.

balbutier *vt* to stammer, babble.

balbuzard *m* osprey.

balcon *m* balcony.

baleine *f* whale.

balistique *f* ballistics.

ballast *m* ballast.

balle *f* bullet; ball.

ballet *m* ballet.

ballon *m* ball; balloon.

ballotter *vt* jolt, shake about.

balourd *adj* stupid; clumsy.

balustrade *f* balustrade; handrail.

bambou *m* bamboo.

banal *adj* banal, trite; **~ement** *adv* tritely.

banalisation *f* vulgarizing; standardization.

banalité *f* banality, triteness.

banane *f* banana.

bancaire *adj* banking, bank.

bancal, *pl* **bancals** *adj* lame; rickety.

bandage *m* bandage.

bande *f* band; tape; ~ **dessinée** strip cartoon.

bandeau *m* headband; blindfold.

bander *vt* to bandage; to stretch.

banderole *f* banner streamer.

bandit *m* bandit.

banlieue *f* suburbs.

bannière *f* banner.

bannir *vt* to banish; to prohibit.

bannissement *m* banishment.

banque *f* bank; banking.

banqueroute *f* bankruptcy.

banquet *m* banquet.

banquette *f* seat, stool.

banquier *m* banker.

banquise *f* ice floe.

baptême *m* baptism.

baptiser *vt* to baptise.

bar *m* bar; (*zool*) bass.

barbare *adj* barbarian; barbaric.

barbarie *f* barbarism; barbarity.

barbarisme *m* (*gr*) barbarism.

barbe *f* beard.

barbelé *adj* barbed.

barbiturique *adj* barbituric; * *m* barbiturate.

barboter *vi* to dabble; to splash.

barbouillage *m* scribble; daub.

barbouiller *vt* to smear; to scrawl.

barbu *adj* bearded; * *m* bearded man.

barème *m* list, schedule.

baril *m* barrel, cask.

bariolé *adj* multicoloured, motley.

baromètre *m* barometer.

baron *m* baron **-ne** *f* baroness.

baroque *adj* baroque; * *m* baroque.

barque *f* small boat.

barrage *m* barrage, barrier, dam.

barre *f* bar, rod.

barré *adj* barred, blocked.

barreau *m* rung; bar (cage).

barrer *vt* to bar, block.

barrette *f* (hair) slide, brooch.

barricader *vt* to barricade; **se** ~ *vr* to barricade o.s.

barrière *f* barrier; fence.

baryton *m* baritone.

bas *adj* low, base; * *n* stocking; sock; **~sement** *adv* basely, meanly.

basalte *m* basalt.

bas-côté *m* verge; aisle.

bascule *f* weighing machine, scales.

basculer *vi* to tip up, topple over.

base *f* base; basis.

baser *vt* to base; **se** ~ **sur** *vr* to depend on, rely on.

bas-fond *m* (*naut*) shallow, shoal.

basilic *m* (*bot*) basil.
basilique *f* basilica.
basket *m* basketball.
basketteur *m* -**euse** *f* basketball player.
bas-relief *m* bas-relief.
basse *f* (*mus*) bass.
basse-cour *f* poultry-yard.
bassesse *f* meanness; vulgarity.
bassin *m* pond, pool; dock.
bassine *f* bowl.
basson *m* bassoon.
bastion *m* bastion.
bas-ventre *m* lower abdomen.
bataille *f* battle.
batailler *vi* (*fig*) to fight, battle.
batailleur *adj* combative, aggressive.
bataillon *m* (*mil*) battalion.
bâtard *adj* bastard, illegitimate.
bateau *m* boat, ship.
batelier *m* boatman.
bâtiment *m* building; ship.
bâtir *vt* to build.
bâtisse *f* building, house.
bâton *m* stick, staff.
batracien *m* batrachian.
battant *m* clapper (bell); shutter.
batte *f* bat.
battement *m* banging; beating.
batterie *f* battery.
batteur *m* drummer; batsman.
battre *vt* to beat, defeat.
battu *adj* beaten.
baudet *m* donkey.
baume *m* balm, balsam.
bauxite *f* bauxite.
bavard *m* -**e** *f* chatterbox; * *adj* talkative, loquacious.
bavardage *m* chatting, gossiping.
bavarder *vi* to chat, gossip.
bave *f* dribble, slobber.
baver *vi* to dribble, drool.
bavure *f* smudge, blunder.
bazar *m* bazaar; general store.
B.D. *f* (**bande dessinée**) strip cartoon.
béant *adj* gaping, wide open.
béat *adj* blissful; -**ement** *adv* rapturously.
béatitude *f* beatitude; bliss.
beau, *f* **belle** *adj* beautiful, lovely.

beaucoup *adv* a lot, a great deal; ~ **de monde** a lot of people; ~ **de temps** a great deal of time.
beau-fils *m* son-in-law; stepson.
beau-frère *m* brother-in-law.
beau-père *m* father-in-law; stepfather.
beauté *f* beauty, loveliness.
beaux-arts *mpl* fine arts.
beaux-parents *mpl* parents-in-law.
bébé *m* baby.
bec *m* beak, bill.
béchamel *f* béchamel (sauce).
bée *adj* open-mouthed, flabbergasted.
bégaiement *m* stammering, faltering.
bégayer *vi* to stammer, stutter.
bégonia *m* begonia.
beige *adj* beige; * *m* beige.
beignet *m* fritter; doughnut.
bêlement *m* bleating.
bêler *vi* to bleat.
Belge *mf* Belgian.
belge *adj* Belgian.
Belgique *f* Belgium.
belle-fille *f* daughter-in-law, stepdaugher.
belle-mère *f* mother-in-law, stepmother.
belle-sœur *f* sister-in-law.
belligérant *m* -**e** *f* belligerent; * *adj* belligerent.
belliqueux *adj* aggressive; warlike.
bémol *m* (*mus*) flat.
bénédictin *m* -**e** *f* Benedictine.
bénédiction *f* benediction, blessing.
bénéfice *m* profit; benefit.
bénéficiaire *mf* beneficiary.
bénéficier *vi* to benefit; to enjoy.
bénévole *adj* voluntary; unpaid; ~**ment** *adv* voluntarily.
bénin, *f* **bénigne** *adj* benign; minor; harmless.
bénir *vt* to bless.
bénit *adj* consecrated, holy.
benne *f* skip; tipper.
benzène *m* benzene.
béquille *f* crutch; prop.
berceau *m* cradle.
bercement *m* rocking.
bercer *vt* to rock, cradle.
berceuse *f* lullaby; rocking chair.
béret *m* beret.
berge *f* riverbank.

berger *m* shepherd, **-ère** *f* shepherdess.
bergerie *f* sheepbarn.
berner *vt* to fool, hoax.
besogne *f* work; job.
besoin *m* need; want; **avoir ~ de** to need.
bestial *adj* bestial; **~ement** *adv* bestially.
bestialité *f* bestiality; brutishness.
bétail *m* livestock; cattle.
bête *adj* stupid, silly; **~ment** *adv* stupidly, foolishly; ** f* animal.
bêtifier *vt* to play the fool; to prattle stupidly.
bêtise *f* stupidity, foolishness.
béton *m* concrete.
betterave *f* beetroot, beet.
beurre *m* butter.
beurrer *vt* to butter.
bévue *f* blunder.
biais *m* slant; angle; bias.
biathlon *m* biathlon.
bibelot *m* curio.
biberon *m* baby's bottle.
bible *f* bible.
bibliographie *f* bibliography.
bibliothécaire *mf* librarian.
bibliothèque *f* library; bookcase.
bicarbonate *m* bicarbonate.
bicentenaire *m* bicentenary.
biceps *m* biceps.
biche *f* doe; darling, pet.
bicolore *adj* bi-coloured, two-tone.
bicyclette *f* bicycle.
bidon *m* tin, can; flask.
bidonville *m* shanty town.
bien *adv* well; properly; very; **c'est ~ cela** that's right; ** n* property, estate.
bien-être *m* well-being.
bienfaisant *adj* beneficial, kind.
bienfaiteur *m* benefactor, **-trice** *f* benefactress.
bienheureux *adj* blessed; lucky; happy.
bientôt *adv* soon.
bienveillant *adj* benevolent, kindly.
bienvenu *adj* welcome.
bienvenue *f* welcome.
bière *f* beer; coffin.
bifteck *m* steak.
bifurcation *f* bifurcation, fork.
bifurquer *vi* to fork, branch off.

bigot *adj* bigoted.
bihebdomadaire *adj* twice-weekly.
bijou *m* jewel.
bijouterie *f* jewellery.
bijoutier *m* **-ière** *f* jeweller.
bilan *m* balance sheet; assessment.
bilatéral *adj* bilateral.
bile *f* bile.
bilingue *adj* bilingual.
billard *m* billiards.
bille *f* marble; billiard ball.
billet *m* ticket; note.
billetterie *f* cash dispenser.
billion *m* billion.
bimensuel *adj* fortnightly.
bimestriel *adj* every two months.
binaire *adj* binary.
biochimie *f* biochemistry.
biochimiste *mf* biochemist.
biodégradable *adj* biodegradable.
bioéthique *f* bioethics.
biographie *f* biography.
biologie *f* biology.
biologique *adj* biological.
biologiste *mf* biologist.
biosphère *f* biosphere.
bioxyde *m* dioxide.
bipède *m* biped.
bipolaire *adj* bipolar.
bisannuel *adj* biennial.
biscornu *adj* crooked, misshapen; odd, outlandish.
biscuit *m* cake; biscuit.
bisexuel *adj* bisexual.
bissextile *adj* bissextile, leap (year).
bistouri *m* bistoury.
bitume *m* bitumen.
bitumer *vt* to asphalt, tarmac.
bizarre *adj* bizarre, strange; **~ment** *adv* strangely, oddly.
bizarrerie *f* strangeness, singularity.
blafard *adj* pale, pallid.
blague *f* joke, trick.
blaguer *vi* to joke.
blagueur *m* **-euse** *f* joker, wag; ** adj* jokey, teasing.
blaireau *m* badger.
blâme *m* blame, rebuke.

blâmer *vt* to blame, rebuke.

blanc *adj*, *f* **blanche** white; * *m* white; blank; * *mf* white person; * *f* (*mus*) minim.

blancheur *f* whiteness.

blanchir *vi* to turn white; to become lighter; * *vt* to whiten; to lighten.

blanchissage *m* laundering; refining.

blanchisserie *f* laundry.

blasé *adj* blasé.

blason *m* blazon, coat of arms.

blasphème *m* blasphemy.

blasphémer *vi* to blaspheme.

blé *m* wheat.

blême *adj* pale, wan.

blêmir *vi* to turn pale.

blessant *adj* cutting, hurtful.

blessé *adj* injured, wounded.

blesser *vt* to injure, wound.

blessure *f* injury, wound.

bleu *adj* blue; * *m* blue; bruise.

bleuet *m* cornflower.

bleuir *vt* *vi* to turn blue.

bleuté *adj* bluish.

blindage *m* armour plating.

blindé *adj* armoured, reinforced.

bloc *m* block, group, unit.

blocage *m* blocking, freezing.

blocus *m* blockade.

blond *adj* blond, fair.

blondir *vi* to turn blond, turn golden; * *vt* to bleach.

bloquer *vt* to block, blockade.

blottir (se) *vr* to curl up, snuggle up.

blouse *f* blouse; overall.

blouson *m* windcheater, bomber jacket.

bobine *f* reel, bobbin.

bocal *m* jar; bowl.

bœuf *m* ox, bullock.

bohémien *m* **-ne** *f* Bohemian.

boire *vt* to drink; * *vi* to drink, tipple.

bois *m* wood.

boisé *adj* wooded.

boisson *f* drink.

boîte *f* box.

boiter *vi* to limp.

boiteux *adj* lame.

boîtier *m* case, body.

boitillant *adj* limping.

boitiller *vi* to hobble slightly.

bol *m* bowl.

bolet *m* boletus.

bombardement *m* bombardment, bombing.

bombarder *vt* to bombard, bomb.

bombe *f* bomb.

bombé *adj* rounded, domed.

bon *adj*, *f* **bonne** good; * *m* slip, coupon, bond.

bonbon *m* sweet, candy.

bond *m* leap; bounce.

bonde *f* stopper, plug.

bondé *adj* packed.

bondir *vi* to jump, leap; to bounce.

bonheur *m* happiness; luck.

bonhomme *m*, *pl* **bonshommes** chap, fellow.

bonification *f* improvement; bonus.

bonifier *vt* to improve; * **se ~** *vr* to improve.

bonjour *m* hello, good morning.

bonnet *m* bonnet, hat.

bonneterie *f* hosiery.

bonsoir *m* good evening.

bonté *f* goodness, kindness.

bon vivant *m* bon vivant.

bord *m* side, edge.

bordé *adj* edged, bordered.

bordée *f* broadside, volley.

border *vt* to edge, border.

bordereau *m* note; invoice.

bordure *f* frame, border.

borgne *adj* one-eyed.

borne *f* boundary; milestone.

borné *adj* narrow-minded.

borner *vt* to restrict, limit.

bosse *f* hump, knob.

bosseler *vt* to dent, emboss.

bossu *m* **-e** *f* hunchback; * *adj* hunchbacked.

botanique *f* botany; * *adj* botanical.

botaniste *f* botanist.

botte *f* boot.

bottine *f* ankle boot, bootee.

bouche *f* mouth.

bouché *adj* cloudy, overcast.

bouchée *f* mouthful.

bouche-à-bouche *m* kiss of life.

boucher *vt* to block, clog up; * **se ~** *vr* to become cloudy; * *m*, **-ère** *f* (woman) butcher.

boucherie *f* butcher's; butchery.
bouchon *m* cork.
boucle *f* curl; buckle.
boucler *vt* to buckle; to surround.
bouclier *m* shield.
bouddhisme *m* Buddhism.
boudeur *adj* sullen, sulky.
boudin *m* (black) pudding.
boue *f* mud.
bouée *f* buoy.
boueur *m* dustman.
bouffée *f* whiff, puff.
bouffi *adj* swollen, puffed up.
bouffon *m* buffoon, clown.
bougeoir *m* candlestick.
bouger *vi* to move; * *vt* to move, shift.
bougie *f* candle.
bouillant *adj* boiling.
bouillir *vi* to boil.
bouilloire *f* kettle.
bouillon *m* broth.
bouillonner *vi* to bubble, foam.
bouillotte *f* hot-water bottle.
boulanger *m* **-ère** *f* baker.
boulangerie *f* bakery.
boule *f* ball, bowl.
boulet *m* cannonball; (*fig*) millstone.
boulevard *m* boulevard.
bouleversant *adj* upsetting, confusing.
bouleversement *m* confusion, disruption.
bouleverser *vt* to confuse, disrupt.
boulimie *f* bulimia.
boulimique *adj* bulimic.
boulon *m* bolt.
bouquet *m* bouquet, posy.
bouquin *m* (*fam*) book.
bouquiniste *mf* second-hand book-seller.
bourbeux *adj* muddy.
bourbier *m* quagmire.
bourdon *m* bumblebee.
bourdonnement *m* buzz, buzzing.
bourdonner *vi* to buzz, hum.
bourg *m* market-town.
bourgeois *m* **-e** *f* bourgeois, middle-class person; * *adj* bourgeois, middle-class.
bourgeoisie *f* bourgeoisie, middle classes.
bourgeon *m* bud.
bourgeonner *vi* to bud.

bourrasque *f* squall, gust.
bourreau *m* torturer, executioner.
bourrelet *m* pad, cushion.
bourrer *vt* to stuff, cram.
bourse *f* purse; **la Bourse** stock exchange.
boursier *m* **-ière** *f* broker; speculator.
boursouflé *adj* bloated, swollen.
bousculade *f* hustle, scramble.
bousculer *vt* to jostle, hustle.
boussole *f* compass.
bout *m* end; piece, scrap.
boutade *f* whim, caprice; jest.
bouteille *f* bottle.
boutique *f* shop, store.
bouton *m* button.
boutonner *vt* to button.
boutonnière *f* buttonhole.
bouture *f* cutting.
bovin *adj* bovine.
boxe *f* boxing.
boxer *vi* to box.
boxeur *m* boxer.
boyau *m* guts, insides.
boycottage *m* boycotting.
boycotter *vt* to boycott.
bracelet *m* bracelet.
braconnier *m* poacher.
brader *vt* to sell at a discount.
braderie *f* discount sale.
braguette *f* fly (trousers).
braise *f* embers.
brancard *m* shaft, stretcher.
branche *f* branch.
branchement *m* branching; connection.
brancher *vt* to connect, link.
branchies *fpl* gills.
brandir *vt* to brandish, flourish.
branlant *adj* loose; shaky.
bras *m* arm.
brasier *m* brazier, furnace.
brasse *f* breaststroke.
brassée *f* armful.
brasser *vt* to brew; to mix.
brasserie *f* bar; brewery.
bravade *f* bravado.
brave *adj* brave, courageous; **~ment** *adv* bravely, courageously.
braver *vt* to brave, defy.

bravoure *f* bravery, courage.

brebis *f* ewe.

brèche *f* breach, gap.

bredouillant *adj* mumbling.

bredouille *adj* empty-handed.

bredouiller *vi* to mumble.

bref *adj*, *f* **brève** brief, concise; **en ~** *adv* in short.

bretelle *f* strap, sling.

brevet *m* licence, patent.

breveté *adj* patented.

bribe *f* bit, scrap.

bric-à-brac *m* bric-a-brac.

bricolage *m* DIY, odd jobs.

bricole *f* small job.

bricoler *vi* to do odd jobs.

bricoleur *m* handyman, **-euse** *f* handywoman.

bride *f* bridle.

bridé *adj* restrained, restricted.

brider *vt* to restrain, restrict.

brièvement *adv* briefly, concisely.

brièveté *f* brevity.

brigade *f* brigade.

brigadier *m* corporal, sergeant (police).

brillamment *adv* brilliantly.

brillant *adj* brilliant, shining.

briller *vi* to shine.

brin *m* stalk, strand.

brindille *f* twig.

brique *f* brick, slab.

briquet *m* lighter.

brise *f* breeze.

briser *vt* to smash, shatter.

brocante *f* second-hand dealing.

brocanteur *m* **-euse** *f* second-hand dealer.

broche *f* brooch.

brochure *f* brochure, booklet.

broder *vt* to embroider, *vi* to embellish, elaborate.

broderie *f* embroidery.

bronche *f* bronchus.

bronchite *f* bronchitis.

bronzage *m* tan.

bronze *m* bronze.

bronzer *vi* to get a tan.

brosse *f* brush.

brosser *vt* to brush.

brouette *f* wheelbarrow.

brouillard *m* fog, mist.

brouiller *vt* to blur, confuse.

brouillon *m* rough copy, draft; * *adj* untidy.

broussaille *f* brushwood, undergrowth.

broussailleux *adj* bushy, overgrown.

brousse *f* undergrowth, bush.

brouter *vt vi* to graze.

broyer *vt* to grind, pulverize.

broyeur *adj* crushing, grinding.

bruine *f* drizzle.

bruissement *m* rustle.

bruit *m* noise, sound.

bruitage *m* sound-effects.

brûlant *adj* burning, scorching.

brûler *vt vi* to burn.

brûlure *f* burn.

brume *f* haze, mist.

brumeux *adj* hazy, misty.

brun *m* dark-haired man, **brune** *f* brunette; * *adj* brown.

brusque *adj* brusque, abrupt; **~ment** *adv* brusquely, abruptly.

brusquer *vt* to offend; to hasten.

brut *adj* crude, raw.

brutal *adj* brutal, rough; **~ement** *adv* brutally, roughly.

brutaliser *vt* to brutalize; to bully.

brutalité *f* brutality.

brute *f* brute; beast.

bruyamment *adv* noisily.

bruyant *adj* noisy.

bruyère *f* heather.

bûche *f* log.

bûcheron *m* **-ne** *f* woodcutter, lumberjack.

budget *m* budget.

budgétaire *adj* budgetary.

buée *f* condensation; steam.

buffet *m* sideboard, buffet.

buisson *m* bush.

bulbe *m* bulb.

bulle *f* bubble; blister.

bulletin *m* bulletin.

buraliste *mf* tobacconist.

bureau *m* office; desk.

bureaucrate *mf* bureaucrat.

bureaucratie *f* bureaucracy.

bureaucratique *adj* bureaucratic.

burin *m* chisel.

bus *m* bus.
buste *m* bust, chest.
but *m* objective, goal.
butane *m* butane.
buté *adj* stubborn.
butin *m* booty, loot.

butte *f* knoll, mound.
buvable *adj* drinkable.
buvard *m* blotting paper.
buvette *f* refreshment-room.
buveur *m* **-euse** *f* drinker.

C

ça *pn* that; it; ~ **va?** How goes it?; ~ **y est** that's it; **qui ~?** who (do you mean)?; **comment ~?** how (do you mean)?; ~ **alors!** you don't say!
cabale *f* cabal, intrigue.
cabane *f* cabin, shed.
cabanon *m* cottage; chalet.
cabaret *m* cabaret; tavern.
cabine *f* cabin, cab; cockpit.
cabinet *m* surgery; office, study.
câble *m* cable.
câbler *vt* to cable.
cabosser *vt* to dent.
cabotage *m* coastal navigation.
cabriolet *m* convertible.
cacahuète *f* peanut.
cacao *m* cocoa.
cache *m* cache; mask; hiding place.
caché *adj* hidden, secluded.
cache-col *m invar* scarf.
cache-nez *m invar* scarf, muffler.
cacher *vt* to hide, conceal; **se ~** *vr* to hide o.s.
cacheter *vt* to seal.
cachette *f* hideout, hiding place.
cachot *m* dungeon, prison cell.
cachottier *m* **-ière** *f* secretive.
cactus *m* cactus.
cadavre *m* corpse.
cadeau *m* present.
cadenas *m* padlock.
cadenasser *vt* to padlock.
cadence *f* rhythm, time, cadence.
cadet *m* **-te** *f* youngest child.
cadrage *m* framing.
cadran *m* dial, face.
cadre *m* frame; context; scope.
cadrer *vt* to centre; to fit with.
caduc *adj*, *f* **caduque** null and void; obsolete.

cafard *m* hypocrite; cockroach.
café *m* coffee.
cafétéria *f* cafeteria.
cafetière *f* coffeepot.
cage *f* cage.
cageot *m* crate.
cagoule *f* cowl; balaclava.
cahier *m* notebook.
cahot *m* jerk, jolt.
caillot *m* clot.
caillou *m* stone; pebble.
caisse *f* box; till; fund.
caissier *m* **-ière** *f* cashier.
cajoler *vt* to cajole, coax; to pet.
cajou *m* cashew.
calamité *f* calamity.
calcaire *m* calcareous, chalky.
calcination *f* calcination.
calciner *vt* to calcine; to char.
calcium *m* calcium.
calcul *m* sum, calculation.
calculateur *adj*, *f* **-trice** calculating.
calculatrice, calculette *f* calculator.
calculer *vt* to calculate, reckon; * *vi* to budget carefully.
cale *f* (*mar*) wedge, hold.
caleçon *m* shorts, pants.
calembour *m* pun.
calendrier *m* calendar.
calepin *m* notebook.
caler *vi* to stall; to give up; to wedge.
calfeutrer *vt* to make airtight, draughtproof.
calibre *m* calibre, bore.
calibrer *vt* to calibrate.
calice *m* chalice.
câlin *m* cuddle; * *adj* cuddly.
câliner *vt* to cuddle.
calligraphie *f* calligraphy.

callosité *f* callosity.

calmant *m* tranquillizer, sedative; * *adj* tranquillizing.

calmar *m* squid.

calme *m* calm, stillness; * *adj* calm, still; ~**ment** *adv* calmly, quietly.

calmer *vt* calm, soothe, pacify.

calomnie *f* slander, calumny.

calomnier *vt* to slander; to libel.

calomnieux *adj* slanderous, calumnious.

calorie *f* calorie.

calorifique *adj* calorific.

calque *m* tracing; copy.

calquer *vt* to trace; to copy.

calvaire *m* calvary; ordeal.

calvitie *f* baldness.

camarade *mf* companion, friend.

camaraderie *f* camaraderie, friendship.

cambouis *m* dirty grease.

cambré *adj* arched.

cambriolage *m* burglary.

cambrioler *vt* to burgle.

cambrioleur *m* -**euse** *f* burglar.

caméléon *m* chameleon.

camélia *m* camellia.

caméra *f* camera.

camion *m* lorry.

camionneur *m* lorry driver, trucker.

camomille *f* camomile.

camouflage *m* camouflage.

camoufler *vt* to camouflage.

camp *m* camp.

campagnard *m* countryman, -**e** *f* countrywoman; * *adj* country, rustic.

campagne *f* country, countryside.

campement *m* camp, encampment.

camper *vi* to camp.

campeur *m* -**euse** *f* camper.

canal *m* canal, channel.

canalisation *f* canalization; mains.

canaliser *vt* to channel, funnel.

canapé *m* sofa, settee.

canard *m* duck.

cancer *m* cancer.

cancéreux *adj* cancerous.

candeur *f* ingeniousness.

candidat *m* -**e** *f* candidate.

candidature *f* candidature, candidacy.

candide *adj* guileless, ingenuous; ~**ment** *adv* openly, ingenuously.

canevas *m* canvas; framework.

canicule *m* heatwave.

canif *m* penknife.

canine *f* eye tooth.

caniveau *m* gutter.

canne *f* cane, rod.

cannelle *f* cinnamon.

canoè *m* canoe.

canon *m* cannon, gun.

canot *m* boat, dinghy.

cantate *f* cantata.

cantatrice *f* opera singer.

cantine *f* canteen.

cantique *m* canticle, hymn.

canton *m* canton.

cantonner (se) *vr* to take up position in.

caoutchouc *m* rubber.

cap *f* cape; course.

capable *adj* capable, competent.

capacité *f* capacity.

cape *f* cloak.

capillaire *adj* capillary.

capitaine *m* captain.

capital *adj* capital, cardinal, major; * *m* capital, stock.

capitale *f* capital (letter, city).

capitalisme *m* capitalism.

capitaliste *mf* capitalist.

capiteux *adj* heady, strong.

capitonner *vt* to pad.

capitulation *f* capitulation.

capituler *vt* to capitulate.

caporal *m* corporal.

capot *m* bonnet, hood.

capote *f* great-coat, hood.

capoter *vt* to capsize, overturn.

câpre *m* caper.

caprice *m* caprice, whim.

capricieusement *adv* capriciously.

capricieux *adj* capricious.

capricorne *m* capricorn.

capsule *f* capsule.

capter *vt* to catch; to pick up.

capteur *m* captor; pick-up.

captif *m* -**ive** *f* captive; * *adj* captive.

captivant *adj* enthralling, captivating.

captiver *vt* to captivate, enthral.

captivité *f* captivity.

capture *f* capture.

capturer *vt* to capture.

capuche *f* hood.

car *conj* for; because; * *m* bus; van.

carabine *f* carbine, rifle.

caractère *m* character, disposition.

caractérisé *adj* marked, blatant.

caractériser *vt* to characterize.

caractéristique *f* characteristic, feature; * *adj* characteristic.

carafe *f* carafe.

carambolage *m* pile-up (car).

caramel *m* caramel.

caraméliser *vt* to caramelize.

carapace *f* carapace, shell.

carat *m* carat.

caravane *f* caravan.

caravelle *f* caravel.

carbonate *m* carbonate.

carbone *m* carbon.

carbonique *adj* carbonic.

carboniser *vt* to carbonize; to char.

carburant *m* motor-fuel.

carburateur *m* carburettor.

carburation *f* carburation.

carbure *m* carbide.

carcasse *f* carcass.

carcéral *adj* prison.

cardiaque *adj* cardiac.

cardigan *m* cardigan.

cardinal *m* cardinal; * *adj* cardinal.

cardiologie *f* cardiology.

cardiologue *m* cardiologist.

cardio-vasculaire *adj* cardiovascular.

carême *m* fast, fasting.

carence *f* deficiency; insolvency.

caressant *adj* affectionate.

caresse *f* caress.

caresser *vt* to caress, fondle.

cargaison *f* cargo, freight.

cargo *m* cargo-boat.

caricatural *adj* caricatural; grotesque.

caricature *f* caricature.

caricaturer *vt* to caricature.

caricaturiste *m* caricaturist.

carie *f* decay; caries.

carié *adj* decayed.

carillon *m* carillon, chime, peal.

caritatif *adj* charitable.

carnage *m* carnage.

carnassier *m* carnivore, **-ière** *f* gamebag; * *adj* carnivorous.

carnaval *m* carnival.

carnet *m* notebook.

carnivore *mf* carnivore; *adj* carnivorous.

carotide *f* carotid.

carotte *f* carrot.

carpe *f* carp.

carpette *f* rug, doormat.

carré *m* square; * *adj* square; straightforward.

carreau *m* tile; pane.

carrefour *m* crossroads.

carrelage *m* tiling.

carrément *adv* bluntly, directly.

carrière *f* career.

carrosse *m* coach.

carrosserie *f* bodywork, coachwork.

carrossier *m* coachbuilder.

carrure *f* build, stature.

cartable *m* satchel.

carte *f* card; map.

cartel *m* cartel.

cartésien *adj* Cartesian.

cartilage *m* cartilage.

cartilagineux *adj* cartilaginous.

cartomancien *m* **-ne** *f* fortune-teller.

carton *m* cardboard.

cartonner *vt* to bind (book).

cartouche *f* cartridge.

cas *m* case; circumstance.

casanier *m* **-ière** *f* homebody.

cascade *f* waterfall; stunt.

cascadeur *m* **-euse** *f* acrobat, stuntman.

case *f* square; box.

caser *vt* (*fam*) to set up (job, marriage).

caserne *f* barracks.

casier *m* compartment; filing cabinet.

casino *m* casino.

casque *m* helmet.

casquette *f* peaked cap.

cassant *adj* brittle.

casse-croûte *m invar* snack.

casser *vt* to break; **se ~** *vr* to break.

casserole *f* saucepan.

casse-tête *m invar* puzzle, conundrum.

cassette *f* cassette; cash-box.

cassis *m* blackcurrant.

cassure *f* break, crack.

caste *f* caste.

castor *m* beaver.

castration *f* castration.

castrer *vt* to castrate.

cataclysme *m* cataclysm.

catacombe *f* catacomb.

catalogue *m* catalogue.

cataloguer *vt* to catalogue.

catalyseur *m* catalyst.

catalytique *adj* catalytic.

cataplasme *m* cataplasm.

catapulte *f* catapult.

cataracte *f* cataract.

catastrophe *f* catastrophe.

catastrophique *adj* catastrophic.

catéchisme *m* catechism.

catégorie *f* category.

catégorique *adj* categorical; ~**ment** *adv* categorically.

cathédrale *f* cathedral.

cathode *f* cathode.

cathodique *adj* cathodic.

catholicisme *m* Catholicism.

catholique *adj* Catholic.

cauchemar *m* nightmare.

cause *f* cause, reason.

causer *vt* to cause; to chat; * *vi* to talk, chat.

caustique *adj* caustic.

caution *f* deposit; guarantee.

cautionner *vt* to guarantee.

cavalerie *f* cavalry.

cavalier *m* -**ière** *f* rider.

cave *f* cellar.

caveau *m* tomb; small cellar.

caverne *f* cave, cavern.

caverneux *adj* cavernous.

caviar *m* caviar.

cavité *f* cavity.

ce *adj* **cet** (*before vowel and mute h*), *f* **cette**, *pl* **ces** this, these; **cet homme-là** that man; * *pn*: **c'est le facteur** it's the postman; ~ **sont mes lunettes** these are my glasses; ~ **que tu veux** what you want; **c'est ~ dont je**

vous parle that's what I am speaking to you about.

ceci *pn* this.

cécité *f* blindness.

céder *vi* to give in; * *vt* to give up, transfer.

ceindre *vt* to put round, encircle.

ceinture *f* belt, girdle.

ceinturer *vt* to surround.

ceinturon *m* belt.

cela *pn* that; *emphasis* **qui** ~? who? (do you mean)?; **comment** ~? how? (do you mean?).

célébration *f* celebration.

célèbre *adj* famous.

célébrer *vt* to celebrate.

célébrité *f* fame, celebrity.

célérité *f* celerity, speed.

céleste *adj* celestial.

célibat *m* celibacy.

célibataire *mf* single person; * *adj* single, unmarried.

cellulaire *adj* cellular.

cellule *f* cell, unit.

cellulite *f* cellulite.

celluloïd *m* celluloid.

cellulose *f* cellulose.

celui *pn*, *f* **celle** this one, *pl* **ceux** these ones.

cendre *f* ash.

cendrier *m* ashtray.

censé *adj* supposed; deemed.

censure *f* censorship.

censurer *vt* to censor.

cent *adj* a hundred; **tu as** ~ **fois raison** you are absolutely right; **faire les** ~ **pas** to walk up and down; * *m* a hundred; **pour** ~ per cent.

centaine *f* about a hundred, a hundred or so.

centenaire *m* centenarian; * *adj* a hundred years old.

centésimal *adj* centesimal.

centième *mf* hundredth; * *adj* hundredth.

centigrade *m* centigrade.

centigramme *m* centigram.

centime *m* centime.

centimètre *m* centimetre.

central *adj* central.

centraliser *vt* to centralize.

centre *m* centre.

centrer *vt* to centre, focus.

centrifuge *adj* centrifugal.

centuple *adj* centuple, hundredfold; * *mf* centuple.

cependant *conj* however.

céramique *f* ceramic.

cerceau *m* hoop.

cercle *m* circle, ring.

cercueil *m* coffin.

céréale *f* cereal.

cérébral *adj* cerebral.

cérémonial *adj* ceremonial.

cérémonie *f* ceremony.

cérémonieux *adj* ceremonious.

cerf-volant *m* kite.

cerise *f* cherry.

cerisier *m* cherry tree.

cerne *f* ring.

cerner *vt* to circle, encompass.

certain *adj* certain, sure; **~ement** *adv* certainly, most probably; **~s** *pn* some, certain people.

certificat *m* certificate.

certifier *vt* to certify; to guarantee.

certitude *f* certainty, certitude.

cerveau *m* brain.

cervelle *f* brains.

cervical *adj* cervical.

césarienne *f* Caesarean.

cesser *f* to cease, stop.

cessez-le-feu *m* cease-fire.

cet *adj*, *f* **cette** *see* **ce.**

cétacé *m* cetacean.

ceux *see* **ce.**

chacun *pn* each one; **~e d'entre elles** each of them; **~ son tour** each in turn.

chagrin *m* sorrow, grief.

chahut *m* row, uproar.

chahuter *vi* to make a row.

chaîne *f* chain.

chaînon *m* link.

chair *f* flesh.

chaise *f* chair.

châle *m* shawl.

châlet *m* chalet.

chaleur *f* heat.

chaleureusement *adv* warmly.

chaleureux *adj* warm, cordial.

chalumeau *m* blowlamp.

chalutier *m* trawler.

chambre *f* room.

chameau *m* camel.

champ *m* field.

champêtre *adj* rural, country.

champignon *m* mushroom.

champion *m* **-ne** *f* champion.

championnat *m* championship.

chance *f* luck.

chancelant *adj* staggering, tottering.

chanceler *vi* to stagger, totter.

chancelier *m* chancellor.

chanceux *adj* lucky, fortunate.

chandail *m* sweater.

chandeleur *f* Candlemas.

chandelier *m* candlestick.

chandelle *f* candle.

changeant *adj* changeable, variable.

changement *m* change, changing.

changer *vi* to change; * *vt* to change.

chanson *f* song.

chant *m* song; singing.

chantage *m* blackmail.

chanter *vt* *vi* to sing.

chanteur *m* **-euse** *f* singer.

chantier *m* building site.

chantonner *vt* *vi* to hum.

chanvre *m* hemp.

chaos *m* chaos.

chaotique *adj* chaotic.

chapeau *m* hat.

chapelet *m* rosary; string.

chapelle *f* chapel.

chapiteau *m* capital (column).

chapitre *m* chapter.

chaque *adj* each.

char *m* (*mil*) tank; chariot.

charabia *m* gibberish.

charbon *m* coal.

charcuterie *f* pork meat trade.

charcutier *m* **-ière** *f* pork butcher.

chardon *m* thistle.

charge *f* load; responsibility.

chargé *adj* loaded.

chargement *m* loading; freight.

charger *vt* to load; **se ~ de** to take responsibility for, attend to.

chariot *m* waggon; freight car.

charisme *m* charisma.

charitable *adj* charitable, kind; **~ment** *adv* charitably.

charité *f* charity.

charlatan *m* charlatan.

charmant *adj* charming, delightful.

charme *m* charm.

charmer *vt* to charm, beguile.

charmeur *m* **-euse** *f* charmer; * *adj* winning, enchanting.

charnel *adj* carnal.

charnière *f* hinge, pivot.

charnu *adj* fleshy.

charogne *f* carrion.

charpente *f* structure, framework.

charpentier *m* carpenter.

charrette *f* cart.

charrier *vt* to cart, carry.

charrue *f* plough.

chasse *f* hunting; chase.

chasse-neige *m invar* snowplough.

chasser *vt* to hunt, chase.

chasseur *m* **-euse** *f* hunter.

châssis *m* chassis.

chaste *adj* chaste; **~ment** *adv* chastely.

chasteté *f* chastity.

chat *m*, **chatte** *f* cat.

châtaigne *f* chestnut.

châtain *adj* chestnut brown.

château *m* castle.

châtiment *m* chastisement, punishment.

chaton *m* kitten.

chatouiller *vt* to tickle.

chatoyant *adj* shimmering.

châtrer *vt* to castrate.

chaud *adj* warm, hot; **~ement** *adv* warmly, hotly.

chaudière *f* boiler.

chaudron *m* cauldron.

chauffage *m* heating.

chauffard *m* road-hog.

chauffe-eau *m invar* water-heater.

chauffer *vi* to heat; * *vt* to heat up.

chauffeur *m* driver.

chaumière *f* cottage.

chaussée *f* road, street.

chausse-pied *m* shoehorn.

chaussette *f* sock.

chausson *m* slipper.

chaussure *f* shoe.

chauve *adj* bald.

chauve-souris *f* bat.

chauvin *adj*, *f* **chauvine** chauvinistic.

chauvinisme *m* chauvinism.

chaux *f* lime.

chavirer *vi* to capsize, overturn.

chef *m* head, boss; chef.

chef-d'œuvre *m* masterpiece.

chemin *m* way, road; **~ de fer** railway.

cheminée *f* chimney.

cheminement *m* progress; course.

chemise *f* shirt.

chemisier *m* shirtmaker.

chêne *m* oak.

chenil *m* kennel.

chenille *f* caterpillar.

chèque *m* cheque.

chéquier *m* chequebook.

cher *adj*, *f* **chère** dear; expensive.

chercher *vt* to look for.

chercheur *m* **-euse** *f* researcher; seeker.

chéri *m* **-ie** *f* darling, dearest; * *adj* beloved, cherished.

chétif *adj* puny, paltry.

cheval *m* horse.

chevalet *m* easel.

chevalier *m* knight.

chevelu *adj* long-haired.

chevelure *f* hair, head of hair.

chevet *m* chevet; bedside.

cheveu *m* hair.

cheville *f* ankle.

chèvre *f* goat.

chèvrefeuille *m* honeysuckle.

chevreuil *m* roe deer.

chez *prép* at home: **je rentre ~ moi** I'm going home; **~ ta tante** at your aunt's.

chic *m* style, stylishness; **avoir le ~ pour** to have the knack for.

chicorée *f* chicory.

chien *m*, **chienne** *f* dog.

chiffon *m* rag, cloth.

chiffonné *adj* crumpled, rumpled.

chiffre *m* figure.

chignon *m* chignon, bun.

chimère *f* chimera.
chimérique *adj* chimerical, fanciful.
chimie *f* chemistry.
chimique *adj* chemical; **~ment** *adv* chemically.
chimiste *mf* chemist.
chimpanzé *m* chimpanzee.
chiot *m* puppy.
chipoteur *m* **-euse** *f* haggler.
chirurgical *adj* surgical.
chirurgie *f* surgery.
chirurgien *m* surgeon.
chlore *m* chlorine.
chloroforme *m* chloroform.
chlorophyle *f* chlorophyll.
chlorure *m* chloride.
choc *m* shock, crash.
chocolat *m* chocolate.
chœur *m* choir, chorus.
choir *vi* to fall.
choisir *vt* to choose.
choix *m* choice.
choléra *m* cholera.
chômage *m* unemployment.
chômeur *m* **-euse** *f* unemployed person.
choquant *adj* shocking, appalling.
choquer *vt* to shock.
chorale *f* choral.
chorégraphe *mf* choreographer.
choréraphie *f* choreography.
choriste *mf* chorister.
chose *f* thing, matter, object.
chou *m* cabbage.
chouette *f* owl.
chou-fleur *m* cauliflower.
choyer *vt* to cherish.
chrétien *m* **-ne** *f* Christian, *adj* christian.
christianisme *m* Christianity.
chrome *m* chromium.
chromosome *m* chromosome.
chronique *adj* chronic; * *f* chronicle; column; page.
chronologie *f* chronology.
chronologique *adj* chronological; **~ment** *adv* chronologically.
chronomètre *m* chronometer.
chronométrer *vt* to time.
chrysanthème *m* chrysanthemum.

chuchotement *m* whisper, rustling.
chuchoter *vi* to whisper.
chuintement *m* hissing.
chuinter *vi* to hiss.
chute *f* fall, drop.
chuter *vi* to fall.
ci *adv*: **ces fleurs-ci** these flowers; **ci-joint** enclosed; **ci-dessous** below; **ci-contre** opposite; in the margin; annexed.
cible *f* target.
cibler *vt* to target.
cicatrice *f* scar.
cicatrisation *f* cicatrization, healing.
cicatriser *vt* to heal; **se ~** *vr* to heal, form a scar.
cidre *m* cider.
ciel *m*, *pl* **cieux, ciels** sky.
cierge *m* candle.
cigale *f* cicada.
cigare *m* cigar.
cigarette *f* cigarette.
cil *m* eyelash.
ciller *vi* to blink.
cime *f* summit.
ciment *m* cement.
cimenter *vt* to cement.
cimetière *m* cemetery.
cinéaste *mf* film-maker.
cinéma *m* cinema.
cinémathèque *f* film library.
cinématographique *adj* film, cinema.
cinéphile *mf* film enthusiast.
cinétique *adj* kinetic.
cinglant *adj* bitter, lashing, cutting.
cingler *vt* to lash, sting.
cinq *m* five.
cinquantaine *f* about fifty.
cinquante *m* fifty.
cinquantenaire *m* fiftieth anniversary.
cinquantième *mf* fiftieth, *adj* fiftieth.
cinquième *mf* fifth, *adj* fifth; **~ment** *adv* in fifth place.
cintre *m* arch.
cirage *m* polish.
circonférence *f* circumference.
circonscription *f* division, constituency.
circonspect *adj* circumspect.
circonstance *f* circumstance.

circuit *m* circuit, tour.

circulaire *adj* circular; **~ment** *adv* circularly.

circulation *f* circulation; traffic.

circuler *vi* to circulate, move.

cire *f* wax.

cirer *vt* to polish.

cirque *m* circus.

ciseau *m* chisel; **~x** *pl* scissors.

citadelle *f* citadel.

citadin *m* **-e** *f* city dweller; * *adj* town, urban.

citation *f* citation, summons.

cité *f* city.

citer *vt* to quote, cite.

citerne *f* water tank.

citoyen *m* **-ne** *f* citizen.

citron *m* lemon.

citrouille *f* pumpkin.

civière *f* stretcher.

civil *adj* civil; **~ement** *adv* civilly.

civilisation *f* civilization.

civilisé *adj* civilized.

civiliser *vt* to civilize.

civique *adj* civic.

clair *adj* clear, bright; **~ement** *adv* clearly.

clairière *f* clearing, glade.

clairsemé *adj* scattered.

clairvoyance *f* perspicacity; clairvoyance.

clairvoyant *adj* perceptive; clairvoyant.

clameur *f* clamour.

clan *m* clan.

clandestin *adj* clandestine; **~ement** clandestinely.

clandestinité *f* secrecy.

clapoter *vi* to lap (water).

clapotis *m* lapping.

claque *f* slap, smack.

claquement *m* clapping, slamming.

claquer *vi* to bang, slam.

clarifier *vt* to clarify; **se ~** *vr* to become clear.

clarinette *f* clarinet.

clarté *f* light, brightness.

classe *f* class, standing.

classement *m* filing; grading.

classer *vt* to file, classify.

classeur *m* filing cabinet.

classification *f* classification.

classique *adj* classical, standard; **~ment** *adv* classically.

clause *f* clause.

claustrer *vt* to confine.

claustrophobie *f* claustrophobia.

clavecin *m* harpsichord.

clavicule *f* collarbone.

clavier *m* keyboard.

clé, clef *f* key.

clémence *f* clemency, mildness.

clergé *m* clergy.

cliché *m* cliché; negative.

client *m* **-e** *f* client.

clientèle *f* clientele; customers.

cligner *vi* to blink.

clignotant *adj* blinking, flickering; * *m* indicator.

clignotement *m* blinking, flickering.

clignoter *vi* to blink, flicker.

climat *m* climate.

climatique *adj* climatic.

climatisation *f* air-conditioning.

climatiser *vt* to air-condition.

clin d'œil *m* wink.

clinique *f* clinic.

cliqueter *vi* to jingle, clink.

clitoris *m* clitoris.

clochard *m* **-e** *f* tramp.

cloche *f* bell.

clocher *m* steeple, bell tower.

clochette *f* hand-bell.

cloison *f* partition.

cloîtrer (se) *vr* to enter the monastic life.

clore *vt* to close, conclude.

clos *adj* closed, enclosed.

clôture *f* fence, hedge.

clou *m* nail.

clouer *vt* to nail.

club *m* club.

coagulation *f* coagulation.

coaguler *vi* to coagulate.

coaliser *vt vi* to form a coalition.

coalition *f* coalition.

cobalt *m* cobalt.

cobaye *m* guinea-pig.

cobra *m* cobra.

cocaïne *f* cocaine.

coccinelle *f* ladybird.

coccyx *m* coccyx.

cocher *vt* to notch; to tick off.

cochon *m* **-ne** *f* pig.
code *m* code.
coder *vt* to code.
codifier *vt* to codify.
coefficient *m* coefficient.
coéquipier *m* **-ière** *f* team mate.
cœur *m* heart.
coexister *vi* to coexist.
coffre *m* chest; **~-fort** safe.
coffret *m* casket.
cogner *vi* to hammer, bang.
cohabitation *f* cohabitation.
cohabiter *vi* to cohabit.
cohérence *f* coherence.
cohérent *adj* coherent.
cohésion *f* cohesion.
cohue *f* crowd.
coiffer *vt* to arrange sb's hair; **se ~** *vr* to do one's hair.
coiffeur *m* **-euse** *f* hairdresser.
coiffure *f* hairstyle.
coin *m* corner.
coincer *vt* to wedge, jam.
coïncidence *f* coincidence.
coït *m* coitus.
col *m* collar; neck.
colère *f* anger.
colérique *adj* quick-tempered, irascible.
colibri *m* hummingbird.
colique *f* diarrhoea.
colis *m* parcel.
collaborateur *m* **-trice** *f* collaborator, colleague.
collaboration *f* collaboration.
collaborer *vi* to collaborate.
collant *adj* clinging, sticky; * *m* leotard.
collecte *f* collection.
collectif *adj* collective.
collection *f* collection.
collectionner *vt* to collect.
collectionneur *m* **-euse** *f* collector.
collectivement *adv* collectively.
collectivité *f* community; collective ownership.
collège *m* secondary school.
collègue *mf* colleague.
coller *vt* to stick, glue; * *vi* to stick, be sticky.
collier *m* necklace.

colline *f* hill.
collision *f* collision.
colloque *m* colloquium.
colocataire *mf* co-tenant.
colombe *f* dove.
colon *m* colonist.
colonel *m* colonel.
colonie *f* colony.
colonisation *f* colonization.
coloniser *vt* to colonize.
colonne *f* column.
colorant *m* colouring.
coloration *f* colouring, staining.
coloré *adj* coloured.
colorier *vt* to colour in.
coloris *m* colouring, shade.
colossal *adj* colossal.
colporter *vt* to peddle.
colza *m* rape seed.
coma *m* coma.
comateux *adj* comatose.
combat *m* combat, fight.
combatif *adj* combative.
combativité *f* combativeness.
combattant *adj* fighting, combatant.
combattre *vt* to fight, combat; * *vi* to fight.
combien *adv* how much, how many; **~ de temps?** how much time?; **~ sont-ils?** how many are they?
combinaison *f* combination.
combiner *vt* to combine.
comble *m* height, peak.
combler *vt* to fill; to fulfil.
combustible *m* fuel.
combustion *f* combustion.
comédie *f* comedy.
comédien *m* **-ne** *f* actor.
comestible *adj* edible.
comète *f* comet.
comique *adj* comic; **~ment** *adv* comically.
comité *m* committee.
commandant *m* commander.
commande *f* command, order.
commandement *m* command, commandment.
commander *vt* *vi* to order, command.
commanditer *vt* to finance, sponsor.
commando *m* commando.

comme *conj* as, like; ~ **ci** ~ **ça** so-so; ~ **il faut** properly; * *adv* how.

commémoration *f* commemoration.

commémorer *vt* to commemorate.

commencement *m* beginning, start.

commencer *vt vi* to begin, start.

comment *adv* how; ~ **dire?** how shall we say?; ~ **cela?** what do you mean?

commentaire *m* comment; commentary.

commentateur *m* **-trice** *f* commentator.

commenter *vt* to comment.

commérage *m* piece of gossip.

commerçant *m* **-e** *f* merchant, trader.

commerce *m* business, commerce.

commercial *adj* commercial; ~**ement** *adv* commercially.

commercialiser *vt* to market.

commère *f* gossip.

commettre *vt* to commit.

commissaire *m* representative; commissioner.

commissariat *m* police station; commissionership; commissariat.

commission *f* commission, committee.

commissionnaire *m* messenger; agent.

commode *adj* convenient, comfortable.

commodité *f* convenience.

commun *adj* common, joint; ~**ément** *adv* commonly.

communal *adj* council; common, communal.

communautaire *adj* community.

communauté *f* community; joint estate.

commune *f* town, district.

communication *f* communication.

communier *vi* to receive communion.

communion *f* communion.

communiqué *m* communiqué.

communiquer *vt* to communicate, transmit; * *vi* to communicate.

communisme *m* communism.

communiste *mf* communist.

compact *adj* compact, dense.

compagne *f* companion.

compagnie *f* company.

compagnon *m* companion.

comparable *adj* comparable.

comparaison *f* comparison.

comparaître *vi* to appear.

comparativement *adv* comparatively.

comparer *vt* to compare.

compartiment *m* compartment.

compartimenter *vt* to compart, partition.

compas *m* compass.

compassion *f* compassion.

compatibilité *f* compatibility.

compatible *adj* compatible.

compatir *vi* to sympathize.

compatissant *adj* compassionate.

compatriote *mf* compatriot.

compensation *f* compensation.

compenser *vt* to compensate; to offset; **se** ~ *vr* to balance each other, make up for.

compétence *f* competence.

compétent *adj* competent, capable.

compétitif *adj* competitive.

compétition *f* competition.

compétitivité *f* competitiveness.

complaisance *f* kindness; complacency.

complaisant *adj* kind; complacent.

complément *m* complement; extension.

complémentaire *adj* complementary, supplementary.

complet *adj* complete, full.

complètement *adv* completely, fully.

compléter *vt* to complete; **se** ~ *vr* to complement one another.

complexe *adj* complex, complicated.

complexé *adj* mixed up.

complication *f* complication.

complice *mf* accomplice.

complicité *f* complicity, collusion.

compliment *m* compliment.

complimenter *vt* to compliment, congratulate.

compliqué *adj* complicated, intricate.

compliquer *vt* to complicate.

complot *m* plot.

comportement *m* behaviour; performance.

comporter *vt* to consist of, comprise; **se** ~ *vr* to behave.

composant *m* component, constituent.

composante *f* component.

composer *vt* to compose, make up; **se** ~ *vr*: **se** ~ **de** to be made up of.

compositeur *m* **-trice** *f* composer; typesetter.

composition *f* composition, formation.

compréhensible *adj* comprehensible.

compréhensif *adj* comprehensive, understanding.

compréhension *f* comprehension, understanding.

comprendre *vt* to understand; to consist of.

compresse *f* compress.

compresseur *m* compressor.

compression *f* compression; reduction.

comprimé *adj* compressed; restrained; * *m* tablet.

comprimer *vt* to compress; to restrain.

compromettant *adj* compromising.

compromettre *vt* to compromise.

compromis *m* compromise.

comptabilité *f* accountancy.

comptable *adj* accounting; * *mf* accountant.

compte *m* account.

compter *vt vi* to count.

compteur *m* meter.

comptoir *m* counter, bar.

comte *m* count, **comtesse** *f* countess.

concave *adj* concave.

concéder *vt* to grant, concede.

concentration *f* concentration.

concentré *adj* concentrated; reserved.

concentrer *vt* to concentrate; **se ~** *vr* to concentrate.

concept *m* concept.

conception *f* conception, design.

concerner *vt* to concern, regard.

concert *m* concert.

concertation *f* dialogue, consultation.

concession *f* concession; privilege.

concessionnaire *mf* concessionaire, grantee.

concevoir *vt* to imagine, conceive.

concierge *mf* caretaker, concierge.

conciliant *adj* conciliatory.

conciliation *f* conciliation; reconciliation.

concilier *vt* to reconcile; to attract.

concis *adj* concise.

concision *f* conciseness, brevity.

concluant *adj* conclusive, decisive.

conclure *vt* to conclude; to decide; **se ~** *vr* to conclude, come to an end.

conclusion *f* conclusion.

concombre *m* cucumber.

concordance *f* agreement, accord.

concorder *vi* to agree, coincide.

concours *m* competition; conjuncture.

concret *adj* concrete, solid.

concrètement *adv* concretely.

concrétiser *vt* to put in concrete form.

concubin *m* **-e** *f* concubine; cohabitant.

concubinage *m* concubinage; cohabitation.

concurrence *f* competition.

concurrent *m* **-e** *f* concurrent; competitor.

condamnation *f* condemnation; sentencing.

condamné *m* **-e** *f* convict; sentenced person; * *adj* sentenced.

condamner *vt* to condemn; to sentence.

condensation *f* condensation.

condensé *adj* condensed, evaporated.

condenser *vt* to condense, compress.

condescendant *adj* condescending.

condiment *m* condiment.

condition *f* condition, term.

conditionné *adj* conditioned; packaged.

conditionnement *m* conditioning; packaging.

conditionner *vt* to condition; to package.

condoléances *fpl* condolences.

conducteur *m* **-trice** *f* driver; operator.

conduire *vt vi* to lead; to drive.

conduit *m* conduit, pipe.

conduite *f* conduct; driving; behaviour.

cône *m* cone.

confédération *f* confederation.

conférence *f* conference.

conférencier *m* **-ière** *f* speaker; lecturer.

confesser *vt* to confess; **se ~** *vr* to go to confession.

confession *f* confession.

confiance *f* confidence, trust.

confiant *adj* confident; confiding.

confidence *f* confidence; disclosure.

confident *m* **-e** *f* confidant.

confidentiel *adj* confidential; **~lement** *adv* confidentially.

confier *vt* to confide, entrust; **se ~** *vr* to confide in.

confiner *vt* to confine; **se ~** to be confined; *vr*: **se ~ à** to confine o.s. to.

confirmation *f* confirmation.

confirmer *vt* to confirm; **se ~** *vr* to be confirmed.

confiserie *f* confectionery.

confisquer *vt* to confiscate, impound.

confiture *f* jam.

conflictuel *adj* conflicting.

conflit *m* conflict, contention.

confondre *vt* to confuse, mingle.

conforme *adj* consistent; true.

conformément *adv* in accordance with.

conformer *vt* to model; **se ~** *vr* to conform.

conformiste *mf* conformist.

conformité *f* conformity; likeness.

confort *m* comfort.

confortable *adj* comfortable, cosy; **~ment** *adv* comfortably.

confrère *m* colleague.

confrontation *f* confrontation; comparison.

confronter *vt* to confront.

confus *adj* confused, indistinct; **~ément** *adv* confusedly, vaguely.

confusion *f* confusion, disorder.

congé *m* leave; holiday.

congédier *vt* to dismiss.

congélateur *m* freezer.

congeler *vt* to freeze.

congestion *f* congestion; stroke.

congratulation *f* congratulation.

congratuler *vt* to congratulate.

congrégation *f* congregation.

congrès *m* congress, conference.

conifère *m* conifer.

conjoint *m* **-e** *f* spouse; * *adj* joint; linked; **~ement** *adv* jointly.

conjonctivite *f* conjunctivitis.

conjoncture *f* conjuncture; situation.

conjugaison *f* conjugation.

conjugal *adj* conjugal.

conjuguer *vt* to conjugate; to combine.

conjuration *f* conspiracy, plot.

conjurer *vt* to conspire; to implore; to ward off.

connaissance *f* knowledge; consciousness.

connaisseur *m* **-euse** *f* connoisseur; expert.

connaître *vt* to know, be acquainted with.

connecter *vt* to connect.

connecteur *m* connective.

connexion *f* connection, link.

connivence *f* connivance.

connotation *f* connotation.

connu *adj* known; famous.

conquérant *m* **-e** *f* conqueror; * *adj* conquering.

conquérir *vt* to conquer.

conquête *f* conquest.

conquis *adj* conquered, vanquished.

consacrer *vt* to devote, dedicate; **se ~** *vr* to dedicate o.s. to.

consciemment *adv* consciously, knowingly.

conscience *f* consciousness; conscience.

consciencieusement *adv* conscientiously.

consciencieux *adv* conscientious.

conscient *adj* conscious, aware.

consécration *f* consecration.

consécutif *adj* consecutive.

consécutivement *adv* consecutively.

conseil *m* advice, counsel.

conseiller *m* **-ère** *f* counsellor, adviser; * *vt* to advise, counsel.

consentant *adj* consenting, willing.

consentement *m* consent.

consentir *vi* to consent, acquiesce.

conséquence *f* consequence, result.

conséquent *adj* consequent; substantial.

conservateur *m* **-trice** *f* conservative; curator.

conservation *f* conservation.

conservatoire *m* conservatory; academy.

conserve *f* canned food.

conserver *vt* to keep, preserve; **se ~** *vr* to keep.

considérable *adj* considerable; notable; **~ment** *adv* considerably.

considération *f* consideration, respect.

considérer *vt* to consider, regard.

consigne *f* orders, instructions.

consistance *f* consistency; strength.

consister *vi*: **~ en** to consist of; **cela consiste à** that consists in doing.

consolation *f* consolation, solace.

console *f* console.

consoler *vt* to console, comfort.

consolidation *f* consolidation, reinforcement.

consolider *vt* to consolidate, reinforce.

consommateur *m* **-trice** *f* consumer.

consommation *f* consumption; accomplishment.

consommé *adj* consummate, accomplished; * *m* consommé.

consommer *vt* to consume, use.

consonne *f* consonant.

conspirateur *m* **-trice** *f* conspirator.

conspiration *f* conspiracy, plot.

conspirer *vi* to conspire, plot.

constamment *adv* constantly, continually.

constant *adj* constant, continuous.

constante *f* constancy.

constat *m* report; acknowledgement.

constatation *f* authentication, verification.

constater *vt* to record; to verify.

constellation *f* constellation, galaxy.

consternation *f* consternation, dismay.

consterner *vt* to dismay.

constipation *f* constipation.

constituer *vt* to constitute, form.

constitution *f* constitution, formation.

constitutionnel *adj* constitutional; **~lement** *adv* constitutionally.

constructeur *m* **-trice** *f* builder, maker.

constructif *adj* constructive.

construction *f* building, construction.

construire *vt* to construct, build.

consul *m* consul.

consulaire *adj* consular.

consulat *m* consulate.

consultant *m* **-e** *f* consultant; * *adj* consulting.

consultation *f* consultation, advice.

consulter *vt* to consult, take advice from.

consumer *vt* to consume, spend; **se ~** *vr* to be burning, waste away.

contact *m* contact, touch.

contacter *vt* to contact, approach.

contagieux *adj* contagious, infectious.

contamination *f* contamination, pollution.

contaminer *vt* to contaminate, pollute.

conte *m* story, tale.

contemplation *f* contemplation, meditation.

contempler *vt* to contemplate, meditate.

contemporain *adj* contemporary.

contenance *f* capacity, volume.

contenir *vt* to contain.

contentement *m* contentment, satisfaction.

contenter *vt* to please, satisfy; **se ~** *vr*: **se ~ de** to content o.s. with.

contenu *m* contents, enclosure.

contestation *f* dispute, controversy.

contester *vt* to contest, dispute.

contexte *m* context.

contigu *adj*, *f* **contiguè** contiguous, adjacent.

continent *m* continent.

continental *adj* continental.

contingent *m* quota; (*mil*) draft.

continu *adj* continuous, incessant.

continuation *f* continuation.

continuel *adj* continual, continuous; **~le-ment** *adv* continuously, continually.

continuer *vt* to continue, proceed with; * *vi* to continue, go on.

contour *m* contour, outline.

contourner *vt* to bypass, skirt.

contraceptif *adj* contraceptive.

contraception *f* contraception.

contracter *vt* to contract, acquire; **se ~** *vr* to contract, shrink.

contraction *f* contraction.

contradiction *f* contradiction, discrepancy.

contradictoire *adj* contradictory, conflicting.

contraindre *vt* to constrain, compel.

contrainte *f* constraint, compulsion.

contraire *m* opposite, contrary; * *adj* opposite, contrary; **~ment** *adv* contrarily.

contrariant *adj* contrary; perverse.

contrarier *vt* to annoy; to oppose.

contrariété *f* annoyance, disappointment.

contraste *m* contrast.

contrat *m* contract, agreement.

contre *prép* against; **parier à 10 ~ 1** to bet at 10 to 1; **~ toute attente** contrary to all expectations; **par ~** on the other hand.

contre-attaque *f* counter-attack.

contre-attaquer *vi* to counter-attack.

contrebalancer *vt* to counterbalance.

contrebande *f* contraband, smuggling.

contrebandier *m* **-ière** *f* smuggler.

contrebasse *f* double bass.

contrecarrer *vt* to thwart, oppose.

contrecœur: à ~ reluctantly.

contrecoup *m* rebound, repercussion.

contredire *vt* to contradict, refute.

contrefaçon *f* counterfeit, forgery.

contrefaire *vt* to counterfeit, forge.

contre-indication *f* contraindication.

contremaître *m* foreman.

contre-offensive *f* counter-offensive.

contrepartie *f* compensation; consideration.

contre-plaqué *m* plywood.

contrepoison *m* antidote, counter-poison.

contresens *m* nonsense; misunderstanding; mistranslation.

contretemps *m* mishap; contretemps; (*mus*) syncopation.

contribuable *mf* taxpayer.

contribuer *vt vi* to contribute.

contribution *f* contribution; tax.

contrôle *m* control, check.

contrôler *vt* to control, check.

contrôleur *m* **-euse** *f* inspector; auditor.

controverse *f* controversy.

controversé *adj* disputed.

contusion *f* bruise, contusion.

convaincant *adj* convincing.

convaincre *vt* to convince, persuade.

convaincu *adj* convinced, persuaded.

convalescence *f* convalescence.

convenable *adj* fitting, suitable; **~ment** *adv* suitably, fitly.

convenir *vi* to agree, accord.

convention *f* convention, agreement.

conventionnel *adj* conventional; contractual; **~lement** *adv* conventionally.

convenu *adj* agreed; stipulated.

convergent *adj* convergent.

converger *vi* to converge.

conversation *f* conversation, talk.

conversion *f* conversion.

convertir *vt* to convert; **se ~** *vr* to be converted.

convexe *adj* convex.

conviction *f* conviction.

convier *vt* to invite; to urge.

convivial *adj* convivial; user-friendly.

convocation *f* convocation, summoning.

convoi *m* convoy; train.

convoiter *vt* to covet.

convoquer *vt* to convoke, convene.

convulsion *f* convulsion.

coopératif *adj* cooperative.

coopération *f* cooperation.

coopérative *f* cooperative.

coopérer *vi* to cooperate, collaborate.

coordinateur *m* **-trice** *f* coordinator.

coordination *f* coordination; committee.

coordonnées *fpl* coordinates.

coordonner *vt* to coordinate.

copain *m* friend, pal.

copeau *m* shaving, chip.

copie *f* copy, reproduction.

copier *vt* to copy, reproduce.

copieusement *adv* copiously, abundantly.

copieux *adj* copious, abundant.

copilote *m* co-pilot.

copine *f* friend, mate.

coproduction *f* coproduction.

copropriété *f* co-ownership, joint ownership.

coq *m* cock, rooster.

coque *f* (*mar*) hull; shell.

coquelicot *m* poppy.

coquet *adj* stylish, smart; **~tement** *adv* stylishly, smartly.

coquetterie *f* smartness, stylishness.

coquillage *m* shellfish.

coquille *f* shell, scallop.

coquin *m* **-e** *f* naughty, mischievous.

cor *m* (*mus*) horn; corn.

corail *m* coral.

coran *m* Koran.

corbeau *m* crow.

corbeille *f* basket.

corbillard *m* hearse.

cordage *m* rope; rigging.

corde *f* rope; string.

cordée *f* roped mountaineering party.

cordial *adj* cordial, warm; **~ement** *adv* cordially, warmly.

cordialité *f* cordiality, warmth.

cordon *m* cord, string; cordon.

cordonnerie *f* shoemending.

cordonnier *m* **-ière** *f* shoemender, cobbler.

coriace *adj* tough; tight.

coriandre *m* coriander.

corne *f* horn, antler.

cornée *f* cornea.

corneille *f* crow.

cornemuse *f* bagpipes.

cornet *m* cone, cornet.

corniche *f* cornice; ledge.

cornichon *m* gherkin; greenhorn.

corporatif *adj* corporative, corporate.

corporation *f* corporation, guild.

corporatisme *m* corporatism.

corporel *adj* corporal, bodily.

corps *m* body, corpse.

corpulence *f* corpulence.

corpulent *adj* corpulent.

corpus *m* corpus.

correct *adj* correct, accurate; **~ement** *adv* correctly, accurately.

correcteur *m* **-trice** *f* examiner; proofreader.

correction *f* correction; proofreading.

corrélation *f* correlation.

correspondance *f* correspondence, communication.

correspondant *m* **-e** *f* correspondent; * *adj* corresponding.

correspondre *vi* to correspond, communicate.

corridor *m* corridor, passage.

corrigé *m* corrected version, fair copy.

corriger *vt* to correct.

corroborer *vt* to corroborate.

corroder *vt* to corrode.

corrompre *vt* to corrupt, debase.

corrompu *adj* corrupt.

corrosif *adj* corrosive.

corrosion *f* corrosion.

corruption *f* corruption, debasement.

corsage *m* blouse, bodice.

corsaire *m* corsair.

corsé *adj* rich, full-bodied.

corset *m* corset.

cortège *m* cortège, procession.

cortex *m* cortex.

cortical *adj* cortical.

cortisone *f* cortisone.

corvée *f* fatigue duty; forced labour.

cosmétique *m* cosmetic.

cosmique *adj* cosmic.

cosmonaute *mf* cosmonaut.

cosmopolite *adj* cosmopolitan.

cosmos *m* cosmos.

costume *m* costume, dress.

cotation *f* quotation, valuation.

côte *f* coast; rib; slope.

côté *m* side; point.

coteau *m* hill.

côtelé *adj* ribbed.

côtelette *f* cutlet.

coter *vt* to quote; to classify.

côtier *adj* coastal, inshore.

coton *m* cotton.

cotonneux *adj* fleecy, fluffy.

côtoyer *vt* to mix with, skirt.

cou *m* neck.

couchant *adj* setting.

couche *f* layer, coat.

coucher *vt* to put to bed; **se ~** *vr* to go to bed.

coucou *m* cuckoo.

coude *m* elbow.

coudé *adj* angled, bent.

coudoyer *vt* mix with, rub shoulders with.

coudre *vt* *vi* to sew.

couette *f* duvet.

coulant *adj* flowing; smooth.

couler *vi* to flow, run.

couleur *f* colour, shade.

couleuvre *f* grass snake.

coulis *m* sauce, purée.

coulissant *adj* sliding.

coulisse *f* groove; (*thea*) wings.

coulisser *vi* to slide, run.

couloir *m* corridor, passage.

coup *m* blow; shot; **~ sur ~** one after another, incessantly; **tout à ~** suddenly; **après ~** afterwards, after the event; **~ de feu** shot; **jeter un ~ d'œil** to glance; **~ de coude** nudge; **~ de téléphone** phone call; **~ de soleil** sunstroke.

coupable *mf* culprit; * *adj* guilty.

coupant *adj* cutting, sharp.

coupe *f* cut; cutting.

coupe-papier *m invar* paper knife.

couper *vt* to cut, slice.

couple *m* couple, pair.

couplet *m* couplet, verse.

coupole *f* dome.

coupon *m* coupon, voucher, ticket.

coupure *f* cut; break.

cour *f* court, yard, courtyard.

courage *m* courage, daring.

courageusement *adv* courageously.

courageux *adj* courageous.

couramment *adv* fluently; commonly.

courant *adj* current; present; * *m* stream, current.

courbature *f* stiffness; ache.

courbaturé *adj* aching.

courbe *f* curve; contour.

courbé *adj* curved, stooped.

courber *vt* to curve, bend.

coureur *m* **-euse** *f* runner.

courgette *f* courgette.

courir *vi* to run, race.

couronne *f* crown, wreath.

couronnement *m* coronation.

couronner *vt* to crown.

courrier *m* mail, post.

courroie *f* strap, belt.

cours *m* course; flow; path.

course *f* running; race; flight; journey.

coursier *m* **-ière** *f* courier, messenger.

court *adj* short, brief.

court-bouillon *m* court-bouillon, wine sauce.

court-circuit *m* short-circuit.

court-circuiter *vt* to short-circuit.

courtier *m* **-ière** *f* broker, agent.

courtiser *vt* to court.

courtois *adj* courteous; **~ement** *adv* courteously.

courtoisie *f* courtesy, courteousness.

cousin *m* **-e** *f* cousin.

coussin *m* cushion, pillow.

coussinet *m* pad; bearing.

coût *m* cost, charge.

couteau *m* knife.

coûter *vt* *vi* to cost.

coûteusement *adv* expensively.

coûteux *adj* costly, expensive.

coutume *f* custom, habit.

coutumier *adj* customary, usual.

couture *f* sewing, needlework.

couturier *m* couturier, fashion designer.

couturière *f* dressmaker.

couvent *m* convent.

couver *vt* to hatch, incubate; * *vi* to smoulder, lurk.

couvercle *m* lid, cap.

couvert *m* shelter; cover; pretext; * *adj* covered; secret; obscure.

couverture *f* blanket; cover; roofing.

couvre-feu *m* curfew.

couvreur *m* roofer.

couvrir *vt* to cover; **se ~** *vr* to cover up; to become overcast.

crabe *m* crab.

crachement *m* spitting.

cracher *vt* to spit.

crachin *m* drizzle.

craie *f* chalk.

craindre *vt* to fear.

crainte *f* fear, dread.

craintif *adj* timid, cowardly.

crampe *f* cramp.

crampon *m* stud, spike, crampon.

cramponner *vt* to cramp, clamp; **se ~** *vr* to cling, hang on.

cran *m* notch, cog.

crâne *m* cranium, skull.

crânien *adj* cranial.

crapaud *m* toad.

crapule *f* villain.

crapuleux *adj* villainous, vicious.

craquellement *m* cracking.

craquement *m* crack, creaking, snap.

craquer *vi* to creak, squeak, crack.

crasseux *adj* grimy, filthy.

cratère *m* crater.

cravate *f* tie.

créancier *m* **-ière** *f* creditor.

créateur *m* **-trice** *f* creator, author.

créatif *adj* creative.

création *f* creation.

créativité *f* creativity.

créature *f* creature.

crèche *f* crèche; crib.

crédibilité *f* credibility.

crédible *adj* credible.

crédit *m* credit, trust.

crédit-bail *m* lease; leasing.

crédule *adj* credulous, gullible.

crédulité *f* credulity, gullibility.

créer *vt* to create, produce.

crémaillère *f* rack, chimney hook.

crème *f* cream.

crémerie *f* dairy.

crémeux *adj* creamy.

crémier *m* dairyman, **-ière** *f* dairywoman.

créneau *m* battlement.

crêpe *f* pancake; * *m* crepe, crape.

crêperie *f* pancake restaurant.

crépitement *m* crackling; rattling.

crépiter *vi* to crackle; to rattle.

crépu *adj* frizzy, woolly.

crépuscule m twilight, dusk.

cresson m watercress.

crête f crest, comb.

crétin m **-e** f cretin, idiot.

creuser vi to dig, burrow; * vt to dig, hollow.

creuset m crucible.

creux adj hollow, empty.

crevaison f puncture, flat.

crevé adj burst, punctured.

crever vt to burst; to gouge; * vi to burst; to split.

crevette f prawn.

cri m cry, howl, yell.

criant adj crying; striking, glaring.

criard adj yelling; scolding.

crible m riddle, sieve; **passer au ~** to riddle; to examine closely.

cribler vt to sift, riddle.

cric m (auto) jack.

crier vi to cry, shout.

crime m crime, offence.

criminel m **-le** f criminal; * adj criminal.

crin m horsehair.

crinière f mane.

criquet m locust.

crise f crisis, attack.

crisper vt to shrivel; to clench.

cristal m crystal, glassware.

cristallin adj crystalline.

cristallisation f crystallization.

cristalliser vt to crystallize.

critère m criterion, standard.

critiquable adj censurable, open to criticism.

critique adj critical, censorious; * f criticism; critique.

critiquer vt to criticize, censure.

croc m fang; hook.

croche f quaver.

crochet m hook, clasp.

crochu adj hooked, claw-like.

crocodile m crocodile.

croire vt to believe, think.

croisade f crusade.

croisement m crossing, junction.

croiser vt to cross; to fold; **se ~** vr to cross, intersect.

croisière f cruise.

croissance f growth, increase.

croissant adj growing, increasing; * m croissant; crescent.

croître vi to grow, rise.

croix f cross.

croque-monsieur m toasted cheese and ham sandwich.

croquer vt to crunch.

croquette f croquette.

croquis m sketch, outline.

crosse f (rel) crozier; butt, grip.

crotte f manure, dung.

croupir vi to stagnate, wallow.

croustillant adj crusty, crisp.

croustiller vi to be crusty, crispy.

croûte f crust.

croûton m crust, crouton.

croyance f belief.

croyant adj believing.

cru adj raw, uncooked; * m vineyard; wine.

cruauté f cruelty, inhumanity.

cruche f pitcher.

crucial adj crucial, decisive.

crucifix m crucifix.

crucifixion f crucifixion.

crudité f crudity, coarseness.

crue f flood.

cruel adj cruel; **~lement** adv cruelly.

crustacé m crustacean, shellfish.

crypte m crypt.

crypter vt to encode, scramble.

cube m cube, block.

cubique adj cubic.

cubisme m cubism.

cueillette f picking, gathering.

cueillir vt to pick, gather.

cuiller, cuillère f spoon, spoonful.

cuir m leather, hide.

cuirasse f (zool) cuirass, breastplate.

cuirassé adj armoured; * m battleship.

cuire vi to cook.

cuisine f kitchen; cookery.

cuisiner vt vi to cook.

cuisinier m **-ière** f cook.

cuisinière f cooker, stove.

cuisse f thigh.

cuisson f cooking, baking.

cuit adj cooked.

cuivre m copper.

cul *m* (*col*) bottom, ass.
culasse *f* cylinder-head; breech.
cul-de-jatte *mf* legless cripple.
cul-de-sac *m* blind alley, cul-de-sac.
culinaire *adj* culinary.
culminer *vi* to culminate, tower.
culot *m* cheek, nerve.
culotte *f* knickers; underpants; shorts.
culpabiliser *vt* to make sb feel guilty; **se ~** *vr* to feel guilty.
culpabilité *f* guilt, culpability.
culte *m* cult, veneration.
cultivable *adj* cultivable.
cultivateur *m* -**trice** *f* farmer.
cultivé *adj* cultured.
cultiver *vt* to cultivate; **se ~** *vr* to improve o.s.
culture *f* culture; cultivation.
culturel *adj* cultural.
culturisme *m* body-building.
cumin *m* cumin.
cumul *m* pluralism; accumulation.
cumuler *vt* to accumulate; to hold concurrently.
cupide *adj* greedy; ~**ment** *adv* greedily.
cupidité *f* greed, cupidity.
cure *f* cure; treatment.
curé *m* parish priest, parson.
cure-dents *m* toothpick.

curieusement *adv* curiously.
curieux *m* -**euse** *f* inquisitive person; onlooker; * *adj* curious, inquisitive.
curiosité *f* curiosity, inquisitiveness.
cursus *m* degree course.
cutané *adj* skin, cutaneous.
cuve *f* vat, tank.
cuvette *f* basin, bowl.
cyanure *m* cyanide.
cybernétique *f* cybernetics.
cyclable *adj* cycle, for cycling.
cyclamen *m* cyclamen.
cycle *m* cycle; stage.
cyclique *adj* cyclical.
cyclisme *m* cycling.
cycliste *mf* cyclist; * *adj* cycle.
cyclomoteur *m* moped.
cyclone *m* cyclone.
cyclope *m* Cyclops.
cygne *m* swan.
cylindre *m* cylinder.
cylindrée *f* capacity (engine).
cylindrique *adj* cylindrical.
cymbale *f* cymbal.
cynique *adj* cynical; ~**ment** *adv* cynically.
cynisme *m* cynicism.
cytologie *f* cytology.
cytoplasme *m* cytoplasm.

D

dactylographe *mf* typist.
dactylographie *f* typing, typewriting.
dactylographier *vt* to type.
dada *m* (*fam*) hobbyhorse; gee-gee.
dahlia *m* dahlia.
daigner *vt* to deign, condescend.
daim *m* deer.
dalle *f* flagstone, slab.
dalmatien *m* Dalmatian.
daltonien *adj* colour-blind.
dame *f* lady; dame.
damier *m* draughtboard.
damnation *f* damnation.
damné *adj* damned.
damner *vt* to damn.

danger *m* danger, risk.
dangereusement *adv* dangerously.
dangereux *adj* dangerous, risky.
dans *prép* in; into; **il a ~ les trente ans** he's thirty or so.
dansant *adj* dancing.
danse *f* dance; dancing.
danser *vi* to dance.
danseur *m* -**euse** *f* dancer.
dard *m* sting.
datation *f* dating.
date *f* date.
dater *vt* to date.
datif *m* dative.
datte *f* (*bot*) date.

dattier *m* date palm.

dauphin *m* dolphin.

daurade *f* sea bream.

davantage *adv* more.

de *prép* of; from; **une femme ~ quarante ans** a forty-year-old woman; **~ bonne heure** early; **deux ~ plus** two more; * *art* some, any.

dé *m* dice; thimble.

déambuler *vi* to stroll.

débâcle *f* disaster; collapse.

déballage *m* unpacking; display.

déballer *vt* to unpack; to display.

débandade *f* rout, stampede.

débarbouiller *vt* to wash; **se ~** *vr* to wash o.s.

débarcadère *m* landing; wharf.

débardeur *m* docker, stevedore.

débarquement *m* landing, disembarkment.

débarquer *vt* to land, unship; * *vi* to disembark, land.

débarrasser *vt* to clear, rid; **se ~** *vr*: **se ~ de** to rid o.s. of.

débat *m* debate; dispute, contest.

débattre *vi* to debate, discuss.

débauche *f* debauchery, dissoluteness.

débaucher *vt* to debauch, corrupt.

débile *adj* weak, feeble.

débilitant *adj* debilitating, weakening.

débit *m* debit; turnover; flow.

débiter *vt* to debit; to produce.

débiteur *m* **-trice** *f* debtor.

déblayer *vt* to clear away, remove.

déblocage *m* unblocking; freeing, releasing.

débloquer *vt* to release, unlock.

déboisement *m* deforestation.

déboiser *vt* to deforest.

déboîtement *m* dislocation.

débordant *adj* exuberant, overflowing.

débordé *adj* overwhelmed.

débordement *m* overflowing; outflanking.

déborder *vi* to overflow; to outflank.

débouché *m* outlet; issue.

déboucher *vt* to open, uncork; * *vi* to pass out, emerge.

debout *adv* upright, standing; **être ~** to stand.

déboutonner *vt* to unbutton.

débraillé *adj* untidy, disordered.

débrancher *vt* to disconnect.

débrayer *vi* to declutch; to stop work.

débris *m* debris, waste.

débrouiller *vt* to disentangle, unravel; **se ~** *vr* to cope, manage.

début *m* beginning, outset.

débutant *adj* novice.

débuter *vi* to start, begin; * *vt* to lead, start.

décadence *f* decadence, decline.

décadent *adj* decadent.

décaféiné *adj* decaffeinated.

décagone *m* decagon.

décalage *m* gap, interval; discrepancy.

décalcifier *vt* to decalcify.

décaler *vt* to shift; to stagger.

décalitre *m* decalitre.

décamètre *m* decametre.

décaper *vt* to clean, scour.

décapotable *adj* convertible; * *f* convertible.

décapsuler *vt* to take the lid off.

décapsuleur *m* bottle-opener.

décathlon *m* decathlon.

décéder *vi* to die.

décelable *adj* detectable.

déceler *vt* to detect; to disclose.

décembre *m* December.

décemment *adv* decently.

décence *f* decency.

décennal *adj* decennial.

décennie *f* decade.

décent *adj* decent, proper.

décentralisation *f* decentralization.

décentraliser *vt* to decentralize.

déception *f* disappointment; deceit.

décerner *vt* to award, confer.

décès *m* death, decease.

décevant *adj* disappointing; deceptive.

décevoir *vt* to disappoint; to deceive.

déchaîné *adj* wild, unbridled.

déchaîner *vt* to unleash; **se ~** *vr* to break loose, run wild.

décharge *f* discharge; receipt.

déchargement *m* unloading.

décharger *vt* to unload, discharge.

décharné *adj* lean, emaciated.

déchausser *vt* to take off footwear; **se ~** *vr* to take one's shoes off.

déchéance *f* decay, decline.

déchet *m* loss, waste.

déchiffrer *vt* to decipher, decode.

déchiqueter *vt* to tear; to slash; to shred.

déchirant *adj* harrowing, excruciating.

déchirement *m* tearing, ripping.

déchirer *vt* to tear, rip.

déchirure *f* tear, rip.

déchoir *vi* to decline; to sink.

déchu *adj* fallen; declined; deposed.

décibel *m* decibel.

décidé *adj* decided; determined; **~ment** *adv* positively; resolutely; certainly.

décigramme *m* decigram.

décilitre *m* decilitre.

décimal *adj* decimal.

décimètre *m* decimetre.

décisif *adj* decisive, conclusive.

décision *f* decision.

déclamation *f* declamation.

déclamer *vt* to declaim.

déclaré *adj* professed, avowed.

déclarer *vt* to declare, announce; **se ~** *vr* to speak one's mind.

déclenchement *m* release, setting off.

déclencher *vt* to release, set off; **se ~** *vr* to release itself, go off.

déclic *m* click; trigger.

déclin *m* decline, deterioration.

déclinaison *f* declension; declination.

déclinant *adj* declining.

décliner *vi* to decline, refuse.

déclivité *f* declivity, slope.

décloisonner *vt* to decompartmentalize.

décoder *vt* to decode, decipher.

décodeur *m* decoder, decipherer.

décoiffer *vt* to disarrange sb's hair.

décoincer *vt* to loose, release.

décollage *m* take-off, lift-off.

décoller *vi* to unpaste, steam off; to take off; * *vt*: **se ~** *vr* to come unstuck, become detached.

décolleté *adj* low-necked, low-cut; *m* decolletage, low neckline.

décolorant *adj* bleaching, decolorizing; * *m* bleaching substance.

décolorer *vt* to decolour, bleach.

décombres *mpl* rubble, debris.

décomposer *vt* to decompose; to break up; to dissect; **se ~** *vr* to decompose, decay.

décomposition *f* decomposition, breaking up.

décompression *f* decompression.

décomprimer *vt* to decompress.

décompte *m* discount; deduction.

déconcentrer *vt* to devolve; to disperse; **se ~** *vr* to lose concentration.

déconcertant *adj* disconcerting.

déconcerter *vt* to disconcert.

décongeler *vt* to thaw, defrost.

déconnecter *vt* to disconnect.

déconnexion *f* disconnection.

décontenancé *adj* embarrassed; disconcerted.

décontracté *adj* relaxed.

décontracter *vt* to relax; **se ~** *vr* to relax.

décontraction *f* relaxation.

décor *m* scenery; setting.

décorateur *m* **-trice** *f* decorator; set designer.

décoratif *adj* decorative, ornamental.

décoration *f* decoration, embellishment.

décorer *vt* to decorate, adorn.

décortiquer *vt* to husk, shell.

découler *vi* to flow; to ensue.

découpage *m* cutting up, carving.

découper *vt* to carve, cut up.

décourageant *adj* discouraging, disheartening.

découragement *m* discouragement.

décourager *vt* to discourage, dishearten; **se ~** *vr* to become discouraged.

décousu *adj* unsewn; loose; disconnected.

découvert *adj* uncovered; open; * *m* overdraft.

découverte *f* discovery.

découvrir *vt* to discover.

décret *m* decree, enactment.

décréter *vt* to decree, enact.

décrire *vt* to describe.

décrocher *vt* to take down; to unhook.

décroissant *adj* decreasing, lessening.

décroître *vi* to decrease, diminish.

déçu *adj* disappointed.

décupler *vi* to increase tenfold.

dédaigner *vt* to disdain, scorn.

dédaigneusement *adv* disdainfully.

dédaigneux *adj* disdainful, scornful.

dédain *m* disdain, scorn.

dedans *adv* inside, indoors; * *m* inside; **au ~** inside.

dédicace *f* dedication.

dédier *vt* to consecrate, dedicate to.

dédommagement *m* compensation, damages.

dédommager *vt* to compensate, indemnify.

dédouanement *m* customs clearance.

dédoubler *vt* to divide in two; to remove lining.

déduction *f* deduction.

déduire *vt* to deduct; to deduce.

déesse *f* goddess.

défaillance *f* faintness; exhaustion; blackout.

défaillant *adj* faint; weakening.

défaillir *vi* to faint; to weaken.

défaire *vt* to undo, dismantle.

défaite *m* defeat, overthrow.

défaitiste *adj, mf* defeatist.

défaut *m* defect, fault.

défavorable *adj* unfavourable; **~ment** *adv* unfavourably.

défavoriser *vt* to penalize, treat unfairly.

défection *f* defection.

défectueux *adj* defective, faulty.

défendeur *m* **-eresse** *f* defendant.

défendre *vt* to defend, protect; to prohibit; **se ~** *vr* to defend o.s.

défense *f* defence; prohibition.

défenseur *m* defender.

défensif *adj* defensive.

défi *m* defiance; challenge.

défiant *adj* mistrustful, distrustful.

déficience *f* deficiency.

déficient *adj* deficient; weak.

déficit *m* deficit, shortfall.

déficitaire *adj* deficient, in deficit.

défier *vt* to challenge, defy.

défilé *m* procession, parade.

défiler *vi* to parade, march.

défini *adj* definite, precise.

définir *vt* to define, specify.

définitif *adj* definitive, final.

définition *f* definition.

définitivement *adv* definitively, finally.

déflagration *f* deflagration, explosion.

déflation *f* deflation.

défoncer *vt* to smash in; to dig deeply.

déformation *f* deformation, distortion.

déformer *vt* to deform, distort; **se ~** *vr* to bend; to lose its shape.

défoulement *m* outlet; release.

défouler *vt* to unwind, relax; **se ~** *vr* to get rid of one's inhibitions.

défricher *vt* to clear; to reclaim.

défunt *m* **-e** *f* deceased; * *adj* late, deceased.

dégagé *adj* clear; open.

dégagement *m* freeing, clearance.

dégager *vt* to free, clear; **se ~** *vr* to free o.s., extricate o.s.

dégarnir *vt* to empty; to clear.

dégât *m* havoc, damage.

dégel *m* thaw.

dégeler *vt vi* to thaw, melt.

dégénérer *vi* to degenerate, decline.

dégivrer *vt* to de-ice, defrost.

dégonfler *vt* to deflate, empty.

dégourdir *vt* to warm up, revive.

dégourdissement *m* reviving, return of circulation.

dégoût *m* disgust, distaste.

dégoûter *vt* to disgust.

dégradant *adj* degrading.

dégradation *f* degradation, debasement.

dégradé *m* shading off; gradation.

dégrader *vt* to degrade, debase; **se ~** *vr* to become degraded, debased.

dégrafer *vt* to unfasten, unhook.

dégraisser *vt* to remove grease.

degré *m* degree; grade.

dégrèvement *m* reduction; redemption.

dégripper *vt* to unblock; to unchoke.

déguisement *m* disguise.

déguiser *vt* to disguise; **se ~** *vr* to disguise o.s.

dégustation *f* tasting, sampling.

dehors *adv* outside, outdoors; **au ~** outwardly; **en ~ de** outside; apart from; * *m* outside, exterior.

déjà *adv* already.

déjeuner *vi* to lunch; * *m* lunch.

déjouer *vt* to elude; to thwart.

delà *adv*: **au ~ de** beyond; **par ~** beyond.

délabré *adj* dilapidated, ramshackle.

délacer *vt* to unlace, undo.

délai *m* delay; respite; time limit.

délaisser *vt* to abandon, quit.

délassant *adj* relaxing, refreshing.

délasser *vt* to refresh, relax; **se ~** *vr* to rest, relax.

délateur *m* **-trice** *f* informer.

délation *f* denouncement; informing.

délavé *adj* diluted; faded.

délayage *m* dragging-out, spinning-out.

délayer *vt* to thin; to drag out.

délectation *f* delectation, delight.

délecter (se) *vr* to delight, revel.

délégation *f* delegation.

délégué *m* **-e** *f* delegate, representative; * *adj* delegate, delegated.

déléguer *vt* to delegate.

délibération *f* deliberation; resolution.

délibéré *adj* deliberate; resolute; **~ment** *adv* deliberately.

délicat *adj* delicate, dainty; **~ement** *adv* delicately.

délicatesse *f* delicacy, daintiness.

délice *m* delight, pleasure.

délicieux *adj* delicious, delightful.

délier *vt* to unbind, untie.

délimitation *f* delimitation.

délimiter *vt* to delimit, demarcate.

délinquance *f* delinquency.

délinquant *m* **-e** *f* delinquent, offender; * *adj* delinquent.

délirant *adj* delirious, frenzied.

délire *m* delirium, frenzy.

délirer *vi* to be delirious.

délit *m* offence, misdemeanour.

délivrance *f* deliverance; release; delivery.

délivrer *vt* to deliver; to release; **se ~** *vr* to free o.s.

déloger *vt* to evict, dislodge.

déloyal *adj* disloyal, unfaithful; **~ement** *adv* disloyally.

déloyauté *f* disloyalty, treachery.

delta *m* delta.

deltaplane *m* hang-glider.

démagogie *f* demagogy.

démagogique *adj* demagogic.

démagogue *m* demagogue.

demain *adv* tomorrow.

demande *f* request, petition; question.

demander *vt* to ask, request; **se ~** *vr* to wonder.

démangeaison *f* itch; longing.

démaquillant *m* make-up remover; * *adj* make-up removing.

démaquiller *vt* to remove make-up; **se ~** *vr* to take one's make-up off.

démarche *f* gait, walk, step.

démarrage *m* moving off, casting off.

démarrer *vi* to start up, move off; * *vt* to start, get started.

démarreur *m* starter.

démasquer *vt* to unmask, uncover.

démêlage *m* disentangling; combing.

démêler *vt* to disentangle, unravel; comb.

déménagement *m* removal; moving (house).

déménager *vi* to move house.

déménageur *m* removal man.

démener (se) *vr* to struggle, strive.

dément *adj* mad, insane, crazy.

démenti *m* denial, refutation.

démentir *vt* to deny, refute.

démesuré *adj* excessive, inordinate; **~ment** *adv* excessively, inordinately.

démettre *vt* to dislocate; to dismiss.

demeure *f* residence, dwelling place.

demeurer *vi* to live at, reside, stay.

demi *adj* half; **à ~** halfway; * *m* half.

demi-cercle *m* semicircle.

demi-douzaine *f* half-dozen.

demi-droite *f* half-line.

demi-finale *f* semi-final.

demi-frère *m* half-brother.

demi-heure *f* half-hour.

demi-jour *m* half-light.

démilitariser *vt* to demilitarize.

demi-litre *m* half-litre.

demi-lune *f* half-moon.

demi-mesure *f* half-measure.

demi-mot *m*: **à ~** without spelling out.

demi-pension *f* half-board.

demi-sœur *f* half-sister.

démission *f* resignation.

démissionner *vi* to resign.

demi-tarif *m* half-fare.

demi-tour *m* half-turn.

démocrate *mf* democrat.

démocratie *f* democracy.

démocratique *adj* democratic; **~ment** *adv* democratically.

démocratiser *vt* to democratize.

démodé *adj* old-fashioned, out-of-date.

démographie *f* demography.

démographique *adj* demographic.

demoiselle *f* young lady; spinster; damsel.

démolir *vt* to demolish, knock down.

démolition *f* demolition.

démon *m* demon, fiend.

démoniaque *adj* demoniac, fiendish.

démonstrateur *m* **-trice** *f* demonstrator.

démonstratif *adj* demonstrative.

démonstration *f* demonstration; proof.

démontable *adj* collapsible, that can be dismantled.

démonte-pneu *m* tyre lever.

démonter *vt* to dismantle, take down, dismount; **se ~** *vr* to come apart, be nonplussed.

démontrer *vt* demonstrate; to prove.

démoralisant *adj* demoralizing.

démoraliser *vt* to demoralize; **se ~** *vr* to become demoralized.

démouler *vt* to take out of a mould.

démunir *vt* to deprive; to divest.

démystifier *vt* to demystify, disabuse.

dénaturé *adj* denatured, disfigured.

dénégation *f* denial.

déneiger *vt* to clear snow from.

déni *m* denial, refusal.

dénicher *vt* to dislodge; to unearth.

dénier *vt* to deny, disclaim.

dénigrer *vt* to denigrate, disparage.

dénivellation *f* difference in level, unevenness.

dénombrer *vt* to number, enumerate.

dénomination *f* denomination, designation.

dénoncer *vt* to denounce; to inform against.

dénonciation *f* denunciation.

dénouement *m* dénouement; unravelling; outcome.

dénouer *vt* to unravel, untie, undo.

dénoyauter *vt* to stone (fruit).

denrée *f* commodity, provisions, foodstuff.

dense *adj* dense, thick.

densité *f* density, denseness.

dent *f* tooth.

dentaire *adj* dental.

dentelé *adj* jagged, perforated.

dentelle *f* lace.

dentier *m* denture, dental plate.

dentifrice *m* toothpaste.

dentiste *mf* dentist.

dentition *f* dentition, teething.

dénuder *vt* to bare, denude; **se ~** *vr* to strip off.

dénué *adj* devoid, bereft.

dénuement *m* destitution; deprivation.

déodorant *m* deodorant.

déontologie *f* deontology.

dépannage *m* repairing, fixing.

dépanner *vt* to repair, fix.

dépanneur *m* **-euse** *f* breakdown mechanic.

dépanneuse *f* breakdown lorry.

dépareillé *adj* unmatched; odd.

déparer *vt* to spoil; to disfigure.

départ *m* departure; start.

département *m* department.

dépasser *vt* to exceed; to go past.

dépaysé *adj* disoriented, out of one's element.

dépaysement *m* disorientation.

dépêcher *vt* to dispatch, send; **se ~** *vr* to hurry, rush.

dépendance *f* dependence; dependency.

dépendant *adj* dependent.

dépendre *vi* to depend on, be dependent on.

dépens *mpl*: **aux ~ de** at the expense of.

dépense *f* expenditure, outlay.

dépenser *vt* to expend, spend; **se ~** *vr* to exert o.s.

dépérir *vi* to decline, waste away.

dépeupler *vt* to depopulate; to clear.

dépistage *m* tracking; detection.

dépister *vt* to track.

dépit *m* spite; grudge; **en ~ de** in spite of.

dépité *adj* vexed; frustrated.

déplacé *adj* misplaced; ill-timed.

déplacement *m* displacement; removal.

déplacer *vt* to displace; to move; **se ~** *vr* to change residence.

déplaire *vi* to displease; to offend.

déplaisant *adj* disagreeable, unpleasant.

dépliant *m* prospectus, leaflet; * *adj* extendible; folding.

déplier *vt* to unfold; to open out.

déploiement *m* (*mil*) deployment; display.

déplorable *adj* deplorable, disgraceful.

déplorer *vt* to deplore, bewail.

déployer *vt* to deploy; to display.

dépopulation *f* depopulation.

déportation *f* deportation, transportation.

déporté *m* **-e** *f* deportee.

déporter *vt* to deport, transport.

déposer *vt* to lodge, deposit.

dépositaire *mf* depository; trustee.

déposition *f* deposition; evidence.

dépôt *m* deposit; warehouse.

dépouillement *m* scrutiny, perusal; despoiling.

dépouiller *vt* to strip; to despoil; to peruse.

dépourvu *adj* lacking, wanting; **au ~** off guard.

dépoussiérer *vt* to dust.

dépravation *f* depravity, corruption.

dépravé *adj* depraved, corrupt.

dépréciation *f* depreciation.

déprécier *vt* to depreciate; to disparage; **se ~** *vr* to depreciate, fall in value.

dépressif *adj* depressive.

dépression *f* depression, slump; dejection.

déprimant *adj* depressing.

déprimer *vt* to depress; to discourage.

depuis *prép* since, from; after.

député *m* deputy, delegate.

déracinement *m* uprooting.

déraciner *vt* to uproot.

déraillement *m* derailment.

dérailler *vi* to be derailed, run off the rails.

dérailleur *m* (*rail*) derailleur, derailer.

déraisonner *vi* to talk irrationally, rave.

dérangement *m* derangement; inconvenience.

déranger *vt* to upset, unsettle; **se ~** *vr* to move; to put o.s. out.

dérapage *m* skid.

déraper *vi* to skid, slip.

déréglé *adj* out of order; irregular; unruly.

dérèglement *m* disturbance; irregularity; dissoluteness.

dérégler *vt* to disturb; to put out of order; to upset.

dérision *f* derision, mockery.

dérisoire *adj* derisory; pathetic.

dérivation *f* derivation; diversion.

dérive *f* drift; **aller à la ~** to drift away.

dériver *vi* to drift.

dermatologie *f* dermatology.

dermatologue *mf* dermatologist.

derme *m* dermis.

dernier *adj* last; latest; back; * *m* **-ière** *f* last one; latter.

dernièrement *adv* recently; lately.

dérobade *f* sidestepping; evasion.

dérober *vt* to steal; to hide; **se ~** *vr* to steal away, escape.

dérogation *f* derogation; dispensation.

déroger *vi* to derogate; to detract.

déroulement *m* unfolding; pro-gress, development.

dérouler *vt* to unwind, uncoil; **se ~** *vr* to develop; to unfold.

déroutant *adj* disconcerting.

déroute *f* rout, overthrow.

dérouter *vt* to rout, overthrow.

derrière *prép* behind; * *adv*; **par ~** at the back; * *m* bottom; back; **de ~** back, rear.

des *art* = **de les**; *see* **un, une**.

dès *prép* from; since; **~ que** when; as soon as.

désabusé *adj* disenchanted; disabused.

désaccord *m* disagreement, discord.

désaffecté *adj* disused.

désagréable *adj* disagreeable, unpleasant; **~ment** *adv* disagreeably, unpleasantly.

désagréger *vt* to break up, disintegrate; **se ~** *vr* to break up, disintegrate.

désagrément *m* displeasure, annoyance.

désaltérant *adj* thirst-quenching.

désaltérer *vt* to refresh; **se ~** *vi* to quench one's thirst.

désamorcer *vt* to unprime, defuse.

désapprobateur *adj* disapproving.

désapprobation *f* disapproval.

désapprouver *vt* to disapprove, object.

désarçonner *vt* to unsaddle; to nonplus, baffle.

désarmant *adj* disarming.

désarmement *m* disarmament.

désarmer *vt* to disarm; to unload.

désarroi *m* disarray, confusion.

désarticuler *vt* to dislocate; to upset.

désastre *m* disaster.

désastreux *adj* disastrous, unfortunate.
désavantage *m* disadvantage; prejudice.
désavantager *vt* to disadvantage, handicap.
désaveu *m* disavowal, retraction.
désavouer *vt* to disavow, retract.
descendance *f* descent, lineage.
descendant *m* **-e** *f* descendant; * *adj* falling, descending.
descendre *vi* to descend, go down; * *vt* to take down, bring down.
descente *f* descent, way down.
descriptif *adj* descriptive, explanatory.
description *f* description.
désemparé *adj* helpless; distraught.
désenchantement *m* disenchantment; disillusion.
désenfler *vi* to become less swollen.
désensibiliser *vt* to desensitize.
déséquilibre *m* imbalance, unbalance.
déséquilibré *adj* unbalanced, unhinged.
déséquilibrer *vt* to unbalance, throw off balance.
désert *m* desert, wilderness; * *adj* deserted.
déserter *vt* to desert.
déserteur *m* deserter.
désertification *f* desertification.
désertion *f* desertion.
désertique *adj* desert; barren.
désespérant *adj* desperate, hopeless; discouraging.
désespéré *adj* desperate, hopeless; **~ment** *adv* desperately.
désespérer *vi* to despair, give up hope.
désespoir *m* despair, despondency.
déshabiller *vt* to undress; **se ~** *vr* to undress.
désherbage *m* weeding.
désherbant *m* weed killer.
désherber *vt* to weed.
déshériter *vt* to disinherit.
déshonorant *adj* dishonourable, disgraceful.
déshonorer *vt* to dishonour, disgrace.
déshydraté *adj* dehydrated.
déshydrater *vt* to dehydrate; **se ~** *vr* to become dehydrated.
désignation *f* designation, nomination; name.
désigner *vt* to designate, indicate.
désillusion *f* disillusion; disappointment.

désillusionner *vt* to disillusion; to disappoint.
désincarné *adj* disincarnate, disembodied.
désinfectant *m* disinfectant; * *adj* disinfectant.
désinfecter *vt* to disinfect.
désinfection *f* disinfection.
désinformation *f* disinformation.
désintégration *f* disintegration.
désintégrer *vt* to split, break up; **se ~** *vr* to disintegrate.
désintéressé *adj* disinterested, unselfish.
désintéressement *m* disinterestedness, unselfishness.
désintéresser (se) *vr* to lose interest in.
désintoxiquer *vt* to detoxify; to dry out; **se faire ~** *vr* to dry out.
désinvolte *adj* easy, offhand, casual.
désinvolture *f* casualness, offhandedness.
désir *m* desire, wish, longing.
désirable *adj* desirable.
désirer *vt* to desire, wish, long.
désobéir *vi* to disobey.
désobéissance *f* disobedience.
désobéissant *adj* disobedient.
désobligeant *adj* disobliging; uncivil.
désodorisant *m* deodorant; * *adj* deodorizing, deodorant.
désodoriser *vt* to deodorize.
désœuvré *adj* unoccupied, idle.
désœuvrement *m* idleness.
désolation *f* desolation; ruin; grief.
désolé *adj* desolate; disconsolate, grieved.
désordonné *adj* untidy; inordinate; reckless.
désordre *m* disorder, confusion, disturbance.
désorganisation *f* disorganization.
désorienté *adj* disorientated.
désormais *adv* from now on, henceforth.
désossé *adj* boned.
despote *m* despot.
despotique *adj* despotic; **~ment** *adv* despotically.
dessèchement *m* dryness, drying up, withering.
dessécher *vt* to dry, parch, wither; **se ~** *vr* to dry out, become parched.
dessein *m* design, plan, scheme; **à ~** *adv* intentionally.

desserrer *vt* to loosen; to unscrew; to slacken; **se ~** *vr* to work loose, come undone.

dessert *m* dessert, sweet.

desservir *vt* to clear (table); to do a disservice to.

dessin *m* drawing, sketch; draft.

dessinateur *m* **-trice** *f* drawer, draughtsman.

dessiner *vt* to draw, sketch; to design.

dessous *adv* under, beneath; * *m* underside, bottom.

dessus *adv* over, above; * *m*; **prendre le ~** to gain the upper hand; **le ~ du panier** the upper crust, the pick of the bunch.

destabiliser *vt* to destabilize.

destin *m* destiny, fate, doom.

destinataire *mf* addressee, consignee.

destination *f* destination; purpose.

destinée *f* destiny, fate.

destiner *vt* to determine; to intend, destine, aim.

destituer *vt* to dismiss, depose.

destructeur *adj* destructive, ruinous.

destruction *f* destruction.

désuétude *f* disuse **tomber en ~** to fall into disuse.

détachable *adj* detachable.

détachant *m* cleaner, stain remover.

détaché *m* (*mus*) detached.

détachement *m* detachment, indifference.

détacher *vt* (*mus*) to detach; to unfasten; **se ~** *vr* to become detached.

détail *m* detail, particular.

détaillant *m* **-e** *f* retailer.

détailler *vt* to detail; to sell retail.

détartrage *m* descaling.

détartrant *m* descaling substance; * *adj* descaling.

détartrer *vt* to descale.

détaxe *f* reduction in tax.

détecter *vt* to detect.

détecteur *m* detector.

détection *f* detection.

détective *m* detective.

déteindre *vi* to lose colour, fade.

détendre *vt* to release, loosen; **se ~** to relax, calm down.

détendu *adj* slack; relaxed.

détenir *vt* to detain; to hold.

détente *f* relaxation, easing.

détenteur *m* **-trice** *f* holder, possessor.

détergent *m* detergent.

détérioration *f* deterioration.

détériorer *vt* to damage, impair; **se ~** *vr* to deteriorate, worsen.

déterminant *adj* determining, deciding.

détermination *f* determination; resolution.

déterminé *adj* determined, resolute.

déterminer *vt* to determine, decide.

déterrer *vt* to dig up, disinter.

détestable *adj* detestable, odious; **~ment** *adv* detestably.

détester *vt* to detest, hate.

détonateur *m* detonator.

détonation *f* detonation, explosion.

détonner *vi* to clash (colour); to go out of tune.

détour *m* detour; curve; evasion.

détourné *adj* indirect, oblique.

détournement *m* diversion, rerouting.

détourner *vt* to divert, reroute.

détracteur *m* **-trice** *f* detractor, disparager.

détraquer *vt* to upset; to disorder; **se ~** *vr* to become upset; to go wrong.

détresse *f* distress, trouble.

détriment *m*: **au ~ de** to the detriment of.

détritus *m* refuse, rubbish.

détroit *m* strait.

détrôner *vt* to dethrone, depose.

detruire *vt* to destroy, demolish.

dette *f* debt.

deuil *m* mourning, bereavement, grief.

deux *adj* two; * *m* two; **entre les ~** so-so, fair to middling; **en moins de ~** in a jiffy.

deuxième *adj* second; **~ment** *adv* secondly; * *mf* second.

deux-points *m* colon.

deux-roues *m* two-wheeled vehicle.

dévaler *vt* *vi* to hurry down, tear down.

dévaliser *vt* to burgle; to rifle.

dévalorisation *f* depreciation.

dévaloriser *vt* to depreciate, reduce the value of.

dévaluation *f* devaluation.

devancer *vt* to outstrip, outrun; to precede.

devant *prép* in front of, before; * *adv* in front; * *m* front; **prendre les ~s** to make the first move, pre-empt; **aller au-~ de** to anticipate.

devanture *f* display; shop-front.

dévaster *vt* to devastate, lay waste.

développement *m* development; growth; progress.

développer *vt* to develop, expand; **se ~** *vr* to develop, grow.

devenir *vi* to become, grow.

déverrouiller *vt* to unbolt, unlock.

déverser *vt* to pour; to dump.

dévêtir *vt* to undress; **se ~** *vr* to get undressed.

déviation *f* deviation; diversion.

dévier *vi* to deviate; to turn aside; to swerve.

devin *m* **-eresse** *f* seer, soothsayer.

deviner *vt* to guess; to solve; to foretell.

devinette *f* riddle.

devis *m* estimate, quotation.

dévisager *vt* to stare at.

devise *f* currency.

dévisser *vt* to unscrew, undo.

dévoiler *vt* to unveil, disclose.

devoir *m* duty; homework; * *vt* to owe; to have to.

dévorer *vt* to devour, consume.

dévot *adj* devout, pious.

dévotion *f* devotion, piety.

dévoué *adj* devoted, dedicated.

dévouement *m* devotion, dedication.

dévouer (se) *vr* to devote o.s., sacrifice o.s.

dextérité *f* dexterity, adroitness.

diabète *m* diabetes.

diabétique *adj* diabetic.

diable *m* devil.

diablotin *m* imp; cracker (Christmas).

diabolique *adj* diabolical, devilish; **~ment** *adv* diabolically.

diagnostic *m* diagnosis.

diagnostiquer *vt* to diagnose.

diagonale *f* diagonal.

diagramme *m* diagram; graph.

dialecte *m* dialect.

dialectique *f* dialectic; * *adj* dialectic.

dialogue *m* dialogue, conversation.

dialoguer *vt* to write in dialogue form; *vi* to have talks (with).

dialyse *f* dialysis.

diamant *m* diamond.

diamètre *m* diameter.

diaphragme *m* diaphragm.

diarrhée *f* diarrhoea.

dictaphone *m* dictaphone.

dictateur *m* **-trice** *f* dictator.

dictatorial *adj* dictatorial.

dictature *f* dictatorship.

dictée *f* dictating; dictation.

dicter *vt* to dictate, impose.

dictionnaire *m* dictionary.

dicton *m* saying, dictum.

didactique *adj* didactic.

dièse *f* (*mus*) sharp.

diesel *m* diesel.

diète *f* light diet.

diététicien *m* **-ne** *f* dietician.

diététique *adj* dietary.

dieu *m* god.

diffamation *f* defamation, slandering.

diffamer *vt* to defame, slander.

différé *adj* postponed; (*rad*, *TV*) pre-recorded.

différemment *adv* differently.

différence *f* difference.

différenciation *f* differentiation.

différencier *vt* to differentiate.

différend *m* disagreement, difference of opinion.

différent *adj* different; various.

différer *vt* to differ; to vary.

difficile *adj* difficult; awkward, tricky; **~ment** *adv* with difficulty.

difficulté *f* difficulty; problem.

difforme *adj* deformed, misshapen.

difformité *f* deformity.

diffuser *vt* to diffuse, circulate, broadcast.

diffusion *f* diffusion, circulation, broadcasting.

digérer *vt* to digest.

digeste *adj* easily digestible.

digestif *adj* digestive.

digestion *f* digestion.

digital *adj* digital.

digne *adj* worthy; dignified; **~ment** *adv* worthily, deservedly.

dignité *f* dignity.

digression *f* digression.

digue *f* dyke; sea wall.

dilapider *vt* to squander; to embezzle.

dilatation *f* dilation, distension.

dilater *vt* to dilate, distend; **se ~** *vr* to dilate, distend.

dilemme *m* dilemma.

dilettante *mf* dilettante.

diluer *vt* to dilute.

dilution *f* dilution.

dimanche *m* Sunday.

dimension *f* dimension, size.

diminuer *vt* to diminish, reduce; * *vi* to diminish, lessen.

diminutif *m* diminutive.

diminution *f* reduction, lessening.

dinde *f* turkey hen.

dindon *m* turkey cock.

dindonneau *m* young turkey.

dîner *vi* to dine; * *m* dinner.

dinosaure *m* dinosaur.

diocèse *m* diocese.

diode *f* diode.

dioxyde *m* dioxide.

diphtérie *f* diphtheria.

diphtongue *f* diphthong.

diplomate *mf* diplomat.

diplomatie *f* diplomacy.

diplomatique *adj* diplomatic; **~ment** *adv* diplomatically.

diplôme *m* diploma, certificate.

diplômé *m* **-e** *f* graduate; * *adj* qualified.

dire *vt* to say; to tell; **se ~** to say to o.s.; to call o.s; *vr*: **se ~ que** to tell o.s. that.

direct *adj* direct; **~ement** *adv* directly; * *m* (*rail*) express.

directeur *m* **-trice** *f* director.

direction *f* direction, management.

directive *f* directive, order.

dirigeant *m* **-e** *f* leader, ruler; * *adj* ruling, executive.

diriger *vt* to run, direct; **se ~** *vr*: **se ~ vers** to head for, make for.

discernement *m* discernment, judgment.

discerner *vt* to discern, distinguish.

disciple *m* disciple.

disciplinaire *adj* disciplinary.

discipline *f* discipline.

discipliné *adj* disciplined.

discontinu *adj* discontinuous.

discordant *adj* discordant, conflicting.

discorde *f* discord, dissension.

discothèque *f* discotheque.

discours *m* speech, talking.

discourtois *adj* discourteous.

discréditer *vt* to discredit.

discret *adj* discreet.

discrétion *f* discretion, prudence.

discrétionnaire *adj* discretionary.

discrimination *f* discrimination.

discriminer *vt* to distinguish; to discriminate.

disculper *vt* to excuse, exonerate; **se ~** *vr* to justify o.s., excuse o.s.

discussion *f* discussion, debate.

discutable *adj* debatable, questionable.

discuter *vt vi* to discuss, debate.

disgrâce *f* disgrace.

disgracieux *adj* awkward, ungraceful.

disjoncter *vi* to cut off, disconnect.

disjoncteur *m* cutout, circuit breaker.

disparaître *vi* to disappear, vanish.

disparate *adj* disparate, incongruous.

disparité *f* disparity, incongruity.

disparition *f* disappearance; death; extinction.

disparu *adj* vanished; bygone; missing.

dispensaire *m* dispensary.

dispense *f* dispensation, exemption.

dispenser *vt* to dispense, exempt; **se ~** *vr*: **se ~ de** to dispense with; to avoid.

disperser *vt* to spread, scatter; **se ~** *vr* to disperse, scatter.

dispersion *f* dispersal, scattering.

disponibilité *f* availability.

disponible *adj* available; transferable.

dispos *adj* refreshed; alert; in form.

disposer *vt* to arrange, dispose; **se ~** *vr*: **se ~ à** to prepare to do; * *vi* to leave.

dispositif *m* device, mechanism.

disposition *f* arrangement, layout.

disproportionné *adj* disproportionate.

dispute *f* dispute, argument.

disputer *vt* to dispute, rival; **se ~** *vr* to quarrel, argue.

disquaire *mf* record-dealer.

disqualifier *vt* to disqualify.

disque *m* disk; record.

disquette *f* diskette.

dissection *f* dissection.

dissemblable *adj* dissimilar; different.
disséminer *vt* to disseminate, scatter.
dissentiment *m* disagreement, dissent.
disséquer *vt* to dissect.
dissertation *f* dissertation.
dissidence *f* dissidence, dissent.
dissident *adj* dissident.
dissimulation *f* dissimulation, double-dealing.
dissimulé *adj* double-faced, dissembling.
dissimuler *vt* to dissemble, conceal; **se ~** *vr* to conceal o.s.
dissipation *f* dissipation, waste.
dissipé *adj* dissipated, undisciplined.
dissiper *vt* to dispel; to dissipate; **se ~** *vr* to disperse, become undisciplined.
dissociation *f* dissociation.
dissocier *vt* to dissociate.
dissolution *f* dissolution.
dissolvant *m* solvent, dissolvent.
dissonant *adj* dissonant; discordant.
dissoudre *vt* to dissolve.
dissuader *vt* to dissuade.
dissuasif *adj* dissuasive, deterrent.
dissuasion *f* dissuasion.
distance *f* distance, interval.
distancier (se) *vr* to distance o.s. from.
distant *adj* distant.
distendre *vt* to distend, strain; **se ~** *vr* to slacken.
distillation *f* distillation.
distiller *vt* to distil.
distillerie *f* distillery.
distinct *adj* distinct, different; **~ement** *adv* distinctly.
distinctif *adj* distinctive.
distinction *f* distinction.
distingué *adj* distinguished.
distinguer *vt* to distinguish; to discern; **se ~** *vr* to distinguish o.s.
distorsion *f* distortion.
distraction *f* inattention; absentmindedness; abstraction.
distraire *vt* to distract; to amuse; **se ~** *vr* to enjoy o.s.
distrait *adj* inattentive, absent-minded; **~ement** *adv* absent–mindedly.
distrayant *adj* entertaining, diverting.
distribuer *vt* to distribute.

distributeur *m* distributor.
distribution *f* distribution.
district *m* district.
diurétique *adj* diuretic; * *m* diuretic.
divagation *f* wandering, rambling.
divaguer *vi* to ramble, rave.
divan *m* divan.
divergence *f* divergence.
divergent *adj* divergent.
diverger *vi* to diverge, differ.
divers *adj* diverse, varied; **~ement** *adv* diversely.
diversification *f* diversification.
diversifier *vt* to vary, diversify; **se ~** *vr* to diversify.
diversion *f* diversion.
diversité *f* diversity, variety.
divertir *vt* to amuse, entertain; **se ~** *vr* to amuse o.s.
divertissant *adj* amusing, entertaining.
divertissement *m* entertainment, recreation.
dividende *m* dividend.
divin *adj* divine, exquisite; **~ement** *adv* divinely.
divination *f* divination.
divinité *f* divinity.
diviser *vt* to divide, split; **se ~** *vr* to split up, divide into.
division *f* division.
divorce *m* divorce.
divorcé *m* **-e** *f* divorcee; * *adj* divorced.
divorcer *vi* to divorce.
divulgation *f* disclosure, divulgence.
divulguer *vt* to divulge, disclose.
dix *adj, m* ten.
dix-huit *adj, m* eighteen.
dix-huitième *adj, mf* eighteenth.
dixième *adj* tenth; **~ment** *adv* tenthly; * *mf* tenth.
dix-neuf *adj, m* nineteen.
dix-neuvième *adj, mf* nineteenth.
dix-sept *adj, m* seventeen.
dix-septième *adj, mf* seventeenth.
dizaine *f* ten, ten or so.
docile *adj* docile, submissive; **~ment** *adv* docilely.
docilité *f* docility, submissiveness.
dock *m* dock, dockyard.

docteur *m* doctor.

doctorat *m* doctorate.

doctrine *f* doctrine.

document *m* document.

documentaire *adj* documentary.

documentaliste *mf* researcher.

documentation *f* documentation; information.

documenter *vt* to document; **se ~** *vr* to gather information on.

dogmatique *adj* dogmatic.

dogme *m* dogma.

doigt *m* finger; **être à deux ~s de** to come very close to doing; **obéir au ~ et à l'œil** to obey (sb) slavishly.

doigté *m* touch; fingering technique.

domaine *m* domain, estate; to sphere.

domanial *adj* state-owned.

dôme *m* dome, vault.

domestique *adj* domestic, household.

domestiquer *vt* to domesticate, tame.

domicile *m* domicile, address.

domicilié *adj* domiciled.

dominant *adj* dominant, prevailing.

dominante *f* dominant characteristic.

dominateur *adj* governing; domineering.

domination *f* domination.

dominer *vt* to dominate; to prevail; **se ~** to control o.s.

dominical *adj* Sunday.

dommage *m* damage; harm; **c'est ~** it's a pity.

dompter *vt* to tame, train.

dompteur *m* **-euse** *f* trainer, tamer.

don *m* gift; talent.

donateur *m* **-trice** *f* donor.

donation *f* donation.

donc *conj* so, therefore, thus; **pourquoi ~?** why was that?

donné *adj* given; fixed; **étant ~** seeing that, in view of.

donnée *f* datum.

donner *vt* to give; * *vi* to yield (crop).

donneur *m* **-euse** *f* giver, donor; dealer.

dont *pn* whose, of which.

dopage *m* doping.

doper *vt* to dope; **se ~** *vr* to take drugs, dope o.s.

doré *adj* gilded; tanned.

dorénavant *adv* from now on, henceforth.

dorer *vt* to gild; to tan.

dorloter *vt* to pamper, pet.

dormir *vi* to sleep, be asleep; to be still.

dortoir *m* dormitory.

dos *m* back; top; ridge.

dosage *m* mixture; balance; proportioning.

dose *f* dose; amount; quantity.

doser *vt* to measure out, proportion; to strike a balance.

dossier *m* dossier, file; case.

dot *f* dowry.

doter *vt* to provide with a dowry; to endow.

douane *f* customs.

douanier *m* customs officer.

double *adj* double, duplicate, dual; **~ment** *adv* doubly; * *m* copy, double, replica; twice as much.

doubler *vt* *vi* to double, duplicate.

doublure *f* lining; (*thea*) understudy.

doucement *adv* softly, gently.

doucereux *adj* sugary; mawkish; suave.

douceur *f* softness, gentleness.

douche *f* shower.

doucher *vt* to give a shower to; **se ~** *vr* to take a shower.

doué *adj* gifted, endowed with.

douille *f* case; cartridge.

douillet *adj* delicate, tender; soft.

douleur *f* pain, ache; anguish.

douloureusement *adv* painfully, grievously.

douloureux *adj* painful, grievous.

doute *m* doubt; **sans ~** without doubt.

douter *vi* to doubt, question; **se ~** *vr* **se ~ de** to suspect sb; **se ~ que** to suspect that, expect that.

douteux *adj* doubtful, dubious.

doux *adj*, *f* **douce** soft; sweet; mild.

douzaine *f* dozen.

douze *adj*, *m* twelve.

douzième *adj* twelfth; **~ment** *adv* twelfthly; * *mf* twelfth.

doyen *m* **-ne** *f* dean; doyen.

draconien *adj* draconian, drastic.

dragée *f* bonbon, sugared almond.

dragon *m* dragon.

dramatique *adj* dramatic, tragic; **~ment** *adv* dramatically.

dramatiser *vt* to dramatize.

dramaturge *mf* playwright.

drame *m* drama.

drap *m* sheet; **~-housse** fitted sheet; **être dans de beaux ~s** to be in a fine mess.

drapeau *m* flag.

draper *vt* to drape.

dressage *m* taming; pitching.

dresser *vt* to draw up; to put up; **se ~** *vr* to stand up; to rear up.

dresseur *m* **-euse** *f* trainer, tamer.

dribbler *vi* to dribble.

drogue *f* drug.

drogué *m* **-e** *f* drug addict; * *adj* drugged.

droguer *vt* to drug, administer drugs; **se ~** *vr* to dose up; to take drugs.

droguerie *f* hardware trade.

droguiste *mf* hardware storekeeper.

droit *adj* right; straight; sound; honest; **~ement** *adv* uprightly, honestly; * *adv* straight, straight ahead; * *m* right; law; tax.

droite *f* right side; right (wing); straight line.

droitier *adj* right-handed.

droiture *f* uprightness, honesty.

drôle *adj* funny, amusing; peculiar; **~ment** *adv* funnily, peculiarly.

dromadaire *m* dromedary.

dru *adj* thick, dense; sturdy.

du *art* of the.

dû *adj* owed; due; **~ment** *adv* duly.

dualité *f* duality.

dubitatif *adj* doubtful, dubious.

dubitativement *adv* doubtfully, dubiously.

duc *m* duke, **duchesse** *f* duchess.

duché *m* duchy.

duel *m* duel; dual.

duettiste *mf* duettist.

dune *f* dune.

duo *m* duo; duet.

duodénum *m* duodenum.

dupe *adj* easily duped; * *f* dupe.

duper *vt* to dupe, take in.

duplex *m* duplex, two-way.

dupliquer *vt* to duplicate.

dur *adj* hard, tough; difficult; **~ement** *adv* harshly, severely.

durable *adj* durable, lasting; **~ment** *adv* durably.

duralumin *m* duralumin.

durant *prép* during, for.

durcir *vt* *vi* to harden; **se ~** *vr* to become hardened.

durcissement *m* hardening.

durée *f* duration, length.

durer *vi* to last.

dureté *f* hardness; austerity, harshness.

durillon *m* callus, corn.

duvet *m* down.

duveté *adj* downy.

dynamique *f* dynamic; dynamics; * *adj* dynamic; **~ment** *adv* dynamically.

dynamiser *vt* to energize; to potentiate.

dynamisme *m* dynamism.

dynamitage *m* dynamiting.

dynamite *f* dynamite.

dynamiter *vt* to dynamite.

dynamo *f* dynamo.

dynastie *f* dynasty.

dynastique *adj* dynastic.

dysenterie *f* dysentery.

dyslexie *f* dyslexia.

dyslexique *adj* dyslexic.

E

eau *f* water; rain.

eau-de-vie *f* brandy.

ébahir *vt* to astonish, stupefy, dumbfound.

ébahissement *m* astonishment, amazement.

ébauche *f* rough draft, rough outline.

ébaucher *vt* to sketch; to roughcast.

ébène *f* ebony.

ébéniste *m* cabinetmaker.

éblouir *vt* to dazzle; to fascinate.

éblouissant *adj* dazzling; amazing.

éblouissement *m* dazzle; bedazzlement.

ébouillanter *vt* to scald; to blanch; **s'~** *vr* to scald o.s.

éboulement *m* collapse, caving in; fall.

ébouriffé *adj* tousled, ruffled.

ébranler *vt* to shake; to unsettle, disturb.

ébrécher *vt* to chip, indent; to break into (fortune).

ébriété *f* intoxication.

ébrouer (s') *vr* to shake o.s.

ébruiter *vt* to disclose, divulge; **s'~** *vr* to spread, be noised abroad.

ébullition *f* boiling; effervescence; turmoil.

écaille *f* scale; shell.

écailler *vt* to scale; to chip; **s'~** *vr* to flake off, peel off.

écarlate *adj* scarlet.

écart *m* distance; interval; discrepancy; **rester à l'~** to steer clear of.

écarteler *vt* to tear apart; to quarter.

écarter *vt* to separate; to avert; to dismiss; **s'~** *vr* to make way; to swerve.

ecchymose *f* bruise, ecchymosis.

ecclésiastique *adj* ecclesiastical; * *m* ecclesiastic, clergyman.

échafaud *m* scaffold.

échafaudage *m* scaffolding.

échange *m* exchange, barter, trade.

échanger *vt* to exchange.

échantillon *m* sample.

échappée *f* breakaway; glimpse.

échappement *m* exhaust; release.

échapper *vi* to escape, avoid, elude; **s'~** *vr* to escape from; to leak.

écharde *f* splinter, sliver.

écharpe *f* scarf; arm-sling.

échassier *m* wader.

échauffement *m* heating; warm-up; constipation.

échauffer *vt* to heat, overheat; to excite; **s'~** *vr* to warm up; to get worked up.

échéance *f* expiry; maturity date.

échec *m* failure, defeat; chess.

échelle *f* ladder; scale.

échelon *m* rung; grade.

échelonner *vt* to grade; to stagger, set at intervals; **s'~** *vr* to be graduated, staggered.

échine *f* backbone, spine; **courber l'~** to submit.

échiquier *m* chessboard.

écho *m* echo; rumour.

échographie *f* ultrasound scan.

échoir *vi* to fall due; to befall, fall to sb's lot.

échouer *vi* to fail; to end up; to run aground.

éclabousser *vt* to splash, spatter.

éclair *m* flash; lightning flash; spark.

éclairage *m* lighting, light.

éclairagiste *m* electrician; lighting engineer.

éclaircie *f* clear interval, bright spot; glade.

éclaircir *vt* to lighten; to thin down; to brighten up; **s'~** *vr* to clear (up).

éclaircissement *m* clearing up, explanation, elucidation.

éclairer *vt* to light, illuminate; clarify, explain.

éclat *m* brightness, glare; splinter; splendour.

éclatant *adj* bright, blazing; resounding; blatant.

éclatement *m* explosion, bursting, rupture.

éclater *vi* to explode; to break out; to exclaim.

éclectique *adj* eclectic.

éclipse *f* eclipse.

éclipser *vt* to eclipse, overshadow; **s'~** *vr* to disappear, vanish.

éclore *vi* to hatch out; to blossom.

éclosion *f* hatching; blooming; birth.

écluse *f* lock.

écœurant *adj* disgusting, nauseating.

écœurement *m* nausea, disgust; discouragement.

écœurer *vt* to nauseate, disgust.

école *f* school, schooling; sect, doctrine.

écolier *m* schoolgirl, **-ière** *f* schoolgirl.

écologie *f* ecology.

écologique *adj* ecological.

écologiste *mf* ecologist.

économe *adj* thrifty; * *mf* steward, treasurer; (*mar*) bursar.

économie *f* economy, thrift; economics.

économique *adj* economic; **~ment** *adv* economically.

économiser *vt* to economize, save.

écorce *f* bark, peel, skin.

écorchure *f* scratch; graze.

Écossais *m* Scotsman, **-e** *f* Scotswoman.

écossais *adj* Scottish.

Écosse *f* Scotland.

écoulement *m* flow, discharge, outlet; disposal, selling.

écouler *vt* to flow, discharge; to sell; **s'~** *vr* to leak, flow out; to pass by; to sell.

écoute f listening, audience.

écouter vt to listen to.

écran m screen.

écrasant adj crushing; overwhelming.

écraser vt to crush; to overwhelm; to run over; **s'~** vr to crash; to get crushed.

écrémer vt to skim, cream.

écrevisse f crayfish.

écrin m box, casket.

écrire vt to write; to spell.

écrit adj written; * m document; piece of writing.

écriteau m notice, sign.

écriture f writing; handwriting; script.

écrivain m writer.

écrou m nut.

écroulement m collapse, caving in.

écrouler (s') vr to collapse, crumble.

écru adj raw; unbleached; untreated.

ectoplasme m ectoplasm.

écueil m reef, shelf; peril.

écume f foam, froth; scum.

écureuil m squirrel.

écurie f stable.

écusson m badge, shield.

eczéma m eczema.

édification f erection, construction.

édifice m edifice, building.

édifier vt to build, construct; to edify.

éditer vt to publish, produce; to edit.

éditeur m -trice f publisher; editor.

édition f publishing; edition; editing.

éditorial m leading article, editorial.

éducatif adj educational.

éducation f education; upbringing.

édulcorant m sweetener; * adj sweetening.

éduquer vt to educate; to bring up, raise.

effacer vt to delete, erase, wipe off; **s'~** vr to wear away, become obliterated.

effaré adj alarmed, bewildered.

effaroucher vt to frighten off; to alarm.

effectif m staff; size, complement; * adj effective, positive.

effectivement adv effectively, positively.

effectuer vt to effect, execute, carry out.

effervescence f effervescence; excitement, ferment.

effervescent adj effervescent; excited.

effet m effect, impression; spin; bill, note.

efficace adj effective; efficient; **~ment** adv effectively, efficiently.

efficacité f effectiveness, efficiency.

effleurer vt to touch lightly, skim across.

effondrement m collapse, caving in.

effondrer (s') vr to collapse, cave in.

efforcer (s') vr to endeavour, do one's best.

effort m effort, exertion; stress, strain.

effraction f breaking and entering.

effrayant adj frightening, fearsome.

effrayer vt to frighten, scare.

effriter vt to crumble; to exhaust (land); **s'~** vr to crumble away, disintegrate.

effroi m terror, dismay.

effronté adj shameless, impudent, cheeky; **~ment** adv shamelessly, impudently.

effroyable adj horrifying, appalling; **~ment** adv horrifyingly, appallingly.

égal adj equal; even, level; equable; **~ement** adv evenly; equally; also, as well.

égaler vt to equal, match.

égalisation f equalization; levelling.

égaliser vt to equalize; to level out.

égalitaire adj egalitarian.

égalité f equality; equableness; evenness.

égard m consideration, respect; **à l'~ de** concerning, regarding; **à tous ~s** in all respects.

égarer vt to mislead, lead astray; **s'~** vr to get lost; to wander from the point.

égayer vt to enliven, cheer up.

églantine f dog-rose, wild rose.

église f church.

égocentrique adj egocentric, self-centred.

égoïsme m selfishness, egoism.

égoïste mf egotist; * adj egotistic; **~ment** adv egotistically.

égout m sewer.

égoutter vt to strain; to wring out.

égratignure f scratch, scrape.

éjecter vt to eject, throw out.

élaboration f elaboration, development.

élaborer vt to elaborate, develop.

élan m surge, momentum, speed; spirit, elan.

élancer (s') vr to rush, spring, hurl o.s.

élargir vt to widen, stretch; **s'~** vr to get wider.

élargissement *m* widening, stretching, enlarging.

élastique *adj* elastic; flexible; * *m* elastic, elastic band.

électeur *m* **-trice** *f* voter, elector.

élection *f* election; choice.

électoral *adj* electoral.

électorat *m* electorate; constituency; franchise.

électricien *m* electrician.

électricité *f* electricity.

électrique *adj* electric.

électrocardiogramme *m* electrocardiogram.

électrode *f* electrode.

électrolyse *f* electrolysis.

électroménager *m* household appliance; * *adj* electrical (household).

électron *m* electron.

électronicien *m* electronics engineer.

électronique *f* electronics; * *adj* electronic.

élégance *f* elegance, stylishness.

élégant *adj* smart, elegant, stylish.

élément *m* element, component; cell; fact.

élémentaire *adj* elementary; basic.

éléphant *m* elephant.

élevage *m* rearing, breeding.

élève *mf* pupil, student.

élevé *adj* high; heavy; lofty, exalted.

élever *vt* to bring up, raise; to put up, lift up; **s'~** *vr* to rise, go up.

éleveur *m* **-euse** *f* stockbreeder.

éligible *adj* eligible.

élimination *f* elimination.

éliminatoire *adj* eliminatory; * *f* preliminary heat.

éliminer *vt* to eliminate, discard.

élire *vt* to elect.

élite *f* elite.

élitisme *m* elitism.

elle *pn* she; it; her; **c'est à ~** it's up to her; it's hers; **~-même** herself.

elliptique *adj* elliptic; **~ment** *adv* elliptically.

élocution *f* elocution, diction.

éloge *m* praise; eulogy.

élogieux *adj* laudatory, eulogistic.

éloigné *adj* distant, remote.

éloigner *vt* to move away, take away; **s'~** *vr* to go away; to grow distant.

éloquence *f* eloquence.

éloquent *adj* eloquent.

élu *adj* chosen, elected.

élucider *vt* to elucidate, clear up.

émacié *adj* emaciated, wasted.

émail *m* enamel.

émailler *vt* to enamel.

émancipation *f* emancipation, liberation.

émanciper *vt* to emancipate, liberate; **s'~** *vr* to become emancipated, liberated.

émaner *vi* to emanate, issue.

emballage *m* packing paper, wrapping paper.

emballer *vt* to pack up, wrap up.

embarcadère *m* landing stage, pier.

embarcation *f* boat, craft.

embargo *m* embargo.

embarquement *m* loading; embarkation.

embarquer *vt* to embark; to load; * *vi* to embark, go aboard.

embarras *m* embarrassment, confusion; trouble.

embarrassant *adj* embarrassing, uncomfortable.

embarrassé *adj* embarrassed, self-conscious.

embarrasser *vt* to embarrass; to hinder, hamper; **s'~** *vr* to burden o.s. with; to be troubled by.

embaucher *vt* to take on, hire.

embellir *vt* to beautify, make more attractive.

embellissement *m* embellishment, improvement.

embêter *vt* (*fam*) to bore; to get on one's nerves; **s'~** *vr* to be bored, fed up.

emblème *m* symbol, emblem.

emboîter *vt* to fit together; **s'~** *vr* to fit together; to fit into each other.

embonpoint *m* stoutness, plumpness.

embouchure *f* mouth (river); mouthpiece.

embouteillage *m* traffic jam; bottling.

embranchement *m* junction; side road.

embrasser *vt* to kiss, embrace.

embrayage *m* clutch.

embrayer *vi* to engage the clutch.

embrouiller *vt* to tangle up, mix up; **s'~** *vr* to become muddled, confused.

embryon *m* embryo.

embryonnaire *adj* embryonic.

embuscade *f* ambush.

émeraude *f* emerald.

émerger *vi* to emerge; to stand out.

émeri *m* emery.

émerveiller *vt* to astonish, amaze; **s'~** *vr* to marvel at.

émetteur *adj*, *f* **-trice** transmitting.

émettre *vt* to send out, emit, transmit.

émeute *f* riot.

émietter *vt* to crumble; to disperse, break up; **s'~** *vr* to crumble; to disperse, break up.

émigration *f* emigration.

émigré *m* **-e** *f* émigré, expatriate.

émigrer *vi* to emigrate.

éminence *f* hill, elevation; eminence, distinction.

éminent *adj* eminent, distinguished.

émir *m* emir.

émission *f* sending out; transmission; broadcast; emission.

emmêler *vt* to entangle; confuse; **s'~** *vr* to tangle.

emménager *vi* to move in.

emmener *vt* to take away; to lead.

émoi *m* agitation, emotion.

émotif *adj* emotional; emotive.

émotion *f* emotion; commotion.

émotivité *f* emotionalism.

émouvant *adj* moving, touching.

émouvoir *vt* to move, disturb, upset; **s'~** *vr* to be moved; to get worried, upset.

empailler *vt* to stuff.

empaqueter *vt* to parcel up, pack.

emparer (s') *vr* to seize, grab; to take possession of.

empêchement *m* obstacle, hitch; impediment.

empêcher *vt* to prevent, stop; **s'~** *vr*: **s'~ de** to refrain from doing something.

empereur *m* emperor.

empester *vt* to stink out; to poison, infect.

empêtrer *vt* to entangle,; **s'~** *vr* to get involved in, get mixed up in.

emphase *f* pomposity; emphasis, stress.

empiéter *vi* to encroach, overlap.

empiler *vt* to pile up, stack.

empire *m* empire; influence, ascendancy.

empirer *vi* to get worse, deteriorate.

empirique *adj* empirical; **~ment** *adv* empirically.

emplacement *m* site, location.

emploi *m* use; job, employment.

employé *m* **-e** *f* employee.

employer *vt* to use, spend; to employ.

employeur *m*, **euse** *f* employer.

empoisonner *vt* to poison; to annoy.

emporter *vt* to take; to carry off; to involve; **s'~** *vr* to lose one's temper.

empreinte *f* imprint, impression, stamp.

empresser (s') *vi* to rush to; to press around, fuss around.

emprise *f* hold, ascendancy.

emprisonner *vt* to imprison, trap.

emprunt *m* borrowing, loan.

emprunter *vt* to borrow; to assume; to derive.

ému *adj* moved, touched, excited.

émulsion *f* emulsion.

en *prép* in; to; by; on; **~ tant que** as; * *pn* from there; of it, of them; **je n'~ veux plus** I don't want any more of them; **s'~ faire** to worry; **il ~ va de même pour** the same goes for.

encadré *m* box; framed text.

encadrement *m* framing; training; managerial staff.

encadrer *vt* to frame; to train; to surround.

encaissement *m* collection; receipt; cashing.

encaisser *vt* to collect, receive; to cash.

encastrer *vt* to embed, fit in, encase.

enceinte *adj* pregnant.

encens *m* incense.

encenser *vt* (*rel*) to cense; to shower praise on.

encercler *vt* to encircle, surround.

enchaînement *m* linking; link; sequence.

enchaîner *vt* to chain.

enchanté *adj* enchanted, delighted.

enchantement *m* enchantment, delight.

enchanter *vt* to enchant, delight.

enchâsser *vt* to set, imbed.

enchère *f* bid, offer.

enchevêtrement *m* entanglement, confusion.

enclave *f* enclave.

enclencher *vt* to engage; to set in motion.

enclin *adj* inclined, prone.

enclore *vt* to enclose, shut in.

enclume *f* anvil; engine block.

encoder *vt* to encode.

encolure *f* neck; collar size.

encombrant *adj* unwieldy, cumbersome.

encombrement *m* congestion; jumble; obstruction.

encombrer *vt* to clutter, obstruct; **s'~** *vr* to burden o.s.

encore *adv* still; only; again; more; **~ que** even though.

encourageant *adj* encouraging, heartening.

encouragement *m* encouragement.

encourager *vt* to encourage; to incite.

encre *f* ink.

encyclopédie *f* encyclopaedia.

endettement *m* indebtedness; debt.

endetter *vt* to get sb into debt; **s'~** *vr* to get into debt.

endive *f* chicory.

endoctrinement *m* indoctrination.

endoctriner *vt* to indoctrinate.

endommager *vt* to damage.

endormir *vt* to put to sleep; **s'~** *vr* to fall asleep.

endossement *m* endorsement.

endosser *vt* to put on; to shoulder; to endorse.

endroit *m* place; side part; **à l'~** regarding.

enduire *vt* to coat, smear.

enduit *m* coating.

endurance *f* endurance, stamina.

endurci *adj* hardened; hard-hearted.

endurcir *vt* to harden; **s'~** *vr* to become hardened.

endurer *vt* to endure, bear.

énergétique *adj* energy; energising.

énergie *f* energy; spirit, vigour.

énergique *adj* energetic, vigorous; **~ment** *adv* energetically.

énervant *adj* enervating; irritating.

énervement *m* irritation; nervousness.

énerver *vt* to irritate, annoy; to get on one's nerves; **s'~** *vr* to get excited, worked up.

enfance *f* childhood; infancy.

enfant *mf* child; native.

enfanter *vt* to give birth to.

enfantillage *m* childishness.

enfantin *adj* childish, infantile.

enfer *m* hell.

enfermer *vt* to lock up; to confine; to box in.

enfiévrer *vt* to stir up, inflame.

enfiler *vt* to string, thread; to put on.

enfin *adv* at last; in short; after all.

enflammer *vt* to set on fire; to inflame, kindle; **s'~** *vr* to catch fire, ignite.

enflé *adj* swollen; bombastic, turgid.

enfler *vi* to swell up, inflate.

enfoncer *vt* to stick in, thrust; to break open; **s'~** *vr* to sink into, disappear into.

enfouir *vt* to bury.

enfuir (s') *vr* to run away, flee.

engagement *m* agreement, commitment, undertaking; engaging; opening.

engager *vt* to bind; to involve; to insert; to open; **s'~** *vr* to undertake to; to take a job.

engelure *f* chilblain.

engendrer *vt* to create, engender; to father.

engin *m* machine; instrument; contraption.

englober *vt* to include, encompass.

engloutir *vt* to wolf down; to engulf.

engorgement *m* obstruction, clogging; glut.

engouement *m* infatuation; fad, craze.

engouffrer *vt* to devour, swallow up, engulf; **s'~** *vr* to rush into, sweep, surge.

engourdi *adj* numb; dull.

engourdir *vt* to numb; to dull, blunt; **s'~** *vr* to become numb, to grow sluggish.

engourdissement *m* numbness; sleepiness.

engrais *m* fertilizer; manure.

engraisser *vi* to get fatter; * *vt* to fatten; to fertilize.

engrenage *m* gears, gearing.

énigmatique *adj* enigmatic; **~ment** *adv* enigmatically.

énigme *f* enigma, riddle.

enivrer *vt* to intoxicate, make drunk; **s'~** *vr* to get drunk.

enjeu *m* stake.

enjoliver *vt* to ornament; to embroider (truth).

enlacer *vt* to embrace, intertwine.

enlaidir *vt* to make ugly; **s'~** *vr* to become ugly.

enlèvement *m* abduction, kidnapping; removal.

enlever *vt* to remove; to take off; to deprive; to abduct.

enliser *vt* to get stuck (car); **s'~** *vr* to get bogged down, get sucked into.

enneigé *adj* snowy, snowbound.

enneigement *m* snow coverage.

ennemi *m* **-e** *f* enemy.

ennui *m* boredom, tedium, weariness.

ennuyer *vt* to bore, bother; **s'~** *vr* to get bored.

ennuyeux *adj* boring, tedious.

énorme *adj* enormous, huge.

énormément *adv* enormously.

énormité *f* enormity, hugeness; howler.

enquête *f* inquiry, investigation; survey.

enquêter *vi* to hold an inquiry; to investigate.

enraciner *vt* to implant, root; **s'~** *vr* to take root; to settle down somewhere.

enragé *adj* furious; keen.

enregistrement *m* recording; registration.

enregistrer *vt* to record; to register.

enrichi *adj* improved, enriched; nouveau riche.

enrichir *vt* to enrich, expand; **s'~** *vr* to get rich.

enrichissant *adj* enriching.

enrichissement *m* enrichment.

enrober *vt* to wrap, cover, coat.

enrôler *vt* to enlist, enrol.

enrouement *m* hoarseness.

enrouer *vt* to make hoarse.

enrouler *vt* to roll up, wind up.

enseignant *m* **-e** *f* teacher.

enseigne *f* sign; (*mil*) ensign.

enseignement *m* education, training, instruction.

enseigner *vt* to teach.

ensemble *adv* together, at the same time; * *m* unity; whole.

ensoleillé *adj* sunny.

ensorceler *vt* to bewitch, enchant.

ensuite *adv* then, next, afterwards.

entaille *f* cut, gash.

entamer *vt* to start, open, make a hole in.

entassement *m* piling up, heaping up.

entasser *vt* to pile up, heap up.

entendement *m* understanding, comprehension.

entendre *vt* to hear; to intend, mean; to understand; **s'~** *vr* to agree; to know how to.

entendu *adj* agreed; **bien** ~ of course.

entente *f* harmony, understanding; accord.

enterrement *m* burial; funeral.

enterrer *vt* to bury, inter.

en-tête *m* heading, header.

entêté *adj* stubborn, obstinate.

entêtement *m* stubbornness, obstinacy.

entêter *vt* to go to the head of; **s'~** *vr* to persist in.

enthousiasme *m* enthusiasm.

enthousiasmer *vt* to fill with enthusiasm; **s'~** *vr* to be enthusiastic about.

enthousiaste *adj* enthusiastic; * *mf* enthusiast.

entier *adj* entire, whole; intact.

entièrement *adv* entirely, wholly, completely.

entité *f* entity.

entonnoir *m* funnel; swallow hole; shellhole.

entorse *f* sprain.

entortiller *vt* to twist, twine; to hoodwink, wheedle.

entourage *m* set, circle; entourage.

entourer *vt* to surround, frame, encircle; **s'~** *vr*: **s'~ de** to surround o.s. with.

entracte *m* interval, intermission.

entraide *f* mutual aid.

entraider (s') *vr* to help one another.

entrailles *fpl* entrails, guts; womb.

entrain *m* spirit, liveliness.

entraînement *m* training, coaching; force, impetus.

entraîner *vt* to drag; to lead; to train; **s'~** *vr* to train o.s.

entraîneur *m* trainer, coach.

entrave *f* hindrance, obstacle; shackle.

entraver *vt* to hold up; to shackle.

entre *prép* between, among, into.

entrebâiller *vt* to half-open; **s'~** *vr* to be half-open.

entrecôte *f* rib steak.

entrecouper *vt* to intersperse, interrupt with.

entrée *f* entry, entrance; admission; insertion; **~ en matière** introduction; **d'~ de jeu** from the outset.

entrejambes *m* crotch.

entrelacer *vt* to intertwine, interlace.

entremêler *vt* to intermingle, intermix.

entremets *m* sweet, dessert.

entreposer *vt* to store, put into storage.

entrepôt *m* warehouse, bonded warehouse.

entreprenant *adj* enterprising.

entreprendre *vt* to embark upon, undertake.

entrepreneur *m* **-euse** *f* contractor; entrepreneur.

entreprise *f* company; venture, business.

entrer *vi* to enter, go in.

entresol *m* entresol, mezzanine.

entretemps *adv* meanwhile.

entretenir *vt* to maintain, look after; to speak with.

entretien *m* upkeep, maintenance; conversation.

entrevoir *vt* to make out; to glimpse; to anticipate.

entrevue *f* meeting, interview.

entrouvert *adj* half-open.

entrouvrir *vt* to half-open; **s'~** *vr* to half-open; to gape.

énumération *f* enumeration, listing.

énumérer *vt* to enumerate, list.

envahir *vt* to invade, overrun.

envahissant *adj* invasive; intrusive; pervasive.

enveloppe *f* envelope; covering; exterior.

envelopper *vt* to envelop; to wrap up; to veil.

envergure *f* breadth, scope, scale.

envers *prép* towards, to; * *m*; **à l'~** inside out, upside down.

envie *f* desire, longing, inclination; envy.

envier *vt* to envy.

envieux *adj* envious.

environ *adv* about, around; **~s** *mpl* vicinity, neighbourhood.

environnant *adj* surrounding.

environnement *m* environment.

environnemental *adj* environmental.

environner *vt* to surround, encircle.

envisager *vt* to view, envisage.

envoi *m* dispatch, remittance; kick-off.

envol *m* takeoff, flight.

envoler (s') *vr* to fly away; to disappear.

envoûtant *adj* bewitching, entrancing.

envoûter *vt* to bewitch.

envoyé *m* **-e** *f* messenger, envoy.

envoyer *vt* to send, dispatch; hurl, fire.

enzyme *m* enzyme.

épais *adj* thick; deep.

épaisseur *f* thickness; depth.

épaissir *vi* to thicken; to deepen; * *vt*: **s'~** *vr* to thicken, get thicker.

épanoui *adj* radiant, beaming.

épanouir *vt* to brighten, light up; open out; **s'~** *vr* to bloom.

épanouissement *m* blooming; lighting up; opening out.

épargne *f* saving, savings.

épargner *vt* to save; to spare.

éparpiller *vt* to scatter, distribute; **s'~** *vr* to scatter.

épaule *f* shoulder.

épauler *vt* to support, back up.

épave *f* wreck; derelict; ruin.

épée *f* sword.

épeler *vt* to spell.

éperdu *adj* distraught, overcome; **~ment** *adv* frantically, desperately.

éperon *m* spur; (*mar*) ram.

épervier *m* sparrowhawk.

éphémère *adj* ephemeral, fleeting.

épi *m* ear; tuft.

épice *m* spice.

épicé *adj* spicy; juicy.

épicerie *f* grocery trade; grocer's shop.

épicier *m* **-ière** *f* grocer; greengrocer.

épidémie *f* epidemic.

épidémique *adj* epidemic; contagious.

épiderme *m* epidermis; skin.

épier *vt* to spy on.

épiglotte *f* epiglottis.

épilation *f* removal of hair.

épilepsie *f* epilepsy.

épileptique *adj* epileptic.

épiler *vt* to remove hair, pluck.

épilogue *m* epilogue; conclusion.

épinard *m* spinach.

épine *f* spine; thorn.

épineux *adj* thorny, prickly; tricky.

épingle *f* pin.

Épiphanie *f* Epiphany.

épique *adj* epic.

épiscopal *adj* episcopal.

épiscopat *m* episcopate.

épisode *m* episode.

épisodique *adj* occasional; transitory; **~ment** *adv* occasionally.

épitaphe *f* epitaph.

épithète *f* epithet.

éplucher *vt* to clean; to peel; to sift.

épluchure *f* peeling, paring.

éponge *f* sponge.

éponger *vt* to sponge, mop.

épopée *f* epic.

époque *f* time, epoch, age, period.

épouser *vt* to marry, wed; espouse.

épousseter *vt* to dust.

épouvantable *adj* terrible, appalling; **~ment** *adv* terribly, appallingly.

épouvantail *m* scarecrow.

épouvante *f* terror, dread.

épouvanter *vt* to terrify, appall.

époux *m* **épouse** *f* spouse.

éprendre *vr*: **s'~ de** to fall in love with.

épreuve *f* test; ordeal, trial; proof.

éprouvant *adj* trying, testing.

éprouver *vt* to feel, experience.

éprouvette *f* test tube.

épuisé *adj* exhausted; sold out.

épuisement *m* exhaustion.

épuiser *vt* to exhaust, wear out; **s'~** *vr* to run out; to exhaust o.s.

épuisette *f* landing net.

épurer *vt* to purify, refine.

équateur *m* equator.

équation *f* equation.

équatorial *adj* equatorial.

équerre *f* square; bracket.

équestre *adj* equestrian.

équilibre *m* balance, equilibrium; harmony.

équilibrer *vt* to balance; **s'~** *vr* to balance each other.

équipage *m* crew; gear, equipment.

équipe *f* team, crew, gang, staff.

équipement *m* equipment; fitting out, fittings.

équiper *vt* to equip, fit out.

équipier *m* **-ière** *f* team member.

équitable *adj* equitable, fair; **~ment** *adv* equitably, fairly.

équitation *f* equitation, riding.

équivalence *f* equivalence.

équivalent *adj* equivalent, same; * *m* equivalent.

équivoque *adj* equivocal, questionable.

érable *m* maple.

érafler *vt* to scratch, scrape.

ère *f* era.

érection *f* erection; establishment.

éreintant *adj* exhausting, backbreaking.

ergot *m* spur; (*tec*) lug.

ériger *vt* to erect; to establish.

ermite *m* hermit.

éroder *vt* to erode.

érosion *f* erosion.

érotique *adj* erotic.

érotisme *m* eroticism.

errant *adj* wandering, stray.

errer *vi* to wander, roam.

erreur *f* error, mistake, fault.

erroné *adj* erroneous.

éructation *f* eructation.

érudit *adj* erudite, learned; * *m* scholar.

érudition *f* erudition, learning.

éruptif *adj* eruptive.

éruption *f* eruption.

escabeau *m* stool; stepladder.

escadron *m* squadron, platoon.

escalade *f* climbing; escalation.

escalader *vt* to climb, scale.

escale *f* port of call, touchdown.

escalier *m* stairs, steps.

escalope *f* escalope.

escamoter *vt* to dodge, evade; to pilfer.

escapade *f* escapade; prank, jaunt.

escargot *m* snail.

escarpement *m* escarpment; steepness.

esclavage *m* slavery, bondage.

esclavagisme *m* proslavery.

esclave *mf* slave.

escompte *m* discount.

escompter *vt* to discount.

escorte *f* escort; retinue.

escorter *vt* to escort.

escrime *f* fencing.

escrimeur *m* **-euse** *f* fencer.

escroc *m* crook, con man.

escroquer *vt* to swindle, con.

ésotérique *adj* esoteric.

espace *m* space, interval.

espacement *m* spacing, interval.

espacer *vt* to space out.

espadon *m* swordfish.

espadrille *f* espadrille, rope-soled sandal.

espèce *f* sort, kind; species.

espérance *f* hope, expectation.

espérer *vt* to hope.

espion *m* **-ne** *f* spy.

espionnage *m* espionage, spying.

espionner *vt* to spy.

esplanade *f* esplanade.

espoir *m* hope.

esprit *m* mind, intellect; spirit; wit.

esquimau *m* **-de** *f* Eskimo.

esquisse *f* sketch, outline.

esquisser *vt* to sketch, outline.

esquiver *vt* to dodge; to shirk.

essai *m* test, trial; attempt; essay.

essaim *m* swarm.

essayage *m* fitting, trying on.

essayer *vt* to test, try, try on.

essence *f* petrol; essential oil.

essentiel *adj* essential, basic; **-lement** *adv* essentially, basically.

essieu *m* axle.

essorage *m* wringing, mangling.

essorer *vt* to wring, mangle.

essouffler *vt* to wind; **s'~** *vr* to get out of breath.

essuyer *vt* to wipe, mop; **s'~** *vr* to wipe o.s.

est *m* east.

esthète *mf* aesthete.

esthéticien *m* **-ne** *f* beautician.

esthétique *adj* aesthetic; **~ment** *adv* aesthetically; * *f* aesthetics.

estimation *f* valuation; estimation, reckoning.

estime *f* esteem, respect, regard.

estimer *vt* to value, assess, estimate.

estival *adj* summer; summery.

estivant *m* **-e** *f* holidaymaker, summer visitor.

estomac *m* stomach.

estomper *vt* to blur, dim; **s'~** *vr* to become blurred.

estrade *f* platform, rostrum.

estragon *m* tarragon.

et *conj* and.

étable *f* cowshed.

établi *adj* established; * *m* workbench.

établir *vt* to establish, set up; **s'~** *vr* to settle; to set o.s. up as; to become established.

établissement *m* establishing, building; establishment.

étage *m* floor, storey; stage, level.

étagère *f* shelf.

étalage *m* display, display window; stall.

étalagiste *mf* window dresser.

étaler *vt* to spread, strew; to stagger; to display.

étalon *m* stallion.

étanche *adj* waterproof.

étanchéité *f* waterproofness.

étang *m* pond.

étape *f* stage, leg; staging point.

état *m* state, condition; statement.

étatique *adj* under state control.

étatiser *vt* to bring under state control, nationalize.

état-major *m* (*mil*) staff; staff headquarters.

étau *m* vice.

étayer *vt* to prop up, support.

été *m* summer.

éteindre *vt* to put out, extinguish; **s'~** *vr* to go out; to die; to evaporate.

éteint *adj* faded; extinct.

étendard *m* standard, flag.

étendre *vt* to spread, extend; to floor; **s'~** *vr* to spread; to stretch out; to increase.

étendu *adj* extensive, sprawling, wide.

étendue *f* expanse, area; duration.

éternel *adj* eternal, everlasting; **~lement** *adv* eternally.

éterniser *vt* to draw out; to immortalize; **s'~** *vr* to drag on, linger on.

éternité *f* eternity; ages.

éternuer *vi* to sneeze.

éthane *m* ethane.

éther *m* ether.

ethnie *f* ethnic unit.

ethnique *adj* ethnic.

ethnologie *f* ethnology.

ethnologue *mf* ethnologist.

étincelant *adj* sparkling; gleaming.

étinceler *vi* to sparkle, gleam.

étincelle *f* spark; gleam, glimmer.

étiqueter *vt* to label, mark.

étiquette *f* label, tag; etiquette.

étirement *m* stretching.

étirer *vt* to stretch, draw out; **s'~** *vr* to stretch out.

étoffe *f* material, fabric; stuff.

étoile *f* star.

étoilé *adj* starry.

étonnant *adj* astonishing, surprising.

étonné *adj* astonished, surprised.

étonnement *m* surprise, astonishment.

étonner *vt* to astonish, surprise; **s'~** *vr* to be astonished.

étouffant *adj* stifling.

étouffer *vt* to suffocate; to muffle; **s'~** *vr* to be suffocated, to swelter.

étourderie *f* absentmindedness.

étourdi *adj* absentminded; **~ment** *adv* absentmindedly.

étourdir *vt* to stun, daze; to deafen.

étourdissant *adj* deafening; stunning.

étourdissement *m* blackout, dizzy spell; surprise.

étourneau *m* starling.

étrange *adj* strange, funny; **~ment** *adv* strangely, oddly.

étranger *m* **-ère** *f* foreigner, stranger, alien; * *adj* foreign, strange, unknown.

étrangeté *f* strangeness, oddness.

étranglement *m* strangulation; bottleneck.

étrangler *vt* to strangle, stifle; **s'~** *vr* to strangle o.s., choke.

être *vi* to be; **c'est-à-dire** namely, that is to say; * *m* being, person, soul.

étreindre *vt* to embrace, hug; to seize.

étreinte *f* embrace; stranglehold.

étrier *m* stirrup.

étroit *adj* narrow; strict; **~ement** *adv* closely; strictly.

étude *f* study; survey; office.

étudier *vt* to study, examine.

étui *m* case; holster.

étymologie *f* etymology.

étymologique *adj* etymological.

eu = *p.p.* **avoir** had.

eucalyptus *m* eucalyptus.

eucharistie *f* eucharist.

euphémisme *m* euphemism.

euphorie *f* euphoria.

euphorique *adj* euphoric.

européen *m* **-ne** *f* European; * *adj* European.

euthanasie *f* euthanasia.

eux *pn* they, them; **c'est à ~** it's up to them; it's theirs; **~-mêmes** themselves.

évacuation *f* evacuation; emptying.

évacuer *vt* to evacuate, clear.

évader (s') *vr* to escape.

évaluation *f* evaluation, appraisal.

évaluer *vt* to evaluate, appraise.

évangélique *adj* evangelical.

évangéliser *vt* to evangelize.

évangile *m* gospel.

évanouir (s') *vr* to faint, pass out.

évanouissement *m* faint, blackout.

évaporation *f* evaporation.

évaporer (s') *vr* to evaporate.

évasif *adj* evasive.

évasion *f* escape; escapism.

évasivement *adv* evasively.

évêché *m* bishopric.

éveil *m* awakening; dawning.

éveiller *vt* to waken, arouse; **s'~** *vr* to wake up.

événement *m* event, incident.

éventail *m* fan; range.

éventaire *m* tray; stall.

éventualité *f* eventuality, possibility.

éventuel *adj* possible; **~lement** *adv* possibly.

évêque *m* bishop.

évertuer (s') *vr* to strive to.

évidemment *adv* obviously, evidently.

évidence *f* evidence, proof.

évident *adj* obvious, evident.

évier *m* sink.

évincer *vt* to oust; to evict.

éviter *vt* to avoid; to spare.

évocation *f* evocation, recall.

évolué *adj* developed, advanced; enlightened.

évoluer *vi* to evolve, develop.

évolution *f* evolution, development.

évoquer *vt* to evoke, recall.

exacerber *vt* to exacerbate, aggravate.

exact *adj* exact, accurate; **~ement** *adv* exactly.

exactitude *f* exactness, accuracy.

exagération *f* exaggeration.

exagéré *adj* exaggerated, excessive; **~ment** *adv* exaggeratedly.

exagérer *vt* to exaggerate.

exaltation *f* elation; extolling, praising.

exalter *vt* to exalt, glorify; to elate.

examen *m* examination, survey, investigation.

examinateur *m* **-trice** *f* examiner.

examiner *vt* to examine, survey.

exaspération *f* exasperation.

exaspérer *vt* to exasperate.

exaucer *vt* to fulfil, grant.

excédent *m* surplus, excess.

excédentaire *adj* surplus, excess.

excellent *adj* excellent.

exceller *vi* to excel.

excentricité *f* eccentricity.

excentrique *adj* eccentric; **~ment** *adv* eccentrically.

excepté *adj* apart, aside; * *prép* except, but for.

exception *f* exception.

exceptionnel *adj* exceptional; **~lement** *adv* exceptionally.

excès *m* excess, surplus.

excessivement *adv* excessively.

excitant *m* stimulant; * *adj* exciting, stimulating.

excitation *f* excitation, stimulation; incitement.

exciter *vt* to excite, stimulate; **s'~** *vr* to become excited.

exclamation *f* exclamation.

exclamer (s') *vr* to exclaim.

exclu *adj* excluded, outcast.

exclure *vt* to exclude, oust, expel.

exclusif *adj* exclusive.

exclusion *f* exclusion, suspension.

exclusivement *adv* exclusively.

exclusivité *f* exclusive rights.

excrément *m* excrement.

excroissance *f* (*med*) excrescence, outgrowth.

excursion *f* excursion, trip.

excursionniste *mf* tripper; walker.

excuse *f* excuse, pretext.

excuser *vt* to excuse, forgive; **s'~** *vr* to apologize for.

exécrable *adj* execrable, atrocious; **~ment** *adv* atrociously, execrably.

exécration *f* execration, loathing.

exécrer *vt* to execrate, loathe.

exécuter *vt* to execute, carry out, perform; to produce.

exécution *f* execution, carrying out, performance.

exemplaire *m* copy, archetype; * *adj* model, exemplary; **~ment** *adv* exemplarily.

exemple *m* example, model, instance.

exempt *adj* exempt, free from.

exercer *vt* to exercise, perform, fulfil; **s'~** *vr* to practise.

exercice *m* exercise, practice, use; financial year.

exhaustif *adj* exhaustive.

exhaustivement *adv* exhaustively.

exhiber *vt* to exhibit, show; to produce; **s'~** *vr* to show off; to expose o.s.

exhibition *f* exhibition, show; display.

exhibitionniste *mf* exhibitionist.

exhortation *f* exhortation.

exhorter *vt* to exhort, urge.

exigeant *adj* demanding, exacting.

exigence *f* demand, requirement; exigency.

exiger *vt* to demand, require.

exigu *adj*, *f* **exiguè** scanty, exiguous.

exiguïté *f* exiguity, scantiness.

exil *m* exile.

exilé *m* **-e** *f* exile;* *adj* exiled.

exiler *vt* to exile, banish; **s'~** *vr* to go into exile.

existant *adj* existing.

existence *f* existence, life.

exister *vi* to exist; to be.

exode *m* exodus; drift, loss.

exonération *f* exemption.

exonérer *vt* to exempt.

exorbitant *adj* exorbitant, outrageous.

exorciser *vt* to exorcise.

exotique *adj* exotic.

exotisme *m* exoticism.

expansif *adj* expansive, outgoing.

expansion *f* expansion, development.

expatrié *m* **-e** *f* expatriate; * *adj* expatriate.

expatrier *vt* to expatriate; **s'~** *vr* to expatriate o.s.

expectative *f* expectation, hope; **être dans l'~** to be waiting (to see, to hear).

expédier *vt* to send, dispatch; to dispose of.

expéditeur *m* **-trice** *f* sender; shipper, consignor.

expéditif *adj* quick, expeditious.

expédition *f* dispatch; consignment.

expérience *f* experience; experiment.

expérimental *adj* experimental; **~ement** *adv* experimentally.

expérimentateur *m* **-trice** *f* experimenter.

expérimentation *f* experimentation.

expérimenté *adj* experienced.

expérimenter *vt* to test; to experiment with.

expert *adj* expert, skilled in; * *m* expert; connoisseur; assessor.

expertise *f* expertise; expert appraisal.

expiation *f* expiation, atonement.

expier *vi* to expiate, atone for.

expiration *f* expiry; expiration, exhalation.

expirer *vi* to breathe out, expire.

explicatif *adj* explanatory.

explication *f* explanation, analysis.

explicite *adj* explicit **~ment** *adv* explicitly.

expliquer *vt* to explain, account for; to analyse.

exploitant *m* **-e** *f* farmer, smallholder.

exploitation *f* working; exploitation; operating; concern; smallholding.

exploiter *vt* to work, exploit; run, operate.

explorateur *m* **-trice** *f* explorer.

exploration *f* exploration.

explorer *vt* to explore.

exploser *vi* to explode.

explosif *adj* explosive; * *m* explosive.

explosion *f* explosion.

exportateur *m* **-trice** *f* exporter.

exportation *f* export, exportation.

exporter *vt* to export.

exposé *m* exposition, overview, statement.

exposer *vt* to display; to explain, state; to expose; **s'~** *vr* to expose o.s. to, run the risk of.

exposition *f* display; exposition; exposure.

exprès *adj* express.

express *adj* fast; * *m* fast train.

expressif *adj* expressive.

expression *f* expression.

expressionnisme *m* expressionism.

expressionniste *mf* expressionist; * *adj* expressionist, expressionistic.

exprimer *vt* to express, voice; **s'~** *vr* to express o.s.

expropriation *f* expropriation.

expulser *vt* to expel; to evict.

expulsion *f* expulsion; eviction.

exquis *adj* exquisite; **~ément** *adv* exquisitely.

extase *f* ecstasy; rapture.

extasier (s') *vr* to go into ecstasies.

extensible *adj* extensible, extendable.

extension *f* extension; stretching; expansion.

exténuant *adj* exhausting.

exténuer *vt* to exhaust; **s'~** *vr* to exhaust o.s.

extérieur *m* exterior, outside; * *adj* outer, external, exterior; **~ement** *adv* externally, outwardly.

extérioriser *vt* to show, express; to exteriorize.

extermination *f* extermination.

exterminer *vt* exterminate.

externe *adj* external, outer.

extincteur *m* extinguisher.

extinction *f* extinction, extinguishing.

extraction *f* extraction; mining.

extradition *f* extradition.

extraire *vt* to extract; to mine.

extrait *m* extract; *(jur)* abstract.

extraordinaire *adj* extraordinary; **~ment** *adv* extraordinarily.

extraterrestre *mf* extraterrestrial; * *adj* extraterrestrial.

extravagant *adj* extravagant, wild.

extraverti *m* **-e** *f* extrovert; * *adj* extrovert.

extrême *adj* extreme; **~ment** *adv* extremely.

extrémiste *mf, adj* extremist.

extrémité *f* end, extremity, limit.

exubérance *f* exuberance.

exubérant *adj* exuberant.

exulter *vi* to exult.

F

fable *f* fable, story, tale.

fabricant *m* **-e** *f* manufacturer, maker.

fabrication *f* manufacture, production.

fabrique *f* factory.

fabriquer *vt* to manufacture; to forge; to fabricate.

fabuleux *adj* fabulous, mythical, legendary.

façade *f* façade, front.

face *f* face, side, surface, aspect; **en** ~ opposite, over the road; ~ **à** facing; **faire** ~ **à** to confront, face up to; **de** ~ fullface, frontal; ~ **à** ~ face to face.

face à face *m* encounter, interview.

facette *f* facet.

fâché *adj* angry; sorry.

fâcher *vt* to anger, make angry; to grieve; **se** ~ *vr* to get angry.

fâcheux *adj* deplorable, regrettable.

facile *adj* easy; facile; **~ment** *adv* easily.

facilité *f* easiness, ease; ability; facility.

faciliter *vt* to make easier, facilitate.

façon *f* way, fashion; make; imitation; **de toute** ~ at any rate; **non merci, sans** ~ no thanks, honestly; **de** ~ **à** so that, so as to.

façonner *vt* to shape, fashion, model; to till.

fac-similé *m* facsimile.

facteur *m* postman.

factice *adj* artificial, imitation.

faction *f* faction; sentry-duty.

facturation *f* invoicing.

facture *f* bill, invoice; construction, technique.

facturer *vt* to invoice, charge for.

facultatif *adj* optional.

faculté *f* faculty; power, ability; right.

fade *adj* insipid, bland, dull.

fagot *m* faggot, bundle of firewood.

faible *adj* weak, feeble; slight, poor; **~ment** *adv* weakly, faintly, feebly.

faiblesse *f* weakness, feebleness, faintness.

faiblir *vi* to fail, flag, weaken; to wane.

faïence *f* earthenware, crockery.

faille *f* fault; flaw; weakness.

faillir *vi*: to come close to; to fail **j'ai failli tomber** I almost fell.

faillite *f* bankruptcy; collapse.

faim *f* hunger; appetite; famine.

fainéant *m* **-e** *f* idler, loafer.

faire *vt* to do; to make; **rien à** ~**!** nothing doing!; **se** ~ **à** to get used to; **s'en** ~ to worry.

faire-part *m* announcement (birth, marriage, death).

faisable *adj* feasible.

faisan *m* pheasant.

faisceau *m* bundle, stack; beam.

fait *m* event; fact; act.

faîte *m* summit; rooftop.

falaise *f* cliff.

falloir *vi*: to be necessary; **il faut, que tu partes** you must leave.

falsifier *vt* to falsify, alter.

famélique *adj* starving, scrawny.

fameux *adj* famous; excellent.

familial *adj* family, domestic.

familiariser *vt* to familiarize; **se** ~ *vr* to familiarize o.s.

familiarité *f* familiarity.

familier *adj* familiar; colloquial; informal.

familièrement *adv* familiarly, informally.

famille *f* family.

famine *f* famine.

fanatique *adj* fanatic; **~ment** *adv* fanatically; * *mf* fanatic; zealot.

fanatisme *m* fanaticism.

fané *adj* faded, withered.

faner *vt* to turn (hay); to fade; **se** ~ *vr* to wither, fade.

fanfare *f* fanfare, flourish; brass band.

fantaisie *f* whim, extravagance; imagination.

fantasme *m* fantasy.

fantasmer *vi* to fantasize.

fantastique *adj* fantastic; **~ment** *adv* fantastically; eerily.

fantôme *m* ghost, phantom.

faon *m* fawn.

farce *f* joke, prank; farce.

farceur *m* **-euse** *f* joker; clown.

farci *adj* stuffed, crammed, packed.

farcir *vt* to stuff, cram.

fard *m* make-up.

fardeau *m* load, burden.

farder *vt* to make up; to disguise; **se ~** *vr* to make o.s. up.

farine *f* flour.

farineux *adj* floury, powdery; * *m* starchy food.

farouche *adj* shy, timid; unsociable; fierce; **~ment** *adv* fiercely.

fascicule *m* booklet, fascicule, part, instalment.

fascinant *adj* fascinating.

fascination *f* fascination.

fasciner *vt* to fascinate, bewitch.

fascisme *m* fascism.

fasciste *mf, adj* fascist.

faste *m* pomp, ostentation.

fastidieux *adj* tedious, boring.

fastueux *adj* sumptuous, luxurious.

fatal *adj* fatal, deadly; fateful; **~ement** *adv* inevitably, unavoidably.

fataliste *mf* fatalist; * *adj* fatalistic.

fatalité *f* fatality; inevitability.

fatidique *adj* fateful; fatal.

fatigant *adj* tiring, fatiguing.

fatigue *f* fatigue, tiredness.

fatigué *adj* tired, weary; overworked, strained.

fatiguer *vt* to tire; to overwork, strain; **se ~** *vr* to get tired.

faubourg *m* suburb.

faucher *vt* to reap; to flatten, knock down.

faucille *f* sickle.

faucon *m* falcon, hawk.

faufiler *vt* to tack; to insinuate, introduce; **se ~** *vr* to worm one's way in.

faune *f* wildlife, fauna.

faussaire *mf* forger.

faussement *adv* wrongly; falsely.

fausser *vt* to distort, alter; to warp.

fausseté *f* falseness; deceitfulness.

faute *f* mistake, foul, fault; **~ de mieux** for lack of anything better.

fauteuil *m* armchair.

fautif *m* **-ive** *f* culprit, guilty party; * *adj* at fault, guilty; faulty, incorrect.

fauve *m* wild animal; fawn (colour).

faux *adj* false, forged, fake; wrong; bogus.

faux-filet *m* sirloin.

faux-fuyant *m* evasion, equivocation.

faux-semblant *m* sham, pretence.

faveur *f* favour.

favorable *adj* favourable, sympathetic; **~ment** *adv* favourably.

favori *m* **-te** *f* favourite; * *adj* favourite.

favoriser *vt* to favour, further.

fébrile *adj* feverish, febrile; **~ment** *adv* feverishly.

fébrilité *f* feverishness.

fécond *adj* fertile; prolific, fruitful; creative.

fécondation *f* impregnation, fertilization.

féconder *vt* to impregnate; to fertilize, pollinate.

fécondité *f* fertility, fecundity.

fécule *f* starch.

féculent *adj* starchy; * *m* starchy food.

fédéral *adj* federal.

fédération *f* federation.

fée *f* fairy.

féerique *adj* magical, fairy.

feindre *vt* to feign, pretend.

feinte *f* dummy, feint.

fêlé *adj* cracked, hare-brained.

félicitation *f* congratulation.

féliciter *vt* to congratulate.

félin *adj* feline; * *m* feline.

femelle *f* female.

féminin *adj* feminine, female.

féminisme *m* feminism.

féministe *mf* feminist; * *adj* feminist.

féminité *f* femininity.

femme *f* woman; wife; **~ de ménage** cleaning woman; **~ de chambre** chambermaid.

fémur *m* femur.

fendiller *vt* to chink, crack, craze; **se ~** *vr* to be covered in small cracks.

fendre *vt* to split, cleave, crack; **se ~** *vr* to crack.

fenêtre *f* window.

fenouil *m* fennel.

fente *f* crack, fissure; slot.

féodal *adj* feudal.

fer *m* iron, point, blade; **~ à cheval** horseshoe.

férié *adj* public holiday.

ferme *adj* firm, steady; definite; **~ment** *adv* firmly; * *f* farm.

fermé *adj* closed; exclusive; inscrutable.

ferment *m* ferment, leaven.

fermentation *f* fermentation, fermenting.

fermenter *vi* to ferment, work.

fermer *vt* to close; block; turn off; **se ~** *vr* to close, shut up; to close one's mind to.

fermeté *f* firmness, steadiness.

fermeture *f* closing, shutting; latch; fastener.

fermier *m* **-ière** *f* farmer.

féroce *adj* ferocious, savage; **~ment** *adv* ferociously, savagely.

férocité *f* ferocity, fierceness.

ferraille *f* scrap iron.

ferronnerie *f* ironworks; ironwork.

ferroviaire *adj* railway.

fertile *adj* fertile, productive.

fertilisation *f* fertilization.

fertiliser *vt* to fertilize.

fertilité *f* fertility.

fervent *adj* fervent, ardent.

ferveur *f* fervour, ardour.

fesse *f* buttock.

festin *m* feast.

festival *m* festival.

fête *f* feast, holiday.

fêter *vt* to celebrate, fête.

fétichisme *m* fetishism.

fétichiste *mf*; * *adj* fetishist.

fétide *adj* fetid.

feu *m* fire; light; hearth; **en ~** on fire.

feuillage *m* foliage, greenery.

feuille *f* leaf.

feuillet *m* leaf, page, layer.

feuilleté *adj* foliated; laminated.

feuilleter *vt* to leaf through.

feuilleton *m* serial, series.

feutre *m* felt; felt hat.

fève *f* broad bean.

fiabilité *f* accuracy; dependability.

fiable *adj* reliable; dependable.

fiançailles *fpl* engagement, betrothal.

fiancer (se) *vr* to become engaged.

fiasco *m* fiasco.

fibre *f* fibre.

fibreux *adj* fibrous, stringy.

fibrome *m* fibroid, fibroma.

ficeler *vt* to tie up.

ficelle *f* string; stick (bread).

fiche *f* card; sheet; certificate.

ficher *vt* to file, put on file.

fichier *m* catalogue; file.

fictif *adj* fictitious; imaginary.

fiction *f* imagination, fiction.

fidèle *adj* faithful, loyal; **~ment** *adv* faithfully; * *mf* believer.

fidélité *f* fidelity, loyalty.

fief *m* fief; stronghold, preserve.

fier (se) *vr* to trust, rely on.

fier *adj* proud, haughty; noble.

fièrement *adv* proudly.

fierté *f* pride; arrogance.

fièvre *f* fever, temperature; excitement.

fiévreux *adj* feverish.

figer *vt* to congeal, freeze; to clot; **se ~** *vr* to congeal, freeze; to clot.

figue *f* fig.

figuier *m* fig tree.

figurant *m* **-e** *f* extra, walk-on; stooge.

figuratif *adj* figurative, representational.

figure *f* face; figure; illustration, diagram.

figuré *adj* figurative, metaphorical, diagrammatic; * *m*: **au ~** in the figurative sense.

figurer *vt* to represent; * *vi* to appear, feature; **se ~** *vr* to imagine.

figurine *f* figurine.

fil *m* thread; wire; cord; **~ de fer** wire; **~ à plomb** plumb line; **au ~ des jours** with the passing days.

filament *m* filament, strand, thread.

filature *f* spinning; mill; tailing.

file *f* line, queue; **à la ~** in line, in succession; **stationner en double ~** to double-park.

filer *vt* to spin; to tail; to draw out; * *vi* to run, trickle; to fly by; to make off.

filet *m* dribble, trickle; fillet; net.

filiation *f* filiation; relation.

filière *f* path; procedures; network.

fille *f* daughter, girl.

fillette *f* (small) girl.

filleul *m* **-e** *f* godson, godchild.

film *m* film, picture.

filmer *vt* to film.

filon *m* vein, seam.

fils *m* son.

filtre *m* filter.

filtrer *vt* to filter; to screen.

fin *f* end, finish; **prendre ~** to terminate, come to an end; * *adj* thin, fine; delicate; **~ement** *adv* finely, delicately.

final *adj* final; **~ement** *adv* finally.

finale *f* finale.

finance *f* finance.

financement *m* financing.

financer *vt* to finance.

financier *m* **-ière** *f* financier.

financièrement *adv* financially.

finesse *f* fineness; sharpness; neatness; delicacy.

fini *adj* finished, over, complete.

finir *vt* to finish, complete; * *vi* to finish, end; to die.

finition *f* finish, finishing.

fisc *m* tax department.

fiscal *adj* fiscal, tax.

fissure *f* crack, fissure.

fixation *f* fixation; fixing, fastening.

fixe *adj* fixed, permanent, set; **~ment** *adv* fixedly, steadily.

fixer *vt* to fix, fasten; to arrange; **se ~** *vr* to settle.

flacon *m* bottle, flask.

flageolant *adj* shaky.

flageolet *m* flageolet.

flagrant *adj* flagrant, blatant.

flair *m* sense of smell, nose; intuition.

flairer *vt* to smell, sniff; to scent.

flambeau *m* torch; candlestick.

flamboyant *adj* blazing; flamboyant.

flamboyer *vi* to blaze, flash, gleam.

flamme *f* flame; fervour; ardour.

flan *m* custard tart; mould.

flanc *m* flank, side.

flanelle *f* flannel.

flâner *vi* to stroll; to lounge about.

flasque *adj* flaccid; spineless.

flatter *vt* to flatter, gratify; to pander; to delight.

flatterie *f* flattery.

flatteur *m* **-euse** *f* flatterer.

fléau *m* scourge; plague.

flèche *f* arrow.

fléchir *vi* to bend, yield, weaken; * *vt* to bend, sway.

fléchissement *m* bending; flexing; bowing.

flegmatique *adj* phlegmatic.

flegme *m* composure, phlegm.

flétrir *vt* to wither, fade; to stigmatize; **se ~** *vr* to wither, wilt.

fleur *f* flower.

fleuri *adj* in bloom; flowery.

fleurir *vi* to blossom, flower; * *vt* to decorate with flowers.

fleuriste *mf* florist.

fleuve *m* river.

flexibilité *f* flexibility.

flexible *adj* flexible, pliant.

flic *m* (*fam*) cop, policeman.

flocon *m* fleck, flake.

floraison *f* flowering, blossoming.

floral *adj* floral, flower.

flore *f* flora.

florissant *adj* flourishing, blooming.

flot *m* stream, flood; floodtide; wave.

flotte *f* fleet; (*col*) rain.

flottement *m* wavering; vagueness, imprecision.

flotter *vi* to float; to drift; to wander; to waver.

flotteur *m* float.

flou *adj* blurred, hazy.

fluctuant *adj* fluctuating.

fluctuation *f* fluctuation.

fluide *adj* fluid, flowing.

fluidité *f* fluidity.

fluor *m* fluorine.

fluorescent *adj* fluorescent.

fluorure *m* fluoride.

flûte *f* flute; French stick (bread).

flûtiste *mf* flautist.

flux *m* flood; flow; flux.

focaliser *vt* to focus; **se ~** *vr* to be focused on.

foetus *m* foetus.

foi *f* faith, trust.

foie *m* liver.

foin *m* hay.

foire *f* fair, trade fair.

fois *f* time, occasion.

folie *f* madness, insanity; extravagance.

folklore *m* folklore.

folklorique *adj* folk.

follement *adv* madly, wildly.

foncé *adj* dark, deep (colours).

foncer *vi* to hammer along, rush at; * *vt* to make darker; (*tec*) to sink, bore.

foncier *adj* land, landed, property.

foncièrement *adv* fundamentally, basically.

fonction *f* post, duty; function.

fonctionnaire *mf* civil servant.

fonctionnement *m* working, functioning, operation.

fonctionner *vi* to work, function, operate.

fond *m* bottom, back; **au ~** basically, in fact; **à ~** thoroughly, in depth; **dans le ~** in reality, basically; **~ de teint** foundation.

fondamental *adj* fundamental, basic; **~ement** *adv* fundamentally.

fondamentalisme *m* fundamentalism.

fondamentaliste *mf*; * *adj* fundamentalist.

fondant *adj* thawing, melting.

fondateur *m* **-trice** *f* founder.

fondation *f* foundation.

fondement *m* foundation; ground.

fonder *vt* to found; to base.

fondre *vi* to melt; to vanish; to slim; * *vt* to melt; to cast; to merge.

fonds *m* business; fund; money; stock.

fondu *adj* melted; molten; cast.

fontaine *f* fountain, spring.

fonte *f* melting; casting; smelting.

football *m* football, soccer.

forage *m* drilling, boring.

forain *m* **-e** *f* stallholder; fairground entertainer; * *adj* fairground.

force *f* strength, force, violence, energy; **à ~ de** by dint of.

forcé *adj* forced; emergency; **~ment** *adv* inevitably.

forcené *adj* deranged, frenzied.

forcer *vt* to force, compel; track down; * *vi* to overdo, strain; **se ~** *vr* to force o.s. to.

forestier *adj* forest; forestry.

forêt *f* forest.

forfait *m* set price, package; (*sport*) withdrawal.

forfaitaire *adj* fixed, set, inclusive.

forge *f* forge, smithy.

forger *vt* to forge, form, mould.

forgeron *m* blacksmith, smith.

formaliser (se) *vr* to take offence at.

formalité *f* formality.

format *m* format, size.

formation *f* formation; training.

forme *f* form, shape; mould, fitness; **être en ~** to be on form; **en ~ de** forming.

formel *adj* definite, positive; formal; **~lement** *adv* positively, definitely; formally.

former *vt* to form, make up; to train; **se ~** *vr* to form, gather; to train o.s.

formidable *adj* tremendous; fantastic; **~ment** *adv* tremendously, fantastically.

formulaire *m* form.

formule *f* formula; phrase; system.

formuler *vt* to formulate; express.

fort *adj* strong; high; loud; pronounced; **~ement** *adv* strongly; highly; very much; * *adv* loudly; greatly; most; * *m* fort; strong point; (*mus*) forte.

forteresse *f* fortress.

fortifiant *m* tonic; * *adj* fortifying; invigorating.

fortification *f* fortification.

fortifier *vt* to fortify, strengthen; **se ~** *vr* to grow stronger.

fortuit *adj* fortuitous, chance; **~ement** *adv* fortuitously.

fortune *f* fortune, luck.

fortuné *adj* wealthy; fortunate.

fosse *f* pit; grave.

fossé *m* ditch; gulf.

fossette *f* dimple.

fossile *m* fossil.

fou *adj*, *f* **folle** mad, wild; tremendous; erratic.

foudre *f* lightning, thunderbolt.

foudroyant *adj* lightning; thundering; violent.

foudroyer *vt* to strike (lightning).

fouet *m* whip; whisk.

fouetter *vt* to whip, flog.

fougère *f* fern.

fougue *f* ardour, spirit.

fougueux *adj* fiery, ardent.

fouille *f* frisking; excavations.

fouiller *vt* to search, scour.

foulard *m* scarf.

foule *f* crowd; masses, heaps.

four *m* oven; furnace; fiasco.
fourbe *adj* deceitful, two-faced.
fourbu *adj* exhausted.
fourche *f* pitchfork; crotch.
fourchette *f* fork.
fourchu *adj* forked; cloven.
fourgon *m* coach, wagon, van.
fourmi *f* ant.
fourmilière *f* anthill.
fourmillement *m* swarming, milling.
fourmiller *vi* to swarm, teem.
fourneau *m* stove.
fournir *vt* to supply, provide.
fournisseur *m* -euse *f* purveyor, supplier.
fourniture *f* supplying, provision.
fourrage *m* fodder, forage.
fourré *adj* filled; fur-lined; * *m* thicket.
fourrer *vt* to stuff; to line.
fourrière *f* pound (car).
fourrure *f* coat, fur.
foutu *adj* bloody, damned; lousy.
foyer *m* home; fireplace; club; focus.
fracas *m* crash; roar, din.
fraction *f* fraction, part.
fractionnement *m* splitting up, division.
fracture *f* fracture.
fracturer *vt* to fracture, break open.
fragile *adj* fragile, delicate.
fragilité *f* fragility, flimsiness.
fragment *m* fragment.
fragmentation *f* fragmentation; splitting up.
fragmenter *vt* to break up, fragment; **se ~** *vr* to fragment, break up.
fraîcheur *f* freshness, coolness.
frais *mpl* expenses; * *adj*, *f* **fraîche** fresh, cool.
fraise *f* strawberry.
framboise *f* raspberry.
franc *adj*, *f* **franche** frank, open; clear; absolute.
Français *m* Frenchman, -e *f* Frenchwoman.
français *adj* French; * *m* French (language).
France *f* France.
franchement *adv* frankly, openly; boldly; clearly.
franchir *vt* to clear, get over, cross.
franchise *f* frankness, openness; exemption; franchise.

francophone *mf* French-speaker, *adj* French-speaking.
francophonie *f* French-speaking communities.
frange *f* fringe; threshold.
frappant *adj* striking.
frapper *vt* to hit; to strike down; to infringe; * *vi* to strike, knock.
fraternel *adj* fraternal; **~lement** *adv* fraternally.
fraterniser *vi* to fraternize.
fraternité *f* fraternity.
fraude *f* fraud, cheating.
frauduleux *adj* fraudulent.
frayeur *f* fright.
frein *m* brake; check.
freinage *m* braking; slowing down.
freiner *vi* to brake, slow down; * *vt* to slow down; to curb, check.
frêle *adj* flimsy, fragile.
frémir *vi* to quiver, tremble.
frémissant *adj* quivering, trembling.
frémissement *m* shudder, quiver.
frénétique *adj* frenetic; **~ment** *adv* frenetically.
fréquemment *adv* frequently.
fréquence *f* frequency.
fréquent *adj* frequent.
frère *m* brother.
fresque *f* fresco.
friand *adj* partial to, fond of.
friandise *f* delicacy, sweetmeat.
fric *m* (*fam*) cash, lolly.
friction *f* friction.
frigidaire *m* refrigerator.
frigide *adj* frigid.
frileux *adj* susceptible to cold; chilly.
frire *vt* to fry.
frisé *adj* curly, curly-haired.
friser *vi* to curl, be curly; * *vt* to curl; to graze, skim.
frisson *m* shiver, shudder.
frissonnant *adj* shivering, shuddering.
frissonnement *m* shuddering, shivering.
frissonner *vi* to shudder, tremble, shiver.
frite *f* chip.
friteuse *f* chip pan.
friture *f* frying; frying fat.
frivole *adj* frivolous, shallow.

frivolité *f* frivolity.

froid *adj* cold, cool; **~ement** *adv* coldly, coolly; * *m* cold; coolness; refrigeration.

froideur *f* coldness, chilliness.

froissement *m* creasing; rustling, rustle.

froisser *vt* to crease; to offend; **se ~** *vr* to crease; to take offence.

frôler *vt* to brush against; to verge on.

fromage *m* cheese.

front *m* forehead; face; front.

frontal *adj* frontal.

frontalier *adj* border, frontier.

frontière *f* border, frontier.

frottement *m* rubbing, scraping.

frotter *vt* to rub, scrape.

fructifier *vi* to bear fruit.

fructueux *adj* fruitful, profitable.

frugal *adj* frugal; **~ement** *adv* frugally.

frugalité *f* frugality.

fruit *m* fruit, result.

fruité *adj* fruity.

frustration *f* frustration.

frustrer *vt* to frustrate, deprive.

fugace *adj* fleeting, transient.

fugitif *m* **-ive** *f* fugitive; * *adj* fugitive, runaway.

fugue *f* running away.

fuir *vi* to avoid; to flee; to leak.

fuite *f* flight, escape; leak.

fulgurant *adj* lightning; dazzling.

fumant *adj* smoking, fuming.

fumé *adj* smoked.

fumée *f* smoke; vapour.

fumer *vi* to smoke, steam, give off smoke; * *vt* to smoke.

fumet *m* aroma.

fumeur *m* **-euse** *f* smoker.

fumier *m* dung, manure.

funèbre *adj* funeral; funerary.

funérailles *fpl* funeral.

funéraire *adj* funeral, funerary.

funeste *adj* disastrous; harmful.

fureur *f* fury; violence.

furie *f* fury, rage.

furieusement *adv* furiously.

furieux *adj* furious, violent.

furtif *adj* furtive; stealthy.

furtivement *adv* furtively.

fusée *f* rocket, missile.

fusible *m* fuse.

fusil *m* rifle, gun.

fusillade *f* fusillade; gunfire; shoot-out.

fusiller *vt* to shoot.

fusion *f* fusion; melting; merger; blending.

fusionner *vt* to merge, combine.

fût *m* trunk; shaft; barrel.

futé *adj* crafty, cunning.

futile *adj* futile; **~ment** *adv* futilely.

futilité *f* futility.

futur *adj* future; * *m* intended, fiancé; future.

fuyant *adj* fleeting; evasive.

fuyard *m* **-e** *f*, * *adj* runaway.

G

gabarit *m* size, build; calibre.

gâcher *vt* to mix; to waste.

gachette *f* trigger.

gâchis *m* mess.

gadget *m* gadget; gimmick.

gaffe *f* blunder; boat hook.

gage *m* security; pledge; proof.

gagnant *m* **-e** *f* winner; * *adj* winning.

gagner *vt* to earn, to win, beat; to gain; * *vi* to win; to spread.

gai *adj* cheerful, happy, gay; **~ement** *adv* cheerfully, happily.

gaieté *f* cheerfulness, gaiety.

gain *m* earnings; gain, profit, benefit; saving.

gaine *f* girdle; sheath.

gala *m* official reception; gala.

galamment *adv* courteously, gallantly.

galant *adj* gallant, courteous.

galanterie *f* gallantry.

galaxie *f* galaxy.

galère *f* galley.

galerie *f* gallery; tunnel.

galet *m* pebble.

galette *f* pancake.

Gallois *m* Welshman, **-e** *f* Welshwoman.

gallois *adj* Welsh; * *m* Welsh (language).

galon *m* braid; stripe.

galop *m* gallop; canter.

galoper *vi* to gallop; to run wild.

galvaniser *vt* to galvanize.

gamba *f* large prawn.

gamin *m* **-e** *f* kid, street urchin.

gaminerie *f* playfulness; childishness.

gamme *f* range; scale.

ganglion *m* ganglion.

gangrène *f* gangrene.

gant *m* glove.

garage *m* garage.

garagiste *mf* garage owner.

garant *m* **-e** *f* (*jur*) guarantor.

garantie *f* guarantee, surety.

garantir *vt* to guarantee, secure.

garçon *m* boy; assistant; waiter.

garde *f* custody; guard; surveillance; * *m* guard, warder.

garde-à-vous *m* standing to attention.

garde-boue *m* mudguard.

garde-chasse *m* gamekeeper.

garde-fou *m* railing, parapet; safeguard.

garder *vt* to look after; to stay in; to keep on.

garderie *f* day nursery.

garde-robe *f* wardrobe.

gardien *m* **-ne** *f* guard, guardian, warden; protector.

gare *f* rail station; (*mar*) basin; depot.

garer *vt* to park; to dock; **se ~** *vr* to avoid, steer clear of.

gargariser (se) *vr* to gargle; to crow about.

gargarisme *m* gargle.

gargouillement *m* gurgling; rumbling.

gargouiller *vi* to gurgle; to rumble.

garnir *vt* to fit with; to trim, decorate.

garnison *f* (*mil*) garrison.

garniture *f* trimming, lining; garnish.

garrot *m* garrotte; (*med*) tourniquet.

gars *m* (*fam*) lad; bloke.

gaspillage *m* waste; squandering.

gaspiller *vt* to waste, squander.

gastrique *adj* gastric.

gastronome *m* gourmet, gastronome.

gastronomie *f* gastronomy.

gâté *adj* ruined; spoiled.

gâteau *m* cake.

gâter *vt* to ruin; to spoil; **se ~** *vr* to go bad, go off.

gâteux *adj* senile; (*fam*) doddering.

gauche *adj* left; awkward, clumsy; **~ment** *adv* awkwardly; * *f* left; left wing.

gaucher *adj* left-handed.

gauchisant *m* **-e** *f* leftist; * *adj* of leftist tendencies.

gauchiste *mf*; * *adj* leftist.

gaufre *f* waffle.

gaver *vt* to force-feed, fill up; **se ~** *vr* to stuff o.s.; to devour.

gaz *m invar* gas; fizz; wind.

gaze *f* gauze.

gazelle *f* gazelle.

gazeux *adj* gaseous; fizzy.

gazon *m* lawn; turf.

gazouiller *vi* to chirp, warble.

géant *m* giant, **-e** *f* giantess.

geindre *vi* to groan; to whine.

gel *m* frost; gel.

gélatine *f* gelatine.

gelé *adj* frozen; cold, unresponsive.

gelée *f* frost; jelly.

geler *vi* to freeze, be frozen; * *vt* to freeze, turn to ice; to suspend.

gélule *f* capsule.

Gémeaux *mpl* Gemini.

gémir *vi* to groan, moan.

gémissement *m* groan, moan; groaning.

gênant *adj* annoying; awkward.

gencive *f* gum.

gendarme *m* policeman; gendarme.

gendarmerie *f* police force, constabulary.

gendre *m* son-in-law.

gêne *f* discomfort; trouble; embarrassment; **être sans ~** to be inconsiderate.

généalogie *f* genealogy.

généalogique *adj* genealogical.

gêner *vt* to bother; to hinder; to make uneasy; **se ~** *vr* to get in each other's way.

général *adj* general, broad; common; **~ement** *adv* generally; * *m* general, **-e** *f* general's wife; (*thea*) dress rehearsal.

généralisation *f* generalization.

généraliser *vt* to generalize; **se ~** *vr* to become widespread.

généraliste *m* general practitioner; * *adj* general-interest; non-specialized.

généralité *f* majority; general points.

générateur *m* generator.

génération *f* generation.

générer *vt* to generate

généreusement *adv* generously; nobly.

généreux *adj*, *f* **-euse** generous; noble; magnanimous.

générosité *f* generosity; nobility; magnanimity.

génétique *adj* genetic; **~ment** *adv* genetically.

génial *adj* inspired, of genius.

génie *m* genius; spirit; genie.

génital *adj* genital.

génocide *m* genocide.

genou *m* knee.

genre *m* kind, type; gender; genre.

gens *mpl* people, folk.

gentil *adj*, *f* **-le** kind; good; pleasant.

gentillesse *f* kindness; favour.

gentiment *adv* kindly; nicely.

géographe *mf* geographer.

géographie *f* geography.

géographique *adj* geographic.

géologie *f* geology.

géologue *mf* geologist.

géomètre *m* land surveyor.

géométrie *f* geometry.

géométrique *adj* geometric; **~ment** *adv* geometrically.

géranium *m* geranium.

gérant *m* **-e** *f* manager.

gerbe *f* sheaf, bundle; collection.

gercer *vt* to chap, crack; **se ~** *vr* to chap, crack.

gerçure *f* (small) crack.

gérer *vt* to manage, administer.

germe *m* germ; seed.

germer *vi* to sprout, germinate.

gérondif *m* gerundive; gerund.

gésier *m* gizzard.

gestation *f* gestation.

geste *m* gesture; act, deed.

gesticuler *vi* to gesticulate.

gestion *f* management, administration.

gestionnaire *adj* administrative, management.

ghetto *m* ghetto.

gibier *m* game; prey.

gicler *vi* to spurt, squirt.

gicleur *m* jet.

gifle *f* slap, smack.

gifler *vt* to slap, smack.

gigantesque *adj* gigantic, immense.

gigot *m* leg (mutton/lamb), haunch.

gilet *m* waistcoat.

gingembre *m* ginger.

girafe *f* giraffe.

giratoire *adj* gyrating, gyratory.

girouette *f* weather vane.

gisement *m* deposit; mine; pool.

gitan *m* **-e** *f* gipsy.

gîte *m* shelter; home.

givre *m* frost, rime.

givré *adj* covered in frost.

glace *f* ice; ice cream; mirror.

glacé *adj* icy; frozen; glazed; chilly.

glacer *vt* to freeze; to chill; to glaze.

glacial *adj* icy; freezing.

glacier *m* glacier; ice cream maker.

glacière *f* icebox.

glaçon *m* icicle; ice cube.

glaïeul *m* gladiola.

glaise *f* clay.

gland *m* acorn.

glande *f* gland.

glaner *vt* to glean.

glauque *adj* murky; shabby, run-down.

glissade *f* slide, skid.

glissant *adj* slippery.

glissement *m* sliding; gliding; downturn, downswing.

glisser *vi* to slide, slip, skid.

glissière *f* slide; runner.

global *adj* global, overall; **~ement** *adv* globally.

globe *m* globe, sphere; earth.

globulaire *adj* global; (*med*) corpuscular.

globule *m* globule; corpuscle.

globuleux *adj* globular; protruding.

gloire *f* glory; distinction; celebrity.

glorieux *adj* glorious.

glorifier *vt* to glory, honour; **se ~** *vr* to glory in; to boast.

glossaire *m* glossary.

glouton *m* **-ne** *f* glutton; * *adj* gluttonous, ravenous; **~nement** *adv* gluttonously.

gluant *adj* sticky, slimy.

glucide *m* glucide.

glucose *m* glucose.

glycérine *f* glycerine.

gobelet *m* beaker, tumbler.

gober *vt* to swallow; to fall for.

goéland *m* gull.

goinfre *m* pig; * *adj* piggish.

golf *m* golf.

golfeur *m* **-euse** *f* golfer.

gomme *f* gum; rubber, eraser.

gommer *vt* to rub out; to gum.

gond *m* hinge.

gondole *f* gondola.

gondoler *vi* to crinkle, warp, buckle; **se ~** *vr* to crinkle; to split one's sides laughing.

gonflable *adj* inflatable.

gonflement *m* inflation, swelling.

gonfler *vt* to pump up, inflate; **se ~** *vr* to swell; to be puffed up.

gong *m* gong; bell.

gorge *f* throat.

gorgée *f* sip, gulp.

gorille *m* gorilla.

gosier *m* throat, gullet.

gosse *mf* (*fam*) kid.

gothique *m, adj* Gothic.

goudron *m* tar.

goudronner *vt* to tar.

gouffre *m* gulf, chasm, abyss.

goulu *adj* greedy, gluttonous.

goulûment *adv* greedily, gluttonously.

goupille *f* pin.

gourd *adj* numb (with cold).

gourde *f* gourd; flask.

gourdin *m* club, cudgel.

gourmand *adj* greedy.

gourmandise *f* greed, greediness.

gourmet *m* gourmet.

gourmette *f* chain bracelet.

gousse *f* pod.

goût *m* taste; liking; style.

goûter *vt* to taste; to appreciate; * *vi* to have a snack; to taste good; * *m* snack.

goutte *f* drop; dram; gout.

gouttière *f* gutter; drainpipe.

gouvernail *m* rudder; helm.

gouvernement *m* government.

gouvernemental *adj* government, governmental.

gouverner *vt* to govern, rule; to control; to steer.

gouverneur *m* governor.

goyave *f* guava.

grâce *f* grace; favour; mercy; pardon; **~ à** thanks to.

gracier *vt* to pardon.

gracieusement *adv* gracefully; kindly.

gracieux *adj* gracious.

grade *m* rank; grade; degree.

gradé *m* officer; * *adj* promoted.

gradin *m* tier; step; terrace.

graduel *adj* gradual; progressive; **~lement** *adv* gradually.

graduer *vt* to step up; to graduate.

graffiti *mpl* graffiti.

grain *m* grain, seed; bead.

graine *f* seed.

graissage *m* greasing, lubricating.

graisse *f* grease, fat.

graisser *vt* to grease, lubricate.

grammaire *f* grammar.

grammairien *m* **-ne** *f* grammarian.

grammatical *adj* grammatical; **~ement** *adv* grammatically.

gramme *m* gram.

grand *adj* big; tall; great; leading; **pas ~ chose** not a lot, not up to much; **~ement** *adv* greatly; a great deal; nobly.

grandeur *f* size; greatness; magnitude.

grandiose *adj* imposing, grandiose.

grandir *vi* to grow bigger, increase; * *vt* to magnify; exaggerate.

grand-mère *f* grandmother.

grand-père *m* grandfather.

grand-parents *mpl* grandparents

granit(e) *m* granite.

granulé *m* granule; * *adj* granular.

granuleux *adj* granular; grainy.

graphique *m* graph; * *adj* graphic; **~ment** *adv* graphically.

graphite *m* graphite.

grappe *f* cluster, bunch.

gras *adj, f* **-se** fatty; fat; greasy; crude.

gratification *f* gratuity; bonus.

gratin *m* cheese dish, gratin.

gratis *adv* free, gratis.

gratitude *f* gratitude, gratefulness.

gratter *vt* to scratch, scrape.

gratuit *adj* free, gratuitous; disinterested; **~ement** *adv* free; gratuitously.

grave *adj* grave, solemn; **~ment** *adv* gravely, solemnly.

graver *vt* to engrave, imprint.

graveur *m* engraver, woodcutter.

gravier *m* gravel.

gravir *vt* to climb.

gravitation *f* gravitation.

gravité *f* gravity.

gravure *f* engraving, carving.

gré *m*: liking, taste; **au ~ de** depending on, at the mercy of; **bon ~ mal ~** like it or not, willy-nilly; **savoir ~** to be grateful.

greffe *f* transplant, graft.

greffer *vt* to transplant, graft.

grégaire *adj* gregarious.

grêle *f* hail.

grêlon *m* hailstone.

grelotter *vi* to shiver.

grenade *f* pomegranate; grenade.

grenat *m* garnet.

grenier *m* attic, garret.

grenouille *f* frog.

grès *m* sandstone; stoneware.

grésiller *vi* to sizzle; splutter.

grève *f* strike; shore.

gribouillage *m* scrawl, scribble.

gribouiller *vi* to doodle; * *vt* to scribble, scrawl.

grièvement *adv* seriously.

griffe *f* claw.

griffer *vt* to scratch.

griffonner *vt* to scribble, jot down.

grignoter *vi* to nibble at, pick at; * *vt* to nibble at; to eat away.

gril *m* grill pan; rack.

grillade *f* grilled meat.

grillage *m* toasting; grilling.

grille *f* railings; gate; grill.

grille-pain *m invar* toaster.

griller *vt* to toast, scorch; to put bars on; * *vi* to toast, grill.

grillon *m* cricket.

grimace *f* grimace; funny face.

grimper *vi* to climb up.

grincement *m* grating, creaking.

grincer *vi* to grate, creak.

grincheux *adj* grumpy.

griotte *f* Morello cherry; marble.

grippe *f* flu, influenza.

grippé *adj* suffering from flu.

gris *adj* grey.

grisant *adj* exhilarating; intoxicating.

griser *vt* to intoxicate; **se ~** *vr* to get drunk.

grisonnant *adj* greying.

grive *f* thrush.

grog *m* grog.

grognement *m* grunt, grunting.

grogner *vi* to grumble, moan.

grognon *m* grumbler, moaner, *adj* grumpy, surly.

grommeler *vi* to mutter; to grumble; * *vt* to mutter.

grondement *m* rumbling, growling.

gronder *vt* to scold; * *vi* to rumble, growl.

gros *adj*, *f* **-se** big; fat; thick; serious; heavy; coarse; **en ~** in bulk; * *m* bulk; wholesale; fat man.

groseille *f* currant.

grossesse *f* pregnancy.

grosseur *f* thickness; lump; fatness.

grossier *adj* coarse; unrefined; base.

grossièrement *adv* roughly; coarsely.

grossièreté *f* rudeness; coarseness.

grossir *vi* to get fatter; to swell, grow; * *vt* to magnify; to exaggerate.

grossiste *mf* wholesaler.

grotesque *adj* grotesque, ludicrous; **~ment** *adv* grotesquely.

grotte *f* cave; grotto.

grouiller *vi* to mill about; to swarm; **se ~** *vr* (*fam*) to get a move on.

groupe *m* group; party; cluster.

groupement *m* grouping; group.

grouper *vt* to group together; to bulk; **se ~** *vr* to gather.

grue *f* crane.

grumeau *m* lump.

gruyère *m* gruyère (cheese).

guenon *f* female monkey; hag.

guépard *m* cheetah.

guêpe *f* wasp.

guêpier *m* trap; wasp's nest.

guère *adv* hardly, scarcely.

guéri *adj* cured.

guéridon *m* pedestal table.

guérir *vi* to get better; to heal; * *vt* to cure, heal; **se ~** *vr* to get better; to recover from.

guérison *f* recovery; curing.

guérisseur *m* **-euse** *f* healer.

guerre *f* war; warfare.

guerrier *m* **-ière** *f* warrior.

guet *m* watch; **faire le ~** to be on the watch.

guetter *vt* to watch; to lie in wait for.

gueule *f* (*fam*) mouth; face; muzzle.

gueuler *vi* (*fam*) to bawl; bellow.

guichet *m* counter; ticket office, booking office.

guichetier *m* **-ière** *f* counter clerk.

guidage *m* guides; guidance.

guide *m* guide.

guider *vt* to guide; **se ~** *vr* to be guided by.

guidon *m* handlebars.

guignol *m* puppet; puppet show.

guillemet *m* inverted comma; quotation mark.

guillotine *f* guillotine.

guimauve *f* marshmallow.

guindé *adj* stiff, uptight.

guirlande *f* garland.

guise *f* manner, way; **en ~ de** by way of; **à ta ~** as you please.

guitare *f* guitar.

guitariste *mf* guitarist.

guttural *adj* guttural

gymnase *m* gymnasium.

gymnastique *f* gymnastics.

gynécologie *f* gynaecology.

gynécologue, gynécologiste *mf* gynaecologist.

gyrophare *m* revolving light.

H

habile *adj* skilful, skilled; clever; **~ment** *adv* skilfully.

habileté *f* skill, skilfulness; clever move.

habiliter *vt* to qualify; to authorize.

habillement *m* clothing, dress, outfit.

habiller *vt* to dress, clothe; **s'~** *vr* to get dressed.

habit *m* clothes; apparel; dresscoat; outfit

habitable *adj* inhabitable.

habitant *m* **-e** *f* inhabitant; occupant; dweller.

habitat *m* habitat; housing conditions.

habitation *f* dwelling; residence; house.

habité *adj* manned.

habiter *vi* to live; * *vt* to live in; occupy.

habitude *f* habit, custom, routine.

habituel *adj* usual, customary; **~lement** *adv* usually, generally.

habituer *vt* to accustom; to teach; **s'~** *vr* to get used to.

hache *f* axe, hatchet.

hacher *vt* to chop, mince.

hachoir *m* chopper, cleaver.

hachure *f* hatching.

hagard *adj* wild; haggard; distraught.

haie *f* hedge.

haine *f* hatred.

haineux *adj* full of hatred; malevolent.

haïr *vt* to hate, detest.

hâle *m* tan, sunburn.

hâlé *adj* tanned, sunburnt.

haleine *f* breath, breathing.

haletant *adj* panting, gasping.

haleter *vi* to pant, gasp for breath.

hall *m* hall, foyer.

halle *f* covered market; hall.

hallucination *f* hallucination.

halo *m* halo.

halte *f* stop, break; stopping place.

haltère *f* dumbbell.

hamac *m* hammock.

hameçon *m* fish-hook.

hamster *m* hamster.

hanche *f* hip; haunch.

handball *m* handball.

handballeur *m* **-euse** *f* handball player.

handicap *m* handicap.

handicaper *vt* to handicap

hangar *m* shed, barn; hangar.

hanneton *m* maybug.
hanter *vt* to haunt.
happer *vt* to snap up, snatch.
harassant *adj* exhausting, wearing.
harcèlement *m* harassment; pestering.
harceler *vt* to harass; to pester; to plague.
hardi *adj* bold, daring; brazen; ~**ment** *adv* boldly, daringly; brazenly.
hareng *m* herring.
hargne *f* spite.
hargneux *adj* aggressive, belligerent.
haricot *m* bean.
harmonica *m* harmonica.
harmonie *f* harmony; wind section.
harmonieusement *adv* harmoniously.
harmonieux *adj* harmonious; well-matched.
harmoniser *vt* to harmonize; **s'~** *vr* to be in harmony.
harnacher *m* to harness.
harnais *m* harness; equipment.
harpe *f* harp.
harpiste *mf* harpist.
harpon *m* harpoon.
hasard *m* chance; accident; hazard; risk.
hasardeux *adj* hazardous, risky.
hâte *f* haste; impatience.
hâter *vt* to hasten; to quicken; **se ~** *vr* to hurry.
hâtif *adj* precocious; early; hasty.
hâtivement *adv* hastily.
hausse *f* rise, increase.
hausser *vt* to raise; to heighten.
haut *adj* high, tall; upper; superior; ~**ement** *adv* highly.
hautain *adj* haughty, lofty.
hautbois *m* oboe.
hauteur *f* height; elevation; haughtiness; bearing.
haut-parleur *m* loudspeaker.
hebdomadaire *adj*; * *m* weekly.
hébergement *m* accommodation; lodging.
héberger *vt* to accommodate, lodge.
hectare *m* hectare.
hectogramme *m* hectogram.
hectolitre *m* hectolitre.
hectomètre *m* hectometre.
hélice *f* propeller; helix.
hélicoptère *m* helicopter.

hélium *m* helium.
hématome *m* severe bruise, haematoma.
hémicycle *m* semicircle, hemicycle; amphitheatre.
hémiplégique *mf* person paralysed on one side, hemiplegic; * *adj* hemiplegic.
hémisphère *m* hemisphere.
hémoglobine *f* haemoglobin.
hémophile *adj* haemophiliac.
hémophilie *f* haemophilia.
hémorragie *f* bleeding, haemorrhage.
hémorroïde *f* haemorrhoid, pile.
henné *m* henna.
hépatique *adj* hepatic.
hépatite *f* hepatitis.
herbe *f* grass; **en ~** in the blade.
herbivore *m* herbivore; *adj* herbivorous.
herboriste *mf* herbalist.
héréditaire *adj* hereditary.
hérédité *f* heredity; heritage; right of inheritance.
hérésie *f* heresy.
hérétique *adj* heretical.
hérissé *adj* bristling; spiked.
hérisser *vt* to bristle; to spike; * **se ~** *vr* to stand on end; to bristle.
hérisson *m* hedgehog.
héritage *m* inheritance; heritage, legacy.
hériter *vi* to inherit.
héritier *m* heir **-ière** *f* heiress.
hermaphrodite *m* hermaphrodite; * *adj* hermaphrodite.
hermétique *adj* airtight, watertight, hermetic; ~**ment** *adv* hermetically.
hermine *f* ermine; stoat.
hernie *f* hernia, rupture.
héroïne *f* heroine; heroin.
héroïque *adj* heroic; ~**ment** *adv* heroically.
héroïsme *m* heroism.
héron *m* heron.
héros *m* hero.
herpès *m* herpes; cold sore.
hésitant *adj* hesitant.
hésitation *f* hesitation.
hésiter *vi* to hesitate.
hétéroclite *adj* heterogeneous; sundry; eccentric.
hétérogène *adj* heterogeneous.

hétérosexuel *adj* heterosexual.

hêtre *m* beech.

heure *f* hour; time of day; **de bonne ~** early; **tout à l'~** a short time ago, just now.

heureusement *adv* luckily; happily.

heureux *adj* lucky; happy.

heurter *vt* to strike, hit; to jostle.

hexagone *m* hexagon.

hibernation *f* hibernation.

hibou *m* owl.

hideux *adj* hideous.

hier *adv* yesterday.

hiérarchie *f* hierarchy.

hiérarchique *adj* hierarchical; **~ment** *adv* hierarchically

hilarant *adj* hilarious, side-splitting.

hilarité *f* hilarity, laughter.

hindouisme *m* Hinduism.

hippisme *m* riding, equestrianism.

hippocampe *m* sea horse.

hippodrome *m* racecourse.

hippopotame *m* hippopotamus.

hirondelle *f* swallow.

hirsute *adj* dishevelled, tousled.

hisser *vt* to hoist, haul up.

histoire *f* history; story; business; **~ de dire** just to say.

historien *m* **-ne** *f* historian.

historique *adj* historic; historical; **~ment** *adv* historically.

hiver *m* winter.

hivernal *adj* winter; wintry.

HLM (habitation à loyer modéré) *f/m* public sector housing.

hocher *vt* to nod; to shake one's head.

hochet *m* rattle; toy.

holocauste *m* holocaust.

homard *m* lobster.

homéopathe *mf* homeopath.

homéopathie *f* homeopathy.

homicide *m* homicide.

hommage *m* homage, tribute; **rendre ~ à** to pay homage to.

homme *m* man.

homme-grenouille *m* frogman.

homogène *adj* homogeneous.

homogénéiser *vt* to homogenize.

homogénéité *f* homogeneity.

homologue *adj* homologous; equivalent.

homologuer *vt* to ratify; to approve.

homonyme *m* homonym; * *adj* homonymous.

homosexualité *f* homosexuality.

homosexuel *m* **-le** *f* homosexual.

honnête *adj* honest; decent; honourable; **~ment** *adv* honestly, decently.

honnêteté *f* honesty, decency.

honneur *m* honour; integrity; credit; **en l'~ de** in honour of.

honorable *adj* honourable; reputable; **~ment** *adv* honourably.

honoraire *adj* honorary.

honoraires *mpl* fees.

honorer *vt* to honour; to esteem; to do credit to; **s'~** *vr*: **s'~ de** to pride o.s. on.

honte *f* shame, disgrace.

honteusement *adv* shamefully; disgracefully.

honteux *adj* shameful; disgraceful.

hôpital *m* hospital.

hoquet *m* hiccough, hiccup.

horaire *m* timetable; * *adj* hourly.

horizon *m* horizon.

horizontal *adj* horizontal; **~ement** *adv* horizontally.

horloge *f* clock.

horloger *m* **-ère** *f* watchmaker, clockmaker.

hormone *f* hormone.

horoscope *m* horoscope.

horreur *f* horror.

horrible *adj* horrible; dreadful; **~ment** *adv* horribly

horrifier *vt* to horrify.

hors *prép* outside; beyond; save; except; **~ série** incomparable, outstanding; special issue.

hors-bord *m invar* speedboat.

hors-d'œuvre *m invar* hors d'œuvre, starter.

hors-jeu *m invar* offside.

hors-piste *m invar* off-piste.

hortensia *m* hydrangea.

horticulteur *m* horticulturist.

horticulture *f* horticulture.

hospice *m* home, asylum; hospice.

hospitalier *adj* hospital; hospitable.

hospitalisation *f* hospitalization.

hospitaliser *vt* to hospitalize.
hospitalité *f* hospitality.
hostie *f* host.
hostile *adj* hostile; ~**ment** *adv* hostilely.
hostilité *f* hostility.
hôte *m* **hôtesse** *f* host; landlord.
hôtel *m* hotel.
hôtelier *m* -**ière** *f* hotelier; * *adj* hotel.
hôtellerie *f* inn; hotel business.
hotte *f* basket.
houblon *m* hop.
houille *f* coal.
houle *f* swell.
houleux *adj* stormy; turbulent.
houppe *f* tuft; tassel.
housse *f* cover, dust-sheet.
houx *m* holly.
hublot *m* porthole.
huer *vt* to boo.
huile *f* oil; petroleum.
huissier *m* bailiff; usher.
huit *adj, m* eight.
huitaine *f* eight or so.
huitième *adj* eighth; ~**ment** *adv* eighthly; * *mf* eighth.
huître *f* oyster.
humain *adj* human; humane; ~**ement** *adv* humanly; humanely; * *m* human.
humanisme *m* humanism.
humaniste *m* humanist; * *adj* humanist.
humanitaire *adj* humanitarian.
humanité *f* humanity.
humble *adj* humble; modest; ~**ment** *adv* humbly.
humecter *vt* to dampen, moisten.
humeur *f* mood, humour; temper.
humide *adj* humid.
humidité *f* humidity.
humiliant *adj* humiliating.
humiliation *f* humiliation.
humilier *vt* to humiliate.
humilité *f* humility.
humoristique *adj* humorous.
humour *m* humour.

hurlement *m* roar, yell; howl.
hurler *vi*; * *vt* to roar, yell.
hutte *f* hut.
hybride *adj* hybrid; * *m* hybrid.
hydratant *adj* moisturizing.
hydratation *f* hydration; moisturizing.
hydrater *vt* to hydrate; to moisturize.
hydraulique *adj* hydraulic.
hydravion *m* seaplane.
hydrocarbure *m* hydrocarbon.
hydrogène *m* hydrogen.
hydrolyse *f* hydrolysis.
hydrophile *adj* absorbent.
hydroxyde *m* hydroxide.
hyène *f* hyena.
hygiène *f* hygienics; hygiene.
hygiénique *adj* hygienic; ~**ment** *adv* hygienically.
hymne *m* hymn.
hyperbole *f* hyperbole; hyperbola.
hypermarché *m* hypermarket.
hypermétrope *adj* long-sighted; * *mf* long-sighted person.
hypertension *f* hypertension.
hypertrophié *adj* (*med*) enlarged; overdeveloped.
hypnose *f* hypnosis
hypnotique *adj* hypnotic.
hypnotiser *vt* to hypnotize.
hypocondriaque *mf* hypochondriac; * *adj* hypochondriac.
hypocrisie *f* hypocrisy.
hypocrite *mf* hypocrite; * *adj* hypocritical; ~**ment** *adv* hypocritically.
hypophyse *f* pituitary gland, hypophysis.
hypothalamus *m* hypothalamus.
hypothèque *f* mortgage.
hypothéquer *vt* to mortgage.
hypothèse *f* hypothesis; assumption.
hypothétique *adj* hypothetical; ~**ment** *adv* hypothetically.
hystérie *f* hysteria.
hystérique *mf* hysterical; * *adj* hysteric.

I

ibis *m* ibis.

iceberg *m* iceberg.

idéal *adj*; * *m* ideal.

idéaliser *vt* to idealize.

idéaliste *adj* idealistic; * *mf* idealist.

idée *f* idea.

identifier *vt* to identify; **s'~** *vr* to identify with.

identique *adj* identical; **~ment** *adv* identically.

identité *f* identity; similarity.

idéologie *f* ideology.

idiot *m* **-e** *f* idiot, fool; * *adj* idiotic, stupid; **~ement** *adv* idiotically.

idole *f* idol.

igloo *m* igloo.

ignoble *adj* ignoble, mean, base.

ignorance *f* ignorance.

ignorant *adj* ignorant; unacquainted; uninformed.

ignorer *vt* to be ignorant of; to be unaware of; to ignore.

iguane *m* iguana.

il *pn* he, it.

île *f* island, isle.

illégal *adj* illegal; unlawful; **~ement** *adv* illegally.

illégalité *f* illegality.

illégitime *adj* illegitimate; unwarranted.

illettré *adj* illiterate.

illicite *adj* illicit; **~ment** *adv* illicitly.

illimité *adj* unlimited; limitless.

illisible *adj* illegible, unreadable.

illogique *adj* illogical.

illumination *f* illumination, lighting.

illuminer *vt* to light up, illuminate; to enlighten.

illusion *f* illusion

illusoire *adj* illusory; illusive; **~ment** *adv* illusorily.

illustration *f* illustration.

illustre *adj* illustrious, renowned.

illustrer *vt* to illustrate.

îlot *m* islet; block (flats).

image *f* image, picture; reflection.

imagé *adj* colourful; full of imagery.

imaginaire *adj* imaginary.

imagination *f* imagination.

imaginer *vt* to imagine; to suppose; to devise; **s'~** *vr* to imagine o.s.; to think.

imbattable *adj* unbeatable.

imbécile *mf* idiot, imbecile; * *adj* stupid, idiotic.

imbiber *vt* to soak, moisten.

imbriquer *vt* to fit into; to overlap; **s'~** *vr* to be linked.

imbuvable *adj* undrinkable; unbearable.

imitation *f* imitation; mimicry; forgery.

imiter *vt* to imitate.

immaculé *adj* spotless, immaculate.

immangeable *adj* inedible.

immatriculation *f* registration.

immatriculer *vt* to register.

immédiat *adj* immediate; instant; **~ement** *adv* immediately, instantly.

immense *adj* immense, boundless.

immensément *adv* immensely; hugely.

immensité *f* immensity; immenseness.

immergé *adj* submerged.

immersion *f* immersion; submersion.

immeuble *m* building; block of flats; real estate.

immigrant *m* **-e** *f* immigrant.

immigration *f* immigration.

immigré *m* **-e** *f* immigrant.

imminent *adj* imminent, impending.

immobile *adj* motionless, still.

immobilier *adj* property; * *m* property business.

immobiliser *vt* to immobilize; to bring to a standstill; **s'~** *vr* to stop, stand still.

immobilité *f* stillness; immobility; permanence.

immonde *adj* squalid; base, vile.

immoral *adj* immoral.

immoralité *f* immorality.

immortaliser *vt* to immortalize.

immortel *adj* immortal.

immuable *adj* unchanging, immutable; **~ment** *adv* immutably.

immuniser *vt* to immunize.
immunité *f* immunity.
impact *m* impact.
impair *adj* odd, uneven.
impalpable *adj* impalpable.
impardonnable *adj* unforgivable, unpardonable.
imparfait *adj* imperfect; **~ement** *adv* imperfectly.
impartial *adj* impartial; **~ement** *adv* impartially.
impartialité *f* impartiality.
impasse *f* dead end, cul-de-sac; impasse.
impassible *adj* impassive.
impatiemment *adv* impatiently.
impatience *f* impatience.
impatient *adj* impatient.
impatienter *vt* to irritate, annoy; **s'~** *vr* to grow, get impatient.
impeccable *adj* perfect; faultless, impeccable; **~ment** *adv* perfectly, impeccably.
impénétrable *adj* impenetrable; inscrutable.
impensable *adj* unthinkable.
impératif *adj* imperative; mandatory; * *m* requirement; demand; constraint.
impératrice *f* empress.
imperceptible *adj* imperceptible; **~ment** *adv* imperceptibly.
imperfection *f* imperfection.
impérial *adj* imperial.
impérialisme *m* imperialism.
imperméable *adj* impermeable, waterproof; **~ à** impervious to.
impersonnel *adj* impersonal.
impertinence *f* impertinence.
impertinent *adj* impertinent.
imperturbable *adj* unshakeable; imperturbable; **~ment** *adv* imperturbably.
impétueux *adj* impetuous.
impitoyable *adj* merciless, pitiless; **~ment** *adv* mercilessly, pitilessly.
implacable *adj* implacable; **~ment** *adv* implacably.
implantation *f* implantation; establishment; introduction.
implanter *vt* to introduce; to establish; to implant; **s'~** *vr* to be established; to become implanted.

implication *f* implication; involvement.
implicite *adj* implicit; **~ment** *adv* implicitly.
impliquer *vt* to imply; to necessitate; to implicate; **s'~** *vr* to get involved in one's work.
impoli *adj* impolite, rude.
impolitesse *f* impoliteness, rudeness.
impopulaire *adj* unpopular.
importance *f* importance, significance; size.
important *adj* important, significant; sizeable.
importateur *m* **-trice** *f* importer; * *adj* importing.
importation *f* import, importation.
importer *vt* to import; * *vi* to matter; **que m'importe que** what does it matter to me that; **peu importe** whatever; **n'importe qui** anybody; **n'importe quoi** anything; **n'importe comment** anyhow; **n'importe quel** any.
importuner *vt* to importune, bother.
imposant *adj* imposing; stately.
imposer *vt* to impose, lay down; **s'~** *vr* to be essential; to assert o.s.
impossibilité *f* impossibility.
impossible *adj* impossible.
imposteur *m* impostor.
impôt *m* tax, duty.
impotent *adj* disabled, crippled.
imprégner *vt* impregnate; to permeate; to imbue; **s'~** *vr* to become impregnated with; to become imbued with.
impresario *m* manager, impresario.
impression *f* feeling, impression.
impressionnant *adj* impressive; upsetting.
impressionner *vt* to impress; to upset.
impressionisme *m* impressionism.
impressioniste *mf*; * *adj* impressionist.
imprévisible *adj* unforeseeable; unpredictable.
imprévoyant *adj* improvident.
imprévu *adj* unforeseen, unexpected.
imprimante *f* printer.
imprimé *adj* printed; * *m* printed form; printed material.
imprimer *vt* to print.
imprimerie *f* printing works; printing house.
imprimeur *m* printer.
improbable *adj* improbable, unlikely.
improductif *adj* unproductive.

improvisation *f* improvisation.
improviser *vt* to improvise.
improviste *adv*: **à l'~** unexpectedly.
imprudence *f* carelessness, imprudence.
imprudent *adj* careless, imprudent.
impudence *f* impudence; shamelessness.
impudique *adj* immodest, shameless.
impuissance *f* powerlessness, helplessness.
impuissant *adj* powerless, helpless.
impulsif *adj* impulsive.
impulsion *f* impulse; impetus.
impulsivement *adv* impulsively.
impunément *adv* with impunity.
impur *adj* impure; mixed.
impureté *f* impurity.
inacceptable *adj* unacceptable.
inaccessible *adj* inaccessible; obscure; incomprehensible.
inaccoutumé *adj* unusual.
inachevé *adj* unfinished, uncompleted.
inactif *adj* inactive, idle.
inaction *f* inactivity, idleness.
inactivité *f* inactivity.
inadapté *adj* unsuitable; maladjusted.
inadéquat *adj* inadequate.
inadmissible *adj* (*jur*) inadmissible.
inaltérable *adj* stable; unchanging, permanent.
inamovible *adj* irremovable; fixed.
inanimé *adj* inanimate; unconscious.
inaperçu *adj*: unnoticed **passer ~** to go unnoticed.
inappréciable *adj* invaluable, inestimable.
inapte *adj* unfit.
inattaquable *adj* unassailable; irrefutable.
inattendu *adj* unexpected, unforeseen.
inattention *f* inattention, lack of attention.
inauguration *f* inauguration, opening.
inaugurer *vt* to inaugurate, open.
inavouable *adj* shameful; undisclosable.
incapable *adj* incapable; incompetent.
incapacité *f* incompetence; disability; **être dans l'~ de** to be unable to do.
incarcérer *vt* to incarcerate.
incarnation *f* incarnation.
incarner *vt* to incarnate, embody.
incendiaire *adj* incendiary; inflammatory; * *mf* arsonist.
incendie *m* fire, blaze.

incendier *vt* to set alight; to kindle.
incertain *adj* uncertain, unsure.
incertitude *f* uncertainty; **être dans l'~** to feel uncertain.
incessant *adj* incessant, ceaseless.
inceste *m* incest.
incident *m* incident, point of law.
incinération *f* incineration; cremation.
inciser *vt* to incise; (*med*) to lance.
incisive *f* incisive; piercing.
incitation *f* incitement; incentive.
inciter *vt* to incite, urge.
inclinaison *f* incline; gradient.
incliner *vt* to bend; to slope; to bow.
inclure *vt* to include; to insert.
inclus *adj* enclosed; included; **ci-~** herein enclosed.
incohérence *f* incoherence; inconsistency.
incohérent *adj* incoherent; inconsistent.
incolore *adj* colourless; clear.
incommode *adj* inconvenient; awkward.
incommoder *vt* to disturb, bother.
incomparable *adj* incomparable; **~ment** *adv* incomparably.
incompatibilité *f* incompatibility.
incompatible *adj* incompatible.
incompétence *f* incompetence.
incompétent *adj* incompetent; inexpert.
incomplet *adj* incomplete.
incompréhensible *adj* incomprehensible.
incompréhension *f* lack of understanding.
inconcevable *adj* inconceivable.
inconciliable *adj* irreconcilable.
inconditionnel *adj* unconditional; unreserved; unquestioning.
inconfortable *adj* uncomfortable; awkward; **~ment** *adv* uncomfortably.
incongru *adj* unseemly; incongruous.
inconnu *m* **-e** *f* stranger, unknown person; * *m* unknown; * *adj* unknown.
inconsciemment *adv* unconsciously; thoughtlessly.
inconscience *f* unconsciousness; thoughtlessness.
inconscient *adj* unconscious; thoughtless, reckless; * *m* subconscious, unconscious.
inconsidéré *adj* inconsiderate; thoughtless; **~ment** *adv* inconsiderately.

inconsistant *adj* flimsy; colourless; watery.

inconsolable *adj* disconsolate; inconsolable.

inconstant *adj* fickle; variable, inconstant.

incontestable *adj* incontestable, unquestionable; **~ment** *adv* incontestably, unquestionably.

inconvénient *m* drawback, inconvenience.

incorporation *f* incorporation; integration; blending.

incorporer *vt* to incorporate, integrate.

incorrect *adj* faulty, incorrect; **~ement** *adv* incorrectly.

incorrigible *adj* incorrigible.

incorruptible *adj* incorruptible.

incrédule *adj* incredulous; * *mf* unbeliever, non-believer.

incrédulité *f* incredulity, lack of belief.

incroyable *adj* incredible; unbelievable; **~ment** *adv* incredibly, unbelievably.

incruster *vt* to inlay; to superimpose; **s'~** *vr* to become imbedded in; to become rooted in.

inculpation *f* inculcation, instilling.

inculpé *m* **-e** *f* accused; * *adj* accused.

incurable *adj* incurable; **~ment** *adv* incurably, hopelessly.

indécent *adj* indecent, improper.

indéchiffrable *adj* indecipherable; incomprehensible.

indécis *adj* indecisive; unsettled; undefined.

indéfini *adj* undefined; indefinite; **~ment** *adv* indefinitely.

indéfinissable *adj* indefinable.

indemne *adj* unharmed, unhurt.

indemniser *vt* to indemnify; to compensate.

indemnité *f* compensation; indemnity.

indéniable *adj* undeniable, indisputable; **~ment** *adv* undeniably.

indépendance *f* independence.

indépendant *adj* independent.

indestructible *adj* indestructible.

indéterminé *adj* undetermined; unspecified; undecided.

index *m* index; index finger.

indexer *vt* to index.

indicatif *m* signature tune; dialling code; * *adj* indicative.

indication *f* indication; piece of information; instruction.

indice *m* indication; clue; sign.

indifféremment *adv* indiscriminately, equally.

indifférence *f* indifference.

indifférent *adj* indifferent; immaterial.

indigène *mf* native; local; * *adj* indigenous, native.

indigeste *adj* indigestible.

indigestion *f* indigestion.

indigne *adj* unworthy; undeserving.

indigner *vt* to annoy, make indignant; **s'~** *vr* to be indignant.

indiquer *vt* to indicate, point out; to tell.

indirect *adj* indirect; circumstantial; collateral; **~ement** *adv* indirectly.

indiscipliné *adj* undisciplined.

indiscret *adj* indiscreet; inquisitive.

indiscrétion *f* indiscretion; inquisitiveness.

indiscutable *adj* indisputable; unquestionable; **~ment** *adv* indisputably.

indispensable *adj* indispensable; essential.

indisponible *adj* unavailable.

indistinct *adj* indistinct, vague; **~ement** *adv* indistinctly.

individu *m* individual.

individuel *adj* individual; **~lement** *adv* individually.

indolore *adj* painless.

indubitable *adj* indubitable; certain; **~ment** *adv* indubitably.

indulgence *f* indulgence; leniency.

indulgent *adj* indulgent; lenient.

industrialisation *f* industrialization.

industrie *f* industry; dexterity, ingenuity.

industriel *m* **-le** *f* industrialist, manufacturer; * *adj* industrial.

inébranlable *adj* steadfast, unwavering.

inédit *adj* unpublished; original.

inefficace *adj* ineffective; inefficient.

inefficacité *f* ineffectiveness; inefficiency.

inégal *adj* unequal; uneven; irregular; **~ement** *adv* unequally.

inégalité *f* inequality; difference, disparity.

inéluctable *adj* ineluctable, unavoidable; **~ment** *adv* ineluctably.

inépuisable *adj* inexhaustible.

inerte *adj* inert; lifeless.

inertie *f* inertia, apathy.

inespéré *adj* unexpected.
inestimable *adj* inestimable, invaluable.
inévitable *adj* inevitable, unavoidable.
inexact *adj* inexact, inaccurate.
inexactitude *f* inaccuracy.
inexistant *adj* nonexistent.
inexorable *adj* inexorable; ~**ment** *adv* inexorably.
inexpérimenté *adj* inexperienced; inexpert.
inexplicable *adj* inexplicable; ~**ment** *adv* inexplicably.
inexprimable *adj* inexpressible.
infaillible *adj* infallible.
infâme *adj* infamous; base, vile.
infantile *adj* infantile, childish.
infatigable *adj* indefatigable, tireless; ~**ment** *adv* indefatigably.
infect *adj* vile; revolting; filthy.
infecter *vt* to infect; to contaminate; **s'~** *vr* to become infected.
infection *f* infection.
inférieur *adj* inferior; lower.
infériorité *f* inferiority.
infernal *adj* infernal, diabolical.
infester *vt* to infest, overrun.
infidèle *adj* unfaithful, disloyal.
infidélité *f* infidelity.
infiltration *f* infiltration.
infini *adj* infinite; interminable; ~**ment** *adv* infinitely.
infinitif *m* infinitive.
infirme *adj* feeble; crippled, disabled.
infirmerie *f* infirmary; sick bay.
infirmier *m* **-ière** *f* nurse.
infirmité *f* disability; infirmity.
inflammation *f* inflammation.
inflation *f* inflation.
inflexible *adj* inflexible, rigid.
infliger *vt* to inflict; to impose.
influence *f* influence.
influencer *vt* to influence, sway.
informaticien *m* **-ne** *f* computer scientist.
information *f* piece of information; information; inquiry.
informatique *f* computing; data processing; * *adj* computer.
informer *vt* to inform, tell; **s'~** *vr* to find out, inquire.

infraction *f* infraction, infringement; offence.
infranchissable *adj* impassable; insuperable.
infrarouge *adj* infrared.
infrastructure *f* infrastructure; substructure.
infructueux *adj* fruitless, unsuccessful.
infusion *f* infusion, herb tea.
ingénieur *m* engineer.
ingénieux *adj* ingenious, clever.
ingénu *adj* ingenuous, naive.
ingrat *adj* ungrateful; unprofitable.
ingratitude *f* ingratitude.
ingrédient *m* ingredient; component.
inhabité *adj* uninhabited, unoccupied.
inhabituel *adj* unusual, unaccustomed.
inhumain *adj* inhuman.
inimaginable *adj* unimaginable.
inimitable *adj* inimitable.
ininterrompu *adj* uninterrupted; unbroken.
initial *adj* initial; ~**ement** *adv* initially.
initiation *f* initiation.
initiative *f* initiative; enterprise.
initier *vt* to initiate.
injecter *vt* to inject.
injection *f* injection.
injure *f* injury; insult.
injurier *vt* to abuse; insult.
injuste *adj* unjust, unfair; ~**ment** *adv* unjustly.
injustice *f* injustice.
injustifié *adj* unjustified.
inné *adj* innate, inborn.
innocence *f* innocence.
innocent *m* **-e** *f* innocent person; simpleton; * *adj* innocent.
innocenter *vt* to clear, prove innocent.
innovation *f* innovation.
innover *vi* to innovate, make innovations.
inodore *adj* odourless, scentless.
inoffensif *adj* inoffensive, harmless.
inondation *f* flood.
inonder *vt* to flood, inundate.
inopportun *adj* ill-timed, inopportune.
inoubliable *adj* unforgettable.
inouï *adj* unprecedented, unheard of.
inox *m* stainless steel.
inqualifiable *adj* unspeakable.
inquiet *adj* worried, anxious, uneasy.
inquiéter *vt* to worry, disturb; **s'~** *vr* to get worried.

inquiétude *f* restlessness, uneasiness.

insaisissable *adj* elusive; imperceptible.

insalubre *adj* insalubrious; unhealthy.

insatiable *adj* insatiable; **~ment** *adv* insatiably.

insatisfaction *f* dissatisfaction.

inscription *f* inscription; registration; matriculation.

inscrire *vt* to inscribe; to enter; to set down; to register; **s'~** *vr* to join; to register, enrol.

insecte *m* insect.

insecticide *m* insecticide.

insémination *f* insemination.

insensé *adj* insane, demented.

insensible *adj* insensible, unfeeling, insensitive; imperceptible; **~ment** *adv* imperceptibly; insensibly.

inséparable *adj* inseparable.

insérer *vt* to insert.

insertion *f* insertion, inserting.

insidieux *adj* insidious

insignifiant *adj* insignificant, trifling.

insinuation *f* insinuation.

insinuer *vt* to insinuate, imply; **s'~** *vr* to insinuate o.s. into; to creep into.

insipide *adj* insipid, tasteless.

insister *vi* to insist, be insistent; to stress.

insolence *f* insolence.

insolent *adj* insolent; brazen.

insolite *adj* unusual; strange.

insomnie *f* insomnia.

insouciance *f* unconcern; carelessness.

insouciant *adj* carefree; careless.

insoutenable *adj* unbearable; untenable.

inspecter *vt* to inspect, examine.

inspecteur *m* **-trice** *f* inspector

inspection *f* inspection.

inspiration *f* inspiration; suggestion.

inspirer *vt* to inspire; to breathe in; **s'~** *vr*: **s'~ de** to be inspired by.

instable *adj* unstable; unsettled.

installation *f* installation; installing.

installer *vt* to install; to fit out; **s'~** *vr* to set o.s. up; to settle down.

instant *m* moment, instant.

instantané *adj* instant, instantaneous; **~ment** *adv* instantly.

instaurer *vt* to institute; to impose.

instinct *m* instinct.

instinctif *adj* instinctive.

instinctivement *adv* instinctively.

institut *m* institute; school.

instituteur *m* **-trice** *f* teacher.

institution *f* institution; establishment.

instructif *adj* instructive.

instruction *f* instruction; education; inquiry.

instruire *vt* to instruct; to teach; to conduct an inquiry; **s'~** *vr* to educate o.s.; to obtain information.

instrument *m* instrument, implement.

insuffisance *f* insufficiency, inadequacy.

insuffisant *adj* insufficient, inadequate.

insuline *f* insulin.

insulte *f* insult.

insulter *vt* to insult, affront.

insupportable *adj* unbearable, intolerable; **~ment** *adv* unbearably, intolerably.

insurrection *f* insurrection, revolt.

intact *adj* intact.

intégral *adj* integral; uncut; complete; **~ement** *adv* integrally; in full.

intégralité *f* whole; entirety.

intégrer *vt* to integrate; **s'~** *vr* to become integrated; to fit in.

intégrité *f* integrity.

intellectuel *m* **-le** *f* intellectual; * *adj* intellectual, mental.

intelligence *f* intelligence; understanding.

intelligent *adj* intelligent, shrewd, bright.

intelligible *adj* intelligible.

intempéries *fpl* bad weather.

intendant *m* **-e** *f* bursar; steward, stewardess.

intense *adj* intense; severe.

intensément *adv* intensely.

intensif *adj* intensive.

intensifier *vt* to intensify; **s'~** *vr* to intensify.

intensité *f* intensity; severity.

intention *f* intention; purpose, intent.

interaction *f* interaction.

intercaler *vt* to intercalate; to interpolate.

intercepter *vt* to intercept.

interchangeable *adj* interchangeable.

interdiction *f* interdiction, prohibition, ban.

interdire *vt* to forbid, ban, prohibit.

interdit *adj* forbidden, prohibited; dumbfounded.

intéressant *adj* interesting; attractive, worthwhile.

intéresser *vt* to interest; to concern; *vr*: **s'~ à** to be interested in.

intérêt *m* interest; significance, importance.

interférence *f* interference; conjunction.

intérieur *adj* interior, internal, inland; **à l'~** inside; within; **~ement** *adv* inwardly.

intérimaire *adj* interim; acting; temporary.

interligne *m* line space; interlining; lead.

interlocuteur *m* **-trice** *f* interlocutor, speaker.

intermède *m* interlude.

intermédiaire *adj* intermediate; intermediary.

interminable *adj* interminable; endless; **~ment** *adv* interminably, endlessly.

intermittent *adj* intermittent, sporadic.

international *adj* international.

interne *adj* internal; * *mf* boarder; house doctor.

interpeller *vt* to call out to; (*police*) to interpellate.

interphone *m* intercom, entryphone.

interposer *vt* to interpose; **s'~** *vr* to intervene.

interprétation *f* interpretation, rendering.

interprète *mf* interpreter.

interpréter *vt* to interpret; to perform.

interrogation *f* interrogation, questioning; question.

interrogatoire *m* questioning; cross-examination.

interroger *vt* to question; to interrogate; **s'~** *vr* to wonder.

interrompre *vt* to interrupt, break; **s'~** *vr* to break off, interrupt o.s.

interrupteur *m* switch.

interruption *f* interruption, break.

intervalle *m* interval; space, distance.

intervenir *vi* to intervene; to take part in.

intervention *f* intervention; operation.

intestinal *adj* intestinal

intestin *m* intestine.

intime *adj* intimate; private; **~ment** *adv* intimately; * *mf* close friend.

intimider *vt* to intimidate.

intimité *f* intimacy; privacy.

intituler *vt* to call, entitle; **s'~** *vr* to be called; to call o.s.

intolérable *adj* intolerable.

intolérance *f* intolerance.

intolérant *adj* intolerant.

intonation *f* intonation.

intoxication *f* poisoning; indoctrination.

intransigeant *adj* intransigent, uncompromising.

intransitif *adj* intransitive.

intrépide *adj* intrepid, fearless; **~ment** *adv* intrepidly.

intrigant *adj* scheming.

introduction *f* introduction; launching; (*jur*) institution.

introduire *vt* to introduce, insert; to present; **s'~** *vr* to find one's way in; to be introduced.

introuvable *adj* undiscoverable; not to be found.

introverti *m* **-e** *f* introvert; * *adj* introverted.

intrus *m* **-e** *f* intruder; * *adj* intruding, intrusive.

intuitif *adj* intuitive.

intuition *f* intuition.

inutile *adj* useless; unavailing; pointless; **~ment** *adv* uselessly, needlessly.

inutilisable *adj* unusable.

invalide *adj* disabled; (*jur*) invalid.

invariable *adj* invariable; unvarying; **~ment** *adv* invariably.

invasion *f* invasion.

inventaire *m* inventory; stocklist.

inventer *vt* to invent; to devise; to make up.

inventeur *m* **-trice** *f* inventor.

invention *f* invention; inventiveness.

inverse *adj* opposite; * *m* opposite, reverse.

inverser *vt* to reverse, invert.

inversion *f* inversion; reversal.

investir *vt* to invest; to surround.

investissement *m* investment; investing.

invincible *adj* invincible, indomitable.

invisible *adj* invisible; unseen.

invitation *f* invitation.

invité *m* **-e** *f* guest.

inviter *vt* to invite, ask.

involontaire *adj* involuntary; unintentional; **~ment** *adv* involuntarily.

invoquer *vt* to invoke; to call up; to plead.

invraisemblable *adj* unlikely, improbable; **~ment** *adv* improbably.

invulnérable *adj* invulnerable.
iode *m* iodine.
ion *m* ion.
iris *m* iris.
Irlandais *m* Irishman, **-e** *f* Irishwoman
irlandais *adj* Irish.
Irlande *f* Ireland.
ironie *f* irony.
ironique *adj* ironic; **~ment** *adv* ironically.
irradiation *f* irradiation; radiation.
irrationnel *adj* irrational.
irrécupérable *adj* irretrievable.
irréel *adj* unreal.
irréfléchi *adj* unconsidered; hasty.
irrégularité *f* irregularity; variation; unevenness.
irrégulier *adj* irregular; varying; uneven.
irrégulièrement *adv* irregularly; unevenly.
irrémédiable *adj* irreparable; incurable; **~ment** *adv* irreparably.
irremplaçable *adj* irreplaceable.

irréparable *adj* irreparable; irretrievable; **~ment** *adv* irreparably.
irrésistible *adj* irresistible; **~ment** *adv* irresistibly.
irresponsable *adj* irresponsible
irréversible *adj* irreversible; **~ment** *adv* irreversibly.
irrigation *f* irrigation.
irriguer *vt* to irrigate.
irriter *vt* to irritate; to provoke.
irruption *f* irruption.
Islam *m* Islam.
isolement *m* loneliness; isolation; insulation.
isoler *vt* to isolate; to insulate; **s'~** *vr* to cut o.s. off.
issu *adj* descended from; stemming from.
issue *f* outlet; solution; outcome.
ivoire *m* ivory.
ivre *adj* drunk, inebriated.
ivresse *f* drunkenness.
ivrogne *mf* drunkard.

J

jachère *f* fallow; leaving land lying fallow.
jade *m* jade.
jadis *adv* formerly, long ago.
jaguar *m* jaguar.
jaillir *vi* to spout, gush; to spring.
jalon *m* staff; landmark, milestone.
jalonner *vt* to mark out.
jalousie *f* jealousy, envy.
jaloux *m* **-ouse** *f* jealous person; * *adj* jealous, envious.
jamais *adv* never, not ever; **à ~** for ever.
jambe *f* leg.
jambon *m* ham.
janvier *m* January.
jardin *m* garden.
jardinage *m* gardening.
jardiner *vi* to garden.
jardinier *m* **-ière** *f* gardener.
jargon *m* jargon, slang; gibberish.
jarret *m* hock; (*zool*) hollow of the knee.
jaser *vi* to chatter; to twitter; to babble.

jasmin *m* jasmine.
jauge *f* gauge; capacity; tonnage.
jauger *vt* to gauge the capacity of; to size up.
jaunâtre *adj* yellowish.
jaune *adj* yellow; * *m* yellow.
jaunir *vi* to yellow, turn yellow; * *vt* to make yellow.
jaunisse *f* jaundice.
jazz *m* jazz.
je, j' *pn* I.
jésuite *m* Jesuit.
jet *m* jet, spurt; throwing.
jetable *adj* disposable.
jetée *f* pier.
jeter *vt* to throw; to discard; to give out; **se ~** *vr* to throw o.s.; to rush at.
jeton *m* token; counter.
jeu *m* play; game; gambling; **~ de jambes** footwork; **~ de mots** pun, play on words; **cacher son ~** to conceal one's intentions.
jeudi *m* Thursday.

jeun *adv*: **à ~** on an empty stomach.

jeune *adj* young; junior; new; youthful; * *m* youth, young man; *f* young girl.

jeûne *m* fast.

jeûner *vi* to fast.

jeunesse *f* youth, youthfulness.

joaillerie *f* jewellery.

joaillier *m* **-ière** *f* jeweller.

joie *f* joy, happiness; pleasure.

joindre *vt* to join, link; to attach; **se ~** *vr* to join, join in.

joint *m* joint; join.

jointure *f* (*anat*) joint.

joli *adj* pretty; good, handsome; **~ment** *adv* nicely, attractively.

jonc *m* rush; cane.

joncher *vt* to strew with.

jonction *f* junction.

jongler *vi* to juggle.

jongleur *m* **-euse** *f* juggler.

jonquille *f* daffodil, jonquil.

joue *f* cheek

jouer *vi* to play; to gamble; to act.

jouet *m* toy.

joueur *m* **-euse** *f* player; gambler.

joufflu *adj* chubby; round-faced.

joug *m* yoke.

jouir *vi* to enjoy; to delight in.

jouissance *f* enjoyment; use.

jour *m* day; daylight; **tous les ~s** every day; **à ~** up to date; **vivre au ~ le ~** to live from day to day; **~ férié** public holiday; **mise à ~** updating; update; **du ~ au lendemain** overnight.

journal *m* newspaper; bulletin, journal; **~ de bord** logbook; **~ télévisé** television news.

journalisme *m* journalism.

journaliste *mf* journalist.

journée *f* day; day's work.

jovial *adj* jovial, jolly.

jovialité *f* joviality.

joyau *m* jewel, gem.

joyeusement *adv* joyfully, cheerfully.

joyeux *adj* joyful, cheerful.

jubiler *vi* to be jubilant, exult.

judaïsme *m* Judaism.

judiciaire *adj* judicial, legal.

judicieusement *adv* judiciously.

judicieux *adj* judicious.

judo *m* judo

judoka *mf* judoka.

juge *m* judge.

jugement *m* judgment; sentence; opinion.

juger *vt* to judge; to decide; to consider.

juif *m* Jew; Jewish; **juive** *f* Jewess; * *adj* Jewish.

juillet *m* July.

juin *m* June.

jumeau *m* **-elle** *f* twin; * *adj* twin; double.

jumelage *m* twinning.

jumelé *adj* twinned, twin.

jumelle(s) *f(pl)* binoculars.

jument *f* mare.

jungle *f* jungle.

jupe *f* skirt.

jurer *vt* to swear, pledge.

juridiction *f* jurisdiction; court of law.

juridique *adj* legal, juridical; **~ment** *adv* juridically, legally.

jurisprudence *f* case law, jurisprudence.

juriste *m* lawyer; jurist.

juron *m* oath, curse.

jury *m* jury; board of examiners.

jus *m* juice.

jusque, jusqu' *prép* to, as far as; until.

justaucorps *m* jerkin; leotard.

juste *adj* just, fair; exact; sound; **~ment** *adv* exactly, precisely.

justesse *f* accuracy; aptness; soundness.

justice *f* justice, fairness.

justicier *m* **-ière** *f* justiciary; dispenser of justice.

justificatif *adj* supporting, justificatory.

justification *f* justification; proof.

justifier *vt* to justify, prove; **se ~** *vr* to justify o.s.

jute *m* jute.

juteux *adj* juicy; lucrative.

juvénile *adj* young, youthful.

juxtaposer *vt* to juxtapose.

juxtaposition *f* juxtaposition.

K

kaki *adj* khaki.
kaléidoscope *m* kaleidoscope.
kangourou *m* kangaroo.
karaté *m* karate.
kayac, kayak *m* kayak.
képi *m* kepi.
kermesse *f* fair; bazaar.
kérosène *m* kerosene, aviation fuel.
kidnapper *vt* to kidnap, abduct.
kidnappeur *m* **-euse** *f* kidnapper.
kilogramme *m* kilogram.
kilohertz *m* kilohertz.

kilométrage *m* total kilometres travelled (mileage).
kilomètre *m* kilometre.
kimono *m* kimono.
kinésithérapeute *mf* physiotherapist.
kiosque *m* kiosk, stall.
kiwi *m* kiwi, Chinese gooseberry.
klaxon *m* horn.
klaxonner *vi* to sound one's horn.
kleptomane *mf* kleptomaniac.
kleptomanie *f* kleptomania.
koala *m* koala.
kyste *m* cyst.

L

la *art pn: see* **le**.
là *adv* there; over there; then; **par ~** that way; **~-dedans** inside, in there; **~-dessous** underneath, under there; **~-dessus** on that; thereupon; **~-haut** up there, up on top; **celui-~** that one.
label *m* label; seal.
labeur *m* labour, toil.
laboratoire *m* laboratory.
laborieux *adj* laborious, toilsome.
labourer *vt* to plough; to dig over; to rip open.
labyrinthe *m* labyrinth.
lac *m* lake.
lacer *vt* to lace up; to tie up.
lacérer *vt* to lacerate; to tear.
lacet *m* lace.
lâche *adj* slack; loose; lax; cowardly; **~ment** *adv* loosely; in a cowardly manner; * *mf* coward.
lâcher *vt* to loosen; to release.
lâcheté *f* cowardice; meanness.
laconique *adj* laconic; **~ment** *adv* laconically.
lacté *adj* milky, lacteal.
lactique *adj* lactic.
lacune *f* lacuna; gap.

lagon *m* lagoon.
lagune *f* lagoon.
laïc *m* layman, **laïque** *f* laywoman; * **laïque** *adj* lay, civil.
laid *adj* ugly, unsightly.
laideur *f* ugliness, unsightliness.
lainage *m* woollen article.
laine *f* wool.
laisse *f* leash, string, lead.
laisser *vt* to leave; to let; **~ tomber** to drop; **se ~ aller** to let o.s. go.
laisser-passer *m invar* pass, permit.
lait *m* milk.
laitage *m* milk; milk products.
laiton *m* brass.
laitue *f* lettuce.
lama *m* (*zool*) llama; lama.
lambeau *m* shred; tatter.
lambris *m* plastering; panelling.
lame *f* blade; strip; metal plate.
lamelle *f* slide; small strip.
lamentable *adj* lamentable, distressing; **~ment** *adv* lamentably.
lamentation *f* lamentation; wailing.
lamenter (se) *vr* to lament, bewail.
laminer *vt* to laminate.
lampadaire *m* standard-lamp; street lamp.

lampe *f* lamp, light; bulb.

lance *f* lance, spear.

lance-flammes *m invar* flamethrower.

lancement *m* launching; starting up; throwing.

lance-pierres *m invar* catapult.

lancer *vt* to throw; to launch; **se ~** *vr* to leap, jump; to embark on.

lancinant *adj* nagging; haunting.

lande *f* moor.

langage *m* language, speech.

langoureux *adj* languid, languorous.

langouste *f* spiny lobster.

langoustine *f* Dublin bay prawn.

langue *f* tongue; language.

languette *f* tongue; tongue-like strip.

langueur *f* languor.

languir *vi* to languish; to linger.

lanière *f* thong; lash.

lanoline *f* lanolin.

lanterne *f* lantern; lamp.

lapin *m* **-e** *f* rabbit.

lapsus *m* slip, mistake.

laque *f* hairspray; lacquer; * *m* lacquer ware.

lard *m* fat; bacon.

lardon *m* bacon cube.

large *adj* wide; generous; lax; great; **~ment** *adv* widely; greatly.

largeur *f* width, breadth.

larguer *vt* to loose, release; cast off.

larme *f* tear.

larmoyant *adj* tearful, weeping.

larve *f* larva, grub.

laryngite *f* laryngitis.

larynx *m* larynx.

las *adj*, *f* **-se** weary, tired.

lasagne *f* lasagne.

laser *m* laser.

lasser *vt* to tire; **se ~** *vr* to grow tired.

lassitude *f* tiredness, weariness.

latent *adj* latent.

latéral *adj* lateral, side; **~ement** *adv* laterally.

latex *m* latex.

latin *adj* Latin; * *m* Latin.

latitude *f* latitude; margin.

latte *f* lath.

lauréat *m* **-e** *f* prize winner.

laurier *m* bay-tree, laurel.

lavabo *m* washbasin.

lavage *m* washing; bathing.

lavande *f* lavender.

lave *f* lava.

lavement *m* enema.

laver *vt* to wash; to cleanse; **se ~** *vr* to wash o.s.

laverie *f* laundry.

lave-vaisselle *m invar* dishwasher.

laxatif *adj* laxative; * *m* laxative.

laxisme *m* laxness.

layette *f* baby clothes.

le *art*, *f* **la**, *devant voyelle* **l'**, *pl* **les** the; * *pn* him, her, them.

lécher *vt* to lick.

leçon *f* lesson; reading; class.

lecteur *m* **-trice** *f* reader.

lecture *f* reading; perusal.

légal *adj* legal, lawful; **~ement** *adv* legally.

légaliser *vt* to legalize.

légalité *f* legality, lawfulness.

légendaire *adj* legendary.

légende *f* legend; inscription.

léger *adj* light; slight; faint; inconsiderate.

légèrement *adv* lightly; thoughtlessly.

légèreté *f* lightness; nimbleness; thoughtlessness.

légion *f* legion.

législatif *adj* legislative; * *m* legislature.

législation *f* legislation, laws.

légitime *adj* legitimate, lawful; **~ment** *adv* legitimately.

légitimité *f* legitimacy.

legs *m* legacy, bequest.

léguer *vt* to bequeath; (*jur*) to devise.

légume *m* vegetable.

lendemain *m* next day, day after.

lent *adj* slow; tardy; sluggish; **~ement** *adv* slowly.

lente *f* (*zool*) nit.

lenteur *f* slowness.

lentille *f* lentil; lens.

léopard *m* leopard.

lèpre *f* leprosy.

lépreux *m* **-euse** *f* leper; * *adj* leprous.

lequel *pn*, *f* **laquelle**, *pl* **lesquels, lesquelles** who, whom, which.

lesbienne *f* lesbian.

léser *vt* to wrong; to damage.

lésion *f* wrong; lesion, wound.

lessive *f* washing powder.

leste *adj* nimble, agile; **~ment** *adv* nimbly.

lester *vt* to fill; to ballast.

léthargie *f* lethargy.

léthargique *adj* lethargic.

lettre *f* letter, note; literature; **en toutes ~s** in black and white; **suivre à la ~** to carry out to the letter; **avant la ~** in advance, premature.

leucémie *f* leukaemia.

leucocyte *m* leucocyte.

leur *pn* them; **le ~, la ~, les ~s** theirs.

leurrer *vt* to deceive; to lure; **se ~** *vr* to delude o.s.

levain *m* leaven.

lever *vt* to lift, raise; to levy; **se ~** *vr* to get up; * *m* rising; getting up.

levier *m* lever.

lèvre *f* lip.

lévrier *m* greyhound.

levure *f* yeast.

lexique *m* vocabulary, lexis.

lézard *m* lizard.

lézarde *f* crack.

liaison *f* affair; connection; liaison, link.

liasse *f* bundle.

libellule *f* dragonfly.

libéral *adj* liberal; **~ement** *adv* liberally; * *m* liberal.

libéraliser *vt* to liberalize.

libéralisme *m* liberalism.

libéralité *f* liberality, generosity.

libération *f* release, liberation.

libérer *vt* to release; to liberate; **se ~** *vr* to free o.s.

liberté *f* liberty, freedom.

libido *f* libido.

libraire *mf* bookseller.

librairie *f* bookshop; bookselling.

libre *adj* free; independent; **~ment** *adv* freely.

licence *f* degree; permit; licentiousness.

licenciement *m* redundancy; dismissal.

licencier *vt* to make redundant; to dismiss.

lichen *m* lichen.

licorne *f* unicorn.

lie *f* dregs, sediment.

liège *m* cork.

lien *m* bond; link, connection; tie.

lier *vt* to bind; to link; **se ~** *vr*: **se ~ avec** to make friends.

lierre *m* ivy.

lieu *m* place, position; cause; occasion; **avoir ~** to take place; **en premier ~** in the first place; **au ~ de** instead of.

lieutenant *m* (*mil*) lieutenant.

lièvre *m* hare.

ligament *m* ligament

ligature *f* ligature; tying up.

ligne *f* line; row; range.

lignée *f* lineage; offspring.

lignite *m* lignite.

ligoter *vt* to bind hand and foot.

ligue *f* league.

lilas *m* lilac; * *adj* lilac.

limace *f* slug.

limande *f* dab.

lime *f* file.

limer *vt* to file down.

limitation *f* limitation, restriction.

limite *f* boundary, limit; **à la ~** ultimately.

limiter *vt* to limit, restrict; **se ~** *vr* to limit o.s. to.

limitrophe *adj* border.

limon *m* silt.

limonade *f* lemonade.

limpide *adj* limpid, clear.

limpidité *f* limpidity, clearness.

lin *m* flax; linen.

linceul *m* shroud.

linéaire *adj* linear.

linge *m* linen; washing.

lingerie *f* linen room; underwear, lingerie.

lingot *m* ingot.

linguiste *mf* linguist.

linguistique *f* linguistics; * *adj* linguistic.

lion *m* lion, **lionne** *f* lioness.

lionceau *m* lion cub.

lipide *m* lipid.

liquéfier *vt* to liquefy; **se ~** *vr* to liquefy.

liqueur *f* liqueur; liquid.

liquidation *f* liquidation; winding up; elimination.

liquide *m* liquid.

liquider *vt* to settle; to wind up; to eliminate

lire *vt* to read.

lis *m* lily.

lisible *adj* legible; readable; ~**ment** *adv* legibly.

lisière *f* edge; border; outskirts.

lisse *adj* smooth, glossy.

lisser *vt* to smooth, gloss.

liste *f* list; (*jur*) schedule.

lit *m* bed; layer.

litanie *f* litany.

literie *f* bedding.

lithographie *f* lithography.

litière *f* litter.

litige *m* lawsuit; dispute.

litigieux *adj* litigious.

litre *m* litre.

littéraire *adj* literary.

littéral *adj* literal; ~**ement** *adv* literally.

littérature *f* literature; writing.

littoral *m* coast; * *adj* coastal, littoral.

liturgie *f* liturgy.

livide *adj* livid, pale.

livraison *f* delivery; number, issue.

livre *m* book; * *f* pound (weight, currency).

livrer *vt* to deliver, hand over; to give away; **se ~** *vr* to abandon o.s.

livret *m* (*mus*) libretto; booklet.

livreur *m* delivery man, **-euse** *f* delivery woman.

lobe *m* lobe.

lobotomie *f* lobotomy.

local *adj* local; ~**ement** *adv* locally.

localisation *f* localization.

localiser *vt* to localize.

localité *f* locality; town.

locataire *mf* tenant; lodger.

location *f* renting; lease, leasing.

locomotion *f* locomotion.

locomotive *f* locomotive, engine; dynamo.

locution *f* locution, idiom.

logarithme *m* logarithm.

loge *f* lodge; dressing room; box.

logement *m* housing; accommodation.

loger *vt* to accommodate; to billet; * *vi* to live in.

logiciel *m* software.

logique *f* logic; * *adj* logical; ~**ment** *adv* logically.

logistique *f* logistics.

logo *m* logo.

loi *f* law; act, statute; rule.

loin *adv* far, a long way; * *m*: distance; background **au ~** in the distance; **de ~** from a distance.

lointain *adj* distant, remote; * *m* distance; background.

loir *m* dormouse.

loisir *m* leisure, spare time.

lombaire *adj* lumbar; * *f* lumbar vertebra.

lombric *m* earthworm.

long *adj*, *f* **-ue** long, lengthy; ~**uement** *adv* at length.

longer *vt* to border; to walk along.

longévité *f* longevity.

longitude *f* longitude.

longtemps *adv* for a long time.

longueur *f* length.

longue-vue *f* telescope.

loquace *adj* loquacious, talkative.

loque *f* rag.

loquet *m* latch; clasp.

lorgner *vt* to leer, ogle.

lors *adv* then; **~ de** at the time of; **dès ~** from that time.

lorsque *conj* when.

losange *m* lozenge, diamond.

lot *m* prize; lot; portion.

loterie *f* lottery; raffle.

lotion *f* lotion.

lotissement *m* allotment; site, housing development.

lotus *m* lotus.

louange *f* praise, commendation.

louche *adj* dubious; suspicious, shady.

loucher *vi* to squint; to ogle.

louer *vt* to rent, lease; to book.

loup *m* wolf.

loupe *f* magnifying glass.

louper *vt* (*fam*) to botch, bungle; to flunk.

lourd *adj* heavy; sultry; unwieldy; ~**ement** *adv* heavily.

lourdeur *f* heaviness.

loutre *f* otter.

louve *f* she-wolf.

louveteau *m* wolf-cub.

loyal *adj* loyal, faithful; ~**ement** *adv* loyally.

loyauté *f* loyalty.
loyer *m* rent.
lubrifiant *m* lubricant; * *adj* lubricating.
lubrifier *vt* to lubricate.
lubrique *adj* lustful, lecherous; ~**ment** *adv* lustfully.
lucarne *f* skylight.
lucide *adj* lucid, clear; ~**ment** *adv* lucidly.
lucidité *f* lucidity, clearness.
lucratif *adj* lucrative.
ludique *adj* play.
lueur *f* glimmer, gleam; glimpse.
luge *f* sledge, toboggan.
lugubre *adj* lugubrious, gloomy; ~**ment** *adv* lugubriously.
lui *pn* him, her, it; **c'est à ~** it is his; ~**-même** himself, itself.
luire *vt* to shine, gleam.
luisant *adj* gleaming, shining.
lumbago *m* lumbago.
lumière *f* light; daylight; lamp; insight.
lumineux *adj* luminous; illuminated.
lunaire *adj* lunar, moon.
lunatique *adj* fantastical, whimsical, quirky.
lundi *m* Monday.
lune *f* moon.
lunette *f* telescope; ~**s** glasses.

lustré *adj* glossy; shiny.
luth *m* lute.
luthérien *adj* Lutheran.
luthiste *mf* lutanist.
lutin *m* imp;goblin.
lutte *f* struggle; contest; strife.
lutter *vi* to struggle, fight.
lutteur *m* -**euse** *f* wrestler, fighter.
luxation *f* dislocation, luxation.
luxe *m* luxury, excess.
luxueusement *adv* luxuriously.
luxueux *adj* luxurious.
luxure *f* lust.
luxuriance *f* luxuriance.
luxuriant *adj* luxuriant.
luzerne *f* lucerne, alfalfa.
lycée *m* secondary school.
lycéen *m* secondary school boy, -**ne** *f* secondary school girl.
lymphatique *adj* lymphatic.
lymphe *f* lymph.
lymphocyte *m* lymphocyte.
lyncher *vt* to lynch.
lynx *m* lynx.
lyre *f* lyre.
lyrique *adj* lyric; ~**ment** *adv* lyrically.
lyrisme *m* lyricism.

M

macabre *adj* macabre.
macadam *m* tarmac.
macaque *m* macaque.
macédoine *f* medley, hotchpotch; macedoine.
macérer *vt* to macerate; to mortify o.s.; * *vi* to macerate, steep.
mâche *f* corn-salad.
mâcher *vt* to chew.
machiavélique *adj* Machiavellian.
machin *m* (*fam*) gadget; thingamajig.
machinal *adj* mechanical, automatic; ~**ement** *adv* mechanically.
machination *f* machination, plot.
machine *f* machine; engine; apparatus.
machinerie *f* machinery, plant.
machiniste *m* machinist; driver; stagehand.

mâchoire *f* jaw.
maçon *m* builder, mason.
maçonnerie *f* masonry; building.
macrobiotique *adj* macrobiotic; * *f* macrobiotics
madame *f* Madam; Mrs; lady.
madeleine *f* madeleine.
mademoiselle *f* Miss; young lady.
magasin *m* shop, store; warehouse.
magazine *m* magazine.
mage *m* magus; seer.
magicien *m* -**ne** *f* magician.
magie *f* magic
magique *adj* magic; magical; ~**ment** *adv* magically.
magistral *adj* masterly; authoritative; ~**ement** *adv* in a masterly fashion.

magistrat *m* magistrate.

magistrature *f* magistracy; magistrature.

magnanime *adj* magnanimous; ~**ment** *adv* magnanimously.

magnanimité *f* magnanimity.

magnat *m* magnate.

magnésium *m* magnesium.

magnétique *adj* magnetic.

magnétiser *vt* to magnetize; to hypnotize.

magnétisme *m* magnetism; hypnotism.

magnétophone *m* tape recorder.

magnétoscope *m* video recorder; videotape.

magnifique *adj* magnificent; sumptuous; ~**ment** *adv* magnificently.

magnolia *m* magnolia.

magot *m* (*fam*) savings, hoard, nest egg.

magouille *f* (*fam*) fiddle, scam; scheming.

mai *m* May.

maigre *adj* thin; meagre, scarce; ~**ment** *adv* meagrely.

maigreur *f* thinness; meagreness; sparseness.

maigrir *vi* to get thinner; to waste away.

maille *f* stitch; mesh; link.

maillet *m* mallet.

maillon *m* link; shackle.

maillot *m* jersey; leotard.

main *f* hand; **avoir la ~** to have the lead; **passer la ~** to make way for sb.

main-d'œuvre *f* workforce.

maintenance *f* maintenance, servicing.

maintenant *adv* now; **à partir de ~** from now on.

maintenir *vt* to keep, maintain; preserve; **se ~** *vr* to persist; to hold one's own.

maintien *m* maintenance; preservation; keeping up.

maire *m* mayor, *f* mayoress.

mairie *f* mayoralty; town hall.

mais *conj* but.

maïs *m* maize; corn.

maison *f* house; home; building; premises.

maître *m* -**esse** *f* master; ruler; lord; proprietor.

maîtresse *f* mistress; teacher.

maîtrise *f* mastery; control; expertise.

maîtriser *vt* to control; to master; **se ~** *vr* to control o.s.

majesté *f* majesty, grandeur.

majestueusement *adv* majestically.

majestueux *adj* majestic.

majeur *adj* major; main; chief; superior; * *m* major *mf* adult.

majoration *f* increased charge; overestimation.

majordome *m* majordomo, butler.

majorer *vt* to increase, raise.

majorette *f* majorette.

majoritaire *adj* majority.

majorité *f* majority.

majuscule *f* capital letter.

mal *adv* wrong, badly; * *m* evil, wrong; harm; pain.

malachite *f* malachite.

malade *adj* sick, ill; diseased; * *mf* invalid, sick person.

maladie *f* illness; malady, complaint; disorder.

maladresse *f* clumsiness; awkwardness.

maladroit *adj* clumsy, awkward; ~**ement** *adv* clumsily.

malaise *m* uneasiness, discomfort; indisposition.

malchance *f* ill luck; misfortune; mishap.

malchanceux *adj* unlucky, unfortunate.

mâle *m* male; * *adj* male; manly, virile.

malédiction *f* malediction, curse.

maléfique *adj* hurtful; malignant; baleful.

malencontreux *adj* unfortunate, untoward.

malentendu *m* misunderstanding.

malfaisant *adj* malevolent; harmful; wicked.

malfaiteur *m* criminal; malefactor.

malgré *prép* in spite of; despite.

malheur *m* misfortune; calamity.

malheureusement *adv* unfortunately.

malheureux *adj* unfortunate; unlucky; unhappy.

malhonnête *adj* dishonest, crooked; uncivil; ~**ment** *adv* dishonestly.

malhonnêteté *f* dishonesty; incivility.

malice *f* malice, spite; mischievousness.

malicieux *adj* malicious, spiteful; mischievous.

malin *adj* shrewd, cunning, crafty; malignant.

malintentionné *adj* ill-disposed, spiteful.

malle *f* trunk.

malléable *adj* malleable.

malmener *vt* to ill-treat, maltreat.

malnutrition *f* malnutrition.

malsain *adj* unhealthy, unwholesome; immoral.

malt *m* malt.

maltraiter *vt* to abuse; to handle roughly.

malveillance *f* malevolence, spite.

malveillant *adj* malevolent, spiteful.

maman *f* mother, mummy, mum.

mamelle *f* breast; udder.

mamelon *m* nipple, teat.

mammifère *m* mammal.

manche *f* sleeve; game, round; * *m* handle, shaft.

manchot *m* **-e** *f* one-armed person; * *adj* one-armed; * *m* penguin.

mandarin *m* mandarin; Mandarin.

mandarine *f* tangerine.

mandat *m* mandate; money order; proxy.

mandataire *mf* proxy; representative.

mandibule *f* mandible, jaw.

mandoline *f* mandolin.

manège *m* roundabout, merry-go-round.

manette *f* lever, tap.

manganèse *m* manganese.

mangeable *adj* edible.

manger *vt* to eat; to consume.

mangeur *m* **-euse** *f* eater.

mangouste *f* mongoose.

mangue *f* mango.

maniable *adj* handy, workable, tractable; amenable.

maniaque *adj* eccentric; fussy.; * *mf* maniac; fusspot; fanatic.

manie *f* mania.

maniement *m* handling; management, use.

manier *vt* to handle; to manipulate.

manière *f* manner, way, style.

maniéré *adj* affected.

manifestation *f* demonstration; expression, manifestation.

manifeste *adj* manifest, evident, obvious; **~ment** *adv* manifestly, obviously; * *m* manifesto.

manifester *vt* to display, make known; to demonstrate; **se ~** *vr* to make o.s. known; to appear; to express o.s.

manigancer *vt* to contrive; to scheme.

manipulation *f* handling; manipulation.

manipuler *vt* to handle; to manipulate

manivelle *f* crank.

mannequin *m* model; dummy.

manœuvre *f* manoeuvre, operation; scheme; * *m* labourer.

manœuvrer *vt* to manoeuvre; to operate; * *vi* to manoeuvre, move.

manoir *m* manor.

manomètre *m* manometer.

manquant *adj* missing.

manque *m* lack, shortage; shortcoming, deficiency.

manquer *vt* to miss; to fail; to be absent.

mansarde *f* attic, garret.

manteau *m* coat; mantle, blanket; cloak.

manuel *m* manual, handbook; * *adj* manual; **~lement** *adv* manually.

manufacture *f* factory; manufacture.

manufacturier *m* **-ière** *f* factory owner; manufacturer; * *adj* manufacturing.

manuscrit *m* manuscript; typescript; * *adj* handwritten.

manutention *f* handling.

mappemonde *f* map of the world.

maquereau *m* mackerel.

maquette *f* model; mock-up; dummy; sketch.

maquillage *m* make-up.

maquiller *vt* to make up; to fake; to fiddle; **se ~** *vr* to put make-up on.

marais *m* marsh, swamp.

marasme *m* stagnation; depression, slump.

marathon *m* marathon.

marbre *m* marble; marble statue.

marbré *adj* marbled; mottled, blotchy.

marbrier *m* marble-cutter; monumental mason.

marchand *m* **-e** *f* shopkeeper; dealer; merchant; * *adj* market, trade.

marchandage *m* bargaining, haggling.

marchander *vi* to bargain over, haggle.

marchandise *f* merchandise, commodity; goods.

marche *f* walk; journey; progress; movement; **mettre en ~** to start up; to turn on.

marché *m* market; transaction, contract.

marcher *vi* to walk, march; to progress; to work.

marcheur *m* **-euse** *f* walker, pedestrian.

mardi *m* Tuesday.

mare *f* pool, pond.

marécage *m* marsh, swamp.

maréchal *m* marshal.

marée *f* tide.

margarine *f* margarine.

marge *f* margin; latitude, freedom; mark-up.

marginal *adj* marginal.

marginaliser *vt* to marginalize.

marguerite *f* daisy.

mari *m* husband.

mariage *m* marriage.

marié *m* bridegroom; * *adj* married.

marier *vt* to marry; blend, harmonize; **se ~** *vr* to get married.

marin *m* sailor.

marine *f* navy; seascape; marine.

mariner *vi* to marinate; to hang about; * *vt* to marinate.

marionnette *f* puppet; puppet show.

maritime *adj* maritime; seaboard.

marjolaine *f* marjoram.

marmelade *f* stewed fruit; marmalade.

marmite *f* pot.

marmonner *vt* to mumble, mutter.

marmotte *f* marmot.

maroquinerie *f* tannery; fine leather craft.

maroquinier *m* leather craftsman; dealer in fine leather.

marquant *adj* outstanding, vivid.

marque *f* mark, sign; brand; make.

marquer *vt* to mark; to note down; to score.

marquis *m* marquis, **-e** *f* marchioness.

marraine *f* godmother; sponsor.

marron *m* chestnut; brown; * *adj* brown.

marronnier *m* chestnut tree.

mars *m* March.

marsouin *m* porpoise.

marteau *m* hammer; knocker.

marteler *vt* to hammer; to beat.

martial *adj* martial, warlike.

martin-pêcheur *m* kingfisher.

martyr *m* **-e** *f* martyr; * *adj* martyred.

martyre *m* martyrdom.

martyriser *vt* to torture, martyrize.

mascarade *f* farce, mascarade.

masculin *adj* masculine.

masochisme *m* masochism.

masochiste *mf* masochist; * *adj* masochistic.

masque *m* mask; facade, front.

masquer *vt* to mask, conceal; to disguise.

massacre *m* massacre; slaughter.

massacrer *vt* to massacre, slaughter.

massage *m* massage.

masse *f* mass, heap; bulk; mob.

masser *vt* to mass, assemble; to massage.

masseur *m* masseur, **-euse** *f* masseuse.

massif *adj* massive, solid, heavy; * *m* massif; clump.

massivement *adv* en masse, massively, heavily.

massue *f* club.

mastic *m* mastic; cement; putty.

mastiquer *vt* to chew, masticate.

masturbation *f* masturbation.

masturber *vi* **se ~** *vr* to masturbate.

mat *adj* matt, dull; dead, dull-sounding.

mât *m* mast; pole.

match *m* match; game.

matelas *m* mattress.

matelassé *adj* stuffed; padded, cushioned.

matelot *m* sailor; seaman.

mater *vt* to subdue; to control, curb; to spy on; to ogle.

matérialiser *vt* to embody; **se ~** *vr* to materialize.

matériaux *mpl* material, materials.

matériel *adj* material, physical; practical; **~lement** *adv* materially, practically.

maternel *adj* maternal, motherly; **~lement** *adv* maternally.

maternité *f* motherhood; pregnancy; maternity hospital.

mathématicien *m* **-ne** *f* mathematician.

mathématique *adj* mathematical; **~ment** *adv* mathematically; * *f* mathematics.

matière *f* material, matter; subject; **~ pre-mière** raw material.

matin *m* morning; dawn.

matinal *adj* morning.

matinée *f* morning; matinée.

matraque *f* truncheon; cosh.

matrice *f* womb; mould; matrix.

matricule *m* reference number; * *f* roll, register.

matrimonial *adj* matrimonial, marriage.

maturation *f* maturing; maturation.

maturité *f* maturity; prime.

maudire *vt* to curse.

maudit *adj* cursed; blasted, damned.

maussade *adj* sulky, sullen; **~ment** *adv* sulkily, sullenly.

mauvais *adj* bad; wicked; faulty; hurtful; poor.

mauve *adj* mauve; * *f* mallow.

maximal *adj* maximal.

maxime *f* maxim.

maximum *m* maximum.

mayonnaise *f* mayonnaise.

me, m' *pn* me; myself.

mécanicien *m* **-ne** *f* mechanic; engineer.

mécanique *f* mechanics; mechanical engineering; * *adj* mechanical; **~ment** *adv* mechanically.

mécanisme *m* mechanism, working.

mécène *m* patron.

méchamment *adv* spitefully; wickedly.

méchanceté *f* spitefulness; wickedness; mischievousness.

méchant *adj* spiteful; wicked; mischievous.

mèche *f* wick, fuse; tuft.

méconnaissable *adj* unrecognizable.

méconnu *adj* unrecognized; misunderstood.

mécontent *adj* discontent, displeased.

mécontentement *m* discontent; displeasure.

médaille *f* medal; stain, mark.

médaillon *m* medallion; locket.

médecin *m* doctor, physician.

médecine *f* medicine

médiateur *m* **-trice** *f* mediator; arbitrator.

médiatique *adj* media.

médical *adj* medical; **~ement** *adv* medically.

médicament *m* medicine, drug.

médicinal *adj* medicinal.

médiéval *adj* medieval.

médiocre *adj* mediocre; passable; indifferent; **~ment** *adv* indifferently; poorly.

médisant *adj* slanderous.

méditation *f* meditation.

méditer *vi* to meditate; * *vt* to contemplate, have in mind.

médium *m* medium.

méduse *f* jellyfish.

méfiance *f* distrust, mistrust.

méfiant *adj* distrustful, mistrustful.

méfier (se) *vr* to mistrust, distrust; to be suspicious.

mégalomane *adj* megalomaniac; * *mf* megalomaniac.

mégaphone *m* megaphone.

mégot *m* cigarette-end, stub.

meilleur *adj* better, preferable; **le ~, la ~e** the best.

mélancolie *f* melancholy, gloom.

mélancolique *adj* melancholy; melancholic; **~ment** *adv* melancholically.

mélange *m* mixing, blending; mixture.

mélanger *vt* to mix, blend; to muddle.

mêlée *f* melée, fray; scrum.

mêler *vt* to mix; to combine; **se ~** *vr* to mix, mingle; **se ~ à** to join; **se ~ de** to meddle in.

mélisse *f* lemon balm.

mélodie *f* melody, tune.

mélodieusement *adv* melodiously, tunefully.

mélodieux *adj* melodious, tuneful.

mélomane *mf* music lover.

melon *m* melon.

membrane *f* membrane.

membre *m* member; limb.

même *adv* even; **tout de ~** nevertheless, all the same; * *adj* same, identical; * *pn*: **le ~, la ~, les ~s** the same, the same ones.

mémoire *f* memory; * *m* memorandum, report.

mémorable *adj* memorable.

mémoriser *vt* to memorize.

menaçant *adj* menacing, threatening.

menace *f* threat; intimidation; danger.

menacer *vt* to threaten, menace; to impend.

ménage *m* housework, housekeeping; household.

ménager *vt* to treat with caution; to manage; to arrange.; **se ~** *vr* to take care of o.s.; * *adj* household, domestic.

ménagère *f* housewife.

ménagerie *f* menagerie.

mendiant *m* **-e** *f* beggar.

mendier *vt* to beg; to implore.

mener *vt* to lead, guide; to steer; to manage.

meneur *m* **-euse** *f* leader; agitator.

menhir *m* menhir, standing stone.

méningite f meningitis.

ménopause f menopause.

menottes fpl handcuffs.

mensonge m lie, falsehood; error, illusion.

menstruation f menstruation.

mensuel adj monthly.

mental adj mental; **~ement** adv mentally.

mentalité f mentality.

menteur m **-euse** f liar; * adj lying, deceitful.

menthe f mint.

menthol m menthol.

mention f mention; comment; grade.

mentionner vt to mention.

mentir vi to lie; to be deceptive.

menton m chin.

menu m menu; meal; * adj slender, thin; petty, minor.

menuiserie f joinery, carpentry.

menuisier m joiner, carpenter.

mépris m contempt, scorn.

méprisant adj contemptuous, scornful.

mépriser vt to scorn, despise.

mer f sea; tide.

mercenaire m mercenary.

mercerie f haberdashery.

merci m thank you; * f mercy; **sans ~** merciless; **être à la ~ de** to be at the mercy of.

mercredi m Wednesday.

mercure m mercury.

mère f mother.

méridien m meridian; midday.

méridional adj southern.

meringue f meringue.

merisier m wild cherry.

mérite m merit, worth; quality.

mériter vt to deserve, merit.

merlan m whiting.

merle m blackbird.

merveille f marvel, wonder.

merveilleusement adv marvellously, wonderfully.

merveilleux adj marvellous, wonderful.

mésange f (orn) tit.

mésentente f misunderstanding.

mesquin adj mean, niggardly; petty; **~ement** adv meanly, pettily.

message m message.

messager m **-ère** f messenger.

messagerie f parcels office, parcels service.

messe f mass.

messie m messiah.

mesure f measure; gauge; measurement; moderation; step; **au fur et à ~** as; one by one; **sans commune ~ avec** there is no possible comparison with; **dans la mesure où** insofar as; **en ~** in time.

mesurer vt to measure; to assess; to limit; **se ~** vr to try one's strength; **se ~ à** to pit o.s. against, measure one's strength against.

métabolisme m metabolism.

métal m metal.

métallique adj metallic.

métallisé adj metallic, metallized.

métallurgie f metallurgy.

métallurgiste m steelworker, metalworker.

métamorphose f metamorphosis.

métamorphoser vt to transform, metamorphose; **se ~** vr to be metamorphosed.

métaphore f metaphor.

métaphorique adj metaphorical; **~ment** adv metaphorically.

métaphysique adj metaphysical; * f metaphysics.

météore m meteor.

météorite m/f meteorite.

météorologue, météorologiste mf meteorologist.

méthane m methane.

méthode f method, way.

méthodique adj methodical; **~ment** adv methodically.

méthylène m methyl alcohol; methylene.

méticuleusement adv meticulously.

méticuleux adj meticulous

métier m job; occupation; **~ à tricoter** knitting machine; **~ à tisser** weaving loom.

métis m **-se** f half-caste; hybrid; mongrel; * adj half-caste; hybrid, mongrel.

mètre m metre.

métro m underground, metro.

métronome m metronome.

métropole f metropolis.

métropolitain adj metropolitan; underground.

mets m dish.

metteur en scène m (cin) director.

mettre *vt* to put, place; to put on; ~ **en marche** to start up; **se ~** *vr* to place o.s.; to sit down; **se ~ à** to begin to; **se ~ en route** to start off.

meuble *m* piece of furniture.

meubler *vt* to furnish.

meule *f* millstone; grindstone.

meurtrier *m* murderer, **-ière** *f* murderess.

meurtrir *vt* to bruise.

meute *f* pack.

mezzanine *f* mezzanine.

mi- *adj* half; **à ~chemin** halfway; **~clos** half-closed; **à ~jambe** up to the knees; **à ~voix** in a low voice.

miauler *vi* to mew.

miche *f* round loaf.

microbe *m* germ, microbe.

microbien *adj* microbial, microbic.

microclimat *m* microclimate.

microfilm *m* microfilm.

micro-informatique *f* micro-computing.

micro-onde *f* microwave; * *m* **micro-ondes** microwave oven.

micro-ordinateur *m* microcomputer.

microphone *m* microphone.

microprocesseur *m* microprocessor.

microscope *m* microscope.

microscopique *adj* microscopic.

midi *m* midday, noon.

mie *f* crumb, soft part of a loaf.

miel *m* honey.

mien *pn*, *f* **mienne**: **le ~, la mienne, les ~s, les miennes** mine, my own.

miette *f* crumb; remnant; morsel.

mieux *m* improvement; **le ~** the best; **de ~ en ~** better and better.

mignon *adj* sweet, pretty.

migraine *f* headache; migraine.

migrateur *m* migrant.

migration *f* migration.

mijoter *vi* to simmer, be brewing; * *vt* to simmer; to scheme, plot.

milice *f* militia.

milieu *m* middle, centre; medium; environment.

militaire *m* serviceman; * *adj* military, army.

militant *m* **-e** *f* militant; * *adj* militant.

militer *vi* to militate; to be a militant.

mille *m* one thousand; * *adj* one thousand.

millénaire *m* millennium, a thousand years; thousandth anniversary; * *adj* thousand-year-old; millennial.

mille-pattes *m* millipede, centipede.

millésime *m* year, date; vintage.

millet *m* millet.

milliard *m* thousand million; billion.

milliardaire *adj* worth (many) millions; * *mf* multimillionaire.

milliardième *adj* thousand millionth; * *m* thousand millionth.

millième *adj* thousandth; * *m* thousandth.

millier *m* thousand.

milligramme *m* milligram.

millilitre *m* millilitre.

millimètre *m* millimetre.

million *m* million.

millionième *adj* millionth; * *m* millionth.

millionnaire *adj* millionaire; worth millions; * *mf* millionaire.

mime *m* mime; * *mf* mimic.

mimer *vt* to mime; to mimic, imitate.

mimétisme *m* mimicry; mimetism.

mimosa *m* mimosa.

minable *adj* seedy, shabby; **~ment** *adv* shabbily.

mince *adj* thin, slender; meagre, trivial.

mincir *vi* to get slimmer, get thinner.

mine *f* expression; appearance; mine; **avoir bonne ~** to look good.

minerai *m* ore.

minéral *adj* mineral; inorganic; * *m* mineral.

minéralogique *adj* mineralogical.

mineur *m* **-e** *f* minor; * *adj* minor; * *m* miner.

miniature *f* miniature.

mini-jupe *f* miniskirt.

minimal *adj* minimal, minimum.

minime *adj* minor, minimal.

minimum *m* minimum.

ministère *m* ministry; agency.

ministériel *adj* ministerial.

ministre *m* minister; clergyman.

minoritaire *adj* minority.

minorité *f* minority.

minuit *m* midnight.

minuscule *adj* minuscule, tiny, minute.

minute *f* minute, moment.

minuterie *f* time switch; regulator.

minutieux *adj* meticulous.

mirabelle *f* mirabelle.

miracle *m* miracle, wonder.

miraculeux *adj* miraculous.

mirage *m* mirage.

miroir *m* mirror, reflection.

misanthrope *mf* misanthrope; misanthropist; * *adj* misanthropic.

mise *f* putting, placing; stake; deposit; investment; ~ **en scène** production, staging; ~ **en liberté** release; ~ **en ordre** ordering, arrangement; ~ **en œuvre** implementation.

miser *vt* to stake, to bet.

misérable *adj* miserable; destitute; pitiable; ~**ment** *adv* miserably.

misère *f* misery; poverty; destitution.

miséricorde *f* mercy, forgiveness.

misogyne *mf* misogynist; * *adj* misogynous.

missile *m* missile.

mission *f* mission, assignment.

missionnaire *m* missionary.

mi-temps *f* half-time; half.

miteux *adj* dingy, shabby, poverty-stricken.

mitigé *adj* mitigated; lukewarm.

mitoyen *adj* common; semi-detached.

mitrailler *vt* to machine-gun.

mitraillette *f* submachine gun.

mitrailleuse *f* machine gun.

mixer *vt* to mix; to blend.

mixte *adj* mixed; joint; combined.

mixture *f* mixture, concoction.

mobile *adj* moving; movable; mobile; nimble; * *m* motive; moving body.

mobilier *m* furniture; * *adj* movable; personal; transferable.

mobilisation *f* mobilization, calling up.

mobilité *f* mobility.

mobylette *f* moped.

moche *adj* (*fam*) ugly, lousy.

mode *f* fashion; custom; * *m* form, mode; way.

modèle *m* model; pattern; design; example.

modeler *vt* to model; to shape; **se ~** *vr*: **se ~ sur** to model o.s. on.

modem *m* modem.

modération *f* moderation; diminution.

modéré *adj* moderate; ~**ment** *adv* in moderation.

modérer *vt* moderate, restrained; **se ~** *vr* to control o.s., keep one's temper.

moderne *adj* modern, up-to-date.

moderniser *vt* to modernize.

modeste *adj* modest, simple; unassuming; ~**ment** *adv* modestly.

modestie *f* modesty.

modification *f* modification.

modifier *vt* to modify, alter; **se ~** *vr* to be modified.

modulation *f* modulation; adjustment.

moelle *f* marrow; core.

moelleux *adj* mellow; soft; smooth.

mœurs *fpl* morals; customs.

moi *pn* me, I; **c'est à ~** it is mine, it is my turn; ~-**même** myself.

mois *m* month.

moisi *adj* mouldy, mildewed; * *m* mould.

moisir *vi* to go mouldy.

moisissure *f* mould, mildew.

moisson *f* harvest.

moissonner *vt* to reap, harvest.

moite *adj* moist, damp.

moitié *f* half.

molaire *f* molar.

molécule *f* molecule.

mollement *adv* softly; gently.

mollusque *m* mollusc.

moment *m* moment, instant, while; time; opportunity.

momentané *adj* momentary; brief; ~**ment** *adv* momentarily.

momie *f* mummy.

mon *pn*, *f* **ma**, *pl* **mes** my, my own.

monarchie *f* monarchy.

monastère *m* monastery.

mondain *adj* worldly, mundane; society, fashionable.

monde *m* world, earth; society, company; **il y a du ~** there are some people there.

mondial *adj* world, world-wide; ~**ement** *adv* the world over.

monétaire *adj* monetary.

moniteur *m* **-trice** *f* instructor, coach; supervisor.

monnaie *f* currency; coin; change.

monoculture *f* single-crop farming, monoculture.

monologue *m* monologue.

monopole *f* monopoly.

monopoliser *vt* to monopolize.

monotone *adj* monotonous.

monotonie *f* monotony, sameness.

monseigneur *m* my lord, your grace.

monsieur *m* sir, gentleman, Mr, *pl* **messieurs** gentlemen, Messrs.

monstre *m* monster.

monstrueux *adj* monstrous.

mont *m* mountain; mount.

montage *m* assembly; setting up; editing.

montagnard *m* **-e** *f* mountain dweller.

montagne *f* mountain.

montagneux *adj* mountainous.

montant *m* upright; total, total sum; * *adj* upward, rising; upstream.

montée *f* climb, climbing; ascent; rise.

monter *vi* to go up, ascend; get into (vehicle); * *vt* to go up; to carry/bring up.

monteur *m* **-euse** *f* fitter; editor.

montre *f* watch.

montrer *vt* to show, point to; to prove; **se ~** *vr* to appear; to prove o.s.

monture *f* mount; setting; frame.

monument *m* monument, memorial.

monumental *adj* monumental, colossal.

moquer (se) *vr* to make fun, jeer, laugh at.

moqueur *m* **-euse** *f* mocker, scoffer; * *adj* mocking.

moral *adj* moral, ethical; intellectual; **~ement** *adv* morally.

moralité *f* morals, morality.

morbide *adj* morbid, unhealthy.

morceau *m* piece, morsel, fragment; extract.

mordant *adj* cutting, mordant; * *m* mordant.

mordre *vt* to bite, gnaw; to grip.

morgue *f* morgue; mortuary.

morille *f* morel.

morne *adj* gloomy, dismal.

morose *adj* sullen, morose.

morphine *f* morphine.

morphologie *f* morphology.

morse *m* Morse; walrus.

morsure *f* bite.

mort *m* dead man, **-e** *f* dead woman; * *adj* dead; * *f* death.

mortalité *f* mortality; death rate.

mortel *adj* mortal; fatal; **~lement** *adv* mortally.

mortier *m* mortar.

mortuaire *adj* mortuary; funeral.

morue *f* cod.

mosaïque *f* mosaic.

mosquée *f* mosque.

mot *m* word; saying; **~s croisés** crossword.

moteur *m* engine, motor; * *adj* motor, driving.

motif *m* motive, grounds; motif, design.

motion *f* motion; **~ de censure** censure motion.

motivation *f* motivation.

motiver *vt* to justify; to motivate.

moto *f* motorbike.

moto-cross *m* motocross, scrambling.

motte *f* clod, lump; slab.

mou *adj*, *f* **molle** soft; gentle; muffled.

mouche *f* fly.

moucher *vt* to wipe sb's nose; **se ~** *vr* to blow one's nose.

moucheron *m* midge, gnat.

moucheté *adj* speckled; flecked.

mouchoir *m* handkerchief.

moudre *vt* to mill, grind.

moue *f* pout; **faire la ~** to pout.

mouette *f* gull.

moufle *f* mitten.

mouillé *adj* wet, soaked.

mouiller *vt* to wet; to water down; **se ~** *vr* to get wet.

moulage *m* moulding, casting.

moule *m* mould; * *f* mussel.

mouler *vt* to mould; to model.

moulin *m* mill.

moulu *adj* ground; bruised.

mourant *m* dying man, **-e** *f* dying woman; * *adj* dying.

mourir *vi* to die.

mousse *f* moss; foam, froth.

mousser *vi* to froth, foam.

mousseux *adj* sparkling; frothy; * *m* sparkling wine.

moustache *f* moustache; whiskers.

moustachu *adj* moustached; * *m* moustached man.

moustiquaire *f* mosquito net.

moustique *m* mosquito.

moutarde *f* mustard.

mouton *m* sheep; mutton.

mouvement *m* movement, motion; animation.

mouvementé *adj* eventful; turbulent.

mouvoir *vt* to drive, power; **se ~** *vr* to move.

moyen *m* means; way; * *adj* average, medium, moderate; **~nement** *adv* fairly, moderately; **~ âge** Middle Ages.

moyenne *f* average.

moyeu *m* hub; boss.

mue *f* moulting; shedding.

muer *vi* to moult; to slough.

muet *m* mute (man), **muette** *f* mute (woman); * *adj* dumb; silent, mute.

mufle *m* muffle; muzzle.

muguet *m* lily-of-the-valley; (*med*) thrush.

mule *f* she-mule.

mulet *m* mule.

multicolore *adj* multicoloured.

multinationale *f* multinational.

multiple *adj* numerous, multiple; * *m* multiple.

multiplication *f* multiplication.

multiplier *vt* **se ~** *vr* to multiply, increase.

multitude *f* multitude, crowd.

municipal *adj* municipal; local.

municipalité *f* town, municipality.

munir *vt* to provide, equip with; **se ~** *vr* to equip o.s.

munition *f* munition, ammunition.

mur *m* wall.

mûr *adj* ripe, mature; worn out.

muraille *f* city wall, rampart.

mûre *f* blackberry.

mûrir *vi* to ripen, mature.

murmure *m* murmur; muttering; grumbling.

murmurer *vi* to murmur; to whisper; grumble; to babble * *vt* to murmur.

muscle *m* muscle.

musclé *adj* muscular, brawny.

musculaire *adj* muscular.

muse *f* muse.

museau *m* muzzle, snout.

musée *m* art gallery, museum.

musicien *m* **-ne** *f* musician; * *adj* musical.

musique *f* music.

musulman *m* **-e** *f* Muslim; * *adj* Muslim.

mutant *m* **-e** *f* mutant; * *adj* mutant.

mutation *f* transfer; transformation; mutation.

muter *vt* to transfer, move.

mutilation *f* mutilation, maiming.

mutiler *vt* to mutilate; **se ~** *vr* to injure o.s.

mutisme *m* silence; dumbness, muteness.

mutuel *adj* mutual; **~lement** *adv* mutually.

mutuelle *f* mutual insurance company.

mycose *f* mycosis.

mygale *f* tarantula.

myope *mf* short-sighted person; * *adj* short-sighted.

myopie *f* short-sightedness, myopia.

myosotis *m* forget-me-not.

myrtille *f* bilberry, blueberry.

mystère *m* mystery.

mystérieusement *adv* mysteriously.

mystérieux *adj* mysterious.

mystifier *vt* to mystify; to hoax.

mystique *adj* mystical; * *mf* mystic.

mythe *m* myth.

mythique *adj* mythical.

mythologie *f* mythology.

N

nacre *f* mother-of-pearl.

nacré *adj* nacreous, pearly, iridescent.

nageoire *f* fin, flipper.

nager *vi* to swim.

nageur *m* **-euse** *f* swimmer; rower.

naïf *adj* naïve, artless, ingenuous.

nain *m* **-e** *f* dwarf; * *adj* dwarfish, dwarf.

naissance *f* birth, extraction; dawn, beginning.

naître *vi* to be born; to arise, spring up.

naïvement *adv* naïvely.

naïveté *f* naïvety, artlessness, gullibility.

nanti *m* rich man, *adj* rich, well-to-do.

nappe *f* tablecloth; layer; sheet, expanse.

napper *vt* to top with.

napperon *m* tablemat.

narcisse *m* narcissus.

narcotique *m* drug, narcotic; * *adj* narcotic.

narguer *vt* to flout, defy; to cheek.

narine *f* nostril.

narrateur *m* **-trice** *f* narrator.

narration *f* narration, narrative.

nasal *adj* nasal.

naseau *m* nostril.

natalité *f* birth rate.

natation *f* swimming.

nation *f* nation.

national *adj* national; domestic.

nationaliser *vt* to nationalize.

nationaliste *mf* nationalist; * *adj* nationalist.

nationalité *f* nationality.

natte *f* plait, braid.

naturalisation *f* nationalization.

naturaliste *mf* naturalist; taxidermist; * *adj* naturalistic.

nature *f* nature; kind, sort; temperament.

naturel *adj* natural; native; unsophisticated; **~lement** *adv* naturally; of course.

naufrage *m* shipwreck; ruin, foundering.

nausée *f* nausea.

nautique *adj* nautical, water.

naval *adj* naval, shipbuilding.

navet *m* turnip.

navette *f* shuttle; **faire la ~** to shuttle between.

navigateur *m* navigator, sailor.

navigation *f* sailing, navigation.

navire *m* ship, vessel.

navrant *adj* distressing, upsetting.

ne *adv* no, not.

né *adj* born.

néanmoins *adv* nevertheless.

néant *m* nothing, nothingness, emptiness.

nécessaire *adj* necessary; requisite; indispensable; **~ment** *adv* necessarily.

nécessité *f* necessity; need; inevitability.

nécessiter *vt* to require, necessitate.

nécropole *f* necropolis.

nectar *m* nectar.

nectarine *f* nectarine.

néfaste *adj* harmful; unlucky; ill-fated.

négatif *adj* negative.

négation *f* negation; negative.

négativement *adv* negatively.

négligemment *adv* negligently; carelessly; nonchalantly.

négligence *f* negligence, carelessness.

négligent *adj* negligent, careless; nonchalant.

négliger *vt* to neglect; to be negligent about.

négociant *m* **-e** *f* merchant.

négociation *f* negotiation.

négocier *vi* to negotiate; to trade; * *vt* to negotiate.

neige *f* snow.

neiger *vi* to snow, be snowing.

nénuphar *m* water-lily.

néophyte *mf* neophyte; novice; * *adj* newly converted.

nerf *m* nerve.

nerveusement *adv* nervously; irritably.

nerveux *adj* nervous; vigorous; excitable.

nervosité *f* nervousness; excitability.

nervure *f* nervure, vein; rib.

net *adj*, *f* **-te** clean; clear; plain; sharp; net; **~tement** *adv* cleanly; clearly; plainly.

netteté *f* neatness; clearness; sharpness.

nettoyage *m* cleaning; clearing up.

nettoyer *vt* to clean; to ruin, clean out.

neuf *adj* nine; * *m* nine.

neurologie *f* neurology.

neurone *m* neurone.

neutraliser *vt* to neutralize.

neutralité *f* neutrality.

neutre *adj* neutral; neuter.

neutron *m* neutron.

neuvième *adj* ninth; **~ment** *adv* ninthly; * *mf* ninth.

neveu *m* nephew.

névralgie *f* neuralgia.

névrose *f* neurosis.

nez *m* nose; flair; **avoir du ~** to have flair.

niais *adj* silly, simple, inane; **~ement** *adv* inanely.

niche *f* niche, nook; kennel; trick.

nickel *m* nickel.

nicotine *f* nicotine.

nid *m* nest; den; berth.

nièce *f* niece.

nier *vt* to deny; to repudiate.

nigaud *m* -e *f* simpleton.

nitrate *m* nitrate.

nitroglycérine *f* nitroglycerine.

niveau *m* level; standard; par; gauge.

niveler *vt* to level; to even out, equalize.

noble *adj* noble, dignified; ~ment *adv* nobly.

noblesse *f* nobleness, nobility.

noce *f* wedding, wedding feast; marriage ceremony.

nocif *adj* noxious, harmful.

noctambule *mf* night reveller, night owl; sleepwalker; * *adj* enjoying night life; noctambulant.

nocturne *adj* nocturnal, night; * *f* evening fixture; late night opening.

nodule *m* nodule.

Noèl *m* Christmas.

nœud *m* knot, bow; crux.

noir *adj* black; dark; * *m* black; darkness; black man.

noircir *vt* to blacken; to dirty; **se ~** *vr* to darken, grow black.

noire *f* black woman.

noisetier *m* hazel tree.

noisette *f* hazel.

noix *f* walnut.

nom *m* name; fame; noun.

nomade *mf* nomad.

nombre *m* number, quantity.

nombreux *adj* numerous, frequent.

nombril *m* navel.

nomenclature *f* list, catalogue; nomenclature.

nominal *adj* nominal; noun; ~ement *adv* nominally.

nominatif *m* nominative.

nomination *f* appointment; nomination.

nommer *vt* to appoint; nominate.

non *adv* no; not.

nonchalance *f* nonchalance.

nonchalant *adj* nonchalant.

non-conformiste *mf* nonconformist; * *adj* nonconformist.

non-lieu *m* (*jur*) no ground for prosecution.

non-sens *m* nonsense.

non-violence *f* non-violence.

nord *m* north, northerly (wind).

nordique *adj* Nordic; Scandinavian.

normal *adj* normal, usual; standard-sized; ~ement *adv* normally, usually.

norme *f* norm; standard.

nostalgie *f* nostalgia.

nostalgique *adj* nostalgic.

notable *adj* notable; noteworthy; ~ment *adv* notably.

notaire *m* notary; solicitor.

notamment *adv* notably; in particular.

note *f* note; minute; mark; bill.

noter *vt* to note down; to notice; to mark.

notice *f* note; directions; instructions.

notion *f* notion, idea.

notoire *adj* notorious; well-known, acknowledged; ~ment *adv* notoriously.

notoriété *f* notoriety; fame.

notre *adj*, *pl* **nos** ours, our own.

nôtre *pn*: **le ~, la ~, les ~s** ours, our own.

nouer *vt* to tie, knot; **se ~** *vr* to join together.

nouille *f* (piece of) pasta.

nourrice *f* child-minder, nanny.

nourrir *vt* to feed, provide for; to stoke; **se ~** *vr* to feed o.s.

nourrissant *adj* nourishing, nutritious.

nourrisson *m* infant, nursling.

nourriture *f* food; sustenance.

nous *pn* we; us; **c'est à ~** it's ours; it's our turn; ~-**mêmes** ourselves.

nouveau *adj* new; recent; additional.

nouveau-né *m* -e *f* new-born child.

nouveauté *f* novelty; newness.

nouvelle *f* piece of news; short story.

novembre *m* November.

novice *mf* novice, beginner; * *adj* novice, unpractised, inexperienced.

noyade *f* drowning, drowning incident.

noyau *m* stone, pit; core; nucleus.

noyer *vt* to drown; to flood; **se ~** *vr* to drown, drown o.s.; * *m* walnut (tree).

nu *adj* naked, nude; plain, unadorned.

nuage *m* cloud.

nuageux *adj* cloudy, overcast.

nuance *f* shade, hue; faint difference, nuance.

nucléaire *adj* nuclear; * *m* nuclear energy.

nudiste *mf* nudist; * *adj* nudist.

nudité *f* nakedness, nudity.

nuée *f* dense cloud; horde, swarm.

nuire *vi* to harm, injure; to prejudice.

nuisible *adj* harmful; noxious; **~ment** *adv* harmfully.

nuit *f* night, darkness.

nul *adj* no; nil; null and void; nonexistent; **~lement** *adv* not at all, not in the least.

nullité *f* nullity; uselessness.

numéral *adj* numeral; * *m* numeral.

numérique *adj* numerical; digital.

numéro *m* number; issue.

numérotation *f* numbering, numeration.

numéroter *vt* to number.

nuptial *adj* nuptial, wedding.

nuque *f* nape (of the neck).

nutritif *adj* nutritious, nourishing.

nutrition *f* nutrition.

nylon *m* nylon.

nymphe *f* nymph.

O

oasis *m* oasis.

obéir *vt* to obey, be obedient; to comply.

obéissance *f* obedience; compliance.

obéissant *adj* obedient.

obèse *adj* obese.

obésité *f* obesity.

objecter *vt* to object.

objectif *adj* objective, unbiased; * *m* objective, target.

objection *f* objection.

objectivement *adv* objectively.

objet *m* object, thing; purpose; matter.

obligation *f* obligation, duty; bond.

obligatoire *adj* obligatory, compulsory; **~ment** *adv* obligatorily.

obligé *adj* obliged, compelled; inevitable; necessary.

obliger *vt* to oblige, require; (*jur*) to bind.

oblique *adj* oblique, sidelong.

oblitérer *vt* to obliterate; to cancel (stamp).

obscène *adj* obscene.

obscénité *f* obscenity.

obscur *adj* obscure, dark, gloomy; **~ément** *adv* obscurely.

obscurcir *vt* to darken; to obscure; **s'~** *vr* to get dark.

obscurité *f* obscurity; darkness.

obséder *vt* to obsess, haunt.

obsèques *fpl* funeral.

observateur *m* **-trice** *f* observer; * *adj* observant.

observation *f* observation; remark.

observatoire *m* observatory.

observer *vt* to observe, watch; to notice; to comply with.

obsession *f* obsession.

obstacle *m* obstacle, hindrance.

obstétrique *f* obstetrics.

obstination *f* obstinacy, stubbornness.

obstiné *adj* obstinate, stubborn; **~ment** *adv* obstinately.

obstiner (s') *vr* to insist, persist.

obtenir *vt* to obtain, procure, get; to achieve.

obturation *f* stopping, closing up, obturation.

obus *m* shell.

occasion *f* occasion, opportunity; cause; bargain; **d'~** second-hand.

occident *m* west.

occidental *adj* western; Occidental.

occulte *adj* occult.

occupant *m* **-e** *f* occupant, occupier.

occupation *f* occupation, pursuit; work; occupancy.

occuper *vt* to occupy; to employ; to inhabit; **s'~** *vr* to keep busy.

océan *m* ocean.

ocre *m* ochre; * *adj* ochre.

octane *m* octane.

octave *f* octave.

octet *m* byte.

octobre *m* October.

octroyer *vt* to grant, bestow; **s'~** *vr* to allow o.s.

oculaire *adj* ocular.

odeur *f* smell, odour.

odieux *adj* hateful, obnoxious.

odorat *m* smell (sense).

oedème *m* oedema.

œil *m, pl* **yeux** eye; look; bud.

œillet *m* carnation.

œsophage *m* oesophagus.

œuf *m* egg.

œuvre *f* work; action, deed; production.

offense *f* offence; injury, wrong.

offenser *vt* to offend; to injure, shock; **s'~** *vr* to take offence.

offensif *adj* offensive; forceful, aggressive.

offensive *f* offensive, attack.

office *m* office, bureau; duty; function.

officiel *adj* official; **~lement** *adv* officially.

officier *m* officer.

officieusement *adv* officiously; unofficially.

officieux *adj* officious, over-obliging; unofficial.

offrande *f* offering.

offre *f* offer, tender, bid.

offrir *vt* to offer.

offusquer *vt* to offend; **s'~** *vr* to take offence; to be offended.

ogive *f* ogive, pointed arch.

ogre *m* ogre, **-sse** *f* ogress.

ohm *m* ohm.

oie *f* goose.

oignon *m* onion; bulb.

oiseau *m* bird.

oisif *adj* idle.

oisiveté *f* idleness.

oléagineux *adj* oleaginous, oily.

oléoduc *m* oil pipeline.

olfactif *adj* olfactory.

oligarchie *f* oligarchy.

oligo-élément *m* trace element.

olive *f* olive.

olivier *m* olive tree.

olympique *adj* Olympic.

ombilical *adj* umbilical.

ombragé *adj* shaded, shady.

ombre *f* shade, shadow.

omelette *f* omelette.

omettre *vt* to leave out, miss out.

omission *f* omission.

omnibus *m* local train; omnibus.

omnipotent *adj* omnipotent.

omniprésent *adj* omnipresent.

omoplate *f* shoulder blade.

on *pn* one; someone, anyone.

once *f* ounce.

oncle *m* uncle.

onctueux *adj* smooth, creamy.

onde *f* wave.

ondoyant *adj* undulating, flowing; changeable.

ondulation *f* undulation; wave.

onduler *vi* to undulate; to ripple.

onéreux *adj* onerous; expensive, costly.

ongle *m* nail; claw, talon; hoof.

onomatopée *f* onomatopoeia.

onyx *m* onyx.

onze *adj* eleven; * *m* eleven.

onzième *adj* eleventh; **~ment** *adv* in eleventh place; * *mf* eleventh.

opale *f* opal.

opaque *adj* opaque; impenetrable.

opéra *m* opera.

opération *f* operation, performance; transaction, deal.

opérationnel *adj* operational.

opératoire *adj* operating; operative, surgical.

opérer *vt* to operate; to carry out, implement.

opérette *f* operetta, light opera.

ophtalmie *f* ophthalmia.

opiniâtre *adj* stubborn; persistent; **~ment** *adv* stubbornly; persistently.

opinion *f* opinion, view.

opium *m* opium.

opportun *adj* timely, opportune; **~ément** *adv* opportunely.

opportuniste *mf* opportunist; * *adj* opportunist.

opportunité *f* opportuneness, expediency, timeliness.

opposant *m* **-e** *f* opponent; * *adj* opposing.

opposé *adj* opposite, contrary; facing; * *m* opposite; **à l'~** contrary to.

opposer *vt* to oppose; to contrast; to object; **s'~** *vr* to be opposed to; to clash, conflict.

opposition *f* opposition; conflict.

oppresser *vt* to oppress, weigh down.

oppressif *adj* oppressive.

oppression *f* oppression.

opprimer *vt* to oppress, crush.

opticien *m* **-ne** *f* optician.

optimisme *m* optimism.

optimiste *mf* optimist; * *adj* optimistic.

option *f* option, choice.

optionnel *adj* optional.

optique *adj* optical; * *f* optics.

opulence f opulence, wealth.

opulent adj opulent, wealthy.

or m gold; * conj now.

oracle m oracle.

orage m storm, tempest, thunderstorm.

orageux adj stormy.

oral adj oral, verbal; ~**ement** adv orally.

orange f orange; * adj invar orange.

oranger m orange tree.

orang-outan(g) m orang-utang.

orateur m **-trice** f orator.

orbite f orbit; socket; sphere.

orchestral adj orchestral.

orchestre m orchestra.

orchestrer vt to orchestrate, score.

orchidée f orchid.

ordinaire adj ordinary, common, usual; ~**ment** adv ordinarily, usually; * m custom, usual routine; **d'~, à l'~** ordinarily, usually.

ordinateur m computer.

ordonnance f prescription, order, edict.

ordonner vt to arrange; to order; to prescribe.

ordre m order, command; class.

ordure f filth, dirt; excrement; rubbish.

oreille f ear; hearing; wing; handle.

oreiller m pillow.

oreillons mpl mumps.

orfèvre m silversmith, goldsmith.

orfèvrerie f silversmith's (goldsmith's) craft.

organe m organ; instrument; medium.

organigramme m organizational chart.

organique adj organic.

organisateur m **-trice** f organizer.

organisation f organization.

organiser vt to organize, arrange; **s'~** vr to organize o.s.

organisme m organism.

organiste mf organist.

orgasme m orgasm.

orge f barley.

orgie f orgy.

orgue m (mus) organ.

orgueil m pride, arrogance.

orgueilleux adj proud, arrogant.

orient m orient, east.

oriental adj eastern, oriental.

orientation f orientation; positioning; directing; trend.

orienter vt to orientate; to position; to direct; **s'~** vr to ascertain one's position; to turn towards.

orifice m orifice; aperture, opening.

originaire adj originating from, native to; ~**ment** adv originally, primitively.

original adj original, novel; peculiar, bizarre; * m original; top copy.

originalité f originality; oddness.

origine f origin, source, derivation; **à l'~** originally.

originel adj original, primitive.

orme m elm.

ornement m ornament, embellishment.

ornemental adj ornamental.

orner vt to adorn, decorate.

ornière f rut.

ornithologie f ornithology.

ornithologiste, ornithologue mf ornithologist.

orphelin m **-e** f orphan.

orphelinat m orphanage.

orteil m toe.

orthodoxe adj orthodox; * mf orthodox.

orthogonal adj orthogonal.

orthographe f spelling.

orthopédie f orthopaedics.

orthopédique adj orthopaedic.

ortie f nettle.

orvet m slow-worm.

os m bone.

oscillation f oscillation, swinging.

osciller vi to oscillate, swing.

oseille f sorrel.

oser vt to dare.

osier m osier, willow, wicker.

osmose f osmosis.

ossature f skeleton; framework.

ossements mpl bones.

ostensible adj open, conspicuous; ~**ment** adv openly; conspicuously.

ostentation f ostentation.

ostéopathe mf osteopath.

ostracisme m ostracism.

otage m hostage.

otarie f sea-lion.

ôter vt to take away, remove; to deprive, deduct.

otite f ear infection.

oto-rhino-laryngologie *f* oto-rhinolaryngology.

oto-rhino(-laryngologiste) *mf* ear, nose and throat specialist.

ou *conj* or.

où *adv* where, in which; * *pn* where.

ouate *f* cotton wool.

oubli *m* forgetfulness; oblivion; oversight, omission.

oublier *vt* to forget; to omit, neglect.

oubliette *f* oubliette.

ouest *m* west; *adj* west.

oui *adv* yes.

ouïe *f* hearing (sense).

ouragan *m* hurricane, whirlwind.

ourlet *m* hem.

ours *m* **-e** *f* bear.

oursin *m* sea urchin.

ourson *m* bear cub.

outil *m* tool, implement.

outillage *m* (set of) tools; equipment.

outiller *vt* to equip; to provide with tools.

outrage *m* outrage, insult, wrong.

outrageant *adj* outrageous, insulting.

outre *prép* as well as, besides; **en ~** moreover; **~ mesure** to excess, inordinately; **passer ~** to go on, to take no notice; * *f* goatskin, leather bottle.

outré *adj* excessive, exaggerated.

outremer *m* ultramarine.

outrepasser *vt* to exceed; to transgress.

ouvert *adj* open; exposed; frank; **~ement** *adv* openly, overtly.

ouverture *f* opening; mouth; overture; means, way.

ouvrable *adj* working, business.

ouvrage *m* work; piece of work.

ouvre-boîte *m* tin-opener.

ouvre-bouteille *m* bottle-opener.

ouvrier *m* **-ière** *f* worker; * *adj* working-class; industrial; labour.

ouvrir *vt* to open; to unlock; to broach; **s'~** *vr* to open; to open one's mind; to cut o.s.

ovaire *m* ovary.

ovale *adj* oval; * *m* oval.

ovation *f* ovation.

ovni *m* UFO.

ovulation *f* ovulation.

ovule *m* ovum; ovule.

oxydation *f* oxidation.

oxyde *m* oxide.

oxyder *vt* to oxidize; **s'~** *vr* to become oxidized.

oxygène *m* oxygen.

ozone *f* ozone.

P

pacifier *vt* to pacify.

pacifique *adj* peaceful, pacific; **~ment** *adv* peacefully, pacifically.

pacifiste *mf* pacifist; * *adj* pacifist.

pacte *m* pact, treaty.

pactiser *vt* to treat with sb; to come to terms with.

pagaie *f* paddle.

pagayer *vi* to paddle.

page *f* page; passage.

pagne *m* loincloth.

paiement *m* payment.

païen *m* **-ne** *f* pagan; * *adj* pagan.

paillasse *f* straw mattress.

paillasson *m* doormat.

paille *f* straw.

paillette *f* sequin; spangle.

pain *m* bread; loaf; bar.

pair *adj* even; * *m* peer; par; **hors ~** outstanding, matchless.

paire *f* pair; yoke; brace.

paisible *adj* peaceful; calm; **~ment** *adv* peacefully; calmly.

paître *vi* to graze.

paix *f* peace; quiet; stillness; tranquillity.

palais *m* palace; law courts; palate.

palan *m* hoist.

pâle *adj* pale, pallid.

palette *f* palette; pallet; paddle.

pâleur *f* paleness, pallor.

palier *m* landing; level; degree.

pâlir *vi* to turn pale; to dim; to fade.

palissade *f* fence; boarding; stockade.
palliatif *m* palliative; * *adj* palliative.
pallier *vt* to palliate; to offset.
palmarès *m* prize list; medal record.
palme *f* palm leaf; palm.
palmé *adj* palmate; webbed.
palmeraie *f* palm grove.
palmier *m* palm tree.
palmipède *m* palmiped.
palpable *adj* palpable.
palper *vt* to feel, touch; to palpate.
palpitation *f* palpitation; throbbing; quivering.
palpiter *vi* to palpitate; to beat; to race.
paludisme *m* malaria.
pamplemousse *m* grapefruit.
panache *m* panache; gallantry.
panaché *adj* variegated; motley.
pancarte *f* sign, notice; placard.
pancréas *m* pancreas.
panda *m* panda.
pané *adj* covered in breadcrumbs.
panier *m* basket; pannier (mode).
panique *f* panic.
paniquer *vi* to panic, get panicky.
panne *f* breakdown; fault, problem.
panneau *m* panel; sign, notice.
panoplie *f* outfit; display.
panorama *m* panorama.
panoramique *adj* panoramic.
pansement *m* dressing, bandage.
panser *vt* to dress, bandage.
pantalon *m* trousers; pants; knickers.
panthéon *m* pantheon.
panthère *f* panther.
pantin *m* jumping-jack; puppet.
pantomime *f* pantomime; mime.
pantoufle *f* slipper.
paon *m* peacock.
papa *m* dad; daddy.
papauté *f* papacy.
papaye *f* papaya.
pape *m* pope.
papeterie *f* stationery; stationer's shop; paper mill.
papetier *m* **-ière** *f* stationer; paper-maker.
papier *m* paper; article; wrapper.
papillon *m* butterfly.

papillote *f* sweet wrapper.
papoter *vi* to chatter.
Pâques *fpl* Easter.
paquebot *m* liner, steamer.
pâquerette *f* daisy.
paquet *m* packet, pack; bag; parcel.
par *prép* by, with, through; from; along; **~-ci**, **~-là** here and there, now and then; **~-derrière** round the back; **~-dessous** underneath; **~-dessus** over, above.
parabole *f* (*math*) parabola; parable.
parachever *vt* to perfect; to complete.
parachute *m* parachute.
parachuter *vt* to parachute.
parachutiste *mf* parachutist.
parade *f* parade, show; parry.
paradis *m* paradise; (*thea*) gallery.
paradoxal *adj* paradoxical; **~ement** *adv* paradoxically.
paradoxe *m* paradox.
paraffine *f* paraffin.
parages *mpl* vicinity; **dans les ~** in the area.
paragraphe *m* paragraph; section.
paraître *vi* to appear; to be published; to look, seem; **il paraît que** apparently.
parallèle *adj* parallel; **~ment** *adv* parallel; at the same time.
paralyser *vt* to paralyse.
paralysie *f* paralysis.
paralytique *mf* paralytic; * *adj* paralytic.
paramètre *m* parameter.
paranoïa *f* paranoia.
paranoïaque *adj* paranoiac, paranoid; * *mf* paranoiac, paranoid.
paraphraser *vt* to paraphrase.
parapluie *m* umbrella.
parasite *m* parasite, sponger.
parasol *m* parasol; sunshade.
paratonnerre *m* lightning conductor.
paravent *m* folding screen, partition.
parc *m* park; grounds; depot.
parcelle *f* fragment, particle; parcel.
parce que *conj* because.
parchemin *m* parchment.
parcimonie *f* parsimony.
parcmètre *m* meter (parking).
parcourir *vt* to travel through; to scour; to traverse.

pardon *m* pardon, forgiveness.

pardonner *vt* to pardon; to excuse, overlook.

pare-brise *m invar* windscreen.

pare-chocs *m invar* bumper.

pareil *m* **-le** *f* equal; match; **sans ~** unparalleled, unequalled; * *adj* like, equal, similar; identical; **~lement** *adv* likewise, equally.

parent *m* **-e** *f* relative, relation; **~s** (*pl*) parents.

parental *adj* parental.

parenté *f* relationship, kinship.

parenthèse *f* parenthesis, digression.

parer *vt* to adorn, deck out; to ward off; to parry; **~ à** to deal with, overcome.

paresse *f* laziness; sluggishness.

paresseux *m* **-euse** *f* lazy person, loafer; * *adj* lazy.

parfaire *vt* to perfect, bring to perfection.

parfait *adj* perfect, flawless; **~ement** *adv* perfectly; completely, absolutely.

parfois *adv* sometimes, occasionally.

parfumer *vt* to perfume, scent; **se ~** *vr* to put perfume on.

parfumerie *f* perfumery.

parfumeur *m* **-euse** *f* perfumer.

pari *m* bet, wager.

parier *vt* to bet, wager.

parking *m* car park; parking.

parlement *m* Parliament.

parlementaire *adj* parliamentary; * *mf* member of parliament.

parler *vi* to talk, speak; * *vt* to speak.

parmesan *m* parmesan.

parmi *prép* among.

parodie *f* parody.

paroi *f* wall; surface.

paroisse *f* parish.

parole *f* word; speech; voice; lyrics.

paroxysme *m* paroxysm; crisis.

parquer *vt* to park; to enclose, pen.

parquet *m* floor, floorboards.

parrain *m* godfather; patron; promoter.

parrainage *m* sponsorship; promoting; patronage.

parrainer *vt* to sponsor; propose.

parsemer *vt* to sprinkle, strew.

part *f* part; share; portion; **prendre ~ à** to participate in; **faire ~ de** to announce; **de sa part** for his part; **autre ~** elsewhere; **nulle ~** nowhere; **d'autre ~** moreover.

partage *m* sharing, distribution; portion.

partager *vt* to divide up, share out.

partenaire *mf* partner.

parti *m* party; option; match.

partial *adj* partial, biased; **~ement** *adv* in a biased way.

participant *m* **-e** *f* participant, member; * *adj* participant, participating.

participation *f* participation; involvement.

participe *m* participle.

participer *vi* to take part in, participate.

particularité *f* particularity, characteristic.

particule *f* particle.

particulier *adj* particular, specific; peculiar, characteristic; * *m* person, private individual; character.

particulièrement *adv* particularly, especially.

partie *f* part; subject; game; party; **faire ~ de** to be a part of.

partiel *adj* part, partial; **~lement** *adv* partially, in part.

partir *vi* to leave, set off; to start up; **à ~ de** from.

partisan *m* **-e** *f* partisan, supporter, proponent.

partition *f* partition; score.

partout *adv* everywhere.

parvenir *vi*: **~ à** to reach; to achieve.

pas *m* step; pace; footprint; gait; * *adv* no, not.

passable *adj* passable, tolerable; **~ment** *adv* tolerably; reasonably.

passage *m* passage, passing by; transit.

passager *m* **-ère** *f* passenger; * *adj* passing, transitory.

passant *m* **-e** *f* passer-by, wayfarer; * *adj* much-frequented, busy.

passe *f* pass; permit; channel.

passé *m* past.

passeport *m* passport.

passer *vi* to pass; to elapse; to disappear, fade; **se ~** *vr* to pass; to take place; **se ~ de** to do without.

passerelle *f* footbridge; bridge; gangway.

passe-temps *m invar* pastime.

passif *adj* passive; * *m* passive.

passion f passion; fondness.

passionnant adj fascinating; exciting.

passionné adj passionate, impassioned; **~ment** adv passionately.

passionner vt to fascinate; to interest deeply, impassion; **se ~** vr to be fascinated by, have a passion for.

passivement adv passively.

passivité f passivity, passiveness.

pastel m pastel.

pastèque f watermelon.

pasteur m minister, pastor.

pasteuriser vt to pasteurize.

pastiche m pastiche.

pastille f pastille, lozenge.

patate f (fam) spud; sweet potato.

patauger vi to wade about, splash about.

pâte f pastry, pasta, dough, batter.

pâté m pâté.

paternel adj paternal, fatherly; **~lement** adv paternally.

paternité f paternity; fatherhood.

pathétique adj pathetic.

patiemment adv patiently.

patience f patience, endurance.

patient adj patient, enduring.

patienter vi to wait.

patin m skate; **~ à glace** ice skate; **~ à roulettes** roller skate.

patinage m skating; slipping; spinning.

patiner vi to skate; to slip; to spin.

patineur m **-euse** f skater.

patinoire f ice rink.

pâtisserie f cake shop, confectioner's.

pâtissier m **-ière** f pastry cook, confectioner.

patois m patois, provincial dialect.

patrie f homeland, country.

patrimoine m inheritance, patrimony.

patriote mf patriot; * adj patriotic.

patriotisme m patriotism.

patron m **-ne** f owner, boss, proprietor.

patronat m employers.

patronner vt to patronize, sponsor.

patrouille f patrol.

patte f leg, paw, foot.

pâturage m pasture, pasturage, grazing.

pâture f pasture; food.

paume f palm.

paumer vt (fam) to lose; **se ~** vr to get lost.

paupière f eyelid.

paupiette f stuffed slice of meat.

pause f pause; half-time.

pauvre adj poor; indigent; scanty; weak; **~ment** adv poorly; * mf poor person, pauper.

pavé m cobblestone, paving stone.

pavillon m house; pavilion; flag.

pavot m poppy.

paye f pay, wages.

payer vt to pay, settle; to reward.

pays m country; region; village; land.

paysage m landscape; scenery.

paysan m countryman, farmer; **-ne** f countrywoman.

PDG (président-directeur général) m chairman and managing director.

péage m toll; tollgate.

peau f skin; hide, pelt.

pêche f peach; fishing.

pécher vi to sin.

pêcher vt to fish; to catch; * m peach tree.

pécheur m **-eresse** f sinner.

pêcheur m fisherman, **-euse** f fisherwoman.

pectoral adj pectoral; cough.

pectoraux mpl pectorals.

pédagogie f education; educational methods.

pédagogue mf teacher; educationalist; * adj pedagogic.

pédale f pedal; treadle.

pédaler vi to pedal.

pédalier m pedal-board, crank-gear.

pédestre adj pedestrian.

pédiatre mf paediatrician.

pédicure mf chiropodist.

peigne m comb.

peigner vt to comb; to card; **se ~** vr to comb one's hair.

peignoir m dressing gown.

peindre vt to paint; to depict, portray.

peine f effort; sadness; pain; punishment; difficulty.

peiner vi to toil; to struggle.

peintre m painter; portrayer.

peinture f painting, picture; paintwork.

péjoratif adj pejorative.

pelage m coat, fur.

peler vi to peel.

pèlerin *m* pilgrim; peregrine falcon.

pèlerinage *m* pilgrimage.

pélican *m* pelican.

pelle *f* shovel; spade.

pellicule *f* film; thin layer.

pelote *f* ball; pelota ball.

peloton *m* pack; squad; platoon.

pelouse *f* lawn, field; ground.

pelure *f* peeling, piece of peel.

pénal *adj* penal; criminal.

pénaliser *vt* to penalize.

pénalité *f* penalty.

penalty *m* penalty (kick).

pencher *vi* to lean; to tilt; (*mar*) to list; * *vt* to tip up; tilt; **se ~** *vr* to bend down; to study, look at.

pendant *prép* during; for; **~ que** while, whilst; * *adj* hanging, drooping; pending.

pendentif *m* pendant; pendentive.

pendre *vi* to hang, dangle; * *vt* to hang; **se ~** *vr* to hang o.s.

pendule *f* clock; * *m* pendulum.

pénétrant *adj* penetrating, piercing; searching; acute.

pénétration *f* penetration; perception.

pénétrer *vi* to enter, penetrate; * *vt* to penetrate, pierce; to pervade.

pénible *adj* hard, tiresome; difficult; laborious; **~ment** *adv* painfully; with difficulty.

péniche *f* barge.

péniciline *f* penicillin.

péninsule *f* peninsula.

pénis *m* penis.

pénitence *f* penitence, penance; punishment.

pénitencier *m* prison, penitentiary.

pénitent *m* **-e** *f* penitent; * *adj* penitent.

pénombre *f* half-light; penumbra (astronomy).

pensée *f* thought; thinking; mind.

penser *vt* to think, suppose, believe; * *vi* to think.

pensif *adj* pensive, thoughtful.

pension *f* pension; boarding house.

pensionnaire *mf* boarder; lodger.

pensionnat *m* boarding school.

pensivement *adv* pensively, thoughtfully.

pentagone *m* pentagon.

pentathlon *m* pentathlon.

pente *f* slope; gradient.

Pentecôte *f* Pentecost, Whitsun.

pénurie *f* shortage, scarcity; penury.

pépère *m* granddad, grandpa.

pépin *m* pip; snag, hitch.

pépinière *f* tree nursery; breeding-ground.

pépite *f* nugget.

perçant *adj* piercing, shrill.

percée *f* opening, clearing; breach; breakthrough.

perce-oreille *m* earwig.

perception *f* perception; collection.

percer *vt* to pierce; to drill; to see through.

percevoir *vt* to perceive, detect; to collect.

percher *vt* to stick; to place on; **se ~** *vr* to perch.

percussion *f* percussion.

percussionniste *mf* percussionist.

percuter *vt* to strike; to crash into.

perdant *m* **-e** *f* loser; * *adj* losing.

perdre *vt* to lose; to waste; to miss; * *vi* to lose; **se ~** *vr* to lose one's way.

perdrix *f* partridge.

perdu *adj* lost; wasted; missed.

père *m* father; sire.

péremptoire *adj* peremptory.

perfection *f* perfection.

perfectionnement *m* perfection, perfecting; improvement.

perfectionner *vt* to improve, perfect; **se ~** *vr* to improve, improve o.s.

perfectionniste *mf* perfectionist; * *adj* perfectionist.

perfide *adj* perfidious, treacherous; **~ment** *adv* perfidiously.

perforation *f* perforation.

perforer *vt* to perforate; to pierce.

performance *f* result, performance.

performant *adj* outstanding; high-performance, high-return.

péricliter *vi* to collapse; to be in jeopardy.

péril *m* peril, danger.

périlleux *adj* perilous.

périmé *adj* out-of-date; expired.

périmètre *m* perimeter.

période *f* period; epoch, era; wave, spell.

périodique *adj* periodic; **~ment** *adv* periodically.

péripétie *f* event, episode.

périphérie *f* periphery.

périphérique *adj* peripheral, outlying; * *m* ring road; peripheral.

périple *m* voyage; journey.

périr *vi* to perish, die.

périscope *m* periscope.

périssable *adj* perishable.

perle *f* pearl; bead; gem.

permanence *f* permanence; permanency.

permanent *adj* permanent, continuous.

permanente *f* perm.

permanenter *vt* to perm.

perméable *adj* permeable; pervious.

permettre *vt* to allow, permit; **se ~** *vr* to allow o.s.

permis *adj* permitted; * *m* permit, licence.

permission *f* permission; leave.

permutation *f* permutation.

permuter *vt* to change, switch round; to permutate.

pernicieux *adj* pernicious.

perpendiculaire *adj* perpendicular; ~**ment** *adv* perpendicularly.

perpétuel *adj* perpetual; permanent; ~**lement** *adv* perpetually.

perpétuer *vt* to perpetuate, carry on; **se ~** *vr* to be perpetuated; to survive.

perpétuité *f* perpetuity.

perplexe *adj* perplexed, confused.

perplexité *f* perplexity, confusion.

perquisition *f* search.

perquisitionner *vt* to make a search.

perron *m* flight of steps.

perroquet *m* parrot.

perruche *f* budgerigar; chatterbox.

perruque *f* wig.

persécuter *vt* to persecute; to harass.

persécution *f* persecution.

persévérance *f* perseverance.

persévérant *adj* persevering.

persévérer *vi* to persevere; to persist in.

persil *m* parsley.

persistance *f* persistence.

persistant *adj* persistent; evergreen.

persister *vi* to persist, keep up.

personnage *m* character, individual.

personnaliser *vt* to personalize.

personnalité *f* personality.

personne *f* person; self; appearance; **en ~** in person; * *pn* anyone, anybody; nobody.

personnel *adj* personal; selfish; ~**lement** *adv* personally.

personnifier *vt* to personify.

perspective *f* perspective; view; angle.

perspicace *adj* shrewd, perspicacious.

perspicacité *f* insight, perspicacity.

persuader *vt* to persuade; to convince.

persuasif *adj* persuasive; convincing.

persuasion *f* persuasion; conviction.

perte *f* loss, losing; ruin.

pertinent *adj* pertinent.

perturbation *f* disruption; perturbation.

perturber *vt* to disrupt, disturb.

pervenche *f* periwinkle.

pervers *adj* perverse; perverted.

perversité *f* perversity.

pesant *adj* heavy, weighty.

pesanteur *f* gravity; heaviness.

pèse-personne *m* scales.

peser *vt* to weigh; to press; to evaluate; * *vi* to weigh, weigh down; to hang over; **se ~** to weigh o.s.

pessimisme *m* pessimism.

pessimiste *mf* pessimist; * *adj* pessimistic.

peste *f* pest, nuisance; plague.

pesticide *m* pesticide.

pétale *f* petal.

pétanque *f* petanque.

pétard *m* firecracker; detonator; charge; racket, row.

pétillant *adj* bubbly, fizzy.

pétiller *vi* to crackle; to bubble; to sparkle.

petit *adj* small, tiny; slim; young.

petitesse *f* smallness, modesty; meanness.

petit-fils *m* grandson.

petite-fille *f* granddaughter.

pétition *f* petition.

petits-enfants *mpl* grandchildren.

pétrifié *adj* petrified; transfixed; fossilized.

pétrin *m* kneading trough; scrape, mess, tight spot.

pétrir *vt* to knead; to mould, shape.

pétrole *m* oil, petroleum.

pétrolier *m* oil tanker; * *adj* petroleum, oil, oil-producing.

pétrolifère *adj* oil-bearing.
pétunia *m* petunia.
peu *adv* little, not much, few; **un petit ~** a little bit; **quelque ~** a little; **pour ~ que** however little; **~ de** little, few.
peuplade *f* tribe, people.
peuple *m* people, nation; crowd.
peuplement *m* populating; stocking.
peupler *vt* to populate, stock; to plant.
peuplier *m* poplar.
peur *f* fear, terror, apprehension; **avoir ~** to be afraid.
peureux *adj* fearful, timorous.
peut-être *adv* perhaps.
phalange *f* phalanx.
phallocrate *m* male chauvinist.
pharaon *m* pharaoh.
phare *m* lighthouse; headlight.
pharmaceutique *adj* pharmaceutical.
pharmacie *f* pharmacy; pharmacology.
pharmacien *m* **-ne** *f* pharmacist; chemist.
pharynx *m* pharynx.
phase *f* phase, stage.
phénoménal *adj* phenomenal.
phénomène *m* phenomenon; freak; character.
philanthrope *mf* philanthropist.
philatélie *f* philately, stamp collecting.
philologie *f* philology.
philosophe *mf* philosopher; * *adj* philosophical.
philosopher *vi* to philosophize.
philosophie *f* philosophy.
philosophique *adj* philosophical; **~ment** *adv* philosophically.
phobie *f* phobia.
phonétique *f* phonetics; * *adj* phonetic; **~ment** *adv* phonetically.
phoque *m* seal; sealskin.
phosphate *m* phosphate.
phosphore *m* phosphorus.
phosphorescent *adj* luminous, phosphorescent.
photo *f* photo.
photocopie *f* photocopy.
photocopier *vt* to photocopy.
photocopieur *m*, **-euse** *f* photocopier.
photogénique *adj* photogenic.

photographe *mf* photograph.
photographie *f* photography.
photographier *vt* to photograph.
photographique *adj* photographic.
phrase *f* sentence; phrase.
physicien *m* **-ne** *f* physicist.
physiologie *f* physiology.
physiologique *adj* physiological.
physionomie *f* countenance, physiognomy.
physionomiste *adj* good at remembering faces.
physiothérapie *f* physiotherapy.
physique *f* physics; * *adj* physical; **~ment** *adv* physically.
pianiste *mf* pianist.
piano *m* piano.
pic *m* peak; **à ~** vertically, sheer.
pichet *m* pitcher, jug.
picorer *vt* to peck; to nibble.
picot *m* picot; (*bot*) burr; (*tec*) tooth.
picotement *m* tickle; prickling.
picoter *vt* to tickle; to prickle; to smart, sting.
pictural *adj* pictorial.
pie *f* magpie; chatterbox.
pièce *f* piece; object; component; room; paper, document.
pied *m* foot; track; hoof; bottom; **à ~** on foot; **être sur ~** to be underway.
pied-à-terre *m invar* pied-à-terre.
piédestal *m* pedestal.
piège *m* trap; pit; snare.
piéger *vt* to trap, set a trap.
pierre *f* stone.
piété *f* piety.
piétiner *vi* to stamp (one's foot); * *vt* to trample on.
piéton *m* pedestrian; * *adj* pedestrian.
pieu *m* post, stake, pile.
pieusement *adv* piously, devoutly.
pieux *adj* pious, devout.
pigeon *m* pigeon; dupe, mug.
pigment *m* pigment.
pigmentation *f* pigmentation.
pignon *m* gable; cogwheel.
pile *f* pile; pier; battery; * *adv* dead; just, right, exactly.
piler *vt* to crush, pound.
pilier *m* pillar.

pillage *m* pillaging, looting.
piller *vt* to pillage, loot.
pilon *m* pestle; wooden leg.
pilote *m* pilot; driver.
piloter *vt* to pilot, fly; to drive.
pilotis *m* stilts; pilotis.
pilule *f* pill.
piment *m* hot pepper, capsicum.
pimenter *vt* to add spice.
pin *m* pine.
pince *f* pliers, crowbar; pincer; dart.
pinceau *m* brush, paintbrush.
pincée *f* pinch.
pincer *vt* to pinch, nip; to grip.
pinède *f* pine forest.
pingouin *m* penguin.
ping-pong *m* table tennis.
pintade *f* guinea-fowl.
pinte *f* pint.
pioche *f* pick, pickaxe.
piocher *vt* to use a pick; to swot.
piolet *m* ice axe.
pion *m* pawn; draught.
pionnier *m* pioneer.
pipe *f* pipe.
pipette *f* pipette.
piquant *adj* prickly; pungent; piquant; * *m* quill, spine; prickle.
pique *f* pike, lance.
pique-nique *m* picnic.
pique-niquer *vi* to picnic.
piquer *vt* to sting, bite; to goad; to puncture.
piquet *m* post, picket.
piqûre *f* prick; sting; bite.
pirate *m* pirate.
pire *adj* worse; **le ~, la ~, les ~s** the worst.
pirogue *f* pirogue, dugout canoe.
pirouette *f* pirouette; about-turn.
pis *m* udder.
pis-aller *m invar* last resort, stopgap.
piscine *f* swimming pool.
pissenlit *m* dandelion.
pistache *f* pistachio.
piste *f* track, trail; course; runway; lead, clue.
pistolet *m* pistol, gun.
piston *m* piston.
pistonner *vt* to pull strings for, recommend.
piteux *adj* pitiful, pathetic.

pitié *f* pity, mercy.
pitoyable *adj* pitiful, pitiable.
pittoresque *adj* picturesque.
pivoine *f* peony.
pivot *m* pivot; mainspring.
pivoter *vi* to revolve, pivot.
placard *m* cupboard; poster, notice.
place *f* place; square; seat; space; position; **à la ~ de** instead of.
placebo *m* placebo.
placement *m* placing; investment.
placenta *m* placenta; afterbirth.
placer *vt* to place, put; to fit; to seat; to sell; to invest; **se ~** *vr* to take up position; to stand; to find a job.
placide *adj* placid, calm.
placidité *f* placidity, calmness.
plafond *m* ceiling; roof.
plafonner *vi* to reach a ceiling/maximum.
plage *f* beach.
plagiat *m* plagiarism, plagiary.
plagier *vt* to plagiarize.
plaider *vt* to plead; to defend; * *vi* to plead for, go to court.
plaidoirie *f* defence speech; plea.
plaidoyer *m* defence speech; plea.
plaie *f* wound, cut; scourge.
plaignant *m* **-e** *f* plaintiff.
plaindre *vt* to pity; to begrudge; **se ~** *vr* to complain.
plaine *f* plain.
plainte *f* complaint; moan, groan.
plaintif *adj* plaintive, complaining.
plaire *vi* to please, be pleasant; **se ~** *vr* to enjoy, take pleasure in.
plaisant *adj* pleasant, agreeable.
plaisanter *vi* to joke, jest.
plaisanterie *f* joking; pleasantry; humour.
plaisir *m* pleasure; delight; entertainment; **faire ~** to please.
plan *m* plan, scheme, project; plane, level.
planche *f* plank, board; plate; shelf.
plancher *m* floor.
planchette *f* small board, small shelf.
plancton *m* plankton.
planer *vi* to glide, soar; to hover over.
planétaire *adj* planetary.
planète *f* planet.

planeur *m* glider.

planifier *vt* to plan.

planisphère *m* planisphere.

planning *m* programme, schedule.

plantation *f* plantation; planting.

plante *f* plant.

planter *vt* to plant; to hammer in; to stick, dump.

plantureux *adj* copious, ample.

plaque *f* sheet, plate; plaque; slab.

plaqué *adj* plated.

plaquer *vt* to plate, veneer; to jilt; to tackle.

plaquette *f* plaque; tablet; slab.

plasma *m* plasma.

plastifier *vt* to coat with plastic.

plastique *m* plastic; * *adj* plastic.

plat *adj* flat; straight; dull, insipid; **~ement** *adv* dully, insipidly; * *m* plate, dish; course.

platane *m* plane tree.

plateau *m* tray; turntable; plateau; stage.

plate-bande *f* border, flower-bed.

plate-forme *f* platform.

platine *m* platinum; * *f* deck; turntable; stage.

platitude *f* platitude; flatness, dullness.

platonique *adj* platonic.

plâtre *m* plaster.

plâtrer *vt* to plaster; to set in plaster.

plâtrier *m* plasterer.

plausible *adj* plausible.

plébiscite *m* plebiscite.

plébisciter *vt* to elect by plebiscite.

plein *adj* full; entire, whole; busy; **~ement** *adv* fully, in full; wholly; * *m* filling up; full house; height, middle.

plénitude *f* plenitude, fullness.

pléonasme *m* pleonasm.

pleur *m* tear, sob; **en ~s** in tears.

pleurer *vi* to cry, weep; * *vt* to mourn for, lament.

pleurésie *f* pleurisy.

pleuvoir *vi* to rain; to shower down, rain down.

plexus *m* plexus.

pli *m* fold; crease; wrinkle; envelope.

pliant *adj* collapsible, folding.

plier *vt* to fold; to bend; * *vi* to bend; to yield; **se ~** *vr* to fold up; to submit.

plinthe *f* plinth; skirting board.

plissement *m* creasing, folding; puckering.

plisser *vt* to pleat, fold; to pucker; * *vi* to become creased.

pliure *f* fold; bend.

plomb *m* lead; sinker; fuse.

plombage *m* weighting; leading; filling.

plomber *vt* to weight; to fill.

plomberie *f* plumbing.

plombier *m* plumber.

plongée *f* diving, dive.

plongeoir *m* diving board.

plongeon *m* dive.

plonger *vi* to dive; to plunge, dip sharply.

plongeur *m* **-euse** *f* diver; washer-up.

ployer *vi* to bend, to sag.

pluie *f* rain; shower.

plumage *m* plumage, feathers.

plume *f* feather.

plumeau *m* feather duster.

plumer *vt* to pluck.

plupart *f* most, most part, majority; **la ~ de** most of.

pluriel *m* plural; * *adj* plural.

plus *adv* more, most; **~ grand que** bigger than; **de ~ en ~** more and more; **de ~** besides, moreover; **non ~** neither, not either.

plusieurs *adj* several.

plus-que-parfait *m* pluperfect.

plus-value *f* appreciation; increase in value.

plutonium *m* plutonium.

plutôt *adv* rather, quite, fairly; sooner.

pluvieux *adj* rainy, wet.

pneu *m* tyre.

pneumatique *adj* pneumatic; * *m* tyre.

pneumonie *f* pneumonia.

poche *f* pocket; pouch; bag.

pocher *vt* to poach.

pochette *f* pocket handkerchief; wallet; envelope.

pochoir *m* stencil.

podium *m* podium.

poêle *m* stove; * *f* frying pan.

poème *m* poem.

poésie *f* poetry.

poète *m* poet.

poétique *adj* poetic; **~ment** *adv* poetically.

poids *m* weight, influence; **~ lourd** heavyweight; **~ plume** featherweight.

poignant *adj* poignant.

poignard *m* dagger.

poignarder *vt* to stab.

poigne *f* grip; hand.

poignée *f* handful; ~ **de mains** handshake.

poignet *m* wrist; cuff.

poil *m* hair; coat; bristle.

poilu *adj* hairy.

poinçon *m* hallmark, style; awl.

poinçonner *vt* to stamp; to hallmark.

poindre *vi* to break, dawn.

poing *m* fist; **coup de ~** punch.

point *m* point, spot; stage; full stop; **mettre au ~** to finalize; to perfect; **faire le ~** (*mar*) to take bearings; **être sur le ~ de** to be about to; **à~** medium, just right, when due; **~-virgule** semicolon; **~ de vue** point of view.

pointage *m* checking off; sighting; scrutiny.

pointe *f* point, head; spike; tack; **tailler en ~** to cut to a point; **sur la ~ des pieds** on tiptoe.

pointer *vi* to clock in; to soar up; to peep out; * *vt* to check off; to clock in; to stick into.

pointillé *m* stipple engraving; dotted line.

pointilleux *adj* particular, fastidious.

pointu *adj* pointed, sharp; subtle.

pointure *f* size, number.

poire *f* pear.

poireau *m* leek.

poirier *m* pear tree.

pois *m* pea; ~ **chiche** chickpea; **petits ~** garden peas.

poison *m* poison.

poisseux *adj* sticky.

poisson *m* fish.

poissonnerie *f* fishmonger's, fish shop.

poissonnier *m* **-ière** *f* fishmonger.

poitrail *m* breast, chest.

poitrine *f* chest, breast; bosom.

poivre *m* pepper.

poivrer *vt* to pepper, put pepper in.

poivrière *f* pepperpot.

poivron *m* green pepper, capsicum.

polaire *adj* polar.

polariser *vt* to polarize; to attract.

polarité *f* polarity.

polaroïd *m* polaroid; * *adj* polaroid.

pôle *m* pole; centre.

polémique *f* controversy, polemic; * *adj* controversial, polemic.

poli *adj* polite; polished, smooth; **~ment** *adv* politely.

police *f* police; policing; regulations.

polichinelle *m* buffoon.

policier *m* policeman, **-ière** *f* policewoman.

poliomyélite *f* poliomyelitis.

polir *vt* to polish; to refine.

politesse *f* politeness, courtesy.

politicien *m* **-ne** *f* politician; * *adj* (*pej*) politicking.

politique *f* politics; policy; * *adj* political; **~ment** *adv* politically.

politiser *vt* to politicize; to make a political issue of.

pollen *m* pollen.

polluant *adj* polluting; * *m* pollutant.

polluer *vt* to pollute.

pollution *f* pollution.

polo *m* polo.

poltron *m* **-ne** *f* coward; * *adj* cowardly, craven.

polyamide *m* polyamide.

polycopier *vt* to duplicate, stencil.

polyester *m* polyester.

polygame *m* polygamist.

polygamie *f* polygamy.

polyglotte *adj* polyglot; * *mf* polyglot.

polygone *m* polygon.

polymère *m* polymer; * *adj* polymeric.

polyvalent *adj* polyvalent; varied; versatile.

pommade *f* ointment.

pomme *f* apple.

pomme de terre *f* potato.

pommette *f* cheekbone.

pommier *m* apple tree.

pompe *f* pump.

pomper *vt* to pump.

pompeux *adj* pompous; pretentious.

pompier *m* fireman.

pompiste *mf* pump attendant.

poncer *vt* to sand down, rub down.

ponction *f* (*med*) puncture.

ponctualité *f* punctuality.

ponctuation *f* punctuation.

ponctuel *adj* punctual; **~lement** *adv* punctually.

ponctuer *vt* to punctuate; to phrase.

pondéré *adj* weighted; levelheaded.

pondre *vt* to lay; to produce.

poney *m* pony.

pont *m* bridge; deck; axle.

ponte *f* laying; clutch.

pontifical *adj* pontifical.

ponton *m* pontoon; landing stage.

populaire *adj* popular; working-class; vernacular.

populariser *vt* to popularize.

popularité *f* popularity.

population *f* population.

porc *m* pig; pork.

porcelaine *f* porcelain, china.

porc-épic *m* porcupine.

porche *m* porch.

porcherie *f* pigsty.

pore *m* pore.

poreux *adj* porous.

pornographique *adj* pornographic.

port *m* port, harbour; carrying, wearing.

portail *m* portal, gate.

portatif *adj* portable.

porte *f* door; gate; threshold.

porte-avions *m invar* aircraft carrier.

porte-bagages *m invar* luggage rack.

porte-bonheur *m invar* lucky charm.

porte-clefs, porte-clés *m invar* key ring.

porte-documents *m invar* briefcase.

portée *f* reach, range; capacity; impact, significance; **à la ~ de** within reach; **hors de ~** out of reach.

portefeuille *m* wallet; portfolio.

porte-jarretelles *m invar* suspender belt.

portemanteau *m* coat hanger; hat stand.

porte-parole *m invar* spokesperson.

porte-plume *m invar* penholder.

porter *vt* to carry; to take; to wear; to hold, keep; **se ~** *vr* to put o.s. forward; to go.

porteur *m* **-euse** *f* porter; carrier; * *adj* booster; strong, buoyant.

portier *m* commissionaire.

portière *f* door.

portillon *m* gate, barrier.

portion *f* portion, share.

portique *m* portico.

portrait *m* portrait.

portraitiste *mf* portraitist.

pose *f* pose, posture; laying, fitting, setting.

poser *vt* to put; to install; to set out; to ask; **se ~** *vr* to land, settle; to come up, arise.

positif *adj* positive, definite.

position *f* position; situation; state; stance.

positionner *vt* to position, locate.

positivement *adv* positively.

posologie *f* posology.

posséder *vt* to possess, have; to know inside out.

possesseur *m* possessor, owner.

possessif *adj* possessive.

possession *f* possession, ownership.

possibilité *f* possibility; potential.

possible *adj* possible, feasible; potential; * *m:* **faire son ~** to do one's best.

postal *adj* postal, mail.

poste *f* post office, post; * *m* post, position; station; job.

poster *vt* to post, mail; to station; **se ~** *vr* to take up a position.

postérieur *adj* later, subsequent; back, posterior.

postérité *f* posterity; descendants.

posthume *adj* posthumous.

postiche *adj* false; postiche; pretended; * *m* hairpiece; toupee.

postier *m* **-ière** *f* post office worker.

postillon *m* postilion.

postulant *m* **-e** *f* applicant.

postuler *vt* to apply for; to postulate.

posture *f* posture, position.

pot *m* jar; pot; can.

potable *adj* drinkable; passable.

potage *m* soup.

potager *m* kitchen garden; * *adj* vegetable, edible.

potassium *m* potassium.

pot-au-feu *m invar* stew.

pot-de-vin *m* bribe.

poteau *m* post, stake.

potée *f* hotpot.

potelé *adj* plump, chubby.

potence *f* gallows; bracket.

potentiel *adj* potential; * *m* potential.

poterie *f* pottery, piece of pottery.

potiche *f* vase, mere, puppet.

potier *m* potter.

potion *f* potion.
potiron *m* pumpkin.
pou *m* louse.
poubelle *f* dustbin.
pouce *m* thumb; big toe; inch.
poudre *f* powder, dust.
poudrer *vt* to powder.
poudrière *f* powder magazine.
poulailler *m* henhouse.
poulain *m* foal; protegé.
poule *f* hen, fowl.
poulet *m* chicken.
poulie *f* pulley.
poulpe *m* octopus.
pouls *m* pulse.
poumon *m* lung.
poupe *f* stern.
poupée *f* doll.
poupon *m* baby.
pouponnière *f* day nursery, crèche.
pour *prép* for; to; in favour of; on account of; in order; **~ que** so that, in order that; **être ~** to be in favour of.
pourboire *m* tip.
pourceau *m* pig, swine.
pourcentage *m* percentage.
pourchasser *vt* to pursue; to harry.
pourparlers *mpl* talks, negotiations.
pourpre *adj* crimson; * *m* crimson.
pourquoi *adv* why; **~ pas?** why not?; * *m* reason, question.
pourri *adj* rotten, decayed; corrupt; * *m* rotten part, rottenness.
pourrir *vi* to rot, go rotten; to deteriorate.
pourriture *f* rot, rottenness.
poursuite *f* pursuit; prosecution.
poursuivant *m* **-e** *f* pursuer; plaintiff.
poursuivre *vt* to pursue; to seek; to prosecute.
pourtant *adv* however, yet, nevertheless.
pourtour *m* circumference, perimeter.
pourvoir *vt* to provide, equip.
pourvu *conj*: **~ que** provided that.
pousse *f* shoot; sprouting.
poussée *f* pressure, pushing; thrust; upsurge.
pousser *vt* to push; to drive; to incite; * *vi* to push; to grow, expand; **se ~** *vr* to move, shift.

poussette *f* pushchair.
poussière *f* dust.
poussiéreux *adj* dusty.
poussin *m* chick; junior.
poutre *f* beam.
pouvoir *vi* can, be able; may, be allowed; * *m* power, ability; authority; proxy.
pragmatique *adj* pragmatic.
prairie *f* meadow, prairie.
pralin *m* praline.
praline *f* sugared almond.
praticable *adj* practicable; passable.
pratiquant *m* **-e** *f* churchgoer; * *adj* practising.
pratique *f* practice; exercise; observance; * *adj* practical; **~ment** *adv* practically.
pratiquer *vt* to practise, exercise; to carry out.
pré *m* meadow.
préalable *adj* preliminary; previous; **~ment** *adv* previously, first.
préambule *m* preamble, prelude.
préau *m* covered playground; inner yard.
préavis *m* notice, advance warning.
précaire *adj* precarious.
précarité *f* precariousness.
précaution *f* precaution; care.
précautionneux *adj* cautious, careful.
précédent *adj* previous, preceding; * *m* precedent.
précéder *vt* to precede, go before.
précepte *m* precept.
prêcher *vt* to preach; * *vi* to preach, sermonize.
prêcheur *m* **-euse** *f* preacher.
précieux *adj* precious; invaluable.
précipice *m* precipice; abyss.
précipitamment *adv* hurriedly, hastily.
précipitation *f* haste, violent hurry.
précipiter *vt* to throw, push down; to hasten, precipitate; **se ~** *vr* to rush forward; to speed up.
précis *adj* precise, exact; **~ément** *adv* precisely.
préciser *vt* to specify; to clarify; **se ~** *vr* to become clear.
précision *f* precision, preciseness.
précoce *adj* precocious, premature.

préconçu *adj* preconceived.

préconiser *vt* to recommend; to advocate.

précurseur *m* forerunner, precursor; * *adj* precursory, preceding.

prédateur *m* predator.

prédécesseur *m* predecessor.

prédestiné *adj* predestined, fated.

prédiction *f* prediction.

prédire *vt* to predict, foretell.

prédisposition *f* predisposition.

prédominance *f* predominance.

prédominant *adj* predominant.

prédominer *vi* to predominate.

préfabriqué *adj* prefabricated.

préface *f* preface, prelude.

préfecture *f* prefecture.

préférable *adj* preferable; better; **~ment** *adv* preferably.

préféré *m* **-e** *f* favourite; *adj* favourite, preferred.

préférence *f* preference.

préférer *vt* to prefer.

préfet *m* prefect.

préfigurer *vt* to prefigure.

préhistoire *f* prehistory.

préhistorique *adj* prehistoric.

préjudice *m* loss; harm; wrong; damage.

préjudiciable *adj* prejudicial, detrimental.

préjudicier *vt* to be prejudicial.

préjugé *m* prejudice.

prélasser (se) *vr* to sprawl, lounge.

prélèvement *m* taking; levying; imposition.

prélever *vt* to take; to levy; to deduct.

préliminaire *m* preliminary; * *adj* preliminary.

prélude *m* prelude; warm-up.

prématuré *adj* premature; untimely; **~ment** *adv* prematurely.

préméditation *f* premeditation.

prémédité *adj* premeditated.

premier *m* first, first floor, **-ière** *f* first, first gear; * *adj* first; former; chief; early; primary.

première *f* première.

premièrement *adv* firstly, in first place.

prémonition *f* premonition.

prémonitoire *adj* premonitory.

prénatal *adj* prenatal.

prendre *vt* to take; to pick up; to catch; * *vi* to take root; to harden; to start; **se ~** *vr* to consider o.s.; **s'y ~ mal** to set about the wrong way; **s'en ~ à** to set upon, take it out on.

prénom *m* first name, forename.

préoccuper *vt* to worry; to preoccupy; **se ~** *vr* to concern o.s.

préparatif *m* preparation.

préparation *f* preparation; making up; training.

préparatoire *adj* preparatory.

préparer *vt* to prepare, get ready; to train; **se ~** *vr* to prepare o.s.

prépondérant *adj* preponderant, dominating.

préposition *f* preposition.

prérogative *f* prerogative.

près *adv* near, close; nearly, almost; **de ~** closely; **à peu ~** just about, near enough; **à peu de choses ~** more or less.

présage *m* omen; harbinger.

presbytère *m* presbytery.

presbytie *f* long-sightedness, presbyopia.

prescrire *vt* to prescribe; to stipulate.

présélection *f* preselection.

présence *f* presence.

présent *m* present, gift; **-e** *f* this letter, the present letter; * *adj* present; * *m* present; **à ~** just now.

présentable *adj* presentable.

présentateur *m* **-trice** *f* host, compère; presenter.

présentation *f* presentation; introduction; **faire les ~s** to make the introductions.

présenter *vt* to introduce; to present; to explain; **se ~** *vr* to appear; to come forward; to introduce o.s.

présentoir *m* display shelf.

préservatif *m* condom.

préserver *vt* to preserve; to protect; **se ~** *vr* to protect o.s.

présidence *f* presidency; chairmanship.

président *m* **-e** *f* president.

présidentiel *adj* presidential.

présider *vt* to preside, chair; to direct.

présomption *f* presumption, assumption.

présomptueux *adj* presumptuous.

presque *adv* almost, nearly; hardly, scarcely.

presqu'île *f* peninsula.

pressant *adj* urgent, pressing.

presse *f* press, newspapers; throng.

pressé *adj* hurried, urgent.

presse-citron *m invar* lemon squeezer.

pressentiment *m* presentiment, foreboding, premonition.

pressentir *vt* to have a presentiment of.

presse-papiers *m invar* paperweight.

presser *vt* to press; to squeeze; to hurry up; **se ~** *vr* to hurry; to crowd around.

pression *f* pressure.

pressoir *m* press (wine, cider).

prestation *f* benefit; service; payment; allowance.

prestidigitateur *m* **-trice** *f* conjurer; magician.

prestige *m* prestige.

prestigieux *adj* prestigious.

présumer *vt* to presume, assume.

prêt *adj* ready; prepared, willing; * *m* loan, lending.

prêt-à-porter *m* ready-to-wear.

prétendant *m* **-e** *f* candidate.

prétendre *vt* to claim, maintain; to want; to intend, mean.

prétendu *adj* so-called, supposed; **~ment** *adv* supposedly, allegedly.

prétentieux *adj* pretentious.

prétention *f* pretension, claim; pretentiousness.

prêter *vt* to lend; to attribute; to give.

prétérit *m* preterite tense.

prétexte *m* pretext, excuse.

prêtre *m* priest.

preuve *f* proof, evidence.

prévaloir *vi* to prevail.

prévenant *adj* considerate, thoughtful.

prévenir *vt* to prevent; to warn, inform; to anticipate.

préventif *adj* preventive.

prévention *f* prevention.

prévisible *adj* foreseeable.

prévision *f* prediction; forecast.

prévoir *vt* to anticipate; to plan; to provide for.

prévoyance *f* foresight, forethought.

prévoyant *adj* provident.

prévu *adj* provided for.

prier *vi* to pray; * *vt* to pray to; to beg; to invite.

prière *f* prayer; entreaty.

primaire *adj* primary; elementary.

primate *m* primate.

primauté *f* primacy.

prime *f* premium, subsidy; free gift.

primer *vi* to dominate; to take first place; * *vt* to outdo, prevail.

primeurs *fpl* early fruit and vegetable.

primevère *f* primrose.

primitif *adj* primitive.

primordial *adj* primordial, essential.

prince *m* prince.

princesse *f* princess.

principal *m* principal; headmaster; * *adj* main, principal; **~ement** *adv* principally.

principe *m* principle; origin; element; **en ~** in principle.

printanier *adj* spring.

printemps *m* spring.

prioritaire *adj* having priority, priority.

priorité *f* priority.

pris *adj* taken; busy, engaged.

prise *f* hold, grip; catch; plug; dose; **lâcher ~** to let go one's hold; **~ de sang** blood sample; **~ de courant** plug, power point; **~ de conscience** awareness, realization.

prisme *m* prism.

prison *f* prison; jail.

prisonnier *m* **-ière** *f* prisoner; * *adj* captive.

privation *f* deprivation; forfeiture.

privatiser *vt* to privatize.

privé *adj* private; unofficial; independent.

priver *vt* to deprive; **se ~** *vr* to go without.

privilège *m* privilege.

privilégié *m* **-e** *f* privileged person; * *adj* privileged, favoured.

privilégier *vt* to favour.

prix *m* price, cost; prize.

probabilité *f* probability, likelihood.

probable *adj* probable, likely; **~ment** *adv* probably.

problématique *adj* problematical; * *f* problem; problematics.

problème *m* problem, issue.

procédé *m* process; behaviour.

procéder *vi* to proceed.

procédure *f* procedure; proceedings.

procès *m* proceedings; lawsuit, trial.

procession *f* procession.

processus *m* process; progress.

procès-verbal *m* minutes; report.

prochain *adj* next; imminent; **~ement** *adv* soon, shortly; * *m* neighbour.

proche *adj* nearby; close, imminent.

proclamation *f* proclamation.

proclamer *vt* to proclaim, declare.

procuration *f* proxy, power of attorney.

procurer *vt* to procure, provide; **se ~** *vr* to procure, obtain for o.s.

procureur *m* prosecutor.

prodige *m* marvel, wonder.

prodigieusement *adv* prodigiously, incredibly.

prodigieux *adj* prodigious.

prodiguer *vt* to be lavish, be unsparing; to squander.

producteur *m* **-trice** *f* producer; * *adj* producing, growing.

productif *adj* productive.

production *f* production; generation; output.

productivité *f* productivity.

produire *vt* to produce; to grow; to generate; **se ~** *vr* to happen, take place.

produit *m* product; goods; yield, profit.

proéminent *adj* prominent.

profane *adj* secular, profane; * *mf* layman, lay person.

profaner *vt* to profane; to defile.

proférer *vt* to utter, pronounce.

professeur *m* teacher, professor.

profession *f* profession; occupation, trade.

professionnel *m* **-le** *f* professional; skilled worker; * *adj* professional; occupational; technical; **~lement** *adv* professionally.

profil *m* profile, outline.

profiler *vt* to profile; to streamline; **se ~** *vr* to stand out, be profiled.

profit *m* profit; advantage, benefit.

profitable *adj* profitable; **~ment** *adv* profitably.

profiter *vi* to profit; to thrive.

profiteur *m* **-euse** *f* profiteer.

profond *adj* deep, profound; heavy; **~ément** *adv* deeply, profoundly.

profondeur *f* depth; profundity.

profusion *f* profusion, wealth; **à ~** plenty, in profusion.

programme *m* program; syllabus; schedule.

programmer *vt* to program; to schedule.

progrès *m* progress; improvement; advance.

progresser *vi* to progress; to advance.

progression *f* progress; progression, spread.

progressivement *adv* progressively.

prohiber *vt* to prohibit, ban.

proie *f* prey, victim.

projecteur *m* projector; spotlight, floodlight.

projectile *m* projectile; missile.

projection *f* projection, casting; showing.

projet *m* plan; draft.

projeter *vt* to plan; to throw out; to cast, project.

prolétaire *mf* proletarian.

prolétariat *m* proletariat.

prolifération *f* proliferation.

proliférer *vi* to proliferate.

prologue *m* prologue.

prolongation *f* prolongation, extension.

prolongement *m* continuation, extension.

prolonger *vt* to prolong, extend; **se ~** *vr* to go on, persist.

promenade *f* walk, stroll; drive, spin.

promener *vt* to take out for a walk; **se ~** *vr* to go for a walk.

promeneur *m* **-euse** *f* walker.

promesse *f* promise.

prometteur *adj* promising.

promettre *vt* to promise.

promontoire *m* promontory, headland.

promoteur *m* **-trice** *f* promoter, instigator.

promotion *f* promotion; advancement.

promouvoir *vt* to promote, upgrade.

prompt *adj* prompt; swift; ready; **~ement** *adv* promptly; swiftly.

promptitude *f* promptness; swiftness.

promulgation *f* promulgation.

promulguer *vt* to promulgate.

prôner *vt* to advocate.

pronom *m* pronoun.

prononcer *vt* to pronounce, utter; **se ~** *vr* to reach a verdict.

prononciation *f* pronunciation.

pronostic *m* forecast; prognosis; tip.

pronostiquer *vt* to forecast, prognosticate.

propagande *f* propaganda.

propagation *f* propagation; spreading.

propager *vt* to propagate, spread; **se** ~ *vr* to spread, be propagated.

propane *m* propane.

prophète *m* prophet.

prophétie *f* prophecy.

prophétique *adj* prophetic.

prophétiser *vt* to prophesy.

propice *adj* propitious, favourable.

proportion *f* proportion, ratio.

proportionné *adj* proportional; proportionate.

proportionnel *adj* proportional; ~**lement** *adv* proportionally.

propos *m* talk, remarks; intention; **à** ~ **de** about, on the subject of; **hors de** ~ irrelevant.

proposer *vt* to propose, suggest; **se** ~ *vr* to offer one's services; to intend to.

proposition *f* proposition, suggestion.

propre *adj* clean, neat; honest; own; peculiar; suitable; ~**ment** *adv* cleanly; exactly; specifically.

propreté *f* cleanliness; tidiness.

propriétaire *mf* owner; landlord.

propriété *f* ownership, property; appropriateness, suitability.

propulser *vt* to propel, power.

propulsion *f* propulsion.

prorogation *f* prorogation; deferment; extension.

proroger *vt* to prorogue; to defer; to extend.

prosaïque *adj* mundane, prosaic.

proscrire *vt* to proscribe; to prohibit.

prose *f* prose.

prospecter *vt* to prospect; to canvass.

prospecteur *m* **-trice** *f* prospector.

prospection *f* prospecting; canvassing.

prospectus *m* leaflet; prospectus.

prospère *adj* prosperous, flourishing.

prospérer *vi* to prosper, flourish.

prospérité *f* prosperity.

prostate *f* prostate.

prosterner (se) *vr* to prostrate o.s.

prostituée *f* prostitute.

prostitution *f* prostitution.

prostré *adj* prostrate, prostrated.

protagoniste *m* protagonist.

protecteur *m* **-trice** *f* protector; patron; * *adj* protective; patronizing.

protection *f* protection; patronage.

protectionnisme *m* protectionism.

protégé *m* **-e** *f* favourite, protegé; * *adj* protected, sheltered.

protéger *vt* to protect; to patronize; **se** ~ *vr* to protect o.s.

protéine *f* protein.

protestant *m* **-e** *f* Protestant; * *adj* Protestant.

protestantisme *m* Protestantism.

protestation *f* protest, protestation.

protester *vi* to protest; to affirm.

prothèse *f* prosthesis; prosthetics.

protocole *m* protocol; etiquette.

prototype *m* prototype.

protubérance *f* protuberance, bulge.

proue *f* prow; bows.

prouesse *f* prowess.

prouver *vt* to prove; to demonstrate.

provenir *vi* to come from; to be due to.

proverbe *m* proverb.

proverbial *adj* proverbial.

providence *f* providence.

providentiel *adj* providential.

province *f* province.

provincial *m* **-e** *f* provincial; * *adj* provincial.

provision *f* provision; supply, stock.

provisoire *adj* provisional, temporary; ~**ment** *adv* provisionally.

provocant *adj* provocative.

provocation *f* provocation.

provoquer *vt* to provoke; to cause.

proximité *f* proximity, closeness; imminence.

prudemment *adv* prudently, carefully.

prudence *f* prudence, care.

prudent *adj* prudent, careful.

prune *f* plum.

pruneau *m* prune.

prunelle *f* sloe; pupil, eye.

prunier *m* plum tree.

psaume *m* psalm.

pseudonyme *m* pseudonym; pen name; alias.

psoriasis *m* psoriasis.

psychanalyse *f* psychoanalysis.

psychanalyser *vt* to psychoanalyse.

psychanalyste *mf* psychoanalyst.

psychédélique *adj* psychedelic.
psychiatre *mf* psychiatrist.
psychiatrie *f* psychiatry.
psychiatrique *adj* psychiatric.
psychique *adj* psychic, mental.
psychisme *m* psyche, mind.
psychologie *f* psychology.
psychologique *adj* psychological; **~ment** *adv* psychologically.
psychologue *mf* psychologist; * *adj* psychological.
psychopathe *mf* psychopath; mentally ill person.
psychose *f* psychosis; obsessive fear.
psychosomatique *adj* psychosomatic.
psychothérapie *f* psychotherapy.
puberté *f* puberty.
pubis *m* pubis.
public *adj*, *f* **publique** public, state; * *m* public, audience; public sector.
publication *f* publication, publishing.
publicité *f* publicity.
publier *vt* to publish; to make public.
publiquement *adv* publicly.
puce *f* flea.
puceron *m* aphid, greenfly.
pudeur *f* modesty, decency.
pudique *adj* modest; chaste; **~ment** *adv* modestly.
puer *vi* to stink; * *vt* to stink.
puéricultrice *f* paediatric nurse.
puéril *adj* puerile, childish; **~ement** *adv* puerilely, childishly.
puérilité *f* puerility, childishness.
puis *adv* then, next.
puiser *vt* to draw from, extract.
puisque *conj* since; as, seeing that.

puissance *f* power, strength; output; force.
puissant *adj* powerful; potent.
puits *m* well; shaft.
pull-over *m* pullover, sweater.
pulluler *vi* to swarm, pullulate.
pulmonaire *adj* pulmonary, lung.
pulpe *f* pulp.
pulsation *f* beat; beating; pulsation.
pulsion *f* drive, urge.
pulvériser *vt* to pulverize; to powder.
puma *m* puma.
punaise *f* bug; drawing pin.
punir *vt* to punish.
punition *f* punishment.
pupille *f* pupil; ward.
pupitre *m* desk; console; lectern.
pur *adj* pure; neat; clear; **~ement** *adv* purely.
purée *f* mashed potatoes; purée.
pureté *f* purity, pureness.
purge *f* purge; purgative; draining.
purger *vt* to purge; to drain.
purifier *vt* to purify, cleanse.
purin *m* liquid manure, slurry.
puritain *m* **-e** *f* puritan; * *adj* puritan.
puritanisme *m* puritanism.
pur-sang *m invar* thoroughbred.
purulent *adj* purulent.
pus *m* pus.
putois *m* polecat; skunk.
putréfaction *f* putrefaction.
putréfier *vt* to putrefy, rot.
pyjama *m* pyjamas.
pylône *m* pylon.
pyramide *f* pyramid.
pyrex *m* Pyrex.
pyromane *mf* pyromaniac; arsonist.
python *m* python.

Q

quadragénaire *adj mf* forty-year-old.
quadrangle *m* quadrangle.
quadrature *f* quadrature.
quadriceps *m* quadriceps.
quadrilatère *m* quadrilateral.
quadrillage *m* covering, control; check pattern.

quadriller *vt* to mark out in squares; to cover, control.
quadrupède *adj m* quadruped.
quadruple *adj m* quadruple.
quai *m* quay, wharf; platform.
qualificatif *adj* qualifying.
qualification *f* qualification.

qualifier *vt* to describe; to qualify; **se ~** *vr* to qualify for; to call o.s.

qualitatif *adj* qualitative.

qualitativement *adv* qualitatively.

qualité *f* quality; skill; position.

quand *conj* when, whenever, while.

quant *prép*: **~ à lui** as for him/it.

quantifier *vt* to quantify.

quantitatif *adj* quantitative.

quantitativement *adv* quantitatively.

quantité *f* quantity, amount.

quarantaine *f* about forty; **avoir la ~** to be in one's forties.

quarante *adj, m inv* forty.

quarantième *adj, mf* fortieth.

quart *m* quarter; beaker; watch.

quartette *m* quartet.

quartier *m* district, neighbourhood; quarters; quarter.

quartz *m* quartz.

quasi *adv* almost, nearly.

quasiment *adv* almost, nearly.

quaternaire *adj* quaternary. * *m* Quaternary.

quatorze *adj, m* fourteen.

quatorzième *adj, mf* fourteenth; **~ment** *adv* in fourteenth place.

quatre *adj, m* four.

quatre-vingt(s) *adj, m* eighty.

quatre-vingt-dix *adj, m* ninety.

quatre-vingtième *adj, mf* eightieth.

quatrième *adj, mf* fourth; **~ment** *adv* in fourth place.

quatuor *m* quartet.

que *conj* that; than; * *pn* that; whom; what; which.

quel, *f* **quelle** *adj* who, what, which.

quelconque *adj* some, any; least, slight; poor, indifferent.

quelque *adj* some; **~ part** somewhere.

quelque chose *pn* something.

quelquefois *adv* sometimes

quelqu'un, *f* **-une** someone, somebody, *pl* **quelques-uns, -unes** *pn* some, a few; **il y a ~?** is there someone there?

quémander *vt* to beg for.

querelle *f* quarrel; row; debate.

quereller (se) *vr* to quarrel, squabble.

question *f* question; matter, issue.

questionnaire *m* questionnaire.

questionner *vt* to question.

quête *m* quest, search; collection; **en ~ de** in search of.

quêter *vi* to seek; to collect money.

queue *f* tail; stalk; queue; **faire la ~** to queue.

qui *pn* who, whom; which.

quiche *f* quiche.

quiconque *pn* whoever, whosoever.

quiétude *f* quiet; peace; tranquillity.

quille *f* skittle; (*mar*) keel.

quincaillerie *f* hardware, ironmongery.

quinine *f* quinine.

quinquagénaire *adj mf* fifty-year-old.

quinquennal *adj* five-year, quinquennial.

quinquina *m* cinchona.

quinte *f* (*mus*) fifth; coughing fit.

quintette *m* quintet.

quintuple *adj* quintuple; * *m* quintuple.

quintupler *vt* to multiply by five; * *vi* to quintuple, increase fivefold.

quintuplés *mpl* **-ées** *fpl* quintuplets.

quinzaine *f* about fifteen; fortnight.

quinze *adj, m* fifteen.

quinzième *adj, mf* fifteenth; **~ment** *adv* in fifteenth place.

quiproquo *m* mistake; misunderstanding.

quittance *f* receipt; bill.

quitte *adj* even, quits; **être ~ envers** to be quits, all square with; **~ à** even if it means, although it may mean; **~ ou double** double or quits.

quitter *vt* to leave; to give up; **se ~** *vr* to part company, separate.

quoi *pn* what; **~ que** whatever.

quoique *conj* although, though.

quolibet *m* gibe, jeer.

quote-part *f* share.

quotidien *adj* daily, everyday; **~nement** *adv* daily, every day; * *m* everyday life.

quotient *m* quotient; quota.

R

rabâcher *vi* to harp on, keep on; * *vt* to rehearse, harp on.

rabais *m* reduction, discount; **au ~** at a reduced price.

rabaisser *vt* to humble, disparage; to reduce; **se ~** *vr* to belittle o.s.

rabattre *vt* to close; to pull down; to reduce; **se ~** *vr* to cut across, pull in front of; **se ~ sur** to fall back on.

rabbin *m* rabbi.

rabot *m* plane.

raboter *vt* to plane; to scrape.

rabougri *adj* stunted, puny.

racaille *f* rabble, scum.

raccommodage *m* mending, repairing.

raccommoder *vt* to mend, repair.

raccompagner *vt* to see back to; to accompany home.

raccord *m* join; link; pointing.

raccordement *m* linking; joining; connecting.

raccorder *vt* to link up, join up; **se ~** *vr* to link, join up.

raccourci *m* shortcut; **en ~** in short.

raccourcir *vt* to shorten, curtail; * *vi* to shrink; to grow shorter.

raccrocher *vt* to ring off; to hang up; to grab; **se ~** *vr* to catch; to cling to.

race *f* race; stock; breed.

rachat *m* repurchase, purchase.

racheter *vt* to repurchase; to redeem; to ransom.

rachitique *adj* rachitic; scrawny.

racial *adj* racial.

racine *f* root; **~ carrée** square root.

racisme *m* racism.

raciste *mf* racist; * *adj* racist.

racler *vt* to scrape; to rake.

racoler *vt* to accost; to solicit.

raconter *vt* to tell, recount.

radar *m* radar.

rade *f* (*mar*) harbour, roads.

radeau *m* raft.

radiateur *m* radiator; heater.

radiation *f* radiation.

radical *adj* radical; **~ement** *adv* radically.

radieux *adj* radiant, dazzling.

radin *m* **-e** *f* skinflint; * *adj* mean, stingy.

radio *f* radio; X-ray.

radioactif *adj* radioactive.

radioactivité *f* radioactivity.

radiodiffuser *vt* to broadcast (radio).

radiodiffusion *f* broadcasting (radio).

radiographie *f* radiography; X-ray photography.

radiologie *f* radiology.

radiologue *mf* radiologist.

radiophonique *adj* radio.

radioscopie *f* radioscopy.

radio-taxi *m* radio taxi.

radis *m* radish.

radium *m* radium.

radoter *vi* to ramble; to dote.

radoucir *vt* to soften; **se ~** *vr* to calm down; to mellow.

rafale *f* gust, blast; flurry.

raffermir *vt* to harden; to strengthen; **se ~** *vr* to become strengthened.

raffinage *m* refining.

raffiné *adj* refined, sophisticated.

raffinement *m* refinement, sophistication.

raffiner *vt* to refine.

raffoler *vi*: **~ de** to be crazy about.

rafle *f* raid, round-up.

rafraîchir *vt* to cool, freshen, chill; **se ~** *vr* to freshen up; to get colder.

rafraîchissant *adj* refreshing, cooling.

rafraîchissement *m* cooling; cold drink.

rage *f* rage, fury; mania; rabies.

rageur *adj* quick-tempered; bad-tempered.

ragot *m* (*fam*) malicious gossip.

ragoût *m* ragout; stew.

raid *m* raid; trek.

raide *adj* stiff; steep; rough; (*col*) broke.

raideur *f* stiffness; steepness; roughness.

raidir *vt* to stiffen; to tighten; to harden.

raie *f* line; furrow; scratch.

raifort *m* horseradish.

rail *m* rail; railway.

railler *vt* to scoff at, mock.

raillerie *f* mockery, scoffing.

railleur *adj* mocking, scoffing.

rainette *f* tree frog.

raisin *m* grape.

raison *f* reason; motive; sense; ground; ratio; **avoir ~** to be right; **en ~ de** because of.

raisonnable *adj* reasonable, sensible; **~ment** *adv* reasonably.

raisonnement *m* reasoning; argument.

raisonner *vi* to reason; to argue.

rajeunir *vi* to feel younger; to be modernized; * *vt* to rejuvenate.

rajouter *vt* to put in; to add; **en ~** to exaggerate.

rajuster *vt* to readjust, rearrange; to tidy up.

râle *m* groan; death rattle.

ralenti *adj* slow; slackened; * *m* slow motion; **au ~** ticking over, idling.

ralentir *vi* to slow down, let up; * *vt* to slow down, check.

ralentissement *m* slowing down; slowing up.

râler *vi* to groan, moan.

ralliement *m* rallying, winning over; uniting.

rallier *vt* to rally; to win over; **se ~** *vr* to join; to side with.

rallonge *f* extension, lengthening; extension lead.

rallumer *vt* to relight; to switch on again; to revive.

ramadan *m* Ramadan.

ramage *m* song; foliage.

ramassage *m* collection; gathering.

ramasser *vt* to pick up; to collect, gather.

rambarde *f* guardrail.

rame *f* oar; underground train; stake.

rameau *m* branch; ramification.

ramener *vt* to bring back, restore.

ramer *vi* to row.

rameur *m* **-euse** *f* rower.

ramification *f* ramification.

ramifier (se) *vr* to ramify; to branch out.

ramollir *vt* to soften; to weaken; **se ~** *vr* to go soft.

ramoner *vt* to sweep.

ramoneur *m* chimney sweep.

rampant *adj* crawling, creeping.

rampe *f* ramp, slope; gradient.

ramper *vi* to crawl, slither.

rance *adj* rancid, rank.

rancœur *f* rancour, resentment.

rançon *f* ransom.

rancune *f* grudge, resentment.

rancunier *adj* rancorous, spiteful.

randonnée *f* drive; ride; ramble.

randonneur *m* **-euse** *f* hiker, rambler.

rang *m* row, line; rank; class.

rangée *f* row, range, tier.

rangement *m* arranging, putting in order.

ranger *vt* to arrange, array; to put in order; **se ~** *vr* to line up; to make room; to park.

ranimer *vt* to reanimate, revive; to rekindle.

rapace *m* bird of prey.

rapatrié *m* **-e** *f* repatriate; * *adj* repatriated.

rapatriement *m* repatriation.

rapatrier *vt* to repatriate.

râpe *f* rasp, rough file.

râper *vt* to grate; to rasp.

râpeux *adj* rough.

rapide *adj* rapid, quick; steep; **~ment** *adv* rapidly, quickly.

rapidité *f* rapidity, quickness.

rapiécer *vt* to patch up.

rappel *m* recall; reminder.

rappeler *vt* to recall; to remind; **se ~** *vr* to remember.

rapport *m* report; relation; reference; profit; **en ~ avec** in touch with.

rapporter *vt* to report; to bring back; to yield; **se ~** *vr*: **se ~ à** to relate to.

rapporteur *m* **-euse** *f* reporter; tell-tale; * *adj* tell-tale; * *m* (*math*) protractor.

rapprochement *m* drawing closer; reconciliation.

rapprocher *vt* to bring nearer; to reconcile; **se ~** *vr* to approach; to come together, be reconciled.

rapt *m* abduction.

raquette *f* racket.

rare *adj* rare; few, odd; exceptional; **~ment** *adv* rarely, seldom.

raréfier (se) *vr* to rarefy; become scarce.

rareté *f* rarity; scarcity; infrequency.

rarissime *adj* extremely rare.

ras *adj* close-shaven, shorn; **à ~** short; level with; **à ~ bords** to the brim; **en avoir ~ le bol** (*fam*) to be fed up.

rasage *m* shaving; shearing.

raser *vt* to shave off; to scrape; to raze; **se ~** *vr* to have a shave.

rasoir *m* razor.

rassasier *vt* to fill sb up.

rassemblement *m* assembling, mustering; crowd; political group.

rassembler *vt* to rally, gather together; **se ~** *vr* to gather, assemble.

rasseoir (se) *vr* to sit down again.

rasséréner *vt* to clear up, restore serenity to.

rassis *adj* settled; calm; stale.

rassurant *adj* reassuring, comforting.

rassurer *vt* to reassure; to comfort; **se ~** *vr* to be reassured.

rat *m* rat.

ratatiner *vt* to shrivel; to wrinkle; **se ~** *vr* to become wrinkled.

ratatouille *f* ratatouille.

rate *f* spleen.

raté *m* **-e** *f* failure; * *m* misfire.

râteau *m* rake.

râtelier *m* rack; denture.

rater *vt* to miss; to spoil; to fail; * *vi* to misfire; to miss.

ratification *f* ratification.

ratifier *vt* to ratify, confirm.

ration *f* ration, allowance.

rationnel *adj* rational.

rationnement *m* rationing.

rationner *vt* to ration, put on rations; **se ~** *vr* to ration o.s.

ratisser *vt* to rake; to comb.

rattacher *vt* to refasten; to attach; to link.

rattraper *vt* to catch again, retake; to recover; **se ~** *vr* to catch hold of; to make up for.

rature *f* crossing-out.

raturer *vt* to cross out.

rauque *adj* hoarse, raucous.

ravage *m* havoc; ravaging, laying waste.

ravager *vt* to ravage; devastate.

ravaler *vt* to swallow again; to restore.

ravi *adj* delighted.

ravin *m* ravine, gully.

ravir *vt* to delight.

raviser (se) *vr* to think better of it, change one's mind.

ravissant *adj* ravishing, delightful.

ravitaillement *m* supplies; refuelling.

ravitailler *vt* to resupply; **se ~** *vr* to be resupplied; to refuel.

raviver *vt* to revive, reanimate; **se ~** *vr* to be revived.

rayer *vt* to scratch; to cross out.

rayon *m* ray, beam; spoke; shelf.

rayonnant *adj* radiant, beaming.

rayonnement *m* radiance, effulgence; influence.

rayonner *vi* to radiate, shine; to be influential.

rayure *f* stripe; streak; groove.

réaccoutumer *vt* to reaccustom; **se ~** *vr* to become reaccustomed.

réacteur *m* reactor; jet-engine.

réaction *f* reaction.

réactionnaire *adj* reactionary; * *mf* reactionary.

réactiver *vt* to reactivate.

réadaptation *f* rehabilitation; readjustment.

réadapter *vt* to readjust; to rehabilitate.

réagir *vi* to react.

réalisateur *m* **-trice** *f* director, film-maker.

réalisation *f* realization; achievement.

réaliser *vt* to realize; to carry out; to achieve; **se ~** *vr* to be realized, come true.

réalisme *m* realism.

réaliste *adj* realistic; * *mf* realist.

réalité *f* reality; **en ~** in fact, in reality.

réanimation *f* resuscitation.

réanimer *vt* to reanimate; to resuscitate.

réapparaître *vi* to reappear.

rébarbatif *adj* stern, grim, forbidding.

rebattu *adj* hackneyed.

rebelle *mf* rebel; * *adj* rebel, rebellious.

rebeller (se) *vr* to rebel.

rébellion *f* rebellion.

reboisement *m* reafforestation.

reboiser *vt* to reafforest.

rebondir *vi* to bounce; to rebound.

rebondissement *m* rebound; bouncing.

rebord *m* rim, edge; hem.

rebrousser *vt* to brush back; **~ chemin** to turn back.

rébus *m* rebus, puzzle.

rebut *m* scrap; repulse, rebuff.

récalcitrant *adj* recalcitrant, stubborn.

récapituler *vt* to recapitulate, sum up.

receler *vt* to receive; to harbour.

récemment *adv* recently.

recensement *m* census, inventory.

recenser *vt* to make a census of; to record.

récent *adj* recent; new.

récépissé *m* receipt.

récepteur *m* receiver.

réceptif *adj* receptive.

réception *f* reception, welcome; receipt.

réceptionniste *mf* receptionist.

récession *f* recession.

recette *f* recipe; formula; receipt.

receveur *m* **-euse** *f* recipient; collector.

recevoir *vt* to receive, welcome; to take, collect.

rechange *m*: change; spare; **de ~** spare.

recharge *f* recharging; reloading.

rechargeable *adj* rechargeable; reloadable; refillable.

recharger *vt* to recharge; to reload; to refill.

réchaud *m* stove; dish-warmer.

réchauffer *vt* to reheat; to warm up; **se ~** *vr* to get warmer.

rêche *adj* rough, harsh.

recherche *f* search; inquiry; investigation; research; **être à la ~ de** to be in search of.

recherché *adj* sought after, in demand; choice, exquisite.

rechercher *vt* to seek; to investigate.

rechigner *vt* to balk; to grumble.

rechute *f* relapse; lapse.

récidive *f* second offence, relapse into crime; (*med*) recurrence.

récidiver *vi* to reoffend; to recur.

récidiviste *mf* recidivist, habitual criminal.

récif *m* reef.

récipient *m* container, receptacle.

réciproque *adj* reciprocal, mutual; **~ment** *adv* reciprocally.

récit *m* account, story.

récital *m*, *pl* **-als** recital.

récitation *f* recitation; recital.

réciter *vt* to recite.

réclamation *f* complaint; demand; claim.

réclame *f* advertisement; publicity; **en ~** on offer.

réclamer *vt* to claim, demand, ask for; * *vi* to complain.

reclus *adj* shut up, secluded.

réclusion *f* reclusion; confinement.

recoiffer *vt* to do sb's hair; **se ~** *vr* to do one's hair.

recoin *m* corner, nook.

recoller *vt* to restick.

récolte *f* harvest; collection; result.

récolter *vt* to harvest; to collect.

recommandation *f* recommendation, reference.

recommander *vt* to recommend; to commend; to register (letter).

recommencement *m* renewal; fresh beginning.

recommencer *vi* to begin again; * *vt* to begin again, resume.

récompense *f* reward; award.

réconciliation *f* reconciliation.

réconcilier *vt* to reconcile; **se ~** *vr* to become reconciled.

reconduire *vt* to bring back; to see home, escort.

réconfort *m* comfort.

réconfortant *adj* comforting; tonic.

réconforter *vt* to comfort; to fortify; **se ~** *vr* to take some refreshment.

reconnaissance *f* recognition; acknowledgement; gratitude.

reconnaissant *adj* grateful.

reconnaître *vt* to recognize; to acknowledge; to be grateful.

reconnu *adj* recognized, accepted.

reconquérir *vt* to reconquer; to recover.

reconsidérer *vt* to reconsider.

reconstituer *vt* to reconstitute; rebuild, restore.

reconstitution *f* reconstitution; rebuilding, restoration.

reconstruire *vt* to reconstruct, rebuild.

reconversion *f* reconversion, redeployment.

recopier *vt* to copy out.

record *m* record.

recoudre *vt* to sew up.

recoupement *m* crosscheck.

recourbé *adj* curved, hooked.

recourir *vi* to run again; **~ à** to resort to.

recours *m* recourse; redress; (*jur*) appeal.

recouvrir *vt* to cover again; to cover up.

récréatif *adj* recreative; entertaining.

récréation *f* recreation; break.

récrimination *f* recrimination, remonstration.

récriminer *vi* to recriminate, remonstrate.

recroqueviller (se) *vr* to shrivel up.

recrudescence *f* recrudescence; upsurge; further outbreak.

recrue *f* recruit.

recrutement *m* recruiting, recruitment.

recruter *vt* to recruit.

rectal *adj* rectal.

rectangle *m* rectangle.

rectangulaire *adj* rectangular.

recteur *m* priest, rector.

rectificatif *m* correction; * *adj* corrected, rectified.

rectification *f* rectification; correction.

rectifier *vt* to rectify, correct; to adjust.

rectiligne *adj* straight; rectilinear.

recto *m* recto, first side; front.

rectum *m* rectum.

reçu *pp* **recevoir** accepted, successful; * *m* receipt.

recueil *m* collection, miscellany.

recueillement *m* meditation.

recueillir *vt* to gather, collect; to record; **se ~** *vr* to collect one's thoughts.

recul *m* retreat; recession; decline.

reculer *vi* to fall back, retreat; * *vt* to move back; to defer.

récupération *f* recovery; retrieval.

récupérer *vt* to recover, retrieve; to recuperate; * *vi* to recover.

récurer *vt* to scour.

recycler *vt* to recycle.

rédacteur *m* **-trice** *f* editor, compiler; drafter; writer; sub-editor.

rédaction *f* drafting, drawing up.

rédemption *f* redemption.

redescendre *vi* to go down again; * *vt* to bring down again.

redevable *adj* indebted, owing; liable.

redevance *f* rent; tax; fees.

rediffusion *f* repeat, reshowing.

rédiger *vt* to write; to compile; to draft.

redire *vt* to repeat, say again; **trouver à ~ à** to find fault with.

redoubler *vt* to increase, intensify; * *vi* to increase, intensify; **~ de** to redouble.

redoutable *adj* redoubtable, formidable.

redouter *vt* to dread, fear.

redresser *vt* to rectify; to true; to set up again; **se ~** *vr* to stand up; to right o.s.

réduction *f* reduction; discount; mitigation.

réduire *vt* to reduce, diminish; **se ~** *vr*: **se ~ à** to boil down to.

réduit *adj* reduced, limited; miniature; * *m* retreat; recess; small room.

rééducation *f* re-education; rehabilitation.

rééduquer *vt* to re-educate; to rehabilitate.

réel *adj* real, genuine; **~lement** *adv* really.

réélire *vt* to re-elect.

rééquilibrer *vt* to restabilize.

réévaluer *vt* to revalue.

refaire *vt* to redo; to remake; to renew.

réfectoire *m* canteen, refectory.

référence *f* reference.

référendum *m* referendum.

refermer *vt* to close again.

réfléchi *adj* well-considered; reflective, thoughtful.

réfléchir *vi* to think, reflect; * *vt* to realize; to mirror.

reflet *m* reflection; reflex.

refléter *vt* to reflect, mirror.

réflexe *m* reflex.

réflexion *f* thought, reflection; remark; **à la ~** on reflection, **~ faite** all things considered.

reflux *m* reflux, ebb.

réforme *f* reform, amendment; discharge.

réformer *vt* to reform, correct; to invalid out; to scrap.

refouler *vt* to drive back, repel.

réfraction *f* refraction.

refrain *m* refrain, chorus.

réfréner *vt* to curb, hold in check.

réfrigérateur *m* refrigerator.

réfrigérer *vt* to refrigerate.

refroidir *vt* to cool; * *vi* to cool down, get cold.

refroidissement *m* cooling; chill.

refuge *m* refuge, shelter; lay-by.

réfugié *m* **-e** *f* refugee; * *adj* refugee.

réfugier (se) *vr* to take refuge.

refus *m* refusal.

refuser *vt* to refuse; to reject; to deny; **se ~** *vr* to deny o.s.; **se ~ à** to reject.

réfuter *vt* to refute.

regagner *vt* to regain, win back.

regain *m* renewal; revival.

régal *m* delight, treat.

régaler *vt* to regale; to treat; **se ~** *vr* to treat o.s.

regard *m* look; glance; expression; peephole.

regardant *adj* particular, meticulous; stingy.

regarder *vt* to look at; to glance; to be opposite; to concern; **~ à** to think about.

régates *fpl* regattas.

régénération *f* regeneration.

régénérer *vt* to regenerate, revive.

régent *m* **-e** *f* regent.

régenter *vt* to rule over, domineer.

régie *f* administration; state control.

régime *m* system, régime; scheme; diet; rate, speed.

régiment *m* regiment.

région *f* region, area.

régional *adj* regional.

régir *vt* to govern, rule.

régisseur *m* manager; steward; bailiff.

registre *m* register, record; style; compass.

réglable *adj* adjustable.

réglage *m* regulation, adjustment; tuning.

règle *f* rule; order; regularity; period.

règlement *m* regulation, rules; settlement.

réglementaire *adj* regulation; statutory.

réglementation *f* regulations; control.

réglementer *vt* to regulate, control.

régler *vt* to settle, pay; to regulate.

réglisse *f* liquorice.

règne *m* reign.

régner *vi* to reign; to prevail.

regorger *vi*: **~ de** to overflow with, abound in.

régresser *vi* to regress; to recede.

régression *f* regression.

regret *m* regret, yearning; **à ~** regretfully.

regrettable *adj* regrettable.

regretter *vt* to regret, be sorry; to miss.

regroupement *m* gathering together; merger.

regrouper *vt* to group together; to reassemble; **se ~** *vr* to gather together.

régulariser *vt* to regularize; straighten out.

régularité *f* regularity; consistency.

régulier *adj* regular; consistent; steady; even; legitimate.

régulièrement *adv* regularly; consistently; lawfully.

réhabilitation *f* rehabilitation; discharge; reinstatement.

réhabiliter *vt* to rehabilitate; to discharge; to reinstate.

réhabituer *vt* to reaccustom sb to; **se ~** *vr* to reaccustom o.s. to.

rehausser *vt* to heighten, raise.

rein *m* kidney.

réincarnation *f* reincarnation.

reine *f* queen.

reine-claude *f* greengage.

réinsertion *f* reinsertion, reintegration.

réintégrer *vt* to reinstate; to return to.

réitérer *vt* to reiterate, repeat.

rejaillir *vi* to gush out; to rebound on.

rejet *m* rejection, dismissal; throwing up.

rejeter *vt* to reject, dismiss; throw up.

rejoindre *vt* to rejoin; to catch up with.

rejouer *vt* to replay; to perform again; * *vi* to play again.

réjouir *vt* to delight; to entertain; **se ~** *vr* to rejoice, be delighted.

réjouissance *f* rejoicing, merry-making.

relâche *f* intermission, respite; **faire ~** to be closed; **sans ~** relentlessly.

relâchement *m* relaxation, loosening; laxity.

relâcher *vt* to relax, slacken; **se ~** *vr* to relax; to become lax.

relais *m* relay; shift; staging post.

relatif *adj* relative; relating to.

relation *f* relation, relationship; reference; acquaintance; account; **être en ~ avec** to be in contact with.

relativement *adv* relatively.

relativisme *m* relativism.

relativité *f* relativity.

relaxant *adj* relaxing.

relaxation *f* relaxation.

relaxer *vt* to relax; to acquit; to release; **se ~** *vr* to relax.

relayer *vt* to relieve, take the place of; to relay; **se ~** *vr* to take turns.

relecture *f* rereading.

reléguer *vt* to relegate; to banish.

relève *f* relief; relief party.

relevé *m* statement; list; bill; * *adj* turned up, rolled up; elevated.

relever *vt* to set up again, raise again; to rebuild; to relieve; **se** ~ *vr* to stand up again; to get up.

relief *m* relief; contours; depth.

relier *vt* to link up, connect; to bind.

religieux *m* monk, **-euse** *f* nun; * *adj* religious.

religion *f* religion.

relique *f* relic.

relire *vt* to reread.

reliure *f* binding; bookbinding.

reluire *vi* to gleam, shine.

remaniement *m* recasting; altering; revision; amendment.

remanier *vt* to recast, revise; to amend.

remarquable *adj* remarkable, notable; **~ment** *adv* remarkably.

remarque *f* remark, comment.

remarquer *vt* to remark; to notice.

rembourrer *vt* to stuff; to pad.

remboursement *m* reimbursement, repayment.

rembourser *vt* to reimburse, pay back.

remède *m* remedy, cure.

remédier *vi*: ~ **à** to remedy, cure.

remerciement *m* thanks; thanking.

remercier *vt* to thank.

remettre *vt* to put back; to replace; to restart; to revive; **se** ~ *vr* to recover, get better; **se** ~ **à** to start doing sth again; **se** ~ **de** to get over sth.

réminiscence *f* reminiscence.

remise *f* delivery; remittance; discount; deferment; **~ en état** repairing; **~ à neuf** restoration; **~ en jeu** throw-in; **~ en question** calling into question; **~ en cause** calling into question; **~ de peine** remission.

remmener *vt* to take back.

remontant *m* tonic; * *adj* invigorating, fortifying.

remonte-pente *m* ski tow.

remonter *vi* to go up again; to rise, increase; to return; * *vt* to go up; to take up.

remontrance *f* remonstrance.

remords *m* remorse.

remorque *f* trailer; towrope.

remorquer *vt* to tow.

remorqueur *m* tug.

rémouleur *m* knife-grinder.

remous *m* back-wash; eddy, swirl.

rempailler *vt* to reseat (chair).

rempart *m* rampart; defence.

remplaçant *m* **-e** *f* substitute.

remplacement *m* replacing; substitution.

remplacer *vt* to replace, stand in for.

remplir *vt* to fill; to fill in; to fulfil; **se** ~ *vr* to fill up.

remplissage *m* filling up; padding.

remporter *vt* to take away.

remuant *adj* restless, fidgety.

remue-ménage *m invar* commotion; hullabaloo.

remuer *vi* to move; to fidget; * *vt* to move, shift; to stir; **se** ~ *vr* to move; to shift o.s.

rémunération *f* remuneration, payment.

rémunérer *vt* to remunerate, pay.

renaissance *f* rebirth, Renaissance.

renaître *vi* to be reborn; to be revived; to reappear.

renard *m* fox.

renchérir *vi* to go further, go one better; to bid higher.

renchérissement *m* increase in price.

rencontre *f* meeting, encounter; conjuncture; collision.

rencontrer *vt* to meet; to find; to strike; **se** ~ *vr* to meet each other.

rendement *m* yield; output.

rendez-vous *m* appointment; date; meeting place.

rendormir *vt* to put to sleep again; **se** ~ *vr* to go back to sleep.

rendre *vt* to render; to give back, return; to yield; **se** ~ *vr* to surrender; to give way.

rêne *f* rein.

renfermé *adj* withdrawn, close; * *m* fusty/close smell.

renfermer *vt* to contain, hold.

renflement *m* bulge.

renflouer *vt* to refloat; to bail out.

renfoncement *m* recess.

renfoncer *vt* to drive further in; to recess.

renforcer *vt* to strengthen, reinforce.

renfort *m* reinforcement; help.

renfrogné *adj* frowning, glum.

renier *vt* to repudiate, disown.

renifler *vt* to sniff, snuffle.

renne *m* reindeer.

renom *m* renown, fame.

renommée *f* renowned, famed.

renoncement *m* renouncement; renunciation.

renoncer *vi* to renounce, give up.

renonciation *f* renunciation; waiver.

renouer *vt* to retie; to renew.

renouveau *m* spring; renewal.

renouveler *vt* to renew; to revive; **se ~** *vr* to be renewed.

renouvellement *m* renewal; revival.

rénovation *f* renovation; renewal.

rénover *vt* to renovate.

renseignement *m* information; intelligence.

renseigner *vt* to inform, give information to; **se ~** *vr* to ask for information.

rentabiliser *vt* to make profitable.

rentable *adj* profitable.

rente *f* rent; profit; annuity.

rentier *m* **-ière** *f* stockholder, fundholder; rentier.

rentrée *f* reopening; reassembly; reappearance.

rentrer *vi* to re-enter; to return home; to begin again; * *vt* to bring in.

renversement *m* inversion; reversal; overturning.

renverser *vt* to turn upside down; to reverse; to overturn.

renvoi *m* sending back; returning; dismissal.

renvoyer *vt* to send back; to return; to dismiss.

réorganisation *f* reorganization.

réorganiser *vt* to reorganize.

réouverture *f* reopening.

repaire *m* den, lair.

répandre *vt* to pour out; to scatter, spread; **se ~** *vr* to spread; to be spilled.

répandu *adj* widespread.

réparateur *m* **-trice** *f* repairer.

réparation *f* repairing; restoration.

réparer *vt* to repair; to restore; to make up for.

repartie *f* retort; **avoir de la ~** to have a quick wit.

repartir *vi* to set off again; to start up again.

répartir *vt* to share out; to distribute; **se ~** *vr* to share out.

répartition *f* sharing out; allocation.

repas *m* meal.

repassage *m* ironing; grinding, sharpening.

repasser *vt* to iron; to cross again; to resit; * *vi* to go past again.

repêcher *vt* to fish out, retrieve.

repeindre *vt* to repaint.

repenti *adj* repentant.

repentir *m* repentance, contrition.

repentir (se) *vr* to repent, rue.

répercussion *f* repercussion.

répercuter *vt* to reverberate; to echo; **se ~** *vr* to reverberate; to echo.

repère *m* line, mark; **point de ~** indication, reference mark.

repérer *vt* to spot, pick out; to mark out.

répertoire *m* index, catalogue; repertory.

répertorier *vt* to itemize; to index.

répéter *vt* to repeat; to rehearse; **se ~** *vr* to repeat o.s.; to reoccur.

répétitif *adj* repetitive.

répétition *f* repetition; rehearsal.

repiquer *vt* to plant out, transplant.

répit *m* respite, rest.

repli *m* fold, coil, meander; withdrawal; downturn.

replier *vt* to fold up; to withdraw; **se ~** *vr* to coil up, curl up.

réplique *f* reply, retort; counterattack.

répliquer *vt* to reply; to retaliate.

répondant *m* **-e** *f* guarantor; bail, surety.

répondeur *m* answering machine.

répondre *vt* to answer, reply.

réponse *f* response, reply.

report *m* postponement, deferment; carrying forward.

reportage *m* report; commentary; reporting.

reporter *vt* to postpone; to carry forward; to transfer; * *m* reporter.

repos *m* rest; tranquillity; landing.

reposant *adj* restful, refreshing.

reposer *vt* to put back; to rest; to ask again; **se ~** *vr* to rest.

repoussant *adj* repulsive; repellent.

repousser *vt* to push back; to repel.

reprendre *vt* to retake, recapture; to resume; **se ~** *vr* to correct o.s.; to pull o.s. together.

représailles *fpl* reprisals; retaliation.

représentant *m* representative.
représentatif *adj* representative.
représentation *f* representátion; performance.
représenter *vt* to represent, depict; to perform; to symbolize.
répressif *adj* repressive.
répression *f* repression.
réprimande *f* reprimand, rebuke.
réprimander *vt* to reprimand, rebuke.
réprimer *vt* to repress; to quell.
reprise *f* resumption; recapture, taking back; **à plusieurs ~s** several times.
repriser *vt* to darn.
réprobation *f* reprobation.
reproche *m* reproach; objection.
reprocher *vt* to reproach, blame.
reproduction *f* reproduction; copy; duplicate.
reproduire *vt* to reproduce, copy; to repeat; **se ~** *vr* to reproduce, breed.
reptile *m* reptile.
repu *adj* full, satiated.
républicain *m* **-e** *f* republican; * *adj* republican.
république *f* republic.
répudier *vt* to repudiate; to renounce.
répugnance *f* repugnance, disgust.
répugnant *adj* repugnant, disgusting, revolting.
répulsion *f* repulsion, repugnance.
réputation *f* reputation; character; fame.
réputé *adj* reputable, renowned; supposed, reputed.
requérir *vt* to call for, request.
requête *f* petition, request.
requin *m* shark.
requis *adj* required, requisite.
réquisition *f* requisition; conscription.
réquisitionner *vt* to requisition; to conscript.
rescapé *m* **-e** *f* survivor.
réseau *m* network, net.
réservation *f* reservation, booking.
réserve *f* reserve; reservation, caution.
réservé *f* reserved.
réserver *vt* to reserve, save; to book; to lay by.
réservoir *m* tank; reservoir.

résidence *f* residence; apartment block.
résidentiel *adj* residential.
résider *vi* to reside, dwell.
résidu *m* residue.
résignation *f* resignation.
résigner (se) *vr* to resign o.s.
résilier *vt* to terminate; to annul.
résine *f* resin.
résistance *f* resistance.
résistant *adj* resistant; tough, unyielding.
résister *vi* to resist, withstand.
résolu *adj* resolved, determined; **~ment** *adv* resolutely.
résolution *f* resolution, determination.
résonner *vi* to resound, resonate.
résorber *vt* to reduce; to absorb; **se ~** *vr* to be reduced.
résoudre *vt* to solve; to resolve; to annul; **se ~** *vr*: **se ~ à** to decide to do.
respect *m* respect, regard, deference.
respectable *adj* respectable; sizeable.
respecter *vt* to respect; to comply with.
respectif *adj* respective.
respectivement *adv* respectively.
respectueusement *adv* respectfully.
respectueux *adj* respectful.
respirable *adj* breathable.
respiration *f* breathing, respiration.
respiratoire *adj* respiratory.
respirer *vi* to breathe, respire; to rest; * *vt* to breathe in.
resplendissant *adj* shining, radiant.
responsabilité *f* responsibility; liability.
responsable *adj* responsible; liable; * *mf* official, manager.
resquiller *vi* to sneak in; to take a free ride.
ressaisir (se) *vr* to regain one's self-control.
ressemblance *f* resemblance, likeness; similarity.
ressemblant *adj* lifelike.
ressembler *vi* to resemble, be like; **se ~** *vr* to be alike.
ressemelage *m* soling, resoling.
ressentiment *m* resentment.
ressentir *vt* to feel, experience; **se ~** *vr*: **se ~ de** to feel the effects of.
resserrement *m* contraction, tightening; narrowing.

resserrer *vt* to tighten; to strengthen; **se ~** *vr* to grow tighter.

ressort *m* spring; motivation.

ressortir *vi* to go out again; to stand out.

ressortissant *m* **-e** *f* national.

ressource *f* resource, resort, expedient.

ressusciter *vi* to revive, reawaken; to come back to life; * *vt* to resuscitate; to revive.

restant *adj* remaining; * *m* rest, remainder.

restaurant *m* restaurant.

restaurateur *m* **-trice** *f* restaurateur; restorer.

restauration *f* restoration, rehabilitation; catering.

restaurer *vt* to restore; to feed; **se ~** *vr* to eat.

reste *m* rest, left-over, remainder; **du ~** besides; **être en ~** to be outdone.

rester *vi* to remain, stay; to be left; to continue; to pause.

restituer *vt* to return, restore; to refund.

restitution *f* restoration; restitution.

restreindre *vt* to restrict, curtail; **se ~** *vr* to restrain o.s.

restreint *adj* restricted, limited.

restrictif *adj* restrictive.

restriction *f* restriction, limitation; reserve.

restructurer *vt* to restructure.

résultat *m* result, outcome; profit.

résulter *vi*: **~ de** to result, follow from, ensue.

résumé *m* summary, recapitulation; **en ~** in brief.

résumer *vt* to sum up; **se ~** *vr*: **se ~ à** to amount to.

résurrection *f* resurrection.

rétablir *vt* to re-establish, restore; **se ~** *vr* to recover, get well again.

rétablissement *m* re-establishment, restoring.

retard *m* lateness; delay; **être en ~** to be late; to be behind; to be backward.

retardataire *mf* latecomer; * *adj* obsolete.

retardé *adj* backward, slow.

retarder *vt* to delay; to hinder; to put back; * *vi* to be out of touch.

retenir *vt* to hold back, retain; to remember; **se ~** *vr* to control o.s.

rétention *f* retention; withholding.

retentir *vi* to resound; to ring.

retentissant *adj* resounding; ringing.

retenue *f* discretion; deduction, stoppage; reservoir.

réticence *f* reticence.

réticent *adj* reticent.

rétine *f* retina.

retiré *adj* remote, isolated.

retirer *vt* to take off; to take out, withdraw; to redeem; **se ~** *vr* to retire, withdraw; to stand down.

retombée *f* fallout; repercussions.

retomber *vi* to fall again; to have a relapse; **~ sur** to come across again.

rétorquer *vt* to retort.

retouche *f* touching up; alteration.

retoucher *vt* to touch up; to alter.

retour *m* return; recurrence; vicissitude, reversal; **être de ~** to be back.

retournement *m* reversal; turnaround.

retourner *vt* to reverse, turn over; to return; * *vi* to return, go back; **se ~** *vr* to turn over; to overturn.

rétracter *vt* to retract, take back; **se ~** *vr* to retract, withdraw one's evidence.

retrait *m* ebb; retreat; withdrawal; **être en ~** to be set back.

retraite *f* retreat; retirement; refuge; **à la ~** retired.

retraité *m* **-e** *f* pensioner; * *adj* retired.

retranchement *m* curtailment; entrenchment.

retrancher *vt* to curtail; to entrench.

retransmettre *vt* to retransmit.

retransmission *f* retransmission.

rétrécir *vi* to narrow; to shrink; * *vt* to take in, make narrower; **se ~** *vr* to narrow; to shrink.

rétrécissement *m* narrowing; shrinking.

rétribuer *vt* to remunerate.

rétribution *f* retribution.

rétroactif *adj* retrospective; retroactive.

rétroaction *f* retroaction; retrospective action.

rétrograde *adj* reactionary, backward.

rétrograder *vi* to go backward, regress.

rétroprojecteur *m* overhead projector.

rétrospectif *adj* retrospective.

rétrospective *f* retrospective.

rétrospectivement *adv* retrospectively.

retrousser *vt* to roll up, hitch up.

retrouvailles *fpl* reunion.

retrouver *vt* to find again, to regain; to recover; to recognize; **se ~** *vr* to meet up; to end up in.

rétroviseur *m* rear-view mirror.

réunifier *vt* to reunify.

réunion *f* reunion, gathering.

réunir *vt* to unite; to collect, gather; to combine; **se ~** *vr* to meet; to assemble.

réussir *vi* to succeed, be a success; * *vt* to make a success of.

réussite *f* success, successful outcome.

revanche *f* revenge; **en ~** on the other hand.

rêvasser *vi* to daydream.

rêve *m* dream, dreaming; illusion.

réveil *m* waking, awaking; alarm clock.

réveiller *vt* to wake; **se ~** *vr* to awaken.

réveillon *m* midnight feast.

révélation *f* revelation, disclosure; developing.

révéler *vt* to reveal, disclose; **se ~** *vr* to be revealed; to prove to be.

revenant *m* **-e** *f* ghost.

revendeur *m* **-euse** *f* retailer; dealer.

revendication *f* claiming; claim; demand.

revendiquer *vt* to claim; to demand.

revendre *vt* to resell.

revenir *vi* to come back, reappear; to happen again; **ne pas en ~** to not recover from, not pull through; **~ à soi** to come round.

revenu *m* income, revenue.

rêver *vi* to dream; to muse; * *vt* to dream of.

réverbération *f* reverberation.

réverbère *m* street lamp.

révérence *f* bow, curtsey.

révérend *adj* reverend.

révérer *vt* to revere.

rêverie *f* reverie, musing.

revers *m* back, reverse; counterpart.

réversible *adj* reversible.

revêtement *m* coating, surface.

revêtir *vt* to don; to assume.

rêveur *m* **-euse** *f* dreamer; * *adj* dreamy.

revigorer *vt* to invigorate; to revive.

revirement *m* change of mind; reversal; turnaround.

réviser *vt* to review; to revise.

révision *f* review; auditing; revision.

revivre *vt* to relive; * *vi* to live again, come alive again.

révocation *f* removal; dismissal; revocation.

revoir *vt* to see again; **se ~** *vr* to meet each other again.

révoltant *adj* revolting, appalling.

révolte *f* revolt, rebellion.

révolter *vt* to revolt, outrage; **se ~** *vr* to rebel, revolt.

révolu *adj* past, bygone.

révolution *f* revolution.

révolutionnaire *mf* revolutionary; * *adj* revolutionary.

révolutionner *vt* to revolutionize; to upset.

revolver *m* revolver.

révoquer *vt* to revoke; to dismiss.

revue *f* review; inspection.

rez-de-chaussée *m invar* ground floor.

rhabiller *vt* to dress (sb) again; to fit (sb) out again; **se ~** *vr* to get dressed again.

rhésus *m* rhesus.

rhétorique *f* rhetoric; * *adj* rhetorical.

rhinocéros *m* rhinoceros.

rhododendron *m* rhododendron.

rhubarbe *f* rhubarb.

rhum *m* rum.

rhumatisme *m* rheumatism.

rhume *m* cold.

riant *adj* smiling; cheerful.

ribambelle *f* swarm, herd.

ricanement *m* snigger, sniggering.

ricaner *vi* to snigger, giggle.

riche *adj* rich, wealthy; abundant; **~ment** *adv* richly; * *mf* rich person.

richesse *f* richness; wealth; abundance.

ricochet *m* ricochet; rebound.

rictus *m* grin; grimace.

ride *f* wrinkle; ripple; ridge.

ridé *adj* wrinkled.

rideau *m* curtain.

ridicule *adj* ridiculous; * *m* ridiculousness; absurdity; ridicule.

ridiculiser *vt* to ridicule.

rien *pn* nothing; **de ~** don't mention it; **il n'en est ~** it's nothing of the sort; * *m* nothingness; mere nothing; pinch, shade; **en un ~ de temps** in no time; **pour un ~** at the slightest little thing.

rieur *adj* cheerful; laughing.
rigide *adj* rigid; **~ment** *adv* rigidly.
rigidité *f* rigidity, stiffness.
rigole *f* channel; rivulet.
rigoler *vi* (*fam*) to have a good laugh.
rigoureusement *adv* harshly, rigorously.
rigoureux *adj* rigorous, harsh.
rigueur *f* rigour; harshness, severity.
rime *f* rhyme.
rimer *vi* to rhyme (with).
rince-doigts *m invar* finger-bowl.
rincer *vt* to rinse out; to rinse.
ring *m* boxing ring.
riposte *f* riposte, retort.
riposter *vi* to answer back, retaliate.
rire *vi* to laugh; to smile; to joke; * *m* laughter, laugh.
risée *f* laugh; ridicule; mockery, derision.
risible *adj* laughable, ridiculous.
risque *m* risk, hazard.
risqué *adj* risky, hazardous; risqué.
risquer *vt* to risk; to venture; **se ~** *vr* to venture, dare.
ristourne *f* discount, rebate.
rite *m* rite.
rituel *adj* ritual.
rivage *m* shore.
rival *m* **-e** *f* rival; **sans ~** unrivalled; * *adj* rival.
rivaliser *vi* to rival, compete with; **~ de** to vie with.
rivalité *f* rivalry.
rive *f* shore, bank.
river *vt* to clinch; to rivet.
riverain *m* **-e** *f* lakeside resident; riverside resident; * *adj* lakeside, riverside.
rivière *f* river.
riz *m* rice.
robe *f* dress; gown; **~ de chambre** dressing gown.
robinet *m* tap.
robot *m* robot.
robotique *f* robotics.
robuste *adj* robust.
robustesse *f* robustness.
roc *m* rock.
rocaille *f* loose stones; rocky ground.
rocailleux *adj* rocky.

roche *f* rock.
rocher *m* rock, boulder.
rodage *m* grinding; running in, breaking in.
roder *vt* to grind; to run in.
rôder *vi* to roam; to prowl about.
rôdeur *m* **-euse** *f* prowler.
rogner *vt* to pare, prune, clip.
rognon *m* kidney.
roi *m* king.
rôle *m* role, character; roll, catalogue.
roman *m* novel; romance.
romancier *m* **-ière** *f* novelist.
romanesque *adj* fabulous; storybook; fictional.
romantique *adj* romantic.
romantisme *m* romanticism.
rompre *vt* to break; to snap; to dissolve; * *vi* to break; to burst.
ronce *f* bramble.
rond *m* circle, ring; slice, round; * *adj* round; chubby, plump; frank, **~ement** *adv* briskly, frankly.
ronde *f* patrol; round; beat.
rondelle *f* slice, round; disc.
rondeur *f* plumpness; roundness.
rondin *m* log.
rond-point *m* roundabout.
ronflement *m* snore, snoring; humming; roaring.
ronfler *vi* to snore; to hum; to roar.
ronger *vt* to gnaw.
ronronner *vi* to purr; to hum.
rosbif *m* roast beef.
rose *f* rose; * *adj* pink; * *m* pink.
roseau *m* reed.
rosée *f* dew.
rosier *m* rosebush.
rossignol *m* nightingale.
rot *m* belch, burp.
roter *vi* to belch, burp.
rotation *f* rotation; turnover.
rôti *m* joint, roast.
rotin *m* rattan.
rôtir *vt* to roast.
rôtisserie *f* rotisserie, steak-house.
rotonde *f* rotunda; roundhouse.
rotule *f* kneecap, patella.
rouage *m* cog; gearwheel.

roucouler *vi* to coo; to bill.

roue *f* wheel.

rouge *adj* red; * *m* red; ~ **à lèvres** lipstick.

rouge-gorge *m* robin.

rougeole *f* measles.

rougeur *f* redness, blushing.

rougir *vi* to blush, go red; * *vt* to make red, redden.

rouille *f* rust.

rouiller *vi* to rust; * *vt* to make rusty.

roulant *adj* on wheels; moving.

rouleau *m* roll; roller.

roulement *m* rotation; movement; rumble, rumbling.

rouler *vt* to wheel, roll along; * *vi* to go, run (train); to drive.

roulette *f* castor; trundle; roulette.

roulis *m* rolling.

roulotte *f* caravan.

rouquin *m* **-e** *f* redhead; * *adj* red-haired.

route *f* road; way; course, direction.

routier *adj* road; * *m* lorry driver; transport café.

routine *f* routine.

routinier *adj* humdrum, routine.

roux *m*, **rousse** *f* redhead; * *adj* red, auburn.

royal *adj* royal, regal; ~**ement** *adv* royally.

royaliste *mf* royalist; * *adj* royalist.

royaume *m* kingdom.

royauté *f* monarchy.

ruade *f* kick (horse).

ruban *m* ribbon; tape, band.

rubéole *f* rubella.

rubis *m* ruby.

rubrique *f* column; heading, rubric.

ruche *f* hive.

rude *adj* rough; hard; unrefined; ~**ment** *adv* roughly, harshly.

rudesse *f* roughness; harshness.

rudiment *m* rudiment; principle.

rudimentaire *adj* rudimentary.

rudoyer *vt* to treat harshly.

rue *f* street.

ruée *f* rush, stampede.

ruelle *f* alley.

ruer *vi* to kick (horse); **se ~** *vr* to pounce on.

rugby *m* rugby.

rugbyman *m* rugby player.

rugir *vi* to roar.

rugissement *m* roar, roaring.

rugueux *adj* rough; coarse.

ruine *f* ruin; wreck.

ruiner *vt* to ruin.

ruineux *adj* ruinous; extravagant.

ruisseau *m* stream, brook.

ruisseler *vi* to stream, flow.

ruissellement *m* streaming; cascading.

rumeur *f* rumour; murmur; hum.

ruminer *vt* to ruminate; to brood over.

rupture *f* break, rupture; breach; split.

rural *adj* rural, country.

ruse *f* cunning, slyness.

rusé *adj* cunning, crafty.

rustine ® *f* rubber repair patch.

rustique *adj* rustic.

rutilant *adj* gleaming, rutilant.

rythme *m* rhythm; rate, speed.

rythmique *adj* rhythmic.

S

sabbatique *adj* sabbatical.

sable *m* sand.

sablé *m* shortbread biscuit; * *adj* sandy, sanded.

sablier *m* hourglass, sandglass.

sabot *m* clog; hoof.

sabotage *m* sabotage.

saboter *vt* to sabotage; to mess up.

saboteur *m* **-euse** *f* saboteur; bungler.

sabre *m* sabre

sac *m* bag, sack; ~ **à main** handbag; ~ **de voyage** travelling bag.

saccade *f* jerk, jolt.

saccadé *adj* jerky, broken, staccato.

saccager *vt* to sack; to wreck, devastate.

saccharine *f* saccharin.

sacerdoce *m* priesthood.

sacerdotal *adj* priestly, sacerdotal.

sachet *m* bag; sachet; packet.

sacoche *f* saddlebag, satchel.

sacre *m* coronation; consecration.

sacré *adj* sacred, holy; damned, confounded.

Sacré-Cœur *m* Sacred Heart.

sacrer *vt* to crown; to consecrate.

sacrifice *m* sacrifice.

sacrifier *vt* to sacrifice; to give up; **se ~** *vr* to sacrifice o.s.

sacrilège *m* sacrilege.

sacristie *f* sacristy.

sacrum *m* sacrum.

sadique *adj* sadistic; * *mf* sadist.

sadisme *m* sadism.

sadomasochiste *adj* sadomasochistic; * *mf* sadomasochist.

safari *m* safari.

safran *m* saffron.

saga *f* saga.

sagace *adj* sagacious, shrewd.

sagacité *f* sagacity, shrewdness.

sage *adj* wise, sensible; well-behaved; **~ment** *adv* wisely, sensibly; * *m* sage, wise man.

sage-femme *f* midwife.

sagesse *f* wisdom, sense; good behaviour.

sagittaire *m* archer; Sagittarius.

saignant *adj* bleeding; underdone.

saignement *m* bleeding.

saigner *vi* to bleed; * *vt* to bleed; to stick.

saillant *adj* prominent, protruding.

saillie *f* projection; sally; flash of wit.

saillir *vi* to gush out; to project, jut.

sain *adj* healthy; sound; sane; **~ement** *adv* healthily; soundly.

saindoux *m* lard.

saint *m* **-e** *f* saint; * *adj* holy, saintly; **Saint-Sylvestre** New Year's Eve; **Saint-Esprit** Holy Spirit.

saint-bernard *m* St Bernard.

sainteté *f* saintliness; holiness.

saisie *f* (*jur*) seizure, distraint; capture.

saisir *vt* to take hold of; (jur) to seize, distrain; to capture.

saisissant *adj* gripping, startling, striking.

saison *f* season.

saisonnier *adj* seasonal.

salade *f* salad; jumble, miscellany.

saladier *m* salad bowl.

salaire *m* salary, pay; reward.

salamandre *f* salamander.

salarié *m* **-e** *f* salaried employee; * *adj* salaried.

sale *adj* dirty, filthy; obscene; nasty; **~ment** *adv* dirtily.

salé *adj* salty, salted; savoury.

saler *vt* to salt, add salt.

saleté *f* dirtiness, dirt; rubbish; obscenity.

salière *f* saltcellar.

salin *adj* saline.

salir *vt* to make dirty, soil; **se ~** *vr* to get dirty.

salissant *adj* dirty; that gets dirty easily.

salive *f* saliva.

saliver *vi* to salivate; to drool.

salle *f* room; hall; theatre; audience; **~ de séjour** living room; **~ à manger** dining room; **~ de bain** bathroom; **~ de cinéma** cinema; **~ des ventes** saleroom.

salon *m* lounge, sitting room; exhibition.

salopette *f* overalls.

salpêtre *m* saltpetre.

salsifis *m* salsify.

salubre *adj* healthy, salubrious.

saluer *vt* to greet; to salute.

salut *m* safety, salvation; welfare; wave (hand); salute.

salutaire *adj* salutary; profitable; healthy.

salutation *f* salutation, greeting.

samedi *m* Saturday.

sanatorium *m* sanatorium.

sanctifier *vt* to sanctify, bless.

sanction *f* sanction, penalty; approval.

sanctionner *vt* to punish; to sanction, approve.

sanctuaire *m* sanctuary.

sandale *f* sandal.

sandwich *m* sandwich.

sang *m* blood; race; kindred.

sang-froid *m* sangfroid, cool, calm.

sanglant *adj* bloody, gory; bloodshot; blood-red.

sangle *f* strap; girth.

sanglier *m* wild boar.

sanglot *m* sob.

sangloter *vi* to sob.

sangsue *f* leech.

sanguinaire *adj* sanguinary, bloodthirsty.

sanitaire *adj* health, sanitary.

sans-abris *mf invar* homeless person.

sans-gêne *adj* inconsiderate; * *m invar* inconsiderate type.

santal *m* sandalwood.

santé *f* health, healthiness.

saper *vt* to undermine, sap.

sapeur-pompier *m* fireman.

saphir *m* sapphire.

sapin *m* fir tree, fir.

sarcasme *m* sarcasm.

sarcastique *adj* sarcastic.

sarcler *vt* to weed; to hoe.

sarcophage *m* sarcophagus.

sardine *f* sardine.

sardonique *adj* sardonic

SARL (société à responsabilité limitée) *f* limited liability company.

sarrasin *m* buckwheat.

sas *m* airlock; sieve.

satanique *adj* satanic, diabolical.

satellite *m* satellite.

satiété *f* satiety, satiation; **à ~** ad nauseam.

satin *m* satin.

satiné *adj* satiny, satin-smooth; glazed.

satire *f* satire, lampoon.

satirique *adj* satirical.

satisfaction *f* satisfaction; gratification; appeasement.

satisfaire *vt* to satisfy; to gratify; to appease.

satisfaisant *adj* satisfactory; satisfying.

satisfait *adj* satisfied.

saturation *f* saturation.

saturé *adj* saturated; overloaded, jammed.

saturer *vt* to saturate; to surfeit; to congest.

satyre *m* satyr.

sauce *f* sauce, dressing.

saucière *f* sauceboat.

saucisse *f* sausage.

saucisson *m* large sausage; salami.

sauf *prép* save, except; unless; * *adj* safe, unhurt.

sauge *f* sage.

saugrenu *adj* preposterous, absurd.

saule *m* willow.

saumon *m* salmon.

sauna *m* sauna.

saupoudrer *vt* to sprinkle; to dust.

saut *m* jump, bound; waterfall.

sauté *adj* sauté.

sauter *vi* to jump, leap; to blow up; to get sacked.

sauterelle *f* grasshopper.

sautiller *vi* to hop, skip.

sauvage *adj* savage, wild; unsociable; **~ment** *adv* savagely.

sauvegarde *f* safeguard; backup.

sauvegarder *vt* to safeguard.

sauver *vt* to save, rescue; to preserve; **se ~** *vr* to save o.s.; to escape.

sauvetage *m* rescue; salvage.

sauveteur *m* rescuer.

savant *adj* learned; expert; skilled; * *m* scientist, scholar.

savate *f* old shoe.

saveur *f* flavour; savour.

savoir *vt* to know; to be aware; to understand; to be able; * *m* learning, knowledge.

savoir-faire *m* know-how.

savoir-vivre *m* good manners, good breeding.

savon *m* soap.

savonner *vt* to soap, lather.

savonnette *f* bar of soap.

savoureux *adj* tasty, savoury.

saxophone *m* saxophone.

saxophoniste *mf* saxophonist.

scabreux *adj* scabrous; dangerous; improper.

scalpel *m* scalpel.

scandale *m* scandal.

scandaleux *adj* scandalous.

scandaliser *vt* to scandalize, shock deeply; **se ~** *vr* to be scandalized.

scanner *m* scanner.

scaphandre *m* diving suit.

scarabée *m* beetle, scarab.

scarlatine *f* scarlet fever.

sceau *m* seal.

scélérat *m* **-e** *f* villain, rascal; * *adj* villainous, wicked.

sceller *vt* to seal.

scénario *m* scenario; screenplay.

scénariste *mf* scriptwriter.

scène *f* stage; scenery, scene.

scepticisme *m* scepticism.

sceptique *adj* sceptical; * *mf* sceptic.

sceptre *m* sceptre.

schéma *m* diagram, sketch; outline.

schématique *adj* diagrammatic, schematic; ~**ment** *adv* diagrammatically.

schématiser *vt* to schematize.

schisme *m* schism; split.

schiste *m* schist, shale.

schizophrène *mf* schizophrenic; * *adj* schizophrenic.

schizophrénie *f* schizophrenia.

sciatique *f* sciatica.

scie *f* saw; bore.

sciemment *adv* knowingly, on purpose.

science *f* science; skill; knowledge.

science-fiction *f* science fiction.

scientifique *adj* scientific; ~**ment** *adv* scientifically.

scierie *f* sawmill.

scinder *vt* to split, divide up.

scintillant *adj* sparkling, glistening.

scintillement *m* sparkling, glistening.

scintiller *vi* to sparkle, glisten.

scission *f* split, scission.

sciure *f* sawdust.

sclérose *f* sclerosis.

scléroser (se) *vr* to become sclerotic.

scolaire *adj* school; academic.

scolariser *vt* to send to school; to provide schools.

scolarité *f* schooling.

scoliose *f* scoliosis, curvature of the spine.

scooter *m* scooter.

score *m* score.

scorie *f* slag, scoria.

scorpion *m* scorpion.

scout *m* scout, boy scout.

script *m* printing; script.

scrupule *m* scruple, qualm, doubt.

scrupuleusement *adv* scrupulously.

scrupuleux *adj* scrupulous.

scruter *vt* to scrutinize, scan.

scrutin *m* ballot, poll.

sculpter *vt* to sculpt; to carve.

sculpteur *m* sculptor.

sculpture *f* sculpture.

se *pn* oneself, himself, herself, itself, themselves.

séance *f* meeting, sitting, session; seat.

seau *m* bucket, pail.

sec *adj, f* **sèche** dry, arid; barren; unfeeling; curt; neat.

sécateur *m* secateurs.

séchage *m* drying; seasoning.

sèche-cheveux *m invar* hair-drier

sèchement *adv* dryly; curtly.

sécher *vi* to dry, dry out; * *vt* to dry, wipe.

sécheresse *f* drought; dryness.

séchoir *m* drying room; ~ **à linge** clothes horse.

second *adj* second, in second place; * *m* second; second floor; second in command; * *f* second.

secondaire *adj* secondary.

seconder *vt* to assist, help.

secouer *vt* to shake, toss; **se ~** *vr* to shake o.s.

secourir *vt* to help, assist.

secouriste *mf* first-aid worker.

secours *m* help, assistance; relief; rescue.

secousse *f* jolt, bump.

secret *m* secret; privacy; mystery; * *adj* secret; private; discreet.

secrétaire *mf* secretary; * *m* writing desk.

secrétariat *m* office of secretary; secretariat.

secrètement *adv* secretly.

secréter *vt* to secrete, exude.

sécrétion *f* secretion.

secte *f* sect.

secteur *m* sector, section, district.

section *f* section, division; branch.

sectionner *vt* to sever; to divide into sections.

séculaire *adj* secular, century-old, once a century.

sécurisant *adj* reassuring, lending security.

sécuriser *vt* to make sb feel secure.

sécuritaire *adj* security.

sécurité *f* security; safety.

sédatif *m* sedative; * *adj* sedative.

sédentaire *adj* sedentary; * *m* sedentary.

sédiment *m* sediment.

sédimentation *f* sedimentation.

séducteur *m* seducer **-trice** *f* seductress.

séduction *f* seduction; captivation.

séduire *vt* to seduce; to charm, captivate.

séduisant *adj* seductive; enticing, attractive.

segment *m* segment.

segmenter *vt* to segment.

ségrégation *f* segregation.

seigle *m* rye.

seigneur *m* lord, nobleman; master.

sein *m* breast, bosom; womb; **au ~ de** within.

séisme *m* earthquake, seism.

seize *adj, m* sixteen.

seizième *adj, mf* sixteenth; **~ment** *adv* in sixteenth place.

séjour *m* stay, sojourn; abode; **salle de ~** living room.

séjourner *vi* to stay, sojourn.

sel *m* salt; wit.

sélecteur *m* selector; gear lever.

sélectif *adj* selective.

sélection *f* choosing, selection.

sélectionner *vt* to select, pick.

sélectivement *adv* selectively.

self-service *m* self-service restaurant.

selle *f* saddle.

selon *prép* according to; pursuant to.

semaine *f* week.

semblable *adj* like, similar, alike; such.

semblant *m* appearance, look; pretence; **faire ~ (de)** to pretend to.

sembler *vi* to seem, appear.

semelle *f* sole.

semence *f* seed; semen.

semer *vt* to sow; to scatter, strew.

semestre *m* half-year; semester.

semestriel *adj* half-yearly; semestral.

semi-conducteur *m* semiconductor.

séminaire *m* seminary; seminar.

semi-remorque *f* trailer, semitrailer.

semis *m* seedling; sowing; seedbed.

semoule *f* semolina.

sénat *m* senate.

sénateur *m* senator.

sénile *adj* senile.

sénilité *f* senility.

sens *m* sense; judgement; consciousness; meaning; direction; **bon ~** good sense.

sensation *f* sensation, feeling.

sensationnel *adj* fantastic, sensational.

sensé *adj* sensible.

sensibiliser *vt* to make sensitive to, heighten awareness of.

sensibilité *f* sensitivity, sensitiveness.

sensible *adj* sensitive; perceptive; appreciable; **~ment** *adv* approximately; noticeably.

sensoriel *adj* sensory.

sensualité *f* sensuality.

sensuel *adj* sensual.

sentence *f* sentence; maxim.

sentencieux *adj* sententious.

sentier *m* path, track.

sentiment *m* feeling, sentiment; emotion.

sentimental *adj* sentimental.

sentimentalisme *m* sentimentalism.

sentinelle *f* sentry, sentinel.

sentir *vt* to feel; to perceive, guess; to smell.

séparation *f* separation; division; pulling apart.

séparatiste *mf* separatist.

séparément *adv* separately.

séparer *vt* to separate, divide; to pull off; to split; **se ~** *vr* to separate, divide; to part with.

sept *adj, m* seven.

septembre *m* September

septième *adj, mf* seventh; **~ment** *adv* in seventh place.

sépulture *f* sepulture, burial.

séquelle *f* after-effect.

séquence *f* sequence.

séquestre *m* sequestration, confiscation.

séquestrer *vt* to sequester, impound.

serein *adj* serene, calm; **~ement** *adv* serenely.

sérénade *f* serenade.

sérénité *f* serenity, calmness.

sergent *m* sergeant; **~ de ville** police constable.

série *f* series, string; class; rank.

sérieusement *adv* seriously, responsibly.

sérieux *adj* serious; responsible; * *m* seriousness, reliability.

seringue *f* syringe.

serment *m* oath; pledge.

sermon *m* sermon.

sermonner *vt* to lecture, reprimand.

séropositif *adj* HIV positive, seropositive.

serpe *f* billhook, bill.

serpent *m* serpent, snake.

serpenter *vi* to meander, wind.

serpentin *m* coil; streamer.

serre *f* greenhouse; claw.

serré *adj* tight; close, compact.

serrer *vt* to tighten, fasten; to clench; **se ~** *vr* to crowd, huddle.

serrure *f* lock.

serrurerie *f* locksmithing.

serrurier *m* locksmith.

sérum *m* serum.

servante *f* servant, maidservant.

serveur *m* waiter, **-euse** *f* waitress.

serviable *adj* obliging, helpful.

service *m* service; function; department; operation; **rendre ~** to do a favour; **~ militaire** national service.

serviette *f* towel; serviette, napkin.

servile *adj* servile, slavish; **~ment** *adv* servilely, slavishly.

servilité *f* servility.

servir *vi* to be of use, be useful; * *vt* to serve, attend to; **se ~** *vr* to help o.s.; **se ~ de** to use, make use of.

servitude *f* servitude; (*jur*) easement.

sésame *m* sesame.

session *f* session, sitting.

seuil *m* threshold.

seul *adj* alone; single; sole; **~ement** *adv* only; but; solely.

sève *f* sap; pith, vigour.

sévère *adj* severe, austere; **~ment** *adv* severely; strictly.

sévérité *f* severity; strictness.

sévir *vi* to deal severely; to rage, hold sway.

sevrer *vt* to wean; to deprive.

sexe *m* sex; genitals.

sexiste *mf* sexist; * *adj* sexist.

sexualité *f* sexuality.

sexuel *adj* sexual, sex; **~lement** *adv* sexually.

sexy *adj* sexy.

seyant *adj* becoming.

shampooing *m* shampoo.

shooter *vt* to shoot, make a shot.

shopping *m* shopping.

short *m* shorts.

si *adv* so, so much, however much; yes; * *conj* if; whether.

siamois *adj* Siamese.

sida *m* Aids.

sidéral *adj* sidereal.

sidérer *vt* to flabbergast, stagger.

sidérurgie *f* steel metallurgy

sidérurgique *adj* steel-making.

sidérurgiste *mf* steel maker.

siècle *m* century; period.

siège *m* seat, bench; head office.

siéger *vi* to sit; to be located.

sien *pn*, *f* **sienne: le ~** his, its, his own, its own, **la sienne** her, its, her own, its own, **les ~s, les siennes** their, their own.

sieste *f* nap, snooze; siesta.

sifflement *m* whistling; hissing.

siffler *vi* to whistle; to hiss; * *vt* to whistle for; to hiss, boo.

sifflet *m* whistle; catcall.

sigle *m* abbreviation; acronym.

signal *m* signal, sign.

signalement *m* description, particulars.

signaler *vt* to signal, indicate; to point out.

signalisation *f* signalling system; installing signs.

signature *f* signature; signing.

signe *m* sign; mark; indication; symptom.

signer *vt* to sign; to hallmark.

signet *m* bookmark.

significatif *adj* significant, revealing.

signification *f* significance; meaning.

signifier *vt* to mean, signify; to make known; to serve notice.

silence *m* silence; stillness.

silencieusement *adv* silently.

silencieux *adj* silent; still.

silhouette *f* silhouette, outline.

silice *f* silica.

silicone *f* silicone.

sillage *m* wake; slipstream; trail.

sillon *m* furrow; fissure.

sillonner *vt* to plough, furrow; to criss-cross.

silo *m* silo.

similaire *adj* similar.

similarité *f* similarity.

similitude *f* similitude.

simple *adj* simple; mere; single; common; **~ment** *adv* simply, merely.

simplicité *f* simplicity; simpleness.

simplification *f* simplification.

simplifier *vt* to simplify.

simpliste *adj* simplistic.

simulation *f* simulation.

simuler *vt* to simulate, feign.

simultané *adj* simultaneous; **~ment** *adv* simultaneously.

sincère *adj* sincere, honest; **~ment** *adv* sincerely.

sincérité *f* sincerity, honesty.

singe *m* monkey.

singulariser *vt* to singularize; make conspicuous; **se ~** *vr* to make o.s. conspicuous.

singularité *f* singularity; peculiarity.

singulier *adj* singular; peculiar; remarkable.

singulièrement *adv* singularly; remarkably.

sinistre *m* disaster; accident; * *adj* sinister; **~ment** *adv* in a sinister way.

sinistré *m* **-e** *f* disaster victim; * *adj* disaster-stricken.

sinon *conj* otherwise, if not; except.

sinueux *adj* sinuous, winding.

sinus *m* sinus; (*math*) sine.

sinusite *f* sinusitis.

siphon *m* siphon.

sirène *f* mermaid; siren, hooter.

sirop *m* syrup.

sirupeux *adj* syrupy.

sismique *adj* seismic.

site *m* setting, beauty spot.

sitôt *adv* so soon, as soon; **pas de ~** not for a while; **~ que** as soon as.

situation *f* situation, position; state of affairs.

situer *vt* to site, situate; **se ~** *vr* to place o.s.; to be situated.

six *adj*, *m* six.

sixième *adj*, *mf* sixth; **~ment** *adv* in sixth place.

sketch *m* sketch.

ski *m* ski, skiing.

skier *vi* to ski.

skieur *m* **-euse** *f* skier.

slalom *m* slalom.

slip *m* briefs, panties, swimming trunks.

slogan *m* slogan.

snack(-bar) *m* snack bar.

snob *adj* snobbish.

snobisme *m* snobbery, snobbishness.

sobre *adj* sober, temperate; **~ment** *adv* soberly, temperately.

sobriété *f* sobriety, temperance.

sobriquet *m* nickname.

sociable *adj* sociable; social.

social *adj* social; **~ement** *adv* socially.

social-démocrate *mf* social democrat; * *adj* social democrat.

socialisme *m* socialism.

socialiste *mf* socialist; * *adj* socialist.

sociétaire *mf* member.

société *f* society; company; partnership.

socio-économique *adj* socio-economic.

sociologie *f* sociology.

sociologique *adj* sociological; **~ment** *adv* sociologically.

sociologue *mf* sociologist.

socle *m* pedestal, plinth; base.

socquette *f* ankle sock.

sodium *m* sodium.

sodomie *f* sodomy.

sœur *f* sister; nun.

sofa *m* sofa.

soi *pn* one(self); self; **~-même** oneself, himself, herself, itself; **~-disant** so called.

soie *f* silk.

soif *f* thirst.

soigné *adj* neat, well-kept.

soigner *vt* to look after, care for; **se ~** *vr* to take care of o.s.

soigneusement *adv* neatly; carefully.

soigneux *adj* neat; careful.

soin *m* care; attention; trouble.

soir *m* evening; night.

soirée *f* evening; evening party.

soit *conj* either; or; whether; * *adv* granted; that is to say.

soixantaine *f* about sixty.

soixante *adj*, *m* sixty.

soixantième *adj*, *mf* sixtieth.

soja *m* soya.

sol *m* ground; floor; soil.

solaire *adj* solar.

soldat *m* soldier.

solde *f* pay; * *m* balance; clearance sale.

solder *vt* to pay; to settle, discharge; **se ~** *vr*: **se ~ par** to show (profit, loss).

sole *f* sole; hearth.

soleil *m* sun, sunshine; sunflower.

solennel *adj* solemn; **~lement** *adv* solemnly.

solfège *m* musical theory; sol-fa.

solidaire *adj* jointly liable; interdependent; **~ment** *adv* jointly.

solidarité *f* solidarity.

solide *adj* solid; stable; sound; **~ment** *adv* solidly; soundly.

solidifier *vt* **se ~** *vr* to solidify.

solidité *f* solidity; soundness.

soliste *mf* soloist.

solitaire *mf* recluse, hermit; * *adj* solitary, lone; **~ment** *adv* alone.

solitude *f* solitude; loneliness.

sollicitation *f* entreaty, appeal.

solliciter *vt* to seek, solicit; to appeal to.

sollicitude *f* solicitude, concern.

solo *m* solo.

solstice *m* solstice.

soluble *adj* soluble, solvable.

solution *f* solution; solving; answer.

solvable *adj* solvent; creditworthy.

solvant *m* solvent.

somatique *adj* somatic.

sombre *f* dark; gloomy, dismal.

sombrer *vi* to sink, founder.

sommaire *m* summary, argument; * *adj* basic, brief, summary; **~ment** *adv* basically, summarily.

sommation *f* summons; demand.

somme *m* nap, snooze.

sommeil *m* sleep; sleepiness, drowsiness.

sommeiller *vi* to slumber, doze.

sommelier *m* wine waiter.

sommet *m* summit; top; crest; apex.

sommier *m* springs, divan base; ledger (construction).

sommité *f* leading light, eminent person.

somnambule *mf* sleepwalker; * *adj* sleepwalking.

somnifère *m* sleeping pill; * *adj* soporific.

somnolent *adj* sleepy, drowsy.

somnoler *vi* to doze, drowse.

somptueux *adj* sumptuous, lavish.

son *m* sound; * *adj*, *f* **sa**; *pl* **ses** his, her, its.

sonate *f* sonata.

sondage *m* drilling; probing; sounding.

sonde *f* sounding line; probe; drill.

sonder *vt* to sound; to probe; to drill.

songe *m* dream.

songer *vt* to dream; to imagine; to consider.

songeur *adj* pensive.

sonner *vi* to ring; to go off; * *vt* to ring, sound.

sonnerie *f* ringing, bells; chimes.

sonnette *f* small bell; house-bell.

sonore *adj* resonant, deep-toned.

sonorisation *f* sound recording; sound system.

sonorité *f* sonority, tone; resonance.

sophistiqué *adj* sophisticated.

soporiphique *m* sleeping drug; soporific; * *adj* soporific.

soprano *mf* soprano.

sorbet *m* sorbet, water ice.

sorcellerie *f* witchcraft, sorcery.

sorcier *m* sorcerer.

sorcière *f* witch, sorceress.

sordide *adj* sordid, squalid; **~ment** *adv* sordidly, squalidly.

sort *m* fate, destiny, lot.

sortant *adj* outgoing, retiring.

sorte *f* sort, kind, manner.

sortie *f* exit, way out; trip; sortie; outburst; export.

sortilège *m* spell (magical).

sortir *vi* to go out, emerge; to result; to escape; **se ~** *vr* to get out of; to extricate o.s.; **s'en ~** to get over, pull through.

sosie *m* double, second self.

sot *adj*, *f* **-te** silly, foolish; **~tement** *adv* foolishly, stupidly.

sottise *f* stupidity; stupid remark, action.

sou *m* five centimes; cent.

soubresaut *m* jolt; start.

souche *f* stump; stock.

souci *m* worry; concern.

soucier (se) *vr*: **se ~ de** to care about.

soucieux *adj* concerned, worried.

soucoupe *f* saucer.

soudain *adj* sudden, unexpected; **~ement** *adv* suddenly.

soude *f* soda.

souder *vt* to solder; to weld.

soudeur *m* **-euse** *f* solderer; welder.

soudoyer *vt* to bribe, buy over.

soudure *f* soldering, welding.

souffle *m* blow, puff; breath.

soufflé *m* soufflé; * *adj* flabbergasted.

souffler *vi* to blow; to breathe; to puff.
soufflerie *f* bellows.
soufflet *m* slap in the face; affront; bellows.
souffrance *f* suffering; pain.
souffrant *adj* suffering; in pain.
souffrir *vi* to suffer, be in pain.
souhait *m* wish.
souhaitable *adj* desirable.
souhaiter *vt* to wish for, desire.
souiller *vt* to soil, dirty; to tarnish.
soulagement *m* relief.
soulager *vt* to relieve, soothe.
soulèvement *m* uprising.
soulever *vt* to lift, raise; to excite, stir up; **se ~** *vr* to rise; to revolt.
soulier *m* shoe.
souligner *vt* to underline.
soumettre *vt* to subdue, subjugate; to submit, deliver; **se ~** *vr* to subject o.s. to.
soumis *adj* submissive.
soumission *f* submission.
soupape *f* valve; safety valve.
soupçon *m* suspicion, conjecture; hint.
soupçonner *vt* to suspect, surmise.
soupçonneux *adj* suspicious.
soupe *f* soup.
soupeser *vt* to feel the weight of; to weigh up.
soupière *f* soup tureen.
soupir *m* sigh; gasp.
soupirail *m* basement window.
soupirer *vi* to sigh; to gasp.
souple *adj* supple; pliable; **~ment** *adv* supply, flexibly.
souplesse *f* suppleness; flexibility.
source *f* source; origin; spring.
sourcil *m* eyebrow.
sourd *m* **-e** *f* deaf person; * *adj* deaf; muted; veiled; **~ement** *adv* dully; silently.
sourdine *f* mute.
sourd(e)-muet(te) *m(f)* deaf-mute; * *adj* deaf and dumb.
souriant *adj* smiling, cheerful.
sourire *m* smile, grin.
souris *f* mouse.
sournois *adj* deceitful; sly; **~ement** *adv* deceitfully.
sous *prép* under, beneath, below.

sous-alimenté *adj* undernourished.
sous-bois *m* undergrowth.
sous-chef *m* second-in-command.
souscrire *vi* to subscribe.
sous-développé *adj* underdeveloped.
sous-directeur *m* **-trice** *f* sub-manager.
sous-entendre *vt* to imply, infer.
sous-entendu *m* innuendo, understood.
sous-estimer *vt* to underestimate.
sous-jacent *adj* subjacent, underlying.
sous-louer *vt* to sublet.
sous-marin *m* submarine; * *adj* underwater.
sous-multiple *m* submultiple.
sous-officier *m* non-commissioned officer.
sous-préfecture *f* sub-prefecture.
sous-préfet *m* sub-prefect.
soussigné *adj* undersigned.
sous-sol *m* subsoil; basement.
sous-titre *m* subtitle.
sous-titrer *vt* to subtitle.
soustraction *f* subtraction.
soustraire *vt* to subtract; to remove; **se ~** *vr*: **se ~ à** to escape, elude.
sous-traitance *f* subcontracting.
sous-traitant *m* subcontractor.
sous-traiter *vi* to subcontract.
sous-vêtement *m* undergarment.
soutane *f* cassock, soutane.
soute *f* hold; baggage hold.
soutenir *vt* to hold up; to sustain; to endure.
souterrain *m* underground passage; * *adj* underground.
soutien *m* support.
soutien-gorge *m* bra.
soutirer *vt* to extract from.
souvenir *m* memory; recollection; reminder.
souvenir (se) *vr* to remember, recollect.
souvent *adv* often, frequently.
souverain *m* **-e** *f* sovereign; * *adj* sovereign; supreme; **~ement** *adv* supremely.
soyeux *adj* silky.
spacieux *adj* spacious, roomy.
spaghetti *mpl* spaghetti.
sparadrap *m* sticking plaster.
spasme *m* spasm.
spasmophilie *f* spasmophilia.
spatial *adj* spatial; space.
spatule *f* spatula.

spécial *adj* special, particular; **~ement** *adv* specially.

spécialisation *f* specialization.

spécialiser *vt* to specialize; **se ~** *vr* to be a specialist in sth.

spécialiste *mf* specialist.

spécialité *f* speciality; specialism.

spécieux *adj* specious.

spécification *f* specification.

spécifier *vt* to specify, determine.

spécifique *adj* specific; **~ment** *adv* specifically.

spécimen *m* specimen; sample.

spectacle *m* spectacle, scene.

spectaculaire *adj* spectacular.

spectateur *m* **-trice** *f* spectator.

spectre *m* ghost.

spéculateur *m* **-trice** *f* speculator.

spéculation *f* speculation.

spéculer *vi* to speculate.

spéléologie *f* speleology; caving.

spermatozoïde *m* sperm; spermatozoon.

sperme *m* sperm, semen.

sphère *f* sphere.

sphérique *adj* spherical.

sphinx *m* sphinx.

spirale *f* spiral.

spiritisme *m* spiritualism.

spiritualité *f* spirituality.

spirituel *adj* witty; spiritual; **~lement** *adv* wittily; spiritually.

splendeur *f* splendour, brilliance.

splendide *adj* splendid, magnificent; **~ment** *adv* splendidly.

spongieux *adj* spongy.

sponsoriser *vt* to sponsor.

spontané *adj* spontaneous; **~ment** *adv* spontaneously.

sporadique *adj* sporadic.

sport *m* sport.

sportif *m* sportsman, **-ive** *f* sportswoman; * *adj* sports; competitive; athletic.

square *m* (public) square.

squatter *vi* to squat in.

squelette *m* skeleton.

squelettique *adj* skeleton-like, scrawny.

stabiliser *vt* to stabilize, consolidate; **se ~** *vr* to stabilize, become stabilized.

stabilité *f* stability.

stable *adj* stable, steady.

stade *m* stadium; stage.

stage *m* training course; probation.

stagiaire *mf* trainee.

stagnation *f* stagnation.

stagner *vi* to stagnate.

standard *m* standard; switchboard; * *adj* standard.

standardiser *vt* to standardize.

standardiste *mf* switchboard operator.

starter *m* choke.

station *f* station; stage, stop; resort; posture.

stationnaire *adj* stationary.

stationnement *m* parking.

stationner *vi* to park.

station-service *f* service station.

statique *adj* static.

statistique *f* statistics; * *adj* statistical.

statue *f* statue.

statuer *vt* to rule, give a verdict.

statu quo *m* status quo.

statut *m* statute, ordinance; status.

statutaire *adj* statutory; **~ment** *adv* statutorily.

stencil *m* stencil.

sténodactylo *mf* shorthand typist.

sténographie *f* shorthand.

stentor *m*: **une voix de ~** stentorian voice.

steppe *f* steppe.

stère *f* stere.

stéréo(phonique) *adj* stereophonic.

stéréotype *m* stereotype.

stérile *adj* sterile, infertile.

stérilet *m* coil, IUD.

stériliser *vt* to sterilize.

stérilité *f* sterility.

sternum *m* breastbone, sternum.

stéroïde *adj* steroidal; * *m* steroid.

stigmate *m* mark, scar; stigmata.

stimulant *adj* stimulating; * *m* stimulant, stimulus.

stimulation *f* stimulation.

stimuler *vt* to stimulate, spur on.

stipuler *vt* to stipulate, specify.

stock *m* stock, supply.

stockage *m* stocking; stockpiling.

stocker *vt* to stock, stockpile.

stoïcisme *m* stoicism.

stoïque *adj* stoical; **~ment** *adv* stoically; * *mf* stoic.

stop *m* stop; stop sign; brake-light.

stopper *vt* to stop, halt; * *vi* to stop, halt.

store *m* blind, shade.

strabisme *m* squinting; strabismus.

strapontin *m* foldaway seat; minor role.

stratégie *f* strategy.

stratégique *adj* strategic; **~ment** *adv* strategically.

stratifié *adj* stratified.

stress *m* stress.

stressant *adj* stressful.

stresser *vt* to cause stress to.

strict *adj* strict, severe; **~ement** *adv* strictly.

strident *adj* strident, shrill.

strié *adj* streaked, striped, ridged.

stroboscope *m* stroboscope.

strophe *f* verse, stanza.

structural *adj* structural.

structure *f* structure.

structurel *adj* structural.

structurer *vt* to structure; **se ~** *vr* to develop a structure.

stuc *m* stucco.

studieux *adj* studious.

studio *m* studio; film theatre.

stupéfaction *f* stupefaction, amazement.

stupéfait *adj* astounded, dumbfounded.

stupéfiant *adj* astounding, amazing; drug, narcotic.

stupéfier *vt* to stupefy; to astound.

stupeur *f* amazement; stupor.

stupide *adj* stupid, foolish; **~ment** *adv* stupidly.

stupidité *f* stupidity.

style *m* style; stylus.

stylet *m* stiletto.

styliste *mf* designer; stylist.

stylo *m* pen.

su *m* knowledge.

suave *adj* suave, smooth.

subalterne *mf* subordinate; * *adj* subordinate.

subconscient *m* subconscious; * *adj* subconscious.

subdiviser *vt* to subdivide.

subdivision *f* subdivision.

subir *vt* to sustain, support; to undergo, suffer.

subit *adj* sudden; **~ement** *adv* suddenly.

subjectif *adj* subjective.

subjectivement *adv* subjectively.

subjectivité *f* subjectivity.

subjonctif *m* subjunctive; * *adj* subjunctive.

subjuguer *vt* to subjugate; to captivate.

sublime *adj* sublime; * *m* sublime.

sublimer *vt* to sublimate.

subliminal *adj* subliminal.

submerger *vt* to submerge, flood; to engulf.

submersible *m* submersible; * *adj* submersible.

subordination *f* subordination.

subordonné *m* **-e** *f* subordinate; * *adj* subordinate.

subordonner *vt* to subordinate.

subreptice *adj* surreptitious; **~ment** *adv* surreptitiously.

subséquent *adj* subsequent.

subside *m* grant.

subsidiaire *adj* subsidiary.

subsistance *f* subsistence, maintenance, sustenance.

subsister *vi* to subsist; to live on.

substance *f* substance.

substantiel *adj* substantial; **~lement** *adv* substantially.

substantif *m* noun, substantive; * *adj* substantival, nominal.

substituer *vt* to substitute, replace.

substitut *m* substitute.

substitution *f* substitution.

subterfuge *m* subterfuge.

subtil *adj* subtle; **~ement** *adv* subtly.

subtiliser *vt* to steal, spirit away.

subtilité *f* subtlety.

subvenir *vi*: **~ à** to provide for.

subvention *f* grant, subsidy.

subventionner *vt* to subsidize.

subversif *adj* subversive.

suc *m* sap; juice.

succéder *vi*: **~ à** to succeed, follow; * **se ~** *vr* to succeed one another.

succès *m* success; hit.

successeur *m* successor.

successif *adj* successive.

succession f succession; inheritance, estate.
successivement adv successively.
succinct adj succinct; ~ement adv succinctly.
succomber vi to succumb, give way.
succulent adj succulent, delicious.
succursale f branch.
sucer vt to suck.
sucette f lollipop; dummy.
suçon m love bite.
sucre m sugar.
sucrer vt to sugar, sweeten.
sucrerie f sugar refinery.
sucrier m sugar bowl; * adj sugar; sugar-producing.
sud m south.
suer vi to sweat, perspire.
sueur f sweat.
suffire vi to suffice, be sufficient; **il suffit de** it is enough to, it only takes.
suffisamment adv sufficiently, enough.
suffisant adj sufficient, adequate.
suffoquer vi to choke, suffocate; * vt to choke, stifle.
suffrage m suffrage; vote; commendation, approval.
suggérer vt to suggest, put forward.
suggestion f suggestion.
suicidaire adj suicidal; * mf person with suicidal tendencies.
suicide m suicide.
suicider (se) vr to commit suicide.
suie f soot.
suif m tallow.
suintement m oozing; sweating.
suinter vi to ooze; to sweat.
suite f rest; sequel; continuation; series; connection; progress; **tout de** ~ at once; **deux fois de** ~ two times in a row; **et ainsi de** ~ and so on; **à la suite de** after, behind; **par la** ~ afterwards; **donner** ~ **à** to follow up.
suivant m -e f next one; attendant; * adj following, next; * prép according to; ~ **que** according to whether.
suivi adj steady, regular; widely adopted; * m follow-up.
suivre vt to follow; to attend, accompany; to exercise; ~ **son cours** to take its course; **à**

suivre to be continued; **se** ~ vr to follow each other; to be continuous.
sujet m subject, topic; ground; reason; * adj: **être** ~ **à** to be subject to, liable to.
sujétion f subjection; constraint.
sulfate m sulphate.
sulfater vt to apply copper sulphate.
sulfure m sulphur.
sulfureux adj sulphurous.
sulfurique adj sulphuric.
sultan m sultan, -e f sultana.
summum m climax, height.
super m super, four-star petrol; * adj (fam) ultra, super.
superbe adj superb, splendid; ~ment adv superbly.
supercarburant m high-octane petrol.
supercherie f trick, trickery.
superficie f area, surface.
superficiel adj superficial; ~lement adv superficially.
superflu adj superfluous.
supérieur adj upper; superior; higher, greater; ~ment adv exceptionally well.
supériorité f superiority.
superlatif m superlative; * adj superlative.
superposer vt to superpose, stack; to superimpose; **se** ~ vr to be superimposed.
superposition f superposing; superimposition.
supersonique adj supersonic.
superstitieux adj superstitious.
superstition f superstition.
superviser vt to supervise.
supplanter vt to supplant, oust.
suppléant m -e f substitute, understudy; * adj substitute.
supplément m supplement; extra charge.
supplémentaire adj supplementary, additional.
suppliant adj beseeching, entreating.
supplication f supplication; entreaty.
supplice m corporal punishment; torture.
supplier vt to beseech, entreat.
support m support, prop; stand.
supporter vt to support; to endure, bear.
supporter m supporter.
supposer vt to suppose; to assume; to imply.

supposition *f* supposition, surmise.

suppositoire *m* suppository.

suppression *f* suppression; deletion; cancellation.

supprimer *vt* to suppress; to cancel.

suppurer *vi* to suppurate.

suprématie *f* supremacy.

suprême *adj* supreme.

sur *prép* on; over, above; into; out of, from.

sûr *adj* sure, certain; secure; ~ **de soi** self-assured; **bien ~** of course; **à coup ~** for sure; **~ement** *adv* surely, certainly.

surabondance *f* overabundance.

suranné *adj* outmoded, outdated.

surcharge *f* overloading; excess; surcharge.

surcharger *vt* to overload.

surchauffe *f* overheating.

surcroît *m*: surplus, excess; **de ~** in addition.

surdité *f* deafness.

sureau *m* elder (tree).

surélever *vt* to raise, heighten.

surenchérir *vi* to outbid.

surestimer *vt* to overestimate; to overvalue.

sûreté *f* safety; guarantee, surety; **être en ~** to be safe.

surexcité *adj* overexcited.

surface *f* surface.

surgeler *vt* to deep-freeze.

surgir *vi* to rise, appear; to arise, crop up.

surhomme *m* superman.

surintendant *m* superintendent.

surlendemain *m* day after tomorrow.

surmenage *m* overwork; overtaxing.

surmener *vt* to overwork; **se ~** *vr* to overwork.

surmonter *vt* to surmount, overcome.

surnager *vi* to float.

surnaturel *adj* supernatural.

surnom *m* nickname.

surnommer *vt* to nickname.

surpasser *vt* to surpass, outdo.

surplomb *m* overhang; **en ~** overhanging.

surplomber *vt* to overhang.

surplus *m* surplus, remainder, excess.

surpopulation *f* overpopulation.

surprenant *adj* surprising, amazing.

surprendre *vt* to surprise, amaze.

surprise *f* surprise.

surproduction *f* overproduction.

surréalisme *m* surrealism.

surréaliste *mf* surrealist; * *adj* surrealistic.

sursaut *m* start, jump.

sursauter *vi* to start, jump.

sursis *m* reprieve; deferment.

sursitaire *adj* deferred; suspended.

surtaxe *f* surcharge.

surtout *adv* especially; above all.

surveillance *f* surveillance; supervision; inspection.

surveillant *m* **-e** *f* warder, guard.

surveiller *vt* to watch; to supervise; to inspect.

survenir *vi* to take place, occur.

survêtement *m* tracksuit.

survie *f* survival.

survivant *m* **-e** *f* survivor; * *adj* surviving.

survivre *vi* to survive.

survoler *vt* to fly over.

susceptible *adj* sensitive; susceptible; capable; likely; **être ~ de** to be liable to.

susciter *vt* to arouse, incite.

suspect *m* **-e** *f* suspect; * *adj* suspicious, suspect.

suspecter *vt* to suspect.

suspendre *vt* to hang up; to suspend, defer.

suspendu *adj* hanging; suspended.

suspens *m*: **en ~** in abeyance; shelved.

suspense *m* suspense.

suspension *f* suspension; deferment; adjournment.

suspicieux *adj* suspicious.

suspicion *f* suspicion.

susurrer *vt* to whisper.

suture *f* suture; **points de ~** stitches.

svelte *adj* svelte, slim.

SVP *abrév* de **s'il vous plaît** please.

syllabe *f* syllable.

sylvestre *adj* forest.

symbole *m* symbol.

symbolique *adj* symbolic; token; nominal; **~ment** *adv* symbolically.

symboliser *vt* to symbolize.

symbolisme *m* symbolism.

symétrie *f* symmetry.

symétrique *adj* symmetrical; **~ment** *adv* symmetrically.

sympa *adj invar* (*fam*) nice, friendly.
sympathie *f* liking; fellow feeling; sympathy.
sympathique *adj* likeable, nice; friendly.
sympathisant *m* **-e** *f* sympathizer; * *adj* sympathizing.
sympathiser *vi* to get on well with.
symphonie *f* symphony.
symphonique *adj* symphonic.
symptomatique *adj* symptomatic.
symptôme *m* symptom.
synagogue *f* synagogue.
synchronisation *f* synchronization.
synchroniser *vt* to synchronize.
syncope *f* blackout, syncope.
syncopé *adj* syncopated.
syndical *adj* trade-union.
syndicalisme *m* trade unionism.

syndicaliste *mf* trade unionist; * *adj* trade union.
syndicat *m* trade union; association.
syndiquer *vt* to unionize; **se ~** *vr* to form a trade union.
syndrome *m* syndrome.
synonyme *m* synonym; * *adj* synonymous.
syntaxe *f* syntax.
synthèse *f* synthesis.
synthétique *adj* synthetic.
synthétiser *vt* to synthesize.
synthétiseur *m* synthesizer.
syphilis *f* syphilis.
systématique *adj* systematic; **~ment** *adv* systematically.
système *m* system.

T

tabac *m* tobacco.
tabagisme *m* nicotine addiction.
tabatière *f* snuffbox; skylight.
table *f* table; **~ de nuit** bedside table; **~ ronde** round-table conference.
tableau *m* table; chart; timetable; scene; **~ de bord** dashboard.
tablette *f* bar; tablet; block.
tablier *m* apron; pinafore; overall.
tabou *m* taboo.
tabouret *m* stool.
tache *f* mark; stain; spot.
tâche *f* task, assignment; work.
taché *adj* stained, blemished.
tâcher *vi* to endeavour.
tacheté *adj* spotted; freckled.
tachycardie *f* tachycardia.
tacite *adj* tacit; **~ment** *adv* tacitly.
taciturne *adj* taciturn, silent.
tact *m* tact; **avoir du ~** to have tact, be tactful.
tactile *adj* tactile.
tactique *f* tactics; * *adj* tactical.
taffetas *m* taffeta.
tagliatelles *fpl* tagliatelli.
taillader *vt* to slash, gash.
taille *f* waist; height, stature, size; **de ~** considerable, sizeable; **être de ~ à** to be up to it.

taille-crayons *m* pencil sharpener.
tailler *vt* to cut; to carve; to sharpen; **se ~** *vr* (*fam*) to clear off, split.
tailleur *m* tailor; cutter, hewer.
taillis *m* copse, coppice.
taire *vt* to hush up; to conceal; **se ~** *vr* to be quiet; to fall silent.
talc *m* talc, talcum powder.
talent *m* talent, ability.
talentueux *adj* talented.
talisman *m* talisman.
talon *m* heel; end; pile.
talonner *vt* to follow closely; to hound.
talquer *vt* to put talcum powder on.
talus *m* embankment.
tambour *m* drum; barrel.
tambourin *m* tambourine.
tambouriner *vi* to drum; to beat, hammer.
tamis *m* sieve; riddle.
tamiser *vt* to sieve; to sift.
tampon *m* stopper, plug; tampon; buffer.
tamponner *vt* to mop up; to stamp.
tam-tam *m* tom-tom; row.
tandem *m* tandem; duo.
tandis *conj*: **~ que** while; whereas.
tangent *adj* tangent, tangential.
tangible *adj* tangible.

tango *m* tango.

tanguer *vi* to pitch (ship).

tanière *f* den, lair.

tank *m* tank.

tanné *adj* tanned; weathered.

tanner *vt* to tan, weather.

tanneur *m* tanner.

tant *adv* so much; ~ **que** as long as; ~ **soit peu** ever so slightly; ~ **mieux** so much the better; that's a good job; ~ **pis** too bad; ~ **bien que mal** as well as can be expected.

tante *f* aunt.

tantôt *adv* sometimes; this afternoon; shortly.

taon *m* horsefly, gadfly.

tapage *m* din, uproar, racket.

tapageur *adj* noisy, rowdy; showy.

tape *f* slap.

taper *vi* to hit, tap, stamp; to beat down; * *vt* to beat; to slap; to type.

tapioca *m* tapioca.

tapir (se) *vr* to crouch; to hide away.

tapir *m* tapir.

tapis *m* carpet; rug; cloth.

tapisser *vt* to wallpaper; to cover; to carpet.

tapisserie *f* tapestry; tapestry-making; **faire** ~ to be a wallflower.

tapoter *vt* to pat; to tap; to strum.

taquin *adj* teasing.

taquiner *vt* to tease; to plague.

tarauder *vt* to tap; to torment.

tard *adv* late.

tarder *vi* to delay, put off; to dally.

tardif *adj* late; tardy; slow; backward.

tardivement *adv* late; tardily.

tare *f* tare; defect, flaw.

taré *adj* tainted, corrupt; sickly.

tari *adj* dried up.

tarif *m* tariff; price-list.

tarir *vt* to dry up; to exhaust; **se** ~ *vr* to dry up.

tarot *m* tarot.

tartare *adj* Tartar.

tarte *f* tart, flan.

tartelette *f* tartlet, tart.

tartine *f* slice of buttered bread.

tartiner *vt* to spread with butter, jam, etc.

tartre *m* tartar; fur, scale.

tas *m* heap, pile; lot, set.

tasse *f* cup.

tassement *m* settling, sinking.

tasser *vt* to heap up; **se** ~ *vr* to sink; subside.

tata *f* auntie.

tâter *vt* to feel, try; **se** ~ *vr* to feel o.s.

tâtonnement *m* trial and error; experimentation.

tâtonner *vi* to feel one's way, grope along.

tatouage *m* tattooing; tattoo.

tatouer *vt* to tattoo.

taudis *m* hovel, slum.

taupe *f* mole.

taureau *m* bull.

tauromachie *f* bullfighting.

taux *m* rate; ratio; ~ **de change** exchange rate.

taverne *f* tavern.

taxation *f* taxation, taxing.

taxe *f* tax; duty; rate.

taxer *vt* to tax; to fix the price of.

taxi *m* taxi.

tchin-tchin! *interj* cheers!

te *pn* you, yourself.

technicien *m* **-ne** *f* technician.

technique *f* technique; * *adj* technical; **~ment** *adv* technically.

technocrate *m* technocrat.

technocratie *f* technocracy.

technologie *f* technology.

technologique *adj* technological.

téflon *m* teflon.

teigne *f* moth; ringworm.

teindre *vt* to dye.

teint *m* complexion, colouring.

teinte *f* tint, colour, shade.

teinter *vt* to tint; to stain.

teinture *f* dye; dyeing.

teinturerie *f* dyeing; dye-works; dry cleaner's.

teinturier *m* **-ère** *f* dyer; dry cleaner.

tel *adj* such; like, similar; ~ **quel** such as it is; **en tant que** ~ as such, in such a capacity; **il n'y a rien de** ~ there's nothing like…

télé *f* TV, telly.

télécarte *f* phonecard.

télécommande *f* remote control.

télécommunication *f* telecommunication.

télécopie *f* facsimile transmission, fax.

télécopieur *m* fax machine.

télédiffusion *f* television broadcasting.

téléphérique *m* cableway; cable-car.

télégramme *m* telegram; cable.

télégraphier *vt* to telegraph, cable.

téléguider *vt* to radio-control.

télématique *f* telematics.

téléobjectif *m* telephoto lens.

télépathie *f* telepathy.

téléphone *m* telephone.

téléphoner *vi* to telephone.

téléphonique *adj* telephone; telephonic.

télescope *m* telescope.

télescopique *adj* telescopic.

télésiège *m* chairlift.

téléski *m* lift, ski tow.

téléspectateur *m* **-trice** *f* television viewer.

téléviseur *m* television set.

télévision *f* television.

télex *m* telex.

tellement *adv* so, so much; ~ **de** so many, so much.

téméraire *adj* rash, reckless; ~**ment** *adv* rashly; recklessly.

témérité *f* rashness; recklessness.

témoignage *m* testimony; evidence; certificate.

témoigner *vi* to testify.

témoin *m* witness; evidence; proof.

tempérament *m* constitution; temperament; character.

tempérance *f* temperance.

température *f* temperature.

tempéré *adj* temperate; tempered.

tempérer *vt* to temper; to assuage, soothe.

tempête *f* tempest.

temple *m* temple.

tempo *m* tempo, pace.

temporaire *adj* temporary; ~**ment** *adv* temporarily.

temporel *adj* worldly, temporal.

temporiser *vi* to temporize, delay.

temps *m* time; while; tense; beat; weather; **de** ~ **en** ~ from time to time; **entre** ~ meanwhile.

tenace *adj* tenacious, stubborn, persistent.

ténacité *f* tenacity; stubbornness.

tenaille *f* pincers; tongs.

tenailler *vt* to torture; to rack.

tendance *f* tendency; leaning; trend.

tendancieux *adj* tendentious.

tendinite *f* tendinitis.

tendon *m* tendon, sinew.

tendre *adj* tender, soft; delicate; ~**ment** *adv* tenderly, affectionately.

tendresse *f* tenderness; fondness.

tendu *adj* tight; stretched; concentrated; delicate, fraught.

ténèbres *fpl* darkness, gloom.

ténébreux *adj* dark, gloomy.

teneur *f* terms; content; grade.

tenir *vt* to hold, keep; to stock; to run; * *vi* to hold, stay in place; ~ **à** to value, care about; ~ **de** to take after; **se** ~ *vr* to hold on to; to behave; **s'en** ~ **à** to limit o.s. to, stick to.

tennis *m* tennis; ~ **de table** table tennis.

ténor *m* tenor; leading light.

tentacule *m* tentacle.

tentant *adj* tempting, inviting.

tentation *f* temptation.

tentative *f* attempt, bid.

tente *f* tent.

tenter *vt* to tempt.

tenture *f* hanging; curtain.

tenue *f* holding; session; deportment, good behaviour; dress, appearance.

tergal *m* terylene.

tergiverser *vi* to procrastinate, beat about the bush.

terme *m* term; termination, end; word, expression; **au** ~ **de** at the end of.

terminaison *f* ending.

terminal *adj* terminal; * *m* terminal.

terminer *vt* to terminate; to finish off; **se** ~ *vr* to terminate; to come to an end.

terminologie *f* terminology.

termite *m* termite.

terne *adj* colourless; lustreless, drab; spiritless.

ternir *vt* to tarnish, dull.

terrain *m* ground, soil, earth; plot; position; site; field.

terrasse *f* terrace.

terrasser *vt* to floor, knock down; to strike down, overcome.

terre *f* earth; world; ground; land; **mettre pied à** ~ to land, alight.

terre à terre *adj* down to earth, commonplace.

terreau *m* compost.

terre-plein *m* (*mil*) terreplein; platform; central reservation.

terrer (se) *vr* to crouch down; to lie low, go to ground.

terrestre *adj* land; terrestrial.

terreur *f* terror, dread.

terreux *adj* earthy; dirty; ashen.

terrible *adj* terrible, dreadful; terrific, great; ~**ment** *adv* terribly.

terrien *m* countryman; earthling; **-ne** *f* countrywoman; earthling.

terrier *m* burrow; earth; terrier.

terrifiant *adj* terrifying, fearsome.

terrifier *vt* to terrify.

terrine *f* earthenware dish, terrine.

territoire *m* territory, area.

territorial *adj* land, territorial.

terroir *m* land.

terroriser *vt* to terrorize.

terrorisme *m* terrorism.

terroriste *mf* terrorist; * *adj* terrorist.

tertiaire *adj* tertiary.

test *m* test.

testament *m* will, testament.

tester *vt* to test; to make out one's will.

testicule *m* testicle, testis.

tétanos *m* tetanus; lockjaw.

tétard *m* tadpole.

tête *f* head; face; front; top; sense, judgment; **tenir** ~ to stand up to sb; **faire la** ~ to pout, sulk; ~ **de turc** whipping boy; ~ **de mort** skull and crossbones; **être en** ~ to head.

tête à tête *m* private conversation; **en** ~ in the lead.

tétée *f* feeding; nursing.

téter *vt* to suck.

tétine *f* teat; udder; dummy.

téton *m* breast.

têtu *adj* headstrong, stubborn.

texte *m* text.

textile *adj* textile.

textuel *adj* textual, literal, exact; ~**lement** *adv* literally; word for word.

texture *f* texture.

thé *m* tea.

théâtral *adj* theatrical, dramatic.

théâtre *m* theatre; drama.

théière *f* teapot.

thématique *adj* thematic.

thème *m* theme.

théologie *f* theology.

théorème *m* theorem.

théoricien *m* **-ne** *f* theoretician, theorist.

théorie *f* theory.

théorique *adj* theoretical; ~**ment** *adv* theoretically.

thérapeute *mf* therapist.

thérapie *f* therapy.

thermal *adj* thermal; hydropathic.

thermique *adj* thermal; thermic.

thermomètre *m* thermometer.

thermos *f/m* thermos.

thermostat *m* thermostat.

thésaurus *m* thesaurus.

thèse *f* thesis.

thon *m* tuna.

thoracique *adj* thoracic; **cage** ~ ribcage.

thorax *m* thorax.

thrombose *f* thrombosis.

thym *m* thyme.

thyroïde *f* thyroid.

tibia *m* tibia.

tic *m* twitch, tic; mannerism.

ticket *m* ticket.

tiède *adj* lukewarm, tepid.

tien *pn*, *f* **tienne**: **le** ~, **la tienne**, **les** ~**s**, **les tiennes** yours, your own.

tiers *adj* third; ~~**monde** Third World; * *m* third; third party.

tige *f* stem, stalk.

tigre *m* tiger.

tigresse *f* tigress.

tilleul *m* lime, linden.

timbale *f* kettledrum.

timbre *m* stamp; postmark; bell; tone, timbre.

timbré *adj* stamped; resonant.

timbrer *vt* to stamp; to postmark.

timide *adj* timid, shy; ~**ment** *adv* timidly.

timidité *f* timidity, shyness.

timonier *m* (*mar*) helmsman.

tintamarre *m* hubbub, uproar.

tintement *m* ringing; chiming; toll.

tinter *vi* to ring, toll; to chime.

tique *f* tick.

tiquer *vi* to wince.

tir *m* shooting, firing, fire; shot; ~ **à l'arc** archery.

tirade *f* tirade; monologue.

tirage *m* drawing, drawing off; printing; circulation; friction.

tiraillement *m* tugging; pulling.

tirailler *vt* to tug; to plague; to pester.

tire-bouchon *m* corkscrew.

tire-fesses *m* ski tow.

tirelire *f* moneybox.

tirer *vt* to pull; to draw; to extract; **se ~** *vr* (*fam*) to clear off; **bien s'en ~** to make a good job of sth.

tiret *m* dash; hyphen.

tireur *m* **-euse** *f* gunner, sharpshooter; printer; drawer (cheque).

tiroir *m* drawer.

tison *m* brand.

tisonnier *m* poker.

tissage *m* weaving.

tisser *vt* to weave.

tissu *m* texture, fabric; tissue.

titan *m* titan.

titane *m* titanium.

titanesque *adj* titanic.

titre *m* title; heading; denomination; claim, right; deed; **à ~ de** by right of; **à juste ~** deservedly, justly; **en ~** titular, acknowledged.

tituber *vi* to stagger.

titulaire *mf* incumbent, holder; * *adj* titular; entitled.

toast *m* slice of toast; toast; **porter un ~** to drink a toast.

toboggan *m* toboggan.

toc *m* tap, knock; sham jewellery etc.; **en ~** imitation, fake.

toi *pn* you; **~-même** yourself; **c'est à ~** it's your's; it's your turn.

toile *f* cloth; canvas; sheet

toilette *f* cleaning, grooming; washstand; **faire sa ~** to wash o.s.; **cabinet de ~** bathroom.

toiser *vt* to survey; to evaluate.

toison *f* fleece.

toit *m* roof; home.

toiture *f* roof, roofing.

tôle *f* sheet metal.

tolérable *adj* tolerable, bearable.

tolérance *f* tolerance.

tolérant *adj* tolerant.

tolérer *vt* to tolerate; to put up with.

tomate *f* tomato.

tombe *f* tomb; grave.

tombeau *m* tomb.

tomber *vi* to fall; to sink; to decay; **laisser ~** to drop; **~ malade** to fall sick; **~ amoureux** to fall in love; **~ sur** to come across; **bien/mal ~** to be lucky/unlucky.

tombola *f* tombola.

tome *m* book; volume.

ton *adj*, *f* **ta**, *pl* **tes** your; * *m* tone; pitch; shade.

tonalité *f* tonality; key.

tondeuse *f* clippers, shears; mower.

tondre *vt* to shear, clip; mow.

tonifiant *m* tonic; * *adj* bracing; invigorating.

tonifier *vt* to tone up; to invigorate.

tonique *adj* tonic; fortifying; invigorating *m* tonic.

tonitruant *adj* thundering.

tonnage *m* tonnage; displacement.

tonne *f* ton.

tonneau *m* barrel, cask.

tonnelle *f* bower, arbour.

tonnerre *m* thunder.

tonton *m* (*fam*) uncle.

tonus *m* tone; energy.

top *m* pip, stroke.

topaze *f* topaz.

topographie *f* topography.

toquade *f* infatuation; fad, craze.

toque *f* fur hat; cap.

toquer *vi* to tap, rap.

torche *f* torch.

torcher *vt* to wipe, mop up; **se ~** *vr* to wipe o.s.

torchon *m* cloth; duster.

tordre *vt* to twist, contort; **se ~** *vr* to bend, twist; to sprain.

tordu *adj* twisted, crooked, bent.

tornade *f* tornado.

torpeur *f* torpor.

torpille *f* torpedo.

torpiller *vt* to torpedo.

torréfaction *f* roasting; toasting.

torrent *m* torrent.

torrentiel *adj* torrential.

torride *adj* torrid; scorching.

torsade *f* twist; cable moulding.

torse *m* chest; torso.

torsion *f* twisting; torsion.

tort *m* fault; wrong; prejudice; **avoir ~** to be wrong; **en ~** in the wrong; **à ~ ou à raison** wrongly or rightly; **faire du ~** to harm; **à ~ et à travers** wildly; here, there and everywhere.

torticolis *m* stiff neck; torticollis.

tortiller *vt* to twist; **se ~** *vr* to wriggle; to squirm.

tortionnaire *mf* torturer; * *adj* pertaining to torture.

tortue *f* tortoise.

tortueux *adj* tortuous, winding, meandering.

torture *f* torture.

torturer *vt* to torture.

tôt *adv* early; soon, quickly; **au plus ~** as soon as possible; **plus ~** sooner.

total *adj* total; absolute; **~ement** *adv* totally.

totaliser *vt* to totalize, add up.

totalitaire *adj* totalitarian.

totalitarisme *m* totalitarianism.

totalité *f* totality; whole.

totem *m* totem.

touchant *adj* touching, moving.

touche *f* touch; trial; stroke; key.

toucher *vt* to touch; to feel; * *m* touch, feeling.

touffe *f* tuft, clump.

touffu *adj* bushy, thick.

toujours *adv* always; still; all the same; **pour ~** for ever; **~ est-il que** the fact remains that.

toupet *m* quiff, tuft; cheek.

toupie *f* spinning top.

tour *f* tower; * *m* turn, round; circuit; tour; trick; **faire un ~** to take a stroll; **faire le tour de** to go around; **fermer à double ~** to double-lock; **jouer un ~** to play a trick; **~ à ~** by turns.

tourbe *f* peat.

tourbillon *m* whirlwind, whirlpool.

tourbillonner *vi* to whirl, eddy.

tourisme *m* tourism.

touriste *mf* tourist.

touristique *adj* tourist.

tourment *m* torment, agony.

tourmente *f* storm, tempest.

tourmenter *vt* to rack, torment; **se ~** *vr* to fret; to worry.

tournage *m* turning; (*cin*) shooting.

tournant *m* bend; turning point; * *adj* revolving, swivelling; winding.

tournedos *m* fillet steak.

tournée *f* tour; round.

tourner *vt* to turn; to round; * *vi* to turn; to work; to change; **se ~** *vr* to turn round; to change.

tournesol *m* sunflower.

tourneur *m* turner.

tournevis *m* screwdriver.

tourniquet *m* tourniquet; turnstile.

tournis *m* (*vet*) sturdy, staggers; **avoir le ~** to feel giddy.

tournoi *m* tournament.

tournoyer *vi* to whirl, swirl.

tournure *f* turn; turn of phrase.

tourte *f* pie.

tourerelle *f* turtledove.

tourtière *f* pie tin.

Toussaint *f* All Saints' Day.

tousser *vi* to cough.

tout *adj, pl* **tous, toutes** all; whole; every; **~ le monde** everybody; * *pn* everything; all; **c'est ~** that is all; * *m* whole, only thing; **pas du ~** not at all; **du ~ au ~** completely; * *adv* entirely, quite; **~ droit** straight on; **~ à fait** completely, quite; **~ de suite** immediately.

toutefois *adv* however.

tout-puissant *adj* all-powerful.

toux *f* cough.

toxicomane *mf* drug addict; * *adj* drug addicted.

toxicomanie *f* drug addiction.

toxine *f* toxin.

toxique *adj* toxic.

trac *m* nerves, stage fright.

tracas *m* bustle, turmoil; worry.

tracasser *vt* to worry; to harass.

trace *f* track, impression; outline, sketch; vestige, trace.

tracé *m* layout, plan.

tracer *vt* to draw, trace; to open up.

trachée *f* trachea, windpipe.

tract *m* leaflet, tract.

tractation *f* transaction; bargaining.

tracteur *m* tractor.

traction *f* traction; pulling.

tradition *f* tradition.

traditionaliste *mf* traditionalist; * *adj* traditionalist.

traditionnel *adj* traditional; usual; **~lement** *adv* traditionally.

traducteur *m* **-trice** *f* translator.

traduction *f* translation.

traduire *vt* to translate.

trafic *m* traffic; trading; dealings.

trafiquant *m* **-e** *f* trafficker.

trafiquer *vi* to fiddle, tamper with.

tragédie *f* tragedy.

tragédien *m* **-ne** *f* tragedian, tragic actor.

tragique *adj* tragic; **~ment** *adv* tragically.

trahir *vt* to betray.

trahison *f* betrayal, treason.

train *m* train; pace, rate; **être en ~ de** to be in the act of doing sth.

traînasser *vi* to dawdle; to loiter.

traîne *f* dragging; train; **être à la ~** to be in tow.

traîneau *m* sleigh, sledge.

traînée *f* trail, track; drag.

traîner *vi* to lag, dawdle; to drag on; * *vt* to drag, pull; to protract; **se ~** *vr* to drag o.s.; to crawl along.

train-train *m* humdrum routine.

traire *vt* to milk.

trait *m* trait, feature; deed; relation; **avoir ~ à** to have reference; **~ d'union** hyphen, connecting link.

traite *f* trade; draft; bill; milking.

traité *m* treaty; treatise, tract.

traitement *m* treatment; salary; processing.

traiter *vt* to treat; to process; * *vi* to treat, negotiate.

traiteur *m* caterer; trader.

traître *m* traitor **-sse** *f* traitress.

traîtrise *f* treachery, treacherousness.

trajectoire *f* trajectory.

trajet *m* distance; journey; course, path.

trame *f* framework; web.

tramer *vt* to plot; to weave.

trampoline *m* trampoline.

tramway *m* tram, tramway.

tranchant *adj* sharp, cutting.

tranche *f* slice; edge; section.

tranchée *f* trench; cutting.

trancher *vt* to cut, sever; to conclude; to settle; * *vi* to cut; to resolve; to stand out.

tranquille *adj* quiet, tranquil; **~ment** *adv* quietly, tranquilly.

tranquillisant *m* tranquillizer; * *adj* soothing, tranquillizing.

tranquilliser *vt* to reassure.

tranquillité *f* tranquillity.

transaction *f* transaction, arrangement.

transatlantique *m* transatlantic liner; * *adj* transatlantic.

transcendant *adj* transcendent; transcendental.

transcender *vt* to transcend.

transcription *f* transcription; copy.

transcrire *vt* to transcribe; copy out.

transe *f* trance.

transept *m* transept.

tranférer *vt* to transfer.

transfert *m* transfer; conveyance.

transfiguration *f* transfiguration.

transfigurer *vt* to transfigure.

transformateur *m* transformer.

transformation *f* transformation.

transformer *vt* to transform, change; **se ~** *vr* to be transformed; to change.

transfuge *mf* defector.

transfuser *vt* to transfuse.

transfusion *f* transfusion.

transgresser *vt* to transgress, infringe.

transgression *f* transgression, infringement.

transi *adj* numb, paralysed.

transiger *vi* to compromise, come to terms.

transistor *m* transistor.

transit *m* transit.

transiter *vi* to pass in transit.

transitif *adj* transitive.

transition *f* transition.

transitoire *adj* transitory.

translucide *adj* translucent.

transmettre *vt* to transmit; to pass on, hand down.

transmissible *adj* transmissible.

transmission *f* transmission; passing on; handing down.

transmuter *vt* to transmute.

transparaître *vi* to show through.

transparence *f* transparency.

transparent *adj* transparent.

transpercer *vt* to pierce; to penetrate.

transpiration *f* transpiration; perspiration.

transpirer *vi* to perspire; to come to light.

transplanter *vt* to transplant.

transport *m* carrying; transport; conveyance; transfer.

transportable *adj* transportable.

transporter *vt* to carry; to transport.

transporteur *m* haulier; carrier.

transposer *vt* to transpose.

transposition *f* transposition.

transsexuel *adj* transsexual.

transvaser *vt* to decant.

transversal *adj* transverse; **~ement** *adv* crosswise; transversely.

transvider *vt* to pour into another container.

trapèze *m* trapeze.

trapéziste *mf* trapeze artist.

trappe *f* trap door.

trappeur *m* trapper.

trapu *adj* squat; thickset.

traquer *vt* to track; to hunt down.

traumatisant *adj* traumatizing.

traumatiser *vt* to traumatize.

traumatisme *m* traumatism.

travail *m* work; job, occupation; labour; *pl* **travaux** work, labour.

travailler *vi* to work; to endeavour; * *vt* to work, shape; to cultivate; to fatigue.

travailleur *m* **-euse** *f* worker; * *adj* diligent; hard-working.

travers *m* breadth; irregularity; fault; **à ~** through, across; **de ~** obliquely, askew; **en ~** across, crosswise.

traversée *f* crossing, going through; traverse.

traverser *vt* to cross, traverse.

traversin *m* bolster.

travesti *m* drag artist; transvestite; * *adj* disguised.

trébucher *vi* to stumble, trip up.

trèfle *m* clover.

tréfonds *m* subsoil, bottom.

treille *f* climbing vine.

treillis *m* trellis; wire mesh.

treize *adj, m* thirteen.

treizième *adj, mf* thirteenth; **~ment** *adv* in thirteenth place.

tréma *m* dieresis.

tremblant *adj* trembling, shaking.

tremblement *m* trembling; shiver; vibration; **~ de terre** earthquake.

trembler *vi* to tremble, shake.

trembloter *vi* to tremble slightly, flicker.

trémousser (se) *vr* to wriggle.

tremper *vt* to soak; to dip; * *vi* to soak; to take part in.

tremplin *m* springboard; ski-jump.

trentaine *f* about thirty.

trente *adj, m* thirty.

trentième *adj, mf* thirtieth.

trépasser *vi* to pass away.

trépidant *adj* pulsating, quivering.

trépied *m* tripod.

trépigner *vi* to stamp one's feet.

très *adv* very; most; very much.

trésor *m* treasure.

trésorerie *f* treasury.

trésorier *m* **-ière** *f* treasurer.

tressaillir *vi* to thrill; to shudder.

tressauter *vi* to start, jump.

tresse *f* plait, braid.

tresser *vt* to plait, braid.

tréteau *m* trestle.

treuil *m* winch.

trêve *f* truce; respite, rest.

tri *m* sorting out; selection; grading.

triage *m* sorting out.

triangle *m* triangle.

triangulaire *adj* triangular.

triathlon *m* triathlon.

tribal *adj* tribal.

tribord *m* starboard.

tribu *f* tribe.

tribunal *m* court, tribunal.

tribune *f* gallery, stand; rostrum.

tribut *m* tribute.

tributaire *adj* dependent, tributary.

tricher *vi* to cheat.

tricheur *m* **-euse** *f* cheater.

trichloréthylène *m* trichlorethylene.

tricolore *adj* three-coloured, tricolour.

tricot *m* jumper; knitting.

tricoter *vt* to knit.

tridimensionnel *adj* three-dimensional.

triennal *adj* triennial; three-yearly.

trier *vt* to sort out; to pick over.

trifouiller *vi* (*fam*) to rummage about; * *vt* to rummage about in.

trigonométrie *f* trigonometry.

trilingue *adj* trilingual.

trilogie *f* trilogy.

trimer *vi* to slave away.

trimestre *m* quarter; term.

trimestriel *adj* quarterly; three-monthly.

tringle *f* rod.

trinité *f* trinity.

trinquer *vi* to toast; to booze.

trio *m* trio.

triomphal *adj* triumphal; **~ement** *adv* triumphantly.

triomphant *adj* triumphant.

triomphe *m* triumph, victory.

triompher *vi* to triumph.

triparti, **tripartite** *adj* tripartite.

tripe *f* tripe; guts.

triple *adj* triple, treble.

tripler *vi* to triple, increase threefold; * *vt* to triple, treble.

tripoter *vt* to play with, speculate with.

trique *f* cudgel.

triste *adj* sad, melancholy; **~ment** *adv* sadly.

tristesse *f* sadness; melancholy.

triton *m* triton; tritone.

triturer *vt* to grind up, triturate.

trivial *adj* mundane, trivial; coarse, crude.

trivialité *f* triviality; crudeness.

troc *m* exchange; barter.

troglodyte *m* cave dweller, troglodyte.

trognon *m* core; stalk.

trois *adj*, *m* three.

troisième *adj*, *mf* third; **~ment** *adv* thirdly.

trombe *f*: **~ d'eau** cloudburst, downpour; **entrer/sortir en ~** to dash in/out.

trombone *m* trombone.

trompe *f* trumpet; trunk, snout.

trompe-l'œil *m invar* trompe-l'oeil.

tromper *vt* to deceive, trick; **se ~** *vr* to be mistaken.

tromperie *f* deception, deceit.

trompette *f* trumpet.

trompettiste *mf* trumpet player.

trompeur *adj* deceitful; deceptive.

tronc *m* trunk, shaft.

tronçon *m* section, part.

tronçonner *vt* to cut up, cut into sections.

tronçonneuse *f* chain saw.

trône *m* throne.

trôner *vi* to sit on the throne.

tronquer *vt* to truncate, curtail.

trop *adv* too; too much, unduly; *m* **~** too much, too many.

trophée *m* trophy.

tropical *adj* tropical.

tropique *m* tropic.

trop-plein *m* overflow; excess.

troquer *vt* to barter, swap.

trot *m* trot.

trotter *vi* to trot; to run about; to toddle.

trottiner *vi* to jog along; to trot along.

trottinette *f* scooter.

trottoir *m* pavement.

trou *m* hole; gap; cavity.

troublant *adj* disturbing, disquieting.

trouble *adj* unclear; murky, suspicious; * *m* disturbance, confusion; disorder.

trouble-fête *mf* spoilsport, killjoy.

troubler *vt* to disturb, disconcert; to cloud, darken; **se ~** *vr* to become cloudy; to become flustered.

trouer *vt* to make a hole in; to pierce.

trouille *f*: **avoir la ~** to have the wind up.

troupe *f* troupe; troop, band.

troupeau *m* herd, drove.

trousse *f* case, kit; wallet.

trousseau *m* trousseau; outfit.

trouvaille *f* windfall; inspired idea.

trouver *vt* to find, detect; to think; **se ~** *vr* to find o.s.; to be located; **il se trouve que** it happens that.

truand *m* (*fam*) gangster; tramp.

truc *m* (*fam*) trick; gadget, thingummy.

truculent *adj* truculent; colourful, vivid.

truelle *f* trowel.

truffe *f* truffle.

truie *f* sow.

truite *f* trout.

truquage *m* rigging, fixing; fiddling.

truquer *vt* to rig, fix; to fiddle.

tsar *m* tsar.
tu *pn* you.
tuant *adj* exhausting; exasperating.
tuba *m* tuba, snorkel.
tube *m* tube, pipe; duct.
tuberculose *f* tuberculosis.
tuer *vt* to kill; **se ~** *vr* to be killed; to kill o.s.
tuerie *f* slaughter.
tueur *m* **-euse** *f* killer.
tuile *f* tile.
tulipe *f* tulip.
tulle *m* tulle.
tuméfié *adj* puffed-up, swollen.
tumeur *f* tumour.
tumulte *m* tumult, commotion.
tumultueux *adj* tumultuous, stormy.
tungstène *m* tungsten.
tunique *f* tunic; smock.
tunnel *m* tunnel.
turban *m* turban.
turbine *f* turbine.

turbo *m* turbo.
turbulence *f* turbulence; excitement.
turbulent *adj* turbulent.
turpitude *f* turpitude, baseness.
tutelle *f* guardianship, supervision.
tuteur *m* **-trice** *f* guardian; * *m* stake, prop.
tutoyer *vt* to address sb as '*tu*'.
tuyau *m* pipe.
tuyauterie *f* piping.
TVA (taxe à la valeur ajoutée) *f* VAT.
tympan *m* eardrum, tympanum.
type *m* type; model; sample; bloke, chap.
typé *adj* typical.
typhoïde *f* typhoid; * *adj* typhoid.
typhon *m* typhoon.
typhus *m* typhus.
typique *adj* typical; **~ment** *adv* typically.
tyran *m* tyrant.
tyrannie *f* tyranny.
tyrannique *adj* tyrannical.
tyranniser *vt* to tyrannize.

U

ulcère *m* ulcer.
ulcérer *vt* to sicken; to embitter.
ultérieur *adj* later, subsequent; **~ement** *adv* later, subsequently.
ultimatum *m* ultimatum.
ultime *adj* ultimate, final.
ultra-violet *m* ultraviolet ray; * *adj* ultraviolet.
un, une *art* a, an; (number) one; **l'~ l'autre, les ~s les autres** one another.
unanime *adj* unanimous; **~ment** *adv* unanimously.
uni *adj* plain, self-coloured; close; smooth; **~ment** *adv* plainly, smoothly.
unification *f* unification; standardization.
unifier *vt* to unify; to standardize.
uniforme *adj* uniform, regular; * *m* uniform.
uniformément *adv* uniformly, regularly.
uniformité *f* uniformity; regularity.
unilatéral *adj* unilateral.
union *f* union; combination, blending.
unique *adj* only, single; unique; **~ment** *adv* only, solely, exclusively; merely.

unir *vt* to unite; to join; to combine; **s'~** *vr* to unite; to be joined in marriage.
unisson *m* unison; **à l'~** in unison.
unitaire *adj* unitary, unit.
unité *f* unity; unit.
univers *m* universe; world.
universalité *f* universality.
universel *adj* universal; all-purpose; **~lement** *adv* universally.
universitaire *adj* university; * *mf* academic.
université *f* university.
uranium *m* uranium.
urbain *adj* urban, city.
urbanisation *f* urbanization.
urbaniser *vt* to urbanize.
urbanisme *m* town planning.
urbaniste *mf* town planner.
urée *f* urea.
urgence *f* urgency; emergency.
urgent *adj* urgent.
urinaire *adj* urinary.
urine *f* urine.

uriner *vi* to urinate.

urne *f* ballot box; urn.

urticaire *f* hives, urticaria.

usage *m* use; custom; usage; practice; wear; **faire ~ de** to exercise; to make use of.

usagé *adj* worn, old.

usager *m* **-ère** *f* user.

usé *adj* worn; threadbare; banal, trite.

user *vt* to make use of, enjoy; to wear out; **~ de** to exercise; to employ; **s'~** *vr* to wear out.

usine *f* factory.

usiner *vt* to machine; to manufacture.

usité *adj* in common use, common.

ustensile *m* implement; utensil.

usuel *adj* ordinary; everyday; **~lement** *adv* ordinarily.

usufruit *m* (*jur*) usufruct.

usure *f* usury.

usurier *m* **-ière** *f* usurer.

usurper *vt* to usurp.

utérus *m* womb, uterus.

utile *adj* useful; **~ment** *adv* usefully.

utilisateur *m*, **-trice** *f* user.

utilisation *f* use, utilization.

utiliser *vt* to use, utilize; to make use of.

utilitaire *adj* utilitarian.

utilité *f* usefulness; use; profit.

utopie *f* utopia.

utopique *adj* utopian.

V

vacance *f* vacancy; **~s** holiday, vacation.

vacancier *m* **-ière** *f* holidaymaker.

vacant *adj* vacant, unoccupied.

vacarme *m* racket, row.

vaccin *m* vaccine.

vaccination *f* vaccination.

vacciner *vt* to vaccinate.

vache *f* cow; cowhide.

vachement *adv* (*fam*) damned, bloody.

vacher *m* **-ère** *f* cowherd.

vacherie *f* (*fam*) rottenness, meanness; nasty remark/trick.

vaciller *vi* to sway, totter; to falter.

va-et-vient *m invar* comings and goings; to and fro.

vagabond *m* **-e** *f* tramp, vagabond.

vagabondage *m* wandering, roaming; (*jur*) vagrancy.

vagabonder *vi* to wander, roam.

vagin *f* vagina.

vaginal *adj* vaginal.

vague *adj* vague, hazy, indistinct; **~ment** *adv* vaguely; * *m* vagueness; * *f* wave.

vaguer *vi* to wander, roam.

vaillamment *adv* bravely, courageously.

vaillant *adj* brave, courageous.

vain *adj* vain; empty, hollow; shallow; **en ~** in vain; **~ement** *adv* vainly.

vaincre *vt* to defeat, overcome.

vaincu *adj* defeated, beaten.

vainqueur *m* conqueror, victor.

vaisseau *m* vessel; ship.

vaisselle *f* crockery; dishes; **faire la ~** to do the washing up.

valable *adj* valid, legitimate; worthwhile.

valet *m* valet; servant.

valeur *f* value, worth; security, share; meaning.

valide *adj* able, able-bodied; **~ment** *adv* validly.

valider *vt* to validate.

validité *f* validity.

valise *f* suitcase.

vallée *f* valley.

vallon *m* vale, dale.

vallonné *adj* undulating, hilly.

valoir *vt* to be worth; to be valid; **il vaut mieux** it is better to; **~ la peine** to be worth the trouble.

valoriser *vt* to valorize.

valse *f* waltz.

valser *vi* to waltz.

valve *f* valve.

vampire *m* vampire.

vandale *mf* vandal.

vandalisme *m* vandalism.

vanille f vanilla.

vanité f vanity, conceit.

vaniteux adj vain, conceited.

vanne f gate, sluice.

vannerie f basketry; wickerwork.

vantard adj boastful, bragging.

vantardise f boastfulness; boast.

vanter vt to praise, vaunt; **se ~** vr to boast, brag.

vapeur f haze, vapour.

vaporeux adj filmy, vaporous.

vaporisateur m spray, atomizer.

vaporiser vt to spray; to vaporize.

varappe f rock-climbing.

variable adj variable, changeable.

variante f variant; variation.

variation f variation, change.

varice f varicose vein.

varicelle f chickenpox.

varié adj varied; variegated; various.

varier vi to vary, change; * vt to vary.

variété f variety, diversity.

variole f smallpox.

vasculaire adj vascular.

vase m vase, bowl; * f silt, mud.

vaseline f vaseline.

vaseux adj woolly, muddled; muddy, silty.

vasistas m fanlight.

vaste adj vast, huge.

vaudeville m vaudeville.

vaudou m voodoo.

vaurien m **-ne** f good-for-nothing.

vautour m vulture.

vautrer (se) vr to wallow in.

veau m calf; veal.

vecteur m vector.

vécu adj real, true-life; lived; * m real-life.

vedette f star; (mar) launch.

végétal adj vegetable.

végétarien m **-ne** f vegetarian; * adj vegetarian.

végétatif adj vegetative.

végétation f vegetation.

végéter vi to vegetate; to stagnate.

véhémence f vehemence.

véhément adj vehement.

véhicule m vehicle.

veille f wakefulness; watch; eve.

veillée f evening; evening meeting.

veiller vi to stay up, sit up.

veilleur m watchman.

veilleuse f night light; sidelight.

veinard m **-e** f lucky person; * adj lucky, jammy.

veine f vein, seam; inspiration; luck.

vêler vi to calve.

velléité f vague desire, vague impulse.

vélo m bike.

vélodrome m velodrome.

vélomoteur m moped.

velours m velvet.

velouté adj velvety, downy.

velu adj hairy.

vénal adj venal, mercenary.

vendange f wine harvest.

vendanger vt to harvest grapes from; * vi to harvest the grapes.

vendangeur m **-euse** f grape-picker.

vendetta f vendetta.

vendeur m **-euse** f seller, salesperson.

vendre vt to sell.

vendredi m Friday.

vénéneux adj poisonous.

vénérable adj venerable.

vénération f veneration.

vénérer vt to venerate.

vénérien adj venereal.

vengeance f vengeance, revenge.

venger vt to avenge; **se ~** vr to avenge o.s.

venimeux adj venomous, poisonous; vicious.

venin m venom; poison.

venir vi to come; to happen; to grow; **~ de** to come from; to derive from; **~ au monde** to be born.

vent m wind; breath; emptiness.

vente f sale; selling; auction; **en ~** for sale.

ventilateur m ventilator, fan.

ventiler vt to ventilate; to divide up.

ventouse f sucker; suction disc.

ventre m stomach, belly; womb.

ventricule m ventricle.

ventriloque mf ventriloquist; * adj ventriloquial.

venue f coming.

ver m worm; grub; **~ de terre** earthworm.

véracité f veracity; truthfulness.

véranda *f* veranda.

verbal *adj* verbal; **~ement** *adv* verbally.

verbe *m* verb; language, word.

verbiage *m* verbiage.

verdeur *f* vigour, vitality.

verdict *m* verdict.

verdir *vi* to go green; * *vt* to turn green.

verdure *f* greenery, verdure.

verge *f* stick, cane.

verger *m* orchard.

verglas *m* black ice.

véridique *adj* truthful, veracious; **~ment** *adv* truthfully.

vérification *f* check; verification.

vérifier *vt* to verify, check; to audit.

véritable *adj* real, genuine; **~ment** *adv* really, genuinely.

vérité *f* truth; truthfulness, sincerity; **en ~** really, actually.

vermeil *adj* vermilion, ruby, cherry; * *m* vermeil.

vermicelle *m* vermicelli.

vermillon *m* vermilion; scarlet.

vermine *f* vermin.

vermisseau *m* small worm.

vermoulu *adj* worm-eaten.

verni *adj* varnished.

vernis *m* varnish; glaze; shine.

vernissage *m* varnishing; glazing.

verre *m* glass; lens; drink.

verrerie *f* glassworks; glass-making.

verrière *f* window; glass roof.

verrou *m* bolt.

verrouillage *m* bolting; locking.

verrouiller *vt* to bolt; to lock.

verrue *f* wart, verruca.

vers *prép* towards; around; about; * *m* line, verse.

versatile *adj* versatile.

verse *f*: **pleuvoir à ~** to pour down.

Verseau *m* Aquarius.

verser *vt* to pour, shed; to pay; (*mil*) to assign.

verset *m* verse.

version *f* version.

verso *m* back.

vert *m* green; * *adj* green; **langue ~e** slang; **~ement** *adv* sharply, brusquely.

vertébral *adj* vertebral.

vertèbre *f* vertebra.

vertical *adj* vertical; **~ement** *adv* vertically.

vertige *m* vertigo; dizziness.

vertigineux *adj* vertiginous, breathtaking.

vertu *f* virtue; courage; **en ~ de** in accordance with.

vertueux *adj* virtuous.

verve *f* verve, vigour.

verveine *f* verbena.

vésicule *f* vesicle; gall bladder.

vessie *f* bladder.

veste *f* jacket.

vestiaire *m* cloakroom; changing-room.

vestibule *m* hall, vestibule.

vestige *m* relic; trace, vestige.

veston *m* jacket.

vêtement *m* garment.

vétéran *m* veteran.

vétérinaire *mf* veterinary surgeon; * *adj* veterinary.

vêtir *vt* to clothe, dress; **se ~** *vr* to dress o.s.

veto *m* veto.

vêtu *adj* dressed; clad, wearing.

vétuste *adj* dilapidated, ancient.

veuf *m* widower; * *adj* widowed.

veule *adj* spineless.

veuve *f* widow; * *adj* widowed.

vexant *adj* annoying, vexing.

vexer *vt* to annoy; to hurt.

viable *adj* viable.

viaduc *m* viaduct.

viande *f* meat.

vibration *f* vibration.

vibrer *vi* to vibrate; to quiver.

vibromasseur *m* vibrator.

vicaire *m* curate, vicar.

vice *m* vice; fault, defect.

vice-président *m* vice-president; deputy chairman.

vice-versa *adv* vice versa.

vicieux *adj* licentious; dissolute; incorrect.

vicissitude *f* vicissitude, change; trial.

vicomte *m* viscount, **-esse** *f* viscountess.

victime *f* victim, casualty; **être ~ de** to be the victim of.

victoire *f* victory.

victorieusement *adv* victoriously.

victorieux *adj* victorious.

vidange *f* emptying; waste outlet.

vidanger *vt* to empty; to drain off.

vide *adj* empty, vacant, devoid; * *m* vacuum; gap; void.

vidéo *f* video; * *adj invar* video.

vidéocassette *f* videocassette.

vide-ordures *m invar* rubbish chute.

vider *vt* to empty; to drain; to vacate; to gut.

videur *m* bouncer.

vie *f* life; living; **être en ~** to be alive.

vieillard *m* old man.

vieillesse *f* old age; the elderly; oldness.

vieillir *vi* to get old; * *vt* to age; to put years on.

vieillissement *m* ageing; obsolescence.

vierge *f* virgin; * *adj* virgin; blank; unexposed.

vieux *adj*, *f* **vieille** old; ancient; obsolete.

vif *adj* alive, lively; quick; eager, passionate.

vigilance *f* vigilance.

vigilant *adj* vigilant.

vigile *m* vigil.

vigne *f* vine; vineyard.

vigneron *m* **-ne** *f* wine grower.

vignette *f* vignette; illustration; seal.

vignoble *m* vineyard.

vigoureusement *adv* vigorously, energetically.

vigoureux *adj* vigorous.

vigueur *f* vigour, strength, energy.

vil *adj* vile; lowly.

vilain *m* naughty boy, **-e** *f* naughty girl.

villa *f* villa, detached house.

village *m* village.

villageois *adj* village, rustic.

ville *f* town, city.

villégiature *f* holiday; vacation.

vin *m* wine.

vinaigre *m* vinegar.

vinaigrette *f* vinaigrette, oil and vinegar dressing, French dressing.

vindicatif *adj* vindictive.

vingt *adj*, *m* twenty.

vingtaine *f* about twenty; score.

vingtième *adj*, *mf* twentieth; **~ment** *adv* in twentieth place.

vinicole *adj* wine, wine-growing.

vinyl *m* vinyl.

viol *m* rape.

violation *f* violation; transgression.

violemment *adv* violently.

violence *f* violence; force, duress.

violent *adj* violent; considerable, excessive.

violer *vt* to violate, desecrate; to rape.

violet *adj* purple, violet; * *m* purple, violet.

violette *f* (*bot*) violet.

violeur *m* rapist.

violon *m* violin.

violoncelle *m* cello, violoncello.

violoncelliste *mf* cello player.

violoniste *mf* violinist.

vipère *f* viper, adder.

virage *m* turn, bend; tacking.

viral *adj* viral.

virement *m* turning, tacking; transfer, clearance.

virer *vt* to transfer; * *vi* to turn, tack.

virevolter *vi* to spin round, pirouette.

virginité *f* virginity; purity.

virgule *f* comma; (*math*) point.

viril *adj* virile; male, masculine; **~ement** *adv* in a virile way.

virilité *f* virility; masculinity.

virtuel *adj* virtual; potential; **~lement** *adv* virtually.

virtuose *mf* virtuoso, master.

virulence *f* virulence, viciousness.

virulent *adj* virulent, vicious.

virus *m* virus.

vis *f* screw.

visa *m* stamp, visa.

visage *m* face; expression.

vis-à-vis *prép*: opposite; **~ de** towards; as regards; * *m* encounter; person opposite; **en ~** opposite each other.

viscéral *adj* visceral; deep-rooted.

viscère *f* viscera; intestines.

viser *vt* to aim, target; to visa.

viseur *m* sight; viewfinder.

visibilité *f* visibility.

visible *adj* visible; evident, obvious; **~ment** *adv* visibly; obviously.

visière *f* peak; eyeshade; visor.

vision *f* eyesight; vision.

visionnaire *mf* visionary; * *adj* visionary.

visite *f* visit; visiting, inspection; visitor.

visiter *vt* to visit; to examine, inspect.

visiteur *m* **-euse** *f* visitor; representative.

vison *m* mink.

visqueux *adj* viscous, thick.

visser *vt* to screw on.

visuel *adj* visual.

vital *adj* vital.

vitalité *f* energy, vitality.

vitamine *f* vitamin.

vite *adv* quickly, fast; soon; * *adj* swift; quick.

vitesse *f* speed, swiftness; gear.

viticole *adj* wine, wine-growing.

viticulteur *m* wine grower.

vitrage *m* glazing; windows.

vitrail *m* stained-glass window.

vitre *f* pane, window.

vitreux *adj* glassy, glazed, vitreous.

vitrier *m* glazier.

vitrine *f* shop window; display cabinet.

vitriol *m* vitriol.

vitupérer *vi* to vituperate, reprimand.

vivace *adj* hardy, perennial; enduring.

vivacité *f* vivacity, liveliness; vividness; acuteness.

vivant *adj* alive, living; lively.

vivement *adv* quickly, briskly; keenly, acutely.

vivier *m* fishpond.

vivifiant *adj* refreshing, invigorating.

vivifier *vt* to enliven, invigorate, refresh.

vivre *vi* to live, be alive; to last, endure; **vive la mariée!** three cheers for the bride; * *vt* to live, spend; to live through.

vivres *mpl* victuals, supplies.

VO (version originale) *f* original version.

vocabulaire *m* vocabulary.

vocal *adj* vocal; **~ement** *adv* vocally.

vocalise *f* singing exercise.

vocation *f* vocation, calling.

vociférer *vi* to vociferate, bawl.

vœu *m* vow; wish.

vogue *f* fashion, vogue; **en ~** in fashion.

voici *prép* here is, here are; ago; past.

voie *f* way, road; means; process; **~ ferrée** railway; **~ d'eau** leak; **en ~ de** in the process of.

voilà *prép* there is, there are; ago; **et ~!** so there!

voile *f* sail; * *m* veil.

voilé *adj* veiled; hazy, blurred.

voiler *vt* to veil, shroud; **se ~** *vr* to wear a veil; to mist over.

voilier *m* sailing boat, yacht.

voir *vt* to see; to deal with; to understand; **avoir à ~ avec** to have to do with; **se ~** *vr* to find o.s.; to show.

voisin *m* **-e** *f* neighbour; fellow; * *adj* neighbouring, next.

voisinage *m* neighbourhood, vicinity.

voiture *f* car; carriage; cart.

voix *f* voice; vote; **parler à ~ basse/haute** to speak in a low/high voice.

vol *m* flight; flock; **à ~ d'oiseau** as the crow flies.

volaille *f* fowl, poultry.

volant *m* steering wheel; * *adj* flying.

volatile *adj* volatile.

volatiliser *vt* to volatilize; to extinguish; **se ~** *vr* to volatilize; to vanish.

volcan *m* volcano.

volcanique *adj* volcanic.

volée *f* flight; volley; **à la ~** in mid-air; rashly, at random; **demi-~** half-volley.

voler *vi* to fly; **~ en éclats** to smash into pieces; * *vt* to steal; to rob.

volet *m* shutter; flap, paddle.

voleur *m* **-euse** *f* thief; * *adj* dishonest, thieving.

volley-ball *m* volleyball.

volleyeur *m* **-euse** *f* volleyball player.

volontaire *adj* voluntary; intentional; **~ment** *adv* voluntarily; intentionally.

volonté *f* will, wish; willingness; willpower.

volontiers *adv* willingly; gladly.

volt *m* volt.

volte-face *f invar* volte-face, about-turn; **faire ~** to turn round.

voltige *f* acrobatics; trick riding.

voltiger *vi* to flutter about.

volubile *adj* voluble.

volume *m* volume.

volumineux *adj* voluminous, bulky.

volupté *f* voluptuousness, sensual pleasure.

voluptueux *adj* voluptuous.

volute *f* volute, scroll; wreath.

vomir *vi* to vomit, be sick; * *vt* to vomit, bring up.

vomissement *m* vomiting.
vorace *adj* voracious; **~ment** *adv* voraciously.
voracité *f* voracity, voraciousness.
vos = *pl* **votre**.
votant *m* **-e** *f* voter.
vote *m* vote; voting.
voter *vi* to vote.
votre *adj*, *pl* **vos** your, your own.
vôtre *pn*: **le ~, la ~, les ~s** yours, your own.
vouer *vt* to vow; to devote, dedicate.
vouloir *vt* to want, wish; to require; to try; **~ du mal à** to wish sb harm; **en ~ à** to bear a grudge against sb; **bien ~** to be happy that.
voulu *adj* required; deliberate.
vous *pn* you, yourself.
voûte *f* vault.
voûté *adj* vaulted.
vouvoyer *vt* to use the '*vous*' form.
voyage *m* journey, trip; travelling.
voyager *vi* to travel, journey.
voyageur *m* **-euse** *f* traveller, passenger.
voyant *m* **-e** *f* visionary, seer; * *m* signal light; * *adj* gaudy, showy.

voyelle *f* vowel.
voyeur *m* **-euse** *f* voyeur.
voyou *m* lout, loafer, hoodlum.
vrac *adv*: **en ~** in bulk.
vrai *adj* true, genuine; **~ment** *adv* truly, really.
vraisemblable *adj* likely, probable; **~ment** *adv* probably.
vrille *f* tendril; spiral; **descendre en ~** to come down in a spin.
vrombir *vi* to roar, hum.
vu *adj* seen; considered, regarded; **être bien/ mal ~** to be well/ poorly thought of; **ni ~ ni connu** you won't discover anything; * *prép* in view of.
vue *f* sight, eyesight; **en ~ de** with a view to; **avoir des ~s sur** to have designs on.
vulgaire *adj* vulgar, crude; **~ment** *adv* vulgarly.
vulgariser *vt* to popularize; to coarsen.
vulgarité *f* vulgarity, coarseness.
vulnérable *adj* vulnerable.
vulve *f* vulva.

WXYZ

wagon *m* wagon, truck, freight car; wagonload.
wagon-citerne *m* tanker.
wagon-lit *m* sleeper.
wagon-restaurant *m* restaurant car.
water-polo *m* water polo.
watt *m* watt.
W-C (water-closet) *mpl* lavatory.
week-end *m* weekend.
western *m* western.
whisky *m* whisky.
xénophobe *mf* xenophobe; * *adj* xenophobic.
xénophobie *f* xenophobia.
xylophone *m* xylophone.
yacht *m* yacht.
yang *m* yang.
yaourt *m* yoghurt.
yard *m* yard.
yeux *pl* = **œil**.
yin *m* yin.
yoga *m* yoga.

yogi *m* yogi.
yogourt *m* = **yaourt**.
yo-yo *m* yo-yo.
yucca *m* yucca.
yuppie *mf* yuppy.
zèbre *m* zebra.
zébu *m* zebu.
zèle *m* zeal.
zélé *adj* zealous.
zen *m* Zen.
zénith *m* zenith.
zéro *m* zero, nought, nothing.
zézayer *vi* to lisp.
zigzag *m* zigzag.
zigzaguer *vi* to zigzag.
zinc *m* zinc.
zizanie *f* ill-feeling.
zizi *m* (*fam*) willy.
zodiaque *m* zodiac.
zona *m* shingles.

zone *f* zone, area.

zoo *m* zoo.

zoologie *f* zoology.

zoologiste *mf* zoologist.

zoom *m* zoom; zoom lens.

zoophile *adj* zoophilic, zoophilous.

zozoter *vi* (*fam*) to lisp.

ZUP (zone à urbaniser en priorité) *f* urban development zone.

zut *interj* damn! rubbish! shut up!

English-French
Anglais-Français

A

a *art* un, une.

aback *adv* **to be taken** ~ *vi* être décontenancé.

abacus *n* abaque, boulier *m*.

abandon *vt* abandonner, laisser.

abandonment *n* abandon *m*.

abase *vt* avilir; humilier.

abasement *n* avilissement *m*; humiliation *f*.

abash *vt* couvrir de honte.

abate *vt* baisser; * *vi* baisser; se calmer.

abatement *n* baisse, réduction *f*.

abbess *n* abbesse *f*.

abbey *n* abbaye *f*.

abbot *n* abbé *m*.

abbreviate *vt* abréger, raccourcir.

abbreviation *n* abréviation *f*.

abdicate *vt* abdiquer; renoncer à.

abdication *n* abdication *f*; renonciation *f*.

abdomen *n* abdomen *m*.

abdominal *adj* abdominal.

abduct *vt* kidnapper, enlever.

abductor *n* abducteur *m*.

abed *adv* au lit.

aberrant *adj* aberrant.

aberration *n* aberration *f*.

abet *vt*: **to aid and** ~ être complice de.

abeyance *n* suspension *f*.

abhor *vt* abhorrer, exécrer.

abhorrence *n* exécration, horreur *f*.

abhorrent *adj* exécrable.

abide *vt* supporter, souffrir.

ability *n* capacité, aptitude *f*; **abilities** *pl* talents *mpl*.

abject *adj* misérable; abject, méprisable; **~ly** *adv* misérablement.

abjure *vt* abjurer; renoncer à.

ablative *n* (*gr*) ablatif *m*.

ablaze *adj* enflammé.

able *adj* capable; **to be** ~ pouvoir.

able-bodied *adj* robuste.

ablution *n* ablution *f*.

ably *adv* habilement.

abnegation *n* renoncement *m*.

abnormal *adj* anormal.

abnormality *n* anomalie *f*.

aboard *adv* à bord.

abode *n* domicile *m*.

abolish *vt* abolir, supprimer.

abolition *n* abolition, suppression *f*.

abominable *adj* abominable; **~bly** *adv* abominablement.

abomination *n* abomination *f*.

aboriginal *adj* aborigène.

aborigines *npl* aborigènes *mpl*.

abort *vi* avorter.

abortion *n* avortement *m*.

abortive *adj* raté.

abound *vi* abonder; ~ **with** abonder en.

about *prep* au sujet de; vers; **I carry no money** ~ **me** je n'ai pas d'argent sur moi; * *adv* çà et là; **to be** ~ **to** être sur le point de; **to go** ~ aller de- ci de- là; **to go** ~ **a thing** entreprendre qch; **all** ~ partout.

above *prep* au-dessus de; * *adv* au-dessus; ~ **all** surtout, principalement; ~ **mentioned** mentionné ci-dessus.

aboveboard *adj* franc.

abrasion *n* écorchure *f*.

abrasive *adj* abrasif.

abreast *adv* de front.

abridge *vt* abréger, raccourcir.

abridgment *n* abrégement *m*; version abrégée *f*.

abroad *adv* à l'étranger; **to go** ~ se rendre à l'étranger.

abrogate *vt* abroger.

abrogation *n* abrogation *f*.

abrupt *adj* abrupt; brusque; **~ly** *adv* brusquement; rudement.

abscess *n* abcès *m*.

abscond *vi* s'enfuir.

absence *n* absence *f*.

absent *adj* absent; * *vi* s'absenter.

absentee *n* absent *m* -e *f*.

absenteeism *n* absentéisme *m*.

absent-minded *adj* distrait.

absolute *adj* absolu; ~ly *adv* absolument.

absolution *n* absolution *f*.

absolutism *n* absolutisme *m*.

absolve *vt* absoudre.

absorb *vt* absorber.

absorbent *adj* absorbant.

absorbent cotton *n* coton hydrophile *m*.

absorption *n* absorption *f*.

abstain *vi* s'abstenir.

abstemious *adj* sobre; ~ly *adv* sobrement.

abstemiousness *n* sobriété *f*.

abstinence *n* abstinence *f*.

abstinent *adj* abstinent.

abstract *adj* abstrait; * *n* abrégé *m*; **in the ~** dans l'abstrait.

abstraction *n* abstraction *f*; extraction *f*.

abstractly *adv* abstraitement.

abstruse *adj* abstrus, obscur; ~ly *adv* obscurément.

absurd *adj* absurde; ~ly *adv* absurdement.

absurdity *n* absurdité *f*.

abundance *n* abondance *f*.

abundant *adj* abondant; ~ly *adv* abondamment.

abuse *vt* abuser de; insulter; maltraiter; * *n* abus *m*; injures *fpl*; mauvais traitements *mpl*.

abusive *adj* injurieux; ~ly *adv* injurieusement.

abut *vi* être contigu.

abysmal *adj* abominable.

abyss *n* abîme *m*.

acacia *n* acacia *m*.

academic *adj* universitaire; scolaire; théorique.

academician *n* académicien *m* -ne *f*.

academy *n* académie *f*.

accede *vi* accéder.

accelerate *vt* accélérer.

accelerator *n* accélérateur *m*.

acceleration *n* accélération *f*.

accent *n* accent *m*; * *vt* accentuer.

accentuate *vt* accentuer.

accentuation *n* accentuation *f*.

accept *vt* accepter.

acceptable *adj* acceptable.

acceptability *n* acceptabilité *f*.

acceptance *n* acceptation *f*.

access *n* accès *m*.

accessible *adj* accessible.

accession *n* augmentation *f*; accession *f*.

accessory *n* accessoire *m*; (*law*) complice *m*.

accident *n* accident *m*; hasard *m*.

accidental *adj* accidentel; ~ly *adv* par hasard.

acclaim *vt* acclamer.

acclamation *n* acclamation *f*.

acclimate *vt* (US) acclimater.

accommodate *vt* loger; accommoder.

accommodating *adj* obligeant.

accommodations *npl* logement *m*.

accompaniment *n* (*mus*) accompagnement *m*.

accompanist *n* (*mus*) accompagnateur *m* -trice *f*.

accompany *vt* accompagner.

accomplice *n* complice *mf*.

accomplish *vt* accomplir.

accomplished *adj* accompli.

accomplishment *n* accomplissement *m*; ~s *pl* talents *mpl*.

accord *n* accord *m*; **with one ~** d'un commun accord; **of one's own ~** de son propre chef.

accordance *n*: **in ~ with** conformément à.

according *prep* selon; **~ as** selon que; ~ly *adv* en conséquence.

accordion *n* (*mus*) accordéon *m*.

accost *vt* accoster.

account *n* compte *m*; **on no ~** en aucun cas; **on ~ of** en raison de; **to call to ~** demander des comptes; **to turn to ~** mettre à profit; * *vt* **~ for** expliquer; représenter.

accountability *n* responsabilité *f*.

accountable *adj* responsable.

accountancy *n* comptabilité *f*.

accountant *n* comptable *mf*.

account book *n* livre *m* de comptes.

account number *n* numéro de compte *m*.

accrue *vi* s'accumuler; revenir.

accumulate *vt* accumuler; * *vi* s'accumuler.

accumulation *n* accumulation *f*.

accuracy *n* exactitude *f*.

accurate *adj* exact; ~ly *adv* exactement.

accursed *adj* maudit.

accusation *n* accusation *f*.

accusative *n* (*gr*) accusatif *m*.

accusatory *adj* accusateur.

accuse *vt* accuser.

accused *n* accusé *m* -e *f*.

accuser *n* accusateur *m* -trice *f*.

accustom *vt* accoutumer.

accustomed *adj* accoutumé.

ace *n* as *m*; **within an ~ of** à deux doigts de.

acerbic *adj* acerbe.

acetate *n* (*chem*) acétate *m*.

ache *n* douleur *f*; * *vi* faire mal.

achieve *vt* réaliser; obtenir.

achievement *n* réalisation *f*; exploit *m*.

acid *adj* acide; aigre; * *n* acide *m*.

acidity *n* acidité *f*.

acknowledge *vt* reconnaître, admettre.

acknowledgment *n* reconnaissance *f*.

acme *n* apogée *m*.

acne *n* acné *f*.

acorn *n* gland *m*.

acoustics *n* acoustique *f*.

acquaint *vt* informer, aviser.

acquaintance *n* connaissance *f*.

acquiesce *vi* acquiescer, consentir.

acquiescence *n* consentement *m*.

acquiescent *adj* consentant.

acquire *vt* acquérir.

acquisition *n* acquisition *f*.

acquit *vt* acquitter.

acquittal *n* acquittement *m*.

acre *n* acre *f*.

acrid *adj* âcre; acerbe.

acrimonious *adj* acrimonieux.

acrimony *n* acrimonie *f*.

across *adv* en travers, d'un côté à l'autre; * *prep* à travers; **to come ~** tomber sur.

act *vt* jouer; * *vi* agir; jouer la comédie; * *n* acte *m*; **~s of the apostles** Actes des Apôtres *mpl*.

acting *adj* intérimaire.

action *n* action *f*; combat *m*.

action replay *n* répétition *f*.

activate *vt* activer.

active *adj* actif; **~ly** *adv* activement.

activity *n* activité *f*.

actor *n* acteur *m*.

actress *n* actrice *f*.

actual *adj* réel; concret; **~ly** *adv* en fait; réellement.

actuary *n* actuaire *mf*.

acumen *n* perspicacité *f*.

acute *adj* aigu; perspicace; **~ accent** *n* accent aigu *m*; **~ angle** *n* angle aigu *m*; **~ly** *adv* vivement; avec perspicacité.

acuteness *n* finesse *f*, intensité *f*.

ad *n* annonce *f*.

adage *n* adage *m*.

adamant *adj* inflexible.

adapt *vt* adapter, ajuster.

adaptability *n* adaptabilité *f*.

adaptable *adj* adaptable.

adaptation *n* adaptation *f*.

adaptor *n* adaptateur *m*.

add *vt* ajouter; **~ up** additionner.

addendum *n* addendum *m*.

adder *n* vipère *f*.

addict *n* intoxiqué *m* -e *f*.

addiction *n* dépendance *f*.

addictive *adj* qui crée une dépendance.

addition *n* addition *f*.

additional *adj* additionnel; **~ly** *adv* de plus.

additive *n* additif *m*.

address *vt* adresser; s'adresser à; * *n* adresse *f*; discours *m*.

adduce *vt* mentionner, citer.

adenoids *npl* végétations *fpl*.

adept *adj* expert.

adequacy *n* suffisance *f*; capacité *f*.

adequate *adj* adéquat; suffisant; **~ly** *adv* convenablement; suffisamment.

adhere *vi* adhérer.

adherence *n* adhérence *f*.

adherent *n* adhérent, partisan *m*.

adhesion *n* adhérence *f*; adhésion *f*.

adhesive *adj* adhésif.

adhesive tape *n* (*med*) sparadrap *m*; papier *m* collant.

adhesiveness *n* adhérence *f*.

adieu *adv* adieu; * *n* adieux *mpl*.

adipose *adj* adipeux.

adjacent *adj* adjacent, contigu.

adjectival *adj* adjectival; **~ly** *adv* adjectivalement.

adjective *n* adjectif *m*.

adjoin *vi* être contigu.
adjoining *adj* contigu.
adjourn *vt* reporter, remettre.
adjournment *n* ajournement *m*.
adjudicate *vt* décider; juger.
adjunct *n* subalterne *mf*; annexe *f*.
adjust *vt* ajuster, adapter.
adjustable *adj* ajustable, adaptable.
adjustment *n* ajustement *m*; réglage *m*.
adjutant *n* (*mil*) adjudant *m*.
ad lib *vt* improviser.
administer *vt* administrer; distribuer; ~ **an oath** faire prêter serment.
administration *n* administration *f*; gouvernement *m*.
administrative *adj* administratif.
administrator *n* administrateur *m* -trice *f*.
admirable *adj* admirable; **~bly** *adv* admirablement.
admiral *n* amiral *m*.
admiralship *n* amirauté *f*.
admiralty *n* ministère de la Marine *m*.
admiration *n* admiration *f*.
admire *vt* admirer.
admirer *n* admirateur *m* -trice *f*.
admiringly *adv* avec admiration.
admissible *adj* admissible.
admission *n* admission, entrée *f*.
admit *vt* admettre; ~ **to** reconnaître, avouer.
admittance *n* admission *f*.
admittedly *adv* il est vrai (que).
admixture *n* mélange *m*.
admonish *vt* admonester, réprimander.
admonition *n* admonestation *f*; conseil *m*.
admonitory *adj* d'admonestation.
ad nauseam *adv* à saturation.
ado *n* agitation *f*.
adolescence *n* adolescence *f*.
adopt *vt* adopter.
adopted *adj* adoptif.
adoption *n* adoption *f*.
adoptive *adj* adoptif.
adorable *adj* adorable.
adorably *adv* adorablement.
adoration *n* adoration *f*.
adore *vt* adorer.
adorn *vt* orner.
adornment *n* ornement *m*.

adrift *adv* à la dérive.
adroit *adj* adroit, habile.
adroitness *n* adresse *f*.
adulation *n* adulation *f*.
adulatory *adj* adulateur.
adult *adj* adulte; * *n* adulte *mf*.
adulterate *vt* falsifier; * *adj* falsifié.
adulteration *n* falsification *f*.
adulterer *n* adultère *m*.
adulteress *n* adultère *f*.
adulterous *adj* adultère.
adultery *n* adultère *m*.
advance *vt* avancer; * *vi* avancer; faire des progrès; * *n* avance *f*.
advanced *adj* avancé.
advancement *n* avancement *m*.
advantage *n* avantage *m*; **to take ~ of** profiter de.
advantageous *adj* avantageux; **~ly** *adv* avantageusement.
advantageousness *n* avantage *m*.
advent *n* venue *f*; **Advent** *n* Avent *m*.
adventitious *adj* accidentel.
adventure *n* aventure *f*.
adventurer *n* aventurier *m* -ière *f*.
adventurous *adj* aventureux; **~ly** *adv* aventureusement.
adverb *n* adverbe *m*.
adverbial *adj* adverbial; **~ly** *adv* adverbialement.
adversary *n* adversaire *mf*.
adverse *adj* défavorable, contraire.
adversity *n* adversité *f*; malheur *m*.
advertise *vt* faire de la publicité pour; mettre une annonce pour.
advertisement *n* publicité *f*; annonce *f*.
advertising *n* publicité *f*.
advice *n* conseil *m*; avis *m*.
advisability *n* opportunité *f*.
advisable *adj* prudent, conseillé.
advise *vt* conseiller; aviser.
advisedly *adv* de manière avisée.
advisory *adj* consultatif.
advocacy *n* défense *f*.
advocate *n* avocat *m*; * *vt* plaider pour.
aerial *n* antenne *f*.
aerobics *npl* aérobic *m*.
aerometer *n* aéromètre *m*.

aeroplane *n* avion *m*.
aerosol *n* aérosol *m*.
aerostat *n* aérostat *m*.
aesthetic *adj* esthétique; **~s** *npl* esthétique *f*.
afar *adv* au loin; **from ~** de loin.
affability *n* affabilité *f*.
affable *adj* affable; **~bly** *adv* affablement.
affair *n* affaire *f*.
affect *vt* toucher; affecter.
affectation *n* affectation *f*.
affected *adj* affecté; **~ly** *adv* avec affectation.
affectingly *adv* avec émotion.
affection *n* affection *f*.
affectionate *adj* affectueux; **~ly** *adv* affectueusement.
affidavit *n* déclaration sous serment *f*.
affiliate *vt* affilier.
affiliation *n* affiliation *f*.
affinity *n* affinité *f*.
affirm *vt* affirmer, déclarer.
affirmation *n* affirmation *f*.
affirmative *adj* affirmatif; **~ly** *adv* affirmativement.
affix *vt* coller; apposer; * *n* (*gr*) affixe *m*.
afflict *vt* affliger.
affliction *n* affliction *f*.
affluence *n* abondance *f*.
affluent *adj* riche; abondant.
afflux *n* afflux *m*, affluence *f*.
afford *vt* fournir; **to be able to ~** avoir les moyens d'acheter.
affray *n* (*law*) rixe *f*.
affront *n* affront *m*, injure *f*; * *vt* affronter; insulter.
aflame *adv* en flammes.
afloat *adv* à flot.
afore *prep* avant; * *adv* d'abord.
afraid *adj* apeuré; **I am ~** j'ai peur.
afresh *adv* à nouveau.
aft *adv* (*mar*) en poupe.
after *prep* après; * *adv* après; **~ all** après tout.
afterbirth *n* placenta *m*.
after-crop *n* deuxième récolte *f*.
after-effects *npl* répercussions *fpl*.
afterlife *n* vie après la mort *f*.
aftermath *n* conséquences *fpl*.
afternoon *n* après-midi *mf*.
afterpains *npl* tranchées utérines *fpl*.

aftershave *n* après-rasage *m*.
aftertaste *n* arrière-goût *m*.
afterward(s) *adv* ensuite.
again *adv* à nouveau; **~ and** de nombreuses fois; **as much ~** encore autant.
against *prep* contre; **~ the grain** à contre fil; de mauvaise volonté.
agate *n* agate *f*.
age *n* âge *m*; vieillesse *f*; **under ~** mineur; * *vt* vieillir.
aged *adj* âgé.
agency *n* agence *f*.
agenda *n* ordre du jour *m*.
agent *n* agent *m*.
agglomerate *vt* agglomérer.
agglomeration *n* agglomération *f*.
aggrandizement *n* avancement *m*.
aggravate *vt* aggraver; énerver.
aggravation *n* aggravation *f*; énervement *m*.
aggregate *n* agrégat *m*.
aggregation *n* agrégation *f*.
aggression *n* agression *f*.
aggressive *adj* agressif.
aggressor *n* agresseur *m*.
aggrieved *adj* offensé.
aghast *adj* horrifié.
agile *adj* agile; adroit.
agility *n* agilité *f*; adresse *f*.
agitate *vt* agiter.
agitation *n* agitation *f*.
agitator *n* agitateur *m* -trice *f*.
ago *adv*: **how long ~?** il y a combien de temps?
agog *adj* en émoi; impatient.
agonizing *adj* atroce, angoissant.
agony *n* douleur *f* atroce; angoisse *f*.
agrarian *adj* agraire.
agree *vt* convenir; * *vi* être d'accord.
agreeable *adj* agréable; **~bly** *adv* agréablement; **~ with** conforme à.
agreeableness *n* caractère agréable *m*.
agreed *adj* convenu; **~!** *adv* d'accord!
agreement *n* accord *m*.
agricultural *adj* agricole.
agriculture *n* agriculture *f*.
agriculturist *n* agriculteur *m*.
aground *adv* (*mar*) échoué.
ah! *excl* ah!

ahead *adv* en avant; à l'avance; (*mar*) sur l'avant.

ahoy! *excl* (*mar*) ohé!

aid *vt* aider, secourir; **~ and abet** être complice de; * *n* aide *f*, secours *m*; aide *mf*.

aide-de-camp *n* (*mil*) aide de camp *m*.

AIDS *n* SIDA *m*.

ail *vt* affliger.

ailing *adj* souffrant.

ailment *n* maladie *f*.

aim *vt* pointer; viser; aspirer à; * *n* but *m*; cible *f*.

aimless *adj* sans but; **~ly** à la dérive, sans but.

air *n* air *m*; * *vt* aérer.

air balloon *n* ballon *m*.

airborne *adj* aéroporté.

air-conditioned *adj* climatisé.

air-conditioning *n* climatisation *f*.

aircraft *n* avion *m*.

air cushion *n* coussin d'air *m*.

air force *n* armée de l'air *f*.

air freshener *n* appareil de conditionnement d'air *m*.

air gun *n* carabine à air comprimé *f*.

air hole *n* trou d'aération *m*.

airiness *n* aération, ventilation *f*.

airless *adj* mal aéré, mal ventilé.

airlift *n* pont aérien *m*.

airline *n* ligne aérienne *f*.

airmail *n*: **by ~** par avion.

airport *n* aéroport *m*.

air pump *n* compresseur *m*.

airsick *adj*: **to be ~** avoir le mal de l'air.

airstrip *n* piste d'atterrissage *f*.

air terminal *n* aérogare *f*.

airtight *adj* hermétique.

airy *adj* aéré; léger.

aisle *n* nef d'église *f*.

ajar *adj* entrouvert.

akimbo *adj* les poings sur les hanches.

akin *adj* ressemblant.

alabaster *n* albâtre *m*; * *adj* d'albâtre.

alacrity *n* vivacité *f*.

alarm *n* alarme *f*; * *vt* alarmer; inquiéter.

alarm bell *n* sonnette d'alarme *f*.

alarmist *n* alarmiste *mf*.

alas *adv* hélas.

albeit *conj* bien que.

album *n* album *m*.

alchemist *n* alchimiste *m*.

alchemy *n* alchimie *f*.

alcohol *n* alcool *m*.

alcoholic *adj* alcoolisé; * *n* alcoolique *mf*.

alcove *n* alcôve *f*.

alder *n* aulne *m*.

ale *n* bière *f*.

alehouse *n* taverne, brasserie *f*.

alert *adj* vigilant; vif; * *n* alerte *f*.

alertness *n* vigilance *f*; vivacité *f*.

algae *npl* algues *fpl*.

algebra *n* algèbre *f*.

algebraic *adj* algébrique.

alias *adj* alias.

alibi *n* (*law*) alibi *m*.

alien *adj* étranger; * *n* étranger *m* -ère *f*; extra-terrestre *mf*.

alienate *vt* aliéner.

alienation *n* aliénation *f*.

alight *vi* mettre pied à terre; * *adj* en feu.

align *vt* aligner.

alike *adj* semblable, égal; * *adv* de la même façon.

alimentary *n* (*med*) digestif *m*.

alimony *n* (*law*) pension *f* alimentaire.

alive *adj* en vie, vivant; actif.

alkali *n* alcali *m*.

alkaline *adj* alcalin.

all *adj* tout; * *adv* totalement; **~ at once**, **~ of a sudden** soudain; **~ the same** cependant; **~ the better** tant mieux; **not at ~!** pas du tout!; il n'y a pas de quoi!; **once and for ~** une fois pour toutes; * *n* tout *m*.

allay *vt* apaiser.

all clear *n* feu vert *m*.

allegation *n* allégation *f*.

allege *vt* alléguer.

allegiance *n* loyauté, fidélité *f*.

allegorical *adj* allégorique; **~ly** *adv* allégoriquement.

allegory *n* allégorie *f*.

allegro *n* (*mus*) allegro *m*.

allergy *n* allergie *f*.

alleviate *vt* alléger.

alleviation *n* allègement *m*.

alley *n* ruelle *f*.

alliance *n* alliance *f*.
allied *adj* allié.
alligator *n* alligator *m*.
alliteration *n* allitération *f*.
all-night *adj* ouvert toute la nuit.
allocate *vt* allouer.
allocation *n* allocation *f*.
allot *vt* assigner.
allow *vt* permettre; accorder; ~ **for** tenir compte de.
allowable *adj* admissible, permis.
allowance *n* allocation *f*; concession *f*.
alloy *n* alliage *m*.
all right *adv* bien.
all-round *adj* complet.
allspice *n* piment *m* de la Jamaïque.
allude *vi* faire allusion à.
allure *n* charme, attrait *m*.
alluring *adj* attrayant; ~**ly** *adv* avec charme.
allurement *n* attrait *m*.
allusion *n* allusion *f*.
allusive *adj* allusif; ~**ly** *adv* par allusion.
alluvial *adj* alluvial.
ally *n* allié *m* -e *f*; * *vt* allier.
almanac *n* almanach *m*.
almighty *adj* omnipotent, tout-puissant.
almond *n* amande *f*.
almond-milk *n* lait d'amandes *m*.
almond tree *n* amandier *m*.
almost *adv* presque.
alms *n* aumône *f*.
aloft *prep* en l'air; en haut.
alone *adj* seul; * *adv* seul; **to leave ~** laisser tranquille.
along *adv* le long (de); ~ **side** à côté.
aloof *adj* distant.
aloud *adj* à voix haute.
alphabet *n* alphabet *m*.
alphabetical *adj* alphabétique; ~**ly** *adv* par ordre alphabétique, alphabétiquement.
alpine *adj* alpin.
already *adv* déjà.
also *adv* aussi.
altar *n* autel *m*.
altarpiece *n* retable *m*.
alter *vt* modifier.
alteration *n* modification *f*.
altercation *n* altercation *f*.

alternate *adj* alterné; * *vt* alterner; ~**ly** *adv* alternativement.
alternating *adj* alterné.
alternation *n* alternance *f*.
alternator *n* alternateur *m*.
alternative *n* alternative *f*; * *adj* alternatif; ~**ly** *adv* sinon.
although *conj* bien que, malgré.
altitude *n* altitude *f*.
altogether *adv* complètement.
alum *n* alun *m*.
aluminium *n* aluminium *m*.
aluminous *adj* alumineux.
always *adv* toujours.
a.m. *adv* du matin.
amalgam *n* amalgame *m*.
amalgamate *vt* amalgamer; *vi* s'amalgamer.
amalgamation *n* amalgamation *f*.
amanuensis *n* copiste *mf*.
amaryllis *n* (*bot*) amaryllis *f*.
amass *vt* accumuler, amasser.
amateur *n* amateur *m*.
amateurish *adj* d'amateur.
amatory *adj* amoureux; galant.
amaze *vt* stupéfier.
amazement *n* stupéfaction *f*.
amazing *adj* stupéfiant; ~**ly** *adv* incroyablement.
amazon *n* amazone *f*.
ambassador *n* ambassadeur *m*.
ambassadress *n* ambassadrice *f*.
amber *n* ambre *m*; * *adj* ambré.
ambidextrous *adj* ambidextre.
ambient *adj* ambiant.
ambiguity *n* ambiguïté *f*.
ambiguous *adj* ambigu; ~**ly** *adv* de manière ambiguè.
ambition *n* ambition *f*.
ambitious *adj* ambitieux; ~**ly** *adv* ambitieusement.
amble *vi* marcher tranquillement.
ambulance *n* ambulance *f*.
ambush *n* embuscade *f*; **to lie in ~** être embusqué; * *vt* tendre une embuscade à.
ameliorate *vt* améliorer.
amelioration *n* amélioration *f*.
amenable *adj* responsable.
amend *vt* modifier; amender.

amendable *adj* réparable, corrigible.

amendment *n* modification *f*; amendement *m*.

amends *npl* compensation *f*.

amenities *npl* commodités *fpl*.

America *n* Amérique *f*.

American *adj* américain.

amethyst *n* améthyste *f*.

amiability *n* amabilité *f*.

amiable *adj* aimable.

amiableness *n* amabilité *f*.

amiably *adv* aimablement.

amicable *adj* amical; **~bly** *adv* amicalement.

amid(st) *prep* entre, parmi.

amiss *adv*: **something's** ~ quelque chose ne va pas.

ammonia *n* ammoniaque *m*.

ammunition *n* munitions *fpl*.

amnesia *n* amnésie *f*.

amnesty *n* amnistie *f*.

among(st) *prep* entre, parmi.

amoral *adj* amoral.

amorous *adj* amoureux; **~ly** *adv* amoureusement.

amorphous *adj* informe.

amount *n* montant *m*; quantité *f*; * *vi* s'élever (à).

amp(ere) *n* ampère *m*.

amphibian *n* amphibie *m*.

amphibious *adj* amphibie.

amphitheatre *n* amphithéâtre *m*.

ample *adj* spacieux; abondant, gros.

ampleness *n* abondance *f*.

amplification *n* amplification *f*.

amplifier *n* amplificateur *m*.

amplify *vt* amplifier.

amplitude *n* amplitude *f*.

amply *adv* amplement.

amputate *vt* amputer.

amputation *n* amputation *f*.

amulet *n* amulette *f*.

amuse *vt* distraire, divertir.

amusement *n* distraction *f*, divertissement *m*.

amusing *adj* divertissant; **~ly** *adv* de manière divertissante.

an *art* un, une.

anachronism *n* anachronisme *m*.

anaemia *n* anémie *f*.

anaemic *adj* (*med*) anémique.

anaesthetic *n* anesthésique *m*.

analog *adj* (*comput*) analogique.

analogous *adj* analogue.

analogy *n* analogie *f*.

analyse *vt* analyser.

analysis *n* analyse *f*.

analyst *n* analyste *mf*.

analytical *adj* analytique; **~ly** *adv* analytiquement.

anarchic *adj* anarchique.

anarchist *n* anarchiste *mf*.

anarchy *n* anarchie *f*.

anatomical *adj* anatomique; **~ly** *adv* anatomiquement.

anatomize *vt* disséquer.

anatomy *n* anatomie *f*.

ancestor *n* ancêtre *mf*.

ancestral *adj* ancestral.

ancestry *n* ascendance *f*.

anchor *n* ancre *f*; * *vi* jeter l'ancre.

anchorage *n* ancrage *m*.

anchovy *n* anchois *m*.

ancient *adj* ancien, antique; **~ly** *adv* anciennement.

ancillary *adj* auxiliaire.

and *conj* et.

anecdotal *adj* anecdotique.

anecdote *n* anecdote *f*.

anemone *n* (*bot*) anémone *f*.

anew *adv* de nouveau.

angel *n* ange *m*.

angelic *adj* angélique.

anger *n* colère *f*; * *vt* mettre en colère, irriter.

angle *n* angle *m*; * *vi* pêcher à la ligne.

angled *adj* anguleux.

angler *n* pêcheur à la ligne *m*.

anglicism *n* anglicisme *m*.

angling *n* pêche à la ligne *f*.

angrily *adv* avec colère.

angry *adj* en colère, irrité.

anguish *n* angoisse *f*.

angular *adj* angulaire.

angularity *n* caractère anguleux *m*.

animal *n adj* animal *m*.

animate *vt* animer; * *adj* vivant.

animated *adj* animé.

animation *n* animation *f*.

animosity *n* animosité *f.*
animus *n* haine *f.*
anise *n* anis *m.*
aniseed *n* graine d'anis *f.*
ankle *n* cheville *f;* ~**bone** astragale *m.*
annals *n* annales *fpl.*
annex *vt* annexer; * *n* annexe *f.*
annexation *n* annexion *f.*
annihilate *vt* annihiler, anéantir.
annihilation *n* anéantissement *m.*
anniversary *n* anniversaire (de) *m.*
annotate *vt* annoter.
annotation *n* annotation *f.*
announce *vt* annoncer.
announcement *n* annonce *f.*
announcer *n* présentateur *m* -trice *f.*
annoy *vt* ennuyer.
annoyance *n* ennui *m.*
annoying *adj* ennuyeux.
annual *adj* annuel; ~**ly** *adv* annuellement.
annuity *n* rente viagère *f.*
annul *vt* annuler, abroger.
annulment *n* annulation *f.*
annunciation *n* annonciation *f.*
anodyne *adj* calmant.
anoint *vt* oindre.
anomalous *adj* anormal.
anomaly *n* anomalie, irrégularité *f.*
anon *adv* = **anonymous.**
anonymity *n* anonymat *m.*
anonymous *adj* anonyme; ~**ly** *adv* anonymement.
anorexia *n* anorexie *f.*
another *adj* un autre; **one** ~ l'un l'autre.
answer *vt* répondre à; ~ **for** répondre de; ~ **to** répondre à; * *n* réponse *f.*
answerable *adj* responsable.
answering machine *n* répondeur téléphonique *m.*
ant *n* fourmi *f.*
antagonism *n* antagonisme *m;* rivalité *f.*
antagonist *n* antagoniste *mf.*
antagonize *vt* provoquer.
antarctic *adj* antarctique.
anteater *n* fourmilier *m.*
antecedent *n:* ~**s** *pl* antécédents *mpl.*
antechamber *n* antichambre *f.*
antedate *vt* antidater.

antelope *n* antilope *f.*
antenna *n* antenne *f.*
anterior *adj* antérieur, précédent.
anthem *n* hymne *m.*
anthill *n* fourmilière *f.*
anthology *n* anthologie *f.*
anthracite *n* anthracite *m.*
anthropology *n* anthropologie *f.*
antiaircraft *adj* antiaérien.
antibiotic *n* antibiotique *m.*
antibody *n* anticorps *m.*
Antichrist *n* Antéchrist *m.*
anticipate *vt* prévoir.
anticipation *n* attente *f;* prévision *f.*
anticlockwise *adv* dans le sens contraire des aiguilles d'une montre.
antidote *n* antidote *m.*
antifreeze *n* antigel *m.*
antimony *n* antimoine *m.*
antipathy *n* antipathie *f.*
antipodes *npl* antipodes *fpl*
antiquarian *n* antiquaire *mf.*
antiquated *adj* vieux; suranné.
antique *n* meuble *m* ancien.
antiquity *n* antiquité *f.*
antiseptic *adj* antiseptique.
antisocial *adj* antisocial.
antithesis *n* antithèse *f.*
antler *n* corne *f.*
anvil *n* enclume *f.*
anxiety *n* anxiété *f;* désir *m.*
anxious *adj* anxieux; ~**ly** *adv* anxieusement.
any *adj pn* n'importe quel, n'importe quelle; un, une; tout; ~**body** quelqu'un; n'importe qui; personne; ~**how** de toute façon; de n'importe quelle manière; ~**more** plus; ~**place** n'importe où; nulle part; ~**thing** quelque chose; n'importe quoi; rien.
apace *adv* rapidement.
apart *adv* séparément.
apartment *n* appartement *m.*
apartment house *n* immeuble *m.*
apathetic *adj* apathique.
apathy *n* apathie *f.*
ape *n* singe *m;* * *vt* singer.
aperture *n* ouverture *f.*
apex *n* sommet *m;* apex *m.*
aphorism *n* aphorisme *m.*

apiary *n* rucher *m*.
apiece *adv* chacun, chacune.
aplomb *n* aplomb *m*.
Apocalypse *n* Apocalypse *f*.
apocrypha *npl* apocryphes *mpl*.
apocryphal *adj* apocryphe.
apologetic *adj* d'excuse.
apologist *n* apologiste *mf*.
apologize *vt* excuser.
apology *n* apologie, défense *f*.
apoplexy *n* apoplexie *f*.
apostle *n* apôtre *m*.
apostolic *adj* apostolique.
apostrophe *n* apostrophe *f*.
apotheosis *n* apothéose *f*.
appall *vt* horrifier, atterrer.
appalling *adj* horrible.
apparatus *n* appareil *m*.
apparel *n* vêtements *mpl*.
apparent *adj* évident, apparent; ~**ly** *adv* apparemment.
apparition *n* apparition, vision *f*.
appeal *vi* faire appel; * *n* (*law*) appel *m*.
appealing *adj* attrayant.
appear *vi* paraître.
appearance *n* apparence *f*.
appease *vt* apaiser.
appellant *n* (*law*) appelant *m*.
append *vt* annexer.
appendage *n* appendice *m*.
appendicitis *n* appendicite *f*.
appendix *n* appendice *m*.
appertain *vi* appartenir (à).
appetite *n* appétit *m*.
appetizing *adj* appétissant.
applaud *vt vi* applaudir.
applause *n* applaudissements *mpl*.
apple *n* pomme *f*.
apple pie *n* tourte aux pommes *f*; **in ~ order** parfaitement en ordre.
apple tree *n* pommier *m*.
appliance *n* appareil *m*.
applicability *n* applicabilité *f*.
applicable *adj* applicable.
applicant *n* candidat *m* -e *f*.
application *n* application *f*; candidature *f*.
applied *adj* appliqué.
apply *vt* appliquer; * *vi* s'adresser.

appoint *vt* nommer.
appointee *n* personne nommée *f*.
appointment *n* rendez-vous *m*; nomination *f*.
apportion *vt* répartir.
apportionment *n* répartition *f*.
apposite *adj* approprié, juste.
apposition *n* apposition *f*.
appraisal *n* estimation *f*.
appraise *vt* évaluer.
appreciable *adj* appréciable, sensible.
appreciably *adv* sensiblement.
appreciate *vt* apprécier; être conscient de.
appreciation *n* appréciation *f*.
appreciative *adj* reconnaissant.
apprehend *vt* appréhender.
apprehension *n* appréhension *f*; arrestation *f*.
apprehensive *adj* appréhensif.
apprentice *n* apprenti *m*; * *vt* mettre en apprentissage.
apprenticeship *n* apprentissage *m*.
apprise *vt* informer.
approach *vi* (s')approcher; * *vt* (s')approcher de; * *n* approche *f*.
approachable *adj* accessible, approchable.
approbation *n* approbation *f*.
appropriate *vt* s'approprier; * *adj* approprié, adéquat.
approval *n* approbation *f*.
approve (of) *vt* approuver.
approximate *vi* s'approcher; * *adj* approximatif; ~**ly** *adv* approximativement.
approximation *n* approximation *f*.
apricot *n* abricot *m*.
April *n* avril *m*.
apron *n* tablier *m*.
apse *n* abside *f*.
apt *adj* idéal; susceptible; ~**ly** *adv* opportunément.
aptitude *n* aptitude *f*.
aqualung *n* scaphandre autonome *m*.
aquarium *n* aquarium *m*.
Aquarius *n* Verseau *m* (signe du zodiaque).
aquatic *adj* aquatique.
aqueduct *n* aqueduc *m*.
aquiline *adj* aquilin.
arabesque *n* arabesque *f*.
arable *adj* arable.
arbiter *n* arbitre *m* (de la mode).

arbitrariness *n* caractère arbitraire *m*.

arbitrary *adj* arbitraire.

arbitrate *vt* arbitrer.

arbitration *n* arbitrage *m*.

arbitrator *n* arbitre *m*.

arbour *n* tonnelle *f*.

arcade *n* galerie *f*.

arch *n* arc *m*; * *adj* malicieux.

archaic *adj* archaïque.

archangel *n* archange *m*.

archbishop *n* archevêque *m*.

archbishopric *n* archevêché *m*.

archeological *adj* archéologique.

archeology *n* archéologie *f*.

archer *n* archer *m*.

archery *n* tir à l'arc *m*.

architect *n* architecte *mf*.

architectural *adj* architectural.

architecture *n* architecture *f*.

archives *npl* archives *fpl*.

archivist *n* archiviste *mf*.

archly *adv* malicieusement.

archway *n* arcade, voûte *f*.

arctic *adj* arctique.

ardent *adj* ardent; ~**ly** *adv* ardemment.

ardour *n* ardeur *f*.

arduous *adj* ardu, difficile.

area *n* région *f*; domaine *m*.

arena *n* arène *f*.

arguably *adv* peut-être, sans doute.

argue *vi* se disputer; * *vt* soutenir.

argument *n* argument *m*; dispute *f*.

argumentation *n* argumentation *f*.

argumentative *adj* raisonneur.

aria *n* (*mus*) aria *f*.

arid *adj* aride.

aridity *n* aridité *f*.

Aries *n* Bélier *m* (signe du zodiaque).

aright *adv* correctement; **to set** ~ rectifier.

arise *vi* se lever; survenir.

aristocracy *n* aristocratie *f*.

aristocrat *n* aristocrate *mf*.

aristocratic *adj* aristocratique; ~**ally** *adv* aristocratiquement.

arithmetic *n* arithmétique *f*.

arithmetical *adj* arithmétique; ~**ly** *adv* arithmétiquement.

ark *n* arche *f*.

arm *n* bras *m*; arme *f*; * *vt* armer; * *vi* (s')armer.

armament *n* armement *m*.

armchair *n* fauteuil *m*.

armed *adj* armé.

armful *n* brassée *f*.

armhole *n* emmanchure *f*.

armistice *n* armistice *m*.

armour *n* armure *f*.

armoured car *n* voiture blindée *f*.

armoury *n* arsenal *m*.

armpit *n* aisselle *f*.

armrest *n* accoudoir *m*.

army *n* armée *f*.

aroma *n* arôme *m*.

aromatic *adj* aromatique.

around *prep* autour de; * *adv* autour.

arouse *vt* éveiller; exciter.

arraign *vt* traduire en justice.

arraignment *n* accusation *f*; procès criminel *m*.

arrange *vt* arranger, organiser.

arrangement *n* arrangement *m*.

arrant *adj* fieffé.

array *n* série *f*.

arrears *npl* arriéré *m*; retard *m*.

arrest *n* arrestation *f*; * *vt* arrêter.

arrival *n* arrivée *f*.

arrive *vi* arriver.

arrogance *n* arrogance *f*.

arrogant *adj* arrogant; ~**ly** *adv* avec arrogance.

arrogate *vt* s'arroger.

arrogation *n* usurpation *f*.

arrow *n* flèche *f*.

arsenal *n* (*mil*) arsenal *m*.

arsenic *n* arsenic *m*.

arson *n* incendie criminel *m*.

art *n* art *m*.

arterial *adj* artériel.

artery *n* artère *f*.

artesian well *n* puits artésien *m*.

artful *adj* malin, astucieux.

artfulness *n* astuce *f*; habileté *f*.

art gallery *n* musée d'art *m*.

arthritis *n* arthrite *f*.

artichoke *n* artichaut *m*.

article *n* article *m*.

articulate *vt* articuler.

articulated *adj* articulé.

articulation *n* articulation *f*.

artifice *n* artifice *m*.

artificial *adj* artificiel; **~ly** *adv* artificielle-
ment.

artificiality *n* caractère artificiel *m*.

artillery *n* artillerie *f*.

artisan *n* artisan *m*.

artist *n* artiste *mf*.

artistic *adj* artistique.

artistry *n* habileté *f*.

artless *adj* naturel, simple; **~ly** *adv* naturellement, simplement.

artlessness *n* simplicité *f*, naturel *m*.

art school *n* école des beaux-arts *f*.

as *conj* comme; pendant que; aussi; **~ for, ~
to** quant à.

asbestos *n* asbeste *m*, amiante *f*.

ascend *vi* monter.

ascendancy *n* ascendant *m*.

ascension *n* ascension *f*.

ascent *n* montée *f*.

ascertain *vt* établir.

ascetic *adj* ascétique; * *n* ascète *mf*.

ascribe *vt* attribuer.

ash *n* (*bot*) frêne *m*; cendre *f*.

ashamed *adj* honteux.

ashbin *n* poubelle *f*.

ashore *adv* à terre; **to go ~** débarquer.

ashtray *n* cendrier *m*.

Ash Wednesday *n* mercredi des Cendres *m*.

aside *adv* de côté.

ask *vt* demander; **~ after** demander des nouvelles de; **~ for** demander; **~ out** inviter à
sortir.

askance *adv* avec méfiance.

askew *adv* de côté.

asleep *adj* endormi; **to fall ~** s'endormir.

asparagus *n* asperge *f*.

aspect *n* aspect *m*.

aspen *n* (*bot*) tremble *m*.

aspersion *n* calomnie *f*.

asphalt *n* asphalte *m*.

asphyxia *n* (*med*) asphyxie *f*.

asphyxiate *vt* asphyxier.

asphyxiation *n* asphyxie *f*.

aspirant *n* aspirant *m* -e *f*.

aspirate *vt* aspirer; * *n* aspirée *f*.

aspiration *n* aspiration *f*.

aspire *vi* aspirer, désirer.

aspirin *n* aspirine *f*.

ass *n* âne *m*; **she ~** ânesse *f*.

assail *vt* assaillir, attaquer.

assailant *n* assaillant, agresseur *m*.

assassin *n* assassin *m*.

assassinate *vt* assassiner.

assassination *n* assassinat *m*.

assault *n* assaut *m*; agression *f*; * *vt* agresser.

assemblage *n* assemblage *m*.

assemble *vt* assembler; * *vi* s'assembler.

assembly *n* assemblée *f*.

assembly line *n* chaîne de montage *f*.

assent *n* assentiment *m*; * *vi* donner son assentiment.

assert *vt* soutenir; affirmer.

assertion *n* assertion *f*.

assertive *adj* péremptoire.

assess *vt* évaluer.

assessment *n* évaluation *f*.

assessor *n* assesseur *m*.

assets *npl* biens *mpl*.

assiduous *adj* assidu; **~ly** *adv* assidûment.

assign *vt* assigner.

assignation *n* rendez-vous *m*; (*law*) cession
f.

assignment *n* (*law*) cession *f*; mission *f*.

assimilate *vt* assimiler.

assimilation *n* assimilation *f*.

assist *vt* assister, aider; secourir.

assistance *n* assistance, aide *f*; secours *m*.

assistant *n* aide *mf*, assistant *m* -e *f*.

associate *vt* associer; * *adj* associé; * *n* associé *m* -e *f*.

association *n* association *f*.

assonance *n* assonance *f*.

assorted *adj* assorti.

assortment *n* assortiment *m*.

assuage *vt* calmer, adoucir.

assume *vt* assumer; supposer.

assumption *n* supposition *f*; **Assumption** *n*
Assomption *f*.

assurance *n* assurance *f*.

assure *vt* assurer.

assuredly *adv* assurément.

asterisk *n* astérisque *m*.

astern *adv* (*mar*) en poupe.

asthma *n* asthme *m*.

asthmatic *adj* asthmatique.

astonish *vt* surprendre, stupéfier.

astonishing *adj* stupéfiant; **~ly** *adv* incroyablement.

astonishment *n* surprise, stupéfaction *f*.

astound *vt* ébahir.

astray *adv*: **to go ~** s'égarer; **to lead ~** détourner du droit chemin.

astride *adv* à califourchon.

astringent *adj* astringent.

astrologer *n* astrologue *mf*.

astrological *adj* astrologique.

astrology *n* astrologie *f*.

astronaut *n* astronaute *mf*.

astronomer *n* astronome *mf*.

astronomical *adj* astronomique.

astronomy *n* astronomie *f*.

astute *adj* malin.

asylum *n* asile, refuge *m*.

at *prep* à; en; **~ once** tout de suite; **~ all** du tout; **~ all events** en tout cas; **~ first** au début, d'abord; **~ last** enfin.

atheism *n* athéisme *m*.

atheist *n* athée *mf*.

athlete *n* athlète *mf*.

athletic *adj* athlétique.

atlas *n* atlas *m*.

atmosphere *n* atmosphère *f*.

atmospheric *adj* atmosphérique.

atom *n* atome *m*.

atom bomb *n* bombe atomique *f*.

atomic *adj* atomique.

atone *vt* expier.

atonement *n* expiation *f*.

atop *adv* en haut.

atrocious *adj* atroce; **~ly** *adv* atrocement.

atrocity *n* atrocité, énormité *f*.

atrophy *n* (*med*) atrophie *f*.

attach *vt* joindre.

attaché *n* attaché *m* -e *f*.

attachment *n* attachement *m*.

attack *vt* attaquer; * *n* attaque *f*.

attacker *n* attaquant *m* -e *f*.

attain *vt* atteindre, obtenir.

attainable *adj* accessible.

attempt *vt* essayer; * *n* essai *m*, tentative *f*.

attend *vt* servir; assister à; **~ to** s'occuper de; * *vi* faire attention.

attendance *n* service *m*; assistance *f*; présence *f*.

attendant *n* serviteur *m*.

attention *n* attention *f*; soin *m*.

attentive *adj* attentif; **~ly** *adv* attentivement.

attenuate *vt* atténuer.

attest *vt* attester.

attic *n* grenier *m*.

attire *n* atours *mpl*.

attitude *n* attitude *f*.

attorney *n* avocat *m*.

attract *vt* attirer.

attraction *n* attraction *f*; attrait *m*.

attractive *adj* attrayant.

attribute *vt* attribuer; * *n* attribut *m*.

attrition *n* usure *f*.

auburn *adj* auburn.

auction *n* vente aux enchères *f*.

auctioneer *n* commissaire-priseur *m*.

audacious *adj* audacieux, téméraire; **~ly** *adv* audacieusement.

audacity *n* audace, témérité *f*.

audible *adj* audible; **~ly** *adv* audiblement.

audience *n* audience *f*; auditoire *m*.

audit *n* audit *m*; * *vt* vérifier.

auditor *n* vérificateur(-trice) de comptes *m*(*f*); auditeur *m* -trice *f*.

auditory *adj* auditif.

augment *vt vi* augmenter.

augmentation *n* augmentation *f*.

August *n* août *m*.

august *adj* auguste, majestueux.

aunt *n* tante *f*.

au pair *n* (jeune fille) au pair *f*.

aura *n* aura *f*.

auspices *npl* auspices *mpl*.

auspicious *adj* favorable, propice; **~ly** *adv* favorablement.

austere *adj* austère, sévère; **~ly** *adv* austèrement.

austerity *n* austérité *f*.

authentic *adj* authentique; **~ally** *adv* authentiquement.

authenticate *vt* légaliser.

authenticity *n* authenticité *f*.

author *n* auteur *m*.

authoress *n* femme auteur *f*.

authoritarian *adj* autoritaire.

authoritative *adj* autoritaire; **~ly** *adv* autoritairement.

authority *n* autorité *f*.

authorization *n* autorisation *f*.

authorize *vt* autoriser.

authorship *n* paternité *f* (d'un livre).

auto *n* voiture *f*.

autocrat *n* autocrate *mf*.

autocratic *adj* autocratique.

autograph *n* autographe *m*.

automated *adj* automatisé.

automatic *adj* automatique.

automaton *n* automate *m*.

autonomy *n* autonomie *f*.

autopsy *n* autopsie *f*.

autumn *n* automne *m*.

autumnal *adj* automnal.

auxiliary *adj* auxiliaire.

avail *vt*: **to ~ oneself of** profiter de; * *n*: **to no ~** en vain.

available *adj* disponible.

avalanche *n* avalanche *f*.

avarice *n* avarice *f*.

avaricious *adj* avare.

avenge *vt* venger.

avenue *n* avenue *f*.

aver *vt* affirmer, déclarer.

average *vt* atteindre la moyenne de; * *n* moyenne *f*, moyen terme *m*.

aversion *n* aversion *f*, dégoût *m*.

avert *vt* détourner, écarter.

aviary *n* volière *f*.

avoid *vt* éviter; échapper à.

avoidable *adj* évitable.

await *vt* attendre.

awake *vt* réveiller; * *vi* se réveiller; * *adj* éveillé.

awakening *n* réveil *m*.

award *vt* attribuer; * *n* prix *m*; décision *f*.

aware *adj* conscient; au courant.

awareness *n* conscience *f*.

away *adv* absent; loin; **~!** va-t-en!; allez-vous-en! **far and ~** de loin.

away game *n* match à l'extérieur *m*.

awe *n* peur, crainte *f*.

awe-inspiring, awesome *adj* terrifiant; imposant.

awful *adj* horrible, terrible; **~ly** *adv* horriblement, terriblement.

awhile *adv* un moment.

awkward *adj* gauche, maladroit; délicat; **~ly** *adv* maladroitement.

awkwardness *n* maladroitesse *f*; difficulté *f*.

awl *n* alêne *f*.

awning *n* (*mar*) taud *m*.

awry *adv* de travers.

axe *n* hache *f*; * *vt* licencier; supprimer.

axiom *n* axiome *m*.

axis *n* axe *m*.

axle *n* axe *m*.

ay(e) *excl* oui.

B

baa *n* bêlement *m*; * *vi* bêler.

babble *vi* bavarder, babiller; **~, babbling** *n* bavardage, babillage *m*.

babbler *n* bavard *m*.

babe, baby *n* bébé, enfant en bas-âge *m*; nourrisson *m*.

baboon *n* babouin *m*.

baby carriage *n* voiture d'enfant *f*.

babyhood *n* petite enfance *f*.

babyish *adj* enfantin; puéril.

baby linen *n* layette *f*.

bachelor *n* célibataire *m*; (diplôme) licencié *m* -e *f*.

bachelorship *n* célibat *m*.

back *n* dos *m*; * *adv* en arrière, à l'arrière; **a few years ~** il y a quelques années, quelques années en arrière; * *vt* soutenir, appuyer, renforcer.

backbite *vt* médire de, sur.

backbiter *n* détracteur *m* -trice *f*.

backbone *n* colonne vertébrale, épine dorsale *f*.

backdate *vt* antidater.

backdoor *n* porte de derrière *f.*

backer *n* partisan *m* -e *f.*

backgammon *n* (jeu de) jacquet *m.*

background *n* fond *m.*

backlash *n* réaction violente *f.*

backlog *n* accumulation de travail en retard *f.*

back number *n* vieux numéro (magazine, journal) *m.*

backpack *n* sac à dos *m.*

back payment *n* rappel de salaire *m.*

backside *n* derrière *m.*

back-up lights *npl* (*auto*) feux de marche arrière *mpl.*

backward *adj* rétrograde; retardé; lent; * *adv* en arrière.

bacon *n* lard *m.*

bad *adj* mauvais, de mauvaise qualité; méchant; malade; ~ly *adv* mal.

badge *n* plaque *f*, insigne *m*, badge *m*; symbole *m*; signe *m.*

badger *n* blaireau *m*; * *vt* harceler.

badminton *n* badminton *m.*

badness *n* mauvaise qualité *f*; méchanceté *f.*

baffle *vt* déconcerter, confondre.

bag *n* sac *m*; valise *f.*

baggage *n* bagages *mpl*; équipement *m.*

bagpipe *n* cornemuse *f.*

bail *n* mise en liberté sous caution, caution *f*; * *vt* mettre en liberté sous caution; mettre en dépôt.

bailiff *n* huissier *m*; régisseur *m.*

bait *vt* tourmenter; appâter; * *n* appât *m*; amorce *f.*

baize *n* serge *f.*

bake *vt* faire cuire au four.

baker *n* boulanger *m* -ère *f*; ~'s dozen treize à la douzaine.

bakery *n* boulangerie *f.*

baking *n* cuisson *f*; fournée *f.*

baking powder *n* levure *f.*

balance *n* balance *f*; équilibre *m*; solde d'un compte *m*; **to lose one's ~** perdre l'équilibre; * *vt* peser; peser le pour et le contre; solder; équilibrer.

balance sheet *n* bilan *m.*

balcony *n* balcon *m.*

bald *adj* chauve.

baldness *n* calvitie *f.*

bale *n* balle *f*; * *vt* emballer; écoper.

baleful *adj* sinistre, funeste, maléfique; ~ly *adv* sinistrement.

ball *n* balle *f*; boule *f*; ballon *m.*

ballad *n* ballade *f.*

ballast *n* lest *m*; * *vt* lester.

ballerina *n* ballerine *f.*

ballet *n* ballet *m.*

ballistic *adj* balistique.

balloon *n* montgolfière *f*, aérostat *m.*

ballot *n* scrutin *m*; vote *m*; * *vi* voter au scrutin.

ballpoint (pen) *n* stylo à bille *m.*

ballroom *n* salle de bal *f.*

balm, balsam *n* baume *m.*

balmy *adj* balsamique, parfumé; doux.

balustrade *n* balustrade *f.*

bamboo *n* bambou *m.*

bamboozle *vt* (*fam*) embobiner.

ban *n* interdiction *f*; * *vt* interdire.

banal *adj* banal.

banana *n* banane *f.*

band *n* bande *f*; reliure *f*; courroie de transmission *f*; orchestre *m.*

bandage *n* bande *f*, bandage *m*; * *vt* bander.

bandaid *n* pansement *m* adhésif.

bandit *n* bandit *m.*

bandstand *n* kiosque à musique *m.*

bandy *vt* avoir des mots.

bandy-legged *adj* aux jambes arquées.

bang *n* coup violent, claquement *m*, détonation *f*; * *vt* frapper violemment; claquer.

bangle *n* bracelet *m.*

bangs *npl* (US) frange (courte et droite) *f.*

banish *vt* bannir, exiler, chasser, expatrier.

banishment *n* exil, bannissement *m.*

banister(s) *n(pl)* rampe d'escalier *f.*

banjo *n* banjo *m.*

bank *n* rive *f*; remblai *m*; banque *f*; banc *m*; digue *f*; * *vt* déposer de l'argent à la banque; ~ **on** compter sur.

bank account *n* compte en banque *m.*

bank card *n* carte bancaire *f.*

banker *n* banquier *m* -ière *f.*

banking *n* opérations bancaires *fpl.*

banknote *n* billet de banque *m.*

bankrupt *adj* failli; * *n* failli *m.*

bankruptcy *n* banqueroute, faillite *f*.

bank statement *n* relevé de compte *m*.

banner *n* bannière *f*; étendard *m*.

banquet *n* banquet *m*.

baptise *vt* baptiser.

baptism *n* baptême *m*.

baptismal *adj* de baptême, baptismal.

baptistery *n* baptistère *m*.

bar *n* bar *m*; barre *f*; obstacle *m*; (*law*) barreau *m*; * *vt* empêcher; interdire; exclure.

barbarian *n* barbare *mf*; * *adj* barbare, cruel.

barbaric *adj* barbare.

barbarism *n* (*gr*) barbarisme *m*; barbarie *f*.

barbarity *n* barbarie, atrocité *f*.

barbarous *adj* barbare, cruel.

barbecue *n* barbecue *m*.

barber *n* coiffeur (pour hommes) *m*.

bar code *n* code barres *m*.

bard *n* barde *m*; poète *m*.

bare *adj* nu, dépouillé; simple; pur; * *vt* dénuder, découvrir.

barefaced *adj* éhonté, impudent.

barefoot(ed) *adj* aux pieds nus.

bareheaded *adj* nu-tête.

barelegged *adj* aux jambes nues.

barely *adv* à peine, tout juste.

bareness *n* nudité *f*.

bargain *n* affaire *f*; contrat, marché *m*; occasion *f*; * *vi* conclure un marché; négocier; ~ **for** s'attendre à.

barge *n* péniche *f*.

baritone *n* (*mus*) baryton *m*.

bark *n* écorce *f*; aboiement *m*; * *vi* aboyer.

barley *n* orge *m*.

barmaid *n* serveuse *f*.

barman *n* barman *m*.

barn *n* grange *f*; étable *f*.

barnacle *n* anatife *m*, bernacle *f*.

barometer *n* baromètre *m*.

baron *n* baron *m*.

baroness *n* baronne *f*.

baronial *adj* de baron.

barracks *npl* caserne *f*.

barrage *n* barrage *m*; (*fig*) torrent *m*.

barrel *n* tonneau, fût *m*; canon de fusil *m*.

barrelled *adj* (firearms) à canons.

barrel organ *n* orgue de Barbarie *m*.

barren *adj* stérile, infertile, improductif.

barricade *n* barricade *f*; barrière *f*; * *vt* barricader, barrer.

barrier *n* barrière *f*; obstacle *m*.

barring *adv* excepté, sauf.

barrow *n* brouette *f*.

bartender *n* barman *m*.

barter *vi* faire du troc; * *vt* troquer, échanger.

base *n* base *f*; partie inférieure *f*; pied *m*; point de départ *m*; * *vt* fonder sur; * *adj* vil, abject.

baseball *n* baseball *m*.

baseless *adj* sans fondement, injustifié.

basement *n* sous-sol *m*.

baseness *n* bassesse, vilenie *f*.

bash *vt* frapper.

bashful *adj* timide, modeste; **~ly** *adv* timidement.

basic *adj* fondamental, de base; **~ally** *adv* fondamentalement.

basilisk *n* (*zool*) basilic *m*.

basin *n* cuvette *f*; lavabo *m*.

basis *n* base *f*; fondement *m*.

bask *vi* se prélasser.

basket *n* panier *m*, corbeille *f*.

basketball *n* basket-ball *m*.

bass *n* (*mus*) contrebasse *f*.

bassoon *n* basson *m*.

bass viol *n* viole de gambe *f*.

bass voice *n* voix de basse *f*.

bastard *n*, *adj* bâtard *m*.

bastardy *n* bâtardise *f*.

baste *vt* arroser la viande de son jus; bâtir.

basting *n* bâti *m*; jus (de viande) *m*; rossée *f*.

bastion *n* (*mil*) bastion *m*.

bat *n* chauve-souris *f*.

batch *n* fournée *f*.

bath *n* bain *m*.

bathe *vt* (*vi*) (se) baigner.

bathing suit *n* maillot de bain *m*.

bathos *n* platitudes (dans un texte littéraire) *fpl*.

bathroom *n* salle de bain *f*.

baths *npl* piscine *f*.

bathtub *n* baignoire *f*.

baton *n* matraque *f*.

battalion *n* (*mil*) bataillon *m*.

batter *vt* battre; frapper, martyriser; * *n* pâte à frire *f*.

battering ram *n* (*mil*) bélier *m*.

battery *n* pile, batterie *f*.

battle *n* bataille *f*; combat *m*; * *vi* se battre, combattre.

battle array *n* ordre de bataille *m*.

battlefield *n* champ de bataille *m*.

battlement *n* remparts *mpl*.

battleship *n* cuirassé *m*.

bawdy *adj* paillard.

bawl *vi* brailler, (*fam*) gueuler.

bay *n* baie *f*; laurier *m*; * *vi* aboyer, hurler; * *adj* bai.

bayonet *n* baïonnette *f*.

bay window *n* fenêtre en saillie *f*.

bazaar *n* bazar *m*.

be *vi* être.

beach *n* plage *f*.

beacon *n* phare, signal lumineux *m*.

bead *n* perle *f*; ~s *npl* chapelet *m*.

beagle *n* beagle *m*.

beak *n* bec *m*.

beaker *n* gobelet *m*.

beam *n* rayon *m*; poutre *f*; * *vi* rayonner, resplendir.

bean *n* haricot *m*; **French** ~ haricot *m* vert.

beansprouts *npl* germes de soja *mpl*.

bear *vt* porter, supporter, produire; * *vi* se diriger.

bear *n* ours *m*; **she** ~ ourse *f*.

bearable *adj* supportable.

beard *n* barbe *f*.

bearded *adj* barbu.

bearer *n* porteur *m* -euse *f*; arbre fructifère *m*.

bearing *n* relation *f*; maintien, port *m*.

beast *n* bête *f*; brute *f*; ~ **of burden** bête de somme *f*.

beastliness *n* bestialité, brutalité *f*.

beastly *adj* bestial, brutal; abominable; * *adv* terriblement.

beat *vt* battre; * *vi* battre, palpiter; * *n* battement *m*; pulsation *f*.

beatific *adj* béatifique; béat.

beatify *vt* béatifier, sanctifier.

beating *n* correction, raclée *f*; battement *m*.

beatitude *n* béatitude *f*.

beautiful *adj* beau, belle, magnifique; ~**ly** *adv* à la perfection, merveilleusement.

beautify *vt* embellir; décorer.

beauty *n* beauté *f*; ~ **salon** *n* institut de beauté *m*; ~ **spot** *n* site touristique *m*.

beaver *n* castor *m*.

because *conj* parce que; * *prép*: ~ **of** en raison de.

beckon *vi* faire signe.

become *vt* convenir, aller à; * *vi* devenir, se faire.

becoming *adj* convenable, seyant.

bed *n* lit *m*.

bedclothes *npl* couvertures et draps *mpl*.

bedding *n* literie *f*.

bedecked *adj* orné.

bedlam *n* maison *f* de fous; chahut *m*.

bed-post *n* colonne de lit *f*.

bedridden *adj* cloué au lit; grabataire.

bedroom *n* chambre *f*.

bedspread *n* dessus-de-lit *m invar*.

bedtime *n* heure d'aller au lit *f*.

bee *n* abeille *f*.

beech *n* hêtre *m*.

beef *n* bœuf (viande) *m*.

beefburger *n* hamburger *m*.

beefsteak *n* bifteck *m*.

beehive *n* ruche *f*.

beeline *n* ligne droite *f*.

beer *n* bière *f*.

beeswax *n* cire *f*.

beet *n* betterave *f*.

beetle *n* scarabée *m*.

befall *vi* arriver, survenir; * *vt* arriver à.

befit *vt* convenir à.

before *adv, prep* avant; devant; * *conj* avant de, avant que.

beforehand *adv* à l'avance, au préalable.

befriend *vt* traiter en ami; aider.

beg *vt* mendier; solliciter; supplier; * *vi* demander la charité.

beget *vt* engendrer.

beggar *n* mendiant *m* -e *f*.

begin *vt vi* commencer.

beginner *n* débutant *m* -e *f*; novice *mf*.

beginning *n* commencement, début *m*, origine *f*.

begrudge *vt* donner à contrecœur; envier.

behalf *n* faveur *f*, intérêt *m*; nom *m*, part *f*.

behave *vi* se comporter, se conduire.

behaviour *n* conduite *f*; comportement *m*.

behead *vt* décapiter.

behind *prep* derrière; * *adv* derrière, par-derrière, en arrière.

behold *vt* voir; contempler; observer.

behove *vi* (*impers*) incomber à.

beige *adj* beige.

being *n* existence *f*; être *m*.

belated *adj* tardif.

belch *vi* éructer; * *vt* vomir; * *n* éructation *f*, rot *m*.

belfry *n* beffroi, clocher *m*.

belie *vt* démentir, tromper.

belief *n* foi, croyance *f*; conviction, opinion *f*, credo *m*.

believable *adj* croyable.

believe *vt* croire; * *vi* penser, croire.

believer *n* croyant *m* -e *f*; adepte *mf*, partisan *m* -e *f*.

belittle *vt* rabaisser.

bell *n* cloche *f*.

bellicose *adj* belliqueux.

belligerent *adj* belligérant.

bellow *vi* beugler, mugir; hurler; * *n* beuglement, mugissement *m*.

bellows *npl* soufflet *m*.

belly *n* ventre *m*.

bellyful *n* ventrée *f*; ras-le-bol *m*.

belong *vi* appartenir à.

belongings *npl* affaires *fpl*.

beloved *adj* chéri, bien-aimé.

below *adv* en dessous, en bas; * *prep* sous, au-dessous de, en dessous.

belt *n* ceinture *f*.

beltway *n* (US) périphérique *m*.

bemoan *vt* déplorer; pleurer.

bemused *adj* déconcerté.

bench *n* banc *m*.

bend *vt* courber, plier; incliner; * *vi* se courber, s'incliner; * *n* courbe *f*.

beneath *adv* au-dessous; * *prep* sous, au-dessous de.

benediction *n* bénédiction *f*.

benefactor *n* bienfaiteur *m* -trice *f*.

benefice *n* bénéfice *m*; bénéfice ecclésiastique *m*.

beneficent *adj* bienfaisant.

beneficial *adj* profitable, salutaire, utile.

beneficiary *n* bénéficiaire *mf*.

benefit *n* intérêt, avantage *m*; profit *m*; bienfait *m*; * *vt* profiter à; * *vi* bénéficier.

benefit night *n* soirée de bienfaisance *f*.

benevolence *n* bienveillance *f*; générosité *f*.

benevolent *adj* bienveillant; de bienfaisance.

benign *adj* bienveillant, doux, affable; bénin.

bent *n* penchant *m*.

benzine *n* (*chem*) benzine *f*.

bequeath *vt* léguer à.

bequest *n* legs *m*.

bereave *vt* priver.

bereavement *n* perte *f*; deuil *m*.

beret *n* béret *m*.

berry *n* baie *f*.

berserk *adj* fou furieux.

berth *n* (*mar*) couchette *f*.

beseech *vt* supplier, implorer, conjurer.

beset *vt* assaillir.

beside(s) *prep* à côté de; excepté; * *adv* de plus, en outre.

besiege *vt* assiéger, assaillir.

best *adj* le meilleur, la meilleure;
* *adv* le mieux; * *n* le meilleur, le mieux *m*.

bestial *adj* bestial, brutal; **~ly** *adv* bestialement.

bestiality *n* bestialité, brutalité *f*.

bestow *vt* accorder, conférer; consacrer.

bestseller *n* best-seller *m*.

bet *n* pari *m*; * *vt* parier.

betray *vt* trahir.

betrayal *n* trahison *f*.

betroth *vt* promettre en mariage.

betrothal *n* fiançailles *fpl*.

better *adj adv* meilleur, mieux; **so much the** ~ tant mieux; * *vt* améliorer.

betting *n* pari *m*.

between *prep* entre; * *adv* au milieu.

bevel *n* biseau *m*.

beverage *n* boisson *f*.

bevy *n* bande *f*, groupe *m*.

beware *vi* prendre garde.

bewilder *vt* déconcerter, dérouter.

bewilderment *n* perplexité *f*.

bewitch *vt* ensorceler, enchanter.

beyond *prep* au-delà de; au-dessus de; plus de; sauf; * *adv* au-delà, plus loin.

bias *n* préjugé *m*; tendance, inclination *f*.

bib *n* bavoir *m*.

Bible *n* Bible *f*.

biblical *adj* biblique.
bibliography *n* bibliographie *f*.
bicarbonate of soda *n* bicarbonate de soude *m*.
bicker *vi* se chamailler.
bicycle *n* bicyclette *f*.
bid *vt* ordonner, commander; offrir; * *n* offre, tentative *f*.
bidding *n* ordre *m*; enchère, offre *f*.
bide *vt* attendre, supporter.
biennial *adj* biennal, bisannuel.
bifocals *npl* verres à double foyer *mpl*.
bifurcated *adj* divisé en deux branches.
big *adj* grand, gros; important.
bigamist *n* bigame *mf*.
bigamy *n* bigamie *f*.
Big Dipper *n* Grande Ourse *f*.
bigheaded *adj* frimeur.
bigness *n* grandeur, grosseur *f*.
bigot *n* fanatique *mf*.
bigoted *adj* fanatique.
bike *n* vélo *m*.
bikini *n* bikini *m*.
bilberry *n* airelle *f*.
bile *n* bile *f*.
bilingual *adj* bilingue.
bilious *adj* bilieux.
bill *n* bec (d'oiseau) *m*; addition *f*; billet *m*.
billboard *n* panneau d'affichage *m*.
billet *n* logement *m*.
billfold *n* (US) portefeuille *m*.
billiards *npl* billard *m*.
billiard table *n* table de billard *f*.
billion *n* milliard *m*.
billy *n* (US) matraque *f*.
bin *n* coffre *m*.
bind *vt* attacher; lier; entourer; relier.
binder *n* relieur *m* -euse *f*.
binding *n* reliure *f*, extra-fort *m*.
binge *n* beuverie, bringue *f*.
bingo *n* loto *m*.
binoculars *npl* jumelles *fpl*.
biochemistry *n* biochimie *f*.
biographer *n* biographe *mf*.
biographical *adj* biographique.
biography *n* biographie *f*.
biological *adj* biologique.
biology *n* biologie *f*.

biped *n* bipède *m*.
birch *n* bouleau *m*.
bird *n* oiseau *m*.
bird's-eye view *n* vue d'ensemble *f*.
bird-watcher *n* ornithologue *mf*.
birth *n* naissance *f*.
birth certificate *n* extrait de naissance *m*.
birth control *n* limitation des naissances *f*.
birthday *n* anniversaire *m*.
birthplace *n* lieu de naissance *m*.
birthright *n* droit de naissance *m*.
biscuit *n* biscuit *m*.
bisect *vt* couper en deux.
bishop *n* évêque *m*.
bison *n* bison *m*.
bit *n* morceau *m*; peu *m*.
bitch *n* chienne *f*; (*fig*) plainte *f*.
bite *vt* mordre; ~ **the dust** (*fam*) mordre la poussière; * *n* morsure *f*.
bitter *adj* amer, âpre; cuisant, acerbe; glacial; ~**ly** *adv* amèrement; avec amertume; âprement.
bitterness *n* amertume *f*; rancœur *f*.
bitumen *n* bitume *m*.
bizarre *adj* étrange, bizarre.
blab *vi* jacasser; lâcher le morceau.
black *adj* noir, obscur; * *n* noir *m*.
blackberry *n* mûre *f*.
blackbird *n* merle *m*.
blackboard *n* tableau (noir) *m*.
blacken *vt* noircir, ternir.
black ice *n* verglas *m*.
blackjack *n* vingt-et-un *m*.
blackleg *n* jaune *m* (pendant une grève).
blacklist *n* liste noire *f*.
blackmail *n* chantage *m*; * *vt* faire chanter.
black market *n* marché noir *m*.
blackness *n* couleur noire *f*; obscurité *f*; noirceur *f*.
black pudding *n* boudin *m*.
black sheep *n* brebis galeuse *f*.
blacksmith *n* forgeron *m*.
blackthorn *n* épine noire *f*.
bladder *n* vessie *f*.
blade *n* lame *f*.
blame *vt* blâmer; * *n* faute *f*.
blameless *adj* irréprochable; ~**ly** *adv* irréprochablement.

blanch *vt* blanchir.

bland *adj* affable, suave; doux; apaisant.

blank *adj* blanc; vide, déconcerté; * *n* blanc *m*.

blank cheque *n* chèque en blanc *m*.

blanket *n* couverture *f*.

blare *vi* retentir.

blase *adj* blasé.

blaspheme *vt* blasphémer.

blasphemous *adj* blasphématoire.

blasphemy *n* blasphème *m*.

blast *n* souffle d'air *m*; explosion *f*; * *vt* faire sauter.

blast-off *n* lancement *m*, mise à feu *f*.

blatant *adj* flagrant.

blaze *n* flamme *f*; * *vi* flamber; resplendir.

bleach *vt* blanchir; décolorer; * *vi* blanchir; * *n* eau de Javel *f*.

bleached *adj* blanchi; décoloré.

bleachers *npl* gradins *mpl*.

bleak *adj* morne, lugubre, glacial, désolé.

bleakness *n* froid *m*; austérité *f*.

bleary(-eyed) *adj* larmoyant.

bleat *n* bêlement *m*; * *vi* bêler.

bleed *vt* *vi* saigner.

bleeding *n* saignement *m*.

bleeper *n* bip *m*.

blemish *vt* gâter; ternir; * *n* tache *f*; infamie *f*.

blend *vt* mélanger.

bless *vt* bénir.

blessing *n* bénédiction *f*; bienfait *m*.

blight *vt* détruire.

blind *adj* aveugle; ~ **alley** *n* impasse *f*; * *vt* aveugler; éblouir; * *n* aveugle *mf*; **(Venetian)** ~ store vénitien *m*.

blinders *npl* (US) œillères *fpl*.

blindfold *vt* bander les yeux de; ~**ed** *adj* les yeux bandés.

blindly *adv* à l'aveuglette, aveuglément.

blindness *n* cécité *f*.

blind side *n* côté faible de quelqu'un *m*.

blind spot *n* angle mort *m*.

blink *vi* clignoter.

blinkers *npl* clignotants *mpl*.

bliss *n* bonheur extrême *m*; félicité *f*.

blissful *adj* heureux; béat, bienheureux; ~**ly** *adv* heureusement.

blissfulness *n* bonheur extrême *m*, félicité *f*.

blister *n* ampoule *f*, cloque *f*; * *vi* se couvrir de cloques.

blitz *n* bombardement aérien *m*.

blizzard *n* tempête de neige *f*.

bloated *adj* gonflé, boursouflé, bouffi.

blob *n* goutte, tache *f*.

bloc *n* bloc *m*.

block *n* bloc *m*; encombrement, blocage *m*; pâté de maisons *m*; ~ **(up)** *vt* bloquer.

blockade *n* blocus *m*; * *vt* faire le blocus, bloquer.

blockage *n* obstruction *f*.

blockbuster *n* grand succès *m*.

blockhead *n* lourdaud, sot, crétin *m*.

blond *adj* blond; * *n* blond *m* -e *f*.

blood *n* sang *m*.

blood donor *n* donneur(-euse) de sang *m(f)*.

blood group *n* groupe sanguin *m*.

bloodhound *n* limier *m*.

bloodily *adv* cruellement.

bloodiness *n* (*fig*) cruauté *f*.

bloodless *adj* exangue, anémié; sans effusion de sang.

blood poisoning *n* empoisonnement du sang *m*.

blood pressure *n* pression artérielle *f*.

bloodshed *n* effusion de sang *f*; carnage *m*.

bloodshot *adj* injecté de sang.

bloodstream *n* système sanguin *m*.

bloodsucker *n* sangsue *f*; (*fig*) vampire *m*.

blood test *n* analyse de sang *f*.

bloodthirsty *adj* sanguinaire.

blood transfusion *n* transfusion sanguine *f*.

blood vessel *n* veine *f*; vaisseau sanguin *m*.

bloody *adj* sanglant, ensanglanté; cruel; ~ **minded** *adj* pas commode, buté.

bloom *n* fleur *f* (*also fig*); * *vi* éclore, fleurir.

blossom *n* fleur *f*.

blot *vt* tacher; sécher; effacer; * *n* tache *f*.

blotchy *adj* marbré; couvert de taches.

blotting pad *n* buvard *m*.

blotting paper *n* papier buvard *m*.

blouse *n* chemisier *m*.

blow *vi* souffler; sonner; * *vt* souffler; faire voler; jouer de; ~ **up** exploser; * *n* coup *m*.

blowout *n* éclatement *m*.

blowpipe *n* sarbacane *f*.

blubber *n* blanc de baleine *m*; * *vi* pleurnicher.

bludgeon *n* gourdin *m*; matraque *f*.

blue *adj* bleu.

bluebell *n* campanule *f*.

bluebottle *n* (*bot*) bleuet *m*; mouche bleue *f*.

blueness *n* bleu *m*.

blueprint *n* (*fig*) projet *m*.

bluff *n* esbrouffe *f*; * *vt* faire de l'esbrouffe.

bluish *adj* bleuâtre.

blunder *n* gaffe *f*; * *vi* faire une gaffe.

blunt *adj* émoussé, obtus; direct; * *vt* émousser.

bluntly *adv* carrément; sans ménagements.

bluntness *n* brusquerie, rudesse *f*.

blur *n* image *f* floue; * *vt* brouiller.

blurt out *vt* laisser échapper.

blush *n* rougeur *f*; fard à joues *m*; * *vi* rougir.

blustery *adj* de tempête, violent.

boa *n* boa *m* (serpent).

boar *n* verrat *m*; **wild ~** sanglier *m*.

board *n* planche *f*; table *f*; conseil *m*; * *vt* monter à bord de.

boarder *n* pensionnaire *mf*.

boarding card *n* carte d'embarquement *f*.

boarding house *n* internat *m*; pension (de famille) *f*.

boarding school *n* pensionnat *m*.

boast *vi* se vanter; * *n* vantardise *f*; rodomontade *f*.

boastful *adj* vantard.

boat *n* bateau *m*; canot *m*; barque *f*.

boating *n* canotage *m*; promenade en bateau *f*.

bobsleigh *n* bobsleigh *m*.

bode *vt* présager, augurer.

bodice *n* corsage *m*.

bodily *adj adv* physique(ment).

body *n* corps *m*; cadavre *m*; **any ~** n'importe qui; **every ~** tout le monde.

body-building *n* culturisme *m*.

bodyguard *n* garde du corps *m*.

bodywork *n* (*auto*) carrosserie *f*.

bog *n* marécage *m*.

boggy *adj* marécageux.

bogus *adj* faux.

boil *vi* bouillir; * *vt* faire bouillir; * *n* furoncle *m*; ébullition *f*.

boiled egg *n* œuf à la coque *m*.

boiled potatoes *npl* pommes de terre à l'eau *fpl*.

boiler *n* casserole *f*; chaudière *f*.

boiling point *n* point d'ébullition *m*.

boisterous *adj* bruyant; turbulent; tumultueux; **~ly** *adv* bruyamment, tumultueusement.

bold *adj* audacieux, téméraire, osé, hardi; **~ly** *adv* audacieusement, hardiment.

boldness *n* intrépidité *f*; audace *f*; effronterie *f*.

bolster *n* traversin *m*; * *vt* soutenir.

bolt *n* verrou *m*; * *vt* verrouiller, fermer au verrou.

bomb *n* bombe *f*; **~ disposal** déminage *m*.

bombard *vt* (*phys*) bombarder.

bombardier *n* bombardier *m*.

bombardment *n* bombardement *m*.

bombshell *n* (*fig*) bombe *f*.

bond *n* lien *m*; attache *f*; engagement *m*; obligation *f*.

bondage *n* esclavage, asservissement *m*.

bond holder *n* obligataire *mf*.

bone *n* os *m*; * *vt* désosser.

boneless *adj* désossé, sans os.

bonfire *n* feu (de joie) *m*.

bonnet *n* bonnet *m*.

bonny *adj* joli.

bonus *n* prime *f*.

bony *adj* osseux.

boo *vt* huer.

booby trap *n* mine *f*.

book *n* livre *m*; **to bring to ~** *vt* obliger à rendre des comptes.

bookbinder *n* relieur(-euse) de livres *m(f)*.

bookcase *n* bibliothèque *f*.

bookkeeper *n* comptable *mf*.

bookkeeping *n* comptabilité *f*.

bookmaking *n* prise des paris *f*.

bookmarker *n* signet *m*.

bookseller *n* libraire *mf*.

bookstore *n* librairie *f*.

bookworm *n* rat de bibliothèque *m*.

boom *n* grondement *m*; essor *m*; * *vi* gronder.

boon *n* bienfait *m*, aubaine *f*; faveur *f*.

boor *n* rustre *m*; brute *f*.

boorish *adj* rustre, rustique.

boost *n* stimulation *f*; * *vt* stimuler.

booster *n* propulseur *m*.

boot *n* botte *f*; coffre *m*; **to ~** *adv* de plus, de surcroît.

booth *n* cabine *f*; baraque *f*.

booty *n* butin *m*.

booze *vi* se saôuler; * *n* alcool *m*.

border *n* bord *m;* bordure *f;* lisière *f;* frontière *f*; * *vt* border, avoisiner.

borderline *n* limite *f*.

bore *vt* forer, percer; ennuyer; * *n* perceuse *f;* calibre *m;* raseur *m*.

boredom *n* ennui *m*.

boring *adj* ennuyeux.

born *adj* né; originaire.

borrow *vt* emprunter.

borrower *n* emprunteur *m* -euse *f*.

bosom *n* sein *m*, poitrine *f*.

bosom friend *n* ami(e) intime *m(f)*.

boss *n* chef *m;* patron(ne) *m(f)*.

botanic(al) *adj* botanique.

botanist *n* botaniste *mf*.

botany *n* botanique *f*.

botch *vt* cochonner.

both *pn* tou(te)s les deux, l'un(e) et l'autre; * *adj* les deux; * *conj* à la fois; autant que.

bother *vt* ennuyer, déranger; * *n* ennui, problème *m*.

bottle *n* bouteille *f*, * *vt* mettre en bouteille.

bottleneck *n* embouteillage *m;* goulot *m*.

bottle-opener *n* ouvre-bouteille *m invar*.

bottom *n* fond *m;* fondement *m;* * *adj* du bas; dernier.

bottomless *adj* sans fond, insondable; inépuisable.

bough *n* branche *f;* rameau *m*.

boulder *n* gros galet *m*.

bounce *vi* rebondir; bondir, faire des bonds; * *n* bond, rebond *m*.

bound *n* limite *f;* saut *m;* répercussion *f;* * *vi* bondir, sauter; * *adj* à destination de.

boundary *n* limite *f;* frontière *f*.

boundless *adj* illimité, infini.

bounteous, bountiful *adj* abondant; prodigue, généreux; bienfaisant.

bounty *n* libéralité, générosité *f*.

bouquet *n* bouquet *m*.

bourgeois *adj* bourgeois.

bout *n* attaque *f;* accès *m;* combat *m*.

bovine *adj* bovin.

bow *vt* incliner, baisser; * *vi* se courber; faire une révérence; * *n* salut *m*, révérence *f*.

bow *n* arc *m;* archet *m;* nœud *m*.

bowels *npl* intestins *mpl;* entrailles *fpl*.

bowl *n* bol, saladier *m;* boule *f;* * *vi* jouer aux boules.

bowling *n* boules *fpl*.

bowling alley *n* bowling *m*.

bowling green *n* terrain de boules *m*.

bowstring *n* corde (d'arc) *f*.

bow tie *n* nœud papillon *m*.

box *n* boîte, caisse *f;* loge *f;* ~ **on the ear** gifle *f*; * *vt* mettre en boîte; * *vi* boxer.

boxer *n* boxeur *m*.

boxing *n* boxe *f*.

boxing gloves *npl* gants de boxe *mpl*.

boxing ring *n* ring *m*.

box office *n* guichet *m*.

box-seat *n* place à côté du siège du cocher *f*.

boy *n* garçon *m*.

boycott *vt* boycotter; * *n* boycottage *m*.

boyfriend *n* petit ami *m*.

boyish *adj* d'enfant, puéril; de garçon.

bra *n* soutien-gorge *m*.

brace *n* attache *f;* bretelle *f;* appareil dentaire *m*.

bracelet *n* bracelet *m*

bracken *n* (*bot*) fougère *f*.

bracket *n* tranche *f;* parenthèse *f;* crochet *m;* * ~ **with** *vt* réunir par une accolade; mettre ensemble.

bracing *adj* vivifiant, tonifiant.

brag *n* fanfaronnade *f;* * *vi* se vanter, fanfaronner.

braid *n* tresse *f;* * *vt* tresser.

brain *n* cerveau *m;* tête *f;* * *vt* assommer, défoncer le crâne à.

brainchild *n* invention personnelle *f*.

brainless *adj* stupide.

brainwash *vt* faire un lavage de cerveau à.

brainwave *n* idée lumineuse *f*.

brainy *adj* intelligent.

brake *n* frein *m;* * *vi* freiner.

brake fluid *n* liquide de frein *m*.

brake light *n* feu de stop *m*.

bramble *n* ronce *f*.

bran *n* son *m*.

branch *n* branche *f;* ramification *f;* * *vi* se ramifier.

branch line *n* (*rail*) ligne d'embranchement *f*.

brand *n* marque *f;* marque au fer *f;* * *vt* marquer au fer.

brandish *vt* brandir.

brand-new *adj* flambant-neuf.

brandy *n* cognac *m*.

brash *adj* grossier; impertinent.

brass *n* cuivre *m*.

brassiere *n* soutien-gorge *m*.

brat *n* môme, gosse *mf*.

bravado *n* bravade *f*.

brave *adj* courageux, brave, vaillant;   * *vt* braver; * *n* brave *m*; ~**ly** *adv* bravement, courageusement.

bravery *n* bravoure *f*; courage *m*; magnificence *f*.

brawl *n* bagarre, rixe *f*; * *vi* se bagarrer.

brawn *n* muscle *m*; fromage de tête *m*.

bray *vi* braire; * *n* braiment *m*.

braze *vt* souder au laiton.

brazen *adj* de cuivre; impudent, effronté; * *vi* crâner.

brazier *n* brasero *m*.

breach *n* rupture *f*; brèche *f*; violation *f*.

bread *n* pain *m* (*also fig*); **brown** ~ pain bis *m*.

breadbox *n* panière *f*.

breadcrumbs *npl* chapelure *f*.

breadth *n* largeur *f*.

breadwinner *n* soutien de famille *m*.

break *vt* casser; briser; violer; interrompre; * *vi* se casser; ~ **into** entrer par effraction; ~ **out** s'échapper; * *n* cassure, rupture *f*; interruption *f*; ~ **of day** point du jour *m*, aube *f*.

breakage *n* casse *f*.

breakdown *n* panne *f*; dépression nerveuse *f*.

breakfast *n* petit déjeuner *m*; * *vi* déjeuner.

breaking *n* bris *m*; violation *f*; fracture *f*.

breakthrough *n* percée, innovation *f*.

breakwater *n* digue *f*.

breast *n* poitrine *f*, sein *m*; cœur *m*.

breastbone *n* sternum *m*.

breastplate *n* pectoral *m*; plastron *m*.

breaststroke *n* brasse *f*.

breath *n* haleine *f*; respiration *f*; souffle *m*.

breathe *vt vi* respirer; exhaler.

breathing *n* respiration *f*; souffle *m*.

breathing space *n* moment de répit *m*.

breathless *adj* hors d'haleine.

breathtaking *adj* stupéfiant.

breed *n* race, espèce *f*; * *vt* élever, engendrer; produire; éduquer; * *vi* se reproduire.

breeder *n* éleveur *m* -euse *f*.

breeding *n* élevage *m*; éducation *f*.

breeze *n* brise *f*.

breezy *adj* frais.

brethren *npl* frères *mpl*.

breviary *n* bréviaire *m*.

brevity *n* brièveté *f*; concision *f*.

brew *vt* faire infuser; brasser; comploter * *vi* infuser; se tramer; * *n* infusion *f*.

brewer *n* brasseur *m*.

brewery *n* brasserie *f*.

briar, brier *n* ronce *f*; églantier *m*.

bribe *n* pot-de-vin *m*; * *vt* acheter, soudoyer.

bribery *n* corruption *f*.

bric-a-brac *n* bric-à-brac *m*.

brick *n* brique *f*; * *vt* bâtir en briques.

bricklayer *n* maçon *m*.

bridal *adj* de noces, nuptial.

bride *n* mariée *f*.

bridegroom *n* marié *m*.

bridesmaid *n* demoiselle d'honneur *f*.

bridge *n* pont *m*; arête du nez *f*; chevalet *m*; ~ **(over)** *vt* relier par un pont.

bridle *n* bride *f*; frein *m*; * *vt* brider; réfréner.

brief *adj* bref, concis, succint; * *n* affaire *f*; résumé *m*.

briefcase *n* serviette *f*.

briefly *adv* brièvement, en peu de mots.

brigade *n* (*mil*) brigade *f*.

brigadier *n* (*mil*) général de brigade *m*.

brigand *n* bandit, brigand *m*.

bright *adj* clair, brillant, éclatant; ~**ly** *adv* avec éclat.

brighten *vt* faire briller; * *vi* s'éclairer.

brightness *n* éclat, brillant *m*.

brilliance *n* éclat *m*.

brilliant *adj* éclatant; génial; ~**ly** *adv* avec éclat.

brim *n* bord *m*.

brimful *adj* plein jusqu'au bord.

bring *vt* apporter; amener; persuader; ~ **about** entraîner, provoquer; ~ **forth** produire; provoquer; ~ **up** élever.

brink *n* bord *m*.

brisk *adj* vif, rapide, frais.

brisket *n* poitrine *f* (de bœuf).

briskly *adv* vivement; rapidement.

bristle *n* poil *m*; soie *f*; * *vi* se hérisser.

bristly *adj* hérissé.

brittle *adj* cassant, fragile.

broach *vt* aborder.

broad *adj* large.

broadbeans *npl* fèves *fpl*.

broadcast *n* émission *f*; * *vt vi* diffuser, émettre.

broadcasting *n* radiodiffusion *f*; émission de télévision *f*.

broaden *vt* élargir; * *vi* s'élargir.

broadly *adv* généralement.

broad-minded *adj* tolérant, aux idées larges.

broadness *n* largeur *f*.

broadside *n* flanc (d'un navire) *m*; attaque *f* cinglante.

broadways *adv* en large, dans le sens de la largeur.

brocade *n* brocart *m*.

broccoli *n* brocoli *m*.

brochure *n* brochure *f*, dépliant *m*.

brogue *n* accent *m* du terroir.

broil *vt* griller.

broken *adj* cassé; interrompu; ~ **English** mauvais anglais *m*.

broker *n* courtier *m*.

brokerage *n* courtage *m*.

bronchial *adj* des bronches.

bronchitis *n* bronchite *f*.

bronze *n* bronze *m*; * *vt* bronzer, brunir.

brooch *n* broche *f*.

brood *vi* couver; ruminer; * *n* couvée *f*; nichée *f*.

brood-hen *n* couveuse *f*.

brook *n* ruisseau *m*.

broom *n* genêt *m*; balai *m*.

broomstick *n* manche à balai *m*.

broth *n* bouillon de viande et de légumes *m*.

brothel *n* bordel *m*.

brother *n* frère *m*.

brotherhood *n* fraternité *f*.

brother-in-law *n* beau-frère *m*.

brotherly *adj* fraternel; *adv* fraternellement.

brow *n* sourcil *m*; front *m*; sommet *m*.

browbeat *vt* intimider.

brown *adj* marron; brun; ~ **paper** *n* papier d'emballage *m*; ~ **sugar** *n* cassonnade *f*; * *n* marron *m*; * *vt* brunir.

browse *vt* parcourir; * *vi* paître.

bruise *vt* faire un bleu à; * *n* bleu *m*, ecchymose *f*.

brunette *n* brune *f*.

brunt *n* choc *m*.

brush *n* brosse *f*; pinceau *m*; accrochage *m*; * *vt* brosser.

brushwood *n* broussailles *fpl*; brindilles *fpl*.

brusque *adj* brusque.

Brussels sprout *n* chou de Bruxelles *m*.

brutal *adj* brutal; ~**ly** *adv* brutalement.

brutality *n* brutalité *f*.

brutalize *vt* brutaliser.

brute *n* brute *f*; * *adj* bestial, féroce.

brutish *adj* brutal, bestial; féroce; ~**ly** *adv* brutalement.

bubble *n* bulle *f*; * *vi* faire des bulles, bouillonner; pétiller.

bubblegum *n* bubble-gum *m*.

bucket *n* seau *m*.

buckle *n* boucle *f*; * *vt* attacher, boucler; * *vi* se déformer.

bucolic *adj* bucolique.

bud *n* bourgeon, bouton *m*; * *vi* bourgeonner.

Buddhism *n* bouddhisme *m*.

budding *adj* en bouton.

buddy *n* copain *m*.

budge *vi* bouger, remuer; céder.

budgerigar *n* perruche *f*.

budget *n* budget *m*.

buff *n* mordu *m*.

buffalo *n* bison *m*.

buffers *npl* (*rail*) pare-chocs *m invar*.

buffet *n* buffet *m*; * *vt* gifler; frapper.

buffoon *n* bouffon *m*.

bug *n* punaise *f*.

bugbear *n* épouvantail, croquemitaine *m*.

bugle(horn) *n* clairon *m*.

build *vt* construire, bâtir.

builder *n* constructeur *m*; entrepreneur *m*.

building *n* bâtiment *m*; immeuble, édifice *m*.

building society *n* organisme de crédit immobilier *m*.

bulb *n* bulbe *m*; oignon *m*.

bulbous *adj* bulbeux.

bulge *vi* se renfler; * *n* gonflement, renflement *m*.

bulk *n* masse *f*; volume *m*; grosseur *f*; majeure partie *f*; **in** ~ en gros.

bulky *adj* volumineux; encombrant.
bull *n* taureau *m*.
bulldog *n* bouledogue *m*.
bulldozer *n* bulldozer *m*.
bullet *n* balle *f*.
bulletin board *n* panneau d'affichage *m*.
bulletproof *adj* pare-balles, blindé.
bullfight *n* corrida *f*.
bullfighter *n* torero *m*.
bullfighting *n* tauromachie *f*.
bullion *n* or en barre *m*.
bullock *n* bouvillon *m*.
bullring *n* arène *f*.
bull's-eye *n* centre de la cible *m*.
bully *n* tyran *m*; * *vt* tyraniser.
bulwark *n* rempart *m*.
bum *n* clochard *m*.
bumblebee *n* bourdon *m*.
bump *n* heurt *m*; secousse *f*; bosse *f*; * *vt* heurter.
bumpkin *n* rustre *m*; plouc *m*.
bumpy *adj* cahoteux, bosselé.
bun *n* petit pain *m*; chignon *m*.
bunch *n* botte *f*; groupe *m*.
bundle *n* paquet *m*, liasse *f*; ballot *m*; fagot *m*; * *vt* empaqueter, mettre en liasse.
bung *n* bonde *f*; * *vt* boucher.
bungalow *n* bungalow *m*.
bungle *vt* bousiller; * *vi* faire mal les choses.
bunion *n* (*med*) oignon *m*.
bunk *n* couchette *f*.
bunker *n* abri *m*; bunker *m*.
buoy *n* (*mar*) bouée *f*.
buoyancy *n* flottabilité *f*; optimisme *m*.
buoyant *adj* flottable; gai, enjoué.
burden *n* charge *f*; fardeau *m*; * *vt* charger.
bureau *n* commode *f*; bureau *m*.
bureaucracy *n* bureaucratie *f*.
bureaucrat *n* bureaucrate *mf*.
burglar *n* cambrioleur *m* -euse *f*.
burglar alarm *n* signal d'alarme, signal anti-vol *m*.
burglary *n* cambriolage *m*.
burial *n* enterrement *m*; obsèques *fpl*.
burial place *n* lieu de sépulture *m*.
burlesque *n* caricature, parodie *f*; * *adj* burlesque, caricatural.
burly *adj* robuste, de forte carrure.

burn *vt* brûler; incendier, mettre le feu à; * *vi* brûler; * *n* brûlure *f*.
burner *n* brûleur *m*.
burning *adj* brûlant.
burrow *n* terrier *m*; * *vi* se terrer.
bursar *n* intendant(e) *m(f)*.
burst *vi* éclater; ~ **into tears** éclater en sanglots; ~ **out laughing** éclater de rire; * *vt* ~ **into** faire irruption dans; * *n* éclatement *m*; explosion *f*.
bury *vt* enterrer, inhumer.
bus *n* (auto)bus *m*.
bush *n* buisson, taillis *m*.
bushy *adj* touffu, plein de buissons.
busily *adv* activement, avec empressement.
business *n* entreprise *f*; commerce *m*; affaires *fpl*; activité *f*.
businesslike *adj* sérieux.
businessman *n* homme d'affaires *m*.
business trip *n* voyage d'affaires *m*.
businesswoman *n* femme d'affaires *f*.
bust *n* buste *m*.
bus-stop *n* arrêt d'autobus *m*.
bustle *vi* s'affairer; s'activer; * *n* remue-ménage *m*; animation *f*.
bustling *adj* animé.
busy *adj* occupé; actif.
busybody *n* mouche du coche *f*.
but *conj* mais; sauf, excepté, seulement.
butcher *n* boucher *m* -ère *f*; * *vt* abattre, massacrer.
butcher's (shop) *n* boucherie *f*.
butchery *n* boucherie *f*, carnage *m*.
butler *n* majordome *m*.
butt *n* butte *f*; mégot *m*; * *vt* donner un coup de tête à.
butter *n* beurre *m*; * *vt* beurrer.
buttercup *n* (*bot*) bouton d'or *m*.
butterfly *n* papillon *m*.
buttermilk *n* babeurre *m*.
buttocks *npl* fesses *fpl*.
button *n* bouton *m*; * *vt* boutonner.
buttonhole *n* boutonnière *f*.
buttress *n* contre-fort *m*; soutien *m*; * *vt* soutenir.
buxom *adj* bien en chair.
buy *vt* acheter.
buyer *n* acheteur *m* -euse *f*.

buzz *n* bourdonnement, murmure *m*; * *vi* bourdonner.

buzzard *n* buse *f*.

buzzer *n* interphone *m*.

by *prep* à côté de, près de; par; de; ~ **and** ~ bientôt; ~ **the** ~ à propos; ~ **much** de loin; ~ **all means** certainement; * *adv* près.

bygone *adj* passé.

by-law *n* arrêté municipal *m*.

bypass *n* route de contournement *f*.

by-product *n* sous-produit *m*.

by-road *n* chemin de traverse *m*.

bystander *n* spectateur *m* -trice *f*, badaud *m* -e *f*.

byte *n* (*comput*) octet *m*.

byword *n* proverbe, dicton *m*.

C

campaigner *n* militant, candidat en campagne électorale *m*.

camper *n* campeur *m* -euse *f*.

camphor *n* camphre *m*.

campsite *n* camping *m*.

can *v aux* pouvoir; * *n* boîte de conserve *f*.

canal *n* conduit *m*; canal *m*.

cancel *vt* annuler.

cancellation *n* annulation *f*.

cancer *n* cancer *m*.

Cancer *n* Cancer *m* (signe du zodiaque).

cancerous *adj* cancéreux.

candid *adj* candide, simple, sincère; ~**ly** *adv* candidement, franchement.

candidate *n* candidat(e) *m(f)*.

candied *adj* confit.

candle *n* bougie *f*; cierge *m*.

candlelight *n* lueur d'une bougie *f*.

candlestick *n* bougeoir *m*.

candour *n* candeur *f*; sincérité *f*.

candy *n* bonbon *m*.

cane *n* canne *f*; bâton *m*.

canine *adj* canin.

canister *n* boîte *f* métallique.

cannabis *n* cannabis *m*.

cannibal *n* cannibale *mf*; anthropophage *mf*.

cannibalism *n* cannibalisme *m*.

cannon *n* canon *m*.

cannonball *n* boulet de canon *m*.

canny *adj* rusé; prudent.

canoe *n* canoè *m*.

canon *n* canon *m*; règle *f*; ~**law** droit canon *m*.

canonization *n* canonisation *f*.

canonize *vt* canoniser.

can opener *n* ouvre-boîte *m*.

canopy *n* baldaquin *m*, marquise *f*.

cantankerous *adj* acariâtre, atrabilaire.

canteen *n* cantine *f*.

canter *n* petit galop *m*.

canvas *n* toile *f*.

canvass *vt* sonder, examiner; débattre; * *vi* solliciter des voix; faire du démarchage.

canvasser *n* prospecteur *m* -trice *f*, démarcheur *m* -euse *f*.

canyon *n* canyon *m*.

cap *n* casquette *f*.

capability *n* capacité, aptitude, faculté *f*; potentiel *m*.

capable *adj* capable.

capacitate *vt* rendre capable.

capacity *n* capacité, aptitude *f*; potentiel *m*.

cape *n* cap, promontoire *m*.

caper *n* cabriole *f*; gambade *f*; * *vi* cabrioler; gambader.

capillary *adj* capillaire.

capital *adj* capital; principal; * *n* capital *m*; capitale *f*; majuscule *f*.

capitalism *n* capitalisme *m*.

capitalist *n* capitaliste *mf*.

capitalize *vt* capitaliser; ~ **on** profiter de.

capital punishment *n* peine de mort, peine capitale *f*.

Capitol *n* Capitole *m*.

capitulate *vi* capituler.

capitulation *n* capitulation *f*.

caprice *n* caprice *m*.

capricious *adj* capricieux; ~**ly** *adv* capricieusement.

Capricorn *n* Capricorne *m* (signe du zodiaque).

capsize *vt* (*mar*) chavirer.

capsule *n* capsule *f*.

captain *n* capitaine *m*.

captaincy, **captainship** n grade de capitaine m; statut de capitaine m.

captivate vt captiver.

captivation n fascination f.

captive n captif m -ive f, prisonnier m -ière f.

captivity n captivité f.

capture n capture f; * vt prendre, capturer.

car n voiture f, automobile f; wagon m.

carafe n carafe f.

caramel n caramel m.

carat n carat m.

caravan n caravane f.

caraway n (bot) cumin m.

carbohydrates npl hydrates de carbone mpl.

carbon n carbone m.

carbon copy n copie carbone f, double carbone m.

carbonize vt carboniser.

carbon paper n papier carbone m.

carbuncle n escarboucle f; furoncle m, tumeur maligne f.

carburettor n carburateur m.

carcass n cadavre m.

card n carte f.

cardboard n carton m.

card game n jeu de cartes m.

cardiac adj cardiaque.

cardinal adj cardinal, principal; * n cardinal m.

card table n table de jeu f.

care n soin m; souci m; * vi se soucier de, être concerné par; **what do I ~?** qu'est-ce que cela peut me faire?; **~ for** vt soigner; aimer.

career n carrière f; cours m; * vi aller à toute vitesse.

carefree n insouciant.

careful adj soigneux, consciencieux, prudent; **~ly** adv soigneusement.

careless adj insouciant, négligent; indolent; **~ly** adv négligemment.

carelessness n négligence, indifférence f.

caress n caresse f; * vt caresser.

caretaker n gardien m -ne f, concierge mf.

car-ferry n ferry m.

cargo n cargaison de navire f.

car hire n location de voiture f.

caricature n caricature f; * vt caricaturer.

caries n carie f.

caring adj aimant; humanitaire.

Carmelite n carmélite f.

carnage n carnage m.

carnal adj charnel; sensuel; **~ly** adv charnellement.

carnation n œillet m.

carnival n carnaval m.

carnivorous adj carnivore.

carol n chant m (de Noël).

carpenter n charpentier m; **~'s bench** banc de menuisier m.

carpentry n charpenterie f.

carpet n tapis m; * vt recouvrir d'un tapis; moquetter.

carpeting n moquette f.

carriage n port m; voiture f; wagon m.

carriage-free adj franco de port.

carrier n porteur, transporteur m.

carrier pigeon n pigeon voyageur m.

carrion n charogne f.

carrot n carotte f.

carry vt porter; transporter; conduire; * vi porter; **~ the day** être victorieux; **~ on** continuer.

cart n charrette f; chariot m; * vt charrier.

cartel n cartel m.

carthorse n cheval de trait m.

Carthusian n chartreux m.

cartilage n cartilage m.

cartload n charretée f.

carton n pot m; boîte f.

cartoon n dessin animé m.

cartridge n cartouche f.

carve vt tailler, sculpter, ciseler.

carving n sculpture f.

carving knife n couteau à découper m.

car wash n station de nettoyage pour voitures f.

case n boîte f; valise f; cas m; étui m; enveloppe f; **in ~** au cas où.

cash n espèces fpl; * vt encaisser.

cash card n carte bancaire f.

cash dispenser n distributeur automatique de billets m.

cashier n caissier m -ière f.

cashmere n cachemire m.

casing n chambranle m; enveloppe f.

casino n casino m.

cask n tonneau, fût m.

casket n cercueil m.

casserole n cocotte f.

cassette *n* cassette *f*.

cassette player, recorder *n* lecteur de cassettes, magnétophone *m*.

cassock *n* soutane *f*.

cast *vt* jeter, lancer; couler; * *n* coup *m*; moule *m*.

castanets *npl* castagnettes *fpl*.

castaway *n* réprouvé, paria *m*.

caste *n* caste *f*.

castigate *vt* punir sévèrement.

casting vote *n* voix prépondérante *f*.

cast iron *n* fonte *f*.

castle *n* château *m*.

castor oil *n* huile de ricin *f*.

castrate *vt* castrer.

castration *n* castration *f*.

cast steel *n* acier fondu *m*.

casual *adj* accidentel, fortuit; ~**ly** *adv* par hasard, fortuitement.

casualty *n* victime *f*, mort *m* -e *f*.

cat *n* chat *m*, chatte *f*.

catalogue *n* catalogue *m*.

catalyst *n* catalyseur *m*.

cataplasm *n* cataplasme *m*.

catapult *n* catapulte *f*.

cataract *n* cataracte *f*.

catarrh *n* rhume *m*; catarrhe *m*.

catastrophe *n* catastrophe *f*.

catcall *n* sifflet *m*.

catch *vt* attraper, saisir; prendre; surprendre; ~ **cold** attraper froid; ~ **fire** prendre feu; * *n* prise *f*; capture *f*; (*mus*) canon *m*; attrape *f*.

catching *adj* contagieux, communicatif.

catchphrase *n* rengaine *f*.

catchword *n* slogan *m*.

catchy *adj* qui attire l'attention; accrocheur.

catechism *n* catéchisme *m*.

catechize *vt* cathéchiser; interroger.

categorical *adj* catégorique; ~**ly** *adv* catégoriquement.

categorize *vt* classer par catégories.

category *n* catégorie *f*.

cater *vi* approvisionner en nourriture.

caterer *n* fournisseur, traiteur *m*.

catering *n* restauration *f*.

caterpillar *n* chenille *f*.

catgut *n* boyau de chat *m*.

cathedral *n* cathédrale *f*.

catholic *adj n* catholique *mf*.

Catholicism *n* catholicisme *m*.

cattle *n* bétail *m*.

cattle show *n* exposition bovine *f*.

caucus *n* réunion d'un comité électoral *f*.

cauliflower *n* chou-fleur *m*.

cause *n* cause *f*; raison *f*; motif *m*; procès *m*; * *vt* causer.

causeway *n* chaussée *f*.

caustic *adj n* caustique *m/f*.

cauterize *vt* cautériser.

caution *n* prudence, précaution *f*; avertissement *m*; * *vt* avertir.

cautionary *adj* d'avertissement.

cautious *adj* prudent, circonspect.

cavalier *adj* cavalier.

cavalry *n* cavalerie *f*.

cave *n* grotte *f*; caverne *f*.

caveat *n* avertissement *m*; mise en garde *f*; (*law*) notification *f*.

cavern *n* caverne *f*.

cavernous *adj* caverneux.

cavity *n* cavité *f*.

cease *vt* cesser, arrêter; * *vi* cesser.

ceasefire *n* cessez-le-feu *m*.

ceaseless *adj* incessant, continuel; ~**ly** *adv* continuellement.

cedar *n* cèdre *m*.

cede *vt* (*law*) céder.

ceiling *n* plafond *m*.

celebrate *vt* célébrer, fêter.

celebration *n* fête *f*.

celebrity *n* célébrité *f*.

celery *n* céleri *m*.

celestial *adj* céleste, divin.

celibacy *n* célibat *m*.

celibate *adj* célibataire.

cell *n* cellule *f*.

cellar *n* cave *f*; cellier *m*.

cello *n* violoncelle *m*.

cellophane *n* cellophane *f*.

cellular *adj* cellulaire.

cellulose *n* (*chem*) cellulose *f*.

cement *n* ciment *m* (*also fig*); * *vt* cimenter.

cemetery *n* cimetière *m*.

cenotaph *n* cénotaphe *m*.

censor *n* censeur *m*, critique *mf*.

censorious *adj* sévère, critique.

censorship *n* censure *f*.
censure *n* censure, critique *f*; * *vt* censurer, condamner; critiquer.
census *n* recensement *m*.
cent *n* centime *m*.
centenarian *n* centenaire *mf*.
centenary *n* centenaire *m*; * *adj* centenaire.
centennial *adj* centenaire.
centigrade *n* centigrade *m*.
centilitre *n* centilitre *m*.
centimetre *n* centimètre *m*.
centipede *n* mille-pattes *m invar*.
central *adj* central; **~ly** *adv* de façon centralisée; dans le centre.
centralize *vt* centraliser.
centre *n* centre *m*; * *vt* centrer; concentrer; * *vi* se concentrer.
centrifugal *adj* centrifuge.
century *n* siècle *m*.
ceramic *adj* en céramique.
cereals *npl* céréales *fpl*.
cerebral *adj* cérébral.
ceremonial *adj n* cérémonial *m*; rituel *m*.
ceremonious *adj* cérémonieux; **~ly** *adv* solennellement.
ceremony *n* cérémonie *f*; cérémonies *fpl*.
certain *adj* certain, sûr; **~ly** *adv* certainement, sans aucun doute.
certainty, certitude *n* certitude, conviction *f*.
certificate *n* certificat, acte *m*.
certification *n* authentification *f*.
certified mail *n* envoi avec accusé de réception *m*.
certify *vt* certifier, assurer.
cervical *adj* cervical.
cessation *n* cessation *f*.
cesspool *n* cloaque *m*; fosse d'aisances *f*.
chafe *vt* irriter; frotter.
chaff *n* menue paille *f*.
chaffinch *n* pinson *m*.
chagrin *n* dépit *m*.
chain *n* chaîne *f*; série, suite *f*; * *vt* enchaîner; attacher avec une chaîne.
chain reaction *n* réaction en chaîne *f*.
chainstore *n* grand magasin à succursales *m*.
chair *n* chaise *f*; * *vt* présider.
chairman *n* président *m*.
chalice *n* calice *m*.

chalk *n* craie *f*.
challenge *n* défi *m*; * *vt* défier.
challenger *n* provocateur *m* -trice *f*.
challenging *adj* provocateur.
chamber *n* pièce *f*; chambre *f*.
chambermaid *n* femme de chambre *f*.
chameleon *n* caméléon *m*.
chamois leather *n* peau de chamois *f*.
champagne *n* champagne *m*.
champion *n* champion *m* -ne *f*; * *vt* défendre.
championship *n* championnat *m*.
chance *n* hasard *m*; chance *f*; occasion *f*; **by ~** par hasard; * *vt* faire par hasard.
chancellor *n* chancelier *m*.
chancery *n* chancellerie *f*.
chandelier *n* lustre *m*.
change *vt* changer; * *vi* changer, se transformer; * *n* changement *m*, modification *f*; variété *f*; change *m*.
changeable *adj* changeant, variable; inconstant.
changeless *adj* constant, immuable.
changing *adj* variable, changeant.
channel *n* canal *m*; chaîne *f*; * *vt* canaliser.
chant *n* chant *m* scandé; * *vt* scander.
chaos *n* chaos *m*.
chaotic *adj* chaotique.
chapel *n* chapelle *f*.
chaplain *n* chapelain *m*.
chapter *n* chapitre *m*.
char *vt* carboniser.
character *n* caractère *m*; personnage *m*.
characteristic *adj* caractéristique; **~ally** *adv* typiquement.
characterize *vt* caractériser.
characterless *adj* sans caractère.
charade *n* charade *f*.
charcoal *n* charbon de bois *m*.
charge *vt* charger; accuser; * *n* fardeau *m*; accusation *f*; (*mil*) attaque *f*; prix *m*.
chargeable *adj* passible.
charge card *n* carte de crédit *f*.
charitable *adj* caritatif; charitable; **~bly** *adv* charitablement.
charity *n* charité, bienfaisance *f*; aumône *f*.
charlatan *n* charlatan *m*.
charm *n* charme *m*; attrait *m*; * *vt* charmer, enchanter.

charming *adj* charmant.

chart *n* carte de navigation *f*; diagramme *m*.

charter *n* charte *f*; privilège *m*; * *vt* affréter.

charter flight *n* vol charter *m*.

chase *vt* donner la chasse à; poursuivre; * *n* chasse *f*.

chasm *n* abîme *m*.

chaste *adj* chaste; pur; sobre.

chasten *vt* châtier, corriger.

chastise *vt* châtier, punir, corriger.

chastisement *n* châtiment *m*.

chastity *n* chasteté, pureté *f*.

chat *vi* causer; * *n* petite conversation *f*, bavardage *m*.

chatter *vi* bavarder; jacasser; * *n* bavardage *m*; jacasserie *f*.

chatterbox *n* moulin à paroles *m*, pipelette *f*.

chatty *adj* bavard.

chauffeur *n* chauffeur *m*.

chauvinist *n* chauvin *m* -e *f*.

cheap *adj* bon marché, peu cher; ~**ly** *adv* bon marché.

cheapen *vt* baisser le prix de.

cheaper *adj* moins cher.

cheat *vt* tromper, frauder; * *n* fraude, tricherie *f*; tricheur *m* -euse *f*.

check *vt* vérifier; contrôler; réprimer, enrayer; stopper; enregistrer; * *n* contrôle *m*.

checkmate *n* échec et mat *m*.

checkout *n* caisse *f*.

checkpoint *n* poste de contrôle *m*.

checkroom *n* (US) consigne *f*.

checkup *n* bilan de santé *m*.

cheek *n* joue *f*; culot (*fam*) *m*.

cheekbone *n* pommette *f*.

cheer *n* gaieté *f*; joie *f*; applaudissement *m*; * *vt* réconforter, égayer.

cheerful *adj* gai, enjoué, joyeux; ~**ly** *adv* gaiement.

cheerfulness, cheeriness *n* gaieté *f*; bonne humeur *f*.

cheese *n* fromage *m*.

chef *n* chef (de cuisine) *m*.

chemical *adj* chimique.

chemist *n* chimiste *mf*; pharmacien *m* -ne *f*.

chemistry *n* chimie *f*.

cheque *n* chèque *m*.

cheque account *n* compte courant *m*.

chequerboard *n* échiquier *m*.

chequered *adj* à carreaux.

cherish *vt* chérir, aimer.

cheroot *n* petit cigare *m*.

cherry *n* cerise *f*, * *adj* vermeil.

cherrytree *n* cerisier *m*.

cherub *n* chérubin *m*.

chess *n* échecs *mpl*.

chessboard *n* échiquier *m*.

chessman *n* pièce de jeu d'échecs *f*.

chest *n* poitrine *f*; cage thoracique *f*; ~ **of drawers** commode *f*.

chestnut *n* châtaigne *f*.

chestnut tree *n* châtaigner *m*.

chew *vt* mâcher, mastiquer.

chewing gum *n* chewing-gum *m*.

chic *adj* chic.

chicanery *n* chicane, chicanerie *f*.

chick *n* poussin *m*; (*fig*) poulette (*fam*) *f*, nana (*fam*) *f*.

chicken *n* poulet *m*.

chickenpox *n* varicelle *f*.

chickpea *n* pois chiche *m*.

chicory *n* chicorée *f*.

chide *vt* gronder, réprimander.

chief *adj* principal, en chef; ~**ly** *adv* principalement; * *n* chef *m*.

chief executive *n* directeur général *m*.

chieftain *n* chef *m* (de tribu).

chiffon *n* mousseline de soie *f*.

chilblain *n* engelure *f*.

child *n* enfant *m*; **from a ~** tout enfant; **with ~** enceinte.

childbirth *n* accouchement *m*.

childhood *n* enfance *f*.

childish *adj* enfantin, puéril; ~**ly** *adv* puérilement.

childishness *n* enfantillage *m*, puérilité *f*.

childless *adj* sans enfants.

childlike *adj* d'enfant.

children *npl* de **child**: enfants *mpl*.

chill *adj* froid, frais, *f* fraîche; * *n* froid *m*; * *vt* refroidir; glacer.

chilly *adj* froid, très frais.

chime *n* carillon *m*; harmonie *f*; * *vi* sonner; s'accorder.

chimney *n* cheminée *f*.

chimpanzee *n* chimpanzé *m*.

chin n menton m.

china(ware) n porcelaine f.

chink n fente f; tintement m; * vi tinter.

chip vt ébrécher; * vi s'ébrécher; * n fragment, éclat m; puce f; frite f.

chiropodist n pédicure mf.

chirp vi pépier, gazouiller; * n pépiement, gazouillis m.

chirping n chant des oiseaux m.

chisel n ciseau m; * vt ciseler.

chitchat n bavardage, papotage m.

chivalrous adj chevaleresque.

chivalry n chevalerie f.

chives npl ciboulette f.

chlorine n chlore m.

chloroform n chloroforme m.

chock-full adj plein à craquer, comble.

chocolate n chocolat m.

choice n choix m, préférence f; assortiment m; sélection f; * adj de choix, de qualité.

choir n chœur m.

choke vt étrangler; étouffer.

cholera n choléra m.

choose vt choisir, élire.

chop vt trancher, couper, hacher; * n côtelette f; ~s pl (sl) babines fpl.

chopper n hélicoptère m.

chopping block n billot m.

chopsticks npl baguettes fpl.

choral adj choral.

chord n corde f, (mus) accord m.

chore n corvée f; travail routinier m.

chorist, chorister n choriste mf.

chorus n chœur m.

Christ n Jésus-Christ.

christen vt baptiser.

Christendom n christianisme m; chrétienté f.

christening n baptême m.

Christian adj n chrétien m -ne f; ~ name prénom m.

Christianity n christianisme m; chrétienté f.

Christmas n Noël f.

Christmas card n carte de Noël f.

Christmas Eve n veille de Noël f.

chrome n chrome m.

chronic adj chronique.

chronicle n chronique f.

chronicler n chroniqueur m.

chronological adj chronologique; ~ly adv chronologiquement.

chronology n chronologie f.

chronometer n chronomètre m.

chubby adj potelé.

chuck vt lancer, jeter.

chuckle vi rire, glousser.

chug vi souffler, haleter.

chum n copain m, copine f.

chunk n gros morceau m.

church n église f.

churchyard n cimetière m.

churlish adj fruste, grossier; hargneux.

churn n baratte f; * vt baratter.

cider n cidre m.

cigar n cigare m.

cigarette n cigarette f.

cigarette case n étui à cigarettes m.

cigarette end n mégot m.

cigarette holder n fume-cigarette m invar.

cinder n braise f.

cinema n cinéma m.

cinnamon n cannelle f.

cipher n chiffre m (code).

circle n cercle m; groupe m; * vt encercler; tourner autour de; * vi décrire des cercles.

circuit n circuit m; tour m; tournée f.

circuitous adj détourné, indirect.

circular adj circulaire; * n circulaire f.

circulate vi circuler.

circulation n circulation f.

circumcise vt circoncire.

circumcision n circoncision f.

circumference n circonférence f.

circumflex n accent circonflexe m.

circumlocution n circonlocution f.

circumnavigate vt contourner.

circumnavigation n circumnavigation f.

circumscribe vt circonscrire.

circumspect adj circonspect.

circumspection n circonspection f.

circumstance n circonstance, situation f.

circumstantial adj circonstancié; accessoire.

circumstantiate vt détailler.

circumvent vt circonvenir.

circumvention n évitement m; tricherie f.

circus n cirque m.

cistern n citerne f.

citadel n citadelle f.

citation n citation f.

cite vt citer.

citizen n citoyen m -ne f.

citizenship n citoyenneté f.

city n ville f.

civic adj civique.

civil adj civil, courtois; ~**ly** adv poliment.

civil defence n défense passive f.

civil engineer n ingénieur des travaux publics m.

civilian n civil m -e f.

civility n civilité, courtoisie f.

civilization n civilisation f.

civilize vt civiliser.

civil law n droit civil m.

civil war n guerre civile f.

clad adj vêtu, habillé.

claim vt revendiquer, réclamer; * n demande f; réclamation f.

claimant n demandeur m.

clairvoyant n voyant m -e f.

clam n palourde f.

clamber vi grimper (avec difficulté).

clammy adj moite.

clamour n clameur f, cris mpl; * vi vociférer, crier.

clamp n attache f; * vt serrer; imposer; ~ **down on** resserrer le contrôle.

clan n clan, groupe m.

clandestine adj clandestin.

clang n bruit métallique m; * vi faire un bruit métallique.

clap vt vi applaudir.

clapping n applaudissements mpl.

claret n vin rouge de Bordeaux m.

clarification n clarification f, éclaircissement m.

clarify vt clarifier, éclaircir.

clarinet n clarinette f.

clarity n clarté f.

clash vi se heurter; s'entrechoquer; * n choc m; affrontement m.

clasp n fermoir m; boucle f; étreinte f; * vt agrafer; étreindre.

class n classe f; catégorie f; * vt classer, classifier.

classic(al) adj classique; * n auteur classique m.

classification n classification f.

classified advertisement n petite annonce f.

classify vt classifier, classer.

classmate n camarade de classe mf.

classroom n salle de classe f.

clatter vi résonner; cliqueter; * n cliquetis m.

clause n (gr) proposition f; clause f.

claw n griffe f; serre f; pince f; * vt griffer; agripper.

clay n argile m.

clean adj propre; net; * vt nettoyer.

cleaning n nettoyage m.

cleanliness n propreté, pureté f.

cleanly adj propre; * adv proprement, nettement.

cleanness n propreté f.

cleanse vt nettoyer.

clear adj clair; net; transparent; évident; * adv distinctement; * vt clarifier, éclaircir; dégager; disculper; * vi s'éclaircir.

clearance n déblaiement m; autorisation f.

clear-cut adj net.

clearly adv clairement; manifestement.

cleaver n couperet m.

clef n (mus) clé f.

cleft n fissure, crevasse f.

clemency n clémence f.

clement adj clément.

clenched adj serré.

clergy n clergé m.

clergyman n ecclésiastique m.

clerical adj clérical, ecclésiastique.

clerk n ecclésiastique m; employé m.

clever adj intelligent; habile; astucieux; ~**ly** adv intelligemment, habilement.

click vt claquer; * vi faire un bruit sec.

client n client m -e f.

cliff n falaise f.

climate n climat m.

climatic adj climatique.

climax n point culminant m, apogée m.

climb vt grimper, escalader; * vi grimper, escalader.

climber n alpiniste mf.

climbing n alpinisme m.

clinch vt serrer fort.

cling *vi* s'accrocher (à), se cramponner (à); adhérer, (se) coller.

clinic *n* clinique *f*.

clink *vt* faire tinter; * *vi* tinter, résonner; * *n* tintement *m*.

clip *vt* couper; * *n* clip *m*; pince *f*.

clipping *n* coupure *f*.

clique *n* clique *f*.

cloak *n* cape *f*; prétexte *m*; * *vt* masquer.

cloakroom *n* vestiaire *m*.

clock *n* horloge *f*.

clockwork *n* mécanisme d'horloge *m*; * *adj* précis.

clod *n* motte (de terre) *f*.

clog *n* sabot *m*; * *vi* se boucher.

cloister *n* cloître *m*.

close *vt* fermer; clore, conclure; terminer; * *vi* se fermer; * *n* fin *f*; conclusion *f*; * *adj* proche; étroit; ajusté; dense; réservé; * *adv* de près; ~ **by** tout près.

closed *adj* fermé.

closely *adv* étroitement; de près.

closeness *n* proximité *f*; fidélité, exactitude *f*; intimité *f*; minutie *f*.

closet *n* placard *m*.

close-up *n* gros plan *m*.

closure *n* fermeture *f*; clôture *f*.

clot *n* caillot *m*; grumeau *m*.

cloth *n* tissu *m*; chiffon *m*; toile *f*; clergé *m*.

clothe *vt* habiller, vêtir.

clothes *npl* vêtements *mpl*; linge *m*; **bed** ~ draps et couvertures *mpl*.

clothes basket *n* panière à linge *f*.

clotheshorse *n* séchoir à linge *m*.

clothesline *n* corde à linge *f*.

clothespin *n* pince à linge *f*.

clothing *n* vêtements *mpl*.

cloud *n* nuage *m*; nuée *f*; * *vt* rendre trouble; assombrir; * *vi* se couvrir; s'obscurcir.

cloudiness *n* nébulosité *f*; obscurité *f*.

cloudy *adj* nuageux, nébuleux; obscur; sombre, trouble.

clout *n* coup de poing *m*.

clove *n* clou de girofle *m*.

clover *n* trèfle *m*.

clown *n* clown *m*.

club *n* matraque *f*; club *m*.

club car *n* wagon-bar *m* (1ère classe).

clue *n* indice *m*, indication *f*; idée *f*.

clump *n* massif *m*.

clumsily *adv* gauchement.

clumsiness *n* gaucherie *f*.

clumsy *adj* gauche, maladroit; lourd.

cluster *n* bouquet *m*; grappe *f*; groupe *m*; * *vt* grouper; * *vi* se rassembler.

clutch *n* prise *f*; embrayage *m*; * *vt* empoigner, agripper.

clutter *vt* encombrer.

coach *n* autocar *m*; wagon *m*; entraîneur *m*; * *vt* entraîner, donner des cours particuliers à.

coach trip *n* excursion en car *f*.

coagulate *vt* coaguler; agglutiner; * *vi* se coaguler; s'agglutiner.

coal *n* charbon *m*.

coalesce *vi* s'unir, se fondre.

coalfield *n* gisement charbonnier *m*.

coalition *n* coalition *f*.

coalman *n* charbonnier *m*.

coalmine *n* mine de charbon, houillère *f*.

coarse *adj* rude; grossier; **~ly** *adv* grossièrement.

coast *n* côte *f*.

coastal *adj* côtier.

coastguard *n* gendarmerie maritime *f*, garde-côte *m*.

coastline *n* littoral *m*.

coat *n* manteau *m*; pelage *m*; couche *f*; * *vt* enduire, revêtir.

coat hanger *n* cintre *m*.

coating *n* revêtement *m*.

coax *vt* cajôler.

cob *n* épi de maïs *m*.

cobbler *n* cordonnier *m*.

cobbles, cobblestones *npl* pavés ronds *mpl*.

cobweb *n* toile d'araignée *f*.

cocaine *n* cocaïne *f*.

cock *n* coq *m*; (*zool*) mâle *m*; * *vt* armer; dresser.

cock-a-doodle-doo *n* cocorico *m*.

cockcrow *n* chant du coq *m*.

cockerel *n* jeune coq *m*.

cockfight(ing) *n* combat de coqs *m*.

cockle *n* (*zool*) coque *f*.

cockpit *n* cabine de pilotage *f*.

cockroach *n* cafard *m*.

cocktail *n* cocktail *m*.

cocoa *n* cacao *m*.

coconut *n* noix de coco *f*.

cocoon *n* cocon *m*.

cod *n* morue *f*.

code *n* code *m*; indicatif *m*.

cod-liver oil *n* huile de foie de morue *f*.

coefficient *n* coefficient *m*.

coercion *n* coercition, contrainte *f*.

coexistence *n* coexistence *f*.

coffee *n* café *m*.

coffee break *n* pause-café *f*.

coffee house *n* café *m*.

coffeepot *n* cafetière *f*.

coffee table *n* table basse *f*.

coffer *n* coffre *m*; caisse *f*.

coffin *n* cercueil *m*.

cog *n* dent d'engrenage *f*.

cogency *n* puissance, force *f*.

cogent *adj* convaincant, puissant; **~ly** *adv* d'une manière convaincante.

cognac *n* cognac *m*.

cognate *adj* apparenté.

cognisance *n* connaissance *f*; compétence *f*.

cognisant *adj* instruit; (*law*) compétent.

cognition *n* connaissance *f*; cognition *f*.

cogwheel *n* roue dentée *f*.

cohabit *vi* cohabiter.

cohabitation *n* cohabitation *f*.

cohere *vi* se tenir; être cohérent.

coherence *n* cohérence *f*.

coherent *adj* cohérent; logique.

cohesion *n* cohésion *f*.

cohesive *adj* cohésif.

coil *n* rouleau *m*; bobine *f*; * *vt* enrouler.

coin *n* pièce de monnaie *f*; * *vt* frapper.

coincide *vi* coïncider.

coincidence *n* coïncidence *f*.

coincident *adj* coïncident.

coke *n* coke *m*.

colander *n* passoire *f*.

cold *adj* froid; indifférent; **~ly** *adv* froidement; avec froideur; * *n* froid *m*; rhume *m*.

cold-blooded *adj* insensible.

coldness *n* froideur *f*.

cold sore *n* bouton de fièvre *m*.

coleslaw *n* salade de chou cru *f*.

colic *n* coliques *fpl*.

collaborate *vi* collaborer.

collaboration *n* collaboration *f*.

collapse *vi* s'écrouler; * *n* écroulement; (*med*) évanouissement *m*.

collapsible *adj* pliant.

collar *n* col *m*.

collarbone *n* clavicule *f*.

collate *vt* collationner, confronter.

collateral *adj* concomitant; parallèle; * *n* nantisse ment *m*.

collation *n* collation *f*.

colleague *n* collègue *mf*, confrère *m*, consœur *f*.

collect *vt* rassembler; collectionner.

collection *n* collection *f*.

collective *adj* collectif; **~ly** collectivement.

collector *n* collectionneur *m* -euse *f*.

college *n* faculté *f*.

collide *vi* entrer en collision, se heurter.

collision *n* collision *f*, heurt *m*.

colloquial *adj* familier; parlé; **~ly** *adv* familièrement.

colloquialism *n* expression familière *f*.

collusion *n* collusion *f*.

colon *n* deux-points *m invar*; (*med*) colon *m*.

colonel *n* (*mil*) colonel *m*.

colonial *adj* colonial.

colonist *n* colon *m*.

colonize *vt* coloniser.

colony *n* colonie *f*.

colossal *adj* colossal.

colossus *n* colosse *m*.

colour *n* couleur *f*; prétexte *m*; **~s** *pl* drapeau *m*; * *vt* colorer; * *vi* se colorer.

colour-blind *adj* daltonien.

colourful *adj* coloré.

colouring *n* teint *m*; coloris *m*.

colourless *adj* sans couleur, incolore.

colour television *n* télévision en couleur *f*.

colt *n* poulain *m*.

column *n* colonne *f*.

columnist *n* chroniqueur *m*.

coma *n* coma *m*.

comatose *adj* comateux.

comb *n* peigne *m*; * *vt* peigner.

combat *n* combat *m*; **single ~** duel *m*; * *vt* combattre.

combatant *n* combattant *m* -e *f*.

combative *adj* combatif.

combination *n* combinaison, association *f*.

combine *vt* combiner; * *vi* s'unir.

combustion *n* combustion *f*.

come *vi* venir; ~ across, ~ upon *vt* rencontrer par hasard, tomber sur; ~ by *vt* obtenir; ~ down *vi* descendre; se résumer à, baisser (prices); ~ from *vt* provenir de; être originaire de; ~ in for *vt* être l'objet de; ~ into *vt* hériter de; ~ round, ~ to *vi* revenir à soi; ~ up with *vt* suggérer.

comedian *n* comédien *m*; comique *m*.

comedienne *n* comédienne *f*; comique *f*.

comedy *n* comédie *f*.

comet *n* comète *f*.

comfort *n* confort *m*; aises *fpl*; commodités *fpl*; consolation *f*; * *vt* réconforter; soulager; consoler.

comfortable *adj* confortable; réconfortant.

comfortably *adv* confortablement; agréablement.

comforter *n* personne qui réconforte *f*; édredon *m*.

comic(al) *adj* comique; ~ly *adv* comiquement.

coming *n* venue, arrivée *f*; * *adj* à venir.

comma *n* (*gr*) virgule *f*.

command *vt* ordonner, commander; * *n* ordre *m*.

commander *n* commandant *m*.

commandment *n* commandement *m*.

commando *n* commando *m*.

commemorate *vt* commémorer.

commemoration *n* commémoration *f*.

commence *vt vi* commencer.

commencement *n* commencement *m*.

commend *vt* recommander, confier à; louer.

commendable *adj* louable.

commendably *adv* élogieusement.

commendation *n* louange *f*; recommandation *f*.

commensurate *adj* proportionné.

comment *n* commentaire *m*; * *vt* commenter.

commentary *n* commentaire *m*; observation *f*.

commentator *n* commentateur *m* -trice *f*.

commerce *n* commerce *m*, affaires *fpl*; relations *fpl*.

commercial *adj* commercial.

commiserate *vt* compatir.

commiseration *n* commisération, pitié *f*.

commissariat *n* (*mil*) intendance *f*, ravitaillement *m*.

commission *n* commission *f*; * *vt* commissionner; commander.

commissioner *n* commissionnaire, coursier *m*.

commit *vt* commettre; confier à; engager.

commitment *n* engagement *m*.

committee *n* comité *m*.

commodity *n* produit *m*, denrée *f*.

common *adj* commun; ordinaire; in ~ en commun; * *n* terrain communal *m*.

commoner *n* roturier *m* -ière *f*.

common law *n* droit coutumier *m*.

commonly *adv* communément, généralement.

commonplace *n* lieux communs *mpl*; * *adj* banal.

common sense *n* bon sens *m*.

Commonwealth *n* Commonwealth *m*.

commotion *n* vacarme *m*; perturbation *f*.

commune *vi* discuter avec sincérité.

communicable *adj* communicable, transmissible.

communicate *vt* communiquer, transmettre; * *vi* communiquer.

communication *n* communication *f*.

communicative *adj* communicatif.

communion *n* communion *f*.

communiqué *n* communiqué *m*.

communism *n* communisme *m*.

communist *n* communiste *mf*.

community *n* communauté *f*.

community centre *n* centre social *m*.

community chest *n* fonds commun *m*.

commutable *adj* interchangeable, permutable.

commutation ticket *n* carte d'abonnement *f*.

commute *vt* échanger.

compact *adj* compact, serré, dense; * *n* accord, contrat *m*; ~ly *adv* de façon compacte; en peu de mots.

compact disc *n* disque compact *m*.

companion *n* compagnon *m*, compagne *f*.

companionship *n* camaraderie *f*; compagnie *f*.

company *n* compagnie, fréquentation *f*; société *f*.

comparable *adj* comparable.

comparative *adj* comparatif; ~ly *adv* comparativement.

compare *vt* comparer.

comparison *n* comparaison *f*.

compartment *n* compartiment *m*.

compass *n* boussole *f*.

compassion *n* compassion *f*.

compassionate *adj* compatissant.

compatibility *n* compatibilité *f*.

compatible *adj* compatible.

compatriot *n* compatriote *mf*.

compel *vt* contraindre, obliger, forcer.

compelling *adj* irrésistible.

compensate *vt* compenser.

compensation *n* compensation *f*; dédommagement *m*.

compère *n* animateur *m* -trice *f*.

compete *vi* rivaliser (avec), faire concurrence (à).

competence *n* compétence *f*; aptitude *f*.

competent *adj* compétent; suffisant; **~ly** *adv* avec compétence.

competition *n* compétition *f*; concurrence *f*.

competitive *adj* concurrentiel, compétitif.

competitor *n* concurrent *m* -e *f*.

compilation *n* compilation *f*.

compile *vt* compiler.

complacency *n* suffisance *f*.

complacent *adj* suffisant.

complain *vi* se plaindre; déposer une plainte.

complaint *n* plainte *f*; réclamation *f*.

complement *n* complément *m*.

complementary *adj* complémentaire.

complete *adj* complet; achevé; **~ly** *adv* complètement; * *vt* achever, mener à bien, compléter.

completion *n* achèvement *m*.

complex *adj* complexe.

complexion *n* teint *m*; aspect *m*.

complexity *n* complexité *f*.

compliance *n* conformité *f*; soumission *f*.

compliant *adj* docile, soumis.

complicate *vt* compliquer.

complication *n* complication *f*.

complicity *n* complicité *f*.

compliment *n* compliment *m*; * *vt* complimenter.

complimentary *adj* flatteur; à titre gracieux.

comply *vi* se soumettre, se plier, se conformer.

component *adj* composant.

compose *vt* composer; constituer.

composed *adj* calme, posé.

composer *n* auteur *m*; compositeur *m* -trice *f*.

composite *adj* composite, composé.

composition *n* composition *f*.

compositor *n* compositeur *m* -trice *f*.

compost *n* compost *m*.

composure *n* maîtrise de soi *f*, calme *m*, sangfroid *m*.

compound *vt* composer, combiner; * *adj* composé *m*.

comprehend *vt* comprendre; englober.

comprehensible *adj* compréhensible; **~ly** *adv* intelligiblement.

comprehension *n* compréhension *f*; inclusion *f*.

comprehensive *adj* global; complet; compréhensif; **~ly** *adv* globalement.

compress *vt* comprimer, concentrer; * *n* compresse *f*.

comprise *vt* comprendre, embrasser.

compromise *n* compromis *m*; * *vt* compromettre; * *vi* adopter un compromis.

compulsion *n* contrainte *f*; compulsion *f*.

compulsive *adj* compulsif; **~ly** *adv* compulsivement.

compulsory *adj* obligatoire.

compunction *n* remords, scrupule *m*.

computable *adj* computable, calculable.

computation *n* computation *f*, calcul *m*.

compute *vt* calculer.

computer *n* ordinateur *m*.

computerize *vt* traiter par ordinateur, informatiser.

computer programming *n* programmation *f*.

computer science *n* informatique *f*.

comrade *n* camarade *mf*, compagnon *m*, compagne *f*.

comradeship *n* camaraderie *f*.

con *vt* duper; * *n* duperie *f*.

concave *adj* concave.

concavity *n* concavité *f*.

conceal *vt* cacher, dissimuler.

concealment *n* dissimulation *f*; recel *m*.

concede *vt* concéder, accorder.

conceit *n* vanité *f*; trait d'esprit *m*.

conceited *adj* vaniteux, prétentieux.

conceivable *adj* concevable.

conceive *vt* concevoir; * *vi* concevoir.

concentrate *vt* concentrer.

concentration *n* concentration *f*.

concentration camp *n* camp de concentration *m*.

concentric *adj* concentrique.

concept *n* concept *m*.

conception *n* conception *f*.

concern *vt* concerner, toucher; * *n* affaire *f*; souci *m*.

concerning *prep* en ce qui concerne, concernant.

concerto *n* concerto *m*.

concession *n* concession *f*.

conciliate *vt* concilier.

conciliation *n* conciliation *f*.

conciliatory *adj* conciliateur, conciliant.

concise *adj* concis, succinct; **~ly** *adv* avec concision.

conclude *vt* conclure; décider; déduire.

conclusion *n* conclusion, déduction *f*; fin *f*.

conclusive *adj* décisif, concluant; **~ly** *adv* de façon concluante.

concoct *vt* confectionner, fabriquer.

concoction *n* préparation *f*; élaboration *f*.

concomitant *adj* concomitant.

concord *n* entente, harmonie *f*.

concordance *n* accord *m*.

concordant *adj* concordant.

concourse *n* rassemblement *m*; carrefour *m*; foule *f*.

concrete *n* béton *m*; * *vt* bétonner.

concubine *n* concubine *f*.

concur *vi* coïncider; s'entendre.

concurrence *n* consentement *m*, coïncidence *f*; union *f*.

concurrently *adv* simultanément.

concussion *n* commotion *f*.

condemn *vt* condamner; désapprouver.

condemnation *n* condamnation *f*.

condensation *n* condensation *f*.

condense *vt* condenser.

condescend *vi* condescendre; daigner.

condescending *adj* condescendant.

condescension *n* condescendance *f*.

condiment *n* condiment *m*.

condition *vt* conditionner; * *n* condition, situation *f*; état *m*.

conditional *adj* conditionnel, hypothétique; **~ly** *adv* conditionnellement.

conditioned *adj* conditionné.

conditioner *n* après-shampoing *m*.

condolences *npl* condoléances *fpl*.

condom *n* préservatif *m*.

condominium *n* condominium *m*, copropriété *f*.

condone *vt* pardonner, fermer les yeux sur.

conducive *adj* propice, opportun.

conduct *n* conduite *f*; comportement *m*; * *vt* conduire, mener.

conductor *n* receveur *m*; chef d'orchestre *m*; conducteur *m*.

conduit *n* conduit *m*; tuyau *m*.

cone *n* cône *m*.

confection *n* sucrerie, confiserie *f*; confection *f*.

confectioner *n* confiseur *m* -euse *f*.

confectioner's (shop) *n* confiserie *f*; pâtisserie *f*.

confederacy *n* confédération *f*.

confederate *vi* se confédérer; * *adj n* confédéré *m*.

confer *vt vi* conférer.

conference *n* conférence *f*.

confess *vt* confesser; * *vi* se confesser.

confession *n* confession *f*.

confessional *n* confessionnal *m*.

confessor *n* confesseur *m*.

confidant *n* confident *m* -e *f*.

confide *vt* confier; **~ in** se confier à.

confidence *n* confiance *f*; assurance *f*.

confidence trick *n* abus de confiance *m*, escroquerie *f*.

confident *adj* confiant, assuré, sûr (de soi).

confidential *adj* confidentiel.

configuration *n* configuration *f*.

confine *vt* limiter; emprisonner.

confinement *n* détention *f*; alitement *m*.

confirm *vt* confirmer; ratifier.

confirmation *n* confirmation *f*; ratification *f*; corroboration *f*.

confirmed *adj* invétéré, endurci.

confiscate *vt* confisquer.

confiscation *n* confiscation *f*.

conflagration *n* incendie *m*; conflagration *f*.

conflict *n* conflit *m*; lutte *f*; dispute *f*.

conflicting *adj* contradictoire.

confluence *n* confluence *f*; rencontre *f*.

conform *vt* conformer, adapter; * *vi* se conformer (à), s'adapter (à).

conformity *n* conformité *f*, accord *m*.

confound *vt* confondre.

confront *vt* confronter; affronter.

confrontation *n* affrontement *m*, confrontation *f*.

confuse *vt* confondre; embarrasser; embrouiller.

confusing *adj* déroutant.

confusion *n* confusion *f*; désordre *m*.

congeal *vt* solidifier, congeler; * *vi* se solidifier, se congeler.

congenial *adj* sympathique; similaire.

congenital *adj* congénital.

congested *adj* encombré, congestionné.

congestion *n* encombrement *m*, congestion *f*.

conglomerate *vt* conglomérer, agglomérer; * *adj* aggloméré; * *n* (*com*) conglomérat *m*.

conglomeration *n* conglomération *f*.

congratulate *vt* complimenter, féliciter.

congratulations *npl* félicitations *fpl*.

congratulatory *adj* de félicitations.

congregate *vt* rassembler, réunir.

congregation *n* assemblée *f*, rassemblement *m*.

congress *n* congrès *m*; conférence *f*.

congressman *n* membre du Congrès *m*.

congruity *n* congruence *f*.

congruous *adj* congru, approprié.

conic(al) *adj* conique.

conifer *n* conifère *m*.

coniferous *adj* (*bot*) conifère.

conjecture *n* conjecture, supposition *f*; * *vt* conjecturer, supposer.

conjugal *adj* conjugal.

conjugate *vt* (*gr*) conjuguer.

conjugation *n* conjugaison *f*.

conjunction *n* conjonction *f*; union *f*.

conjuncture *n* conjoncture *f*; occasion *f*.

conjure *vt* conjurer; exorciser.

conjurer *n* magicien *m* -ne *f*, illusionniste *mf*.

con man *n* escroc *m*.

connect *vt* relier, joindre, rattacher.

connection *n* liaison, connexion *f*.

connivance *n* connivence *f*.

connive *vi* fermer les yeux (sur); être de connivence.

connoisseur *n* connaisseur *m* -euse *f*.

conquer *vt* conquérir; vaincre.

conqueror *n* vainqueur *m*; conquérant *m*.

conquest *n* conquête *f*.

conscience *n* conscience *f*.

conscientious *adj* consciencieux; de conscience; **~ly** *adv* consciencieusement.

conscious *adj* conscient; intentionnel; **~ly** *adv* consciemment, sciemment.

consciousness *n* conscience *f*.

conscript *n* conscrit *m*.

conscription *n* conscription *f*.

consecrate *vt* consacrer.

consecration *n* consécration *f*.

consecutive *adj* consécutif; **~ly** *adv* consécutivement.

consensus *n* consensus *m*.

consent *n* consentement *m*; assentiment *m*; * *vi* consentir.

consequence *n* conséquence *f*; importance *f*.

consequent *adj* consécutif; **~ly** *adv* par conséquent.

conservation *n* conservation *f*.

conservative *adj* conservateur.

conservatory *n* conservatoire *m*.

conserve *vt* conserver; * *n* conserve *f*.

consider *vt* considérer, examiner; * *vi* penser, délibérer.

considerable *adj* considérable; important; **~bly** *adv* considérablement.

considerate *adj* prévenant, attentionné; prudent; **~ly** *adv* avec prévenance; prudemment.

consideration *n* considération *f*; réflexion *f*; estime *f*; rémunération *f*.

considering *conj* étant donné que; **~ that** vu que; étant donné que.

consign *vt* confier, remettre, expédier.

consignment *n* expédition *f*, envoi *m*.

consist *vi* consister (en).

consistency *n* consistance *f*; cohérence *f*; constance *f*.

consistent *adj* constant; cohérent; compatible; **~ly** *adv* régulièrement.

consolable *adj* consolable.

consolation *n* consolation *f*; réconfort *m*.

consolatory *adj* consolateur.

console *vt* consoler.

consolidate *vt* consolider, grouper; * *vi* se consolider.

consolidation *n* consolidation *f.*

consonant *adj* en accord; * *n* (*gr*) consonne *f.*

consort *n* consort *m*; associé *m* -e *f.*

conspicuous *adj* voyant, manifeste; notable; **~ly** *adv* manifestement.

conspiracy *n* conspiration *f.*

conspirator *n* conspirateur *m* -trice *f.*

conspire *vi* conspirer.

constancy *n* constance, fermeté d'âme *f*; persévérance *f.*

constant *adj* constant; persévérant; **~ly** *adv* constamment.

constellation *n* constellation *f.*

consternation *n* consternation *f.*

constipated *adj* constipé.

constituency *n* électorat *m*; circonscription *f.*

constituent *n* composant *m*; * *adj* constituant.

constitute *vt* constituer; établir.

constitution *n* constitution *f.*

constitutional *adj* constitutionnel.

constrain *vt* contraindre, forcer, obliger.

constraint *n* contrainte *f.*

constrict *vt* serrer; gêner.

construct *vt* construire, bâtir.

construction *n* construction *f.*

construe *vt* interpréter, analyser.

consul *n* consul *m.*

consular *adj* consulaire.

consulate, consulship *n* consulat *m.*

consult *vt* consulter; * *vi* (se) consulter.

consultation *n* consultation, délibération *f.*

consume *vt* consommer; dissiper; consumer, brûler; * *vi* se consommer.

consumer *n* consommateur *m* -trice *f.*

consumer goods *npl* biens de consommation *mpl.*

consumerism *n* consumérisme *m.*

consumer society *n* société de consommation *f.*

consummate *vt* consommer, accomplir; perfectionner; * *adj* accompli, consommé.

consummation *n* consommation *f*; perfection *f.*

consumption *n* consommation *f.*

contact *n* contact *m.*

contact lenses *npl* lentilles de contact *fpl.*

contagious *adj* contagieux.

contain *vt* contenir, renfermer; refréner.

container *n* récipient *m.*

contaminate *vt* contaminer; **~d** *adj* contaminé.

contamination *n* contamination *f.*

contemplate *vt* contempler.

contemplation *n* contemplation *f.*

contemplative *adj* contemplatif.

contemporaneous,contemporary *adj* contemporain.

contempt *n* mépris, dédain *m.*

contemptible *adj* méprisable, vil; **~bly** *adv* vilement.

contemptuous *adj* méprisant, dédaigneux; **~ly** *adv* dédaigneusement.

contend *vi* combattre, lutter; * *vt* affirmer.

content *adj* content, satisfait; * *vt* contenter, satisfaire; * *n* contentement *m*; **~s** *pl* contenu *m*; table des matières *f.*

contentedly *adv* avec contentement.

contention *n* querelle, altercation *f.*

contentious *adj* litigieux; querelleur; **~ly** *adv* en chicanant.

contentment *n* contentement *m*, satisfaction *f.*

contest *vt* contester, discuter, disputer; * *n* concours *m*; altercation *f.*

contestant *n* concurrent *m* -e *f.*

context *n* contexte *m.*

contiguous *adj* contigu, voisin.

continent *adj* continent, chaste; * *n* continent *m.*

continental *adj* continental.

contingency *n* contingence *f*; événement imprévu *m*; éventualité *f.*

contingent *n* contingent *m*; * *adj* contingent, éventuel; **~ly** fortuitement.

continual *adj* continuel; **~ly** *adv* continuellement.

continuation *n* continuation, reprise, suite *f.*

continue *vt vi* continuer.

continuity *n* continuité *f.*

continuous *adj* continu; **~ly** *adv* sans interruption.

contort *vt* tordre, déformer.

contortion *n* contorsion *f*.

contour *n* contour *m*.

contraband *n* contrebande *f*; * *adj* de contrebande.

contraception *n* contraception *f*.

contraceptive *n* contraceptif *m*; * *adj* contraceptif.

contract *vt* contracter; * *vi* se contracter; * *n* contrat *m*.

contraction *n* contraction *f*.

contractor *n* entrepreneur *m*.

contradict *vt* contredire.

contradiction *n* contradiction *f*.

contradictory *adj* contradictoire.

contraption *n* gadget, bidule (*fam*) *m*.

contrariness *n* esprit de contradiction *m*.

contrary *adj* contraire, opposé; * *n* contraire *m*; **on the ~** au contraire.

contrast *n* contraste *m*; * *vt* contraster, mettre en contraste.

contrasting *adj* contrasté, opposé.

contravention *n* infraction *f*.

contributary *adj* contributif.

contribute *vt* contribuer.

contribution *n* contribution *f*; cotisation *f*.

contributor *n* souscripteur(-trice), collaborateur(-trice) *m(f)*.

contributory *adj* contribuant.

contrite *adj* contrit, repentant.

contrition *n* contrition *f*, repentir *m*.

contrivance *n* dispositif *m*; invention *f*.

contrive *vt* inventer, combiner; trouver le moyen de.

control *n* contrôle *m*; maîtrise *f*; autorité *f*; * *vt* maîtriser; réguler; contrôler; gouverner.

control room *n* salle des commandes *f*.

control tower *n* tour de contrôle *f*.

controversial *adj* polémique.

controversy *n* polémique *f*.

contusion *n* contusion *f*.

conundrum *n* énigme *f*.

conurbation *n* conurbation *f*.

convalesce *vi* être en convalescence.

convalescence *n* convalescence *f*.

convalescent *adj* convalescent.

convene *vt* convoquer; réunir; * *vi* se réunir.

convenience *n* commodité, convenance *f*.

convenient *adj* commode, pratique; qui convient; **~ly** *adv* commodément.

convent *n* couvent *m*.

convention *n* convention *f*; contrat *m*; assemblée *f*.

conventional *adj* conventionnel.

converge *vi* converger.

convergence *n* convergence *f*.

convergent *adj* convergent.

conversant *adj* au courant; compétent.

conversation *n* conversation *f*.

converse *vi* converser.

conversely *adv* inversement, réciproquement.

conversion *n* conversion; transformation *f*.

convert *vt* convertir; * *n* converti *m* -e *f*.

convertible *adj* convertible; * *n* décapotable *f*.

convex *adj* convexe.

convexity *n* convexité *f*.

convey *vt* transporter; transmettre, communiquer.

conveyance *n* transport *m*; transfert *m*; cession *f*.

conveyancer *n* notaire *m*.

convict *vt* déclarer coupable; * *n* détenu *m* -e *f*.

conviction *n* condamnation *f*; conviction *f*.

convince *vt* convaincre, persuader.

convincing *adj* convaincant.

convincingly *adv* de façon convaincante.

convivial *adj* jovial.

conviviality *n* jovialité *f*.

convoke *vt* convoquer.

convoy *n* convoi *m*.

convulse *vt* ébranler, convulser.

convulsion *n* convulsion *f*; bouleversement *m*; forte agitation *f*.

convulsive *adj* convulsif; **~ly** *adv* convulsivement.

coo *vt vi* roucouler.

cook *n* cuisinier *m* -ière *f*; * *vt* cuire; falsifier; * *vi* faire la cuisine, cuisiner.

cookbook *n* livre de cuisine *m*.

cooker *n* cuisinière *f*.

cookery *n* cuisine *f*.

cookie *n* gâteau *m* sec.

cool *adj* frais; calme; * *n* fraîcheur *f*; * *vt* rafraîchir, refroidir.

coolly *adv* fraîchement; de sang-froid.

coolness *n* fraîcheur *f*; froideur *f*; sang-froid *m*.

cooperate *vi* coopérer.

cooperation *n* coopération *f*.

cooperative *adj* coopératif.

coordinate *vt* coordonner.

coordination *n* coordination *f*.

cop *n* (*fam*) flic *m*.

copartner *n* coassocié *m* -e *f*.

cope *vi* se débrouiller.

copier *n* photocopieuse *f*.

copious *adj* copieux, abondant; **~ly** *adv* abondamment.

copper *n* cuivre *m*.

coppice, copse *n* taillis *m*.

copulate *vi* copuler.

copy *n* copie *f*; reproduction *f*; exemplaire *m*; * *vt* copier; imiter.

copybook *n* cahier *m*.

copying machine *n* photocopieuse *f*.

copyist *n* copiste *mf*.

copyright *n* droit d'auteur *m*.

coral *n* corail *m*.

coral reef *n* récif de corail *m*.

cord *n* cordon *m*, corde *f*.

cordial *adj* cordial, chaleureux; **~ly** *adv* cordialement.

corduroy *n* velours côtelé *m*.

core *n* trognon *m*; noyau, centre, cœur *m*.

cork *n* liège *m*; bouchon *m*; * *vt* boucher.

corkscrew *n* tire-bouchon *m*.

corn *n* maïs *m*; grain *m*; blé *m*.

corncob *n* épi de maïs *m*.

cornea *n* cornée *f*.

corned beef *n* corned-beef *m*.

corner *n* coin *m*; angle *m*.

cornerstone *n* pierre angulaire *f*.

cornet *n* cornet *m*.

cornfield *n* champ de maïs *m*.

cornflakes *npl* flocons de maïs, cornflakes *mpl*.

cornice *n* corniche *f*.

cornstarch *n* (US) farine de maïs *f*.

corollary *n* corollaire *m*.

coronary *n* infarctus *m*.

coronation *n* couronnement *m*.

coroner *n* coroner *m*.

coronet *n* couronne *f*.

corporal *n* caporal *m*.

corporate *adj* en commun; d'entreprise.

corporation *n* corporation *f*; société par actions *f*.

corporeal *adj* corporel.

corps *n* (*mil*) corps *m*.

corpse *n* cadavre *m*.

corpulent *adj* corpulent.

corpuscle *n* corpuscule *m*; électron *m*.

corral *n* corral *m*.

correct *vt* corriger; rectifier; * *adj* correct, juste; **~ly** *adv* correctement.

correction *n* correction *f*; rectification *f*.

corrective *adj* correcteur, correctif; * *n* rectificatif *m*.

correctness *n* correction *f*.

correlation *n* corrélation *f*.

correlative *adj* corrélatif.

correspond *vi* correspondre.

correspondence *n* correspondance *f*.

correspondent *adj* correspondant; * *n* correspondant *m* -e *f*.

corridor *n* couloir, corridor *m*.

corroborate *vt* corroborer.

corroboration *n* corroboration *f*.

corroborative *adj* qui corrobore.

corrode *vt* corroder.

corrosion *n* corrosion *f*.

corrosive *adj* n corrosif *m*.

corrugated iron *n* tôle ondulée *f*.

corrupt *vt* corrompre; * *vi* se corrompre, se pourrir; * *adj* corrompu; dépravé.

corruptible *adj* corruptible.

corruption *n* corruption *f*; dépravation *f*.

corruptive *adj* qui corrompt.

corset *n* corset *m*, gaine *f*.

cortege *n* cortège *m*.

cosily *adv* confortablement, douillettement.

cosmetic *adj* n cosmétique *m*.

cosmic *adj* cosmique.

cosmonaut *n* cosmonaute *mf*.

cosmopolitan *adj* cosmopolite.

cosset *vt* dorloter.

cost *n* prix, coût *m*; * *vi* coûter.

costly *adj* coûteux, cher.

costume *n* costume *m*.

cosy *adj* douillet.

cottage *n* cottage *m*.

cotton *n* coton *m*.

cotton candy *n* barbe à papa *f*.

cotton mill *n* filature de coton *f*.

cotton wool *n* coton hydrophile *m*.

couch *n* canapé, divan *m*.

couchette *n* couchette *f*.

cough *n* toux *f*; * *vi* tousser.

council *n* conseil *m*.

councillor *n* membre du conseil *m*; conseiller *m* -ère *f*.

counsel *n* conseil *m*; avocat *m*.

counsellor *n* conseiller *m* -ère *f*; avocat *m*.

count *vt* compter, dénombrer; calculer; ~ **on** compter sur; * *n* compte *m*; calcul *m*; chef d'accusation *m*; comte *m*.

countdown *n* compte à rebours *m*.

countenance *n* visage *m*; aspect *m*; mine *f*.

counter *n* comptoir *m*; pion *m*.

counteract *vt* contrecarrer; neutraliser; contrebalancer.

counterbalance *vt* contrebalancer; compenser; * *n* contrepoids *m*.

counterfeit *vt* contrefaire; * *adj* faux.

countermand *vt* annuler.

counterpart *n* contrepartie *f*; homologue *mf*.

counterproductive *adj* qui va à l'encontre du but visé.

countersign *vt* contresigner.

countess *n* comtesse *f*.

countless *adj* innombrable.

countrified *adj* rustique; campagnard.

country *n* pays *m*; patrie *f*; campagne *f*; région *f*; * *adj* rustique; campagnard.

country house *n* maison de campagne *f*.

countryman *n* campagnard *m*; compatriote *m*.

county *n* comté *m*.

coup *n* coup *m* d'État.

coupé *n* coupé *m*.

couple *n* couple *m*; **a ~ of** deux; * *vt* unir, associer.

couplet *n* distique *m*; couplet *m*.

coupon *n* coupon *m*, bon *m*.

courage *n* courage *m*.

courageous *adj* courageux; **~ly** *adv* courageusement.

courier *n* messager *m*; guide *m*.

course *n* cours *m*; route *f*; chemin *m*; plat *m*; marche à suivre *f*; **of ~** bien sûr, naturellement.

court *n* cour *f*; tribunal *m*; * *vt* courtiser; solliciter.

courteous *adj* courtois; poli; **~ly** *adv* courtoisement.

courtesan *n* courtisane *f*.

courtesy *n* courtoisie *f*.

courthouse *n* palais de justice *m*.

courtly *adj* élégant, raffiné.

court-martial *n* conseil de guerre *m*.

courtroom *n* salle de tribunal *f*.

courtyard *n* cour *f*.

cousin *n* cousin *m* -e *f*; **first ~ cousin(e)** germain(e) *m(f)*.

cove *n* (*mar*) crique, anse *f*.

covenant *n* contrat *m*; convention *f*; * *vi* convenir, stipuler par contrat.

cover *n* couverture *f*; abri *m*; prétexte *m*; * *vt* (re)couvrir; dissimuler; protéger.

coverage *n* reportage *m*, couverture *f*.

coveralls *npl* bleu de travail *m*.

covering *n* couverture *f*; couche *f*.

cover letter *n* lettre explicative *f*.

covert *adj* voilé; caché; secret; **~ly** *adv* secrètement.

cover-up *n* dissimulation *f*.

covet *vt* convoiter.

covetous *adj* avide, cupide.

cow *n* vache *f*.

coward *n* lâche *mf*.

cowardice *n* lâcheté *f*.

cowardly *adj* lâche; *adv* lâchement.

cowboy *n* cowboy *m*.

cower *vi* se tapir.

cowherd *n* vacher *m*.

coy *adj* timide; coquet; évasif; **~ly** *adv* évasivement.

coyness *n* timidité *f*; modestie *f*.

crab *n* crabe *m*.

crab-apple *n* pomme sauvage *f*; **crab-apple tree** *n* pommier sauvage *m*.

crack *n* craquement *m*; fente, fissure *f*; * *vt* fêler, craquer; **~ down on** sévir; * *vi* se fêler; craquer.

cracker *n* pétard *m*; biscuit salé *m*.

crackle *vi* crépiter, pétiller.

crackling n crépitement m; friture f.
cradle n berceau m; * vt bercer.
craft n habileté f; métier manuel m; barque f.
craftily adv astucieusement.
craftiness n astuce, ruse f.
craftsman n artisan m.
craftsmanship n artisanat m.
crafty adj astucieux, rusé.
crag n rocher escarpé m.
cram vt bourrer; fourrer; * vi s'entasser.
crammed adj bourré.
cramp n crampe f; * vt entraver.
cramped adj à l'étroit.
crampon n crampon m.
cranberry n canneberge f.
crane n grue f.
crash vi s'écraser; * n fracas m; collision f.
crash helmet n casque m.
crash landing n atterrissage en catastrophe m.
crass adj grossier, crasse.
crate n caisse f; cageot m.
crater n cratère m.
cravat n foulard m, cravate f.
crave vt avoir extrêmement besoin de.
craving n désir extrême m, soif f.
crawfish n écrevisse f.
crawl vi ramper; ~ **with** grouiller de.
crayfish n écrevisse f.
crayon n crayon de couleur m.
craze n manie f, engouement m.
craziness n folie f.
crazy adj fou.
creak vi grincer, craquer.
cream n crème f; * adj crème.
creamy adj crémeux.
crease n pli m; * vt froisser.
create vt créer; causer.
creation n création f.
creative adj créatif.
creator n créateur m -trice f.
creature n créature f.
credence n créance f; crédit m.
credentials npl lettres de créance fpl; preuves d'identité fpl.
credibility n crédibilité f.
credible adj crédible.
credit n crédit m; honneur m; reconnaissance f; * vt croire, reconnaître; créditer.

creditable adj estimable, honorable; ~**bly** adv honorablement.
credit card n carte de crédit f.
creditor n créancier m -ière f.
credulity n crédulité f.
credulous adj crédule; ~**ly** adv avec crédulité.
creed n credo m.
creek n ruisseau m.
creep vi ramper; avancer lentement.
creeper n (bot) plante grimpante f.
creepy adj terrifiant, qui donne la chair de poule.
cremate vt incinérer.
cremation n incinération, crémation f.
crematorium n crématoire m.
crescent adj croissant; * n croissant de lune m.
cress n cresson m.
crest n crête f.
crested adj à crête.
crestfallen adj découragé, abattu.
crevasse n crevasse f.
crevice n fissure, lézarde f.
crew n bande, équipe f; équipage m.
crib n berceau m; mangeoire f.
cricket n grillon m.
crime n crime m; délit m.
criminal adj criminel; ~**ly** adv criminellement; * n criminel m -le f.
criminality n criminalité f.
crimson adj n cramoisi m.
cripple n, adj invalide mf; * vt estropier; (fig) paralyser.
crisis n crise f.
crisp adj frais; croquant.
crispness n croquant m.
criss-cross adj entrecroisé.
criterion n critère m.
critic n critique m.
critical adj critique; exigeant, sévère; ~**ly** adv d'un œil critique; sévèrement.
criticism n critique f.
criticize vt critiquer.
croak vi coasser, croasser.
crochet n crochet m; * vt faire au crochet; vi faire du crochet.
crockery n poterie f.

crocodile *n* crocodile *m*.

crony *n* copain *m* (copine *f*) de longue date.

crook *n* escroc *m*; filou *m*.

crooked *adj* tordu; malhonnête.

crop *n* culture *f*; récolte *f*; * *vt* récolter.

cross *n* croix *f*; croisement *m*; * *adj* de mauvaise humeur, fâché; * *vt* traverser, croiser; ~ **over** traverser.

crossbar *n* barre transversale *f*.

crossbreed *n* hybride *m*.

cross-country *n* cross-country *m*.

cross-examine *vt* soumettre à un contre-interrogatoire.

crossfire *n* feux croisés *mpl*.

crossing *n* traversée *f*; passage pour piétons *m*.

cross-purpose *n* malentendu *m*; quiproquo *m*; **to be at ~s** comprendre (quelqu'un) de travers.

cross-reference *n* renvoi *m*, référence *f*.

crossroad *n* carrefour *m*.

crosswalk *n* (US) passage clouté *m*.

crotch *n* entre-jambes *m*.

crouch *vi* s'accroupir, se tapir.

crow *n* corbeau *m*; chant du coq *m*; * *vi* chanter victoire.

crowd *n* foule *f*; monde *m*; * *vt* entasser; * *vi* s'entasser.

crown *n* couronne *f*; sommet *m*; * *vt* couronner.

crown prince *n* prince héritier *m*.

crucial *adj* crucial.

crucible *n* creuset *m*.

crucifix *n* crucifix *m*.

crucifixion *n* crucifixion *f*.

crucify *vt* crucifier.

crude *adj* brut, grossier; ~**ly** *adv* crûment.

cruel *adj* cruel; ~**ly** *adv* cruellement.

cruelty *n* cruauté *f*.

cruet *n* huilier-vinaigrier *m*.

cruise *n* croisière *f*; * *vi* croiser.

cruiser *n* croiseur *m*.

crumb *n* miette *f*.

crumble *vt* émietter; effriter; * *vi* s'émietter; se désintégrer.

crumple *vt* froisser.

crunch *vt* croquer; * *n* (*fig*) crise *f*.

crunchy *adj* croquant.

crusade *n* croisade *f*.

crush *vt* écraser; opprimer; * *n* cohue *f*.

crust *n* croûte *f*.

crusty *adj* croustillant; hargneux, bourru.

crutch *n* béquille *f*.

crux *n* cœur *m* (d'une question).

cry *vt* *vi* crier; pleurer; * *n* cri *m*; sanglot *m*.

crypt *n* crypte *f*.

cryptic *adj* énigmatique.

crystal *n* cristal *m*.

crystal-clear *adj* clair comme de l'eau de roche.

crystalline *adj* cristallin; pur.

crystallize *vi* se cristalliser; * *vt* cristalliser.

cub *n* petit *m* (animal).

cube *n* cube *m*.

cubic *adj* cubique.

cuckoo *n* coucou *m*.

cucumber *n* concombre *m*.

cud *n*: **to chew the ~** ruminer (*also fig*).

cuddle *vt* embrasser; * *vi* s'enlacer; * *n* étreinte *f*, câlin *m*.

cudgel *n* gourdin *m*, trique *f*.

cue *n* queue de billard *f*.

cuff *n* manchette *f*; revers de pantalon *m*.

culinary *adj* culinaire.

cull *vt* sélectionner; éliminer.

culminate *vi* culminer.

culmination *n* point culminant *m*.

culpability *n* culpabilité *f*.

culpable *adj* coupable; blâmable; ~**bly** *adv* coupablement.

culprit *n* coupable *mf*.

cult *n* culte *m*.

cultivate *vt* cultiver; améliorer, perfectionner.

cultivation *n* culture *f*.

cultural *adj* culturel.

culture *n* culture *f*.

cumbersome *adj* encombrant; lourd, pesant.

cumulative *adj* cumulatif.

cunning *adj* astucieux, rusé; ~**ly** *adv* astucieusement; habilement; * *n* astuce, finesse *f*.

cup *n* tasse, coupe *f*; (*bot*) corolle *f*.

cupboard *n* placard *m*.

curable *adj* guérissable.

curate *n* vicaire *m*.

curator *n* conservateur *m*; curateur *m*.

curb *n* frein *m*; bord du trottoir *m*; * *vt* freiner, juguler, modérer.

curd *n* lait caillé *m*.

curdle *vt* cailler, figer; *vi* se cailler, se figer.

cure *n* remède *m*; cure *f*; * *vt* guérir.

curfew *n* couvre-feu *m*.

curing *n* salaison *f*.

curiosity *n* curiosité *f*.

curious *adj* curieux; ~**ly** *adv* avec curiosité; curieusement.

curl *n* boucle de cheveux *f*; * *vt* boucler; friser; * *vi* friser.

curling iron *n*, **curling tongs** *npl* fer à friser *m*.

curly *adj* frisé, bouclé.

currant *n* raisin *m* sec.

currency *n* monnaie *f*; circulation *f*; cours *m*.

current *adj* courant; actuel; * *n* cours *m*; tendance *f*; courant *m*.

current affairs *npl* actualité *f*; problèmes actuels *mpl*.

currently *adv* actuellement.

curriculum vitae *n* curriculum vitae *m*.

curry *n* curry *m*.

curse *vt* maudire; * *vi* jurer; * *n* malédiction *f*.

cursor *n* curseur *m*.

cursory *adj* superficiel; hâtif.

curt *adj* succinct; sec.

curtail *vt* réduire; écourter.

curtain *n* rideau *m*.

curtain rod *n* tringle à rideaux *f*.

curtsy *n* révérence *f*; * *vi* faire une révérence.

curvature *n* courbure *f*.

curve *vt* courber; * *n* courbe *f*.

cushion *n* coussin *m*.

custard *n* crème anglaise *f*.

custodian *n* gardien *m* -ne *f*.

custody *n* garde *f*; emprisonnement *m*.

custom *n* coutume *f*, usage *m*.

customary *adj* habituel, coutumier, ordinaire.

customer *n* client *m* -e *f*.

customs *npl* douane *f*.

customs duty *n* droits de douane *mpl*.

customs officer *n* douanier *m*.

cut *vt* découper; couper; tailler; réduire; blesser; ~ **short** écourter; interrompre; ~ **a tooth** percer une dent; * *vi* couper; se couper; * *n* coupe *f*; coupure *f*; réduction *f*; ~ **and dried** *adj* arrangé.

cutback *n* réduction *f*.

cute *adj* mignon.

cutlery *n* couverts *mpl*.

cutlet *n* côtelette *f*.

cut-rate *adj* à prix réduit.

cut-throat *n* assassin *m*; * *adj* acharné.

cutting *n* coupure *f*; * *adj* coupant; tranchant.

cyanide *n* cyanure *m*.

cycle *n* cycle *m*; bicyclette *f*; * *vi* aller à bicyclette.

cycling *n* cyclisme *m*.

cyclist *n* cycliste *mf*.

cyclone *n* cyclone *m*.

cygnet *n* jeune cygne *m*.

cylinder *n* cylindre *m*; rouleau *m*.

cylindric(al) *adj* cylindrique.

cymbals *n* cymbale *f*.

cynic(al) *adj* cynique; sceptique; * *n* cynique *mf*.

cynicism *n* cynisme *m*.

cypress *n* cyprès *m*.

cyst *n* kyste *m*.

czar *n* tsar *m*.

D

dab *n* petit peu *m*; touche *f*.

dabble *vi* barboter.

Dacron *n* dacron *m*.

dad(dy) *n* papa *m*.

daddy-long-legs *n* (*zool*) cousin *m*.

daffodil *n* narcisse *m*, jonquille *f*.

dagger *n* poignard *m*.

daily *adj* quotidien; * *adv* quotidiennement, tous les jours; * *n* quotidien *m*.

daintily *adv* délicatement.

daintiness *n* élégance *f*; délicatesse *f*.

dainty *adj* délicat; élégant.

dairy *n* laiterie *f*.

dairy farm *n* laiterie *f*.

dairy produce *n* produits laitiers *mpl*.
daisy *n* marguerite *f*.
daisy wheel *n* marguerite *f*.
dale *n* vallée *f*.
dally *vi* traîner.
dam *n* barrage *m*; * *vt* endiguer.
damage *n* dommage *m*; tort *m*; * *vt* endommager; faire du tort à.
damask *n* damas *m*; * *adj* damassé.
dame *n* dame *f*; fille *f*.
damn *vt* condamner; * *adj* maudit.
damnable *adj* maudit; ~**bly** *adv* terriblement.
damnation *n* damnation *f*.
damning *adj* accablant.
damp *adj* humide; * *n* humidité *f*; * *vt* humidifier.
dampen *vt* humidifier.
dampness *n* humidité *f*.
damson *n* prune de Damas *f*.
dance *n* danse *f*; soirée dansante *f*; * *vt vi* danser.
dance hall *n* dancing *m*.
dancer *n* danseur *m* -éuse *f*.
dandelion *n* pissenlit *m*.
dandruff *n* pellicules *fpl*.
dandy *adj* génial.
danger *n* danger *m*.
dangerous *adj* dangereux; ~**ly** *adv* dangereusement.
dangle *vi* pendre.
dank *adj* humide.
dapper *adj* soigné.
dappled *adj* tacheté.
dare *vi* oser; * *vt* défier.
daredevil *n* casse-cou *m invar*.
daring *n* audace *f*; * *adj* audacieux; ~**ly** *adv* audacieusement.
dark *adj* sombre, obscur; * *n* obscurité *f*; ignorance *f*.
darken *vt* assombrir, obscurcir;
* *vi* s'assombrir, s'obscurcir.
dark glasses *npl* lunettes de soleil *fpl*.
darkness *n* obscurité *f*.
darkroom *n* chambre noire *f*.
darling *n*, *adj* chéri *m* -e *f*.
darn *vt* repriser.
dart *n* dard *m*.
darts *n* jeu de fléchettes *m*.

dash *vi* se dépêcher; * *n* goutte *f*; tiret, trait *m*; **at one** ~ tout d'un coup.
dashboard *n* tableau de bord *m*.
dashing *adj* impétueux; élégant.
dastardly *adj* infâme.
data *n* données *fpl*.
database *n* base de données *f*.
data processing *n* traitement de données *m*.
date *n* date *f*; rendez-vous *m*; (*bot*) datte *f*;
* *vt* dater; sortir avec.
dated *adj* démodé.
dative *n* (*gr*) datif *m*.
daub *vt* barbouiller.
daughter *n* fille *f*; ~ **in-law** belle-fille *f*.
daunting *adj* décourageant.
dawdle *vi* traîner.
dawn *n* aube *f*; * *vi* se lever.
day *n* jour *m*, journée *f*; **by** ~ de jour; ~ **by** ~ de jour en jour.
daybreak *n* aube *f*.
day laborer *n* (US) journalier *m*.
daylight *n* lumière du jour, lumière naturelle *f*; ~ **saving time** *n* heure d'été *f*.
daytime *n* journée *f*, jour *m*.
daze *vt* étourdir.
dazed *adj* étourdi.
dazzle *vt* éblouir.
dazzling *adj* éblouissant.
deacon *n* diacre *m*.
dead *adj* mort; ~**wood** *n* bois mort *m*; ~ **silence** *n* silence de mort *m*; **the** ~ *npl* les morts *mpl*.
dead-drunk *adj* ivre-mort.
deaden *vt* amortir.
dead heat *n* arrivée ex-aequo *f*.
deadline *n* date limite *f*.
deadlock *n* impasse *f*.
deadly *adj* mortel; * *adv* terriblement.
dead march *n* marche funèbre *f*.
deadness *n* inertie *f*.
deaf *adj* sourd.
deafen *vt* assourdir.
deaf-mute *n* sourd(e)-muet(te) *mf*.
deafness *n* surdité *f*.
deal *n* accord *m*; marché *m*; **a great** ~ beaucoup; **a good** ~ pas mal; * *vt* distribuer, donner; * *vi* ~ **in** être dans le commerce de; ~ **with** avoir affaire à.

dealer *n* commerçant *m*; trafiquant *m*; donneur *m*.

dealings *npl* rapports *mpl*; transactions *fpl*.

dean *n* doyen *m*.

dear *adj* ~**ly** *adv* cher.

dearness *n* cherté *f*.

dearth *n* pénurie *f*.

death *n* mort *f*.

deathbed *n* lit de mort *m*.

deathblow *n* coup mortel *m*.

death certificate *n* acte de décès *m*.

death penalty *n* peine de mort *f*.

death throes *npl* agonie *f*.

death warrant *n* condamnation à mort *f*.

debacle *n* débâcle *f*.

debar *vt* exclure.

debase *vt* dégrader.

debasement *n* dégradation *f*.

debatable *adj* discutable.

debate *n* débat *m*; * *vt* discuter; examiner.

debauched *adj* débauché.

debauchery *n* débauche *f*.

debilitate *vt* débiliter.

debit *n* débit *m*; * *vt* (*com*) débiter.

debt *n* dette *f*; **to get into** ~ s'endetter.

debtor *n* débiteur *m* -trice *f*.

debunk *vt* démystifier.

decade *n* décennie *f*.

decadence *n* décadence *f*.

decaffeinated *adj* décaféiné.

decanter *n* carafe *f*.

decapitate *vt* décapiter.

decapitation *n* décapitation *f*.

decay *vi* décliner; pourrir; * *n* déclin *m*; pourrissement *m*; carie *f*.

deceased *adj* décédé.

deceit *n* tromperie *f*.

deceitful *adj* trompeur; ~**ly** *adv* faussement.

deceive *vt* tromper.

December *n* décembre *m*.

decency *n* décence *f*; pudeur *f*.

decent *adj* décent; bien, bon; ~**ly** *adv* décemment.

deception *n* tromperie *f*.

deceptive *adj* trompeur.

decibel *n* décibel *m*.

decide *vt* decider; * *vi* se décider.

decided *adj* décidé.

decidedly *adv* décidément.

deciduous *adj* (*bot*) à feuilles caduques.

decimal *adj* décimal.

decimate *vt* décimer.

decipher *vt* déchiffrer.

decision *n* décision, détermination *f*.

decisive *adj* décisif; ~**ly** *adv* avec décision.

deck *n* pont *m*; * *vt* orner.

deckchair *n* chaise longue *f*.

declaim *vt vi* déclamer.

declamation *n* déclamation *f*.

declaration *n* déclaration *f*.

declare *vt* déclarer.

declension *n* déclinaison *f*.

decline *vt* (*gr*) décliner; refuser; * *vi* décliner; * *n* déclin *m*; décadence *f*.

declutch *vi* débrayer.

decode *vt* décoder.

decompose *vt* décomposer.

decomposition *n* décomposition *f*.

decor *n* décor *m*; décoration *f*.

decorate *vt* décorer, orner.

decoration *n* décoration *f*.

decorative *adj* décoratif.

decorator *n* décorateur *m* -trice *f*.

decorous *adj* bienséant, convenable; ~**ly** *adv* convenablement.

decorum *n* décorum *m*.

decoy *n* leurre *m*.

decrease *vt* diminuer; * *n* diminution *f*.

decree *n* décret *m*; * *vt* décréter; ordonner.

decrepit *adj* décrépit.

decry *vt* décrier.

dedicate *vt* dédier; consacrer.

dedication *n* dédicace *f*; consacration *f*.

deduce *vt* déduire, conclure.

deduct *vt* déduire, soustraire.

deduction *n* déduction *f*.

deed *n* action *f*; exploit *m*.

deem *vt* juger, considérer.

deep *adj* profond.

deepen *vt* approfondir.

deep-freeze *n* congélateur *m*.

deeply *adv* profondément.

deepness *n* profondeur *f*.

deer *n* cerf *m*.

deface *vt* défigurer.

defacement *n* défiguration *f*.

defamation n diffamation f.

default n défaut m; manque m; * vi manquer à ses engagements.

defaulter n (law) défaillant m -e f.

defeat n défaite f; * vt vaincre; frustrer.

defect n défaut m.

defection n désertion f.

defective adj défectueux.

defend vt défendre; protéger.

defendant n accusé m -e f.

defense n défense f; protection f.

defenseless adj sans défense.

defensive adj défensif; ~ly adv défensivement.

defer vt déférer.

deference n déférence f.

deferential adj respectueux.

defiance n défi m.

defiant adj provocant.

deficiency n défaut m; manque m.

deficient adj insuffisant.

deficit n déficit m.

defile vt souiller.

definable adj définissable.

define vt définir.

definite adj sûr; précis; ~ly adv sans aucun doute.

definition n définition f.

definitive adj définitif; ~ly adv définitivement.

deflate vt dégonfler.

deflect vt dévier.

deflower vt déflorer.

deform vt déformer.

deformity n déformité f.

defraud vt escroquer.

defray vt payer.

defrost vt dégivrer; décongeler.

defroster n dégivreur m.

deft adj habile; ~ly adv habilement.

defunct adj défunt.

defuse vt désamorcer.

degenerate vi dégénérer; * adj dégénéré.

degeneration n dégénération f.

degradation n dégradation f.

degrade vt dégrader.

degree n degré m; diplôme m.

dehydrated adj déshydraté.

de-ice vt dégivrer.

deign vi daigner.

deity n divinité f.

dejected adj découragé.

dejection n découragement m.

delay vt retarder; * n retard m.

delectable adj délectable.

delegate vt déléguer; * n délégué m -e f.

delegation n délégation f.

delete vt effacer.

deliberate vt examiner; * adj délibéré; ~ly adv délibérément, exprès.

deliberation n délibération f.

deliberative adj délibérant.

delicacy n délicatesse f.

delicate adj délicat; ~ly adv délicatement.

delicious adj délicieux, exquis; ~ly adv délicieusement.

delight n délice m; enchantement m; * vt enchanter; * vi adorer.

delighted adj enchanté.

delightful adj charmant; ~ly adv merveilleusement.

delineate vt décrire; délimiter.

delineation n tracé m.

delinquency n délinquance f.

delinquent n délinquant m -e f.

delirious adj délirant.

delirium n délire m.

deliver vt livrer; délivrer; prononcer.

deliverance n libération f.

delivery n livraison f; accouchement m.

delude vt tromper.

deluge n déluge m.

delusion n tromperie f; illusion f.

delve vi creuser; chercher.

demagogue n démagogue m.

demand n demande f; * vt exiger; réclamer.

demanding adj exigeant.

demarcation n démarcation f.

demean vi s'abaisser.

demeanour n conduite f, comportement m.

demented adj dément.

demise n disparition f.

democracy n démocratie f.

democrat n démocrate mf.

democratic adj démocratique.

demolish vt démolir.

demolition *n* démolition *f*.

demon *n* démon, diable *m*.

demonstrable *adj* démontrable; **~bly** *adv* manifestement.

demonstrate *vt* démontrer, prouver; * *vi* manifester.

demonstration *n* démonstration *f*; manifestation *f*.

demonstrative *adj* démonstratif.

demonstrator *n* manifestant *m* -e *f*.

demoralization *n* démoralisation *f*.

demoralize *vt* démoraliser.

demote *vt* rétrograder.

demur *vi* émettre une objection; rechigner.

demure *adj* réservé; **~ly** *adv* avec réserve.

den *n* antre *m*.

denatured alcohol *n* alcool dénaturé *m*.

denial *n* dénégation *f*.

denims *npl* jean *m*.

denomination *n* valeur *f*; dénomination *f*.

denominator *n* (*math*) dénominateur *m*.

denote *vt* dénoter, indiquer.

denounce *vt* dénoncer.

dense *adj* dense, épais.

density *n* densité *f*.

dent *n* bosse *f*; * *vt* cabosser.

dental *adj* dentaire.

dentifrice *n* dentifrice *m*.

dentist *n* dentiste *mf*.

dentistry *n* dentisterie *f*.

denture *n* dentier *m*.

denude *vt* dénuder, dépouiller.

denunciation *n* dénonciation *f*.

deny *vt* nier.

deodorant *n* déodorant *m*.

deodorize *vt* déodoriser.

depart *vi* partir.

department *n* département *m*; service *m*.

department store *n* grand magasin *m*.

departure *n* départ *m*.

departure lounge *n* salle d'embarquement *f*.

depend *vi* dépendre; **~ on/upon** compter sur.

dependable *adj* fiable; sûr.

dependant *n* personne à charge *f*.

dependency *n* dépendance *f*.

dependent *adj* dépendant.

depict *vt* dépeindre, décrire.

depleted *adj* réduit.

deplorable *adj* déplorable, lamentable; **~bly** *adv* déplorablement.

deplore *vt* déplorer, lamenter.

deploy *vt* (*mil*) déployer.

depopulated *adj* dépeuplé.

depopulation *n* dépopulation *f*.

deport *vt* déporter; expulser.

deportation *n* déportation *f*; expulsion *f*.

deportment *n* comportement *m*.

deposit *vt* déposer; * *n* dépôt *m*; caution *f*.

deposition *n* déposition *f*.

depositor *n* déposant *m* -e *f*.

depot *n* dépôt *m*.

deprave *vt* dépraver, corrompre.

depraved *adj* dépravé.

depravity *n* dépravation *f*.

deprecate *vt* désapprouver.

depreciate *vi* se déprécier.

depreciation *n* dépréciation *f*.

depredation *n* déprédation *f*.

depress *vt* déprimer.

depressed *adj* déprimé.

depression *n* dépression *f*.

deprivation *n* privation *f*.

deprive *vt* priver.

deprived *adj* défavorisé.

depth *n* profondeur *f*.

deputation *n* députation *f*.

depute *vt* députer, déléguer.

deputize *vi* remplacer.

deputy *n* remplaçant *m* -e *f*; député *m*; délégué *m* -e *f*.

derail *vt* faire dérailler.

deranged *adj* dérangé.

derby *n* chapeau melon *m*.

derelict *adj* abandonné, en ruines.

deride *vt* se moquer de.

derision *n* dérision *f*.

derisive *adj* ridicule; moqueur.

derivable *adj* déductible.

derivation *n* dérivation *f*.

derivative *n* dérivé *m*.

derive *vt* *vi* dériver.

derogatory *adj* désobligeant.

derrick *n* derrick *m*.

descant *n* (*mus*) déchant *m*.

descend *vi* descendre.

descendant *n* descendant *m* -e *f*.

descent *n* descente *f*.
describe *vt* décrire.
description *n* description *f*.
descriptive *adj* descriptif.
descry *vt* distinguer.
desecrate *vt* profaner.
desecration *n* profanation *f*.
desert *n* désert *m*; * *adj* désert; * *vt* abandonner; déserter.
deserter *n* déserteur *m*.
desertion *n* désertion *f*.
deserve *vt* mériter.
deservedly *adv* à juste titre.
deserving *adj* méritant.
déshabillé *n* déshabillé *m*.
desideratum *n* desideratum *m*.
design *vt* concevoir; dessiner; * *n* dessein *m*; design *m*; dessin *m*.
designate *vt* désigner.
designation *n* désignation *f*.
designedly *adv* exprès, délibérément.
designer *n* créateur *m* -trice *f*; styliste *mf*.
desirability *n* avantage *m*; attrait *m*.
desirable *adj* désirable.
desire *n* désir *m*; * *vt* désirer.
desirous *adj* désireux.
desist *vi* abandonner.
desk *n* bureau *m*.
desolate *adj* désert, désolé.
desolation *n* désolation *f*.
despair *n* désespoir *m*; * *vi* se désespérer.
despairingly *adv* désespérément.
despatch = dispatch.
desperado *n* bandit *m*.
desperate *adj* désespéré; ~ly *adv* désespérément; extrêmement.
desperation *n* désespoir *m*.
despicable *adj* méprisable.
despise *vt* mépriser.
despite *prep* malgré.
despoil *vt* dépouiller.
despondency *n* abattement *m*.
despondent *adj* abattu.
despot *n* despote *m*.
despotic *adj* despotique; ~ally *adv* despotiquement.
despotism *n* despotisme *m*.
dessert *n* dessert *m*.

destination *n* destination *f*.
destine *vt* destiner.
destiny *n* destin, sort *m*.
destitute *adj* indigent.
destitution *n* indigence *f*.
destroy *vt* détruire.
destruction *n* destruction *f*.
destructive *adj* destructeur.
desultory *adj* irrégulier; sans méthode.
detach *vt* séparer, détacher.
detachable *adj* détachable.
detachment *n* (*mil*) détachement *m*.
detail *n* détail *m*; in ~ en détail; * *vt* détailler.
detain *vt* retenir; détenir.
detect *vt* détecter.
detection *n* détection *f*; découverte *f*.
detective *n* détective *m*.
detector *n* détecteur *m*.
detention *n* détention *f*.
deter *vt* dissuader.
detergent *n* détergent *m*.
deteriorate *vt* détériorer.
deterioration *n* détérioration *f*.
determination *n* détermination *f*.
determine *vt* déterminer, décider.
determined *adj* déterminé.
deterrent *n* force de dissuasion *f*.
detest *vt* détester.
detestable *adj* détestable.
dethrone *vt* détrôner.
dethronement *n* détrônement *m*.
detonate *vi* détoner.
detonation *n* détonation *f*.
detour *n* déviation *f*.
detract *vi* nuire à.
detriment *n* détriment *m*.
detrimental *adj* préjudiciable.
deuce *n* deux *m*; égalité *f*.
devaluation *n* dévaluation *f*.
devastate *vt* dévaster.
devastating *adj* dévastateur.
devastation *n* dévastation *f*.
develop *vt* développer.
development *n* développement *m*.
deviate *vi* dévier.
deviation *n* déviation *f*.
device *n* mécanisme *m*.
devil *n* diable, démon *m*.

devilish *adj* diabolique; **~ly** *adv* diaboliquement.

devious *adj* tortueux.

devise *vt* inventer; concevoir.

devoid *adj* dépourvu.

devolve *vt* déléguer.

devote *vt* consacrer.

devoted *adj* dévoué.

devotee *n* partisan *m* -e *f*.

devotion *n* dévotion *f*.

devotional *adj* dévot.

devour *vt* dévorer.

devout *adj* dévot, pieux; **~ly** *adv* pieusement.

dew *n* rosée *f*.

dewy *adj* couvert de rosée; ingénu.

dexterity *n* dextérité *f*.

dexterous *adj* adroit, habile.

diabetes *n* diabète *m*.

diabetic *n* diabétique *mf*.

diabolic *adj* diabolique; **~ally** *adv* diaboliquement.

diadem *n* diadème *m*.

diagnosis *n* (*med*) diagnostic *m*.

diagnostic *adj* diagnostique; * *npl* **~s** diagnostic *m*.

diagonal *adj* diagonal; **~ly** *adv* diagonalement; * *n* diagonale *f*.

diagram *n* diagramme *m*.

dial *n* cadrant *m*.

dial code *n* code *m*.

dialect *n* dialecte *m*.

dialogue *n* dialogue *m*.

dial tone *n* tonalité *f*.

diameter *n* diamètre *m*.

diametrical *adj* diamétral; **~ly** *adv* diamétralement.

diamond *n* diamant *m*.

diamond-cutter *n* tailleur de diamant *m*.

diamonds *npl* (cards) carreaux *mpl*.

diaper *n* couche *f*.

diaphragm *n* diaphragme *m*.

diarrhoea *n* diarrhée *f*.

diary *n* journal *m*.

dice *npl* dés *mpl*.

dictate *vt* dicter; * *n* ordre *m*.

dictation *n* dictée *f*.

dictatorial *adj* dictatorial.

dictatorship *n* dictature *f*.

diction *n* diction *f*.

dictionary *n* dictionnaire *m*.

didactic *adj* didactique.

die *vi* mourir; **~ away** s'affaiblir; **~ down** s'éteindre.

die *n* (*sing de* **dice**) dé *m*.

diehard *n* réactionnaire *mf*.

diesel *n* diesel *m*.

diet *n* diète *f*; régime *m*; * *vi* être au régime.

dietary *adj* diététique.

differ *vi* différer.

difference *n* différence *f*.

different *adj* différent; **~ly** *adv* différemment.

differentiate *vt* différencier.

difficult *adj* difficile.

difficulty *n* difficulté *f*.

diffidence *n* timidité *f*; manque d'assurance *m*.

diffident *adj* timide; mal assuré; **~ly** *adv* avec timidité.

diffraction *n* diffraction *f*.

diffuse *vt* diffuser, répandre; * *adj* diffus.

diffusion *n* diffusion *f*.

dig *vt* creuser; * *n* coup *m*.

digest *vt* digérer.

digestible *adj* digestible.

digestion *n* digestion *f*.

digestive *adj* digestif.

digger *n* excavatrice *f*.

digit *n* chiffre *m*.

digital *adj* digital; numérique.

dignified *adj* digne.

dignitary *n* dignitaire *m*.

dignity *n* dignité *f*.

digress *vi* faire une digression.

digression *n* digression *f*.

dike *n* digue *f*.

dilapidated *adj* délabré.

dilapidation *n* délabrement *m*.

dilate *vt* dilater; * *vi* se dilater.

dilemma *n* dilemme *m*.

diligence *n* assiduité *f*.

diligent *adj* assidu; **~ly** *adv* avec assiduité.

dilute *vt* diluer.

dim *adj* indistinct; faible; sombre; * *vt* affaiblir; troubler.

dime *n* pièce de dix cents *f*.

dimension *n* dimension *f*.

diminish *vt vi* diminuer.

diminution *n* diminution *f*.

diminutive *n* diminutif *m*.

dimly *adv* indistinctement; faiblement.

dimmer *n* interrupteur d'intensité *m*.

dimple *n* fossette *f*.

din *n* vacarme *m*.

dine *vi* dîner.

diner *n* restaurant (économique) *m*; dîneur *m* -euse *f*.

dinghy *n* canot pneumatique *f*.

dingy *adj* sale; miteux.

dinner *n* dîner *m*.

dinner time *n* heure du dîner *f*.

dinosaur *n* dinosaure *m*.

dint *n*: by ~ of à force de.

diocese *n* diocèse *m*.

dip *vt* tremper.

diphtheria *n* diphtérie *f*.

diphthong *n* diphtongue *f*.

diploma *n* diplôme *m*.

diplomacy *n* diplomatie *f*.

diplomat *n* diplomate *m*.

diplomatic *adj* diplomatique.

dipsomania *n* dipsomanie *f*.

dipstick *n* (*auto*) jauge *f*.

dire *adj* atroce, affreux.

direct *adj* direct; * *vt* diriger.

direction *n* direction *f*; instruction *f*.

directly *adv* directement; immédiatement.

director *n* directeur *m* -trice *f*.

directory *n* annuaire *m*.

dirt *n* saleté *f*.

dirtiness *n* saleté *f*.

dirty *adj* sale.

disability *n* incapacité *f*; infirmité *f*.

disabled *adj* infirme.

disabuse *vt* détromper.

disadvantage *n* désavantage *m*; * *vt* désavantager.

disadvantageous *adj* désavantageux.

disaffected *adj* mécontent.

disagree *vi* ne pas être d'accord.

disagreeable *adj* désagréable; ~bly *adv* désagréablement.

disagreement *n* désaccord *m*.

disallow *vt* rejeter.

disappear *vi* disparaître.

disappearance *n* disparition *f*.

disappoint *vt* décevoir.

disappointed *adj* déçu.

disappointing *adj* décevant.

disappointment *n* déception *f*.

disapproval *n* désapprobation *f*.

disapprove *vt* désapprouver.

disarm *vt* désarmer.

disarmament *n* désarmement *m*.

disarray *n* désordre *m*.

disaster *n* désastre *m*.

disastrous *adj* désastreux.

disband *vt* disperser.

disbelief *n* incrédulité *f*.

disbelieve *vt* ne pas croire.

disburse *vt* débourser.

discard *vt* jeter.

discern *vt* discerner, percevoir.

discernible *adj* perceptible.

discerning *adj* perspicace.

discernment *n* perspicacité *f*.

discharge *vt* décharger; régler (une dette); remplir; * *n* décharge *f*; règlement *m*.

disciple *n* disciple *m*.

discipline *n* discipline *f*; * *vt* discipliner.

disclaim *vt* nier.

disclaimer *n* dénégation *f*.

disclose *vt* révéler.

disclosure *n* révélation *f*.

disco *n* discothèque *f*.

discoloration *n* décoloration *f*.

discolour *vt* décolorer.

discomfort *n* incommodité *f*.

disconcert *vt* déconcerter.

disconnect *vt* débrancher.

disconsolate *adj* inconsolable; ~ly *adv* inconsolablement.

discontent *n* mécontentement *m*; * *adj* mécontent.

discontented *adj* mécontent.

discontinue *vt* interrompre.

discord *n* discorde *f*.

discordant *adj* discordant.

discount *n* escompte *m*; remise *f*; * *vt* escompter.

discourage *vt* décourager.

discouraged *adj* découragé.

discouragement *n* découragement *m*.

discouraging *adj* décourageant.

discourse *n* discours *m*.

discourteous *adj* discourtois; **~ly** *adv* de manière discourtoise.

discourtesy *n* manque de courtoisie *m*.

discover *vt* découvrir.

discovery *n* découverte *f*.

discredit *vt* discréditer.

discreditable *adj* peu honorable.

discreet *adj* discret; **~ly** *adv* discrètement.

discrepancy *n* contradiction *f*.

discretion *n* discrétion *f*.

discretionary *adj* discrétionnaire.

discriminate *vt* distinguer; discriminer.

discrimination *n* discrimination *f*.

discursive *adj* discursif.

discuss *vt* discuter.

discussion *n* discussion *f*.

disdain *vt* dédaigner; * *n* dédain, mépris *m*.

disdainful *adj* dédaigneux, méprisant; **~ly** *adv* dédaigneusement, avec mépris.

disease *n* maladie *f*.

diseased *adj* malade.

disembark *vt vi* débarquer.

disembarkation *n* (*mil*) débarquement *m*.

disenchant *vt* désenchanter.

disenchanted *adj* désenchanté.

disenchantment *n* désenchantement *m*.

disengage *vt* dégager.

disentangle *vt* démêler.

disfigure *vt* défigurer.

disgrace *n* honte *f*; scandale *m*; * *vt* déshonorer.

disgraceful *adj* honteux; scandaleux; **~ly** *adv* honteusement.

disgruntled *adj* mécontent.

disguise *vt* déguiser; * *n* déguisement *m*.

disgust *n* dégoût *m*; * *vt* dégoûter.

disgusting *adj* dégoûtant.

dish *n* plat *m*; assiette *f*; * *vt* servir dans un plat; **~ up** servir.

dishcloth *n* torchon à vaisselle *m*.

dishearten *vt* démoraliser.

dishevelled *adj* ébouriffé.

dishonest *adj* malhonnête; **~ly** *adv* malhonnêtement.

dishonesty *n* malhonnêteté *f*.

dishonour *n* déshonneur *m*; * *vt* déshonorer.

dishonourable *adj* déshonorable; **~bly** *adv* de manière déshonorante.

dishtowel *n* torchon à vaisselle *m*.

dishwarmer *n* chauffe-plats *m*.

dishwasher *n* lave-vaisselle *m*; plongeur *m* -euse *f*.

disillusion *vt* désillusionner.

disillusioned *adj* désillusionné.

disincentive *n* élément dissuasif *m*.

disinclination *n* aversion *f*.

disinclined *adj* peu enclin.

disinfect *vt* désinfecter.

disinfectant *n* désinfectant *m*.

disinherit *vt* déshériter.

disintegrate *vi* se désintégrer.

disinterested *adj* désintéressé; **~ly** *adv* de manière désintéressée.

disjointed *adj* déréglé; décousu.

disk *n* disque *m*; disquette *f*.

diskette *n* disque *m*, disquette *f*.

dislike *n* aversion *f*; * *vt* ne pas aimer.

dislocate *vt* disloquer.

dislocation *n* dislocation *f*.

dislodge *vt* déloger.

disloyal *adj* déloyal; **~ly** *adv* déloyalement.

disloyalty *n* déloyauté *f*.

dismal *adj* triste, lugubre.

dismantle *vt* démonter.

dismay *n* consternation *f*.

dismember *vt* démembrer.

dismiss *vt* renvoyer; écarter.

dismissal *n* renvoi *m*; rejet *m*.

dismount *vt* désarçonner; * *vi* descendre.

disobedience *n* désobéissance *f*.

disobedient *adj* désobéissant.

disobey *vt* désobéir.

disorder *n* désordre *m*.

disorderly *adj* en désordre, confus.

disorganization *n* désorganisation *f*.

disorganized *adj* désorganisé.

disorientated *adj* désorienté.

disown *vt* renier.

disparage *vt* dénigrer.

disparaging *adj* désobligeant.

disparity *n* disparité *f*.

dispassionate *adj* impartial; calme.

dispatch *vt* envoyer; * *n* envoi *m*; dépêche *f*.

dispel *vt* dissiper.

dispensary *n* dispensaire *m*.
dispense *vt* dispenser; distribuer.
disperse *vt* disperser.
dispirited *adj* démoralisé.
displace *vt* déplacer.
display *vt* exposer; faire preuve de; * *n* exposition *f*; déploiement *m*.
displeased *adj* mécontent.
displeasure *n* mécontentement *m*.
disposable *adj* à jeter.
disposal *n* disposition *f*.
dispose *vt* disposer.
disposed *adj* disposé.
disposition *n* disposition *f*.
dispossess *vt* déposséder.
disproportionate *adj* disproportionné.
disprove *vt* réfuter.
dispute *n* dispute *f*; controverse *f*; * *vt* mettre en cause.
disqualify *vt* exclure; disqualifier.
disquiet *n* inquiétude *f*.
disquieting *adj* inquiétant.
disquisition *n* dissertation *f*.
disregard *vt* ne pas tenir compte de; mépriser; * *n* dédain *m*.
disreputable *adj* de mauvaise réputation.
disrespect *n* irrévérence *f*.
disrespectful *adj* irrespectueux; ~ly *adv* irrespectueusement.
disrobe *vt* dévêtir.
disrupt *vt* interrompre.
disruption *n* interruption *f*.
dissatisfaction *n* mécontentement *m*.
dissatisfied *adj* mécontent.
dissect *vt* disséquer.
dissection *n* dissection *f*.
disseminate *vt* disséminer.
dissension *n* dissension *f*.
dissent *vi* être en dissension; * *n* dissension *f*.
dissenter *n* dissident *m* -e *f*.
dissertation *n* thèse *f*.
dissident *n* dissident *m* -e *f*.
dissimilar *adj* dissemblable.
dissimilarity *n* dissemblance *f*.
dissimulation *n* dissimulation *f*.
dissipate *vt* dissiper.
dissipation *n* dissipation *f*.

dissociate *vt* dissocier.
dissolute *adj* dissolu.
dissolution *n* dissolution *f*.
dissolve *vt* dissoudre; * *vi* se dissoudre.
dissonance *n* dissonance *f*.
dissuade *vt* dissuader.
distance *n* distance *f*; **at a ~** de loin; * *vt* distancer.
distant *adj* distant.
distaste *n* dégoût *m*.
distasteful *adj* désagréable.
distend *vt* distendre.
distil *vt* distiller.
distillation *n* distillation *f*.
distillery *n* distillerie *f*.
distinct *adj* distinct; ~ly *adv* distinctement.
distinction *n* distinction *f*.
distinctive *adj* distinctif.
distinctness *n* clarté *f*.
distinguish *vt* distinguer; discerner.
distort *vt* déformer.
distorted *adj* déformé.
distortion *n* distortion *f*.
distract *vt* distraire.
distracted *adj* distrait; ~ly *adv* distraitement.
distraction *n* distraction *f*; confusion *f*.
distraught *adj* éperdu.
distress *n* souffrance *f*; détresse *f*; * *vt* désoler; affliger.
distressing *adj* affligeant.
distribute *vt* distribuer, répartir.
distribution *n* distribution *f*.
distributor *n* distributeur *m*.
district *n* district *m*.
district attorney *n* procureur de la République *m*.
distrustful *adj* méfiant.
disturb *vt* déranger.
disturbance *n* dérangement *m*; trouble *m*.
disturbed *adj* troublé.
disturbing *adj* troublant.
disuse *n* désuétude *f*.
disused *adj* abandonné.
ditch *n* fossé *m*.
dither *vi* hésiter.
ditto *adv* idem.
ditty *n* chansonnette *f*.
diuretic *adj* (*med*) diurétique.

dive vi plonger.

diver n plongeur m -euse f.

diverge vi diverger.

divergence n divergence f.

divergent adj divergent.

diverse adj divers, différent; ~ly adv différemment.

diversion n diversion f.

diversity n diversité f.

divert vt dévier; divertir.

divest vt dénuder; dépouiller.

divide vt diviser; * vi se diviser.

dividend n dividende m.

dividers npl (math) compas à pointes sèches m.

divine adj divin.

divinity n divinité f.

diving n plongeon m.

diving board n plongeoir m.

divisible adj divisible.

division n (math) division f.

divisor n (math) diviseur m.

divorce n divorce m; * vi divorcer.

divorced adj divorcé.

divulge vt divulguer.

dizziness n vertige m.

dizzy adj pris de vertige.

DJ n disc-jockey, DJ m.

do vt faire.

docile adj docile.

dock n dock m; * vi entrer aux docks.

docker n docker m.

dockyard n chantier m naval.

doctor n docteur m.

doctrinal adj doctrinal.

doctrine n doctrine f.

document n document m.

documentary adj documentaire.

dodge vt esquiver.

doe n biche f; ~ **rabbit** lapine f.

dog n chien m.

dogged adj tenace; ~ly adv tenacement.

dog kennel n refuge pour chiens m.

dogmatic adj dogmatique; ~ly adv dogmatiquement.

doings npl faits mpl.

do-it-yourself n bricolage m.

doleful adj lugubre, triste.

doll n poupée f.

dollar n dollar m.

dolphin n dauphin m.

domain n domaine m.

dome n dôme m.

domestic adj domestique.

domesticate vt domestiquer.

domestication n domestication f.

domesticity n domesticité f.

domicile n domicile m.

dominant adj dominant.

dominate vi dominer.

domination n domination f.

domineer vi dominer.

domineering adj autoritaire.

dominion n domination f.

dominoes npl domino m.

donate vt donner, faire don de.

donation n donation f.

done p, adj fait; cuit.

donkey n âne m.

donor n donneur m; donateur m.

doodle vi gribouiller.

doom n sort m.

door n porte f.

doorbell n sonnette f.

door handle n poignée de porte f.

doorman n portier m.

doormat n paillasson m.

doorplate n plaque f.

doorstep n pas de porte m.

doorway n entrée f.

dormant adj latent; dormant.

dormer window n lucarne f.

dormitory n dortoir m.

dormouse n loir m.

dosage n dose f; dosage m.

dose n dose f; * vt doser; donner une dose à.

dossier n dossier m.

dot n point m.

dote vi adorer.

dotingly adv avec adoration.

double adj double; * vt doubler; * n double m.

double bed n lit m à deux places.

double-breasted adj croisé.

double chin n double menton m.

double-dealing n duplicité f.

double-edged *adj* à double tranchant.

double entry *n* (*com*) comptabilité en partie double *f*.

double-lock *vt* fermer à double tour.

double room *n* chambre pour deux *f*.

doubly *adv* doublement.

doubt *n* doute *m*; * *vt* douter de.

doubtful *adj* douteux.

doubtless *adv* indubitablement.

dough *n* pâte *f*.

douse *vt* éteindre.

dove *n* colombe *f*.

dovecot *n* colombier *m*.

dowdy *adj* mal habillé.

down *n* duvet *m*; * *prep* en bas; **to sit ~** s'asseoir; **upside ~** à l'envers.

downcast *adj* démoralisé; baissé.

downfall *n* ruine *f*.

downhearted *adj* découragé.

downhill *adv* en descendant, dans la descente.

down payment *n* acompte *m*.

downpour *n* grosse averse *f*.

downright *adj* manifeste.

downstairs *adv* en bas.

down-to-earth *adj* pratique; terre à terre.

downtown *adv* dans le centre, en ville.

downward(s) *adv* vers le bas.

dowry *n* dot *f*.

doze *vi* somnoler.

dozen *n* douzaine *f*.

dozy *adj* somnolent.

drab *adj* gris; morne.

draft *n* brouillon *m*; traite *f*.

drag *vt* tirer; * *n* drague *f*; ennui *m*.

dragnet *n* seine *f*; filet *m*.

dragon *n* dragon *m*.

dragonfly *n* libellule *f*.

drain *vt* drainer; vider; * *n* tuyau d'écoulement *m*.

drainage *n* drainage *m*.

drainboard *n* égouttoir *m*.

drainpipe *n* tuyau d'écoulement *m*.

drake *n* canard mâle *m*.

dram *n* petit verre *m*.

drama *n* drame *m*.

dramatic *adj* dramatique; **~ally** *adv* dramatiquement.

dramatist *n* dramaturge *mf*.

dramatize *vt* dramatiser.

drape *vt* draper.

drapes *npl* tentures *fpl*.

drastic *adj* radical.

draught *n* courant d'air *m*.

draughts *npl* jeu de dames *m*.

draughty *adj* exposé aux courants d'air.

draw *vt* tirer; dessiner; **~ nigh** s'approcher.

drawback *n* désavantage, inconvénient *m*.

drawer *n* tiroir *m*.

drawing *n* dessin *m*.

drawing board *n* planche à dessin *f*.

drawing room *n* salon *m*.

drawl *vi* parler d'une voix traînante.

dread *n* terreur *f*; * *vt* redouter, craindre.

dreadful *adj* horrible; **~ly** *adv* horriblement.

dream *n* rêve *m*; * *vt vi* rêver.

dreary *adj* triste, morne.

dredge *vt* draguer.

dregs *npl* lie *f*.

drench *vt* tremper.

dress *vt* habiller; panser; * *vi* s'habiller; * *n* robe *f*.

dresser *n* buffet *m*.

dressing *n* pansement *m*; sauce *f*.

dressing gown *n* peignoir *m*.

dressing room *n* loge *f*; garde-robe *f*.

dressing table *n* coiffeuse *f*.

dressmaker *n* couturier *m* -ière *f*.

dressy *adj* élégant.

dribble *vi* tomber goutte à goutte.

dried *adj* séché.

drift *n* amoncellement *m*; courant *m*; sens *m*; * *vi* aller à la dérive.

driftwood *n* bois flottant *m*.

drill *n* perceuse *f*; (*mil*) exercice *m*; * *vt* percer.

drink *vt vi* boire; * *n* boisson *f*.

drinkable *adj* potable; buvable.

drinker *n* buveur *m* -euse *f*.

drinking bout *n* beuverie *f*.

drinking water *n* eau potable *f*.

drip *vi* goutter; * *n* goutte *f*; goutte-à-goutte *m*.

dripping *n* graisse *f*.

drive *vt* conduire; pousser; * *vi* conduire; * *n* promenade en voiture *f*; allée, entrée *f*.

drivel n imbécilités fpl; * vi baver; dire des imbécilités.

driver n conducteur m -trice f; chauffeur m.

driveway n allée, entrée f.

driving n conduite f.

driving instructor n moniteur(-trice) d'auto-école m(f).

driving licence n permis m de conduire.

driving school n auto-école f.

driving test n examen m du permis de conduire.

drizzle vi bruiner.

droll adj drôle.

drone n bourdonnement m.

droop vi tomber.

drop n goutte f; * vt laisser tomber; * vi tomber; ~ **out** se retirer; abandonner.

drop-out n marginal m.

dropper n compte-gouttes m invar.

dross n scories fpl.

drought n sécheresse f.

drove n: in ~s en troupe.

drown vt noyer; * vi se noyer.

drowsiness n somnolence f.

drowsy adj somnolent.

drudgery n corvée f.

drug n drogue f; * vt droguer.

drug addict n drogué m -e f.

druggist n pharmacien m -ne f.

drugstore n pharmacie f.

drum n tambour m; * vi jouer du tambour.

drum majorette n majorette f.

drummer n batteur m.

drumstick n baguette de tambour f.

drunk adj ivre.

drunkard n ivrogne mf.

drunken adj ivre.

drunkenness n ivresse f.

dry adj sec; * vt faire sécher; * vi sécher.

dry-cleaning n nettoyage à sec m.

dry-goods store n (US) mercerie f.

dryness n sécheresse f.

dry rot n pourriture f.

dual adj double.

dual-purpose adj à double emploi.

dubbed adj doublé.

dubious adj douteux.

duck n canard m; * vt vi plonger.

duckling n caneton m.

dud adj nul; faux.

due adj dû, f due; * adv exactement; * n droit m; chose due f.

duel n duel m.

duet n (mus) duo m.

dull adj terne; insipide; gris; * vt ternir; atténuer.

duly adv dûment; en temps voulu.

dumb adj muet; ~**ly** adv sans dire un mot.

dumbbell n haltère m; (US) abruti m.

dumbfounded adj interloqué.

dummy n mannequin m; prête-nom m.

dump n tas m; * vt jeter; laisser tomber.

dumping n (com) dumping m.

dumpling n boulette de pâte f.

dumpy adj boulot, -te f.

dunce n cancre m.

dune n dune f.

dung n fumier m.

dungarees npl salopette f.

dungeon n donjon m; cachot m.

dupe n dupe f; * vt duper.

duplex n duplex m.

duplicate n duplicata m; copie f; * vt dupliquer.

duplicity n duplicité f.

durability n durabilité f.

durable adj durable.

duration n durée f.

during prep pendant.

dusk n crépuscule m.

dust n poussière f; * vt épousseter.

duster n chiffon m.

dusty adj poussiéreux.

Dutch courage n courage puisé dans la boisson m.

duteous adj fidèle, loyal.

dutiful adj obéissant, soumis; ~**ly** adv avec obéissance.

duty n devoir m; obligation f.

duty-free adj hors taxe.

dwarf n nain m, naine f; * vt rapetisser.

dwell vi habiter, vivre.

dwelling n habitation f; domicile m.

dwindle vi diminuer.

dye vt teindre; * n teinture f.

dyer n teinturier m.

dyeing *n* teinturerie *f*; teinture *f*.

dye-works *npl* teinturerie *f*.

dying *adj* mourant, agonisant; * *n* mort *f*.

dynamic *adj* dynamique.

dynamics *n* dynamique *f*.

dynamite *n* dynamite *f*.

dynamiter *n* dynamiteur *m* -euse *f*.

dynamo *n* dynamo *f*.

dynasty *n* dynastie *f*.

dysentery *n* dysenterie *f*.

dyspepsia *n* (*med*) dyspepsie *f*.

dyspeptic *adj* dyspeptique.

E

each *pn* chacun(e); ~ **other** les un(e)s les autres.

eager *adj* enthousiaste; ardent; ~**ly** *adv* avec enthousiasme; ardemment.

eagerness *n* enthousiasme *m*; ardeur *f*; désir *m*.

eagle *n* aigle *m*.

eagle-eyed *adj* aux yeux d'aigle.

eaglet *n* aiglon *m*.

ear *n* oreille *f*; ouïe *f*; **by ~** en improvisant.

earache *n* mal d'oreille *m*.

eardrum *n* tympan *m*.

early *adj* premier; *adv* tôt, de bonne heure.

earmark *vt* (*fig*) désigner.

earn *vt* gagner.

earnest *adj* sérieux; ~**ly** *adv* sérieusement.

earnestness *n* sérieux *m*.

earnings *npl* revenus *mpl*.

earphones *npl* écouteurs *mpl*.

earring *n* boucle d'oreille *f*.

earth *n* terre *f*; * *vt* brancher à la terre.

earthen *adj* de terre.

earthenware *n* poterie *f*.

earthquake *n* tremblement de terre *m*.

earthworm *n* ver de terre *m*.

earthy *adj* terreux; truculent.

earwig *n* perce-oreille *m*.

ease *n* aise *f*; facilité *f*; **at ~** à l'aise; * *vt* apaiser; soulager.

easel *n* chevalet *m*.

easily *adv* facilement.

easiness *n* facilité *f*.

east *n* est *m*; orient *m*.

Easter *n* Pâques *fpl*.

Easter egg *n* œuf de Pâques *m*.

easterly *adj* d'est.

eastern *adj* de l'est, oriental.

eastward(s) *adv* vers l'est.

easy *adj* facile; commode; ~ **going** décontracté.

easy chair *n* fauteuil *m*.

eat *vt* *vi* manger.

eatable *adj* comestible; mangeable; * ~**s** *npl* vivres *mpl*.

eau de Cologne *n* eau *f* de Cologne.

eaves *npl* avant-toit *m*.

eavesdrop *vt* espionner; écouter discrètement.

ebb *n* reflux *m*; * *vi* refluer; décliner.

ebony *n* ébène *f*.

eccentric *adj* excentrique.

eccentricity *n* excentricité *f*.

ecclesiastic *adj* ecclésiastique.

echo *n* écho *m*; * *vi* résonner.

eclectic *adj* éclectique.

eclipse *n* éclipse *f*; * *vt* éclipser.

ecology *n* écologie *f*.

economic(al) *adj* économique; économe.

economics *npl* économie *f*.

economist *n* économiste *mf*.

economize *vt* économiser.

economy *n* économie *f*.

ecstasy *n* extase *f*.

ecstatic *adj* extatique; ~**ally** *adv* avec extase.

eczema *n* eczéma *m*.

eddy *n* tourbillon *m*; * *vi* tourbillonner.

edge *n* fil *m*; pointe *f*; bord *m*; acrimonie *f*; * *vt* border; affiler.

edgeways, edgewise *adv* de côté.

edging *n* bordure *f*.

edgy *adj* nerveux.

edible *adj* mangeable; comestible.

edict *n* édit *m*; décret *m*.

edification *n* édification *f*.

edifice *n* édifice *m*.

edify *vt* édifier.

edit *vt* diriger; rédiger; couper.

edition *n* édition *f*.

editor *n* directeur *m* -trice *f*; rédacteur *m* -trice *f*.

editorial *adj* rédactionnel; * *n* éditorial *m*.

educate *vt* éduquer; instruire.

education *n* éducation *f*; instruction *f*.

eel *n* anguille *f*.

eerie *adj* inquiétant; surnaturel.

efface *vt* effacer.

effect *n* effet *m*; réalité *f*; **~s** *npl* biens *mpl*; * *vt* effectuer.

effective *adj* efficace; effectif; **~ly** *adv* effectivement, en effet.

effectiveness *n* efficacité *f*.

effectual *adj* efficace; **~ly** *adv* efficacement.

effeminacy *n* caractère efféminé *m*.

effeminate *adj* efféminé.

effervescence *n* effervescence *f*.

effete *adj* (*bot*) stérile; faible.

efficacy *n* efficacité *f*.

efficiency *n* efficacité *f*.

efficient *adj* efficace.

effigy *n* effigie *f*.

effort *n* effort *m*.

effortless *adj* sans effort.

effrontery *n* effronterie *f*.

effusive *adj* chaleureux; expansif.

egg *n* œuf *m*; * **~ on** *vt* encourager.

eggcup *n* coquetier *m*.

eggplant *n* (US) aubergine *f*.

eggshell *n* coquille d'œuf *f*.

ego(t)ism *n* égoïsme *m*.

ego(t)ist *n* égoïste *mf*.

ego(t)istical *adj* égoïste.

eiderdown *n* édredon *m*.

eight *adj n* huit *m*.

eighteen *adj n* dix-huit *m*.

eighteenth *adj n* dix-huitième *mf*.

eighth *adj n* huitième *mf*.

eightieth *adj n* quatre-vingtième *mf*.

eighty *adj n* quatre-vingt.

either *pn* n'importe lequel, n'importe laquelle; * *conj* ou, soit.

ejaculate *vi* s'exclamer; éjaculer.

ejaculation *n* exclamation *f*; éjaculation *f*.

eject *vt* éjecter, expulser.

ejection *n* éjection, expulsion *f*.

ejector seat *n* siège éjectable *m*.

eke *vt* augmenter; prolonger.

elaborate *vt* élaborer; * *adj* élaboré; compliqué; **~ly** *adv* avec soin.

elapse *vi* s'écouler.

elastic *adj* élastique.

elasticity *n* élasticité *f*.

elated *adj* exultant.

elation *n* exultation *f*.

elbow *n* coude *m*; * *vt* pousser du coude.

elbow-room *n* espace *m*; (*fig*) liberté, latitude *f*.

elder *n* sureau *m*; * *adj* aîné.

elderly *adj* d'un âge avancé.

elders *npl* anciens *mpl*.

eldest *adj* aîné.

elect *vt* élire; choisir; * *adj* élu; choisi.

election *n* élection *f*; choix *m*.

electioneering *n* propagande électorale *f*.

elective *adj* facultatif; électif.

elector *n* électeur *m* -trice *f*.

electoral *adj* électoral.

electorate *n* électorat *m*.

electric(al) *adj* électrique.

electric blanket *n* couverture électrique *f*.

electric cooker *n* cuisinière électrique *f*.

electric fire *n* radiateur électrique *m*.

electrician *n* électricien *m*.

electricity *n* électricité *f*.

electrify *vt* électriser.

electron *n* électron *m*.

electronic *adj* électronique; **~s** *npl* électronique *f*.

elegance *n* élégance *f*.

elegant *adj* élégant; **~ly** *adv* élégamment.

elegy *n* élégie *f*.

element *n* élément *m*.

elemental, elementary *adj* élémentaire.

elephant *n* éléphant *m*.

elephantine *adj* lourd.

elevate *vt* élever, hausser.

elevation *n* élévation *f*; hauteur *f*.

elevator *n* ascenseur *m*.

eleven *adj n* onze *m*.

eleventh *adj n* onzième *mf*.

elf *n* elfe *m*.

elicit *vt* tirer, obtenir.

eligibility *n* éligibilité *f*.

eligible *adj* éligible.

eliminate *vt* éliminer, écarter.

elk *n* élan *m*.

elliptic(al) *adj* elliptique.

elm *n* orme *m*.

elocution *n* élocution *f*.

elocutionist *n* professeur d'élocution *m*.

elongate *vt* allonger.

elope *vi* s'échapper, s'enfuir.

elopement *n* fugue, évasion *f*.

eloquence *n* éloquence *f*.

eloquent *adj* éloquent; ~**ly** *adv* éloquemment.

else *pn* autre.

elsewhere *adv* ailleurs.

elucidate *vt* élucider, expliquer.

elucidation *n* élucidation, explication *f*.

elude *vt* éluder; éviter.

elusive, elusory *adj* insaisissable.

emaciated *adj* émacié.

emanate (from) *vi* émaner (de).

emancipate *vt* émanciper; affranchir.

emancipation *n* émancipation *f*; affranchissement *m*.

embalm *vt* embaumer.

embankment *n* talus *m*; quai *m*.

embargo *n* embargo *m*.

embark *vt* embarquer.

embarkation *n* embarcation *f*.

embarrass *vt* embarrasser.

embarrassed *adj* embarrassé.

embarrassing *adj* embarrassant.

embarrassment *n* embarras *m*.

embassy *n* ambassade *f*.

embed *vt* enchâsser; intégrer.

embellish *vt* embellir, orner.

embellishment *n* ornement *m*.

ember *n* braise *f*.

embezzle *vt* détourner.

embezzlement *n* détournement de fonds *m*.

embitter *vt* rendre amer.

emblem *n* emblème *m*.

emblematic(al) *adj* emblématique, symbolique.

embodiment *n* (*law*) incorporation *f*; incarnation *f*.

embody *vt* (*law*) incorporer; incarner.

embrace *vt* étreindre; comprendre; * *n* étreinte *f*.

embroider *vt* broder.

embroidery *n* broderie *f*.

embroil *vt* impliquer.

embryo *n* embryon *m*.

emendation *n* correction *f*.

emerald *n* émeraude *f*.

emerge *vi* émerger; apparaître.

emergency *n* urgence *f*.

emergency cord *n* sonnette d'alarme *f*.

emergency exit *n* sortie de secours *f*.

emergency landing *n* atterrissage forcé *m*.

emergency meeting *n* réunion extraordinaire *f*.

emery *n* émeri *m*.

emigrant *n* émigré *m* -e *f*.

emigrate *vi* émigrer.

emigration *n* émigration *f*.

eminence *n* hauteur *f*; éminence, excellence *f*.

eminent *adj* élevé; éminent, distingué; ~**ly** *adv* éminemment.

emission *n* émission *f*.

emit *vt* émettre.

emoluments *npl* émoluments *mpl*.

emotion *n* émotion *f*.

emotional *adj* émotionnel; ému.

emotive *adj* émotif.

emperor *n* empereur *m*.

emphasis *n* emphase *f*.

emphasize *vt* souligner, accentuer.

emphatic *adj* emphatique; ~**ally** *adv* avec emphase.

empire *n* empire *m*.

employ *vt* employer.

employee *n* employé *m* -e *f*.

employer *n* employeur *m*.

employment *n* emploi, travail *m*.

emporium *n* grand magasin *m*.

empress *n* impératrice *f*.

emptiness *n* vide *m*; futilité *f*.

empty *adj* vide; vain; * *vt* vider.

empty-handed *adj* les mains vides.

emulate *vt* imiter.

emulsion *n* émulsion *f*.

enable *vt* permettre.

enact *vt* promulguer; représenter.

enamel *n* émail *m*; * *vt* émailler.

enamour *vt* s'éprendre de.

encamp *vi* camper.

encampment *n* campement *m*.

encase *vt* entourer.

enchant *vt* enchanter.

enchanting *adj* enchanteur.

enchantment *n* enchantement *m*.

encircle *vt* encercler.

enclose *vt* entourer; inclure, joindre.

enclosure *n* clôture *f*; enceinte *f*.

encompass *vt* comprendre.

encore *adv* encore.

encounter *n* rencontre *f*; combat *m*; * *vt* rencontrer.

encourage *vt* encourager.

encouragement *n* encouragement *m*.

encroach *vi* empiéter (sur).

encroachment *n* empiètement *m*.

encrusted *adj* incrusté.

encumber *vt* embarrasser.

encumbrance *n* embarras *m*.

encyclical *adj* encyclique.

encyclopedia *n* encyclopédie *f*.

end *n* fin *f*; extrémité *f*; bout *m*; dessein *m*; **to that ~** afin que; **to no ~** en vain; **on ~** debout; * *vt* terminer, conclure; * *vi* terminer.

endanger *vt* mettre en danger.

endear *vt* faire aimer.

endearing *adj* attachant.

endearment *n* expression de tendresse *f*.

endeavour *vi* s'efforcer, tenter; * *n* effort *m*.

endemic *adj* endémique.

ending *n* fin, conclusion *f*; dénouement *m*; terminaison *f*.

endive *n* (*bot*) endive *f*.

endless *adj* infini, perpétuel; **~ly** *adv* sans fin, perpétuellement.

endorse *vt* endosser; approuver.

endorsement *n* endos *m*; approbation *f*.

endow *vt* doter.

endowment *n* dotation *f*.

endurable *adj* supportable.

endurance *n* endurance *f*; patience *f*.

endure *vt* supporter; * *vi* durer.

endways, endwise *adv* debout.

enemy *n* ennemi *mf*.

energetic *adj* énergique, vigoureux.

energy *n* énergie, force *f*.

enervate *vt* débiliter.

enfeeble *vt* affaiblir.

enfold *vt* envelopper.

enforce *vt* mettre en vigueur.

enforced *adj* forcé.

enfranchise *vt* émanciper.

engage *vt* aborder; engager.

engaged *adj* fiancé; occupé.

engagement *n* engagement *m*; combat *m*; fiançailles *fpl*; **~ ring** *n* bague de fiançailles *f*.

engaging *adj* attrayant.

engender *vt* engendrer; produire.

engine *n* moteur *m*; locomotive *f*.

engine driver *n* conducteur *m*.

engineer *n* ingénieur *m*; mécanicien *m*.

engineering *n* ingénierie *f*.

engrave *vt* graver.

engraving *n* gravure *f*.

engrossed *adj* absorbé.

engulf *vt* submerger.

enhance *vt* améliorer; réhausser.

enigma *n* énigme *f*.

enjoy *vt* aimer; jouir de; **~ o.s.** s'amuser.

enjoyable *adj* agréable; amusant.

enjoyment *n* plaisir *m*; jouissance *f*.

enlarge *vt* agrandir; étendre; dilater.

enlargement *n* agrandissement *m*; extension *f*; dilatation *f*.

enlighten *vt* éclairer.

enlightened *adj* éclairé.

Enlightenment *n*: **the ~** le Siècle des lumières *m*.

enlist *vt* recruter.

enlistment *n* recrutement *m*.

enliven *vt* animer; égayer.

enmity *n* inimitié *f*; haine *f*.

enormity *n* énormité *f*; atrocité *f*.

enormous *adj* énorme; **~ly** *adv* énormément.

enough *adv* suffisamment; assez; * *n* assez *m*.

enounce *vt* déclarer.

enquire *vt* = **inquire**.

enrage *vt* rendre furieux.

enrapture *vt* enchanter, enthousiasmer.

enrich *vt* enrichir; orner.

enrichment *n* enrichissement *m*.

enrol *vt* enrôler; inscrire.

enrolment *n* inscription *f*.

en route *adv* en route.

ensign *n* (*mil*) drapeau *m*; porte-étendard *m*; (*mar*) pavillon *m*.

enslave *vt* asservir.

ensue *vi* s'ensuivre.

ensure *vt* assurer.

entail *vt* impliquer, entraîner.

entangle *vt* emmêler, embrouiller.

entanglement *n* emmêlement *m*.

enter *vt* entrer dans; inscrire; ~ **for** se présenter à; ~ **into** commencer; faire partie de.

enterprise *n* entreprise *f*.

enterprising *adj* entreprenant.

entertain *vt* divertir; recevoir; avoir.

entertainer *n* artiste *mf*.

entertaining *adj* divertissant, amusant.

entertainment *n* divertissement, passe-temps *m*.

enthralled *adj* captivé.

enthralling *adj* captivant.

enthrone *vt* introniser.

enthusiasm *n* enthousiasme *m*.

enthusiast *n* enthousiaste *mf*.

enthusiastic *adj* enthousiaste.

entice *vt* tenter; séduire.

entire *adj* entier, complet; parfait; ~**ly** *adv* entièrement.

entirety *n* intégralité *f*.

entitle *vt* intituler; conférer un droit à.

entitled *adj* intitulé; **to be ~ to** avoir le droit de.

entity *n* entité *f*.

entourage *n* entourage *m*.

entrails *npl* entrailles *fpl*.

entrance *n* entrée *f*; admission *f*.

entrance examination *n* examen d'entrée *m*.

entrance fee *n* droit d'inscription *m*.

entrance hall *n* vestibule *m*.

entrance ramp *n* bretelle d'accès *f*.

entrant *n* participant *m* -e *f*; candidat *m* -e *f*.

entrap *vt* piéger.

entreat *vt* implorer, supplier.

entreaty *n* supplication, prière *f*.

entrepreneur *n* entrepreneur *m*.

entrust *vt* confier.

entry *n* entrée *f*.

entry phone *n* interphone *m*.

entwine *vt* entrelacer.

enumerate *vt* énùmérer.

enunciate *vt* énoncer.

enunciation *n* énonciation *f*.

envelop *vt* envelopper.

envelope *n* enveloppe *f*.

enviable *adj* enviable.

envious *adj* envieux; ~**ly** *adv* avec envie.

environment *n* environnement *m*.

environmental *adj* relatif à l'environnement.

environs *npl* environs *mpl*.

envisage *vt* envisager.

envoy *n* envoyé *m* -e *f*.

envy *n* envie *f*; * *vt* envier.

ephemeral *adj* éphémère.

epic *adj* épique; * *n* récit épique *m*.

epidemic *adj* épidémique; * *n* épidémie *f*.

epilepsy *n* épilepsie *f*.

epileptic *adj* épileptique.

epilogue *n* épilogue *m*.

Epiphany *n* Epiphanie *f*.

episcopacy *n* épiscopat *m*.

episcopal *adj* épiscopal.

episcopalian *n* épiscopalien *m* -ne *f*.

episode *n* épisode *m*.

epistle *n* épître *f*.

epistolary *adj* épistolaire.

epithet *n* épithète *f*.

epitome *n* modèle *m*; résumé *m*.

epitomize *vt* incarner; résumer.

epoch *n* époque *f*.

equable *adj* uniforme; ~**bly** *adv* uniformément.

equal *adj* égal; semblable; * *n* égal *m* -e *f*; * *vt* égaler.

equality *n* égalité *f*.

equalize *vt* égaliser.

equalizer *n* point égalisateur *m*.

equally *adv* également.

equanimity *n* équanimité *f*.

equate *vt* comparer; assimiler.

equation *n* équation *f*.

equator *n* équateur *m*.

equatorial *adj* équatorial.

equestrian *adj* équestre.

equilateral *adj* équilatéral.

equilibrium *n* équilibre *m*.

equinox *n* équinoxe *m*.

equip *vt* équiper.

equipment *n* équipement *m*.

equitable *adj* équitable, impartial; **~bly** *adv* équitablement.

equity *n* équité, justice, impartialité *f*.

equivalent *adj* équivalent *m*.

equivocal *adj* équivoque, ambigu; **~ly** *adv* d'une manière équivoque.

equivocate *vt* équivoquer, user d'équivoques.

equivocation *n* faux-fuyants *mpl*.

era *n* ère *f*.

eradicate *vt* supprimer; extirper.

eradication *n* suppression *f*; extirpation *f*.

erase *vt* effacer; gommer.

eraser *n* gomme *f*.

erect *vt* ériger; élever; * *adj* droit, debout.

erection *n* érection *f*; structure *f*.

ermine *n* hermine *f*.

erode *vt* éroder; ronger.

erotic *adj* érotique.

err *vi* se tromper.

errand *n* message *m*; commission *f*.

errand boy *n* garçon de courses, messager *m*.

errata *npl* errata *m*.

erratic *adj* changeant; irrégulier.

erroneous *adj* erroné, faux; **~ly** *adv* erronément, faussement.

error *n* erreur *f*.

erudite *adj* érudit.

erudition *n* érudition *f*.

erupt *vi* entrer en éruption; faire éruption.

eruption *n* éruption *f*.

escalate *vi* monter en flèche; s'intensifier.

escalation *n* montée en flèche *f*; intensification *f*.

escalator *n* escalier roulant *m*.

escapade *n* fredaine *f*.

escape *vt* éviter; échapper à; * *vi* s'évader, s'échapper; * *n* évasion, fuite *f*; **to make one's ~** prendre la fuite.

escapism *n* évasion de la réalité *f*.

eschew *vt* fuir; éviter.

escort *n* escorte *f*; *vt* escorter.

esoteric *adj* ésotérique.

especial *adj* spécial; **~ly** *adv* spécialement.

espionage *n* espionnage *m*.

esplanade *n* (*mil*) esplanade *f*.

espouse *vt* épouser.

essay *n* essai *m*.

essence *n* essence *f*.

essential *n* essentiel *m*; * *adj* essentiel, principal; **~ly** *adv* essentiellement.

establish *vt* établir; fonder; démontrer.

establishment *n* établissement *m*; fondation *f*; institution *f*.

estate *n* état *m*; domaine *m*; biens *mpl*.

esteem *vt* estimer; apprécier; * *n* estime *f*; considération *f*.

esthetic *adj* (US) esthétique; **~s** *npl* esthétique *f*.

estimate *vt* estimer; évaluer.

estimation *n* estimation, évaluation *f*; opinion *f*.

estrange *vt* éloigner, séparer.

estranged *adj* séparé.

estrangement *n* séparation *f*; distance *f*.

estuary *n* estuaire *m*.

etch *vt* graver à l'eau forte.

etching *n* gravure à l'eau forte *f*.

eternal *adj* éternel, perpétuel; **~ly** *adv* éternellement.

eternity *n* éternité *f*.

ether *n* éther *m*.

ethical *adj* éthique, moral; **~ly** *adv* éthiquement.

ethics *npl* éthique *f*.

ethnic *adj* ethnique.

ethos *n* génie *m*, esprit *m*.

etiquette *n* étiquette *f*.

etymological *adj* étymologique.

etymologist *n* étymologiste *mf*.

etymology *n* étymologie *f*.

Eucharist *n* Eucharistie *f*.

eulogy *n* éloge *m*.

eunuch *n* eunuque *m*.

euphemism *n* euphémisme *m*.

evacuate *vt* évacuer.

evacuation *n* évacuation *f*.

evade *vt* éviter; échapper à.

evaluate *vt* évaluer.

evangelic(al) *adj* évangélique.

evangelist *n* évangéliste *m*.

evaporate *vt* faire évaporer; * *vi* s'évaporer; se volatiliser.

evaporated milk *n* lait condensé *m*.

evaporation *n* évaporation *f*.

evasion *n* dérobade *f*.

evasive *adj* évasif; **~ly** *adv* évasivement.

eve *n* veille *f*.

even *adj* égal; uni; pair; * *adv* même; encore; * *vt* égaliser; unir; * *vi*: ~ **out** s'égaliser.

even-handed *adj* impartial, équitable.

evening *n* soir *m*, soirée *f*.

evening class *n* cours du soir *m*.

evening dress *n* robe du soir *f*; tenue de soirée *f*.

evenly *adv* également; uniment.

evenness *n* égalité *f*; uniformité *f*; régularité *f*; impartialité *f*.

event *n* événement *m*; épreuve *f*.

eventful *adj* mouvementé.

eventual *adj* final; **~ly** *adv* finalement, en fin de comptes.

eventuality *n* éventualité *f*.

ever *adv* toujours; jamais; déjà; **for ~ and ~** pour toujours; ~ **since** depuis.

evergreen *adj* à feuilles persistantes; * *n* arbre à feuilles persistantes *m*.

everlasting *adj* éternel.

evermore *adv* toujours.

every *adj* chacun, chacune; ~ **where** partout; ~ **thing** tout; ~ **one**, ~ **body** tout le monde.

evict *vt* expulser.

eviction *n* expulsion *f*.

evidence *n* évidence *f*; témoignage *m*; preuve *f*; * *vt* témoigner de.

evident *adj* évident; manifeste; **~ly** *adv* manifestement, de toute évidence.

evil *adj* mauvais; malveillant; * *n* mal *m*.

evil-minded *adj* malintentionné.

evocative *adj* évocateur.

evoke *vt* évoquer.

evolution *n* évolution *f*.

evolve *vt* développer; * *vi* se développer, évoluer.

ewe *n* brebis *f*.

exacerbate *vt* exacerber.

exact *adj* exact; * *vt* exiger.

exacting *adj* exigeant.

exaction *n* exaction *f*; extorsion *f*.

exactly *adv* exactement.

exactness, exactitude *n* exactitude *f*.

exaggerate *vt* exagérer.

exaggeration *n* exagération *f*.

exalt *vt* exalter; élever.

exaltation *n* exaltation *f*; élévation *f*.

exalted *adj* exalté; élevé.

examination *n* examen *m*.

examine *vt* examiner.

examiner *n* examinateur *m* -trice *f*.

example *n* exemple *m*.

exasperate *vt* exaspérer, irriter.

exasperation *n* exaspération, irritation *f*.

excavate *vt* exhumer, creuser.

excavation *n* excavation *f*.

exceed *vt* excéder, dépasser.

exceedingly *adv* trop; extrêmement.

excel *vt* surpasser; *vi* exceller.

excellence *n* excellence *f*; supériorité *f*.

Excellency *n* Excellence (titre) *f*.

excellent *adj* excellent; **~ly** *adv* excellemment, admirablement.

except *vt* excepter, exclure; **~(ing)** *prep* excepté, à l'exception de.

exception *n* exception *f*.

exceptional *adj* exceptionnel.

excerpt *n* extrait *m*.

excess *n* excès *m*.

excessive *adj* excessif; **~ly** *adv* excessivement.

exchange *vt* échanger; permuter; * *n* échange *m*; change *m*.

exchange rate *n* taux de change *m*.

excise *n* taxe *f*.

excitability *n* excitabilité *f*.

excitable *adj* excitable.

excite *vt* exciter; animer; enthousiasmer; stimuler.

excited *adj* animé, enthousiaste; excité.

excitement *n* animation *f*, enthousiasme *m*.

exciting *adj* passionnant; stimulant.

exclaim *vi* s'exclamer.

exclamation *n* exclamation *f*.

exclamation mark *n* point d'exclamation *m*.

exclamatory *adj* exclamatif.

exclude *vt* exclure.

exclusion *n* exclusion *f*; exception *f*.

exclusive *adj* exclusif; **~ly** *adv* exclusivement.

excommunicate *vt* excommunier.

excommunication *n* excommunion *f*.

excrement *n* excrément *m*.

excruciating *adj* atroce, horrible.

exculpate *vt* disculper; justifier.
excursion *n* excursion *f*; digression *f*.
excusable *adj* excusable.
excuse *vt* excuser; pardonner; * *n* excuse *f*.
execute *vt* exécuter.
execution *n* exécution *f*.
executioner *n* bourreau *m*.
executive *adj* exécutif.
executor *n* exécuteur testamentaire *m*.
exemplary *adj* exemplaire.
exemplify *vt* exemplifier.
exempt *adj* exempt.
exemption *n* exemption *f*.
exercise *n* exercice *m*; * *vi* prendre de l'exercice; * *vt* exercer; montrer.
exercise book *n* cahier *m*.
exert *vt* employer, exercer; ~ **o.s.** s'efforcer.
exertion *n* effort *m*.
exhale *vt* exhaler; expirer.
exhaust *n* échappement *m*; * *vt* épuiser.
exhausted *adj* épuisé.
exhaustion *n* épuisement *m*.
exhaustive *adj* exhaustif, complet.
exhibit *vt* exhiber; montrer; * *n* (*law*) pièce à conviction *f*.
exhibition *n* exposition, présentation *f*.
exhilarating *adj* stimulant, grisant.
exhilaration *n* joie *f* intense.
exhort *vt* exhorter.
exhortation *n* exhortation *f*.
exhume *vt* exhumer, déterrer.
exile *n* exil *m*; * *vt* exiler, déporter.
exist *vi* exister.
existence *n* existence *f*.
existent *adj* existant.
existing *adj* actuel, présent.
exit *n* sortie *f*; * *vi* sortir.
exit ramp *n* bretelle d'accès *f*.
exodus *n* exode *m*.
exonerate *vt* disculper; décharger.
exoneration *n* disculpation *f*; décharge *f*.
exorbitant *adj* exorbitant, excessif.
exorcise *vt* exorciser.
exorcism *n* exorcisme *m*.
exotic *adj* exotique.
expand *vt* étendre; dilater.
expanse *n* étendue *f*.
expansion *n* expansion *f*.

expansive *adj* expansif.
expatriate *vt* expatrier.
expect *vt* attendre; espérer; penser.
expectance, expectancy *n* attente *f*; espoir *m*.
expectant *adj* d'attente.
expectant mother *n* femme enceinte *f*.
expectation *n* expectative *f*; attente *f*.
expediency *n* convenance *f*; opportunité *f*.
expedient *adj* opportun; * *n* expédient *m*; ~**ly** *adv* de manière opportune.
expedite *vt* accélérer; expédier.
expedition *n* expédition *f*.
expeditious *adj* expéditif; ~**ly** *adv* de manière expéditive.
expel *vt* expulser.
expend *vt* dépenser; utiliser.
expendable *adj* jetable; consommable.
expenditure *n* dépense *f*.
expense *n* dépense *f*; coût *m*.
expense account *n* frais *mpl* de représentation.
expensive *adj* cher; coûteux; ~**ly** *adv* de manière coûteuse.
experience *n* expérience *f*; pratique *f*; * *vt* ressentir, éprouver; connaître.
experienced *adj* expérimenté.
experiment *n* expérience *f*; * *vi* expérimenter.
experimental *adj* expérimental; ~**ly** *adv* expérimentalement.
expert *adj* expert.
expertise *n* compétences *fpl*.
expiration *n* expiration *f*.
expire *vi* expirer.
explain *vt* expliquer.
explanation *n* explication *f*.
explanatory *adj* explicatif.
expletive *adj* explétif.
explicable *adj* explicable.
explicit *adj* explicite; ~**ly** *adv* explicitement.
explode *vt* faire exploser; *vi* exploser.
exploit *vt* exploiter; * *n* exploit *m*.
exploitation *n* exploitation *f*.
exploration *n* exploration *f*.
exploratory *adj* exploratoire.
explore *vt* explorer, examiner; sonder.
explorer *n* explorateur *m* -trice *f*.
explosion *n* explosion *f*.

explosive *adj n* explosif *m*.
exponent *n* (*math*) exposant *m*.
export *vt* exporter.
export, exportation *n* exportation *f*.
exporter *n* exportateur *m* -trice *f*.
expose *vt* exposer; dévoiler.
exposed *adj* exposé.
exposition *n* exposition *f*; interprétation *f*.
expostulate *vi* faire des remonstrances.
exposure *n* exposition *f*; temps de pose *m*; cliché *m*.
exposure meter *n* photomètre *m*.
expound *vt* exposer; interpréter.
express *vt* exprimer; * *adj* exprès; * *n* exprès *m*; (*rail*) rapide *m*.
expression *n* expression *f*; locution *f*.
expressionless *adj* inexpressif.
expressive *adj* expressif; ~ly *adv* d'une manière expressive.
expressly *adv* expressément.
expressway *n* autoroute *f*.
expropriate *vt* exproprier.
expropriation *n* (*law*) expropriation *f*.
expulsion *n* expulsion *f*.
expurgate *vt* expurger.
exquisite *adj* exquis; ~ly *adv* exquisément.
extant *adj* existant.
extempore *adv* à l'improviste.
extemporize *vi* improviser.
extend *vt* étendre; élargir; * *vi* s'étendre.
extension *n* extension *f*.
extensive *adj* étendu; important; ~ly *adv* considérablement.
extent *n* extension *f*.
extenuate *vt* atténuer.
extenuating *adj* atténuant.
exterior *adj n* extérieur *m*.
exterminate *vt* exterminer; supprimer.
extermination *n* extermination *f*; suppression *f*.
external *adj* externe; ~ly *adv* extérieurement; ~s *npl* apparence *f*.
extinct *adj* disparu; éteint.
extinction *n* extinction *f*.
extinguish *vt* éteindre; supprimer.

extinguisher *n* extincteur *m*.
extirpate *vt* extirper.
extol *vt* louer, exalter.
extort *vt* extorquer; arracher.
extortion *n* extorsion *f*.
extortionate *adj* exorbitant.
extra *adv* particulièrement; *n* supplément *m*.
extract *vt* extraire; * *n* extrait *m*.
extraction *n* extraction *f*; origine *f*.
extracurricular *adj* périscolaire.
extradite *vt* extrader.
extradition *n* (*law*) extradition *f*.
extramarital *adj* extérieur au mariage.
extramural *adj* extra-muros.
extraneous *adj* superflu; sans rapport.
extraordinarily *adv* extraordinairement.
extraordinary *adj* extraordinaire.
extravagance *n* extravagance *f*; gaspillage *m*.
extravagant *adj* extravagant; exorbitant; gaspilleur; ~ly *adv* de manière extravagante; en gaspillant.
extreme *adj* extrême; suprême; ultime; * *n* extrême *m*; ~ly *adv* extrêmement.
extremist *adj n* extrémiste *mf*.
extremity *n* extrémité *f*.
extricate *vt* extirper, démêler.
extrinsic(al) *adj* extrinsèque.
extrovert *adj n* extraverti *m* -e *f*.
exuberance *n* exubérance *f*.
exuberant *adj* exubérant; ~ly *adv* avec exubérance.
exude *vi* exsuder.
exult *vi* exulter, triompher.
exultation *n* exultation *f*.
eye *n* œil *m*; * *vt* regarder, observer; lorgner.
eyeball *n* globe oculaire *m*.
eyebrow *n* sourcil *m*.
eyelash *n* cil *m*.
eyelid *n* paupière *f*.
eyesight *n* vue *f*.
eyesore *n* monstruosité *f*.
eyetooth *n* canine *f*.
eyewitness *n* témoin oculaire *m*.
eyrie *n* aire *f*, nid *m* d'aigle.

F

fable n fable f; légende f.

fabric n tissu m.

fabricate vt fabriquer; inventer.

fabrication n fabrication f; invention f.

fabulous adj fabuleux; **~ly** adv fabuleusement.

facade n façade f.

face n visage m, figure f; surface f; façade f; mine f; apparence f; * vt faire face à; affronter; **~ up to** faire face à.

face cream n crème pour le visage f.

face-lift n lifting m.

face powder n poudre de riz f.

facet n facette f.

facetious adj facétieux, plaisant, spirituel; **~ly** adv facétieusement.

face value n valeur nominale f.

facial adj facial.

facile adj facile; superficiel.

facilitate vt faciliter.

facility n facilité f; équipement m, infrastructure f.

facing n revers m; * prep en face de.

facsimile n fac-similé m.

fact n fait m; réalité f; **in ~** en fait.

faction n faction f; dissension f.

factor n facteur m.

factory n usine f.

factual adj factuel, basé sur les faits.

faculty n faculté f; le corps enseignant m.

fad n engouement m.

fade vi se faner; perdre son éclat.

fail vt échouer à; omettre; manquer à ses engagements envers; * vi échouer; faiblir; manquer.

failing n défaut m.

failure n échec m; panne f; raté m; faillite f; manquement m.

faint vi s'évanouir, défaillir; * n évanouissement m; * adj faible; **~ly** adv faiblement.

fainthearted adj timide, timoré, pusillanime.

faintness n faiblesse f; légèreté f.

fair adj beau; blond; clair; favorable; juste; équitable; considérable; passable; * adv loyalement; * n foire f.

fairly adv équitablement; absolument.

fairness n beauté f; justice f.

fair play n fair-play, franc-jeu m.

fairy n fée f.

fairy tale n conte de fées m.

faith n foi f; croyance f; fidélité f.

faithful adj fidèle, loyal; **~ly** adv fidèlement.

faithfulness n fidélité, loyauté f.

fake n falsification f; imposteur m; * adj faux; * vt feindre; falsifier.

falcon n faucon m.

falconry n fauconnerie f.

fall vi tomber; s'effondrer; diminuer, baisser; **~ asleep** s'endormir; **~ back** reculer; **~ back on** avoir recours à; **~ behind** être à la traîne; **~ down** tomber; **~ for** se faire avoir; tomber amoureux de; **~ in** s'effondrer; **~ short** échouer; **~ sick** tomber malade; **~ in love** tomber amoureux; **~ off** tomber; diminuer; **~ out** se produire; se quereller; * n chute f; automne m.

fallacious adj fallacieux, trompeur; **~ly** adv d'une manière fallacieuse.

fallacy n erreur f; sophisme m; tromperie f.

fallibility n faillibilité f.

fallible adj faillible.

fallout n retombées fpl.

fallout shelter n abri antiatomique m.

fallow adj en jachère; **~ deer** n daim m.

false adj faux; **~ly** adv faussement.

false alarm n fausse alerte f.

falsehood, falseness n mensonge m; fausseté f.

falsify vt falsifier.

falsity n fausseté f.

falter vi vaciller; faiblir.

faltering adj chancelant.

fame n réputation f; renommée, notoriété f.

famed adj célèbre.

familiar adj familier; domestique; **~ly** adv familièrement.

familiarity n familiarité f.

familiarize vt familiariser.

family n famille f.

family business *n* affaire de famille *f*.

family doctor *n* médecin de famille *m*.

famine *n* famine *f*; disette *f*.

famished *adj* affamé.

famous *adj* célèbre, fameux; **~ly** *adv* fameusement.

fan *n* éventail *m*; ventilateur *m*; jeune admirateur *m* -trice *f*; * *vt* éventer; attiser.

fanatic *adj n* fanatique *mf*.

fanaticism *n* fanatisme *m*.

fan belt *n* courroie de ventilateur *f*.

fanciful *adj* fantasque, capricieux; **~ly** *adv* capricieusement.

fancy *n* fantaisie, imagination *f*; caprice *m*; * *vt* avoir envie de; s'imaginer.

fancydress ball *n* bal masqué *m*.

fancy goods *npl* nouveautés *fpl*.

fanfare *n* (*mus*) fanfare *f*.

fang *n* croc *m*.

fantastic *adj* fantastique; excentrique; **~ally** *adv* fantastiquement.

fantasy *n* imagination *f*.

far *adv* loin; * *adj* lointain, éloigné; **~ and away** de très loin; **~ off** lointain.

faraway *adj* lointain.

farce *n* farce *f*.

farcical *adj* grotesque.

fare *n* prix (du voyage) *m*; tarif *m*; nourriture *f*; voyageur *m* -euse *f*; client *m* -e *f*.

farewell *n* adieu *m*; **~!** *excl* adieu!

farm *n* ferme *f*, exploitation agricole *f*; * *vt* cultiver.

farmer *n* fermier *m*; agriculteur *m*.

farmhand *n* ouvrier agricole *m*.

farmhouse *n* ferme *f*.

farming *n* agriculture *f*.

farmland *n* terres arables *fpl*.

farmyard *n* cour de ferme *f*.

far-reaching *adj* d'une grande portée, considérable.

fart *n* (*sl*) pet *m*; * *vi* péter.

farther *adv* plus loin; * *adj* plus éloigné.

farthest *adv* le plus lointain; le plus loin; au plus.

fascinate *vt* fasciner, captiver.

fascinating *adj* fascinant.

fascination *n* fascination *f*; charme *m*.

fascism *n* fascisme.

fashion *n* manière, façon *f*; forme *f*; coutume *f*; mode *f*; style *m*; **people of ~** personnes élégantes *fpl*; * *vt* façonner, confectionner.

fashionable *adj* à la mode; chic; **the ~ world** le beau monde; **~bly** *adv* à la mode.

fashion show *n* défilé de mode *m*.

fast *vi* jeûner; * *n* jeûne *m*; * *adj* rapide; ferme, stable; * *adv* rapidement; fermement; solidement.

fasten *vt* attacher; fixer; attribuer; * *vi* se fixer, s'attacher.

fastener, fastening *n* attache *f*; fermoir *m*.

fast food *n* restauration rapide *f*.

fastidious *adj* minutieux, méticuleux; **~ly** *adv* minutieusement.

fat *adj* gros, gras; * *n* graisse *f*.

fatal *adj* mortel; néfaste; **~ly** *adv* mortellement.

fatalism *n* fatalisme *m*.

fatalist *n* fataliste *mf*.

fatality *n* accident mortel *m*, fatalité *f*.

fate *n* destin, sort *m*.

fateful *adj* fatidique.

father *n* père *m*.

fatherhood *n* paternité *f*.

father-in-law *n* beau-père *m*.

fatherland *n* patrie *f*.

fatherly *adj* (*adv*) paternel(lement).

fathom *n* brasse (mesure) *f*; * *vt* sonder; pénétrer.

fatigue *n* fatigue *f*; * *vt* fatiguer, lasser.

fatten *vt vi* engraisser.

fatty *adj* gras, graisseux.

fatuous *adj* imbécile, stupide, niais.

faucet *n* (US) robinet *m*.

fault *n* défaut *m*, faute *f*; délit *m*; faille *f*.

faultfinder *n* chicaneur *m* -euse *f*.

faultless *adj* irréprochable.

faulty *adj* défectueux.

fauna *n* faune *f*.

faux pas *n* impair *m*.

favour *n* faveur *f*; approbation *f*; avantage *m*; * *vt* favoriser, préférer.

favourable *adj* favorable, propice; **~bly** *adv* favorablement.

favoured *adj* favorisé.

favourite *n* favori *m*; * *adj* favori.

favouritism *n* favoritisme *m*.

fawn n faon m; * vi flatter servilement.

fawningly adv d'une flatterie servile.

fax n télécopieur, fax m; télécopie f, fax m; * vt envoyer par fax, télécopier.

fear vt craindre; * n crainte f.

fearful adj effrayant; craintif, peureux; ~ly adv terriblement; craintivement.

fearless adj intrépide, courageux; ~ly adv courageusement.

fearlessness n intrépidité f.

feasibility n faisabilité f.

feasible adj faisable, réalisable.

feast n festin, banquet m; fête f; * vi banqueter.

feat n exploit m; prouesse f.

feather n plume f;.

feather bed n lit de plumes m.

feature n caractéristique f; trait m; * vi figurer.

feature film n long métrage m.

February n février m.

federal adj fédéral.

federalist n fédéraliste mf.

federate vt fédérer; * vi se fédérer.

federation n fédération f.

fed-up adj: **to be ~** en avoir marre.

fee n honoraires mpl; frais mpl.

feeble adj faible, frêle.

feebleness n faiblesse f.

feebly adv faiblement.

feed vt nourrir; alimenter; **~ on** se nourrir de; * vi manger; se nourrir; * n nourriture f; alimentation f.

feedback n réaction f, répercussion f.

feel vt sentir; toucher; croire; **~ around** tâtonner, fouiller; * n sensation f; toucher m.

feeler n antenne f; (fig) tentative f.

feeling n sensation f; sentiment m.

feelingly adv avec émotion.

feign vt inventer; feindre, simuler.

feline adj félin.

fellow n homme, type m; membre m.

fellow citizen n concitoyen m -enne f.

fellow countryman n compatriote m.

fellow feeling n sympathie f.

fellow men npl semblables mpl.

fellowship n camaraderie f; association f.

fellow student n copain (copine) de fac m(f).

fellow traveller n compagnon (compagne) de voyage m(f).

felon n criminel m -le f.

felony n crime m.

felt n feutre m.

felt-tip pen n feutre m.

female n femelle f; * adj de sexe féminin, femelle.

feminine adj féminin.

feminist n féministe mf.

fen n marais m.

fence n barrière f; clôture f; * vt clôturer; * vi faire de l'escrime.

fencing n escrime f.

fender n pare-chocs m invar.

fennel n (bot) fenouil m.

ferment n agitation f; * vi fermenter.

fern n (bot) fougère f.

ferocious adj féroce; ~ly adv férocement.

ferocity n férocité f.

ferret n furet m; * vt fureter; **~ out** découvrir, dénicher.

ferry n bac m; ferry m; * vt transporter.

fertile adj fertile, fécond.

fertility n fertilité, fécondité f.

fertilize vt fertiliser.

fertilizer n engrais m.

fervent adj fervent; ardent; ~ly adv avec ferveur.

fervid adj ardent, véhément.

fervour n ferveur, ardeur f.

fester vi suppurer; s'envenimer.

festival n fête f; festival m.

festive adj de fête.

festivity n fête f, réjouissances fpl.

fetch vt aller chercher.

fetching adj charmant, séduisant.

fête n fête f.

fetid adj fétide, nauséabond.

fetus n fœtus m.

feud n rivalité f, dissension f.

feudal adj féodal.

feudalism n féodalité f.

fever n fièvre f.

feverish adj fiévreux.

few adj peu; **a ~** quelques; **~ and far between** rares.

fewer adj moins (de); * adv moins.

fewest *adj* le moins (de).

fiancé *n* fiancé *m*.

fiancée *n* fiancée *f*.

fib *n* bobard *m*; * *vi* raconter des bobards.

fibre *n* fibre *f*.

fibreglass *n* fibre de verre *f*.

fickle *adj* volage, inconstant.

fiction *n* fiction *f*; invention *f*.

fictional *adj* fictif.

fictitious *adj* fictif, imaginaire; feint; **~ly** *adv* fictivement.

fiddle *n* violon *m*; combine *f*; * *vi* jouer du violon.

fiddler *n* violoneux *m*.

fidelity *n* fidélité, loyauté *f*.

fidget *vi* s'agiter, s'impatienter.

fidgety *adj* agité, remuant.

field *n* champ *m*; étendue *f*; domaine *m*.

field day *n* (*mil*) jour de grandes manœuvres *m*.

fieldmouse *n* mulot *m*.

fieldwork *n* recherches sur le terrain *fpl*.

fiend *n* démon *m*; mordu *m*.

fiendish *adj* diabolique.

fierce *adj* féroce, violent; acharné, furieux; **~ly** *adv* férocement.

fierceness *n* férocité, fureur *f*.

fiery *adj* ardent; fougueux.

fifteen *adj n* quinze *m*.

fifteenth *adj n* quinzième *mf*.

fifth *adj n* cinquième *mf*; **~ly** *adv* cinquièmement.

fiftieth *adj n* cinquantième *mf*.

fifty *adj n* cinquante *m*.

fig *n* figue *f*.

fight *vt vi* se battre (contre); combattre; lutter; * *n* bataille *f*; combat *m*; lutte *f*.

fighter *n* combattant *m*; lutteur *m*; chasseur *m*.

fighting *n* combat *m*.

fig-leaf *n* feuille de figuier *f*.

fig tree *n* figuier *m*.

figurative *adj* figuratif; **~ly** *adv* figurativement.

figure *n* figure *f*; forme, silhouette *f*; image *f*; chiffre *m*; * *vi* figurer; avoir du sens; **~ out** comprendre.

figurehead *n* figure de proue *f*.

filament *n* filament *m*; fibre *f*.

filch *vt* chiper.

filcher *n* voleur *m* -euse *f*.

file *n* file *f*; liste *f*; (*mil*) colonne, rangée *f*; lime *f*; dossier *m*; fichier *m*; * *vt* enregistrer; limer; classer; déposer; * *vi* **~ in/out** entrer/sortir en file; **~ past** défiler devant.

filing cabinet *n* classeur (meuble) *m*.

fill *vt* remplir; **~ in** remplir; **~ up** remplir (jusqu'au bord).

fillet *n* filet *m*.

fillet steak *n* filet de bœuf *m*.

filling station *n* station-service *f*.

fillip *n* (*fig*) coup de fouet *m*.

filly *n* pouliche *f*.

film *n* pellicule *f*; film *f*; cellophane *m*; * *vt* filmer; * *vi* s'embuer.

film star *n* vedette de cinéma *f*.

filmstrip *n* film *m*.

filter *n* filtre *m*; * *vt* filtrer.

filter-tipped *adj* à bout filtre.

filth(iness) *n* immondice, ordure *f*; saleté, crasse *f*.

filthy *adj* crasseux, dégoûtant.

fin *n* nageoire *f*.

final *adj* dernier; définitif; **~ly** *adv* finalement.

finale *n* finale *m*.

finalist *n* finaliste *mf*.

finalize *vt* parachever, rendre définitif.

finance *n* finance *f*.

financial *adj* financier.

financier *n* financier *m*.

find *vt* trouver, découvrir; **~ out** découvrir; démasquer; **~ o.s.** se retrouver; * *n* trouvaille *f*.

findings *npl* résultats *mpl*, conclusions *fpl*; verdict *m*.

fine *adj* fin; pur; aigu; raffiné; beau, *f* belle; délicat; subtil; élégant; * *n* amende *f*; * *vt* infliger une amende à.

fine arts *npl* beaux arts *mpl*.

finely *adv* magnifiquement.

finery *n* parure *f*.

finesse *n* finesse, subtilité *f*.

finger *n* doigt *m*; * *vt* toucher, manier.

fingernail *n* ongle *m*.

fingerprint *n* empreinte digitale *f*.

fingertip *n* bout du doigt *m*.

finicky *adj* pointilleux, difficile.

finish *vt* finir, terminer, achever; ~ **off** finir; ~ **up** terminer; * *vi*: ~ **up** se retrouver.

finishing line *n* ligne d'arrivée *f*.

finishing school *n* école privée (pour jeunes filles) *f*.

finite *adj* fini.

fir *n* sapin *m*

fire *n* feu *m*; incendie *m*; * *vt* mettre le feu à; incendier; tirer; * *vi* s'enflammer, faire feu.

fire alarm *n* alarme d'incendie *f*.

firearm *n* arme à feu *f*.

fireball *n* boule de feu *f*.

fire department *n* pompiers *mpl*.

fire engine *n* voiture de pompiers *f*.

fire escape *n* escalier de secours *m*.

fire extinguisher *n* extincteur *m*.

firefly *n* luciole *f*.

fireman *n* pompier *m*.

fireplace *n* cheminée *f*, foyer *m*.

fireproof *adj* ignifugé.

fireside *n* coin du feu *m*.

fire station *n* caserne de pompiers *f*.

firewater *n* eau de vie *f*.

firewood *n* bois de chauffage *m*.

fireworks *npl* feu d'artifice *m*.

firing *n* fusillade *f*.

firing squad *n* peloton d'exécution *m*.

firm *adj* ferme, solide; constant; * *n* (*com*) compagnie *f*; ~**ly** *adv* fermement.

firmament *n* firmament *m*.

firmness *n* fermeté *f*; résolution *f*.

first *adj* premier; * *adv* premièrement; at ~ d'abord; ~**ly** *adv* en premier lieu.

first aid *n* premiers secours *mpl*.

first-aid kit *n* trousse de premiers secours *f*.

first-class *adj* de première classe, de première catégorie.

first-hand *adj* de première main.

First Lady *n* (US) première dame, femme du président d'un pays *f*.

first name *n* prénom *m*.

first-rate *adj* de première qualité.

fiscal *adj* fiscal.

fish *n* poisson *m*; * *vi* pêcher.

fishbone *n* arête *f*.

fisherman *n* pêcheur *m*.

fish farm *n* entreprise de pisciculture *f*.

fishing *n* pêche *f*.

fishing line *n* ligne de pêche *f*.

fishing rod *n* canne à pêche *f*.

fishing tackle *n* attirail de pêche *m*.

fish market *n* marché au poisson *m*.

fishseller *n* poissonnier *m* -ière *f*.

fishstore *n* poissonnerie *f*.

fishy *adj* (*fig*) suspect.

fissure *n* fissure, crevasse *f*.

fist *n* poing *m*.

fit *n* accès *m*, attaque *f*; crise *f*; * *adj* en forme; capable; adapté à, qui convient; * *vt* aller à; ajuster, adapter; ~ **out** équiper; * *vi* (bien) aller; ~ **in** s'accorder avec; être en harmonie avec.

fitment *n* meuble encastré *m*.

fitness *n* forme physique *f*; aptitude *f*.

fitted carpet *n* moquette *f*.

fitted kitchen *n* cuisine encastrée *f*.

fitter *n* monteur *m*.

fitting *adj* qui convient, approprié, juste; * *n* accessoire *m*; ~**s** *pl* installations *fpl*.

five *adj n* cinq *m*.

five spot *n* (*sl*) (US) billet *m* de cinq dollars.

fix *vt* fixer, établir; ~ **up** arranger.

fixation *n* obsession *f*.

fixed *adj* fixe.

fixings *npl* garniture *f*; accessoires *mpl*.

fixture *n* (sport) rencontre *f*.

fizz *vi* pétiller.

fizzy *adj* gazeux.

flabbergasted *adj* abasourdi.

flabby *adj* mou, *f* molle, flasque.

flaccid *adj* flasque, mou, *f* molle.

flag *n* drapeau *m*; (*bot*) iris *m*; * *vi* s'affaiblir.

flagpole *n* mât *m* de drapeau.

flagrant *adj* flagrant.

flagship *n* vaisseau amiral *m*.

flagstop *n* (US) arrêt *m* facultatif.

flair *n* flair *m*; talent *m*.

flak *n* tir antiaérien *m*; critiques *fpl*.

flake *n* flocon *m*; paillette *f*; * *vi* s'effriter, s'écailler.

flaky *adj* floconneux; friable.

flamboyant *adj* flamboyant; ostentatoire.

flame *n* flamme *f*; ardeur *f*.

flamingo *n* flamant *m*.

flammable *adj* inflammable.

flank *n* flanc *m*; (*also mil*); * *vt* flanquer.

flannel *n* flanelle *f*.

flap *n* battement *m*; rabat *m*; * *vt vi* battre.

flare *vi* luire, briller; ~ **up** s'embraser; se mettre en colère; éclater; * *n* flamme *f*.

flash *n* éclat *m*; éclair *m*; * *vt* faire briller; allumer.

flashbulb *n* ampoule de flash *f*.

flash cube *n* cube de flash *m*.

flashlight *n* lampe *f* de poche.

flashy *adj* tape-à-l'œil, voyant.

flask *n* flasque *f*; flacon *m*.

flat *adj* plat; uniforme; insipide; * *n* plaine *f*; plat *m*; (*mus*) bémol *m*; **~ly** *adv* horizontalement; platement; également; catégoriquement.

flatness *n* égalité *f*; monotonie *f*.

flatten *vt* aplanir; aplatir.

flatter *vt* flatter.

flattering *adj* flatteur.

flattery *n* flatterie *f*.

flatulence *n* (*med*) flatulence *f*.

flaunt *vt* étaler, afficher.

flavour *n* saveur *m*; * *vt* parfumer; assaisonner.

flavoured *adj* savoureux; parfumé.

flavourless *adj* insipide.

flaw *n* défaut *m*; imperfection *f*.

flawless *adj* parfait.

flax *n* lin *m*.

flea *n* puce *f*.

flea bite *n* piqûre de puce *f*.

fleck *n* petite tache *f*; particule *f*.

flee *vt* fuir de; * *vi* s'enfuir; fuir.

fleece *n* toison *f*; * *vt* (*sl*) tondre.

fleet *n* flotte *f*; (autos) parc *m*.

fleeting *adj* fugace, fugitif.

flesh *n* chair *f*.

flesh wound *n* blessure superficielle *f*.

fleshy *adj* charnu.

flex *n* cordon *m*; * *vt* fléchir.

flexibility *n* flexibilité *f*.

flexible *adj* flexible, souple.

flick *n* petit coup *m*; * *vt* donner un petit coup à.

flicker *vt* vaciller; trembloter.

flier *n* aviateur *m* -trice *f*.

flight *n* vol *m*; fuite *f*; volée *f*; (*fig*) envolée *f*.

flight attendant *n* steward *m*, hôtesse de l'air *f*.

flight deck *n* cabine de pilotage *f*.

flimsy *adj* léger; fragile.

flinch *vi* sourciller.

fling *vt* lancer, jeter.

flint *n* silex *m*.

flip *vt* lancer.

flippant *adj* désinvolte, cavalier.

flipper *n* nageoire *f*.

flirt *vi* flirter; * *n* charmeur *m* -euse *f*.

flirtation *n* flirt *f*.

flit *vi* voler, voleter.

float *vt* faire flotter; lancer; * *vi* flotter; * *n* flotteur *m*; char (de carnaval) *m*; provision *f*.

flock *n* troupeau *m*; volée *f*; foule *f*; * *vi* affluer.

flog *vt* fustiger.

flogging *n* fustigation, flagellation *f*.

flood *n* inondation *f*; marée haute *f*; déluge *m*; * *vt* inonder.

flooding *n* inondation *f*.

floodlight *n* projecteur *m*.

floor *n* sol *m*; plancher *m*; étage *m*; * *vt* parqueter; déconcerter.

floorboard *n* planche *f*.

floor lamp *n* lampadaire *m*.

floor show *n* spectacle de cabaret *m*.

flop *n* four, fiasco *m*.

floppy *adj* lâche; * *n* disquette *f*.

flora *n* flore *f*.

floral *adj* floral.

florescence *n* floraison *f*.

florid *adj* fleuri.

florist *n* fleuriste *mf*.

florist's (shop) *n* boutique de fleuriste *f*.

flotilla *n* (*mar*) flotille *f*.

flounder *n* flet *m*; * *vi* patauger.

flour *n* farine *f*.

flourish *vi* fleurir; prospérer; * *n* fioriture *f*; (*mus*) fioriture *f*.

flourishing *adj* florissant.

flout *vt* mépriser, se moquer de.

flow *vi* couler; circuler; monter (marée); ondoyer; * *n* flux *m*; écoulement *m*; flot *m*.

flow chart *n* organigramme *m*.

flower *n* fleur *f*; * *vi* fleurir.

flowerbed *n* parterre de fleurs *m*.

flowerpot *n* pot de fleurs *m*.

flowery *adj* fleuri.

flower show *n* exposition de fleurs *f*.

fluctuate *vi* fluctuer.

fluctuation *n* fluctuation *f*.

fluency *n* aisance *f*.

fluent *adj* coulant; facile; ~ly *adv* couramment.

fluff *n* peluche *f*; ~y *adj* duveteux.

fluid *adj n* fluide *m*.

fluidity *n* fluidité *f*.

fluke *n* (*sl*) veine *f*.

fluoride *n* fluorure *m*.

flurry *n* rafale *f*; agitation *f*.

flush *vt*: **to ~ out** nettoyer à grande eau; * *vi* rougir; * *n* rougeur *f*; éclat *m*.

flushed *adj* rouge.

fluster *vt* énerver.

flustered *adj* énervé.

flute *n* flûte *f*.

flutter *vi* voleter; s'agiter; * *n* agitation *f*; émoi *m*.

flux *n* flux *m*.

fly *vt* piloter; transporter par avion; * *vi* voler; fuir; **~ away/off** s'envoler; * *n* mouche *f*; braguette *f*.

flying *n* aviation *f*.

flying saucer *n* soucoupe volante *f*.

flypast *n* défilé aérien *m*.

flysheet *n* feuille volante *f*.

foal *n* poulain *m*.

foam *n* écume *f*; * *vi* écumer.

foam rubber *n* caoutchouc mousse *m*.

foamy *adj* écumeux.

focus *n* foyer *m*; centre *m*.

fodder *n* fourrage *m*.

foe *n* ennemi *m* -e *f*, adversaire *mf*.

fog *n* brouillard *m*.

foggy *adj* brumeux.

fog light *n* feu de brouillard *m*.

foible *n* point faible *m*.

foil *vt* déjouer; * *n* papier d'aluminium *m*; fleuret *m*.

fold *n* pli *m*; parc à moutons *m*; * *vt* plier; **~ up** faire faillite; * *vi*: **~ up** plier, replier.

folder *n* chemise *f*; dépliant *m*.

folding *adj* pliant.

folding chair *n* chaise pliante *f*.

foliage *n* feuillage *m*.

folio *n* folio *m*.

folk *n* gens *mpl*.

folklore *n* folklore *m*.

folk song *n* chant folklorique *m*.

follow *vt* suivre; **~ up** suivre; exploiter; * *vi* suivre, s'ensuivre, résulter.

follower *n* serviteur *m*; disciple *mf*, partisan *m* -e *f*; adhérent *m* -e *f*; admirateur *m* -trice *f*.

following *adj* suivant; * *n* partisans *mpl*.

folly *n* folie, extravagance *f*.

foment *vt* fomenter.

fond *adj* affectueux; **to be ~ of** aimer; ~ly *adv* affectueusement.

fondle *vt* caresser.

fondness *n* prédilection *f*; affection *f*.

font *n* fonts baptismaux *mpl*.

food *n* nourriture *f*.

food mixer *n* mixer *m*.

food poisoning *n* intoxication alimentaire *f*.

food processor *n* robot *m* ménager.

foodstuffs *npl* denrées alimentaires *fpl*.

fool *n* imbécile *mf*, idiot *m* -e *f*; * *vt* duper.

foolhardy *adj* téméraire.

foolish *adj* idiot, insensé; ~ly *adv* bêtement.

foolproof *adj* infaillible.

foolscap *n* papier ministre *m*.

foot *n* pied *m*; patte *f*; **on** *or* **by ~** à pied.

footage *n* métrage *m*.

football *n* football *m*; ballon de football *m*.

footballer *n* footballeur *m* -euse *f*.

footbrake *n* frein à pied *m*.

footbridge *n* passerelle *f*.

foothills *npl* contreforts *mpl*.

foothold *n* prise (pour le pied) *f*.

footing *n* prise (pour le pied) *f*; statut *m*; situation *f*; plan *m*.

footlights *npl* feux de la rampe *mpl*.

footman *n* valet de pied *m*; soldat d'infanterie *m*.

footnote *n* note (de bas de page) *f*.

footpath *n* sentier *m*.

footprint *n* empreinte (de pas) *f*.

footsore *adj* aux pieds endoloris.

footstep *n* pas *m*.

footwear *n* chaussures *fpl*.

for *prep* pour; en raison de; pendant; * *conj*

car; **as ~ me** quant à moi; **what ~?** pourquoi?; pourquoi faire?

forage *n* fourrage *m*; * *vt* fourrager; fouiller.

foray *n* incursion *f*.

forbid *vt* interdire, défendre; empêcher; **God ~!** pourvu que non!

forbidding *adj* menaçant; sévère.

force *n* force *f*; puissance, vigueur *f*; violence *f*; **~s** *pl* forces armées *fpl*; * *vt* forcer, obliger, contraindre; imposer.

forced *adj* forcé.

forced march *n* (*mil*) marche forcée *f*.

forceful *adj* énergique.

forceps *n* forceps *m*.

forcible *adj* énergique, vigoureux, puissant; **~bly** *adv* énergiquement, avec véhémence.

ford *n* gué *m*; * *vt* passer à gué.

fore *n*: **to the ~** en évidence.

forearm *n* avant-bras *m*.

foreboding *n* pressentiment *m*.

forecast *vt* prévoir; * *n* prévision *f*.

forecourt *n* avant-cour *f*.

forefather *n* aïeul, ancêtre *m*.

forefinger *n* index *m*.

forefront *n*: **in the ~ of** au premier plan de.

forego *vt* renoncer à, s'abstenir de.

foregone *adj* passé; anticipé.

foreground *n* premier plan *m*.

forehead *n* front *m*.

foreign *adj* étranger.

foreigner *n* étranger *m* -ère *f*.

foreign exchange *n* devises *fpl*.

foreleg *n* patte de devant *f*.

foreman *n* contremaître *m*; (*law*) premier juré *m*.

foremost *adj* principal.

forenoon *n* matinée *f*.

forensic *adj* médico-légal.

forerunner *n* précurseur *m*; signe avant-coureur *m*.

foresee *vt* prévoir.

foreshadow *vt* présager.

foresight *n* prévoyance *f*; prescience *f*.

forest *n* forêt *f*.

forestall *vt* anticiper; prévenir.

forester *n* garde forestier *m*.

forestry *n* sylviculture *f*.

foretaste *n* avant-goût *m*.

foretell *vt* prédire.

forethought *n* prévoyance *f*; préméditation *f*.

forever *adv* toujours; un temps infini.

forewarn *vt* avertir, prévenir.

foreword *n* préface *f*.

forfeit *n* amende *f*; confiscation *f*; * *vt* perdre.

forge *n* forge *f*; usine métallurgique *f*; * *vt* forger; contrefaire; * *vi*: **~ ahead** aller de l'avant.

forger *n* faussaire *mf*.

forgery *n* contrefaçon *f*.

forget *vt vi* oublier.

forgetful *adj* étourdi; négligent.

forgetfulness *n* étourderie *f*; négligence *f*.

forget-me-not *n* (*bot*) myosotis *m*.

forgive *vt* pardonner.

forgiveness *n* pardon *m*; indulgence *f*.

fork *n* fourchette *f*; fourche *f*; * *vi* bifurquer; **~ out** (*sl*) casquer.

forked *adj* fourchu.

fork-lift truck *n* chariot élévateur *m*.

forlorn *adj* malheureux, abandonné.

form *n* forme *f*; formule *f*; formulaire *m*; formalité *f*; moule *m*; * *vt* former.

formal *adj* formel; méthodique; cérémonieux; **~ly** *adv* formellement.

formality *n* formalité *f*; cérémonie *f*.

format *n* format *m*; * *vt* formater.

formation *n* formation *f*.

formative *adj* formateur *m* -trice *f*.

former *adj* précédent, ancien; **~ly** *adv* autrefois, jadis.

formidable *adj* effrayant, terrible.

formula *n* formule *f*.

formulate *vt* formuler.

forsake *vt* abandonner, renoncer à.

fort *n* fort *m*.

forte *n* fort *m*.

forthcoming *adj* prochain; sociable.

forthright *adj* franc.

forthwith *adv* immédiatement, tout de suite.

fortieth *adj n* quarantième *mf*.

fortification *n* fortification *f*.

fortify *vt* fortifier, renforcer.

fortitude *n* stoïcisme *m*; courage *m*.

fortnight *n* quinze jours *mpl*; deux semaines *fpl*; * *adj* **~ly** bimensuel; * *adv* **~ly** tous les quinze jours.

fortress n (*mil*) forteresse f.

fortuitous adj fortuit; imprévu; ~**ly** adv fortuitement.

fortunate adj chanceux; ~**ly** adv heureusement.

fortune n chance f, sort m; fortune f.

fortune-teller n diseuse de bonne aventure f.

forty adj n quarante m.

forum n forum m, tribune f.

forward adj avancé; précoce; présomptueux; ~**(s)** adv en avant, vers l'avant; * vt transmettre; promouvoir; expédier.

forwardness n précocité f; effronterie f.

fossil adj fossilisé; * n fossile m.

foster vt encourager.

foster child n enfant adoptif m.

foster father n père adoptif m.

foster mother n mère adoptive f.

foul adj infect, ignoble; vil, déloyal; ~ **copy** n copie illisible f; ~**ly** adv salement; ignoblement; * vt polluer.

foul play n jeu déloyal m; meurtre m.

found vt fonder, créer; établir, édifier; fondre.

foundation n foundation f; fondement m.

founder n fondateur m -trice f; fondeur m; * vi (*mar*) couler.

foundling n enfant trouvé(e) mf.

foundry n fonderie f.

fount, fountain n fontaine f.

fountainhead n source, origine f.

four adj n quatre m.

fourfold adj quadruple.

four-poster (bed) n lit à baldaquin m.

foursome n groupe de quatre personnes m.

fourteen adj n quatorze m.

fourteenth adj n quatorzième mf.

fourth adj n quatrième mf; * n quart m; ~**ly** adv quatrièmement.

fowl n volaille f.

fox n renard f; (*fig*) rusé m.

foyer n vestibule m.

fracas n rixe f.

fraction n fraction f.

fracture n fracture f; * vt fracturer.

fragile adj fragile; frêle.

fragility n fragilité f; faiblesse, délicatesse f.

fragment n fragment m.

fragmentary adj fragmentaire.

fragrance n parfum m.

fragrant adj parfumé, odorant; ~**ly** adv en exhalant un parfum.

frail adj frêle, fragile.

frailty n fragilité f; faiblesse f.

frame n charpente f; châssis m, armature f; cadre m; structure f; monture f; * vt encadrer; concevoir; construire; former.

frame of mind n état d'esprit m.

framework n charpente f; structure f, cadre m.

franchise n droit de vote m; franchise f.

frank adj franc, direct.

frankly adv franchement.

frankness n franchise f.

frantic adj frénétique, effréné.

fraternal adj ~**ly** adv fraternel(lement).

fraternity n fraternité f.

fraternize vi fraterniser.

fratricide n fratricide mf.

fraud n fraude, tromperie f.

fraudulence n caractère frauduleux m.

fraudulent adj frauduleux; ~**ly** adv frauduleusement.

fraught adj accablé, tendu.

fray n rixe, bagarre, querelle f.

freak n caprice m; phénomène m.

freckle n tache de rousseur f.

freckled adj couvert de taches de rousseur.

free adj libre; autonome; gratuit; dégagé; * vt affranchir; libérer; débarrasser.

freedom n liberté f.

free-for-all n mêlée générale f.

free gift n prime f.

freehold n propriété libre f.

free kick n coup franc m.

freelance adj indépendant; * adv en indépendant.

freely adv librement; franchement; libéralement.

freemason n franc-maçon m.

freemasonry n franc-maçonnerie f.

freepost n port payé m.

free-range adj de plein air.

freethinker n libre-penseur m -euse f.

freethinking n libre pensée f.

free trade n libre échange m.

freeway n (US) autoroute f.

freewheel *vi* rouler en roue libre.

free will *n* libre arbitre *m*.

freeze *vi* geler; * *vt* congeler; geler.

freeze-dried *adj* lyophilisé.

freezer *n* congélateur *m*.

freezing *adj* gelé.

freezing point *n* point de congélation *m*.

freight *n* cargaison *f*; fret *m*.

freighter *n* affréteur *m*.

freight train *n* train de marchandises *m*.

French bean *n* haricot vert *m*.

French fries *npl* frites *fpl*.

French window *n* porte-fenêtre *f*.

frenzied *adj* fou, frénétique.

frenzy *n* frénésie *f*; folie *f*.

frequency *n* fréquence *f*.

frequent *adj* fréquent; ~ly *adv* fréquemment; * *vt* fréquenter.

fresco *n* fresque *f*.

fresh *adj* frais; nouveau, récent; ~ **water** *n* eau douce *f*.

freshen *vt* rafraîchir; * *vi* se rafraîchir.

freshly *adv* nouvellement; récemment.

freshman *n* nouveau *m*, nouvelle *f*.

freshness *n* fraîcheur *f*.

freshwater *adj* d'eau douce.

fret *vi* s'agiter, se tracasser.

friar *n* moine *m*.

friction *n* friction *f*.

Friday *n* vendredi *m*; **Good ~** Vendredi Saint *m*.

friend *n* ami *m* -e *f*.

friendless *adj* sans amis.

friendliness *n* amitié, bienveillance *f*.

friendly *adj* amical.

friendship *n* amitié *f*.

frieze *n* frise *f*.

frigate *n* (*mar*) frégate *f*.

fright *n* peur, frayeur *f*.

frighten *vt* effrayer.

frightened *adj* effrayé, apeuré.

frightening *adj* effrayant.

frightful *adj* épouvantable, effroyable; ~ly *adv* affreusement, effroyablement.

frigid *adj* froid, glacé; frigide; ~ly *adv* froidement.

fringe *n* frange *f*.

fringe benefits *npl* avantages *mpl* en nature.

frisk *vt* fouiller.

frisky *adj* vif, fringant.

fritter *vt*: **to ~ away** gaspiller.

frivolity *n* frivolité *f*.

frivolous *adj* frivole, léger.

frizz *vt* friser.

frizzle *vt vi* grésiller.

frizzy *adj* frisé.

fro *adv*: **to go to and ~** aller et venir.

frock *n* robe *f*.

frog *n* grenouille *f*.

frolic *vi* folâtrer, gambader.

frolicsome *adj* folâtre, gai.

from *prep* de; depuis; à partir de.

front *n* avant, devant *m*; façade *f*; front *m*; * *adj* de devant; premier.

frontal *adj* de front.

front door *n* porte d'entrée *f*.

frontier *n* frontière *f*.

front page *n* première page *f*.

front-wheel drive *n* (*auto*) traction avant *f*.

frost *n* gel *m*; gelée *f*; * *vt* geler.

frostbite *n* engelure *f*.

frostbitten *adj* gelé.

frosted *adj* gelé, givré.

frosty *adj* glacial; givré.

froth *n* écume *f*; * *vi* écumer.

frothy *adj* mousseux, écumeux.

frown *vt* froncer les sourcils; * *n* froncement de sourcils *m*.

frozen *adj* gelé.

frugal *adj* frugal; économique; simple; ~ly *adv* frugalement.

fruit *n* fruit *m*.

fruiterer *n* fruitier *m* -ière *f*.

fruiterer's (shop) *n* fruiterie *f*.

fruitful *adj* fécond, fertile; fructueux, utile; ~ly *adv* fructueusement.

fruitfulness *n* fertilité *f*; caractère fructueux *m*.

fruition *n* réalisation *f*.

fruit juice *n* jus de fruit *m*.

fruitless *adj* stérile; infécond; ~ly *adv* vainement, inutilement.

fruit salad *n* salade de fruits *f*.

fruit tree *n* arbre fruitier *m*.

frustrate *vt* contrecarrer; frustrer; énerver.

frustrated *adj* frustré.

frustration *n* frustration *f*.

fry *vt* frire.
frying pan *n* poêle *f*.
fuchsia *n* (*bot*) fuchsia *m*.
fudge *n* caramel *m* mou.
fuel *n* combustible, carburant *m*.
fuel tank *n* réservoir à carburant *m*.
fugitive *adj n* fugitif *m* -ive *f*.
fugue *n* (*mus*) fugue *f*.
fulcrum *n* pivot *m*.
fulfil *vt* accomplir; réaliser.
fulfilment *n* accomplissement *m*.
full *adj* plein, rempli; complet; * *adv* pleinement, entièrement.
full-blown *adj* complet.
full-length *adj* en pied; de long métrage.
full moon *n* pleine lune *f*.
fullness *n* plénitude *f*; abondance *f*.
full-scale *adj* grandeur nature; total, complet.
full-time *adj* à plein temps.
fully *adv* pleinement, entièrement.
fully fledged *adj* diplômé, qualifié.
fulsome *adj* exagéré.
fumble *vi* manier gauchement; farfouiller.
fume *vi* exhaler des vapeurs; rager, fumer;
* *~s* *npl* exhalaisons *fpl*.
fumigate *vt* fumiger.
fun *n* amusement *m*; plaisir *m*; **to have ~**
(bien) s'amuser.
function *n* fonction *f*.
functional *adj* fonctionnel.
fund *n* fonds *m*; * *vt* financer.
fundamental *adj* fondamental; *~ly* *adv* fondamentalement.
funeral *n* enterrement *m*.
funeral service *n* service *m* funèbre.

funereal *adj* funèbre, lugubre.
fungus *n* champignon *m*; moisissure *f*.
funnel *n* entonnoir *m*; cheminée *f*.
funny *adj* amusant; curieux.
fur *n* fourrure *f*.
fur coat *n* manteau de fourrure *m*.
furious *adj* furieux; déchaîné; *~ly* *adv* furieusement.
furlong *n* mesure de longueur (220 yards =
201 mètres), furlong *m*.
furnace *n* fourneau *m*; chaudière *f*.
furnish *vt* meubler; fournir; pourvoir.
furnishings *npl* ameublement *m*.
furniture *n* meubles *mpl*.
furrow *n* sillon *m*; * *vt* sillonner; rider.
furry *adj* à poil.
further *adj* supplémentaire; plus lointain;
* *adv* plus loin, plus avant; en outre; de
plus; * *vt* faire avancer; favoriser; promouvoir.
further education *n* formation *f* postscolaire.
furthermore *adv* de plus.
furthest *adv* le plus loin, le plus éloigné.
furtive *adj* furtif; secret; *~ly* *adv* furtivement.
fury *n* fureur *f*; furie *f*; colère *f*.
fuse *vt* fondre; faire sauter; * *vi* fondre, sauter; * *n* fusible *m*; amorce *f*.
fuse box *n* boîte à fusibles *f*.
fusion *n* fusion *f*.
fuss *n* tapage *m*; histoires *fpl*.
fussy *adj* tatillon, chipoteur.
futile *adj* futile, vain.
futility *n* futilité *f*.
future *adj* futur; * *n* futur *m*; avenir *m*.
fuzzy *adj* flou, confus; crépu.

G

gab *n* (*fam*) bavardage *m*.
gabble *vi* baragouiner; * *n* charabia *m*.
gable *n* pignon *m*.
gadget *n* gadget *m*.
gaffe *n* gaffe *f*, bévue *f*.
gag *n* bâillon *m*; blague *f*; * *vt* bâillonner.
gaiety *n* gaieté *f*.
gaily *adv* gaiement.

gain *n* gain *m*; bénéfice *m*; * *vt* gagner; atteindre.
gait *n* démarche *f*; maintien *m*.
gala *n* gala *m*.
galaxy *n* galaxie *f*.
gale *n* grand vent *m*.
gall *n* bile *f*; fiel *m*.
gallant *adj* galant.

gall bladder n vésicule biliaire f.

gallery n galerie f.

galley n galère f; (mar) cuisine f.

gallon n gallon m (mesure).

gallop n galop m; * vi galoper.

gallows n potence f.

gallstone n calcul biliaire m.

galore adv en abondance.

galvanize vt galvaniser.

gambit n stratagème m.

gamble vi jouer; spéculer; * n risque m; pari m.

gambler n joueur m -euse f.

gambling n jeu m (d'argent).

game n jeu m; divertissement m; partie f; gibier m; * vi jouer.

gamekeeper n garde-chasse m.

gaming n jeu m (d'argent).

gammon n jambon m.

gamut n (mus) gamme f.

gander n jars m.

gang n gang m, bande f.

gangrene n gangrène f.

gangster n gangster m.

gangway n passerelle f.

gap n trou m; vide m; intervalle, écart m.

gape vi être bouche bée; bâiller.

gaping adj béant.

garage n garage m.

garbage n ordures fpl.

garbage can n poubelle f.

garbage man n éboueur m.

garbled adj confus.

garden n jardin m.

garden hose n tuyau d'arrosage m.

gardener n jardinier m -ière f.

gardening n jardinage m.

gargle vi se gargariser.

gargoyle n gargouille f.

garish adj tapageur.

garland n guirlande f.

garlic n ail m.

garment n vêtement m.

garnish vt garnir, décorer; * n garniture f.

garret n mansarde f.

garrison n (mil) garnison f; * vt (mil) mettre en garnison; protéger d'une garnison.

garrote vt étrangler, garrotter.

garrulous adj locace, bavard.

garter n jarretelle f.

gas n gaz m; essence f.

gas burner n brûleur à gaz m.

gas cylinder n bouteille de gaz f.

gaseous adj gazeux.

gas fire n radiateur à gaz m.

gash n entaille f; fente f; * vt entailler.

gasket n joint d'étanchéité m.

gasp vi haleter; * n halètements mpl.

gas mask n masque à gaz m.

gas meter n compteur à gaz m.

gasoline n (US) essence f.

gas pedal n (US) accélérateur m.

gas ring n brûleur à gaz m.

gas station n (US) poste d'essence m.

gassy adj gazeux.

gas tap n robinet de gaz m.

gastric adj gastrique.

gastronomic adj gastronomique.

gasworks npl usine à gaz f.

gate n porte f; portail m.

gateway n porte f.

gather vt rassembler; ramasser; comprendre; * vi se rassembler.

gathering n réunion f; récolte f.

gauche adj gauche, maladroit.

gaudy adj criard.

gauge n calibre m; écartement m; * vt mesurer; calibrer.

gaunt adj décharné.

gauze n gaze f.

gay adj gai; vif; homosexuel.

gaze vi contempler, considérer; * n regard m.

gazelle n gazelle f.

gazette n gazette f.

gazetteer n répertoire géographique m.

gear n équipement m, matériel m; appareil m; affaires fpl; vitesse f.

gearbox n boîte de vitesses f.

gear shift n levier de vitesse m.

gear wheel n roue d'engrenage f.

gel n gel m.

gelatin(e) n gélatine f.

gelignite n gélignite f.

gem n pierre précieuse f; perle f.

Gemini n Gémeaux mpl (signe du zodiaque).

gender n genre m.

gene *n* gène *m*.

genealogical *adj* généalogique.

genealogy *n* généalogie *f*.

general *adj* général; commun, usuel; **in ~** en général; **~ly** *adv* généralement; * *n* général *m*; générale *f*.

general delivery *n* (US) poste restante *f*.

general election *n* élections générales *fpl*.

generality *n* généralité; majeure partie *f*.

generalization *n* généralisation *f*.

generalize *vt* généraliser.

generate *vt* engendrer; produire; causer.

generation *n* génération *f*.

generator *n* générateur *m*.

generic *adj* générique.

generosity *n* générosité, libéralité *f*.

generous *adj* généreux.

genetics *npl* génétique *f*.

genial *adj* cordial; doux.

genitals *npl* organes génitaux *mpl*.

genitive *n* (*gr*) génitif *m*.

genius *n* génie *m*.

genteel *adj* distingué.

gentle *adj* doux, *f* douce, modéré.

gentleman *n* gentleman *m*.

gentleness *n* douceur *f*.

gently *adv* doucement.

gentry *n* aristocratie *f*.

gents *n* toilettes pour hommes *fpl*.

genuflexion *n* génuflexion *f*.

genuine *adj* authentique; sincère; **~ly** *adv* authentiquement; sincèrement.

genus *n* genre *m*.

geographer *n* géographe *mf*.

geographical *adj* géographique.

geography *n* géographie *f*.

geological *adj* géologique.

geologist *n* géologue *mf*.

geology *n* géologie *f*.

geometric(al) *adj* géométrique.

geometry *n* géométrie *f*.

geranium *n* (*bot*) géranium *m*.

geriatric *n* malade gériatrique *mf*; * *adj* gériatrique.

germ *n* (*bot*) germe *m*.

germinate *vi* germer.

gesticulate *vi* gesticuler.

gesture *n* geste *m*.

get *vt* avoir; obtenir; atteindre; gagner; attraper; * *vi* devenir; aller; **~ the better** avoir l'avantage, surpasser.

geyser *n* geyser *m*; chauffe-eau *m invar*.

ghastly *adj* affreux; sinistre.

gherkin *n* cornichon *m*.

ghost *n* fantôme, spectre *m*.

ghostly *adj* spectral.

giant *n* géant *m* -e *f*.

gibberish *n* charabia *m*; sornettes *fpl*.

gibe *vi* se moquer; * *n* moquerie *f*.

giblets *npl* abattis (de volaille) *mpl*.

giddiness *n* vertige *m*.

giddy *adj* vertigineux.

gift *n* cadeau *m*; don *m*; talent *m*.

gifted *adj* talentueux; doué.

gift voucher *n* bon-cadeau *m*.

gigantic *adj* gigantesque.

giggle *vi* rire bêtement.

gild *vt* dorer.

gilding, gilt *n* dorure *f*.

gill *n* quart de pinte *m*; **~s** *pl* branchies *fpl*.

gilt-edged *adj* de premier ordre.

gimmick *n* truc *m*.

gin *n* gin *m*.

ginger *n* gingembre *m*.

gingerbread *n* pain d'épice *m*.

ginger-haired *adj* roux, *f* rousse.

giraffe *n* girafe *f*.

girder *n* poutre *f*.

girdle *n* gaine *f*; ceinture *f*.

girl *n* fille *f*.

girlfriend *n* amie *f*; petite amie *f*.

girlish *adj* de fille.

giro *n* virement *m*.

girth *n* sangle *f*; circonférence *f*.

gist *n* essence *f*.

give *vt* donner; offrir; prononcer, faire; consacrer; **~ away** offrir; trahir; révéler; **~ back** rendre; **~ in** *vi* céder; *vt* remettre; **~ off** dégager; **~ out** distribuer; **~ up** *vi* abandonner; *vt* renoncer à.

gizzard *n* gésier *m*.

glacial *adj* glacial.

glacier *n* glacier *m*.

glad *adj* joyeux, content; **I am ~ to see that** je me réjouis de voir que; **~ly** *adv* avec joie, avec plaisir.

gladden *vt* réjouir.

gladiator *n* gladiateur *m*.

glamorous *adj* attrayant, séduisant.

glamour *n* attrait *m*, séduction *f*.

glance *n* regard *m*; * *vi* regarder; jeter un coup d'œil.

glancing *adj* oblique.

gland *n* glande *f*.

glare *n* éclat *m*; regard féroce *m*; * *vi* éblouir, briller; lancer des regards indignés.

glaring *adj* éclatant; évident; furieux.

glass *n* verre *m*; longue-vue *f*; miroir *m*; ~**es** *pl* lunettes *fpl*; * *adj* en verre.

glassware *n* verrerie *f*.

glassy *adj* vitreux, cristallin.

glaze *vt* vitrer; vernisser.

glazier *n* vitrier *m*.

gleam *n* rayon *m*; * *vi* rayonner, briller.

gleaming *adj* brillant.

glean *vt* glaner.

glee *n* joie *f*; exultation *f*.

glen *n* vallée *f*.

glib *adj* facile; volubile; ~**ly** *adv* facilement; volubilement.

glide *vi* glisser; planer.

gliding *n* vol plané *m*.

glimmer *n* lueur *f*; * *vi* luire.

glimpse *n* aperçu *m*; vision *f*; * *vt* entrevoir.

glint *vi* briller, scintiller.

glisten, glitter *vi* luire, briller.

gloat *vi* exulter.

global *adj* global; mondial.

globe *n* globe *m*; sphère *f*.

gloom, gloominess *n* obscurité *f*; mélancolie, tristesse *f*; ~**ily** *adv* sombrement; tristement.

gloomy *adj* sombre, obscur; triste, mélancolique.

glorification *n* glorification *f*.

glorify *vt* glorifier, célébrer.

glorious *adj* glorieux, illustre; ~**ly** *adv* glorieusement.

glory *n* gloire, célébrité *f*.

gloss *n* glose *f*; lustre *m*; * *vt* gloser, interpréter; lustrer; ~ **over** passer sur.

glossary *n* glossaire *m*.

glossy *adj* lustré, brillant.

glove *n* gant *m*.

glove compartment *n* boîte à gants *f*.

glow *vi* rougeoyer; rayonner; * *n* rougeoiement *m*; éclat *m*; feu *m*.

glower *vi* lancer des regards noirs.

glue *n* colle *f*; * *vt* coller.

gluey *adj* gluant, visqueux.

glum *adj* abattu, triste.

glut *n* surabondance *f*.

glutinous *adj* glutineux.

glutton *n* glouton *m* -ne *f*.

gluttony *n* gloutonnerie *f*.

glycerine *n* glycérine *f*.

gnarled *adj* noueux.

gnash *vt*: **to ~ one's teeth** grincer des dents.

gnat *n* moucheron *m*.

gnaw *vt* ronger.

gnome *n* gnome *m*.

go *vi* aller; s'en aller, partir; disparaître; se perdre; ~ **ahead** continuer; ~ **away** s'en aller; ~ **back** repartir; ~ **by** passer; ~ **for** *vt* se lancer sur; aimer; ~ **in** entrer; ~ **off** s'en aller, partir; se passer; se gâter; ~ **on** continuer; se passer; ~ **out** sortir; s'éteindre; ~ **up** monter.

goad *n* aiguillon *m*; * *vt* aiguillonner; stimuler.

go-ahead *adj* entreprenant; * *n* feu vert *m*.

goal *n* but, objectif *m*.

goalkeeper *n* gardien de but *m*.

goalpost *n* poteau de but *m*.

goatherd *n* chevrier *m* -ière *f*.

gobble *vt* engloutir, avaler.

go-between *n* intermédiaire *mf*.

goblet *n* coupe *f*.

goblin *n* lutin *m*.

God *n* Dieu *m*.

godchild *n* filleul *m* -e *f*.

goddaughter *n* filleule *f*.

goddess *n* déesse *f*.

godfather *n* parrain *m*.

godforsaken *adj* perdu.

godhead *n* divinité *f*.

godless *adj* impie, athée.

godlike *adj* divin.

godliness *n* piété, dévotion, sainteté *f*.

godly *adj* pieux, dévot, religieux; droit.

godmother *n* marraine *f*.

godsend *n* don du ciel *m*.

godson *n* filleul *m*.

goggle-eyed *adj* aux yeux exorbités de surprise.

goggles *npl* lunettes *fpl*; lunettes de plongée *fpl*.

going *n* départ *m*; sortie *f*; progrès *m*.

gold *n* or *m*.

golden *adj* doré; d'or; excellent; ~ **rule** *n* règle d'or *f*.

goldfish *n* poisson rouge *m*.

gold-plated *adj* plaqué or.

goldsmith *n* orfèvre *m*.

golf *n* golf *m*.

golf ball *n* balle de golf *f*.

golf club *n* club de golf *m*.

golf course *n* terrain de golf *m*.

golfer *n* golfeur *m* -euse *f*.

gondolier *n* gondolier *m*.

gone *adj* parti; perdu; passé; fini; mort, disparu.

gong *n* gong *m*.

good *adj* bon; bienveillant; favorable; valable; * *adv* bien; * *n* bien *m*; avantage *m*; ~**s** *pl* biens *mpl*; marchandises *fpl*.

goodbye ! *excl* au revoir!

Good Friday *n* Vendredi Saint *m*.

goodies *npl* gourmandises *fpl*.

good-looking *adj* beau.

good nature *n* bon caractère *m*.

good-natured *adj* qui a bon caractère.

goodness *n* bonté *f*; qualité *f*.

goodwill *n* bienveillance *f*.

goose *n* oie *f*.

gooseberry *n* groseille à maquereau *f*.

goosebumps *npl* chair de poule *f*.

goose-step *n* pas de l'oie *m*.

gore *n* sang *m*; * *vt* blesser d'un coup de corne.

gorge *n* (*geogr*) gorge *f*; * *vt* engloutir, avaler.

gorgeous *adj* merveilleux.

gorilla *n* gorille *m*.

gorse *n* ajonc *m*.

gory *adj* sanglant.

goshawk *n* autour *m*.

gospel *n* évangile *m*.

gossamer *n* gaze *f*; toile d'araignée *f*.

gossip *n* commérages, cancans *mpl*; * *vi* cancaner, faire des commérages.

gothic *adj* gothique.

gout *n* goutte *f* (maladie).

govern *vt* gouverner, diriger.

governess *n* gouvernante *f*.

government *n* gouvernement *m*; administration publique *f*.

governor *n* gouverneur *m*.

gown *n* toge *f*; robe *f*; robe de chambre *f*.

grab *vt* saisir.

grace *n* grâce *f*; faveur *f*; pardon *m*; grâces *fpl*; **to say ~** dire le bénédicité; * *vt* orner; honorer.

graceful *adj* gracieux; ~**ly** *adv* gracieusement.

gracious *adj* gracieux; favorable; ~**ly** *adv* gracieusement.

gradation *n* gradation *f*.

grade *n* grade *m*; degré *m*; classe *f*.

grade crossing *n* (US) passage à niveau *m*.

grade school *n* (US) école primaire *f*.

gradient *n* (*rail*) rampe *f*.

gradual *adj* graduel; ~**ly** *adv* graduellement.

graduate *vi* obtenir son diplôme.

graduation *n* remise des diplômes *f*.

graffiti *n* graffiti *mpl*.

graft *n* greffe *f*; * *vt* greffer.

grain *n* grain *m*; graine *f*; céréales *fpl*.

gram *n* gramme *m*.

grammar *n* grammaire *f*.

grammatical *adj* ~**ly** *adv* grammatical(lement).

granary *n* grenier *m*.

grand *adj* grandiose; magnifique.

grandchild *n* petit-fils *m*; petite-fille *f*; **grandchildren** *pl* petits-enfants *mpl*.

grandad *n* pépé *m*.

granddaughter *n* petite-fille *f*; **great~** arrière-petite-fille *f*.

grandeur *n* grandeur *f*; pompe *f*.

grandfather *n* grand-père *m*; **great~** arrière-grand-père *m*.

grandiose *adj* grandiose.

grandma *n* mémé *f*.

grandmother *n* grand-mère *f*; **great~** arrière-grand-mère *f*.

grandparents *npl* grands-parents *mpl*.

grand piano *n* piano à queue *m*.

grandson *n* petit-fils *m*; **great~** arrière-petit-fils *m*.

grandstand *n* tribune *f*.
granite *n* granit *m*.
granny *n* mamie *f*.
grant *vt* accorder; **to take for ~ed** considérer comme acquis; * *n* bourse *f*; allocation *f*.
granulate *vt* granuler.
granule *n* granule *m*.
grape *n* grain *m* de raisin; **bunch of ~s** grappe *f* de raisin.
grapefruit *n* pamplemousse *m*.
graph *n* graphe, graphique *m*.
graphic(al) *adj* graphique; pittoresque; **~ally** *adv* graphiquement.
graphics *n* art graphique *m*; graphiques *mpl*.
grapnel *n* (*mar*) grappin *m*.
grasp *vt* saisir, empoigner; comprendre; * *n* poigne *f*; compréhension *f*; prise *f*.
grasping *adj* avide.
grass *n* herbe *f*.
grasshopper *n* sauterelle *f*.
grassland *n* prés *mpl*.
grass-roots *adj* populaire; de base.
grass snake *n* couleuvre *f*.
grassy *adj* herbeux.
grate *n* grille *f*; * *vt* râper; grincer (des dents); * *vi* grincer.
grateful *adj* reconnaissant; **~ly** *adv* avec reconnaissance.
gratefulness *n* gratitude, reconnaissance *f*.
gratification *n* satisfaction *f*.
gratify *vt* satisfaire; faire plaisir à.
gratifying *adj* réjouissant.
grating *n* grillage *m*; grincement *m*; * *adj* grinçant; énervant.
gratis *adv* gratis, gratuitement.
gratitude *n* gratitude, reconnaissance *f*.
gratuitous *adj* gratuit; volontaire; **~ly** *adv* gratuitement.
gratuity *n* gratification *f*.
grave *n* tombe *f*; * *adj* grave, sérieux; **~ly** *adv* gravement, sérieusement.
grave digger *n* fossoyeur *m*.
gravel *n* gravier *m*.
gravestone *n* pierre tombale *f*.
graveyard *n* cimetière *m*.
gravitate *vi* graviter.
gravitation *n* gravitation *f*.
gravity *n* gravité *f*.

gravy *n* jus de viande *m*; sauce *f*.
graze *vt* paître; effleurer; * *vi* paître.
grease *n* graisse *f*; * *vt* graisser.
greaseproof *adj* (papier) sulfurisé.
greasy *adj* gras.
great *adj* grand; important; fort; **~ly** *adv* énormément.
greatcoat *n* pardessus *m*.
greatness *n* grandeur *f*; importance *f*; pouvoir *m*; noblesse *f*.
greedily *adv* avidement.
greediness, greed *n* avidité *f*; gloutonnerie *f*.
greedy *adj* avide; glouton.
Greek *n* grec *m*; Grec *m* Grecque *f*.
green *adj* vert; inexpérimenté; * *n* vert *m*; verdure *f*; **~s** *npl* légumes verts *mpl*.
greenback *n* (US) billet *m*.
green belt *n* zone verte *f*.
green card *n* carte verte *f*; (US) permis de travail *m*.
greenery *n* verdure *f*.
greengrocer *n* marchand(e) de fruits et légumes *m(f)*.
greenhouse *n* serre *f*.
greenish *adj* verdâtre.
greenness *n* verdure *f*; manque d'expérience *m*.
green room *n* foyer des artistes *m*.
greet *vt* saluer; accueillir.
greeting *n* salutation *f*; accueil *m*.
greeting(s) card *n* carte de vœux *f*.
grenade *n* (*mil*) grenade *f*.
grenadier *n* grenadier *m*.
grey *adj* gris; * *n* gris *m*.
grey-haired *adj* aux cheveux gris.
greyhound *n* lévrier *m*.
greyish *adj* grisâtre; grisonnant.
greyness *n* couleur grise *f*; grisaille *f*.
grid *n* grille *f*; réseau *m*.
gridiron *n* gril *m*; terrain de football américain *m*.
grief *n* chagrin *m*, douleur, peine *f*.
grievance *n* grief *m*; doléance *f*; différend *m*; injustice *f*; tort *m*.
grieve *vt* peiner, affliger; * *vi* se chagriner, s'affliger.
grievous *adj* douloureux; grave, atroce; **~ly** *adv* douloureusement; cruellement.

griffin n griffon m.

grill n gril m; grillade f; * vt faire griller; interroger, cuisiner.

grille n grille f.

grim adj peu engageant; sinistre.

grimace n grimace f; moue f.

grime n saleté f.

grimy adj crasseux.

grin n grimace f; sourire m; * vi grimacer; sourire.

grind vt moudre; piler, broyer; affûter, aiguiser; * vi grincer.

grinder n moulin m; rémouleur m; molaire f.

grip n prise f; poignée f; sac m de voyage; * vt saisir, agripper.

gripping adj passionnant.

grisly adj horrible; sinistre.

gristle n cartilage m.

gristly adj cartilagineux.

grit n gravillon m; cran m.

groan vi gémir; grogner; * n gémissement m; grognement m.

grocer n épicier m -ière f.

groceries npl épicerie f, provisions fpl.

grocer's (shop) n épicerie f.

groggy adj sonné, étourdi.

groin n aine f.

groom n palefrenier m; valet m; marié m; * vt panser; préparer.

groove n rainure f.

grope vt chercher à tâtons; * vi tâtonner.

gross adj gros, corpulent; épais; grossier; brut; ~ly adv énormément.

grotesque adj grotesque.

grotto n grotte f.

ground n terre f, sol m; terrain, territoire m; fondement m; raison fondamentale f; fond m; * vt retenir au sol; fonder; mettre une prise de terre f.

ground floor n rez-de-chaussée m.

grounding n connaissances de base fpl.

groundless adj sans fondement; ~ly adv sans fondement.

ground staff n personnel au sol m.

groundwork n travaux de préparation mpl.

group n groupe m; * vt regrouper.

grouse n grouse f, coq de bruyère m; * vi grogner.

grove n bosquet m.

grovel vi se traîner; ramper.

grow vt cultiver; faire pousser; * vi pousser; grandir; augmenter; ~ up grandir.

grower n cultivateur m -trice f; producteur m -trice f.

growing adj croissant; grandissant.

growl vi grogner; * n grognement m.

grown-up n adulte mf.

growth n croissance f; augmentation f; poussée f.

grub n asticot m.

grubby adj sale.

grudge n rancune f; * vt accorder à contrecœur; vi avoir de la rancune.

grudgingly adv à contrecœur.

gruelling adj difficile, pénible.

gruesome adj horrible.

gruff adj brusque; ~ly adv brusquement.

gruffness n brusquerie f.

grumble vi grogner; grommeler.

grumpy adj ronchon, grincheux.

grunt vi grogner; * n grognement m.

G-string n cache-sexe m.

guarantee n garantie f; * vt garantir.

guard n garde f; garde m; * vt garder; défendre.

guarded adj prudent; surveillé.

guardroom n (mil) corps de garde m.

guardian n tuteur m -trice f; gardien m -ne f.

guardianship n tutelle f.

guerrilla n guérillero m.

guerrilla warfare n guérilla f.

guess vt deviner; supposer; * vi deviner; * n conjecture f.

guesswork n conjectures fpl.

guest n invité m -ée f; client m -e f.

guest room n chambre d'amis f.

guffaw n éclat de rire m.

guidance n guidage m; direction f.

guide vt guider, diriger; * n guide m.

guidebook n guide m.

guide dog n chien d'aveugle m.

guidelines npl directives fpl.

guild n association f; corporation f.

guile n astuce f.

guillotine n guillotine f; * vt guillotiner.

guilt n culpabilité f.

guiltless *adj* innocent.
guilty *adj* coupable.
guinea pig *n* cochon d'Inde, cobaye *m*.
guise *n* apparence *f*.
guitar *n* guitare *f*.
gulf *n* golfe *m*; abîme *m*.
gull *n* mouette *f*.
gullet *n* œsophage *m*.
gullibility *n* crédulité *f*.
gullible *adj* crédule.
gully *n* ravine *f*.
gulp *n* gorgée *f*; * *vt vi* avaler.
gum *n* gomme *f*; gencive *f*; chewing-gum *m*;
  * *vt* coller.
gum tree *n* gommier *m*.
gun *n* pistolet *m*; fusil *m*.
gunboat *n* canonnière *f*.
gun carriage *n* affût de canon *m*.
gunfire *n* coups de feu *mpl*.
gunman *n* homme armé *m*.
gunmetal *n* bronze à canon *m*.
gunner *n* artilleur *m*.
gunnery *n* artillerie *f*.
gunpoint *n*: **at ~** sous la menace d'une arme à
  feu.

gunpowder *n* poudre à canon *f*.
gunshot *n* coup de feu *m*.
gunsmith *n* armurier *m*.
gurgle *vi* gargouiller.
guru *n* gourou *m*.
gush *vi* jaillir; bouillonner; * *n* jaillissement
  m.
gushing *adj* jaillissant; très exubérant.
gusset *n* soufflet *m*.
gust *n* rafale *f*; bouffée *f*.
gusto *n* plaisir *m*, délectation *f*.
gusty *adj* venteux.
gut *n* intestin *m*; **~s** *npl* cœur au ventre *m*; * *vt*
  vider.
gutter *n* gouttière *f*; caniveau *m*.
guttural *adj* guttural.
guy *n* mec, type *m*.
guzzle *vt* bouffer, engloutir; avaler.
gym(nasium) *n* gymnase *m*.
gymnast *n* gymnaste *mf*.
gymnastic *adj* gymnastique; **~s** *npl* gymnastique *f*.
gynaecologist *n* gynécologue *mf*.
gypsy *n* gitan *m* -e *f*.
gyrate *vi* tourner.

H

haberdasher *n* mercier *m* -ière *f*.
haberdashery *n* mercerie *f*.
habit *n* habitude *f*.
habitable *adj* habitable.
habitat *n* habitat *m*.
habitual *adj* habituel; **~ly** *adv* d'habitude, habituellement.
hack *n* coupure, entaille *f*; * *vt* entailler, couper.
hackneyed *adj* rebattu.
haddock *n* aiglefin *m*.
haemorrhage *n* hémorragie *f*.
haemorrhoids *npl* hémorroïdes *fpl*.
hag *n* sorcière *f*.
haggard *adj* exténué; défait.
haggle *vi* marchander.
hail *n* grêle *f*; * *vt* saluer; * *vi* grêler.
hailstone *n* grêlon *m*.

hair *n* cheveux *mpl*; poil *m*.
hairbrush *n* brosse à cheveux *f*.
haircut *n* coupe de cheveux *f*.
hairdresser *n* coiffeur *m* -euse *f*.
hairdryer *n* séchoir à cheveux *m*.
hairless *adj* chauve; sans poils.
hairnet *n* filet à cheveux *m*.
hairpin *n* épingle à cheveux *f*.
hairpin bend *n* virage en épingle à cheveux
  m.
hair remover *n* crème dépilatoire *f*.
hairspray *n* laque à cheveux *f*.
hairstyle *n* coiffure *f*.
hairy *adj* chevelu; poilu.
hale *adj* vigoureux.
half *n* moitié *f*; * *adj* demi; * *adv* à moitié.
half-caste *adj* métis.
half-hearted *adj* peu enthousiaste.

half-hour *n* demi-heure *f*.
half-moon *n* demi-lune *f*.
half-price *adj* à moitié prix.
half-time *n* mi-temps *f*.
halfway *adv* à mi-chemin.
hall *n* vestibule *m*.
hallmark *n* marque *f*.
hallow *vt* consacrer, sanctifier.
hallucination *n* hallucination *f*.
halo *n* halo *m*.
halt *vi* s'arrêter; * *n* arrêt *m*; halte *f*.
halve *vt* couper en deux.
ham *n* jambon *m*.
hamlet *n* hameau *m*.
hammer *n* marteau *m*; * *vt* marteler.
hammock *n* hamac *m*.
hamper *n* panier *m*; * *vt* embarrasser, entraver.
hamstring *vt* couper les jarrets à.
hand *n* main *f*; ouvrier *m* -ière *f*; aiguille *f*; **at ~** à portée de main; * *vt* donner, passer.
handbag *n* sac à main *m*.
handbell *n* sonnette *f*.
handbook *n* manuel *m*.
handbrake *n* frein à main *m*.
handcuff *n* menotte *f*.
handful *n* poignée *f*.
handicap *n* handicap *m*.
handicapped *adj* handicapé.
handicraft *n* artisanat *m*.
handiwork *n* travail manuel *m*.
handkerchief *n* mouchoir *m*.
handle *n* manche *m*, queue *f*; anse *f*; poignée *f*; * *vt* manier; traiter, prendre.
handlebars *npl* guidon *m*.
handling *n* maniement *m*; traitement *m*.
handrail *n* garde-fou *m*.
handshake *n* poignée de mains *f*.
handsome *adj* beau; **~ly** *adv* élégamment.
handwriting *n* écriture *f*.
handy *adj* pratique; adroit.
hang *vt* accrocher; pendre; * *vi* pendre, être accroché; être pendu.
hanger *n* cintre *m*.
hanger-on *n* parasite *m*.
hangings *npl* tapisserie *f*.
hangman *n* bourreau *m*.
hangover *n* gueule de bois *f*.

hang-up *n* complexe *m*.
hanker *vi* avoir envie.
haphazard *adj* fortuit.
hapless *adj* malheureux.
happen *vi* se passer; **I ~ to have one** il se trouve que j'en ai un.
happening *n* événement *m*.
happily *adv* heureusement; gaiement.
happiness *n* bonheur *m*.
happy *adj* heureux.
harangue *n* harangue *f*; * *vt* haranguer.
harass *vt* harceler; tourmenter.
harbinger *n* précurseur *m*.
harbour *n* port *m*; * *vt* héberger; entretenir, nourrir.
hard *adj* dur; pénible; sévère, rigide; **~ of hearing** dur d'oreille; **~ by** tout près.
harden *vt* *vi* durcir.
hard-headed *adj* réaliste.
hard-hearted *adj* au cœur dur, insensible.
hardiness *n* robustesse *f*.
hardly *adv* à peine; **~ ever** presque jamais.
hardness *n* dureté *f*; difficulté *f*; sévérité *f*.
hardship *n* épreuve(s) *f(pl)*.
hard-up *adj* fauché, sans le sou.
hardware *n* matériel *m*; quincaillerie *f*.
hardwearing *adj* résistant.
hardy *adj* fort, robuste; résistant.
hare *n* lièvre *m*.
hare-brained *adj* écervelé.
hare-lipped *adj* qui a un bec de lièvre.
haricot *n* haricot blanc *m*.
harlequin *n* arlequin *m*.
harm *n* mal *m*; tort *m*; * *vt* faire du mal à; nuire à.
harmful *adj* nuisible.
harmless *adj* inoffensif.
harmonic *adj* harmonique.
harmonious *adj* harmonieux; **~ly** *adv* harmonieusement.
harmonize *vt* harmoniser.
harmony *n* harmonie *f*.
harness *n* harnais *m*; * *vt* harnacher.
harp *n* harpe *f*.
harpist *n* harpiste *mf*.
harpoon *n* harpon *m*.
harpsichord *n* clavecin *m*.
harrow *n* herse *f*.

harry *vt* harceler; dévaster.

harsh *adj* dur; austère; rude; **~ly** *adv* sévèrement; durement.

harshness *n* aspérité, dureté *f*; austérité *f*.

harvest *n* récolte *f*; moisson *f*; * *vt* récolter; moissonner.

harvester *n* moissonneur *m* -euse *f*; moissonneuse *f* (machine).

hash *n* hachis *m*; gâchis *m*.

hassock *n* agenouilloir *m*.

haste *n* hâte *f*; **to be in ~** être pressé.

hasten *vt* accélérer, hâter; * *vi* se dépêcher.

hastily *adv* à la hâte, précipitamment.

hastiness *n* précipitation *f*.

hasty *adj* hâtif; irréfléchi.

hat *n* chapeau *m*.

hatbox *n* carton à chapeau *m*.

hatch *vt* couver; faire éclore; tramer; * *n* écoutille *f*.

hatchback *n* (*auto*) voiture à hayon arrière *f*.

hatchet *n* hachette *f*.

hatchway *n* (*mar*) écoutille *f*.

hate *n* haine *f*; * *vt* haïr, détester.

hateful *adj* odieux, détestable.

hatred *n* haine *f*.

hatter *n* chapelier *m* -ière *f*.

haughtily *adv* hautainement.

haughtiness *n* orgueil *m*; hauteur *f*.

haughty *adj* hautain, orgueilleux.

haul *vt* tirer; * *n* prise *f*; butin *m*.

haulier *n* camionneur *m*.

haunch *n* hanche *f*.

haunt *vt* hanter; fréquenter; * *n* repaire *m*.

have *vt* avoir; posséder.

haven *n* refuge *m*.

haversack *n* sac à dos *m*.

havoc *n* ravages *mpl*.

hawk *n* faucon *m*; * *vi* chasser au faucon.

hawthorn *n* aubépine *f*.

hay *n* foin *m*.

hay fever *n* rhume des foins *m*.

hayloft *n* fenil *m*.

hayrick, haystack *n* meule de foin *f*.

hazard *n* risque, danger *m*; * *vt* risquer.

hazardous *adj* risqué, dangereux.

haze *n* brume *f*.

hazel *n* noisetier *m*; * *adj* noisette.

hazelnut *n* noisette *f*.

hazy *adj* brumeux.

he *pn* il.

head *n* tête *f*; chef *m*; esprit *m*; * *vt* conduire; **~ for** se diriger vers.

headache *n* mal de tête *m*.

headdress *n* coiffe *f*.

headland *n* promontoire *m*.

headlight *n* phare *m*.

headline *n* titre *m*.

headlong *adv* à toute allure.

headmaster *n* directeur *m*.

head office *n* siège social *m*.

headphones *npl* écouteurs *mpl*.

headquarters *npl* (*mil*) quartier général *m*; siège social *m*.

headroom *n* hauteur *f*.

headstrong *adj* têtu.

headwaiter *n* maître d'hôtel *m*.

headway *n* progrès *m(pl)*.

heady *adj* capiteux.

heal *vt vi* guérir.

health *n* santé *f*.

healthiness *n* bonne santé *f*.

healthy *adj* en bonne santé; sain.

heap *n* tas *m*; * *vt* entasser.

hear *vt* entendre; écouter; * *vi* entendre; avoir des nouvelles.

hearing *n* ouïe *f*.

hearing aid *n* audiophone *m*.

hearsay *n* rumeur *f*.

hearse *n* corbillard *m*.

heart *n* cœur *m*; **by ~** par cœur; **with all my ~** de tout cœur.

heart attack *n* crise cardiaque *f*.

heartbreaking *adj* à fendre le cœur.

heartburn *n* acidité *f* gastrique.

heart failure *n* arrêt cardiaque *m*.

heartfelt *adj* sincère.

hearth *n* foyer *m*.

heartily *adv* sincèrement, cordialement.

heartiness *n* cordialité, sincérité *f*.

heartless *adj* cruel; **~ly** *adv* cruellement.

hearty *adj* cordial.

heat *n* chaleur *f*; * *vt* chauffer.

heater *n* radiateur *m*.

heather *n* (*bot*) bruyère *f*.

heathen *n* païen *m*, païenne *f*; **~ish** *adj* sauvage, barbare.

heating *n* chauffage *m*.

heatwave *n* onde de chaleur *f*.

heave *vt* lever; tirer; * *n* effort *m*.

heaven *n* ciel *m*.

heavenly *adj* divin.

heavily *adv* lourdement.

heaviness *n* lourdeur *f*.

heavy *adj* lourd, pesant; considérable.

Hebrew *n* hébreu *m* (langue).

heckle *vt* interrompre.

hectic *adj* agité.

hedge *n* haie *f*; * *vt* entourer d'une haie.

hedgehog *n* hérisson *m*.

heed *vt* tenir compte de; * *n* soin *m*; attention *f*.

heedless *adj* inattentif, étourdi; ~**ly** *adv* étourdiment.

heel *n* talon *m*; **to take to one's ~s** prendre ses jambes à son cou.

hefty *adj* costaud, puissant.

heifer *n* génisse *f*.

height *n* hauteur *f*; altitude *f*.

heighten *vt* rehausser; augmenter; intensifier.

heinous *adj* atroce.

heir *n* héritier *m*; ~ **apparent** héritier présomptif *m*.

heiress *n* héritière *f*.

heirloom *n* héritage *m*.

helicopter *n* hélicoptère *m*.

hell *n* enfer *m*.

hellish *adj* infernal.

helm *n* (*mar*) barre *f*.

helmet *n* casque *m*.

help *vt* aider, secourir; **I cannot ~ it** je n'y peux rien; je ne peux pas m'en empêcher; * *n* aide *f*; secours *m*.

helper *n* aide *mf*.

helpful *adj* utile; qui rend service.

helping *n* portion *f*.

helpless *adj* impuissant; ~**ly** *adv* désespérément; sans pouvoir rien faire.

helter-skelter *adv* n'importe comment, en désordre.

hem *n* ourlet *m*; * *vt* ourler.

he-man *n* dur, mâle *m*.

hemisphere *n* hémisphère *m*.

hemp *n* chanvre *m*.

hen *n* poule *f*.

henchman *n* acolyte *m*.

henceforth, henceforward *adv* dorénavant.

hen-house *n* poulailler *m*.

hepatitis *n* hépatite *f*.

her *pn* son, sa, ses; elle; la; lui.

herald *n* héraut *m*.

heraldry *n* héraldique *f*.

herb *n* herbe *f*; ~**s** *pl* fines herbes *fpl*.

herbaceous *adj* herbacé.

herbalist *n* herboriste *mf*.

herbivorous *adj* herbivore.

herd *n* troupeau *m*.

here *adv* ici.

hereabout(s) *adv* dans les environs.

hereafter *adv* plus tard; ci-après.

hereby *adv* par la présente.

hereditary *adj* héréditaire.

heredity *n* hérédité *f*.

heresy *n* hérésie *f*.

heretic *n*, *adj* hérétique *mf*.

herewith *adv* avec ceci.

heritage *n* patrimoine, héritage *m*.

hermetic *adj* hermétique; ~**ly** *adv* hermétiquement.

hermit *n* ermite *m*.

hermitage *n* ermitage *m*.

hernia *n* hernie *f*.

hero *n* héros *m*.

heroic *adj* héroïque; ~**ally** *adv* héroïquement.

heroine *n* héroïne *f*.

heroism *n* héroïsme *m*.

heron *n* héron *m*.

herring *n* hareng *m*.

hers *pn* le sien, la sienne, le(s) sien(ne)s, à elle.

herself *pn* elle-même.

hesitant *adj* hésitant.

hesitate *vi* hésiter.

hesitation *n* hésitation *f*.

heterogeneous *adj* hétérogène.

heterosexual *adj n* hétérosexuel *m* -le *f*.

hew *vt* tailler; couper.

heyday *n* apogée *m*.

hi *excl* salut!

hiatus *n* (*gr*) hiatus *m*.

hibernate *vi* hiberner.

hiccup *n* hoquet *m*; * *vi* avoir le hoquet.

hickory *n* noyer d'Amérique *m*.

hide vt cacher; * n cuir m; peau f.
hideaway n cachette f.
hideous adj hideux; horrible; ~**ly** adv horriblement.
hiding-place n cachette f.
hierarchy n hiérarchie f.
hieroglyphic adj hiéroglyphique; * n hiéroglyphe m.
hi-fi n hi-fi f invar.
higgledy-piggledy adv pêle-mêle.
high adj haut; élevé.
high altar n maître-autel m.
high chair n chaise haute f.
high-handed adj tyrannique.
highlands npl terres montagneuses fpl.
highlight n point fort m.
highly adv extrêmement, hautement.
highness n hauteur f; altesse f.
high school n lycée m.
high-strung adj nerveux, tendu.
high water n marée haute f.
highway n grande route f.
hike vi faire une randonnée.
hijack vt détourner.
hijacker n pirate de l'air m.
hilarious adj hilarant; hilare.
hill n colline f.
hillock n petite colline f.
hillside n coteau m.
hilly adj montagneux.
hilt n poignée f.
him pn lui; le.
himself pn lui-même; soi.
hind adj derrière; * n biche f.
hinder vt gêner, entraver.
hindrance n gêne f, obstacle m.
hindmost adj dernier.
hindquarter n arrière-train m.
hindsight n: with ~ rétrospectivement.
hinge n charnière f; gond m.
hint n allusion f; insinuation f; * vt insinuer; suggérer.
hip n hanche f.
hippopotamus n hippopotame m.
hire vt louer; * n location f.
his pn son, sa, ses; le sien, la sienne, les sien(ne)s; à lui.
Hispanic adj hispanique.

hiss vt vi siffler.
historian n historien m -ne f.
historic(al) adj historique; ~**ally** adv historiquement.
history n histoire f.
histrionic adj théâtral.
hit vt frapper; atteindre; heurter; * n coup m; succès m.
hitch vt accrocher; * n nœud m; anicroche f.
hitchhike vi faire du stop.
hitherto adv jusqu'à présent, jusqu'ici.
hive n ruche f.
hoard n stock m; trésor caché m; * vt accumuler, amasser.
hoarfrost n givre m.
hoarse adj rauque; ~**ly** adv d'une voix rauque.
hoarseness n voix rauque f.
hoax n canular m; * vt faire un canular à.
hobble vi boitiller.
hobby n passe-temps m invar.
hobbyhorse n cheval de bataille m.
hobo n vagabond m.
hockey n hockey m.
hodge-podge n confusion f.
hoe n binette f; * vt biner.
hog n porc m.
hoist vt hisser; * n grue f.
hold vt tenir; détenir; contenir; ~ **on to** se tenir à; * vi valoir; * n prise f; pouvoir m.
holder n détenteur m -trice f; titulaire mf.
holding n possession f.
holdup n hold-up m; retard m.
hole n trou m.
holiday n jour de congé m; jour férié m; ~**s** pl vacances fpl.
holiness n sainteté f.
hollow adj creux; * n creux m; * vt creuser, vider.
holly n (bot) houx m.
hollyhock n rose trémière f.
holocaust n holocauste m.
holster n étui de révolver m.
holy adj saint; bénit; sacré.
holy water n eau bénite f.
holy week n semaine sainte f.
homage n hommage m.
home n maison f; patrie f; domicile m; ~**ly** adj simple.

home address *n* domicile *m*.

homeless *adj* sans abri.

homeliness *n* simplicité *f*.

home-made *adj* fait maison.

homesick *adj* nostalgique, qui a le mal du pays.

homesickness *n* nostalgie *f*, mal du pays *m*.

hometown *n* ville natale *f*.

homeward *adj* vers chez soi; vers son pays.

homework *n* devoirs *mpl*.

homicidal *adj* homicide.

homicide *n* homicide *m*; homicide *mf*.

homoeopathist *n* homéopathe *mf*.

homoeopathy *n* homéopathie *f*.

homogeneous *adj* homogène.

homosexual *adj n* homosexuel *m* -le *f*.

honest *adj* honnête; **~ly** *adv* honnêtement.

honesty *n* honnêteté *f*.

honey *n* miel *m*.

honeycomb *n* rayon de miel *m*.

honeymoon *n* lune de miel *f*.

honeysuckle *n* (*bot*) chèvrefeuille *m*.

honorary *adj* honoraire.

honour *n* honneur *m*; * *vt* honorer.

honourable *adj* honorable.

honourably *adv* honorablement.

hood *n* capot *m*; capuche *f*.

hoodlum *n* truand *m*.

hoof *n* sabot *m*.

hook *n* crochet *m*; hameçon *m*; **by ~ or by crook** coûte que coûte; * *vt* accrocher.

hooked *adj* crochu.

hooligan *n* vandale *m*.

hoop *n* cerceau *m*.

hooter *n* sirène *f*.

hop *n* (*bot*) houblon *m*; saut *m*; * *vi* sauter.

hope *n* espoir *m*, espérance *f*; * *vi* espérer.

hopeful *adj* plein d'espoir; prometteur; **~ly** *adv* avec espoir.

hopefulness *n* bon espoir *m*.

hopeless *adj* désespéré; **~ly** *adv* désespérément.

horde *n* horde *f*.

horizon *n* horizon *m*.

horizontal *adj* horizontal; **~ly** *adv* horizontalement.

hormone *n* hormone *f*.

horn *n* corne *f*.

horned *adj* à cornes.

hornet *n* frelon *m*.

horny *adj* calleux.

horoscope *n* horoscope *m*.

horrendous *adj* horrible.

horrible *adj* horrible.

horribly *adv* horriblement; énormément.

horrid *adj* horrible.

horrific *adj* horrible, affreux.

horrify *vt* horrifier.

horror *n* horreur *f*.

horror film *n* film d'horreur *m*.

hors d'oeuvre *n* hors-d'œuvre *m invar*.

horse *n* cheval *m*.

horseback *adv*: **on ~** à cheval.

horse-breaker *n* dresseur(-euse) de chevaux *m(f)*.

horse chestnut *n* marron d'Inde *m*.

horsefly *n* taon *m*.

horseman *n* cavalier *m*.

horsemanship *n* équitation *f*.

horsepower *n* cheval-vapeur *m*; puissance en chevaux *f*.

horse race *n* course de chevaux *f*.

horseradish *n* raifort *m*.

horseshoe *n* fer à cheval *m*.

horsewoman *n* cavalière *f*.

horticulture *n* horticulture *f*.

horticulturist *n* horticulteur *m* -trice *f*.

hose-pipe *n* tuyau *m*.

hosiery *n* bonneterie *f*.

hospitable *adj* hospitalier.

hospitably *adv* avec hospitalité.

hospital *n* hôpital *m*.

hospitality *n* hospitalité *f*.

host *n* hôte *m*; hostie *f*.

hostage *n* otage *m*.

hostess *n* hôtesse *f*.

hostile *adj* hostile.

hostility *n* hostilité *f*.

hot *adj* chaud; épicé.

hotbed *n* foyer *m*.

hotdog *n* hot-dog *m*.

hotel *n* hôtel *m*.

hotelier *n* hôtelier *m* -ière *f*.

hotheaded *adj* exalté.

hothouse *n* serre *f*.

hotline *n* téléphone rouge *m*.

hotplate n plaque chauffante f.

hotly adv violemment.

hound n chien de chasse m.

hour n heure f.

hourglass n sablier m.

hourly adv toutes les heures.

house n maison f; maisonnée f; * vt loger.

houseboat n péniche f.

housebreaker n cambrioleur m.

housebreaking n cambriolage m.

household n famille f, ménage m.

householder n propriétaire mf; chef de famille m.

housekeeper n gouvernante f.

housekeeping n travaux ménagers mpl.

houseless adv sans abri.

house-warming party n pendaison de crémaillère f.

housewife n ménagère f.

housework n travaux ménagers mpl.

housing n logement m.

housing development n urbanisation f.

hovel n taudis m.

hover vi planer.

how adv comme; comment; ~ **do you do!** enchanté.

however adv de quelque manière que; cependant, néanmoins.

howl vi hurler; * n hurlement m.

hub n centre m; moyeu m.

hubbub n vacarme m.

hubcap n enjoliveur m.

hue n teinte f; nuance f.

huff n: **in a ~** fâché.

hug vt étreindre; * n étreinte f.

huge adj énorme; ~**ly** adv énormément.

hulk n (mar) carcasse f; ponton m.

hull n (mar) coque f.

hum vi chantonner.

human adj humain.

humane adj humain; ~**ly** adv humainement.

humanist n humaniste mf.

humanitarian adj humanitaire.

humanity n humanité f.

humanize vt humaniser.

humanly adv humainement.

humble adj humble, modeste; * vt humilier.

humbleness n humilité f.

humbly adv humblement.

humbug n blagues fpl.

humdrum adj monotone.

humid adj humide.

humidity n humidité f.

humiliate vt humilier.

humiliation n humiliation f.

humility n humilité f.

hummingbird n colibri m.

humorist n humoriste mf.

humorous adj humoristique; ~**ly** adv avec humour.

humour n sens de l'humour m, humour m; * vt complaire à.

hump n bosse f.

hunch n intuition f; ~**backed** adj bossu.

hundred adj cent; * n centaine f.

hundredth adj centième.

hundredweight n quintal m.

hunger n faim f; * vi avoir faim.

hunger strike n grève de la faim f.

hungrily adv avidement.

hungry adj qui a faim, affamé.

hunt vt chasser; poursuivre; chercher; * vi chasser; * n chasse f.

hunter n chasseur m.

hunting n chasse f.

huntsman n chasseur m.

hurdle n haie f.

hurl vt lancer avec violence, jeter.

hurricane n ouragan m.

hurried adj fait à la hâte; précipité; ~**ly** adv hâtivement; précipitamment.

hurry vt presser; * vi se presser, se dépêcher; * n hâte f.

hurt vt faire mal à; blesser; * n mal m.

hurtful adj blessant; ~**ly** adv de manière blessante.

husband n mari m.

husbandry n agriculture f.

hush! chut!, silence!; * vt faire taire; * vi se taire.

husk n coque f (graine).

huskiness n voix rauque f.

husky adj rauque.

hustings n plate-forme électorale f.

hustle vt pousser avec force, bousculer.

hut n cabane, hutte f.

hutch *n* clapier *m*.

hyacinth *n* jacinthe *f*.

hydrant *n* bouche d'incendie *f*.

hydraulic *adj* hydraulique; **~s** *npl* hydraulique *f*.

hydroelectric *adj* hydroélectrique.

hydrofoil *n* hydroptère *m*.

hydrogen *n* hydrogène *m*.

hydrophobia *n* hydrophobie *f*.

hyena *n* hyène *f*.

hygiene *n* hygiène *f*.

hygienic *adj* hygiénique.

hymn *n* hymne *m*.

hyperbole *n* hyperbole *f*.

hypermarket *n* hypermarché *m*.

hyphen *n* (*gr*) trait d'union *m*.

hypochondria *n* hypocondrie *f*.

hypochondriac *adj n* hypocondriaque *mf*.

hypocrisy *n* hypocrisie *f*.

hypocrite *n* hypocrite *mf*.

hypocritical *adj* hypocrite.

hypothesis *n* hypothèse *f*.

hypothetical *adj* **~ly** *adv* hypothétique(ment).

hysterical *adj* hystérique.

hysterics *npl* hystérie *f*; crise de nerfs *f*.

I

I *pn* je, j'; moi

ice *n* glace *f*; * *vt* glacer; geler.

ice-axe *n* piolet *m*.

iceberg *n* iceberg *m*.

ice-bound *adj* fermé par les glaces.

icebox *n* glacière *f*.

ice cream *n* glace *f*.

ice rink *n* patinoire *f*.

ice skating *n* patinage sur glace *m*.

icicle *n* stalactite *f*, glaçon *m*.

iconoclast *n* iconoclaste *mf*.

icy *adj* glacé.

idea *n* idée *f*.

ideal *adj* idéal; **~ly** *adv* idéalement.

idealist *n* idéaliste *mf*.

identical *adj* identique.

identification *n* identification *f*.

identify *vt* identifier.

identity *n* identité *f*.

ideology *n* idéologie *f*.

idiom *n* expression idiomatique *f*.

idiomatic *adj* idiomatique.

idiosyncrasy *n* idiosyncrasie *f*.

idiot *n* imbécile *mf*.

idiotic *adj* idiot, bête.

idle *adj* désœuvré; au repos; inutile.

idleness *n* paresse *f*; oisiveté *f*.

idler *n* paresseux *m* -euse *f*.

idly *adv* oisivement; paresseusement; vainement.

idol *n* idole *f*.

idolatry *n* idôlatrie *f*.

idolize *vt* idôlatrer.

idyllic *adj* idyllique.

i.e. *adv* c.-à-d., c'est-à-dire.

if *conj* si; ~ **not** sinon.

ignite *vt* allumer, enflammer.

ignition *n* (*chem*) ignition *f*; allumage *m*.

ignition key *n* clé de contact *f*.

ignoble *adj* infâme; bas.

ignominious *adj* ignominieux; **~ly** *adv* ignominieusement.

ignominy *n* ignominie, infamie *f*.

ignoramus *n* ignorant *m* -e *f*.

ignorance *n* ignorance *f*.

ignorant *adj* ignorant; **~ly** *adv* par ignorance.

ignore *vt* ne pas tenir compte de.

ill *adj* malade; * *n* mal *m*; dommage *m*; * *adv* mal.

ill-advised *adj* malavisé.

illegal *adj* **~ly** *adv* illégal(ement).

illegality *n* illégalité *f*.

illegible *adj* illisible.

illegibly *adv* illisiblement.

illegitimacy *n* illégitimité *f*.

illegitimate *adj* illégitime; **~ly** *adv* illégitimement.

ill feeling *n* rancœur *f*.

illicit *adj* illicite.

illiterate *adj* analphabète, illettré.

illness *n* maladie *f*.

illogical *adj* illogique.

ill-timed *adj* inopportun.

ill-treat *vt* maltraiter.

illuminate *vt* illuminer.

illumination *n* illumination *f*.

illusion *n* illusion *f*.

illusory *adj* illusoire.

illustrate *vt* illustrer.

illustration *n* illustration *f*.

illustrative *adj* qui illustre.

illustrious *adj* illustre.

ill-will *n* malveillance *f*.

image *n* image *f*.

imagery *n* images *fpl*.

imaginable *adj* imaginable.

imaginary *adj* imaginaire.

imagination *n* imagination *f*.

imaginative *adj* imaginatif.

imagine *vt* imaginer.

imbalance *n* déséquilibre *m*.

imbecile *adj* imbécile, idiot.

imbibe *vt* boire; imbiber; absorber.

imbue *vt* imprégner.

imitate *vt* imiter.

imitation *n* imitation *f*.

imitative *adj* imitatif.

immaculate *adj* immaculé.

immaterial *adj* insignifiant.

immature *adj* pas mûr.

immeasurable *adj* incommensurable.

immeasurably *adv* immensément.

immediate *adj* immédiat; ~**ly** *adv* immédiatement.

immense *adj* immense; énorme; ~**ly** *adv* immensément.

immensity *n* immensité *f*.

immerse *vt* immerger.

immersion *n* immersion *f*.

immigrant *n* immigrant *m* -e *f*.

immigration *n* immigration *f*.

imminent *adj* imminent.

immobile *adj* immobile.

immobility *n* immobilité *f*.

immoderate *adj* immodéré, excessif; ~**ly** *adv* immodérément.

immodest *adj* immodeste.

immoral *adj* immoral.

immorality *n* immoralité *f*.

immortal *adj* immortel.

immortality *n* immortalité *f*.

immortalize *vt* immortaliser.

immune *adj* immunisé.

immunity *n* immunité *f*.

immunize *vt* immuniser.

immutable *adj* immuable.

imp *n* lutin *m*.

impact *n* impact *m*.

impair *vt* diminuer; affaiblir.

impale *vt* empaler.

impalpable *adj* impalpable.

impart *vt* communiquer.

impartial *adj* ~**ly** *adv* impartial(ement).

impartiality *n* impartialité *f*.

impassable *adj* impraticable; infranchissable.

impasse *n* impasse *f*.

impassive *adj* impassible.

impatience *n* impatience *f*.

impatient *adj* impatient; ~**ly** *adv* impatiemment.

impeach *vt* (*law*) mettre en accusation.

impeccable *adj* impeccable.

impecunious *adj* impécunieux.

impede *vt* empêcher; entraver.

impediment *n* obstacle *m*.

impel *vt* pousser.

impending *adj* imminent.

impenetrable *adj* impénétrable.

imperative *adj* impératif.

imperceptible *adj* imperceptible.

imperceptibly *adv* imperceptiblement.

imperfect *adj* ~**ly** imparfait(ement); * *n* (*gr*) imparfait *m*.

imperfection *n* imperfection *f*; défaut *m*.

imperial *adj* impérial.

imperialism *n* impérialisme *m*.

imperious *adj* impérieux; ~**ly** *adv* impérieusement.

impermeable *adj* imperméable.

impersonal *adj* ~**ly** *adv* impersonel(lement).

impersonate *vt* se faire passer pour; imiter.

impertinence *n* impertinence *f*.

impertinent *adj* impertinent; ~**ly** *adv* impertinemment.

imperturbable *adj* imperturbable.

impervious *adj* imperméable; indifférent.

impetuosity *n* impétuosité *f*.

impetuous *adj* impétueux; **~ly** *adv* impétueusement.

impetus *n* élan *m*.

impiety *n* impiété *f*.

impinge (on) *vi* affecter; empiéter (sur).

impious *adj* impie.

implacable *adj* implacable.

implacably *adv* implacablement.

implant *vt* implanter.

implement *n* outil *m*; ustensile *m*.

implicate *vt* impliquer.

implication *n* implication *f*.

implicit *adj* implicite; **~ly** *adv* implicitement.

implore *vt* supplier.

imply *vt* supposer.

impolite *adj* impoli.

impoliteness *n* impolitesse *f*.

impolitic *adj* maladroit; impolitique.

import *vt* importer; * *n* importation *f*.

importance *n* importance *f*.

important *adj* important.

importation *n* importation *f*.

importer *n* importateur *m* -trice *f*.

importunate *adj* importun.

importune *vt* importuner.

importunity *n* importunité *f*.

impose *vt* imposer.

imposing *adj* imposant.

imposition *n* imposition *f*.

impossibility *n* impossibilité *f*.

impossible *adj* impossible.

impostor *n* imposteur *m*.

impotence *n* impotence *f*.

impotent *adj* impotent; **~ly** *adv* faiblement.

impound *vt* confisquer.

impoverish *vt* appauvrir.

impoverished *adj* appauvri.

impoverishment *n* appauvrissement *m*.

impracticability *n* impraticabilité *f*.

impracticable *adj* impraticable.

impractical *adj* peu pratique.

imprecation *n* imprécation, malédiction *f*.

imprecise *adj* imprécis.

impregnable *adj* inexpugnable.

impregnate *vt* imprégner; féconder.

impregnation *n* fécondation *f*; imprégnation *f*.

impress *vt* impressionner.

impression *n* impression *f*; édition *f*.

impressionable *adj* impressionnable.

impressive *adj* impressionnant.

imprint *n* empreinte *f*; * *vt* imprimer; marquer.

imprison *vt* emprisonner.

imprisonment *n* emprisonnement *m*.

improbability *n* improbabilité *f*.

improbable *adj* improbable.

impromptu *adj* impromptu.

improper *adj* indécent; déplacé; impropre; **~ly** *adv* indécemment; de manière déplacée; improprement.

impropriety *n* impropriété *f*; inconvenance *f*.

improve *vt* améliorer; * *vi* s'améliorer.

improvement *n* amélioration *f*.

improvident *adj* imprévoyant.

improvise *vt* improviser.

imprudence *n* imprudence *f*.

imprudent *adj* imprudent.

impudence *n* impudence *f*.

impudent *adj* impudent; **~ly** *adv* impudemment.

impugn *vt* attaquer, contester.

impulse *n* impulsion *f*.

impulsive *adj* impulsif.

impunity *n* impunité *f*.

impure *adj* impur; **~ly** *adv* impurement.

impurity *n* impureté *f*.

in *prep* dans; en.

inability *n* incapacité *f*.

inaccessible *adj* inaccessible.

inaccuracy *n* inexactitude *f*.

inaccurate *adj* inexact.

inaction *n* inaction *f*.

inactive *adj* inactif.

inactivity *n* inactivité *f*.

inadequate *adj* inadéquat.

inadmissible *adj* inadmissible.

inadvertently *adv* par inadvertance.

inalienable *adj* inaliénable.

inane *adj* inepte.

inanimate *adj* inanimé.

inapplicable *adj* inapplicable.

inappropriate *adj* impropre.

inasmuch *adv* attendu que.

inattentive *adj* inattentif.

inaudible *adj* inaudible.

inaugural *adj* inaugural.
inaugurate *vt* inaugurer.
inauguration *n* inauguration *f.*
inauspicious *adj* peu propice.
in-between *adj* intermédiaire.
inborn, inbred *adj* inné.
incalculable *adj* incalculable.
incandescent *adj* incandescent.
incantation *n* incantation *f.*
incapable *adj* incapable.
incapacitate *vt* mettre dans l'incapacité.
incapacity *n* incapacité *f.*
incarcerate *vt* incarcérer.
incarnate *adj* incarné.
incarnation *n* incarnation *f.*
incautious *adj* imprudent; **~ly** *adv* imprudemment.
incendiary *n* bombe incendiaire *f*; incendiaire *mf*
incense *n* encens *m*; * *vt* exaspérer.
incentive *n* stimulant *m*; prime, aide *f*
inception *n* commencement *m.*
incessant *adj* incessant, continuel; **~ly** *adv* continuellement.
incest *n* inceste *m.*
incestuous *adj* incestueux.
inch *n* pouce *m*; **~ by ~** petit à petit.
incidence *n* fréquence *f.*
incident *n* incident *m.*
incidental *adj* fortuit; **~ly** *adv* incidemment.
incinerator *n* incinérateur *m.*
incipient *adj* naissant.
incise *vt* inciser.
incision *n* incision *f.*
incisive *adj* incisif.
incisor *n* incisive *f.*
incite *vt* inciter, encourager.
inclement *adj* inclément.
inclination *n* inclination, propension *f.*
incline *vt* incliner; * *vi* s'incliner.
include *vt* inclure, comprendre.
including *prep* inclus, y compris.
inclusion *n* inclusion *f.*
inclusive *adj* inclus; tout compris.
incognito *adv* incognito.
incoherence *n* incohérence *f.*
incoherent *adj* incohérent; **~ly** *adv* d'une manière incohérente.

income *n* revenu *m*; recettes *fpl.*
income tax *n* impôt sur le revenu *m.*
incoming *adj* entrant; nouveau.
incomparable *adj* incomparable.
incomparably *adv* incomparablement.
incompatibility *n* incompatibilité *f.*
incompatible *adj* incompatible.
incompetence *n* incompétence *f.*
incompetent *adj* incompétent; **~ly** *adv* de manière incompétente.
incomplete *adj* incomplet.
incomprehensibility *n* incompréhensibilité *f.*
incomprehensible *adj* incompréhensible.
inconceivable *adj* inconcevable.
inconclusive *adj* peu concluant; * *adv* d'une manière peu concluante.
incongruity *n* incongruité *f.*
incongruous *adj* incongru; **~ly** *adv* incongrûment.
inconsequential *adj* inconséquent.
inconsiderate *adj* sans considération; inconsidéré; **~ly** *adv* sans considération.
inconsistency *n* inconsistance *f.*
inconsistent *adj* inconsistant.
inconsolable *adj* inconsolable.
inconspicuous *adj* discret.
incontinence *n* incontinence *f.*
incontinent *adj* incontinent.
incontrovertible *adj* indéniable.
inconvenience *n* inconvénient, désagrément *m*; * *vt* incommoder.
inconvenient *adj* incommode; **~ly** *adv* incommodément.
incorporate *vt* incorporer; * *vi* s'incorporer.
incorporated company *n* société constituée *f.*
incorporation *n* incorporation *f.*
incorrect *adj* incorrect, inexact; **~ly** *adv* incorrectement.
incorrigible *adj* incorrigible.
incorruptibility *n* incorruptibilité *f.*
incorruptible *adj* incorruptible.
increase *vt vi* augmenter; * *n* augmentation *f.*
increasing *adj* croissant; *adv* **~ly** de plus en plus.
incredible *adj* incroyable.
incredulity *n* incrédulité *f.*
incredulous *adj* incrédule.

increment n augmentation f.
incriminate vt incriminer.
incrust vt incruster.
incubate vi couver.
incubator n couveuse f.
inculcate vt inculquer.
incumbent adj en exercice; * n titulaire mf.
incur vt encourir.
incurability n incurabilité f.
incurable adj incurable.
incursion n incursion f.
indebted adj endetté; redevable.
indecency n indécence f.
indecent adj indécent; ~ly adv indécemment.
indecision n indécision, irrésolution f.
indecisive adj indécis, irrésolu.
indecorous adj inconvenant.
indeed adv vraiment.
indefatigable adj infatigable.
indefinite adj ~ly adv indéfini(ment).
indelible adj indélébile.
indelicacy n indélicatesse f.
indelicate adj peu délicat.
indemnify vt indemniser.
indemnity n indemnité f.
indent vt bosseler; renfoncer.
independence n indépendance f.
independent adj indépendant; ~ly adv indépendamment.
indescribable adj indescriptible.
indestructible adj indestructible.
indeterminate adj indéterminé.
index n (math) indice m; index m.
index card n fiche f.
indexed adj indexé.
index finger n index m.
indicate vt indiquer.
indication n indication f; indice m.
indicative adj n (gr) indicatif m.
indicator n indicateur m.
indict vt accuser.
indictment n accusation f.
indifference n indifférence f.
indifferent adj indifférent; ~ly adv indifféremment.
indigenous adj indigène.
indigent adj indigent.
indigestible adj indigeste.

indigestion n indigestion f.
indignant adj indigné.
indignation n indignation f.
indignity n indignité f.
indigo n indigo m.
indirect adj indirect; ~ly adv indirectement.
indiscreet adj indiscret; ~ly adv indiscrètement.
indiscretion n indiscrétion f.
indiscriminate adj ~ly adv sans discernement.
indispensable adj indispensable.
indisposed adj indisposé.
indisposition n indisposition f.
indisputable adj indiscutable.
indisputably adv indiscutablement.
indistinct adj indistinct, confus; ~ly adv indistinctement.
indistinguishable adj indiscernable.
individual adj ~ly adv individuel(lement); * n individu m.
individuality n individualité f.
indivisible adj ~bly adv indivisible(ment).
indoctrinate vt endoctriner.
indoctrination n endoctrinement m.
indolence n indolence f.
indolent adj indolent; ~ly adv indolemment.
indomitable adj indomptable.
indoors adv à l'intérieur.
indubitably adv indubitablement.
induce vt persuader; causer, provoquer.
inducement n encouragement m; incitation f.
induction n induction f.
indulge vt céder à; vi se permettre, se laisser aller.
indulgence n indulgence f.
indulgent adj indulgent; ~ly adv avec indulgence.
industrial adj industriel.
industrialist n industriel m.
industrialize vt industrialiser.
industrial park n zone industrielle f.
industrious adj travailleur.
industry n industrie f.
inebriated vt ivre.
inebriation n ivresse f.
inedible adj non comestible.
ineffable adj ineffable.

ineffective, ineffectual *adj* inefficace; **~ly** *adv* inefficacement.

inefficiency *n* inefficacité *f.*

inefficient *adj* inefficace.

ineligible *adj* inéligible.

inept *adj* inepte; déplacé.

ineptitude *n* ineptie *f*; manque d'à-propos *m.*

inequality *n* inégalité *f.*

inert *adj* inerte.

inertia *n* inertie *f.*

inescapable *adj* inévitable.

inestimable *adj* inestimable.

inevitable *adj* inévitable.

inevitably *adv* inévitablement.

inexcusable *adj* inexcusable.

inexhaustible *adj* inépuisable.

inexorable *adj* inexorable.

inexpedient *adj* imprudent, inopportun.

inexpensive *adj* bon marché.

inexperience *n* inexpérience *f.*

inexperienced *adj* inexpérimenté.

inexpert *adj* néophyte.

inexplicable *adj* inexplicable.

inexpressible *adj* indicible; inexprimable.

inextricably *adv* inextricablement.

infallibility *n* infaillibilité *f.*

infallible *adj* infaillible.

infamous *adj* vil, infâme; **~ly** *adv* vilement.

infamy *n* infamie *f.*

infancy *n* enfance *f.*

infant *n* bébé *m*; enfant *mf.*

infanticide *n* infanticide *mf.*

infantile *adj* infantile.

infantry *n* infanterie *f.*

infatuated *adj* fou.

infatuation *n* folie *f*; obsession *f.*

infect *vt* infecter.

infection *n* infection *f.*

infectious *adj* contagieux; infectieux.

infer *vt* inférer.

inference *n* inférence *f.*

inferior *adj* inférieur; * *n* subordonné *m* -e *f.*

inferiority *n* infériorité *f.*

infernal *adj* infernal.

inferno *n* enfer *m.*

infest *vt* infester.

infidel *n* infidèle *mf.*

infidelity *n* infidélité *f.*

infiltrate *vi* s'infiltrer.

infinite *adj* **~ly** *adv* infini(ment).

infinitive *n* (*gr*) infinitif *m.*

infinity *n* infini *m*; infinité *f.*

infirm *adj* infirme.

infirmary *n* infirmerie *f.*

infirmity *n* infirmité *f.*

inflame *vt* enflammer; * *vi* s'enflammer.

inflammation *n* inflammation *f.*

inflammatory *adj* inflammatoire.

inflatable *adj* gonflable.

inflate *vt* gonfler.

inflation *n* inflation *f.*

inflection *n* inflexion *f.*

inflexibility *n* inflexibilité *f.*

inflexible *adj* inflexible.

inflexibly *adv* inflexiblement.

inflict *vt* infliger.

influence *n* influence *f*; * *vt* influencer.

influential *adj* influent.

influenza *n* grippe *f.*

influx *n* afflux *m.*

inform *vt* informer.

informal *adj* informel; simple; familier.

informality *n* simplicité *f.*

informant *n* informateur *m* -trice *f*

information *n* information *f.*

infraction *n* infraction *f.*

infrared *adj* infrarouge.

infrastructure *n* infrastructure *f.*

infrequent *adj* **~ly** *adv* rare(ment).

infringe *vt* enfreindre.

infringement *n* infraction *f.*

infuriate *vt* rendre furieux.

infuse *vt* infuser.

infusion *n* infusion *f.*

ingenious *adj* ingénieux; **~ly** *adv* ingénieuse-ment.

ingenuity *n* ingéniosité *f.*

ingenuous *adj* **~ly** *adv* ingénu(ment); sin-cère(ment).

inglorious *adj* infamant; **~ly** *adv* honteuse-ment.

ingot *n* lingot *m.*

ingrained *adj* invétéré.

ingratiate *vi*: **~ with sb** chercher à entrer dans les bonnes grâces de qn.

ingratitude *n* ingratitude *f.*

ingredient n ingrédient m.
inhabit vt vi habiter.
inhabitable adj habitable.
inhabitant n habitant m -e f.
inhale vt inhaler.
inherent adj inhérent.
inherit vt hériter.
inheritance n héritage m.
inheritor n héritier m -ière f.
inhibit vt inhiber.
inhibited adj inhibé.
inhibition n inhibition f.
inhospitable adj inhospitalier.
inhospitality n inhospitalité f.
inhuman adj inhumain; ~ly adv inhumaine-
    ment.
inhumanity n inhumanité, cruauté f.
inimical adj hostile, ennemi.
inimitable adj inimitable.
iniquitous adj inique, injuste.
iniquity n iniquité, injustice f.
initial adj initial; * n initiale f.
initially adv au début.
initiate vt commencer; initier.
initiation n début, commencement m; initia-
    tion f.
initiative n initiative f.
inject vt injecter.
injection n injection f.
injudicious adj peu judicieux.
injunction n injonction f; ordre m.
injure vt blesser.
injury n blessure f; tort m.
injury time n arrêts de jeu mpl.
injustice n injustice f.
ink n encre f.
inkling n soupçon m.
inkstand n encrier m.
inlaid adj incrusté.
inland adj intérieur; * adv vers l'intérieur,
    dans les terres.
in-laws npl belle-famille f.
inlay vt incruster.
inlet n entrée f; bras de mer m.
inmate n détenu m -e f.
inmost adj le plus profond.
inn n auberge f; hôtel m.
innate adj inné.

inner adj intérieur.
innermost adj le plus profond.
inner tube n chambre à air f.
innkeeper n aubergiste mf, hôtelier m -ière f.
innocence n innocence f.
innocent adj innocent; ~ly adv innocem-
    ment.
innocuous adj inoffensif; ~ly adv de manière
    inoffensive.
innovate vt innover.
innovation n innovation f.
innuendo n allusion f; insinuation f.
innumerable adj innombrable.
inoculate vt inoculer.
inoculation n inoculation f.
inoffensive adj inoffensif.
inopportune adj inopportun.
inordinately adv démesurément.
inorganic adj inorganique.
in-patient n patient(e) hospitalisé(e) m(f).
input n entrée f; consommation f.
inquest n enquête f.
inquire vt vi demander; ~ about s'informer de;
    ~ after vt demander des nouvelles de; ~ into
    vt faire des recherches sur; enquêter sur.
inquiry n demande de renseignements f; en-
    quête f.
inquisition n investigation f.
inquisitive adj curieux.
inroad n incursion f.
insane adj fou, f folle.
insanity n folie f.
insatiable adj insatiable.
inscribe vt inscrire; dédier.
inscription n inscription f; dédicace f.
inscrutable adj impénétrable.
insect n insecte m.
insecticide n insecticide m.
insecure adj peu assuré.
insecurity n insécurité f.
insemination n insémination f.
insensible adj inconscient; insensible.
insensitive adj insensible.
inseparable adj inséparable.
insert vt introduire, insérer.
insertion n insertion f.
inshore adj côtier.
inside n intérieur m; * adv à l'intérieur.

inside out *adv* à l'envers; à fond.

insidious *adj* insidieux; **~ly** insidieusement.

insight *n* perspicacité *f*.

insignia *npl* insignes *mpl*.

insignificant *adj* insignifiant.

insincere *adj* peu sincère.

insincerity *n* manque de sincérité *m*.

insinuate *vt* insinuer.

insinuation *n* insinuation *f*.

insipid *adj* insipide.

insist *vi* insister.

insistence *n* insistance *f*.

insistent *adj* insistant.

insole *n* semelle intérieure *f*.

insolence *n* insolence *f*.

insolent *adj* insolent; **~ly** *adv* insolemment.

insoluble *adj* insoluble.

insolvency *n* insolvabilité *f*.

insolvent *adj* insolvable.

insomnia *n* insomnie *f*.

insomuch *conj* à tel point.

inspect *vt* examiner, inspecter.

inspection *n* inspection *f*.

inspector *n* inspecteur *m* -trice *f*.

inspiration *n* inspiration *f*.

inspire *vt* inspirer.

instability *n* instabilité *f*.

instal *vt* installer.

installation *n* installation *f*.

instalment *n* installation *f*; versement *m*.

instalment plan *n* plan de vente à tempérament *m*.

instance *n* exemple *m*; for ~ par exemple.

instant *adj* instantané; **~ly** *adv* immédiatement; * *n* instant, moment *m*.

instantaneous *adj* **~ly** *adv* instantané(ment).

instead (of) *pr* au lieu, à la place (de).

instep *n* cou-de-pied *m*.

instigate *vt* inciter; susciter.

instigation *n* incitation *f*.

instil *vt* instiller; inspirer.

instinct *n* instinct *m*.

instinctive *adj* instinctif; **~ly** *adv* instinctivement, d'instinct.

institute *vt* instituer; * *n* institut *m*.

institution *n* institution *f*.

instruct *vt* instruire.

instruction *n* instruction *f*.

instructive *adj* instructif.

instructor *n* professeur *m*; moniteur *m* -trice *f*.

instrument *n* instrument *m*.

instrumental *adj* instrumental.

insubordinate *adj* insubordonné.

insubordination *n* insubordination *f*.

insufferable *adj* insupportable.

insufferably *adv* insupportablement.

insufficiency *n* insuffisance *f*.

insufficient *adj* insuffisant; **~ly** *adv* insuffisamment.

insular *adj* insulaire; borné.

insulate *vt* isoler; insonoriser.

insulating tape *n* ruban isolant *m*.

insulation *n* isolation *f*; insonorisation *f*.

insulin *n* insuline *f*.

insult *vt* insulter; * *n* insulte *f*.

insulting *adj* insultant.

insuperable *adj* insurmontable.

insurance *n* (*com*) assurance *f*.

insurance policy *n* police d'assurance *f*.

insure *vt* assurer.

insurgent *n* insurgé, rebelle *m*.

insurmountable *adj* insurmontable.

insurrection *n* insurrection *f*.

intact *adj* intact.

intake *n* admission *f*; consommation *f*.

integral *adj* intégrant; (*chem*) intégral; * *n* intégrale *f*.

integrate *vt* intégrer.

integration *n* intégration *f*.

integrity *n* intégrité *f*.

intellect *n* intellect *m*.

intellectual *adj* intellectuel.

intelligence *n* intelligence *f*.

intelligent *adj* intelligent.

intelligentsia *n* intelligentsia *f*.

intelligible *adj* intelligible.

intelligibly *adv* intelligiblement.

intemperate *adj* **~ly** *adv* immodéré(ment).

intend *vt* avoir l'intention de.

intendant *n* intendant *m* -e *f*.

intended *adj* voulu.

intense *adj* intense; **~ly** *adv* intensément.

intensify *vt* intensifier.

intensity *n* intensité *f*.

intensive *adj* intensif.

intensive care unit *n* service de soins intensifs *m*.

intent *adj* résolu; attentif; **~ly** *adv* attentivement; * *n* intention *f*, dessein *m*.

intention *n* intention *f*, dessein *m*.

intentional *adj* intentionnel; **~ly** *adv* à dessein, intentionnellement.

inter *vt* enterrer.

interaction *n* interaction *f*.

intercede *vi* intercéder.

intercept *vt* intercepter.

intercession *n* intercession *f*.

interchange *n* échange *m*.

intercom *n* interphone *m*.

intercourse *n* relations sexuelles *fpl*.

interest *vt* intéresser; * *n* intérêt *m*.

interesting *adj* intéressant.

interest rate *n* taux d'intérêt *m*.

interfere *vi* s'ingérer.

interference *n* ingérence *f*; interférence *f*.

interim *adj* intérimaire.

interior *adj* intérieur.

interior designer *n* d(écorateur(-trice) d'intérieur *m(f)*.

interjection *n* (*gr*) interjection *f*.

interlock *vi* s'entremêler.

interlocutor *n* interlocuteur *m* -trice *f*.

interloper *n* intrus *m* -e *f*.

interlude *n* intermède *m*.

intermarriage *n* intermariage *m*.

intermediary *n* intermédiaire *mf*.

intermediate *adj* intermédiaire.

interment *n* enterrement *m*.

interminable *adj* interminable.

intermingle *vt* entremêler; * *vi* s'entremêler.

intermission *n* entracte *m*; interruption *f*.

intermittent *adj* intermittent.

intern *n* interne *mf*.

internal *adj* intérieur; interne; **~ly** *adv* intérieurement.

international *adj* international.

interplay *n* interaction *f*.

interpose *vt* interposer.

interpret *vt* interpréter.

interpretation *n* interprétation *f*.

interpreter *n* interprète *mf*.

interregnum *n* interrègne *m*.

interrelated *adj* en corrélation.

interrogate *vt* interroger.

interrogation *n* interrogatoire *m*.

interrogative *adj* interrogatif.

interrupt *vt* interrompre.

interruption *n* interruption *f*.

intersect *vi* se croiser.

intersection *n* croisement *m*.

intersperse *vt* parsemer.

intertwine *vt* entrelacer.

interval *n* intervalle *m*; mi-temps *f*.

intervene *vi* intervenir.

intervention *n* intervention *f*.

interview *n* entrevue *f*; interview *f*; * *vt* faire passer une entrevue à; interviewer.

interviewer *n* interviewer *m*.

interweave *vt* entrelacer.

intestate *adj* intestat.

intestinal *adj* intestinal.

intestine *n* intestin *m*.

intimacy *n* intimité *f*.

intimate *n* intime *mf*; * *adj* **~ly** *adv* intime(ment); * *vt* insinuer, laisser entendre.

intimidate *vt* intimider.

into *prep* dans, en.

intolerable *adj* intolérable.

intolerably *adv* intolérablement.

intolerance *n* intolérance *f*.

intolerant *adj* intolérant.

intonation *n* intonation *f*.

intoxicate *vt* enivrer.

intoxication *n* ivresse *f*.

intractable *adj* intraitable.

intransitive *adj* (*gr*) intransitif.

intravenous *adj* intraveineux.

in-tray *n* courrier à l'arrivée *m*.

intrepid *adj* intrépide; **~ly** *adv* intrépidement.

intrepidity *n* intrépidité *f*.

intricacy *n* complexité *f*.

intricate *adj* complexe, compliqué; **~ly** *adv* de manière compliquée.

intrigue *n* intrigue *f*; * *vi* intriguer.

intriguing *adj* intrigant.

intrinsic *adj* **~ally** *adv* intrinsèque(ment).

introduce *vt* introduire.

introduction *n* introduction *f*.

introductory *adj* d'introduction.

introspection *n* introspection *f*.

introvert *n* introverti *m* -ie *f*.

intrude *vi* s'ingérer, s'immiscer.

intruder *n* intrus *m* -e *f*.

intrusion *n* intrusion *f*.

intuition *n* intuition *f*.

intuitive *adj* intuitif.

inundate *vt* inonder.

inundation *n* inondation *f*.

inure *vt* endurcir.

invade *vt* envahir.

invader *n* envahisseur *m* -euse *f*.

invalid *adj* invalide; * *n* invalide *mf*.

invalidate *vt* invalider, annuler.

invaluable *adj* inappréciable.

invariable *adj* invariable.

invariably *adv* invariablement.

invasion *n* invasion *f*.

invective *n* invective *f*.

inveigle *vt* persuader, entraîner.

invent *vt* inventer.

invention *n* invention *f*.

inventive *adj* inventif.

inventor *n* inventeur *m* -trice *f*.

inventory *n* inventaire *m*.

inverse *adj* inverse.

inversion *n* inversion *f*.

invert *vt* inverser.

invest *vt* investir.

investigate *vt* faire des recherches sur; examiner.

investigation *n* investigation *f*; recherches *fpl*.

investigator *n* investigateur *m* -trice *f*; chercheur *m* -euse *f*.

investment *n* investissement *m*.

inveterate *adj* invétéré.

invidious *adj* odieux; désobligeant.

invigilate *vt* surveiller.

invigorating *adj* vivifiant.

invincible *adj* invincible.

invincibly *adv* invinciblement.

inviolable *adj* inviolable.

invisible *adj* invisible.

invisibly *adv* invisiblement.

invitation *n* invitation *f*.

invite *vt* inviter.

inviting *adj* attrayant, tentant.

invoice *n* (*com*) facture *f*.

invoke *vt* invoquer.

involuntarily *adv* involontairement.

involuntary *adj* involontaire.

involve *vt* impliquer, entraîner.

involved *adj* compliqué; impliqué.

involvement *n* implication *f*; confusion *f*.

invulnerable *adj* invulnérable.

inward *adj* intérieur; intime; ~, ~s *adv* vers l'intérieur.

iodine *n* (*chem*) iode *m*.

IOU (I owe you) *n* reçu *m*.

irascible *adj* irascible.

irate, ireful *adj* irrité.

iris *n* iris *m*.

irksome *adj* fastidieux, ennuyeux.

iron *n* fer *m*; * *adj* de fer; * *vt* repasser.

ironic *adj* ~ally *adv* ironique(ment).

ironing *n* repassage *m*.

ironing board *n* table *f* à repasser.

iron ore *n* minerai de fer *m*.

ironwork *n* ferronnerie *f*; ~s *pl* ferronneries *fpl*.

irony *n* ironie *f*.

irradiate *vt* irradier.

irrational *adj* irrationnel.

irreconcilable *adj* irréconciliable; inconciliable.

irregular *adj* irrégulier; ~ly *adv* irrégulièrement.

irregularity *n* irrégularité *f*.

irrelevant *adj* hors de propos.

irreligious *adj* irréligieux.

irreparable *adj* irréparable.

irreplaceable *adj* irremplaçable.

irrepressible *adj* irrépressible.

irreproachable *adj* irréprochable.

irresistible *adj* irrésistible.

irresolute *adj* ~ly *adv* irrésolu(ment).

irresponsible *adj* irresponsable.

irretrievably *adv* irréparablement.

irreverence *n* irrévérence *f*.

irreverent *adj* irrévérencieux; ~ly *adv* irrévérencieusement.

irrigate *vt* irriguer.

irrigation *n* irrigation *f*.

irritability *n* irritabilité *f*.

irritable *adj* irritable.

irritant *n* (*med*) irritant *m*.

irritate *vt* irriter.

irritating *adj* irritant.

irritation *n* irritation *f*.

Islam *n* Islam *m*.
island *n* île *f*.
islander *n* insulaire *mf*.
isle *n* île *f*.
isolate *vt* isoler.
isolation *n* isolement *m*.
issue *n* sujet *m*, question *f*; * *vt* publier; distribuer; fournir.
isthmus *n* isthme *m*.
it *pn* il, elle; le, la; cela, ça, ce, c'.
italic *n* italique *m*.

itch *n* démangeaison *f*; * *vi* avoir des démangeaisons.
item *n* article *m*.
itemize *vt* détailler.
itinerant *adj* ambulant, itinérant.
itinerary *n* itinéraire *m*.
its *pn* son, sa, ses.
itself *pn* lui-même, elle-même.
ivory *n* ivoire *m*.
ivy *n* lierre *m*.

J

jab *vt* planter, enfoncer.
jabber *vi* baragouiner.
jack *n* cric *m*; valet *m*.
jackal *n* chacal *m*.
jackboots *npl* bottes de militaire *fpl*.
jackdaw *n* choucas *m*.
jacket *n* veste *f*; couverture *f*.
jackknife *vi* se mettre en travers.
jack plug *n* prise à fiche *f*.
jackpot *n* gros lot *m*.
jade *n* jade *m*.
jagged *adj* dentelé.
jaguar *n* jaguar *m*.
jail *n* prison *f*.
jailbird *n* prisonnier *m* -ière *f*.
jailer *n* geôlier *m* -ière *f*.
jam *n* confiture *f*; embouteillage *m*.
jangle *vi* cliqueter.
janitor *n* portier *m*.
January *n* janvier *m*.
jar *vi* se heurter; (*mus*) détonner; grincer; * *n* pot *m*.
jargon *n* jargon *m*.
jasmine *n* jasmin *m*.
jaundice *n* jaunisse *f*.
jaunt *n* promenade *f*.
jaunty *adj* enjoué.
javelin *n* javelot *m*.
jaw *n* mâchoire *f*.
jay *n* geai *m*.
jealous *adj* jaloux.
jealousy *n* jalousie *f*.
jeans *npl* jean *m*.

jeer *vi* se moquer, railler; * *n* raillerie, moquerie *f*.
jelly *n* gelée *f*.
jellyfish *n* méduse *f*.
jeopardize *vt* risquer, mettre en péril.
jerk *n* secousse *f*; * *vt* donner une secousse à.
jerky *adj* saccadé.
jersey *n* jersey *m*, tricot *m*.
jest *n* blague, plaisanterie *f*.
jester *n* bouffon *m*.
jestingly *adv* en plaisantant.
Jesuit *n* jésuite *m*.
Jesus *n* Jésus *m*.
jet *n* avion à réaction *m*; jet *m*; gicleur *m*.
jet engine *n* moteur à réaction *m*.
jettison *vt* se défaire de.
jetty *n* jetée *f*.
Jew *n* Juif *m*.
jewel *n* bijou *m*.
jeweller *n* bijoutier *m* -ière *f*.
jewellery *n* bijoux *mpl*.
jewellery store *n* bijouterie *f*.
Jewess *n* Juive *f*.
Jewish *adj* juif.
jib *n* (*mar*) foc *m*.
jibe *n* raillerie, moquerie *f*.
jig *n* gigue *f*.
jigsaw *n* puzzle *m*.
jilt *vt* laisser tomber.
jinx *n* porte-malheur *m invar*.
job *n* travail *m*.
jockey *n* jockey *m*.
jocular *adj* joyeux; facétieux.

jog *vi* faire du jogging.

join *vt* joindre, unir; ~ **in** participer à; * *vi* se réunir; se joindre.

joiner *n* menuisier *m*.

joinery *n* menuiserie *f*.

joint *n* articulation *f*; * *adj* commun.

jointly *adv* conjointement.

joint-stock company *n* (*com*) société par actions *f*.

joke *n* blague, plaisanterie *f*; * *vi* blaguer, plaisanter.

joker *n* blagueur *m* -euse *f*.

jollity *n* gaieté *f*.

jolly *adj* gai, joyeux.

jolt *vt* secouer; * *n* secousse *f*.

jostle *vt* bousculer.

journal *n* revue *f*.

journalism *n* journalisme *m*.

journalist *n* journaliste *mf*.

journey *n* voyage *m*; * *vi* voyager.

jovial *adj* jovial, gai; ~**ly** *adv* jovialement.

joy *n* joie *f*.

joyful, joyous *adj* joyeux, gai; ~**ly** *adv* joyeusement.

joystick *n* manche à balai *m*.

jubilant *adj* réjoui.

jubilation *n* jubilation *f*.

jubilee *n* jubilé *m*.

Judaism *n* judaïsme *m*.

judge *n* juge *m*; * *vt* juger.

judgment *n* jugement *m*.

judicial *adj* ~**ly** *adv* judiciaire(ment).

judiciary *n* pouvoir judiciaire *m*.

judicious *adj* judicieux.

judo *n* judo *m*.

jug *n* cruche *f*.

juggle *vi* jongler.

juggler *n* jongleur *m* -euse *f*.

juice *n* jus *m*; suc *m*.

juicy *adj* juteux.

jukebox *n* juke-box *m*.

July *n* juillet *m*.

jumble *vt* mélanger; * *n* mélange *m*; fouillis *m*.

jump *vi* sauter; * *n* saut *m*.

jumper *n* pull *m*; sauteur *m* -euse *f*.

jumpy *adj* nerveux.

juncture *n* joncture *f*.

June *n* juin *m*.

jungle *n* jungle *f*.

junior *adj* plus jeune.

juniper *n* (*bot*) genièvre *m*.

junk *n* cochonnerie *f*; bric-à-brac *m invar*.

junta *n* junte *f*.

jurisdiction *n* juridiction *f*.

jurisprudence *n* jurisprudence *f*.

jurist *n* juriste *mf*.

juror, juryman *n* juré *m*.

jury *n* jury *m*.

just *adj* juste; * *adv* justement, exactement; ~ **as** juste quand; ~ **now** tout de suite.

justice *n* justice *f*.

justifiably *adv* légitimement.

justification *n* justification *f*.

justify *vt* justifier.

justly *adv* justement.

justness *n* justesse *f*.

jut *vi*: **to** ~ **out** faire saillie, dépasser.

jute *n* jute *m*.

juvenile *adj* juvénile; pour enfants.

juxtaposition *n* juxtaposition *f*.

K

kaleidoscope *n* kaléidoscope *m*.

kangaroo *n* kangourou *m*.

karate *n* karaté *m*.

kebab *n* brochette *f*.

keel *n* (*mar*) quille *f*.

keen *adj* aiguisé; vif; enthousiaste.

keenness *n* enthousiasme *m*.

keep *vt* garder, conserver; tenir.

keeper *n* gardien *m* -ne *f*.

keepsake *n* souvenir *m*.

keg *n* baril *m*.

kennel *n* niche *f*.

kernel *n* amande *f*; noyau *m*.

kerosene *n* kérosène *m*.

kettle *n* bouilloire *f*.

kettledrum n timbale *f*.

key *n* clé, clef *f*; (*mus*) ton *m*; touche *f*.

keyboard *n* clavier *m*.

keyhole n trou de la serrure m.
keynote n (mus) tonique f.
key ring n porte-clefs m invar.
keystone n clef de voûte f.
khaki n kaki m.
kick vi (vt) donner un coup de pied (à); * n coup de pied m; plaisir m.
kid n gamin m -e f.
kidnap vt kidnapper.
kidnapper n kidnappeur m -euse f.
kidnapping n kidnapping m.
kidney n rein m; rognon m.
killer n assassin m.
killing n assassinat m.
kiln n four m.
kilo n kilo m.
kilobyte n kilo-octet m.
kilogram n kilogramme m.
kilometre n kilomètre m.
kin n parents mpl; **next of ~** parent proche m.
kind adj gentil; * n genre m, sorte f.
kindergarten n jardin d'enfants m.
kind-hearted adj bon.
kindle vt allumer; * vi s'allumer.
kindliness n gentillesse, bonté f.
kindly adj bon, bienveillant.
kindness n bonté f.
kindred adj apparenté.
kinetic adj cinétique.
king n roi m.
kingdom n royaume m.
kingfisher n martin-pêcheur m.
kiosk n kiosque m.
kiss n baiser m; * vt embrasser.
kissing n baisers mpl.
kit n équipement m.

kitchen n cuisine f.
kitchen garden n potager m.
kite n cerf-volant m.
kitten n chaton m.
knack n don, chic m.
knapsack n sac à dos m.
knave n fripouille f; (cards) valet m.
knead vt pétrir.
knee n genou m.
knee-deep adj jusqu'aux genoux.
kneel vi s'agenouiller.
knell n glas m.
knife n couteau m.
knight n chevalier m.
knit vt vi tricoter; **~ the brows** froncer les sourcils.
knitter n tricoteur m -euse f.
knitting pin n aiguille à tricoter f.
knitwear n tricots mpl.
knob n bouton m; nœud m (du bois).
knock vt vi cogner, frapper; **~ down** abattre; * n coup m.
knocker n heurtoir m.
knock-kneed adj aux genoux cagneux.
knock-out n knock-out m.
knoll n butte f.
knot n nœud m; * vt nouer.
knotty adj emmêlé; épineux.
know vt vi savoir; connaître.
know-all n je-sais-tout m.
know-how n savoir-faire m.
knowing adj entendu; **~ly** adv en connaissance de cause.
knowledge n connaissances fpl.
knowledgeable adj bien informé.
knuckle n articulation f.

L

label n étiquette f.
laboratory n laboratoire m.
laborious adj laborieux; pénible; **~ly** adv laborieusement.
labour n travail m; **to be in ~** être en train d'accoucher; * vi travailler.
labourer n ouvrier m.
labour union n syndicat m.

labyrinth n labyrinthe m.
lace n lacet m; dentelle f; * vt lacer.
lacerate vt lacérer.
lack vt manquer de; * vi manquer; * n manque m.
lackadaisical adj nonchalant.
lackey n laquais m.
laconic adj laconique.

lacquer *n* laque *f*.

lad *n* garçon *m*.

ladder *n* échelle *f*.

ladle *n* louche *f*.

ladleful *n* louchée *f*.

lady *n* dame *f*.

ladybird *n* coccinelle *f*.

ladykiller *n* bourreau des cœurs *m*.

ladylike *adj* distingué.

ladyship *n* madame *f*.

lag *vi* se laisser distancer.

lager *n* bière blonde *f*.

lagoon *n* lagune *f*.

laidback *adj* décontracté.

lair *n* repaire *m*.

laity *n* laïcat *m*.

lake *n* lac *m*.

lamb *n* agneau *m*; * *vi* agneler.

lambswool *n* laine d'agneau *f*.

lame *adj* boiteux.

lament *vt* se lamenter sur; * *vi* se lamenter; * *n* lamentation *f*.

lamentable *adj* lamentable, déplorable.

lamentation *n* lamentation *f*.

laminated *adj* laminé.

lamp *n* lampe *f*.

lampoon *n* satire *f*.

lampshade *n* abat-jour *m invar*.

lance *n* lance *f*; bistouri *m*; * *vt* inciser.

lancet *n* bistouri *m*.

land *n* pays *m*; terre *f*; * *vt* débarquer; * *vi* atterrir, débarquer.

land forces *npl* armée de terre *f*.

landholder *n* propriétaire terrien *m*.

landing *n* atterrissage *m*.

landing strip *n* piste d'atterrissage *f*.

landlady *n* propriétaire *f*.

landlord *n* propriétaire *m*.

landlubber *n* marin d'eau douce *m*.

landmark *n* point de repère *m*.

landowner *n* propriétaire terrien *m*.

landscape *n* paysage *m*.

landslide *n* glissement de terrain *m*.

lane *n* allée, ruelle *f*; file *f*.

language *n* langue *f*; langage *m*.

languid *adj* languissant; **~ly** *adv* languissamment.

languish *vi* languir.

lank *adj* raide, plat.

lanky *adj* grand et maigre.

lantern *n* lanterne *f*.

lap *n* genoux *mpl*; * *vt* laper.

lapdog *n* chien *m* de salon.

lapel *n* revers *m*.

lapse *n* laps *m*; défaillance *f*; * *vi* expirer, se périmer; se relâcher.

larceny *n* vol *m*.

larch *n* mélèze *m*.

lard *n* saindoux *m*.

larder *n* garde-manger *m invar*.

large *adj* grand; **at ~** en liberté; **~ly** *adv* en grande partie.

large-scale *adj* à grande échelle.

largesse *n* largesse *f*.

lark *n* alouette *f*.

larva *n* larve *f*.

laryngitis *n* laryngite *f*.

larynx *n* larynx *m*.

lascivious *adj* lascif; **~ly** *adv* lascivement.

laser *n* laser *m*.

lash *n* coup de fouet *m*; * *vt* fouetter; attacher.

lasso *n* lasso *m*.

last *adj* dernier; **at ~** enfin; **~ly** *adv* finalement; * *n* dernier *m*, dernière *f*; forme *f* (de cordonnier); * *vi* durer.

last-ditch *adj* ultime.

lasting *adj* **~ly** *adv* durable(ment).

last-minute *adj* de dernière minute.

latch *n* loquet *m*.

latchkey *n* clef de porte d'entrée *f*.

late *adj* en retard; défunt; (*rail*) **the train is ten minutes ~** le train a dix minutes de retard; * *adv* tard; **~ly** *adv* récemment.

latecomer *n* retardataire *mf*.

latent *adj* latent.

lateral *adj* **~ly** *adv* latérale(ment).

lathe *n* tour *m*.

lather *n* mousse *f*.

latitude *n* latitude *f*.

latrine *n* latrine *f*.

latter *adj* dernier; **~ly** *adv* récemment.

lattice *n* treillis *m*.

laudable *adj* louable.

laudably *adv* louablement.

laugh *vi* rire; **~ at** *vt* rire de, se moquer de; * *n* rire *m*.

laughable *adj* risible; dérisoire.
laughing stock *n* risée *f.*
laughter *n* rires *mpl.*
launch *vt* lancer; * *vi* se lancer; * *n* (*mar*) vedette *f.*
launching *n* lancement *m.*
launching pad *n* rampe de lancement *f.*
launder *vt* laver.
laundrette, laundromat *n* laverie automatique *f.*
laundry *n* lessive *f.*
laurel *n* laurier *m.*
lava *n* lave *f.*
lavatory *n* toilettes *fpl.*
lavender *n* (*bot*) lavande *f.*
lavish *adj* prodigue; **~ly** *adv* avec prodigalité; * *vt* prodiguer.
law *n* loi *f*; droit *m.*
law-abiding *adj* respectueux de la loi.
law and order *n* ordre public *m.*
law court *n* tribunal *m.*
lawful *adj* légal; légitime; **~ly** *adv* légalement.
lawless *adj* anarchique.
lawlessness *n* anarchie *f.*
lawmaker *n* législateur *m* -trice *f.*
lawn *n* pelouse *f*, gazon *m.*
lawnmower *n* tondeuse à gazon *f.*
law school *n* faculté de droit *f.*
law suit *n* procès *m.*
lawyer *n* avocat *m*; juriste *m.*
lax *adj* relâché.
laxative *n* laxatif *m.*
laxity *n* relâchement *m*; flou *m.*
lay *vt* coucher; mettre; pondre; **~ claim** réclamer; prétendre (à); * *vi* pondre.
layabout *n* paresseux *m* -euse *f.*
layer *n* couche *f.*
layette *n* layette *f.*
layman *n* laïc *m.*
layout *n* disposition *f*; présentation *f.*
laze *vi* paresser.
lazily *adv* paresseusement.
laziness *n* paresse *f.*
lazy *adj* paresseux.
lead *n* plomb *m*; * *vt* *vi* conduire, mener.
leader *n* chef *m.*
leadership *n* direction *f.*

leading *adj* principal; premier; ~ **article** *n* article de fond *m.*
leaf *n* feuille *f.*
leaflet *n* feuillet *m*; prospectus *m.*
leafy *adj* feuillu.
league *n* ligue *f*; lieue *f.*
leak *n* fuite *f*; * *vi* (*mar*) faire eau.
leaky *adj* qui fuit.
lean *vt* appuyer; * *vi* s'appuyer; * *adj* maigre.
leap *vi* sauter; * *n* saut *m.*
leapfrog *n* saute-mouton *m.*
leap year *n* année bisextile *f.*
learn *vt* *vi* apprendre.
learned *adj* instruit.
learner *n* élève *mf*; débutant *m* -e *f.*
learning *n* érudition *f.*
lease *n* bail *m*; * *vt* louer.
leasehold *n* bail *m.*
leash *n* laisse *f.*
least *adj* moindre; **at** ~ au moins; **not in the** ~ pas du tout.
leather *n* cuir *m.*
leathery *adj* qui a l'aspect du cuir.
leave *n* permission *f*; congé *m*; **to take** ~ prendre congé; * *vt* laisser.
leaven *n* levain *m*; * *vt* faire lever.
leavings *npl* restes *mpl.*
lecherous *adj* lascif, lubrique.
lecture *n* conférence *f*; * *vi* faire une conférence.
lecturer *n* conférencier *m* -ière *f.*
ledge *n* rebord *m.*
ledger *n* (*com*) registre *m.*
lee *n* (*mar*) côté sous le vent *m.*
leech *n* sangsue *f.*
leek *n* (*bot*) poireau *m.*
leer *vt* regarder d'un œil lascif.
lees *npl* lie *f.*
leeward *adj* (*mar*) sous le vent.
leeway *n* liberté d'action *f.*
left *adj* gauche; **on the** ~ à gauche.
left-handed *adj* gaucher.
left-luggage office *n* consigne *f.*
leftovers *npl* restes *mpl.*
leg *n* jambe *f*; patte *f.*
legacy *n* héritage, legs *m.*
legal *adj* légal, légitime; **~ly** *adv* légalement.
legal holiday *n* jour férié *m.*

legality n légalité, légitimité f.
legalize vt légaliser.
legal tender n monnaie légale f.
legate n légat m.
legatee n légataire mf.
legation n légation f.
legend n légende f.
legendary adj légendaire.
legible adj lisible.
legibly adv lisiblement.
legion n légion f.
legislate vt vi légiférer.
legislation n législation f.
legislative adj législatif.
legislator n législateur m -trice f.
legislature n corps législatif m.
legitimacy n légitimité f.
legitimate adj légitime; ~**ly** adv légitimement; * vt légitimer.
leisure n loisir m; ~**ly** adj tranquille; **at ~** au calme.
lemon n citron m.
lemonade n limonade f.
lemon tea n thé au citron m.
lemon tree n citronnier m.
lend vt prêter.
length n longueur f; durée f; **at ~** longuement; enfin.
lengthen vt allonger; * vi s'allonger.
lengthways, lengthwise adv dans le sens de la longueur.
lengthy adj long.
lenient adj indulgent.
lens n lentille f (optique).
Lent n Carême m.
lentil n lentille f.
Leo n Lion m (signe du zodiaque).
leopard n léopard m.
leotard n justaucorps m.
leper n lépreux m -euse f.
leprosy n lèpre f.
lesbian n lesbienne f.
less adj moins; * adv moins.
lessen vt vi diminuer.
lesser adj moindre.
lesson n leçon f.
lest conj de crainte que.
let vt laisser, permettre; louer.

lethal adj mortel.
lethargic adj léthargique.
lethargy n léthargie f.
letter n lettre f.
letter bomb n lettre piégée f.
letter box boite aux lettres f.
lettering n inscription f.
letter of credit n lettre de crédit f.
lettuce n salade f.
leukaemia n leucémie f.
level adj plat, égal; à niveau; * n niveau m; * vt niveler.
level-headed adj sensé.
lever n levier m.
leverage n effet de levier m; prise f.
levity n légèreté f.
levy n levée f; prélèvement m; * vt prélever.
lewd adj obscène.
lexicon n lexique m.
liability n responsabilité f.
liable adj sujet (à); responsable.
liaise vi effectuer une liaison.
liaison n liaison f.
liar n menteur m -euse f.
libel n diffamation f; * vt diffamer.
libellous adj diffamatoire.
liberal adj libéral; généreux; ~**ly** adv libéralement.
liberality n libéralité, générosité f.
liberate vt libérer.
liberation n libération f.
libertine n libertin m -e f.
liberty n liberté f.
Libra n Balance f (signe du zodiaque).
librarian n bibliothécaire mf.
library n bibliothèque f.
libretto n livret m.
licence n licence f; permis m; permission f.
licentious adj licencieux.
lichen n (bot) lichen m.
lick vt lécher.
lid n couvercle m.
lie n mensonge m; * vi mentir; être allongé.
lieu n: **in ~ of** au lieu de.
lieutenant n lieutenant m.
life n vie f; **for ~** pour toute la vie.
life belt n gilet de sauvetage m.
lifeboat n canot de sauvetage m.

lifeguard n maître nageur m; garde du corps m.

life jacket n gilet de sauvetage m.

lifeless adj mort; sans vie.

lifelike adj naturel.

lifeline n bouée de sauvetage f.

life sentence n condamnation à perpétuité f.

life-sized adj grandeur nature.

lifespan n durée de vie f.

lifestyle n style de vie m.

life-support system n système de respiration artificielle m.

lifetime n vie f.

lift vt lever.

ligament n ligament m.

light n lumière f; * adj léger; clair; * vt allumer; éclairer.

light bulb n ampoule f.

lighten vi s'éclaircir; * vt éclairer; éclaircir; alléger.

lighter n briquet m.

light-headed adj étourdi.

lighthearted adj joyeux.

lighthouse n (mar) phare m.

lighting n éclairage m.

lightly adv légèrement.

lightning n éclair m.

lightning rod n paratonnerre m.

light pen n crayon optique m.

lightweight adj léger.

light year n année-lumière f.

ligneous adj ligneux.

like adj pareil; * adv comme; * vt vi aimer.

likeable adj sympathique.

likelihood n probabilité f.

likely adj probable, vraisemblable.

liken vt comparer.

likeness n ressemblance f.

likewise adv pareillement.

liking n goût m.

lilac n lilas m.

lily n lis m; ~ **of the valley** muguet m.

limb n membre m.

limber adj flexible, souple.

lime n chaux f; lime f; ~ **tree** tilleul m.

limestone n pierre à chaux f.

limit n limite f; * vt limiter.

limitation n limitation f; restriction f.

limitless adj illimité.

limo(usine) n limousine f.

limp vi boiter; * n boitement m; * adj mou.

limpet n patelle f.

limpid adj limpide.

line n ligne f; ride f; * vt rayer; rider.

lineage n lignage m.

linear adj linéaire.

lined adj rayé; ridé.

linen n lin m; linge m de maison.

liner n transatlantique m.

linesman n juge de ligne m.

linger vi traîner.

lingerie n lingerie f.

lingering adj long.

linguist n linguiste mf.

linguistic adj linguistique.

linguistics n linguistique f.

liniment n liniment m.

lining n doublure f.

link n chaînon m; * vt relier.

linnet n linotte f.

linoleum n linoléum m.

linseed n graine de lin f.

lint n peluche f.

lintel n linteau m.

lion n lion m.

lioness n lionne f.

lip n lèvre f; bord m.

lip-read vi lire sur les lèvres.

lip salve n pommade pour les lèvres f.

lipstick n rouge à lèvres m.

liqueur n liqueur f.

liquid adj liquide; * n liquide m.

liquidate vt liquider.

liquidation n liquidation f.

liquidize vt liquéfier.

liquor n spiritueux m.

liquorice n réglisse m/f.

liquor store n magasin de vins et spiritueux m.

lisp vi zézayer; * n zézaiement m.

list n liste f; * vt faire une liste de.

listen vi écouter.

listless adj indifférent.

litany n litanie f.

literal adj ~**ly** adv littéral(ement).

literary adj littéraire.

literate *adj* cultivé.

literature *n* littérature *f*.

lithe *adj* agile.

lithograph *n* lithographie *f*.

lithography *n* lithographie *f*.

litigation *n* litige *m*.

litigious *adj* litigieux.

litre *n* litre *m*.

litter *n* litière *f*; ordures *fpl*; * *vt* recouvrir, joncher.

little *adj* petit; ~ **by** ~ petit à petit; * *n* peu *m*.

liturgy *n* liturgie *f*.

live *vi* vivre; habiter; ~ **on** *vt* se nourrir de; ~ **up to** *vt* faire honneur à; * *adj* vivant.

livelihood *n* moyens de subsistance *mpl*.

liveliness *n* vivacité *f*.

lively *adj* vif.

liven up *vt* animer.

liver *n* foie *m*.

livery *n* livrée *f*.

livestock *n* bétail *m*.

livid *adj* livide; furieux.

living *n* vie *f*; * *adj* vivant.

living room *n* salle de séjour *f*.

lizard *n* lézard *m*.

load *vt* charger; * *n* charge *f*.

loaded *adj* chargé.

loaf *n* pain *m*.

loafer *n* paresseux *m* -euse *f*.

loam *n* terreau *m*.

loan *n* prêt *m*.

loathe *vt* détester.

loathing *n* aversion *f*.

loathsome *adj* répugnant.

lobby *n* vestibule *m*.

lobe *n* lobe *m*.

lobster *n* langouste *f*.

local *adj* local.

local anaesthetic *n* anesthésique local *m*.

local government *n* administration *f* municipale, administration *f* locale.

locality *n* localité *f*.

localize *vt* localiser.

locally *adv* localement.

locate *vt* localiser.

location *n* situation *f*.

lock *n* serrure *f*; * *vt* fermer à clé.

locker *n* casier *m*.

locket *n* médaillon *m*.

lockout *n* grève patronale *f*.

locksmith *n* serrurier *m*.

lock-up *n* cellule *f*.

locomotive *n* locomotive *f*.

locust *n* sauterelle *f*.

lodge *n* loge du gardien *f*; * *vi* se loger.

lodger *n* locataire *mf*.

loft *n* grenier *m*.

lofty *adj* haut.

log *n* bûche *f*.

logbook *n* (*mar*) journal de bord *m*.

logic *n* logique *f*.

logical *adj* logique.

logo *n* logo *m*.

loins *npl* reins *mpl*.

loiter *vi* s'attarder.

loll *vi* se prélasser.

lollipop *n* sucette *f*.

lonely, lonesome *adj* seul, solitaire.

loneliness *n* solitude *f*.

long *adj* long, *f* longue; * *vi* désirer.

long-distance *n*: ~ **call** appel interurbain *m*.

longevity *n* longévité *f*.

long-haired *adj* aux cheveux longs.

longing *n* désir *m*.

longitude *n* longitude *f*.

longitudinal *adj* longitudinal.

long jump *n* saut en longueur *m*.

long-playing record *n* trente-trois tours *m*.

long-range *adj* à longue portée.

long-term *adj* à long terme.

long wave *n* grandes ondes *fpl*.

long-winded *adj* prolixe.

look *vi* regarder; sembler; ~ **after** *vt* s'occuper de; garder; ~ **for** *vt* chercher; ~ **forward to** *vt* attendre avec impatience; ~ **out for** *vt* guetter; * *n* aspect *m*; regard *m*.

looking glass *n* miroir *m*.

look-out *n* (*mil*) sentinelle *f*; vigie *f*.

loom *n* métier à tisser *m*; * *vi* menacer.

loop *n* boucle *f*.

loophole *n* échappatoire *f*.

loose *adj* lâché; desserré; ~**ly** *adv* approximativement; ~, **loosen** *vt* lâcher; desserrer.

loot *vt* piller; * *n* butin *m*.

lop *vt* élaguer.

lopsided *adj* de travers; déséquilibré.

loquacious *adj* loquace.

loquacity *n* loquacité *f*.

lord *n* seigneur *m*.

lore *n* savoir *m* (traditionnel).

lose *vt vi* perdre.

loss *n* perte *f*; **to be at a ~** ne pas savoir que faire.

lost and found *n* objets trouvés *mpl*.

lot *n* sort *f*; lot *m*; **a ~** beaucoup.

lotion *n* lotion *f*.

lottery *n* loterie *f*.

loud *adj* fort, bruyant; **~ly** *adv* bruyamment; haut.

loudspeaker *n* haut-parleur *m*.

lounge *n* salon *m*.

louse *n* (*pl* **lice**) pou *m*.

lousy *adj* minable.

lout *n* vaurien *m*.

lovable *adj* sympathique.

love *n* amour *m*; **to fall in ~** tomber amoureux; * *vt* aimer.

love letter *n* lettre d'amour *f*.

love life *n* vie sentimentale *f*.

loveliness *n* beauté *f*.

lovely *adj* beau.

lover *n* amant *m*.

love-sick *adj* fou amoureux.

loving *adj* affectueux.

low *adj* bas; * *vi* meugler.

low-cut *adj* décolleté.

lower *adj* plus bas; * *vt* baisser.

lowest *adj* le plus bas.

lowland *n* plaine *f*.

lowliness *n* humilité *f*.

lowly *adj* humble.

low-water *n* basse mer *f*.

loyal *adj* loyal, fidèle; **~ly** *adv* loyalement.

loyalty *n* loyauté *f*; fidélité *f*.

lozenge *n* pastille *f*.

lubricant *n* lubrifiant *m*.

lubricate *vt* lubrifier.

lucid *adj* lucide.

luck *n* chance *f*.

luckily *adv* heureusement, par chance.

luckless *adj* malchanceux.

lucky *adj* chanceux, qui a de la chance.

lucrative *adj* lucratif.

ludricrous *adj* absurde.

lug *vt* traîner.

luggage *n* bagages *mpl*.

lugubrious *adj* lugubre, triste.

lukewarm *adj* tiède.

lull *vt* bercer; * *n* répit *m*.

lullaby *n* berceuce *f*.

lumbago *n* lumbago *m*.

lumberjack *n* bûcheron *m*.

lumber room *n* débarras *m*.

luminous *adj* lumineux.

lump *n* bosse *f*; grosseur *f*; morceau *m*; * *vt* réunir.

lump sum *n* somme globale *f*.

lunacy *n* folie *f*.

lunar *adj* lunaire.

lunatic *adj* fou, *f* folle.

lunch, luncheon *n* déjeuner *m*.

lungs *npl* poumons *mpl*.

lurch *n* embardée *f*.

lure *n* leurre *m*; attrait *m*; * *vt* séduire, attirer.

lurid *adj* criard (couleur); horrible.

lurk *vi* être tapi.

luscious *adj* délicieux.

lush *adj* luxuriant.

lust *n* luxure *f*; sensualité *f*; désir *m*; * *vi* désirer; **~ after** *vt* convoiter.

lustful *adj* luxurieux, voluptueux; **~ly** *adv* luxurieusement.

lustily *adv* vigoureusement.

lustre *n* lustre *m*.

lusty *adj* fort, vigoureux.

lute *n* luth *m*.

Lutheran *n* luthérien *m* -ne *f*.

luxuriance *n* exubérance, luxuriance *f*.

luxuriant *adj* exubérant, luxuriant.

luxuriate *vi* pousser de manière exubérante.

luxurious *adj* luxueux; **~ly** *adv* luxueusement.

luxury *n* luxe *m*.

lying *n* mensonges *mpl*.

lymph *n* lymphe *f*.

lynch *vt* lyncher.

lynx *n* linx *m*.

lyrical *adj* lyrique.

lyrics *npl* paroles *fpl*.

M

macaroni *n* macaronis *mpl*.

macaroon *n* macaron *m*.

mace *n* massue *f*; macis *m*.

macerate *vt* macérer.

machination *n* machination *f*.

machine *n* machine *f*.

machine gun *n* mitrailleuse *f*.

machinery *n* machinerie *f*; mécanisme *m*.

mackerel *n* maquereau *m*.

mad *adj* fou, *f* folle; furieux; insensé.

Madam *n* madame *f*.

madden *vt* rendre fou; rendre furieux.

madder *n* (*bot*) garance *f*.

madhouse *n* asile de fous *m*.

madly *adv* à la folie; comme un fou.

madman *n* fou *m*.

madness *n* folie *f*.

magazine *n* magazine *m*, revue *f*; (*mil*) magasin *m*.

maggot *n* asticot *m*.

magic *n* magie *f*; * *adj* ~**ally** *adv* magique(-ment).

magician *n* magicien *m* -ne *f*.

magisterial *adj* ~**ly** *adv* magistral(ement).

magistracy *n* magistrature *f*.

magistrate *n* magistrat *m*.

magnanimity *n* magnanimité *f*.

magnanimous *adj* ~**ly** *adv* magnanime(ment).

magnet *n* aimant *m*.

magnetic *adj* magnétique.

magnetism *n* magnétisme *m*.

magnificence *n* magnificence *f*.

magnificent *adj* ~**ly** *adv* magnifique(ment).

magnify *vt* grossir; exagérer.

magnifying glass *n* loupe *f*.

magnitude *n* magnitude *f*.

magpie *n* pie *f*.

mahogany *n* acajou *m*.

maid *n* bonne *f*.

maiden *n* jeune fille *f*.

maiden name *n* nom de jeune fille *m*.

mail *n* courrier *m*.

mailbox *n* boîte aux lettres *f*.

mail coach *n* malle-poste *f*.

mailing list *n* fichier-clientèle *m*.

mail-order *n* vente par correspondance *f*.

mail train *n* (*rail*) train-poste *m*.

maim *vt* mutiler.

main *adj* principal; essentiel; **in the** ~ en général.

mainland *n* continent *m*.

main line *n* (*rail*) grande ligne *f*.

mainly *adv* principalement, essentiellement.

main street *n* rue principale *f*.

maintain *vt* maintenir; soutenir.

maintenance *n* entretien *m*.

maize *n* maïs *m*.

majestic *adj* majestueux; ~**ally** *adv* majestueusement.

majesty *n* majesté *f*.

major *adj* majeur; * *n* (*mil*) commandant *m*.

majority *n* majorité *f*.

make *vt* faire; ~ **for** se diriger vers; ~ **up** inventer; ~ **up for** compenser; * *n* marque *f*.

make-believe *n* invention *f*.

makeshift *adj* improvisé, de fortune.

make-up *n* maquillage *m*.

make-up remover *n* démaquillant *m*.

malady *n* maladie *f*.

malaise *n* malaise *m*.

malaria *n* malaria *f*.

malcontent *adj n* mécontent *m* -e *f*.

male *adj* mâle; masculin; * *n* mâle *m*.

malevolence *n* malveillance *f*.

malevolent *adj* malveillant; ~**ly** *adv* avec malveillance.

malfunction *n* mauvais fonctionnement *m*.

malice *n* méchanceté *f*.

malicious *adj* méchant; ~**ly** *adv* méchamment.

malign *adj* nocif; * *vt* calomnier.

malignant *adj* malfaisant; ~**ly** *adv* méchamment.

mall *n* centre commercial *m*.

malleable *adj* malléable.

mallet *n* maillet *m*.

mallow *n* (*bot*) mauve *f*.

malnutrition *n* malnutrition *f*.

malpractice *n* malversations *fpl*.

malt *n* malt *m*.

maltreat *vt* maltraiter.

mammal *n* mammifère *m*.

mammoth *adj* gigantesque.

man *n* homme *m*; * *vt* (*mar*) équiper en personnel.

manacle *n* entrave *f*; ~s *pl* menottes *fpl*.

manage *vt* diriger; réussir; * *vi* réussir.

manageable *adj* maniable.

management *n* direction *f*.

manager *n* directeur *m*.

manageress *n* directrice *f*.

managerial *adj* directorial.

managing director *n* directeur *m* général.

mandarin *n* mandarine *f*; mandarin *m*.

mandate *n* mandat *m*.

mandatory *n* obligatoire.

mane *n* crinière *f*.

manfully *adv* vaillamment.

manger *n* mangeoire *f*.

mangle *n* essoreuse *f*; * *vt* mutiler.

mangy *adj* miteux.

manhandle *vt* maltraiter; manutentionner.

manhood *n* âge d'homme *m*; virilité *f*.

man-hour *n* heure *f* de main d'œuvre.

mania *n* manie *f*.

maniac *n* maniaque *mf*.

manic *adj* obsessionnel.

manicure *n* manucure *f*.

manifest *adj* manifeste; * *vt* manifester.

manifestation *n* manifestation *f*.

manifesto *n* manifeste *m*.

manipulate *vt* manipuler.

manipulation *n* manipulation *f*.

mankind *n* humanité *f*.

manlike *adj* viril; d'homme.

manliness *n* virilité *f*; courage *m*.

manly *adj* viril.

man-made *adj* artificiel.

manner *n* manière *f*; attitude *f*; ~s *pl* manières *fpl*.

manoeuvre *n* manœuvre *f*.

manpower *n* main-d'œuvre *f*.

mansion *n* château *m*.

manslaughter *n* homicide involontaire *m*.

mantelpiece *n* manteau de cheminée *m*.

manual *adj n* manuel *m*.

manufacture *n* fabrication *f*; * *vt* fabriquer.

manufacturer *n* fabricant *m*.

manure *n* fumier *m*; engrais *m*; purin *m*; * *vt* fumer.

manuscript *n* manuscrit *m*.

many *adj* beaucoup de; ~ a time de nombreuses fois; how ~? combien?; as ~ as autant que.

map *n* carte *f*; plan *m*; * *vt* dessiner un plan de; ~ out programmer.

maple *n* érable *m*.

mar *vt* gâter, gâcher.

marathon *n* marathon *m*.

marauder *n* maraudeur *m* -euse *f*.

marble *n* marbre *m*; * *adj* marbré.

March *n* mars *m*.

march *n* marche *f*; * *vi* marcher.

marchpast *n* défilé *m*.

mare *n* jument *f*.

margarine *n* margarine *f*.

margin *n* marge *f*; bord *m*.

marginal *adj* marginal.

marigold *n* (*bot*) calendula *f*, souci *m*.

marijuana *n* marijuana *f*.

marinate *vt* mariner.

marine *adj* marin; * *n* fusilier *m* marin.

mariner *n* marin *m*.

marital *adj* matrimonial.

maritime *adj* maritime.

marjoram *n* marjolaine *f*.

mark *n* marque *f*; signe *m*; * *vt* marquer.

marker *n* marque *f*; marqueur *m*.

market *n* marché *m*.

marketable *adj* vendable.

marketing *n* marketing *m*.

marketplace *n* marché *m*.

market research *n* étude de marché *f*.

market value *n* valeur sur le marché *f*.

marksman *n* tireur d'élite *m*.

marmalade *n* confiture d'oranges *f*.

maroon *adj* marron rouge.

marquee *n* tente *f*.

marriage *n* mariage *m*.

marriageable *adj* mariable.

marriage certificate *n* acte de mariage *m*.

married *adj* marié; conjugal.

marrow *n* moelle *f*.

marry *vi* se marier.

marsh *n* marécage *m*.

marshal *n* maréchal *m*.
marshy *adj* marécageux.
marten *n* martre *f*.
martial *adj* martial; ~ **law** *n* loi martiale *f*.
martyr *n* martyr *m* -e *f*.
martyrdom *n* martyre *m*.
marvel *n* merveille *f*; * *vi* s'émerveiller.
marvellous *adj* merveilleux; ~**ly** *adv* merveilleusement.
marzipan *n* massepain *m*, pâte d'amandes *f*.
mascara *n* mascara *m*.
masculine *adj* masculin, viril.
mash *n* bouillie, purée *f*.
mask *n* masque *m*; * *vt* masquer.
masochist *n* masochiste *mf*.
mason *n* maçon *m*.
masonry *n* maçonnerie *f*.
masquerade *n* mascarade *f*.
mass *n* masse *f*; messe *f*; multitude *f*.
massacre *n* massacre *m*; * *vt* massacrer.
massage *n* massage *m*.
masseur *n* masseur *m*.
masseuse *n* masseuse *f*.
massive *adj* énorme.
mass media *npl* média *mpl*.
mast *n* mât *m*.
master *n* maître *m*; * *vt* maîtriser.
masterly *adj* magistral.
mastermind *vt* diriger.
masterpiece *n* chef-d'œuvre *m*.
mastery *n* maîtrise *f*.
masticate *vt* mastiquer.
mastiff *n* mastiff *m*.
mat *n* tapis *m*.
match *n* allumette *f*; match *m*; * *vt* égaler; * *vi* bien aller ensemble.
matchbox *n* boîte d'allumettes *f*.
matchless *adj* incomparable, sans pareil.
matchmaker *n* marieur *m* -euse *f*.
mate *n* camarade *mf*; * *vt* accoupler.
material *adj* ~**ly** *adv* matériel(lement).
materialism *n* matérialisme *m*.
maternal *adj* maternel.
maternity dress *n* robe de grossesse *f*.
maternity hospital *n* maternité *f*.
mathematical *adj* ~**ly** *adv* mathématique(-ment).
mathematician *n* mathématicien *m* -ne *f*.

mathematics *npl* mathématiques *fpl*.
maths *n* maths *fpl*.
matinee *n* matinée *f*.
mating *n* accouplement *m*.
matins *npl* matines *fpl*.
matriculate *vt* immatriculer.
matriculation *n* immatriculation *f*.
matrimonial *adj* matrimonial.
mat(t) *adj* mat.
matted *adj* emmêlé.
matter *n* matière, substance *f*; sujet *m*; affaire *f*; **what is the ~?** que se passe-t-il?; **a ~ of fact** un fait; * *vi* importer.
mattress *n* matelas *m*.
mature *adj* mûr; * *vi* mûrir.
maturity *n* maturité *f*.
maul *vt* meurtrir.
mausoleum *n* mausolée *m*.
mauve *adj* mauve.
maxim *n* maxime *f*.
maximum *n* maximum *m*.
may *v aux* pouvoir; ~**be** peut-être.
May *n* mai *m*.
Mayday *n* le Premier Mai *m*.
mayor *n* maire *m*.
mayoress *n* mairesse *f*.
maze *n* labyrinthe *m*.
me *pn* moi; me.
meadow *n* prairie *f*, pré *m*.
meagre *adj* pauvre.
meagreness *n* pauvreté *f*.
meal *n* repas *m*; farine *f*.
mealtime *n* heure du repas *f*.
mean *adj* avare, mesquin; moyen; **in the ~time, ~while** pendant ce temps-là; ~**s** *npl* moyens *mpl*; * *vt vi* signifier.
meander *vi* serpenter.
meaning *n* sens *m*, signification *f*.
meaningful *adj* significatif.
meaningless *adj* vide de sens.
meanness *n* avarice, mesquinerie *f*.
meantime, meanwhile *adv* pendant ce temps-là.
measles *npl* rougeole *f*.
measure *n* mesure *f*; * *vt* mesurer.
measurement *n* mesure *f*.
meat *n* viande *f*.
meatball *n* boulette de viande *f*.

meaty *adj* riche en viande.
mechanic *n* mécanicien *m*.
mechanical *adj* ~**ly** *adv* mécanique(ment).
mechanics *npl* mécanique *f*.
mechanism *n* mécanisme *m*.
medal *n* médaille *f*.
medallion *n* médaillon *m*.
medallist *n* médaillé *m* -e *f*.
meddle *vi* se mêler des affaires des autres.
meddler *n* fouineur *m* -euse *f*, indiscret *m* -ète *f*.
media *npl* média *mpl*.
median *n* médiane *f*.
mediate *vi* agir en tant que médiateur.
mediation *n* médiation *f*.
mediator *n* médiateur *m* -trice *f*.
medical *adj* médical.
medicate *vt* traiter.
medicated *adj* médical.
medicinal *adj* médicinal.
medicine *n* médecine *f*; médicament *m*.
medieval *adj* médiéval.
mediocre *adj* médiocre.
mediocrity *n* médiocrité *f*.
meditate *vi* méditer.
meditation *n* méditation *f*.
meditative *adj* méditatif.
Mediterranean *adj* méditerranéen.
medium *n* milieu *m*; médium *m*; * *adj* moyen.
medium wave *n* ondes moyennes *fpl*.
medley *n* mélange *m*.
meek *adj* docile; ~**ly** *adv* docilement.
meekness *n* docilité *f*.
meet *vt* rencontrer; ~ **with** retrouver; * *vi* se rencontrer; se retrouver.
meeting *n* réunion *f*; congrès *m*.
megaphone *n* mégaphone *m*.
melancholy *n* mélancolie *f*; * *adj* mélancolique.
mellow *adj* moelleux; doux; * *vi* mûrir.
mellowness *n* moelleux *m*.
melodious *adj* mélodieux; ~**ly** *adv* mélodieusement.
melody *n* mélodie *f*.
melon *n* melon *m*.
melt *vt* faire fondre; * *vi* fondre.
melting point *n* point de fusion *m*.

member *n* membre *m*.
membership *n* adhésion *f*.
membrane *n* membrane *f*.
memento *n* mémento *m*.
memo *n* note de service *f*.
memoir *n* mémoire *m*.
memorable *adj* mémorable.
memorandum *n* mémorandum *m*; note de service *f*.
memorial *n* monument commémoratif, mémorial *m*.
memorize *vt* mémoriser.
memory *n* mémoire *f*; souvenir *m*.
menace *n* menace *f*; * *vt* menacer.
menacing *adj* menaçant.
menagerie *n* ménagerie *f*.
mend *vt* réparer; raccommoder.
mending *n* réparation *f*; raccommodage *m*.
menial *adj* vil.
meningitis *n* méningite *f*.
menopause *n* ménopause *f*.
menstruation *n* menstruation *f*.
mental *adj* mental.
mentality *n* mentalité *f*.
mentally *adv* mentalement.
mention *n* mention *f*; * *vt* mentionner.
menu *n* menu *m*.
mercantile *adj* commercial.
mercenary *adj n* mercenaire *m*.
merchandise *n* marchandise *f*.
merchant *n* négociant *m* -e *f*.
merchantman *n* navire marchand *m*.
merchant marine *n* marine marchande *f*.
merciful *adj* miséricordieux.
merciless *adj* ~**ly** *adv* impitoyable(ment).
mercury *n* mercure *m*.
mercy *n* pitié *f*.
mere *adj* ~**ly** *adv* simple(ment).
merge *vt vi* fusionner.
merger *n* fusion *f*.
meridian *n* méridien *m*.
merit *n* mérite *m*; * *vt* mériter.
meritorious *adj* méritoire.
mermaid *n* sirène *f*.
merrily *adv* joyeusement.
merriment *n* divertissement *m*; réjouissance *f*.
merry *adj* joyeux.

merry-go-round *n* manège *m*.

mesh *n* maille *f*.

mesmerize *vt* hypnotiser.

mess *n* désordre *m*; confusion *f*; (*mil*) mess *m*; ~ **up** *vt* mettre en désordre.

message *n* message *m*.

messenger *n* messager *m* -ère *f*.

metabolism *n* métabolisme *m*.

metal *n* métal *m*.

metallic *adj* métallique.

metallurgy *n* métallurgie *f*.

metamorphosis *n* métamorphose *f*.

metaphor *n* métaphore *f*.

metaphoric(al) *adj* métaphorique.

metaphysical *adj* métaphysique.

metaphysics *npl* métaphysique *f*.

mete (out) *vt* distribuer.

meteor *n* météore *m*.

meteorological *adj* météorologique.

meteorology *n* météorologie *f*.

meter *n* compteur *m*.

method *n* méthode *f*.

methodical *adj* ~**ly** *adv* méthodique(ment).

Methodist *n* méthodiste *mf*.

metre *n* mètre *m*.

metric *adj* métrique.

metropolis *n* métropole *f*.

metropolitan *adj* métropolitain.

mettle *n* courage *m*.

mettlesome *adj* courageux.

mew *vi* miauler.

mezzanine *n* mezzanine *f*.

microbe *n* microbe *m*.

microphone *n* microphone *m*.

microchip *n* microprocesseur *m*, puce *f*.

microscope *n* microscope *m*.

microscopic *adj* microscopique.

microwave *n* four à micro-ondes *m*.

mid *adj* demi; mi-.

midday *n* midi *m*.

middle *adj* moyen; du milieu; * *n* milieu *m*.

middle name *n* deuxième prénom *m*.

middleweight *n* poids moyen *m*.

middling *adj* moyen, passable.

midge *n* moucheron *m*.

midget *n* nain *m* -e *f*.

midnight *n* minuit *m*.

midriff *n* diaphragme *m*; estomac *m*.

midst *n* milieu *m*.

midsummer *n* milieu de l'été *m*.

midway *adv* à mi-chemin.

midwife *n* sage-femme *f*.

midwifery *n* obstétrique *f*.

might *n* force *f*.

mighty *adj* fort, puissant.

migraine *n* migraine *f*.

migrate *vi* émigrer.

migration *n* émigration *f*.

migratory *adj* migratoire.

mike *n* micro *m*.

mild *adj* doux; modéré; ~**ly** *adv* doucement.

mildew *n* moisissure *f*; mildiou *m*.

mildness *n* douceur *f*.

mile *n* mile *m*.

mileage *n* kilométrage *m*.

milieu *n* milieu *m*.

militant *adj* militant.

military *adj* militaire.

militate *vi* militer.

militia *n* milice *f*.

milk *n* lait *m*; * *vt* traire; exploiter.

milkshake *n* milk-shake *m*.

milky *adj* laiteux; **M~ Way** *n* Voie lactée *f*.

mill *n* moulin *m*; * *vt* moudre.

millennium *n* millénaire *m*.

miller *n* meunier *m*.

millet *n* (*bot*) millet *m*.

milligram *n* milligramme *m*.

millilitre *n* millilitre *m*.

millimetre *n* millimètre *m*.

milliner *n* chapelier *m* -ière *f*.

millinery *n* chapellerie *f*.

million *n* million *m*.

millionaire *n* millionaire *mf*.

millionth *adj n* millionième *mf*.

millstone *n* meule *f*.

mime *n* mime *m*.

mimic *vt* mimer.

mimicry *n* mimique *f*.

mince *vt* hacher.

mind *n* esprit *m*; * *vt* prendre soin de; * *vi*: **do you ~?** est-ce que cela vous dérange?

minded *adj* disposé.

mindful *adj* soucieux; attentif.

mindless *adj* insouciant.

mine *pn* le mien, la mienne, les miens, les

miennes; à moi; * *n* mine *f*; * *vi* exploiter la mine.

minefield *n* champ de mines *m*.

miner *n* mineur *m*.

mineral *adj n* minéral *m*.

mineralogy *n* minéralogie *f*.

mineral water *n* eau minérale *f*.

minesweeper *n* dragueur de mines *m*.

mingle *vt* mêler.

miniature *n* miniature *f*.

minimal *adj* minime.

minimize *vt* minimiser.

minimum *n* minimum *m*.

mining *n* exploitation minière *f*.

minion *n* larbin *m*; favorit(te) *m(f)*.

minister *n* ministre *m*; * *vt* servir.

ministerial *adj* ministériel.

ministry *n* ministère *m*.

mink *n* vison *m*.

minnow *n* vairon *m*.

minor *adj* mineur; * *n* mineur *m* -e *f*.

minority *n* minorité *f*.

minstrel *n* ménestrel *m*.

mint *n* (*bot*) menthe *f*; hôtel de la Monnaie *m*; * *vt* frapper la monnaie.

minus *adv* moins.

minute *adj* minuscule; **~ly** *adv* minutieuse-ment.

minute *n* minute *f*.

miracle *n* miracle *m*.

miraculous *adj* miraculeux.

mirage *n* mirage *m*.

mire *n* bourbe *f*.

mirky *adj* trouble; ténébreux.

mirror *n* miroir *m*.

mirth *n* allégresse *f*.

mirthful *adj* joyeux.

misadventure *n* mésaventure *f*.

misanthropist *n* misanthrope *mf*.

misapply *vt* mal appliquer.

misapprehension *n* méprise *f*.

misbehave *vi* se conduire mal.

misbehaviour *n* mauvaise conduite *f*.

miscalculate *vt* mal calculer.

miscarriage *n* fausse couche *f*.

miscarry *vi* faire une fausse couche; échouer.

miscellaneous *adj* divers, varié.

miscellany *n* mélange, assortiment *m*.

mischief *n* mal, tort *m*.

mischievous *adj* mauvais; espiègle.

misconception *n* méprise *f*.

misconduct *n* mauvaise conduite *f*.

misconstrue *vt* mal interpréter.

miscount *vt* mal compter.

miscreant *n* scélérat *m*.

misdeed *n* méfait *m*.

misdemeanour *n* délit *m*.

misdirect *vt* mal diriger.

miser *n* avare *mf*.

miserable *adj* malheureux.

miserly *adj* mesquin, avare.

misery *n* malheur *m*; misère *f*.

misfit *n* inadapté *m* -e *f*.

misfortune *n* infortune *f*.

misgiving *n* doute *m*.

misgovern *vt* mal gouverner.

misguided *adj* malencontreux; malavisé.

mishandle *vt* maltraiter; mal s'y prendre avec.

mishap *n* mésaventure *f*.

misinform *vt* mal renseigner.

misinterpret *vt* mal interpréter.

misjudge *vt* méjuger.

mislay *vt* égarer.

mislead *vt* induire en erreur.

mismanage *vt* mal administrer.

mismanagement *n* mauvaise administration *f*.

misnomer *n* (*law*) nom inapproprié *m*.

misogynist *n* misogyne *mf*.

misplace *vt* égarer.

misprint *vt* mal imprimer; * *n* coquille *f*.

misrepresent *vt* mal représenter.

Miss *n* Mlle, Mademoiselle *f*.

miss *vt* rater; s'ennuyer de.

missal *n* missel *m*.

misshapen *adj* déformé.

missile *n* missile *m*.

missing *adj* perdu; absent.

mission *n* mission *f*.

missionary *n* missionnaire *mf*.

misspent *adj* gaspillé.

mist *n* brouillard *m*.

mistake *vt* confondre; * *vi* se tromper; **to be mistaken** se tromper; * *n* méprise *f*; erreur *f*.

Mister n monsieur m.

mistletoe n (bot) gui m.

mistress n maîtresse f.

mistrust vt se méfier de; * n méfiance f.

mistrustful adj méfiant.

misty adj brumeux.

misunderstand vt mal comprendre.

misunderstanding n malentendu m.

misuse vt faire un mauvais usage de; abuser de.

mitigate vt atténuer.

mitigation n atténuation f.

mitre n mitre f.

mittens npl moufles fpl.

mix vt mélanger.

mixed adj mélangé; mixte.

mixed-up adj confus.

mixer n mixeur m.

mixture n mélange m.

mix-up n confusion f.

moan n gémissement m; * vi gémir; se plaindre.

moat n fossé m.

mob n foule f; masse f.

mobile adj mobile.

mobile home n caravane f.

mobility n mobilité f.

mobilize vt (mil) mobiliser.

moccasin n mocassin m.

mock vt se moquer de.

mockery n moquerie f.

mode n mode m.

model n modèle m; * vt modeler.

moderate adj ~ly adv modéré(ment); * vt modérer.

moderation n modération f.

modern adj moderne.

modernize vt moderniser.

modest adj ~ly adv modeste(ment).

modesty n modestie f.

modicum n minimum m.

modification n modification f.

modify vt modifier.

modulate vt moduler.

modulation n (mus) modulation f.

module n module m.

mogul n magnat m.

mohair n mohair m.

moist adj humide.

moisten vt humidifier.

moisture n humidité f.

molar n molaire f.

molasses npl mélasse f.

mole n taupe f.

molecule n molécule f.

molehill n taupinière f.

molest vt importuner.

mollify vt apaiser.

mollusc n mollusque m.

mollycoddle vt dorloter.

molten adj fondu.

mom, mommy n maman f.

moment n moment m.

momentarily adv momentanément.

momentary adj momentané.

momentous adj capital.

momentum n vitesse f; élan m.

monarch n monarque m.

monarchy n monarchie f.

monastery n monastère m.

monastic adj monastique.

Monday n lundi m.

monetary adj monétaire.

money n argent m; pièce de monnaie f.

money order n mandat m.

mongol n (med) mongolien m -ne f.

mongrel adj n bâtard m -e f.

monitor n moniteur m -trice f.

monk n moine m.

monkey n singe m.

monochrome adj monochrome.

monocle n monocle m.

monologue n monologue m.

monopolize vt monopoliser.

monopoly n monopole m.

monosyllable n monosyllabe m.

monotonous adj monotone.

monotony n monotonie f.

monsoon n mousson f.

monster n monstre m.

monstrosity n monstruosité f.

monstrous adj monstrueux; ~ly adv monstrueusement.

montage n montage m.

month n mois m.

monthly adj mensuel; adv mensuellement.

monument *n* monument *m*.
monumental *adj* monumental.
moo *vi* meugler.
mood *n* humeur *f*.
moodiness *n* mauvaise humeur *f*.
moody *adj* de mauvaise humeur; lunatique.
moon *n* lune *f*.
moonbeams *npl* rayons de lune *mpl*.
moonlight *n* clair de lune *m*.
moor *n* lande *f*; * *vt* (*mar*) amarrer.
moorland *n* lande *f*.
moose *n* élan *m*, orignal *m*.
mop *n* lavette *f*; * *vt* éponger.
mope *vi* se morfondre.
moped *n* vélomoteur *m*.
moral *adj* ~ly *adv* moral(ement); ~s *npl* moralité *f*.
morale *n* moral *m*.
moralist *n* moraliste *mf*.
morality *n* moralité *f*.
moralize *vt vi* moraliser.
morass *n* marais *m*.
morbid *adj* morbide.
more *adj adv* plus; **never** ~ plus jamais; **once** ~ encore une fois; ~ **and** ~ de plus en plus; **so much the** ~ d'autant plus.
moreover *adv* de plus, en outre.
morgue *n* morgue *f*.
morning *n* matin *m*; **good** ~ bonjour.
moron *n* imbécile *mf*.
morose *adj* morose.
morphine *n* morphine *f*.
morse *n* morse *m*.
morsel *n* bouchée *f*; morceau *m*.
mortal *adj* ~ly *adv* mortel(lement); * *n* mortel *m* -le *f*.
mortality *n* mortalité *f*.
mortar *n* mortier *m*.
mortgage *n* hypothèque *f*; * *vt* hypothéquer.
mortgage company *n* banque de prêts hypothécaires *f*.
mortgager *n* débiteur(-trice) hypothécaire *m*(*f*).
mortification *n* mortification *f*.
mortify *vt* mortifier.
mortuary *n* morgue *f*.
mosaic *n* mosaïque *f*.
mosque *n* mosquée *f*.

mosquito *n* moustique *m*.
moss *n* (*bot*) mousse *f*.
mossy *adj* moussu.
most *adj pn* la plupart de; * *adv* extrêmement; **at** ~ au maximum; ~**ly** *adv* surtout, essentiellement.
moth *n* papillon de nuit *m*; mite *f*.
mothball *n* boule de naphtaline *f*.
mother *n* mère *f*.
motherhood *n* maternité *f*.
mother-in-law *n* belle-mère *f*.
motherless *adj* sans mère.
motherly *adj* maternel.
mother-of-pearl *n* nacre *f*.
mother-to-be *n* future maman *f*.
mother tongue *n* langue maternelle *f*.
motif *n* (*art*, *mus*) motif *m*.
motion *n* mouvement *m*.
motionless *adj* immobile.
motion picture *n* film *m*.
motivated *adj* motivé.
motive *n* motif *m*.
motley *adj* bigarré.
motor *n* moteur *m*.
motorbike *n* moto *f*.
motorboat *n* canot à moteur *m*.
motorcycle *n* motocyclette *f*.
motor vehicle *n* automobile *f*.
mottled *adj* marbré, tacheté.
motto *n* devise *f*.
mould *n* moule *m*; * *vt* mouler.
moulder *vi* s'effriter.
mouldy *adj* moisi.
moult *vi* muer.
mound *n* monticule *m*.
mount *n* mont *m*; * *vt* gravir.
mountain *n* montagne *f*.
mountaineer *n* alpiniste *mf*.
mountaineering *n* alpinisme *m*.
mountainous *adj* montagneux.
mourn *vt* pleurer.
mourner *n* personne en deuil *f*.
mournful *adj* ~ly *adv* triste(ment).
mourning *n* deuil *m*.
mouse *n* (*pl* mice) souris *f*.
mouth *n* bouche *f*; embouchure *f*.
mouthful *n* bouchée *f*.
mouth organ *n* harmonica *m*.

mouthpiece n bec m; microphone m.

mouthwash n eau dentifrice f.

mouthwatering adj appétissant.

movable adj mobile.

move vt déplacer; toucher, émouvoir; * vi bouger; * n mouvement m.

movement n mouvement m.

movie n film m.

movie camera n caméra f.

moving adj touchant, émouvant.

mow vt tondre.

mower n tondeuse f.

Mrs n Mme, Madame f.

much adj pn beaucoup; adv beaucoup, très.

muck n saleté f.

mucous adj muqueux.

mucus n mucus m.

mud n boue f.

muddle vt confondre; embrouiller; * n confusion f; désordre m.

muddy adj boueux.

mudguard n garde-boue m invar.

muffle vt assourdir.

mug n tasse f.

muggy adj lourd, étouffant.

mulberry n mûre f; ~ **tree** mûrier m.

mule n mulet m; mule f.

mull vt méditer.

multifarious adj divers.

multiple adj multiple.

multiplication n multiplication f; ~ **table** table de multiplication f.

multiply vt multiplier.

multitude n multitude f.

mumble vt vi grommeler.

mummy n momie f.

mumps npl oreillons mpl.

munch vt mâcher.

mundane adj banal.

municipal adj municipal.

municipality n municipalité f.

munificence n munificence f.

munitions npl munitions fpl.

mural n mural m.

murder n assassinat, meurtre m; homicide volontaire m; * vt assassiner.

murderer n assassin, meurtrier m.

murderess n meurtrière f.

murderous adj meurtrier.

murky adj obscur, glauque.

murmur n murmure m; * vt vi murmurer.

muscle n muscle m.

muscular adj musculaire.

muse vi méditer, rêver.

museum n musée m.

mushroom n (bot) champignon m.

music n musique f.

musical adj musical; mélodieux.

musician n musicien m -ne f.

musk n musc m.

muslin n mousseline f.

mussel n moule f.

must v aux devoir.

mustard n moutarde f.

muster vt rassembler.

musty adj moisi.

mute adj muet, silencieux.

muted adj assourdi.

mutilate vt mutiler.

mutilation n mutilation f.

mutiny n mutinerie f; vi se mutiner, se révolter.

mutter vt vi grommeler, marmonner; * n grommellement m.

mutton n mouton m (viande).

mutual adj ~**ly** adv mutuel(lement), réciproque(ment).

muzzle n muselière f; museau m; * vt museler.

my pn mon, ma, mes.

myriad n myriade f.

myrrh n myrrhe f.

myrtle n myrte m.

myself pn moi-même.

mysterious adj mystérieux; ~**ly** adv mystérieusement.

mystery n mystère m.

mystic(al) adj mystique.

mystify vt mystifier; laisser perplexe.

mystique n mystique f.

myth n mythe m.

mythology n mythologie f.

N

nab *vt* coincer, pincer.

nag *n* bourrin *m*; * *vt* harceler.

nagging *adj* persistant; * *npl* harcèlement *m*.

nail *n* ongle *m*; clou *m*; * *vt* clouer.

nailbrush *n* brosse à ongles *f*.

nailfile *n* lime à ongles *f*.

nail polish *n* vernis à ongles *m*.

nail scissors *npl* ciseaux à ongles *mpl*.

naive *adj* naïf.

naked *adj* nu; dénudé; pur, simple.

name *n* nom *m*; réputation *f*; * *vt* nommer; mentionner.

nameless *adj* anonyme.

namely *adv* à savoir.

namesake *n* homonyme *m*.

nanny *n* nourrice *f*.

nap *n* sieste *f*, somme *m*.

napalm *n* napalm *m*.

nape *n* nuque *f*.

napkin *n* serviette *f*.

narcissus *n* (*bot*) narcisse *m*.

narcotic *adj n* narcotique *m*.

narrate *vt* narrer, raconter.

narrative *adj* narratif; * *n* narration *f*.

narrow *adj* ~**ly** *adv* étroit(ement); * *vt* resserrer; limiter.

narrow-minded *adj* à l'esprit étroit.

nasal *adj* nasal.

nasty *adj* méchant; mauvais; sale.

natal *adj* natal.

nation *n* nation *f*.

national *adj* ~**ly** *adv* national(ement).

nationalism *n* nationalisme *m*.

nationalist *adj n* nationaliste *mf*.

nationality *n* nationalité *f*.

nationalize *vt* nationaliser.

nationwide *adj* au niveau national.

native *adj* natal; * *n* autochtone *mf*.

native language *n* langue maternelle *f*.

Nativity *n* Nativité *f*.

natural *adj* ~**ly** *adv* naturel(lement).

natural gas *n* gaz naturel *m*.

naturalist *n* naturaliste *mf*.

naturalize *vt* naturaliser.

nature *n* nature *f*; sorte *f*.

naught *n* zéro *m*.

naughty *adj* méchant.

nausea *n* nausée, envie de vomir *f*.

nauseate *vt* donner des nausées à.

nauseous *adj* écœurant.

nautic(al), naval *adj* nautique.

nave *n* nef (d'église) *f*.

navel *n* nombril *m*.

navigate *vi* naviguer.

navigation *n* navigation *f*.

navy *n* marine *f*.

Nazi *n* nazi *m* -e *f*.

near *prep* près de; * *adv* près; à côté; * *adj* proche.

nearby *adj* proche.

nearly *adv* presque.

near-sighted *adj* myope.

neat *adj* soigné; net, propre; ~**ly** *adv* proprement; élégamment.

nebulous *adj* nébuleux.

necessarily *adv* nécessairement.

necessary *adj* nécessaire.

necessitate *vt* nécessiter.

necessity *n* nécessité *f*.

neck *n* cou *m*; * *vi* se bécoter.

necklace *n* collier *m*.

necktie *n* cravate *f*.

nectar *n* nectar *m*.

née *adj*: ~ **Brown** née Brown.

need *n* besoin *m*; pauvreté *f*; * *vt* avoir besoin de, nécessiter.

needle *n* aiguille *f*.

needless *adj* superflu, inutile.

needlework *n* couture *f*.

needy *adj* nécessiteux, pauvre.

negation *n* négation *f*.

negative *adj* négatif; ~**ly** *adv* négativement; * *n* négative *f*; négation *f*; négatif *m*.

neglect *vt* négliger; * *n* négligence *f*.

negligee *n* négligé, déshabillé *m*.

negligence *n* négligence *f*; manque de soin *m*.

negligent *adj* négligent; ~**ly** *adv* négligemment.

negligible *adj* négligeable.

negotiate *vt vi* négocier.

negotiation *n* négociation *f*.

Negress *n* Noire *f*.

Negro *adj* noir; * *n* Noir *m*.

neigh *vi* hennir; * *n* hennissement *m*.

neighbour *n* voisin *m* -e *f*; * *vt* être voisin de.

neighbourhood *n* voisinage *m*.

neighbouring *adj* voisin.

neighbourly *adj* sociable.

neither *conj* ni; * *pn* aucun(e), ni l'un(e) ni l'autre.

neon *n* néon *m*.

neon light *n* lumière au néon *f*.

nephew *n* neveu *m*.

nepotism *n* népotisme *m*.

nerve *n* nerf *m*; courage *m*; toupet *m*.

nerve-racking *adj* exaspérant.

nervous *adj* nerveux.

nervous breakdown *n* dépression nerveuse *f*.

nest *n* nid *m*; nichée *f*.

nest egg *n* (*fig*) économies *fpl*.

nestle *vt vi* se blottir.

net *n* filet *m*.

net curtain *n* voile *m*.

netting *n* filet *m*.

nettle *n* ortie *f*.

network *n* réseau *f*.

neurosis *n* névrose *f*.

neurotic *adj n* névrosé *m* -e *f*.

neuter *adj* (*gr*) neutre.

neutral *adj* neutre.

neutrality *n* neutralité *f*.

neutralize *vt* neutraliser.

neutron *n* neutron *m*.

neutron bomb *n* bombe à neutrons *f*.

never *adv* jamais; ~ **mind** ça ne fait rien.

never-ending *adj* interminable.

nevertheless *adv* cependant, néanmoins.

new *adj* neuf; nouveau; dernier; ~**ly** *adv* nouvellement.

newborn *adj* nouveau-né, *f* nouvelle-née.

newcomer *n* nouveau venu *m*, nouvelle venue *f*.

new-fangled *adj* moderne.

news *npl* nouvelles, informations *fpl*.

news agency *n* agence de presse *f*.

newscaster *n* présentateur *m* -trice *f*.

newsdealer *n* (US) marchand(e) de journaux *m*(*f*).

news flash *n* flash d'information *m*.

newsletter *n* bulletin *m*.

newspaper *n* journal *m*.

newsreel *n* actualités *fpl*.

New Year *n* Nouvel An *m*; ~**'s Day** *n* Jour du Nouvel An *m*; ~**'s Eve** Saint-Sylvestre *f*.

next *adj* prochain; **the** ~ **day** le jour suivant; * *adv* ensuite, après.

nib *n* pointe *f*; plume *f*.

nibble *vt* mordiller.

nice *adj* gentil(le) *m*(*f*); agréable; joli; ~**ly** *adv* gentiment; bien.

nice-looking *adj* beau, *f* belle.

niche *n* niche *f*.

nick *n* entaille *f*; * *vt* (*sl*) faucher.

nickel *n* nickel *m*; (US) pièce *f* de cinq cents.

nickname *n* surnom *m*; * *vt* surnommer.

niece *n* nièce *f*.

niggling *adj* insignifiant.

night *n* nuit *f*; **by** ~ de nuit; **good** ~ bonne nuit.

nightclub *n* boîte de nuit *f*.

nightfall *n* tombée de la nuit *f*.

nightingale *n* rossignol *m*.

nightly *adv* tous les soirs; toutes les nuits; * *adj* nocturne.

nightmare *n* cauchemar *m*.

night school *n* cours du soir *mpl*.

night shift *n* équipe de nuit *f*.

night-time *n* nuit *f*.

nihilist *n* nihiliste *mf*.

nimble *adj* léger; agile, souple.

nine *adj n* neuf *m*.

nineteen *adj n* dix-neuf *m*.

nineteenth *adj n* dix-neuvième *mf*.

ninetieth *adj n* quatre-vingt-dixième *mf*.

ninety *adj n* quatre-vingt-dix *m*.

ninth *adj n* neuvième *mf*.

nip *vt* pincer; mordre.

nipple *n* mamelon *m*; tétine *f*.

nit *n* lente *f*.

nitrogen *n* nitrogène *m*.

no *adv* non; * *adj* aucun; pas de.

nobility *n* noblesse *f*.

noble *adj* noble; * *n* noble *mf*.

nobleman *n* noble *m*.

nobody *pn* personne.
nocturnal *adj* nocturne.
nod *n* signe de tête *m*; * *vi* faire un signe de la tête; somnoler.
noise *n* bruit *m*.
noisily *adv* bruyamment.
noisiness *n* bruit, tapage *m*.
noisy *adj* bruyant.
nominal *adj* ~**ly** *adv* nominal(ement).
nominate *vt* nommer.
nomination *n* nomination *f*.
nominative *n* (*gr*) nominatif *m*.
nominee *n* candidat *m* -e *f*.
nonalcoholic *adj* non alcoolisé.
non-aligned *adj* non-aligné.
nonchalant *adj* nonchalant.
noncommittal *adj* réservé.
nonconformist *n* non-conformiste *mf*.
nondescript *adj* quelconque.
none *pn* aucun; personne.
nonentity *n* nullité *f*.
nonetheless *adv* cependant.
nonexistent *adj* inexistant.
nonfiction *n* ouvrages non romanesques *mpl*.
nonplussed *adj* perplexe.
nonsense *n* absurdité *f*.
nonsensical *adj* absurde.
nonsmoker *n* non-fumeur *m*.
nonstick *adj* anti-adhérent.
nonstop *adj* direct; * *adv* sans s'arrêter.
noodles *npl* nouilles *fpl*.
noon *n* midi *m*.
noose *n* nœud coulant *m*.
nor *conj* ni.
normal *adj* normal.
north *n* nord *m*; * *adj* du nord.
North America *n* Amérique du Nord *f*.
northeast *n* nord-est *m*.
northerly, northern *adj* du nord.
North Pole *n* pôle Nord *m*.
northward(s) *adv* vers le nord.
northwest *n* nord-ouest *m*.
nose *n* nez *m*.
nosebleed *n* saignement de nez *m*.
nosedive *n* piqué *m*.
nostalgia *n* nostalgie *f*.
nostril *n* narine *f*.
not *adv* pas; non.

notable *adj* notable.
notably *adv* notamment.
notary *n* notaire *m*.
notch *n* cran *m*, dent *f*; * *vt* denteler.
note *n* note *f*; billet *m*; mot *m*; marque *f*; * *vt* noter, marquer; remarquer.
notebook *n* carnet *m*.
noted *adj* célèbre, connu.
notepad *n* bloc-notes *m*.
notepaper *n* papier à lettres *m*.
nothing *n* rien *m*; **good for** ~ bon à rien.
notice *n* notice *f*; avis *m*; * *vt* remarquer.
noticeable *adj* visible.
notification *n* notification *f*.
notify *vt* notifier.
notion *n* notion *f*; opinion *f*; idée *f*.
notoriety *n* notoriété *f*.
notorious *adj* notoire; ~**ly** *adv* notoirement.
notwithstanding *conj* quoique.
nougat *n* nougat *m*.
nought *n* zéro *m*.
noun *n* (*gr*) nom, substantif *m*.
nourish *vt* nourrir, alimenter.
nourishing *adj* nourrissant.
nourishment *n* nourriture *f*, aliments *mpl*.
novel *n* roman *m*.
novelist *n* romancier *m* -ière *f*.
novelty *n* nouveauté *f*.
November *n* novembre *m*.
novice *n* novice *mf*, débutant(e) *m(f)*.
now *adv* maintenant; ~ **and then** de temps en temps.
nowadays *adv* de nos jours, à l'heure actuelle.
nowhere *adv* nulle part.
noxious *adj* nocif.
nozzle *n* douille *f*.
nuance *n* nuance *f*.
nuclear *adj* nucléaire.
nucleus *n* noyau *m*.
nude *adj* nu.
nudge *vt* donner un coup de coude à.
nudist *n* nudiste *mf*.
nudity *n* nudité *f*.
nuisance *n* ennui *m*; gêne *f*.
nuke *n* (*col*) bombe atomique *f*; * *vt* atomiser.
null *adj* nul.
nullify *vt* annuler; invalider.

numb *adj* engourdi; * *vt* engourdir.

number *n* numéro, nombre *m*; quantité *f*; * *vt* numéroter; compter.

numberplate *n* plaque d'immatriculation *f*.

numbness *n* engourdissement *m*.

numeral *n* chiffre *m*.

numerical *adj* numérique.

numerous *adj* nombreux.

nun *n* religieuse *f*.

nunnery *n* couvent *m*.

nuptial *adj* nuptial; ~s *npl* noces *fpl*.

nurse *n* infirmière *f*; * *vt* soigner; ménager.

nursery *n* crèche *f*; chambre d'enfant *f*.

nursery rhyme *n* comptine *f*.

nursery school *n* (école) maternelle *f*.

nursing home *n* maison de repos *f*.

nurture *vt* élever, soigner.

nut *n* noix *f*.

nutcrackers *npl* casse-noix *m invar*, casse-noisettes.

nutmeg *n* noix de muscade *f*.

nutritious *adj* nutritif.

nut shell *n* coquille de noix *f*.

nylon *n* nylon *m*; * *adj* en nylon.

O

oak *n* chêne *m*.

oar *n* rame *f*.

oasis *n* oasis *f*.

oat *n* avoine *f*.

oath *n* serment *m*.

oatmeal *n* flocons d'avoine *mpl*.

oats *npl* avoine *f*.

obedience *n* obéissance *f*.

obedient *adj* obéissant; ~ly *adv* avec obéissance.

obese *adj* obèse.

obesity *n* obésité *f*.

obey *vt* obéir à.

obituary *n* nécrologie *f*.

object *n* objet *m*; * *vt* objecter.

objection *n* objection *f*.

objectionable *adj* désagréable.

objective *adj n* objectif *m*.

obligation *n* obligation *f*.

obligatory *adj* obligatoire.

oblige *vt* obliger; rendre service à.

obliging *adj* obligeant.

oblique *adj* oblique; indirect; ~ly *adv* obliquement.

obliterate *vt* effacer.

oblivion *n* oubli *m*.

oblivious *adj* oublieux.

obnoxious *adj* odieux.

oboe *n* hautbois *m*.

obscene *adj* obscène.

obscenity *n* obscénité *f*.

obscure *adj* obscur; ~ly *adv* obscurément; * *vt* obscurcir.

obscurity *n* obscurité *f*.

observance *n* observation *f*; observance *f*.

observant *adj* observateur; respectueux.

observation *n* observation *f*.

observatory *n* observatoire *m*.

observe *vt* observer.

observer *n* observateur *m* -trice *f*.

observingly *adv* attentivement.

obsess *vt* obséder.

obsessive *adj* obsédant.

obsolete *adj* désuet.

obstacle *n* obstacle *m*.

obstinate *adj* obstiné; ~ly *adv* obstinément.

obstruct *vt* obstruer; entraver.

obstruction *n* obstruction *f*; encombrement *m*.

obtain *vt* obtenir.

obtainable *adj* disponible.

obtrusive *adj* importun.

obtuse *adj* obtus.

obvious *adj* évident; ~ly *adv* évidemment.

occasion *n* occasion *f*; * *vt* occasionner, causer.

occasional *adj* occasionnel; ~ly *adv* occasionnellement.

occupant, occupier *n* occupant *m* -e *f*; locataire *mf*.

occupation *n* occupation *f*; emploi *m*.

occupy *vt* occuper.

occur *vi* se produire, arriver.

occurrence *n* incident *m*.

ocean *n* océan *m*.

ocean-going *adj* de haute mer.

oceanic *adj* océanique.

ochre *n* ocre *m*.

octave *n* octave *f*.

October *n* octobre *m*.

octopus *n* poulpe *m*.

odd *adj* impair; étrange; quelconque; **~ly** *adv* étrangement.

oddity *n* singularité, particularité *f*.

odd jobs *npl* petits travaux *mpl*.

oddness *n* étrangeté *f*; singularité *f*.

odds *npl* chances *fpl*.

odious *adj* odieux.

odometer *n* (US) odomètre *m*.

odorous *adj* odorant.

odour *n* odeur *f*; parfum *m*.

of *prep* de; à.

off *adj* éteint; fermé; annulé; en congé; **~!** *excl* du vent!

offence *n* offense *f*; injure *f*.

offend *vt* offenser, blesser; choquer; * *vi* pécher.

offender *n* délinquant *m* -e *f*.

offensive *adj* offensant; injurieux; **~ly** *adv* d'une manière offensante.

offer *vt* offrir; * *n* offre *f*.

offering *n* offrande *f*; offre *f*.

offhand *adj* désinvolte; * *adv* soudainement.

office *n* bureau *m*; poste *m*, fonctions *fpl*; service *m*.

office automation *n* bureautique *f*.

office building *n* immeuble de bureaux *m*.

office hours *npl* heures de bureau *fpl*.

officer *n* officier *m*; fonctionnaire *mf*.

office worker *n* employé(e) de bureau *m(f)*.

official *adj* **~ly** *adv* officiel(lement); * *n* employé *m* -e *f*.

officiate *vi* officier.

officious *adj* officieux; **~ly** *adv* officieusement.

off-line *adj adv* hors ligne.

off-peak *adj* aux heures creuses.

off-season *adj adv* hors-saison.

offset *vt* compenser; décaler.

offshoot *n* ramification *f*.

offshore *adj* côtier.

offside *adj* hors jeu.

offspring *n* progéniture *f*; descendance *f*.

offstage *adv* en coulisses.

off-the-rack *adj* prêt-à-porter.

ogle *vt* lorgner.

oil *n* huile *f*; * *vt* huiler.

oilcan *n* burette d'huile *f*; bidon d'huile *m*.

oilfield *n* gisement pétrolifère *m*.

oil filter *n* filtre à huile *m*.

oil painting *n* peinture à l'huile *f*.

oil rig *n* derrick *m*.

oil tanker *n* pétrolier *m*.

oil well *n* puits pétrolifère *m*.

oily *adj* huileux; gras.

ointment *n* onguent *m*.

OK, okay *excl* O.K., d'accord; * *adj* bien; * *vt* approuver.

old *adj* vieux, *f* vieille.

old age *n* vieillesse *f*.

old-fashioned *adj* démodé.

olive *n* olivier *m*; olive *f*.

olive oil *n* huile d'olive *f*.

omelet(te) *n* omelette *f*.

omen *n* augure, présage *m*.

ominous *adj* menaçant.

omission *n* omission *f*; négligence *f*.

omit *vt* omettre.

omnipotence *n* omnipotence *f*.

omnipotent *adj* omnipotent, tout-puissant.

on *prep* sur, dessus; en; pour; * *adj* allumé, branché; ouvert; de service.

once *adv* une fois; **at ~** tout de suite; **all at ~** tout d'un coup; **~ more** encore une fois.

oncoming *adj* qui arrive.

one *adj* un, une; **~ by ~** un par un.

one-day excursion *n* billet d'aller-retour valable une journée *m*.

one-man *adj* individuel.

onerous *adj* lourd; (*law*) dur.

oneself *pn* soi-même.

one-sided *adj* partial.

one-to-one *adj* face à face.

ongoing *adj* continu; en cours.

onion *n* oignon *m*.

on-line *adj adv* en ligne.

onlooker *n* spectateur *m* -trice *f*.

only *adj* seul, unique; * *adv* seulement.

onset, onslaught n début m; attaque f.

onus n obligation f.

onward(s) adv en avant.

ooze vi suinter.

opaque adj opaque.

open adj ouvert; public; déclaré; sincère, franc; ~ly adv ouvertement; * vt ouvrir; * vi s'ouvrir; commencer; ~ on to donner sur; ~ up vt ouvrir; vi s'ouvrir.

opening n ouverture f; (com) débouché m; inauguration f; commencement m.

open-minded adj aux idées larges.

openness n clareté f; franchise, sincérité f.

opera n opéra m.

opera house n théâtre de l'opéra m.

operate vi fonctionner; opérer.

operation n fonctionnement m; opération f.

operational adj opérationnel.

operative adj actif; en vigueur.

operator n opérateur m -trice f; téléphoniste mf.

ophthalmic adj ophtalmique.

opine vt être d'avis (que).

opinion n opinion f; jugement m.

opinionated adj entêté.

opinion poll n sondage m.

opponent n opposant m -e f; adversaire mf.

opportune adj opportun.

opportunist n opportuniste mf.

opportunity n occasion f.

oppose vt s'opposer à.

opposing adj opposé.

opposite adj opposé; contraire; * adv en face; prep en face de; * n contraire m.

opposition n opposition f; résistance f.

oppress vt opprimer.

oppression n oppression f.

oppressive adj oppressif.

oppressor n oppresseur m.

optic(al) adj optique; ~s npl optique f.

optician n opticien m -ne f.

optimist n optimiste mf.

optimistic adj optimiste.

option n option f.

optional adj optionnel; facultatif.

opulent adj opulent.

or conj ou.

oracle n oracle m.

oral adj oral, verbal; ~ly adv oralement.

orange n orange f.

orator n orateur m -trice f.

orbit n orbite f.

orchard n verger m.

orchestra n orchestre m.

orchestral adj orchestral.

orchid n orchidée f.

ordain vt ordonner.

ordeal n épreuve f.

order n ordre m; commande f; mandat m; classe f; * vt ordonner; commander; mettre en ordre.

order form n bon de commande m.

orderly adj ordonné; réglé.

ordinarily adv ordinairement.

ordinary adj ordinaire.

ordination n ordination f.

ordnance n artillerie f.

ore n minerai m.

organ n organe m; orgue m.

organic adj organique.

organism n organisme m.

organist n organiste mf.

organization n organisation f.

organize vt organiser.

orgasm n orgasme m.

orgy n orgie f.

oriental adj oriental.

orifice n orifice m.

origin n origine f.

original adj original; originel; ~ly adv à l'origine; originalement.

originality n originalité f.

originate vi provenir (de); être originaire (de).

ornament n ornement m; * vt ornementer, décorer.

ornamental adj ornemental.

ornate adj ornementé.

orphan adj n orphelin m -e f.

orphanage n orphelinat m.

orthodox adj orthodoxe.

orthodoxy n orthodoxie f.

orthography n orthographe f.

orthopaedic adj orthopédique.

oscillate vi osciller.

osprey n balbuzard pêcheur m.

ostensibly adv selon les apparences.

ostentatious *adj* ostentatoire.
osteopath *n* ostéopathe *mf*.
ostracize *vt* frapper d'ostracisme.
ostrich *n* autruche *f*.
other *pn* autre.
otherwise *adv* autrement.
otter *n* loutre *f*.
ouch *excl* aïe!
ought *v aux* devoir; falloir.
ounce *n* once *f*.
our *pn* notre, *pl* nos.
ours *pn* le nôtre, la nôtre, les nôtres; à nous.
ourselves *pn pl* nous-mêmes.
oust *vt* évincer; déposséder.
out *adv* dehors; éteint.
outback *n* intérieur *m*.
outboard *adj*: ~ **motor** (moteur) hors-bord *m*.
outbreak *n* éruption *f*; explosion *f*.
outburst *n* explosion *f*.
outcast *n* paria *m*.
outcome *n* résultat *m*.
outcry *n* protestations *fpl*.
outdated *adj* démodé; périmé.
outdo *vt* surpasser.
outdoor *adj* de plein air, ~**s** *adv* à l'extérieur.
outer *adj* extérieur.
outermost *adj* extrême; le plus à l'extérieur.
outer space *n* espace *m*.
outfit *n* tenue *f*; équipement *m*.
outfitter *n* confectionneur *m* -euse *f*.
outgoing *adj* extroverti; sortant.
outgrow *vt* devenir plus grand que.
outhouse *n* dépendances *fpl*.
outing *n* excursion *f*.
outlandish *adj* bizarre.
outlaw *n* hors-la-loi *m*; * *vt* proscrire.
outlay *n* dépenses *fpl*, frais *mpl*.
outlet *n* sortie *f*; débouché *m*.
outline *n* contour *m*; grandes lignes *fpl*.
outlive *vt* survivre à.
outlook *n* perspective *f*.
outlying *adj* distant, éloigné.
outmoded *adj* démodé.
outnumber *vt* être plus nombreux que.
out-of-date *adj* périmé; démodé.
out-patient *n* patient(e) en consultation externe *m(f)*.
outpost *n* avant-poste *m*.

output *n* rendement *m*; sortie *f*.
outrage *n* outrage *m*; * *vt* outrager.
outrageous *adj* outrageant; atroce; ~**ly** *adv* outrageusement; atrocement.
outright *adv* absolument, complètement; * *adj* absolu, complet.
outrun *vt* gagner de vitesse, distancer.
outset *n* commencement *m*.
outshine *vt* éclipser.
outside *n* surface *f*; extérieur *m*; apparence *f*; * *adv* dehors; * *prep* en dehors de.
outsider *n* étranger *m* -ère *f*.
outsize *adj* grande taille.
outskirts *npl* périphérie *f*, alentours *mpl*.
outspoken *adj* franc.
outstanding *adj* exceptionnel; en suspens.
outstretch *vi* s'étendre.
outstrip *vt* devancer; surpasser.
out-tray *n* courrier au départ *m*.
outward *adj* extérieur; vers l'extérieur; d'aller; ~**ly** *adv* à l'extérieur, extérieurement.
outweigh *vt* peser plus lourd que; l'emporter sur.
outwit *vt* être plus spirituel que.
oval *n*, *adj* ovale *m*.
ovary *n* ovaire *m*.
oven *n* four *m*.
ovenproof *adj* allant au four.
over *prep* sur, dessus; plus de; pendant; **all ~** de tous côtés; * *adj* fini; en trop, en plus; ~ **again** à nouveau; ~ **and** ~ de nombreuses fois.
overall *adj* total; * *adv* dans l'ensemble; ~**s** *npl* salopette *f*.
overawe *vt* impressionner.
overbalance *vi* perdre l'équilibre.
overbearing *adj* despotique.
overboard *adv* (*mar*) par-dessus bord.
overbook *vt* surréserver.
overcast *adj* couvert.
overcharge *vt* surcharger; faire payer un prix excessif à.
overcoat *n* pardessus *m*.
overcome *vt* vaincre; surmonter.
overconfident *adj* trop confiant.
overcrowded *adj* bondé; surpeuplé.
overdo *vi* exagérer.
overdraft *n* découvert *m*.
overdrawn *adj* à découvert.

overdress *vi* s'habiller trop élégamment.
overdue *adj* en retard; arriéré.
overeat *vi* trop manger.
overestimate *vt* surestimer.
overflow *vt* déborder de; * *vi* déborder; * *n* inondation *f*; surplus *m*.
overgrown *adj* envahi.
overgrowth *n* végétation envahissante *f*.
overhang *vt* surplomber.
overhaul *vt* réviser; * *n* révision *f*.
overhead *adv* en l'air, au-dessus.
overhear *vt* entendre par hasard.
overjoyed *adj* fou de joie.
overkill *n* (*fig*) matraquage *m*.
overland *adj* *adv* par voie de terre.
overlap *vi* se chevaucher.
overleaf *adv* au dos.
overload *vt* surcharger.
overlook *vt* dominer; donner sur; oublier; laisser passer, tolérer; négliger.
overnight *adv* pendant la nuit; * *adj* de nuit.
overpass *n* pont surélevé *m*.
overpower *vt* dominer, écraser.
overpowering *adj* écrasant.
overrate *vt* surévaluer.
override *vt* outrepasser.
overriding *adj* prédominant.
overrule *vt* rejeter; annuler.
overrun *vt* envahir; infester; dépasser.
overseas *adv* à l'étranger; outre-mer; * *adj* étranger.
oversee *vt* inspecter, surveiller.
overseer *n* contremaître *m*.

overshadow *vt* éclipser.
overshoot *vt* dépasser.
oversight *n* oubli *m*; erreur *f*.
oversleep *vi* se réveiller en retard.
overspill *n* excédent de population *m*.
overstate *vi* exagérer.
overstep *vt* dépasser.
overt *adj* ouvert; public; **~ly** *adv* ouvertement.
overtake *vt* doubler.
overthrow *vt* renverser; détruire; * *n* renversement *m*; ruine, déroute *f*.
overtime *n* heures supplémentaires *fpl*.
overtone *n* harmonique *mf*; connotation *f*.
overture *n* ouverture *f*.
overturn *vt* renverser.
overweight *adj* trop lourd.
overwhelm *vt* écraser; submerger.
overwhelming *adj* écrasant; irrésistible.
overwork *vi* se surmener, trop travailler.
owe *vt* devoir; être redevable de.
owing *adj* dû; **~ to** en raison de.
owl *n* chouette *f*.
own *adj* propre; **my ~** mon, ma, mes propre(s); * *vt* posséder; **~ up** *vi* confesser.
owner *n* propriétaire *mf*.
ownership *n* possession *f*.
ox *n* bœuf *m*; **~en** *pl* bœufs *mpl*.
oxidize *vt* oxyder.
oxygen *n* oxygène *m*.
oxygen mask *n* masque à oxygène *m*.
oxygen tent *n* tente à oxygène *f*.
oyster *n* huître *f*.
ozone *n* ozone *m*.

P

pa *n* papa *m*.
pace *n* pas *m*; allure *f*; * *vt* arpenter; * *vi* marcher.
pacemaker *n* meneur *m* -euse *f* de train; (*med*) pacemaker *m*.
pacific(al) *adj* pacifique.
pacification *n* pacification *f*.
pacify *vt* pacifier.
pack *n* paquet *m*; jeu de cartes *m*; bande *f*; * *vt* empaqueter; remplir; * *vi* faire ses valises.

package *n* paquet *m*; accord *m*.
package tour *n* voyage organisé *m*.
packet *n* paquet *m*.
packing *n* emballage *m*.
pact *n* pacte *m*.
pad *n* bloc *m*; coussinet, tampon *m*; plateforme *f*; (*sl*) piaule *f*; * *vt* rembourrer.
padding *n* rembourrage *m*.
paddle *vi* ramer; * *n* pagaie *f*.
paddle steamer *n* vapeur à roues *m*.
paddock *n* paddock *m*.

paddy *n* rizière *f*.

paediatrics *n* pédiatrie *f*.

pagan *adj n* païen *m*, païenne *f*.

page *n* page *f*; page *m*.

pageant *n* grand spectacle *m*.

pageantry *n* pompe *f*.

pail *n* seau *m*.

pain *n* douleur *f*; mal *m*; peine *f*; * *vt* peiner.

pained *adj* peiné.

painful *adj* douloureux; pénible; ~**ly** *adv* douloureusement; péniblement; à grand-peine.

painkiller *n* analgésique *m*.

painless *adj* indolore; sans peine.

painstaking *adj* soigneux.

paint *vt* peindre.

paintbrush *n* pinceau *m*.

painter *n* peintre *m*.

painting *n* peinture *f*; tableau *m*.

paintwork *n* peinture *f*.

pair *n* pair *m*.

pajamas *npl* = **pyjamas**.

pal *n* copain *m*, copine *f*, pote *m*.

palatable *adj* savoureux.

palate *n* palais *m*.

palatial *adj* grandiose.

palaver *n* discussions *fpl*; situation embrouillée *f*.

pale *adj* pâle; clair.

palette *n* palette *f*.

paling *n* palissade *f*.

pall *n* nuage *m* (de fumée); * *vi* perdre sa saveur.

pallet *n* palette *f*.

palliative *adj n* palliatif *m*.

pallid *adj* pâle.

pallor *n* pâleur *f*.

palm *n* (*bot*) palme *f*, palmier *m*.

palmistry *n* chiromancie *f*.

Palm Sunday *n* Dimanche des Rameaux *m*.

palpable *adj* palpable; évident.

palpitation *n* palpitation *f*.

paltry *adj* dérisoire; mesquin.

pamper *vt* gâter, dorloter.

pamphlet *n* pamphlet *m*; brochure *f*.

pan *n* casserole *f*; poêle *f*.

panacea *n* panacée *f*.

panache *n* panache *m*.

pancake *n* crêpe *f*.

pandemonium *n* pandémonium *m*.

pane *n* vitre *f*.

panel *n* panneau *m*; comité *m*.

panelling *n* lambrissage *m*.

pang *n* angoisse *f*; tourment *m*.

panic *adj n* (de) panique *f*.

panicky *adj* paniqué, affolé.

panic-stricken *adj* pris de panique.

pansy *n* (*bot*) pensée *f*.

pant *vi* haleter.

panther *n* panthère *f*.

panties *npl* (petite) culotte *f*.

pantihose *n* collant *m*.

pantry *n* placard *m*.

pants *npl* slip *m*; pantalon *m*.

papacy *n* papauté *f*.

papal *adj* papal.

paper *n* papier *m*; journal *m*; épreuve *f* d'examen; exposé *m*, étude *f*; ~**s** *pl* documents *mpl*; (*com*) fonds *mpl*; * *adj* en papier; * *vt* garnir de papier; tapisser.

paperback *n* livre de poche *m*.

paper bag *n* sac en papier *m*.

paper clip *n* trombone *m*.

paperweight *n* presse-papiers *m*.

paperwork *n* paperasserie *f*.

paprika *n* paprika *m*.

par *n* équivalence *f*; égalité *f*; pair *m*; **at** ~ (*com*) au pair.

parable *n* parabole *f*.

parachute *n* parachute *m*; * *vi* sauter en parachute.

parade *n* parade *f*; (*mil*) défilé *m*; * *vt* faire défiler, faire parader; * *vi* défiler, parader; se pavaner.

paradise *n* paradis *m*.

paradox *n* paradoxe *m*.

paradoxical *adj* paradoxal.

paragon *n* modèle absolu *m*.

paragraph *n* paragraphe *m*.

parallel *adj* parallèle; * *n* parallèle *f*; * *vt* mettre en parallèle; comparer.

paralyse *vt* paralyser.

paralysis *n* paralysie *f*.

paralytic(al) *adj* paralytique.

paramedic *n* auxiliaire médical(e) *m(f)*.

paramount *adj* suprême, supérieur.

paranoid *adj* paranoïaque.

paraphernalia *n* affaires *fpl*; attirail *m*.
parasite *n* parasite *m*.
parasol *n* parasol *m*.
paratrooper *n* parachutiste *m*.
parcel *n* paquet *m*; parcelle *f*; * *vt* empaqueter, emballer.
parch *vt* dessécher.
parched *adj* desséché.
parchment *n* parchemin *m*.
pardon *n* pardon *m*; * *vt* pardonner.
parent *n* parent *m* -e *f*; ~s parents *mpl*.
parentage *n* parenté *f*; origine *f*.
parental *adj* parental.
parenthesis *n* parenthèse *f*.
parish *n* paroisse *f*; * *adj* paroissial.
parishioner *n* paroissien *m* -ne *f*.
parity *n* parité *f*.
park *n* parc *m*; * *vt* garer; *vi* se garer.
parking *n* stationnement *m*.
parking lot *n* parking *m*.
parking meter *n* parcomètre *m*.
parking ticket *n* amende pour stationnement interdit *f*.
parlance *n* langage *m*.
parliament *n* parlement *m*.
parliamentary *adj* parlementaire.
parlour *n* parloir *m*; salon *m*.
parody *n* parodie *f*; * *vt* parodier.
parole *n*: on ~ sur parole.
parricide *n* parricide *m*; parricide *mf*.
parrot *n* perroquet *m*.
parry *vt* parer.
parsley *n* (*bot*) persil *m*.
parsnip *n* (*bot*) navet *m*.
part *n* partie *f*; part *f*; rôle (d'acteur) *m*; raie *f*; ~s *pl* parties *fpl*; parages *mpl*; * *vt* séparer; diviser; * *vi* se séparer; se diviser; ~ with céder; se défaire de; donner; ~ly *adv* en partie.
partial *adj* partial; ~ly *adv* avec partialité; partiellement.
participant *n* participant *m* -e *f*.
participate *vi* participer (à).
participation *n* participation *f*.
participle *n* (*gr*) participe *m*.
particle *n* particule *f*.
particular *adj* particulier, singulier; ~ly *adv* particulièrement; * *n* particulier *m*; particularité *f*.

parting *n* séparation *f*; raie (dans les cheveux) *f*.
partisan *n* partisan *m* -e *f*.
partition *n* partition, séparation *f*; * *vt* diviser en plusieurs parties, partager,
partner *n* associé *m* -e *f*.
partnership *n* association *f*; société *f*.
partridge *n* perdrix *f*.
party *n* parti *m*; fête *f*.
pass *vt* passer; dépasser; adopter; être admis à; * *vi* passer; * *n* permis *m*; passage *m*; ~ away *vi* mourir; ~ by *vi* passer; *vt* négliger, oublier; ~ on *vt* transmettre; passer.
passable *adj* passable; praticable.
passage *n* passage *m*; traversée *f*; couloir *m*.
passbook *n* livret *m* (bancaire).
passenger *n* passager *m* -ère *f*.
passer-by *n* passant *m* -e *f*.
passing *adj* passager.
passion *n* passion *f*; amour *m*; emportement *m*.
passionate *adj* passionné; ~ly *adv* passionnément; ardemment.
passive *adj* passif; ~ly *adv* passivement.
passkey *n* passe-partout *m invar*.
Passover *n* Pâque *f* juive.
passport *n* passeport *m*.
passport control *n* contrôle des passeports *m*.
password *n* mot de passe *m*.
past *adj* passé; * *n* (*gr*) prétérit *m*; passé *m*; * *prep* au-delà de; après.
pasta *n* pâtes *fpl*.
paste *n* pâte *f*; colle *f*; * *vt* coller.
pasteurized *adj* pasteurisé.
pastime *n* passe-temps *m invar*; divertissement *m*.
pastor *n* pasteur *m*.
pastoral *adj* pastoral.
pastry *n* pâtisserie *f*.
pasture *n* pâture *f*.
pasty *adj* pâteux; pâle.
pat *vt* tapoter.
patch *n* pièce *f*; tache *f*; terrain *m*; * *vt* rapiécer; ~ up réparer; se réconcilier.
pâté *n* pâté *m*.
patent *adj* breveté; évident; * *n* brevet *m*; * *vt* faire breveter.
patentee *n* détenteur d'un brevet *m*.

patent leather n cuir verni m.
paternal adj paternel.
paternity n paternité f.
path n chemin, sentier m.
pathetic adj ~ally adv pathétique(ment); lamentable(ment).
pathological adj pathologique.
pathology n pathologie f.
pathos n pathétique m.
pathway n sentier m.
patience n patience f.
patient adj patient; ~ly adv patiemment; * n patient m -e f.
patio n patio m.
patriarch m patriarche m.
patriot n patriote mf.
patriotic adj patriotique.
patriotism n patriotisme m.
patrol n patrouille f; * vi patrouiller.
patrol car n voiture de patrouille f.
patrolman n agent de police m.
patron n protecteur m; client m -e f.
patronage n patronage m; clientèle f.
patronize vt patronner, protéger.
patter n trottinement m; bavardage m; * vi trottiner.
pattern n motif m; modèle m.
paunch n panse f; ventre m.
pauper n pauvre mf.
pause n pause f; * vi faire une pause; hésiter.
pave vt paver; carreler.
pavement n trottoir m.
pavilion n pavillon m.
paving stone n pavé m.
paw n patte f; * vt tripoter.
pawn n pion m; gage m; * vt engager.
pawn broker n prêteur(-euse) sur gages m(f).
pawnshop n mont-de-piété m.
pay vt payer; ~ **back** vt rembourser; ~ **for** payer; ~ **off** vt liquider; vi payer; rapporter; * n paie f; salaire m.
payable adj payable.
pay day n jour de paie m.
payee n bénéficiaire mf.
pay envelope n enveloppe de paie f.
paymaster n caissier m.
payment n paiement m.
pay-phone n téléphone public m.

payroll n liste des employés f.
pea n pois m.
peace n paix f.
peaceful adj paisible; pacifique.
peach n pêche f.
peacock n paon m.
peak n pic m; maximum m.
peak hours, peak period n heures de pointe fpl.
peal n carillon m; grondement m.
peanut n cacahuète f.
pear n poire f.
pearl n perle f.
peasant n paysan m -ne f.
peat n tourbe f.
pebble n caillou m; galet m.
peck n coup de bec m; * vt picoter.
pecking order n hiérarchie f.
peculiar adj étrange, singulier; ~ly adv étrangement.
peculiarity n particularité, singularité f.
pedal n pédale f; * vi pédaler.
pedant n pédant m -e f.
pedantic adj pédant.
peddler n colporteur m.
pedestal n piédestal m.
pedestrian n piéton m -ne f; * adj pédestre.
pediatrics n (US) pédiatrie f.
pedigree n généalogie f; pedigree m; * adj de race.
peek vi regarder à la dérobée.
peel vt peler; éplucher; * vi peler; * n peau f; pelure f.
peer n pair m.
peerless adj incomparable.
peeved adj fâché.
peevish adj maussade, ronchon (fam).
peg n cheville f; piquet m; * vt cheviller.
pelican n pélican m.
pellet n boulette f.
pelt n fourrure f; * vt arroser; * vi pleuvoir à verse.
pen n stylo m; plume f; enclos m.
penal adj pénal.
penalty n peine f; sanction f; amende f.
penance n pénitence f.
pence n = pl of **penny**.
pencil n crayon m.

pencil case n trousse f.
pendant n pendentif m.
pending adj pendant.
pendulum n pendule m.
penetrate vt pénétrer (dans).
penguin n pingouin m.
penicillin n pénicilline f.
peninsula n péninsule f.
penis n pénis m.
penitence n pénitence f.
penitent adj n pénitent m -e f.
penitentiary n pénitencier m.
penknife n canif m.
pennant n fanion m.
penniless adj sans le sou.
penny n penny m.
penpal n correspondant m -e f.
pension n pension f; * vt pensionner.
pensive adj pensif; ~ly adv pensivement.
pentagon n: **the P~** le Pentagone.
Pentecost n la Pentecôte f.
penthouse n appartement situé sur le toit d'un immeuble m.
pent-up adj reprimé, refoulé.
penultimate adj pénultième, avant-dernier.
penury n pénurie f.
people n peuple m; nation f; gens mpl; * vt peupler.
pep n énergie f; ~ **up** vt animer.
pepper n poivre m; * vt poivrer.
peppermint n menthe poivrée f.
per prep par.
per annum adv par an.
per capita adj adv par habitant.
perceive vt percevoir.
percentage n pourcentage m.
perception n perception f; notion f.
perch n perche f.
perchance adv par hasard.
percolate vt filtrer.
percolator n percolateur m.
percussion n percussion f.
perdition n perte, ruine f.
peremptory adj péremptoire; décisif.
perennial adj perpétuel.
perfect adj parfait; idéal; ~ly adv parfaitement; * vt parfaire, perfectionner.
perfection n perfection f.

perforate vt perforer.
perforation n perforation f.
perform vt exécuter; effectuer; * vi donner une représentation, tenir un rôle.
performance n exécution f; accomplissement m; rendement m; représentation f.
performer n exécutant m -e f; acteur m -trice f.
perfume n parfum m; * vt parfumer.
perhaps adv peut-être.
peril n péril, danger m.
perilous adj dangereux; ~ly adv dangereusement.
perimeter n périmètre m.
period n période f; époque f; règles fpl.
periodic(al) adj périodique; ~ally adv périodiquement.
periodical n journal m.
peripheral adj périphérique; * n unité périphérique f.
perish vi périr.
perishable adj périssable.
perjure vt parjurer.
perjury n parjure m.
perk n extra, à-côté m.
perky adj animé, plein d'entrain.
perm n permanente f.
permanent adj permanent; ~ly adv en permanence.
permeate vt pénétrer, traverser.
permissible adj permis.
permission n permission f.
permissive adj permissif.
permit vt permettre; * n permis m.
permutation n permutation f.
perpendicular adj ~ly adv perpendiculaire(ment); * n perpendiculaire f.
perpetrate vt perpétrer, commettre.
perpetual adj perpétuel; ~ly adv perpétuellement.
perpetuate vt perpétuer, éterniser.
perplex vt confondre, laisser perrplexe.
persecute vt persécuter; importuner.
persecution n persécution f.
perseverance n persévérance f.
persevere vi persévérer.
persist vi persister.
persistence n persistance f.

persistent *adj* persistant.
person *n* personne *f*.
personable *adj* attrayant.
personage *n* personnage *m*.
personal *adj* **~ly** *adv* personnel(lement).
personal assistant *n* secrétaire *mf* de direction.
personal column *n* annonces personnelles *fpl*.
personal computer *n* ordinateur individuel *m*.
personality *n* personnalité *f*.
personification *n* personnification *f*.
personify *vt* personnifier.
personnel *n* personnel *m*.
perspective *n* perspective *f*.
perspiration *n* transpiration *f*.
perspire *vi* transpirer.
persuade *vt* persuader.
persuasion *n* persuasion *f*.
persuasive *adj* persuasif; **~ly** *adv* de manière persuasive.
pert *adj* plein d'entrain.
pertaining: ~ to *prep* relatif à.
pertinent *adj* pertinent; **~ly** *adv* de manière pertinente.
pertness *n* impertinence *f*; entrain *m*.
perturb *vt* perturber.
perusal *n* lecture *f*.
peruse *vt* lire; examiner attentivement.
pervade *vt* pénétrer, traverser.
perverse *adj* pervers, dépravé; **~ly** *adv* perversement.
pervert *vt* pervertir, corrompre.
pessimist *n* pessimiste *mf*.
pest *n* insecte nuisible *m*; (*fam*) casse-pieds *mf invar*.
pester *vt* importuner, fatiguer.
pestilence *n* peste *f*.
pet *n* animal domestique *m*; préféré *m* -e *f*; * *vt* gâter; * *vi* (*fam*) se peloter.
petal *n* (*bot*) pétale *m*.
petite *adj* menue.
petition *n* pétition *f*; * *vt* présenter une pétition à; supplier.
petrified *adj* pétrifié.
petroleum *n* pétrole *m*.
petticoat *n* jupon *m*.
pettiness *n* insignifiance *f*.
petty *adj* mesquin; insignifiant.

petty cash *n* argent destiné aux dépenses courantes *m*.
petty officer *n* second maître *m*.
petulant *adj* pétulant.
pew *n* banc *m*.
pewter *n* étain *m*.
phantom *n* fantôme *m*.
Pharisee *n* Pharisien *m*.
pharmaceutic(al) *adj* pharmaceutique.
pharmacist *n* pharmacien *m* -ienne *f*.
pharmacy *n* pharmacie *f*.
phase *n* phase *f*.
pheasant *n* faisan *m*.
phenomenal *adj* phénoménal.
phenomenon *n* phénomène *m*.
phial *n* fiole *f*.
philanthropic *adj* philanthropique.
philanthropist *n* philanthrope *mf*.
philanthropy *n* philanthropie *f*.
philologist *n* philologue *mf*.
philology *n* philologie *f*.
philosopher *n* philosophe *mf*.
philosophical(ly) *adj* (*adv*) philosophique(-ment).
philosophize *vi* philosopher.
philosophy *n* philosophie *f*; **natural ~** physique *f*.
phlegm *n* flegme *m*.
phlegmatic(al) *adj* flegmatique.
phobia *n* phobie *f*.
phone *n* téléphone *m*; * *vt* téléphoner à; **~ back** *vt vi* rappeler; **~ up** *vt* appeler au téléphone.
phone book *n* annuaire *m*.
phone box, phone booth *n* cabine téléphonique *f*.
phone call *n* coup de téléphone *m*.
phosphorus *n* phosphore *m*.
photocopier *n* photocopieuse *f*.
photocopy *n* photocopie *f*.
photograph *n* photo(graphie) *f*; * *vt* photographier.
photographer *n* photographe *mf*.
photographic *adj* photographique.
photography *n* photo(graphie) *f*.
phrase *n* phrase *f*; locution *f*; * *vt* exprimer.
phrase book *n* guide de conversation *m*.
physical *adj* **~ly** *adv* physique(ment).

physical education n éducation physique f.

physician n médecin m.

physicist n physicien m -ne f.

physiological adj physiologique.

physiologist n physiologiste, physiologue mf.

physiology n physiologie f.

physiotherapy n physiothérapie f.

physique n physique m.

pianist n pianiste mf.

pick vt choisir; cueillir; gratter; ~ **on** vt s'en prendre à; ~ **out** vt choisir; ~ **up** vi s'améliorer; se remettre; * vt ramasser; décrocher; arrêter; acheter; * n pic m; choix m.

pickaxe n pic m.

picket n piquet m.

pickle n saumure f; * vt saumurer.

pickpocket n pickpocket m.

pickup n (auto) fourgonnette f.

picnic n pique-nique m.

pictorial adj pictural; illustré.

picture n image f; peinture f; photo f; * vt dépeindre; se figurer.

picture book n livre d'images m.

picturesque adj pittoresque.

pie n gâteau m; tarte f; pâté en croûte m.

piece n morceau m; pièce f; tranche f; * vt raccommoder.

piecemeal adv petit à petit; * adj partiel.

piecework n travail à la pièce m.

pier n jetée f.

pierce vt percer, transpercer.

piercing adj perçant.

piety n piété, dévotion f.

pig n cochon m.

pigeon n pigeon m.

pigeonhole n casier m.

piggy bank n tirelire f.

pigheaded adj têtu.

pigsty n porcherie f.

pigtail n natte f.

pike n brochet m; pique f.

pile n tas m; pile f; amas m; poil m; ~**s** pl hémorroïdes fpl; * vt entasser, empiler.

pile-up n carambolage m.

pilfer vt chaparder.

pilgrim n pèlerin m.

pilgrimage n pèlerinage m.

pill n pilule f.

pillage vt piller, mettre à sac.

pillar n pilier m.

pillion n siège arrière m.

pillow n oreiller m.

pillow case n taie d'oreiller f.

pilot n pilote m; * vt piloter; (fig) mener.

pilot light n témoin m.

pimp n proxénète, maquereau (fam) m.

pimple n bouton m.

pin n épingle f; goupille f; ~**s and needles** npl fourmis fpl; * vt épingler; goupiller.

pinafore n tablier m.

pinball n flipper m.

pincers n tenailles fpl.

pinch vt pincer; (sl) piquer, faucher; * vi serrer; * n pincement m; pincée f.

pincushion n pelote à épingles f.

pine n (bot) pin m; * vi languir.

pineapple n ananas m.

ping n tintement m.

pink adj n rose m.

pinnacle n sommet m.

pinpoint vt préciser; souligner.

pint n pinte f.

pioneer n pionnier m.

pious adj pieux, dévot; ~**ly** adv pieusement.

pip n pépin m.

pipe n tube, tuyau m; pipe f; ~**s** tuyauterie f.

pipe cleaner n cure-pipe m.

pipe dream n rêve impossible m.

pipeline n canalisation f; oléoduc m; gazoduc m.

piper n joueur de cornemuse m.

piping adj bouillant; aigu, f aiguë.

pique n pique f; dépit m.

piracy n piraterie f.

pirate n pirate m.

pirouette n pirouette f; vi pirouetter.

Pisces n Poissons mpl (signe du zodiaque).

piss n (sl) pisse f; * vi pisser.

pistol n pistolet m.

piston n piston m.

pit n noyau m; mine f; fosse f.

pitch n lancement m; ton m; * vt lancer, jeter; * vi tomber; piquer du nez.

pitchblack adj noir comme dans un four.

pitcher n cruche f.

pitchfork *n* fourche *f*.

pitfall *n* piège *m*.

pithy *adj* moelleux; vigoureux.

pitiable *adj* pitoyable; déplorable.

pitiful *adj* pitoyable; lamentable; **~ly** *adv* pitoyablement.

pittance *n* salaire de misère *m*; pitance *f*.

pity *n* pitié *f*; * *vt* avoir pitié de.

pivot *n* pivot, axe *m*.

pizza *n* pizza *f*.

placard *n* affiche *f*.

placate *vt* apaiser.

place *n* endroit, lieu *m*; place *f*; * *vt* placer; mettre.

placid *adj* placide, calme; **~ly** *adv* placidement.

plagiarism *n* plagiat *m*.

plague *n* peste *f*; * *vt* tourmenter; infester.

plaice *n* carrelet *m*.

plaid *n* tartan *m*; plaid *m*.

plain *adj* uni; simple; clair, sincère; commun; évident; **~ly** *adv* simplement; clairement; * *n* plaine *f*.

plaintiff *n* (*law*) plaignant *m* -e *f*.

plait *n* tresse *f*; * *vt* tresser.

plan *n* plan *m*; projet *m*; * *vt* projeter.

plane *n* avion *m*; plan *m*; rabot *m*; * *vt* aplanir; raboter.

planet *n* planète *f*.

planetary *adj* planétaire.

plank *n* planche *f*.

planner *n* planificateur *m* -trice *f*.

planning *n* planification *f*.

plant *n* plante *f*; usine *f*; machinerie *f*; * *vt* planter.

plantation *n* plantation *f*.

plaque *n* plaque *f*.

plaster *n* plâtre *m*; emplâtre *m*; * *vt* plâtrer; emplâtrer.

plastered *adj* (*sl*) bourré, soûl.

plasterer *n* plâtrier *m*.

plastic *adj* plastique.

plastic surgery *n* chirurgie esthétique *f*.

plate *n* assiette *f*; plaque *f*; lame *f*.

plateau *n* (*geol*) plateau *m*.

plate glass *n* vitre *f*.

platform *n* plateforme *f*.

platinum *n* platine *m*.

platitude *n* platitude *f*.

platoon *n* (*mil*) peloton *m*.

platter *n* écuelle *f*; plat *m*.

plaudit *n* applaudissement *m*.

plausible *adj* plausible.

play *n* jeu *m*; pièce de théâtre *f*; * *vt vi* jouer; (*also mus*) **~ down** *vt* rabaisser; minimiser.

playboy *n* playboy *m*.

player *n* joueur *m* -euse *f*; acteur *m* -trice *f*.

playful *adj* enjoué, amusé; **~ly** *adv* d'une manière enjouée; pour s'amuser.

playmate *n* camarade de jeu *mf*.

playground *n* cour de récréation *f*; jardin d'enfants *m*.

playgroup *n* halte-garderie *f*.

play-off *n* prolongation *f* (match).

playpen *n* parc pour enfant *m*.

plaything *n* jouet *m*.

playwright *n* dramaturge *mf*.

plea *n* appel *m*; excuse *f*, prétexte *m*.

plead *vt* plaider; prétexter.

pleasant *adj* agréable; plaisant; aimable; **~ly** *adv* agréablement.

please *vt* faire plaisir à.

pleased *adj* content.

pleasing *adj* agréable, plaisant.

pleasure *n* plaisir *m*; gré *m*, volonté *f*.

pleat *n* pli *m*.

pledge *n* promesse *f*; gage *m*; * *vt* engager; promettre.

plentiful *adj* copieux; abondant.

plenty *n* abondance *f*; **~ of** beaucoup de.

plethora *n* pléthore *f*.

pleurisy *n* pleurésie *f*.

pliable, pliant *adj* pliable, pliant; souple.

pliers *npl* pinces *fpl*.

plight *n* épreuve *f*; situation difficile *f*.

plinth *n* plinthe *f*.

plod *vi* se traîner, avancer péniblement.

plot *n* petit morceau de terrain *m*; complot *m*; intrigue *f*; * *vt* tracer; comploter; conspirer.

plough *n* charrue *f*; * *vt* labourer; **~ back** *vt* réinvestir; **~ through** *vi* se faire un chemin; avancer péniblement.

ploy *n* truc *m*.

pluck *vt* tirer; arracher; déplumer; * *n* courage *m*.

plucky *adj* courageux.

plug *n* tampon *m*; bouchon *m*; bougie *f*; prise *f*; * *vt* boucher.

plum *n* prune *f*.

plumage *n* plumage *m*.

plumb *n* aplomb *m*; * *adv* d'aplomb; * *vt* plomber; sonder.

plumber *n* plombier *m*.

plume *n* plume *f*, panache *m*.

plump *adj* rondouillet, dodu.

plum tree *n* prunier *m*.

plunder *vt* mettre à sac, piller; * *n* pillage *m*; butin *m*.

plunge *vi* plonger; s'élancer.

plunger *n* piston *m*.

pluperfect *n* (*gr*) plus-que-parfait *m*.

plural *adj n* pluriel *m*.

plurality *n* pluralité *f*.

plus *n* signe plus *m*; * *prep* plus.

plush *adj* en peluche.

plutonium *n* plutonium *m*.

ply *vt* manier avec vigueur; * *vi* s'appliquer; (*mar*) faire la navette.

plywood *n* contreplaqué *m*.

pneumatic *adj* pneumatique.

pneumatic drill *n* marteau pneumatique *m*.

pneumonia *n* pneumonie *f*.

poach *vt* pocher; braconner; *vi* braconner.

poached *adj* poché.

poacher *n* braconnier *m*.

poaching *n* braconnage *m*.

pocket *n* poche *f*; * *vt* empocher.

pocketbook *n* portefeuille *m*.

pocket money *n* argent de poche *m*.

pod *n* cosse *f*.

podgy *adj* boudiné.

poem *n* poème *m*.

poet *n* poète *m*.

poetess *n* poétesse *f*.

poetic *adj* poétique.

poetry *n* poésie *f*.

poignant *adj* poignant.

point *n* pointe *f*; point *m*; promontoire *m*; ~ of view *n* point de vue *m*; * *vt* pointer; tailler en pointe; indiquer.

point-blank *adv* à bout portant; directement.

pointed *adj* pointu; acéré; ~ly *adv* subtilement.

pointer *n* auguille *f*; pointer *m*.

pointless *adj* inutile.

poise *n* attitude *f*; équilibre *m*.

poison *n* poison *m*; * *vt* empoisonner.

poisoning *n* empoisonnement *m*.

poisonous *adj* vénéneux.

poke *vt* attiser; donner un coup de coude à; pousser du doigt.

poker *n* tison *m*; poker *m*.

poker-faced *adj* au visage impassible.

poky *adj* exigu, *f* exiguè.

polar *adj* polaire.

pole *n* pôle *m*; mât *m*; perche *f*.

pole bean *n* haricot en rames *m*.

pole vault *n* saut à la perche *m*.

police *n* police *f*.

police car *n* voiture de police *f*.

policeman *n* agent de police *m*.

police state *n* état policier *m*.

police station *n* commissariat *m*.

policewoman *n* femme agent de police *f*.

policy *n* politique *f*; police d'assurance *f*.

polio *n* polio *f*.

polish *vt* polir; cirer; ~ off *vt* parachever; expédier; * *n* poli *m*.

polished *adj* poli; ciré; élégant.

polite *adj* ~ly *adv* poli(ment), courtois(-ement).

politeness *n* politesse, courtoisie *f*.

politic *adj* politique; rusé.

political *adj* politique.

politician *n* homme (femme) politique *m*(*f*).

politics *npl* politique *f*.

polka *n* polka *f*; ~ dot *n* pois *m*.

poll *n* liste électorale *f*; vote *m*; sondage *m*.

pollen *n* (*bot*) pollen *m*.

pollute *vt* polluer; corrompre.

pollution *n* pollution, contamination *f*.

polyester *n* polyester *m*.

polyethylene *n* polyéthylène *m*.

polygamy *n* polygamie *f*.

polystyrene *n* polystyrène *m*.

polytechnic *n* école d'enseignement technique *f*.

pomegranate *n* grenade *f*.

pomp *n* pompe *f*; splendeur *f*.

pompom *n* pompon *m*.

pompous *adj* pompeux.

pond *n* mare *f*; étang *m*.

ponder vt considérer; réfléchir à.

ponderous adj lourd, pesant.

pontiff n pontife m.

pontoon n ponton m.

pony n poney m.

ponytail n queue de cheval f.

pool n flaque d'eau f; piscine f; * vt grouper.

poor adj pauvre; mauvais; ~ly adv pauvrement; **the ~** n les pauvres mpl.

pop n pop m; papa m; boisson gazeuse f; éclatement m; * **~ in/out** vi entrer/sortir un instant.

pop concert n concert de musique pop m.

popcorn n popcorn m.

Pope n pape m.

poplar n peuplier m.

poppy n (bot) pavot m.

popsicle n (US) sucette f glacée.

populace n populace f.

popular adj ~ly adv populaire(ment).

popularity n popularité f.

popularize vt populariser.

populate vi peupler.

population n population f.

populous adj populeux.

porcelain n porcelaine f.

porch n porche m.

porcupine n porc-épic m.

pore n pore m.

pork n porc m (viande).

pornography n pornographie f.

porous adj poreux.

porpoise n marsouin m.

porridge n porridge m, flocons d'avoine mpl.

port n port m; (mar) sabord m; babord m; porto (vin) m.

portable adj portable, portatif.

portal n portail m.

porter n portier m; garçon m.

portfolio n serviette f; carton m; portefeuille m.

porthole n hublot m.

portico n portique m.

portion n portion, part f.

portly adj corpulent.

portrait n portrait m.

portray vt faire le portrait de; dépeindre.

pose n posture f; pose f; * vt vi poser.

posh adj chic; bourgeois.

position n position f; situation f; * vt mettre en position.

positive adj positif; réel; favorable; ~ly adv positivement; assurément.

posse n peloton m, détachement m.

possess vt posséder.

possession n possession f.

possessive adj possessif.

possibility n possibilité f.

possible adj possible; ~ly adv peut-être.

post n courrier m; poste f; emploi m; poste m; pieu m; * vt poster; fixer.

postage n affranchissement m.

postage stamp n timbre m.

postcard n carte postale f.

postdate vt postdater.

posterior n postérieur m.

posterity n postérité f.

postgraduate n licencié m -e f.

posthumous adj posthume.

postman n facteur m.

postmark n cachet de la poste m.

postmaster n receveur des postes m.

post office n poste f, bureau de poste m.

postpone vt remettre; différer.

postscript n post-scriptum m.

posture n posture f.

postwar adj d'après-guerre.

posy n petit bouquet de fleurs m.

pot n pot m; marmite f; (sl) marijuana f; * vt empoter; mettre en pot.

potato n pomme de terre, patate (fam) f.

potato peeler n couteau éplucheur m.

potbellied adj ventru.

potent adj puissant.

potential adj potentiel.

pothole n trou m.

potion n potion f.

potted adj en pot.

potter n potier m.

pottery n poterie f.

potty adj insignifiant; (sl) fou, maboul.

pouch n sac m.

poultice n cataplasme m.

poultry n volaille f.

pound n livre f; livre sterling f; fourrière f; * vt concasser; * vi taper fort.

pour *vt* verser; servir; * *vi* couler; pleuvoir à verse.

pout *vi* faire la moue.

poverty *n* pauvreté *f*.

powder *n* poudre *f*; * *vt* saupoudrer.

powder compact *n* poudrier *m*.

powdered milk *n* lait en poudre *m*.

powder puff *n* houppette *f*.

powder room *n* toilettes *fpl*.

powdery *adj* poudreux.

power *n* pouvoir *m*; puissance *f*; empire *m*; autorité *f*; force *f*; * *vt* propulser.

powerful *adj* puissant; ~**ly** *adv* puissamment; avec force.

powerless *adj* impuissant.

power station *n* centrale électrique *f*.

practicable *adj* praticable; faisable.

practical *adj* ~**ly** *adv* pratique(ment).

practicality *n* faisabilité *f*.

practical joke *n* farce *f*.

practice *n* pratique *f*; usage *m*; entraînement *m*; ~**s** *pl* agissements *mpl*.

practise *vt* pratiquer, exercer; * *vi* s'exercer, s'entraîner.

practitioner *n* médecin *m*.

pragmatic *adj* pragmatique.

prairie *n* prairie *f*.

praise *n* éloge *m*; louange *f*; * *vt* louer.

praiseworthy *adj* digne d'éloges.

prance *vi* cabrioler.

prank *n* folie, extravagance *f*.

prattle *vi* jacasser; * *n* jacasserie *f*.

prawn *n* crevette *f*.

pray *vi* prier.

prayer *n* prière *f*.

prayer book *n* livre de messe *m*.

preach *vt* prêcher.

preacher *n* prédicateur *m*.

preamble *n* préambule *m*.

precarious *adj* précaire, incertain; ~**ly** *adv* précairement.

precaution *n* précaution *f*.

precautionary *adj* préventif.

precede *vt* précéder.

precedence *n* précédence *f*.

precedent *adj n* précédent *m*.

precinct *n* limite *f*; enceinte *f*; circonscription *f*.

precious *adj* précieux.

precipice *n* (*fig*) précipice *m*.

precipitate *vt* précipiter; * *adj* précipité.

precise *n* précis, exact; ~**ly** *adv* précisément, exactement.

precision *n* précision, exactitude *f*.

preclude *vt* exclure, empêcher.

precocious *adj* précoce, prématuré.

preconceive *vt* préconcevoir.

preconception *n* préjugé *m*; idée préconçue *f*.

precondition *n* condition préalable *f*.

precursor *n* précurseur *m*.

predator *n* prédateur *m*.

predecessor *n* prédécesseur *m*.

predestination *n* prédestination *f*.

predicament *n* situation difficile *f*.

predict *vt* prédire.

predictable *adj* prévisible.

prediction *n* prédiction *f*.

predilection *n* prédilection *f*.

predominant *adj* prédominant.

predominate *vt* prédominer.

preen *vt* nettoyer (ses plumes).

prefab *n* maison préfabriquée *f*.

preface *n* préface *f*.

prefer *vt* préférer.

preferable *adj* préférable.

preferably *adv* de préférence.

preference *n* préférence *f*.

preferential *adj* préférentiel.

preferment *n* promotion *f*; préférence *f*.

prefix *vt* préfixer; * *n* (*gr*) préfixe *m*.

pregnancy *n* grossesse *f*.

pregnant *adj* enceinte.

prehistoric *adj* préhistorique.

prejudice *n* (*law*) préjudice, tort *m*; préjugé *m*; * *vt* préjudicier à, faire du tort à.

prejudiced *adj* qui a des préjugés; partial.

prejudicial *adj* préjudiciable.

preliminary *adj* préliminaire.

prelude *n* prélude *m*.

premarital *adj* préconjugal.

premature *adj* ~**ly** *adv* prématuré(ment).

premeditation *n* préméditation *f*.

premier *n* premier ministre *m*.

première *n* (*thea*) première *f*.

premise *n* prémisse *f*.

premises *npl* locaux *mpl*.
premium *n* prix *m*; indemnité *f*; prime *f*.
premonition *n* pressentiment *m*, prémonition *f*.
preoccupied *adj* préoccupé; absorbé.
prepaid *adj* port payé.
preparation *n* préparation *f*.
preparatory *adj* préparatoire.
prepare *vt* préparer; * *vi* se préparer.
preponderance *n* prépondérance *f*.
preposition *n* préposition *f*.
preposterous *adj* ridicule, absurde.
prerequisite *n* condition requise *f*.
prerogative *n* prérogative *f*.
prescribe *vt* prescrire.
prescription *n* prescription *f*; ordonnance *f*.
presence *n* présence *f*.
present *n* cadeau *m*; * *adj* présent; actuel; ~**ly** *adv* actuellement; * *vt* offrir, donner; présenter.
presentable *adj* présentable.
presentation *n* présentation *f*.
present-day *adj* actuel.
presenter *n* présentateur *m* -trice *f*.
presentiment *n* pressentiment *m*, prémonition *f*.
preservation *n* préservation *f*.
preservative *n* préservatif *m*.
preserve *vt* préserver; conserver; faire des conserves de; * *n* conserve *f*; confiture *f*.
preside *vi* présider; diriger.
presidency *n* présidence *f*.
president *n* président *m*.
presidential *adj* présidentiel.
press *vt* appuyer sur; serrer; pressurer; * *vi* se presser; * *n* presse *f*; pressoir *m*; pression *f*.
press agency *n* agence de presse *f*.
press conference *n* conférence de presse *f*.
pressing *adj* pressant; urgent; ~**ly** *adv* de manière pressante; d'urgence.
pressure *n* pression *f*.
pressure cooker *n* autocuiseur *m*.
pressure group *n* groupe de pression *m*.
pressurized *adj* pressurisé.
prestige *n* prestige *m*.
presumable *adj* vraisemblable.
presumably *adv* vraisemblablement.
presume *vt* présumer, supposer.

presumption *n* présomption *f*.
presumptuous *adj* présomptueux.
presuppose *vt* présupposer.
pretence *n* prétexte *m*; simulation *f*; prétention *f*.
pretend *vi* prétendre; faire semblant.
pretender *n* prétendant *m*.
pretension *n* prétention *f*.
pretentious *adj* prétentieux.
preterite *n* prétérit *m*.
pretext *n* prétexte *m*.
pretty *adj* joli, mignon; * *adv* assez; plutôt.
prevail *vi* prévaloir; prédominer.
prevailing *adj* dominant.
prevalent *adj* prédominant.
prevent *vt* prévenir; empêcher; éviter.
prevention *n* prévention *f*.
preventive *adj* préventif.
preview *n* avant-première *f*.
previous *adj* précédent; antérieur; ~**ly** *adv* auparavant.
prewar *adj* d'avant-guerre.
prey *n* proie *f*.
price *n* prix *m*.
priceless *adj* inappréciable.
price list *n* tarif *m*.
prick *vt* piquer; exciter; * *n* piqûre *f*; pointe *f*.
prickle *n* picotement *m*; épine *f*.
prickly *adj* épineux.
pride *n* orgueil *m*; vanité *f*; fierté *f*.
priest *n* prêtre *m*.
priestess *n* prêtresse *f*.
priesthood *n* sacerdoce *m*, prêtrise *f*.
priestly *adj* sacerdotal.
priggish *adj* affecté, bégueule.
prim *adj* prude, affecté.
primacy *n* primauté *f*.
primarily *adv* principalement, surtout.
primary *adj* primaire; principal, premier.
primate *n* primate *m*.
prime *n* (*fig*) fleur *f*; commencement *m*; * *adj* premier; principal; excellent; * *vt* amorcer.
prime minister *n* premier ministre *m*.
primeval *adj* primitif.
priming *n* amorçage *m*.
primitive *adj* primitif; ~**ly** *adv* primitivement.
primrose *n* (*bot*) primevère *f*.
prince *n* prince *m*.

princess *n* princesse *f*.

principal *adj* ~**ly** *adv* principal(ement); * *n* principal *m*.

principality *n* principauté *f*.

principle *n* principe *m*.

print *vt* imprimer; * *n* impression *f*; estampe *f*; caractères imprimés *mpl*; **out of** ~ épuisé (livres).

printed matter *n* imprimés *mpl*.

printer *n* imprimeur *m*; imprimante *f*.

printing *n* impression *f*.

prior *adj* antérieur, précédent; * *n* prieur *m*.

priority *n* priorité *f*.

priory *n* prieuré *m*.

prise *vt*: **to** ~ **open** ouvrir par la force, forcer.

prism *n* prisme *m*.

prison *n* prison *f*.

prisoner *n* prisonnier *m* -ière *f*.

pristine *adj* d'origine; intact.

privacy *n* intimité *f*.

private *adj* privé; secret; particulier; ~ **soldier** *n* simple soldat *m*; ~**ly** *adv* en privé.

private eye *n* détective privé *m*.

privet *n* troène *m*.

privilege *n* privilège *m*.

prize *n* prix *m*; * *vt* apprécier, évaluer.

prize-giving *n* distribution des prix *f*.

prizewinner *n* gagnant *m* -e *f*.

pro *prep* pour.

probability *n* probabilité *f*; vraisemblance *f*.

probable *adj* probable, vraisemblable; ~**bly** *adv* probablement.

probation *n* essai *m*; probation *f*.

probationary *adj* d'essai.

probe *n* sonde *f*; enquête *f*; * *vt* sonder; * *vi* faire des recherches.

problem *n* problème *m*.

problematical *adj* ~**ly** *adv* problématique-(ment).

procedure *n* procédure *f*.

proceed *vi* procéder; provenir; poursuivre; ~**s** *npl* produit *m*; montant *m*; **gross** ~**s** bénéfices bruts *mpl*; **net** ~**s** benéfices nets *mpl*.

proceedings *n* procédure *f*; procédé *m*; procès *m*.

process *n* processus *m*; procédé *m*.

procession *n* procession *f*.

proclaim *vt* proclamer; promulguer.

proclamation *n* proclamation *f*; décret *m*.

procrastinate *vt* différer, retarder.

proctor *n* censeur *m*.

procure *vt* procurer.

procurement *n* obtention *f*.

prod *vt* pousser.

prodigal *adj* prodigue.

prodigious *adj* prodigieux; ~**ly** *adv* prodigieusement.

prodigy *n* prodige *m*.

produce *vt* produire; créer; fabriquer; * *n* produit *m*.

produce dealer *n* revendeur *m* -euse *f*.

producer *n* producteur *m* -trice *f*.

product *n* produit *m*; œuvre *f*; fruit *m*.

production *n* production *f*; produit *m*.

production line *n* chaîne *f* de fabrication.

productive *adj* productif.

productivity *n* productivité *f*.

profane *adj* profane.

profess *vt* professer; exercer; déclarer.

profession *n* profession *f*.

professional *adj* professionnel.

professor *n* professeur *m*.

proficiency *n* capacité *f*.

proficient *adj* compétent.

profile *n* profil *m*.

profit *n* bénéfice, profit *m*; avantage *m*; * *vi* profiter (de).

profitability *n* rentabilité *f*.

profitable *adj* profitable, avantageux.

profiteering *n* exploitation *f*, mercantilisme *m*.

profound *adj* ~**ly** *adv* profond(ément).

profuse *adj* profus; prodigue; ~**ly** *adv* à profusion.

program(me) *n* programme *m*.

programming *n* programmation *f*.

programmer *n* programmeur *m* -euse *f*.

progress *n* progrès *m*; cours *m*; * *vi* progresser.

progression *n* progression *f*; avance *f*.

progressive *adj* progressif; ~**ly** *adv* progressivement.

prohibit *vt* prohiber; défendre.

prohibition *n* prohibition *f*.

project *vt* projeter; * *n* projet *m*.

projectile *n* projectile *m*.

projection *n* projection *f*.

projector *n* projecteur *m*.
proletarian *adj* prolétaire.
proletariat *n* prolétariat *m*.
prolific *adj* prolifique, fécond.
prolix *adj* prolixe.
prologue *n* prologue *m*.
prolong *vt* prolonger.
prom *n* bal *m*; concert-promenade *m*.
promenade *n* promenade *f*.
prominence *n* proéminence *f*; éminence *f*.
prominent *adj* proéminent.
promiscuous *adj* immoral, débauché.
promise *n* promesse *f*; * *vt* promettre.
promising *adj* prometteur.
promontory *n* promontoire *m*.
promote *vt* promouvoir.
promoter *n* promoteur *m*.
promotion *n* promotion *f*.
prompt *adj* ~**ly** *adv* prompt(ement); * *vt* suggérer; inciter; souffler (au théâtre).
prompter *n* souffleur *m* -euse *f*.
prone *adj* enclin (à).
prong *n* dent *f* (fourchette).
pronoun *n* pronom *m*.
pronounce *vt* prononcer; déclarer.
pronounced *adj* marqué, prononcé.
pronouncement *n* déclaration *f*.
pronunciation *n* prononciation *f*.
proof *n* preuve *f*; * *adj* imperméable; résistant.
prop *vt* soutenir; * *n* appui, soutien *m*; tuteur *m*.
propaganda *n* propagande *f*.
propel *vt* propulser.
propeller *n* hélice *f*.
propensity *n* propension, tendance *f*.
proper *adj* propre; convenable; exact; approprié; ~**ly** *adv* convenablement; correctement.
property *n* propriété *f*.
prophecy *n* prophétie *f*.
prophesy *vt* prophétiser, prédire.
prophet *n* prophète *m*.
prophetic *adj* prophétique.
proportion *n* proportion *f*; symétrie *f*.
proportional *adj* proportionnel.
proportionate *adj* proportionné.
proposal *n* proposition *f*; offre *f*.
propose *vt* proposer.
proposition *n* proposition *f*.

proprietor *n* propriétaire *mf*.
propriety *n* propriété *f*.
pro rata *adv* au prorata.
prosaic *adj* prosaïque.
prose *n* prose *f*.
prosecute *vt* poursuivre en justice.
prosecution *n* poursuites *fpl*; accusation *f*.
prosecutor *n* (*law*) procureur *m*.
prospect *n* perspective *f*; espoir *m*; * *vt vi* prospecter.
prospecting *n* prospection *f*.
prospective *adj* probable; futur.
prospector *n* prospecteur *m* -trice *f*.
prospectus *n* prospectus *m*.
prosper *vi* prospérer.
prosperity *n* prospérité *f*.
prosperous *adj* prospère.
prostitute *n* prostituée *f*.
prostitution *n* prostitution *f*.
prostrate *adj* prostré.
protagonist *n* protagoniste *mf*.
protect *vt* protéger; abriter.
protection *n* protection *f*.
protective *adj* protecteur.
protector *n* protecteur *m* -trice *f*.
protégé *n* protégé *m* -e *f*.
protein *n* protéine *f*.
protest *vi* protester; * *n* protestation *f*.
Protestant *n* protestant *m* -e *f*.
protester *n* manifestant *m* -e *f*; protestataire *mf*.
protocol *n* protocole *m*.
prototype *n* prototype *m*.
protracted *adj* prolongé.
protrude *vi* déborder, ressortir.
proud *adj* fier, orgueilleux; ~**ly** *adv* fièrement.
prove *vt* prouver; justifier; * *vi* s'avérer; se révéler.
proverb *n* proverbe *m*.
proverbial *adj* ~**ly** *adv* proverbial(ement).
provide *vt* fournir; ~ **for** pourvoir aux besoins de; prévoir.
provided *conj*: ~ **that** pourvu que.
providence *n* providence *f*.
province *n* province *f*; compétence *f*.
provincial *adj n* provincial *m* -e *f*.
provision *n* provision *f*; disposition *f*.
provisional *adj* ~**ly** *adv* provisoire(ment).
proviso *n* stipulation *f*.

provocation *n* provocation *f*.

provocative *adj* provocateur.

provoke *vt* provoquer.

prow *n* (*mar*) proue *f*.

prowess *n* prouesse *f*.

prowl *vi* rôder.

prowler *n* rôdeur *m* -euse *f*.

proximity *n* proximité *f*.

proxy *n* procuration *f*; délégué *m* -e *f*.

prudence *n* prudence *f*.

prudent *adj* prudent, circonspect; **~ly** *adv* prudemment.

prudish *adj* prude.

prune *vt* tailler; * *n* pruneau *m*.

prussic acid *n* acide prussique *m*.

pry *vi* espionner; **~ open** *vt* (US) forcer.

psalm *n* psaume *m*.

pseudonym *n* pseudonyme *m*.

psyche *n* psyché *f*.

psychiatric *adj* psychiatrique.

psychiatrist *n* psychiatre *mf*.

psychiatry *n* psychiatrie *f*.

psychic *adj* psychique.

psychoanalysis *n* psychanalyse *f*.

psychoanalyst *n* psychanaliste *mf*.

psychological *adj* psychologique.

psychologist *n* psychologue *mf*.

psychology *n* psychologie *f*.

puberty *n* puberté *f*.

public *adj* public; commun; **~ly** *adv* publiquement; * *n* public *m*.

public address system *n* sonorisation *f*.

publican *n* patron(ne) de pub *m(f)*.

publication *n* publication *f*; édition *f*.

publicity *n* publicité *f*.

publicize *vt* faire de la publicité pour.

public opinion *n* opinion publique *f*.

public school *n* école privée *f*.

publish *vt* publier.

publisher *n* éditeur *m* -trice *f*.

publishing *n* édition *f*.

pucker *vt* plisser.

pudding *n* pudding *m*; dessert *m*.

puddle *n* flaque d'eau *f*.

puerile *adj* puéril.

puff *n* souffle *m*; bouffée *f*; * *vt* souffler; dégager; * *vi* souffler; bouffer.

puff pastry *n* pâte feuilletée *f*.

puffy *adj* bouffi, gonflé.

pull *vt* tirer; arracher; **~ down** faire descendre; abattre; **~ in** *vi* s'arrêter; entrer en gare; **~ off** enlever; **~ out** *vi* partir; * *vt* arracher; **~ through** *vi* s'en sortir; se remettre; **~ up** *vi* s'arrêter; * *vt* arracher; arrêter; * *n* tirage *m*; secousse *f*.

pulley *n* poulie *f*.

pulp *n* pulpe *f*.

pulpit *n* chaire *f*.

pulsate *vi* palpiter.

pulse *n* pouls *m*; légumes *mpl* secs.

pulverize *vt* pulvériser.

pumice *n* pierre ponce *f*.

pummel *vt* marteler.

pump *n* pompe *f*; * *vt* pomper; puiser.

pumpkin *n* citrouille *f*.

pun *n* jeu de mots *m*; * *vi* faire des jeux de mots.

punch *n* coup de poing *m*; poinçon *m*; punch *m*; * *vt* cogner; perforer; poinçonner.

punctual *adj* ponctuel, exact; **~ly** *adv* ponctuellement.

punctuate *vt* ponctuer.

punctuation *n* ponctuation *f*.

pundit *n* expert *m*.

pungent *adj* piquant, âcre; mordant.

punish *vt* punir.

punishment *n* châtiment *m*, punition *f*; peine *f*.

punk *n* punk *mf*; minable *mf*; **~ (music)** punk *m*.

punt *n* bateau plat *m*.

puny *adj* chétif, maigrelet.

pup, puppy *n* chiot *m*; * *vi* avoir des chiots, mettre bas.

pupil *n* élève *mf*; pupille *mf*.

puppet *n* marionnette *f*.

purchase *vt* acheter; * *n* achat *m*; acquisition *f*.

purchaser *n* acheteur *m* -euse *f*.

pure *adj* pur; **~ly** *adv* purement.

purée *n* purée *f*.

purge *vt* purger.

purification *n* purification *f*.

purify *vt* purifier.

purist *n* puriste *mf*.

puritan *n* puritain *m* -e *f*.

purity *n* pureté *f*.
purl *n* maille à l'envers *f*.
purple *adj n* pourpre, violet *m*.
purport *vt*: **to ~** to prétendre.
purpose *n* intention *f*; but, dessein *m*; **to the ~** à propos; **to no ~** en vain; **on ~** exprès, à dessein.
purposeful *adj* résolu.
purr *vi* ronronner.
purse *n* sac à main *m*; porte-monnaie *m invar*.
purser *n* commissaire *m* de bord.
pursue *vi* poursuivre; suivre.
pursuit *n* poursuite *f*; occupation *f*.
purveyor *n* fournisseur *m* -euse *f*.
push *vt* pousser; presser; **~ aside** écarter; **~ off** *vi* (*sl*) se casser; **~ on** *vi* continuer; * *n* poussée *f*; impulsion *f*; effort *m*; énergie *f*.

pusher *n* trafiquant de drogues *m*.
push-up *n* (*gymn*) pompe *f*.
put *vt* mettre, poser; proposer; obliger; **~ away** ranger; **~ down** poser par terre; rabaisser; attribuer; **~ forward** avancer; **~ off** remettre; décourager; **~ on** mettre; allumer; prendre; affecter; **~ out** éteindre; faire sortir; déranger; **~ up** lever; augmenter; loger.
putrid *adj* putride.
putt *n* putt *m*;* *vt vi* putter.
putty *n* mastic *m*.
puzzle *n* énigme *f*; casse-tête *m invar*.
puzzling *adj* étrange, mystérieux.
pyjamas *npl* pyjama *m*.
pylon *n* pylône *m*.
pyramid *n* pyramide *f*.
python *n* python *m*.

Q

quack *vi* cancaner; * *n* canard *m*; (*sl*) charlatan *m*.
quadrangle *n* quadrilatère *m*.
quadrant *n* quadrant *m*.
quadrilateral *adj* quadrilatéral.
quadruped *n* quadrupède *m*.
quadruple *adj* quadruple.
quadruplet *n* quadruplé *m* -e *f*.
quagmire *n* marécage *m*.
quail *n* caille *f*.
quaint *adj* désuet; bizarre.
quake *vi* trembler.
Quaker *n* quaker *m*.
qualification *n* qualification *f*; diplôme *m*.
qualified *adj* qualifié; diplômé.
qualify *vt* qualifier; modérer; * *vi* se qualifier.
quality *n* qualité *f*.
qualm *n* scrupule *m*.
quandary *n* incertitude *f*, doute *m*.
quantitative *adj* quantitatif.
quantity *n* quantité *f*.
quarantine *n* quarantaine *f*.
quarrel *n* dispute, querelle *f*; * *vi* se disputer, se quereller.
quarrelsome *adj* querelleur.
quarry *n* carrière *f*.

quarter *n* quart *m*; **a ~ of an hour** un quart d'heure; * *vt* diviser en quatre.
quarterly *adj* trimestriel; * *adv* tous les trimestres.
quartermaster *n* (*mil*) intendant *m*.
quartet *n* (*mus*) quartette *m*; quatuor *m*.
quartz *n* (*min*) quartz *m*.
quash *vt* écraser; annuler.
quay *n* quai *m*.
queasy *adj* qui a des nausées; écœurant.
queen *n* reine *f*; dame *f* (cartes).
queer *adj* extrange; (*sl*) pédale *f*.
quell *vt* étouffer; apaiser.
quench *vt* assouvir; éteindre.
query *n* question *f*; * *vt* demander.
quest *n* recherche *f*.
question *n* question *f*; sujet *m*; doute *m*; * *vt* douter de; mettre en question; questionner.
questionable *adj* discutable; douteux.
questioner *n* interrogateur *m*.
question mark *n* point d'interrogation *m*.
questionnaire *n* questionnaire *m*.
quibble *vi* chicaner.
quick *adj* rapide; vif; prompt; **~ly** *adv* rapidement, vite.
quicken *vt* presser; accélérer; * *vi* s'accélérer.

quicksand *n* sables mouvants *mpl*.
quicksilver *n* mercure *m*.
quick-witted *adj* à l'esprit vif.
quiet *adj* calme; silencieux; ~ly *adv* calmement.
quietness *n* calme *m*, tranquillité *f*; silence *m*.
quinine *n* quinine *f*.
quintet *n* (*mus*) quintette *m*.
quintuple *adj* quintuple.
quintuplet *n* quintuplé *m* -e *f*.
quip *n* sarcasme *m*; * *vt* railler.
quirk *n* particularité *f*.

quit *vt* arrêter de; quitter; * *vi* abandonner; démissionner; * *adj* quitte.
quite *adv* assez; complètement, absolument.
quits *adj* quitte.
quiver *vi* trembler.
quixotic *adj* donquichottesque.
quiz *n* concours *m*; examen *m*; * *vt* interroger.
quizzical *adj* railleur.
quota *n* quota *m*.
quotation *n* citation *f*.
quotation marks *npl* guillemets *mpl*.
quote *vt* citer.
quotient *n* quotient *m*.

R

rabbi *n* rabbi, rabbin *m*.
rabbit *n* lapin *m*.
rabbit hutch *n* clapier *m*.
rabble *n* cohue *f*.
rabid *adj* forcené, enragé.
rabies *n* rage *f*.
race *n* course *f*; race *f*; * *vt* faire une course avec; * *vi* courir; faire une course; aller très vite; foncer.
racer *n* cheval de course *m*.
racial *adj* racial; ~ist *adj* *n* raciste *mf*.
raciness *n* vivacité *f*.
racing *n* courses *fpl*.
rack *n* casier *m*; étagère *f*; * *vt* soumettre au supplice du chevalet; tourmenter.
racket *n* vacarme *m*; raquette *f*.
rack-rent *n* loyer démesuré *m*.
racy *adj* piquant, plein de verve.
radiance *n* rayonnement *m*, éclat *m*.
radiant *adj* rayonnant, radieux.
radiate *vt* *vi* rayonner, irradier.
radiation *n* irradiation *f*.
radiator *n* radiateur *m*.
radical(ly) *adj* (*adv*) radical(ement).
radicalism *n* radicalisme *m*.
radio *n* radio *f*.
radioactive *adj* radioactif.
radish *n* radis *m*.
radius *n* radius *m*.
raffle *n* tombola *f*; * *vt* mettre en tombola.
raft *n* radeau, train de flottage *m*.

rafter *n* chevron *m*.
rag *n* lambeau *m*, loque *f*.
ragamuffin *n* va-nu-pieds *m* *invar*; galopin *m*.
rage *n* rage *f*; fureur *f*; * *vi* être furieux; faire rage.
ragged *adj* déguenillé.
raging *adj* furieux, déchaîné, enragé.
ragman, ~ picker *n* chiffonnier *m*.
raid *n* raid *m*; * *vt* faire un raid sur.
raider *n* raider *m*, pillard *m*.
rail *n* rambarde *f*, garde-fou *m*; (*rail*) rail, chemin de fer *m*; * *vt* entourer d'une barrière.
raillery *n* taquinerie *f*.
railroad, railway *n* chemin de fer *m*.
raiment *n* vêtements *mpl*.
rain *n* pluie *f*; * *vi* pleuvoir.
rainbow *n* arc-en-ciel *m*.
rainwater *n* eau de pluie *f*.
rainy *adj* pluvieux.
raise *vt* lever, soulever; ériger, édifier; élever.
raisin *n* raisin sec *m*.
rake *n* râteau *m*; libertin *m*; * *vt* ratisser.
rakish *adj* libertin, débauché.
rally *vt* (*mil*) rallier; * *vi* se rallier.
ram *n* bélier *m*; navire bélier *m*; * *vt* enfoncer.
ramble *vi* errer; faire une randonnée; * *n* excursion à pied, randonnée *f*.
rambler *n* excursionniste *mf*.
ramification *n* ramification *f*.
ramify *vi* se ramifier.
ramp *n* rampe *f*.

rampant *adj* exubérant.

rampart *n* terre-plein *m*; (*mil*) rempart *m*.

ramrod *n* baguette *f*; refouloir *m*.

ramshackle *adj* délabré.

ranch *n* ranch *m*.

rancid *adj* rance.

rancour *n* rancœur *f*.

random *adj* fortuit, fait au hasard; **at ~** au hasard.

range *vt* ranger, classer; * *vi* s'étendre; * *n* rangée *f*; ordre *m*; portée *f*; chaîne *f*; champ de tir *m*; fourneau de cuisine *m*.

ranger *n* garde forestier *m*.

rank *adj* exubérant; fétide; flagrant; * *n* rang *m*, classe *f*, grade *m*.

rankle *vi* rester sur le cœur.

rankness *n* exubérance *f*; odeur rance *f*.

ransack *vt* saccager, piller.

ransom *n* rançon *f*.

rant *vi* déclamer.

rap *vi* donner un coup sec; * *n* petit coup sec *m*.

rapacious *adj* rapace; **~ly** *adv* avec rapacité.

rapacity *n* rapacité *f*.

rape *n* viol *m*; rapt *m*; (*bot*) colza *m*; * *vt* violer.

rapid *adj* **~ly** *adv* rapide(ment).

rapidity *n* rapidité *f*.

rapier *n* rapière *f*.

rapist *n* violeur *m*.

rapt *adj* extasié; absorbé.

rapture *n* ravissement *m*; extase *f*.

rapturous *adj* de ravissement.

rare *adj* **~ly** *adv* rare(ment).

rarity *n* rareté *f*.

rascal *n* vaurien *m*.

rash *adj* imprudent, téméraire; **~ly** *adv* sans réfléchir; * *n* vague *f*; éruption (cutanée) *f*.

rashness *n* imprudence *f*.

rasp *n* râpe *f*; * *vt* râper.

raspberry *n* framboise *f*; **~ bush** framboisier *m*.

rat *n* rat *m*.

rate *n* taux, prix, cours *m*; classe *f*; vitesse *f*; * *vt* estimer, évaluer.

rather *adv* plutôt; quelque peu.

ratification *n* ratification *f*.

ratify *vt* ratifier.

rating *n* estimation *f*; classement *m*; indice *m*.

ratio *n* rapport *m*.

ration *n* ration *f*; (*mil*) vivres *mpl*.

rational *adj* rationnel; raisonnable; **~ly** *adv* rationnellement.

rationality *n* rationalité *f*.

rattan *n* (*bot*) rotin *m*.

rattle *vi* s'entrechoquer; cliqueter * *vt* faire s'entrechoquer; * *n* fracas *m*; cliquetis *m*.

rattlesnake *n* serpent à sonnettes *m*.

ravage *vt* ravager, piller; dévaster; * *n* ravage *m*.

rave *vi* délirer.

raven *n* corbeau *m*.

ravenous *adj* **~ly** *adv* vorace(ment).

ravine *n* ravin *m*.

ravish *vt* enchanter; ravir.

ravishing *adj* enchanteur.

raw *adj* cru; brut; novice.

rawboned *adj* décharné; maigre.

rawness *n* crudité *f*; inexpérience *f*.

ray *n* rayon *m*; (*fish*) raie *f*.

raze *vt* raser.

razor *n* rasoir *m*.

reach *vt* atteindre; arriver à; * *vi* s'étendre, porter; * *n* portée *f*.

react *vi* réagir.

reaction *n* réaction *f*.

read *vt vi* lire.

readable *adj* lisible.

reader *n* lecteur *m* -trice *f*.

readily *adv* volontiers; facilement.

readiness *n* bonne volonté *f*; empressement *m*.

reading *n* lecture *f*.

reading room *n* salle de lecture *f*.

readjust *vt* réajuster, réadapter.

ready *adj* prêt; enclin; disposé.

real *adj* réel, vrai; **~ly** *adv* vraiment.

realization *n* réalisation *f*.

realize *vt* se rendre compte de; réaliser.

reality *n* réalité *f*.

realm *n* royaume *m*.

ream *n* rame *f* de papier.

reap *vt* moissonner.

reaper *n* moissonneuse *f* (machine).

reappear *vi* réapparaître.

rear *n* arrière *m*; derrière *m*; * *vt* élever, dresser.

rearmament *n* réarmement *m*.

reason *n* raison *f*; cause *f*; * *vt vi* raisonner.

reasonable *adj* raisonnable.

reasonableness *n* bon sens *m*, sagesse *f*.

reasonably *adv* raisonnablement.

reasoning *n* raisonnement *m*.

reassure *vt* rassurer; (*com*) réassurer.

rebel *n* rebelle *mf*; * *vi* se rebeller.

rebellion *n* rébellion *f*.

rebellious *adj* rebelle.

rebound *vi* rebondir.

rebuff *n* rebuffade *f*; * *vt* repousser.

rebuild *vt* reconstruire.

rebuke *vt* réprimander; * *n* réprimande *f*.

rebut *vt* réfuter.

recalcitrant *adj* récalcitrant.

recall *vt* (se) rappeler; retirer; * *n* retrait *m*.

recant *vt* rétracter, désavouer.

recantation *n* rétractation *f*.

recapitulate *vt vi* récapituler.

recapitulation *n* récapitulation *f*.

recapture *n* reprise *f*.

recede *vi* reculer.

receipt *n* reçu *m*; réception *f*; ~s *npl* recettes *fpl*.

receivable *adj* recevable.

receive *vt* recevoir; accueillir.

recent *adj* récent, neuf; ~ly *adv* récemment.

receptacle *n* récipient *m*.

reception *n* réception *f*.

recess *n* (*law*) vacance *f*; renfoncement *m*; recoin *m*.

recession *n* recul *m*; (*com*) récession *f*.

recipe *n* recette *f*.

recipient *n* destinataire *mf*.

reciprocal *adj* ~ly *adv* réciproque(ment).

reciprocate *vi* rendre la pareille.

reciprocity *n* réciprocité *f*.

recital *n* récit *m*; récital *m*.

recite *vt* réciter; exposer, énumérer.

reckless *adj* téméraire; ~ly *adv* imprudemment.

reckon *vt* compter, calculer; * *vi* calculer.

reckoning *n* compte *m*; calcul *m*.

reclaim *vt* assainir; récupérer.

reclaimable *adj* remboursable; récupérable.

recline *vt* reposer; * *vi* être allongé.

recluse *n* reclus *m* -e *f*.

recognition *n* reconnaissance *f*.

recognize *vt* reconnaître.

recoil *vi* reculer.

recollect *vt* se rappeler, se souvenir de.

recollection *n* souvenir *m*.

recommence *vt* recommencer.

recommend *vt* recommander.

recommendation *n* recommandation *f*.

recompense *n* récompense *f*; * *vt* récompenser.

reconcilable *adj* conciliable.

reconcile *vt* réconcilier.

reconciliation *n* réconciliation *f*.

recondite *adj* abstrus, obscur.

reconnoitre *vt* (*mil*) reconnaître.

reconsider *vt* reconsidérer.

reconstruct *vt* reconstruire.

record *vt* enregistrer; consigner par écrit; * *n* rapport *m*, registre *m*; disque *m*; record *m*; ~s *pl* archives *fpl*.

recorder *n* magnétophone *m*, archiviste *mf*; (*mus*) flûte à bec *f*.

recount *vt* raconter.

recourse *n* recours *m*.

recover *vt* retrouver; reprendre; récupérer; * *vi* se remettre, se rétablir.

recoverable *adj* récupérable.

recovery *n* guérison *f*; reprise *f*.

recreation *n* détente *f*; récréation *f*.

recriminate *vi* récriminer.

recrimination *n* récrimination *f*.

recruit *vt* recruter; * *n* (*mil*) recrue *f*.

recruiting *n* recrutement *m*.

rectangle *n* rectangle *m*.

rectangular *adj* rectangulaire.

rectification *n* rectification *f*.

rectify *vt* rectifier.

rectilinear *adj* rectiligne.

rectitude *n* rectitude *f*.

rector *n* pasteur *m*.

recumbent *adj* couché, étendu.

recur *vi* se reproduire.

recurrence *n* répétition *f*.

recurrent *adj* répétitif.

red *adj* rouge; * *n* rouge *m*.

redden *vt vi* rougir.

reddish *adj* rougeâtre.

redeem *vt* racheter, rembourser.

redeemable *adj* rachetable.

Redeemer *n* Rédempteur *m*.

redemption *n* rachat *m*.

redeploy *vt* réaffecter.

redhanded *adj*: **to catch sb ~** prendre quelqu'un la main dans le sac.

redhot *adj* brûlant, ardent.

red-letter day *n* jour à marquer d'une pierre blanche *m*.

redness *n* rougeur, rousseur *f*.

redolent *adj* parfumé, odorant.

redouble *vt vi* redoubler.

redress *vt* réparer; corriger; redresser; * *n* réparation *f*, redressement *m*.

redskin *n* Peau-Rouge *mf*.

red tape *n* (*fig*) paperasserie *f*.

reduce *vt* réduire; diminuer; abaisser.

reducible *adj* réductible.

reduction *n* réduction *f*; baisse *f*.

redundancy *n* licenciement *m*.

redundant *adj* superflu; licencié.

reed *n* roseau *m*.

reedy *adj* couvert de roseaux.

reef *n* (*mar*) ris *m*; récif *m*.

reek *n* puanteur *f*; * *vi* empester; puer.

reel *n* bobine *f*; bande *f*; dévidoir *m*; * *vi* chanceler.

re-election *n* réélection *f*.

re-engage *vt* rengager.

re-enter *vt* rentrer.

re-establish *vt* rétablir; réhabiliter.

re-establishment *n* rétablissement *m*; restauration *f*.

refectory *n* réfectoire *m*.

refer *vt* soumettre, renvoyer; se référer à; * *vi* se référer.

referee *n* arbitre *m*.

reference *n* référence, allusion *f*.

refine *vt* raffiner, affiner.

refinement *n* raffinement *m*; raffinerie *f*; culture *f*.

refinery *n* raffinerie *f*.

refit *vt* réparer (*also mar*).

reflect *vt* réfléchir, refléter; * *vi* réfléchir.

reflection *n* réflexion, pensée *f*.

reflector *n* réflecteur *m*; cataphote *m*.

reflex *adj* réflexe.

reform *vt* réformer; * *vi* se réformer.

reform, reformation *n* réforme *f*.

reformer *n* réformateur *m* -trice *f*.

reformist *n* réformiste *mf*.

refract *vt* réfracter.

refraction *n* réfraction *f*.

refrain *vi*: **to ~ from sth** s'abstenir de qch.

refresh *vt* rafraîchir.

refreshment *n* rafraîchissement *m*.

refrigerator *n* glacière *f*; réfrigérateur *m*.

refuel *vi* se ravitailler (en carburant).

refuge *n* refuge, asile *m*.

refugee *n* réfugié *m* -e *f*.

refund *vt* rembourser; * *n* remboursement *m*.

refurbish *vt* rénover.

refusal *n* refus *m*.

refuse *vt* refuser; * *n* déchets *mpl*.

refute *vt* réfuter.

regain *vt* recouvrer, reprendre.

regal *adj* royal.

regale *vt* régaler.

regalia *n* insignes *mpl*.

regard *vt* considérer; * *n* considération *f*; respect *m*.

regarding *pr* en ce qui concerne.

regardless *adv* quand même, malgré tout.

regatta *n* régate *f*.

regency *n* régence *f*.

regenerate *vt* régénérer; * *adj* régénéré.

regeneration *n* régénération *f*.

regent *n* régent *m*.

regime *n* régime *m*.

regiment *n* régiment *m*.

region *n* région *f*.

register *n* registre *m*; * *vt* enregistrer; **~ed letter** *n* lettre recommandée *f*.

registrar *n* officier d'état civil *m*.

registration *n* enregistrement *m*.

registry *n* enregistrement *m*.

regressive *adj* régressif.

regret *n* regret *m* * *vt* regretter.

regretful *adj* plein de regrets.

regular *adj* régulier; ordinaire; **~ly** *adv* régulièrement; * *n* habitué *m* -e *f*.

regularity *n* régularité *f*.

regulate *vt* régler, réglementer.

regulation *n* règlement *m*; réglementation *f*.

regulator *n* régulateur *m*.

rehabilitate *vt* réhabiliter.

rehabilitation n réhabilitation f.
rehearsal n répétition f.
rehearse vt répéter; raconter.
reign n règne m; * vi régner.
reimburse vt rembourser.
reimbursement n remboursement m.
rein n rêne f; * vt ~ **in** (fig) contenir.
reindeer n renne m.
reinforce vt renforcer.
reinstate vt réintégrer.
reinsure vt (com) réassurer.
reissue n réédition f.
reiterate vt réitérer.
reiteration n réitération, répétition f.
reject vt rejeter.
rejection n refus, rejet m.
rejoice vt réjouir; * vi se réjouir.
rejoicing n réjouissance f.
relapse vi retomber; * n rechute f.
relate vt relater; rapprocher; * vi se rapporter.
related adj apparenté.
relation n rapport m; parent m.
relationship n lien de parenté m; relation f; rapport m.
relative adj relatif; **~ly** adv relativement; * n parent m -e f.
relax vt relâcher; détendre; * vi se relâcher; se détendre.
relaxation n relâchement m; détente f.
relay n relais m; * vt retransmettre.
release vt libérer, relâcher; * n libération f; décharge f.
relegate vt reléguer.
relegation n relégation f.
relent vi s'adoucir.
relentless adj implacable.
relevant adj pertinent.
reliable adj fiable, digne de confiance.
reliance n confiance f.
relic n relique f.
relief n soulagement m; secours m.
relieve vt soulager, alléger; secourir.
religion n religion f.
religious adj religieux; **~ly** adv religieusement.
relinquish vt abandonner, renoncer à.
relish n saveur f; goût m; attrait m; * vt savourer, se délecter de.
reluctance n répugnance f.

reluctant adj peu disposé.
rely vi compter sur, avoir confiance en.
remain vi rester, demeurer.
remainder n reste, restant m.
remains npl restes, vestiges mpl; dépouille f.
remand vt: **to ~ in custody** mettre en détention préventive.
remark n remarque, observation f; * vt (faire) remarquer, (faire) observer.
remarkable adj remarquable, notable.
remarkably adv remarquablement.
remarry vi se remarier.
remedial adj de rattrapage.
remedy n remède, recours m; * vt remédier à.
remember vt se souvenir de; se rappeler.
remembrance n mémoire f; souvenir m.
remind vt rappeler.
reminiscence n réminiscence f.
remiss adj négligent.
remission n rémission f.
remit vt remettre, pardonner; * vi diminuer.
remittance n remise f.
remnant n reste, restant m.
remodel vt remodeler.
remonstrate vi protester.
remorse n remords m.
remorseless adj implacable.
remote adj lointain, éloigné; **~ly** adv au loin, de loin.
remoteness n éloignement m; isolement m.
removable adj amovible.
removal n suppression f; déménagement m.
remove vt enlever; * vi déménager.
remunerate vt rémunérer.
remuneration n rémunération f.
render vt rendre, remettre; traduire; (law) rendre.
rendezvous n rendez-vous m; point de ralliement m.
renegade n renégat m -e f.
renew vt renouveler.
renewal n renouvellement m.
rennet n présure f.
renounce vt renoncer à.
renovate vt rénover.
renovation n rénovation f.
renown n renommée f; célébrité f.
renowned adj célèbre, renommé.

rent *n* loyer *m*; location *f*; * *vt* louer.
rental *n* loyer *m*.
renunciation *n* renonciation *f*.
reopen *vt* rouvrir.
reorganization *n* réorganisation *f*.
reorganize *vt* réorganiser.
repair *vt* réparer; * *n* réparation *f*.
repairable *adj* réparable.
reparation *n* réparation *f*.
repartee *n* répartie, réplique *f*.
repatriate *vt* rapatrier.
repay *vt* rembourser; rendre, récompenser.
repayment *n* remboursement *m*.
repeal *vt* abroger, annuler; * *n* abrogation, annulation *f*.
repeat *vt* répéter.
repeatedly *adv* à plusieurs reprises.
repeater *n* montre à répétition *f*.
repel *vt* repousser, rebuter.
repent *vi* se repentir.
repentance *n* repentir *m*.
repentant *adj* repentant.
repertory *n* répertoire *m*.
repetition *n* répétition, réitération *f*.
replace *vt* replacer; remplacer.
replant *vt* replanter.
replenish *vt* remplir de nouveau.
replete *adj* rempli, rassasié.
reply *n* réponse *f*; * *vt* répondre.
report *vt* rapporter, relater; rendre compte de; * *n* rapport *m*; compte rendu *m*; rumeur *f*.
reporter *n* journaliste *mf*.
repose *vi* (se) reposer; * *n* repos *m*.
repository *n* dépôt *m*.
repossess *vt* reprendre possession de.
reprehend *vt* condamner.
reprehensible *adj* répréhensible.
represent *vt* représenter.
representation *n* représentation *f*.
representative *adj* représentatif; * *n* représentant(e) *m(f)*.
repress *vt* réprimer, contenir.
repression *n* répression *f*.
repressive *adj* répressif.
reprieve *vt* accorder un sursis *ou* un répit à; * *n* sursis *m*.
reprimand *vt* réprimander, blâmer; * *n* blâme *m*; réprimande *f*.

reprint *vt* réimprimer.
reprisal *n* représailles *fpl*.
reproach *n* reproche, opprobre *m*; * *vt* reprocher.
reproachful *adj* réprobateur; ~**ly** *adv* d'un air de reproche.
reproduce *vt* reproduire.
reproduction *n* reproduction *f*.
reptile *n* reptile *m*.
republic *n* république *f*.
republican *adj n* républicain *m* -e *f*.
republicanism *n* républicanisme *m*.
repudiate *vt* renier.
repugnance *n* répugnance f, dégoût *m*.
repugnant *adj* répugnant; ~**ly** *adv* avec répugnance.
repulse *vt* repousser, rejeter; * *n* rebuffade *f*; refus *m*.
repulsion *n* répulsion *f*.
repulsive *adj* répulsif.
reputable *adj* honorable.
reputation *n* réputation *f*.
repute *n* renom *m*.
request *n* demande, requête *f*; * *vt* demander.
require *vt* demander, nécessiter.
requirement *n* besoin *m*; exigence *f*.
requisite *adj* nécessaire, indispensable; * *n* objet(s) nécessaire(s) *m(pl)*.
requisition *n* demande; (*mil*) réquisition *f*.
requite *vt* rembourser.
rescind *vt* annuler, abroger.
rescue *vt* sauver, secourir; * *n* secours *m*, délivrance *f*.
research *vt* faire des/de la recherche(s); * *n* recherche(s) *f(pl)*.
resemblance *n* ressemblance *f*.
resemble *vt* ressembler à.
resent *vt* être contrarié/irrité par.
resentful *adj* plein de ressentiment; amer; ~**ly** *adv* avec ressentiment.
resentment *n* ressentiment *m*.
reservation *n* réserve *f*; réservation *f*.
reserve *vt* réserver; * *n* réserve *f*.
reservedly *adv* avec réserve.
reservoir *n* réservoir *m*.
reside *vi* résider.
residence *n* résidence *f*; séjour *m*.
resident *adj* résidant; * *n* résident *m* -e *f*.

residuary *adj* restant; **~ legatee** *n* (*law*) légataire universel *m*.

residue *n* reste, résidu *m*.

residuum *n* (*chem*) résidu *m*.

resign *vt* démissionner de, renoncer à, céder; se résigner à; * *vi* démissionner.

resignation *n* démission *f*.

resin *n* résine *f*.

resinous *adj* résineux.

resist *vt* résister, s'opposer.

resistance *n* résistance *f*.

resolute *adj* **~ly** *adv* résolu(ment).

resolution *n* résolution *f*.

resolve *vt* résoudre; * *vi* (se) résoudre, (se) décider.

resonance *n* résonance *f*.

resonant *adj* résonant.

resort *vi* recourir; * *n* lieu de vacances *m*; recours *m*.

resound *vi* résonner.

resource *n* ressource(s) *f*(*pl*); expédient *m*.

respect *n* respect *m*; égard *m*; rapport *m*; **~s** *pl* respects *mpl*; * *vt* respecter.

respectability *n* respectabilité *f*.

respectable *adj* respectable; considérable; **~bly** *adv* convenablement.

respectful *adj* respectueux; **~ly** *adv* respectueusement.

respecting *prep* en ce qui concerne.

respective *adj* respectif; **~ly** *adv* respectivement.

respirator *n* respirateur *m*.

respiratory *adj* respiratoire.

respite *n* répit *m*; (*law*) sursis *m*; * *vt* repousser, différer.

resplendence *n* resplendissement *m*, splendeur *f*.

resplendent *adj* resplendissant.

respond *vi* répondre; réagir.

respondent *n* (*law*) défendeur *m* -deresse *f*.

response *n* réponse, réaction *f*.

responsibility *n* responsabilité *f*.

responsible *adj* responsable.

responsive *adj* sensible à, réceptif.

rest *n* repos *m*; (*mus*) pause *f*; reste, restant *m*; * *vt* faire *or* laisser reposer; appuyer; * *vi* se reposer, reposer.

resting place *n* lieu de repos *m*.

restitution *n* restitution *f*.

restive *adj* rétif, récalcitrant; agité.

restless *adj* agité; instable.

restoration *n* restauration *f*.

restorative *adj* fortifiant.

restore *vt* restituer, restaurer.

restrain *vt* retenir, contenir.

restraint *n* contrainte, entrave *f*.

restrict *vt* restreindre, limiter.

restriction *n* restriction *f*.

restrictive *adj* restrictif.

rest room *n* (US) toilettes *fpl*.

result *vi* résulter; * *n* résultat *m*.

resume *vt* reprendre.

resurrection *n* résurrection *f*.

resuscitate *vt* réanimer.

retail *vt* vendre au détail, détailler; * *n* vente au détail *f*.

retain *vt* retenir, conserver.

retainer *n* serviteur *m*; **~s** *pl* arrhes *fpl*; suite *f*.

retake *vt* reprendre.

retaliate *vi* se venger.

retaliation *n* représailles *fpl*.

retardation *n* retard *m*.

retarded *adj* retardé.

retch *vi* avoir des haut-le-cœur.

retention *n* rétention *f*.

retentive *adj* qui retient bien.

reticence *n* réticence *f*.

reticule *n* réticule m.

retina *n* rétine *f*.

retire *vt* mettre à la retraite; * *vi* se retirer; prendre sa retraite.

retired *adj* retraité, à la retraite.

retirement *n* isolement *m*; retraite *f*.

retort *vt* rétorquer; * *n* réplique *f*.

retouch *vt* retoucher.

retrace *vt* retracer.

retract *vt* rétracter; retirer.

retrain *vt* recycler.

retraining *n* recyclage *m*.

retreat *n* repli *m*; * *vi* se retirer.

retribution *n* châtiment *m*; récompense *f*.

retrievable *adj* récupérable; réparable.

retrieve *vt* récupérer, recouvrer.

retriever *n* chien d'arrêt *m*.

retrograde *adj* rétrograde.

retrospect, retrospection n regard rétrospectif m.

retrospective adj rétrospectif.

return vt rendre; restituer; renvoyer; * n retour m; renvoi m; récompense f; revenu m; remboursement m.

reunion n réunion f.

reunite vt réunir; * vi se réunir.

reveal vt révéler.

revel vi faire la fête.

revelation n révélation f.

reveller n fêtard m.

revelry n fête f.

revenge vt venger; * n vengeance f.

revengeful adj vindicatif.

revenue n revenu m; rente f.

reverberate vt réverbérer; * vi résonner, retentir; se réverbérer.

reverberation n répercussion f; réverbération f.

revere vt révérer, vénérer.

reverence n vénération f; * vt révérer.

reverend adj révérend; vénérable; * n curé m.

reverent, reverential adj révérenciel, respectueux.

reversal n renversement m; annulation f.

reverse vt renverser; annuler; * vi faire marche arrière; * n inverse m; contraire m; revers m.

reversible adj révocable; réversible.

reversion n retour m; réversion f.

revert vi revenir; retourner.

review vt revoir; (mil) passer en revue; * n revue f; examen m.

reviewer n critique m.

revile vt vilipender.

revise vt réviser; mettre à jour.

reviser n réviseur m.

revision n révision f.

revisit vt retourner voir.

revival n reprise f; renouveau m.

revive vt ranimer; raviver; * vi reprendre connaissance; reprendre.

revocation n révocation f.

revoke vt révoquer, annuler.

revolt vi se révolter; * n révolte f.

revolting adj exécrable.

revolution n révolution f.

revolutionary adj n révolutionnaire mf.

revolve vt (re)tourner; * vi tourner.

revolving adj tournant.

revue n revue f.

revulsion n écœurement m.

reward n récompense f; * vt récompenser.

rhapsody n r(h)apsodie f.

rhetoric n rhétorique f.

rhetorical adj rhétorique.

rheumatic adj rhumatisant.

rheumatism n rhumatisme m.

rhinoceros n rhinocéros m.

rhombus n rhombe m.

rhomboid n rhomboïd m.

rhubarb n rhubarbe f.

rhyme n rime f; vers mpl; * vi rimer.

rhythm n rythme m.

rhythmical adj rythmique.

rib n côte f.

ribald adj paillard.

ribbon n ruban m; lambeaux mpl.

rice n riz m.

rich adj riche; somptueux; abondant; ~ly adv richement.

riches npl richesse f.

richness n richesse f; abondance f.

rickets n rachitisme m.

rickety adj rachitique.

rid vt débarrasser; se débarrasser de.

riddance n: **good ~!** bon débarras!

riddle n énigme f; crible m; * vt cribler.

ride vi monter à cheval; aller en voiture; * n promenade à cheval ou en voiture f.

rider n cavalier m -ière f.

ridge n arête, crête f; chaîne f; * vt rider, strier.

ridicule n ridicule m; raillerie f; * vt ridiculiser.

ridiculous adj ~ly adv ridicule(ment).

riding n équitation f; monte f.

riding habit n tenue d'amazone f.

riding school n manège m.

rife adj répandu, abondant.

riffraff n racaille f.

rifle vt dévaliser, piller; strier, rayer; * n fusil m.

rifleman n fusilier m.

rig vt équiper; truquer; (mar) gréer; * n gréement m; plateforme de forage f.

rigging n (mar) gréement m.

right *adj* droit, bien; juste; équitable; ~! bien!, bon!; **~ly** *adv* bien; correctement; à juste titre; * *n* justice *f*; raison *f*; droit *m*; droite *f*; * *vt* redresser.

righteous *adj* droit, vertueux; **~ly** *adv* vertueusement.

righteousness *n* droiture *f*; vertu *f*.

rigid *adj* rigide; sévère, strict; **~ly** *adv* rigidement.

rigidity *n* rigidité *f*; sévérité *f*.

rigmarole *n* galimatias *m*.

rigorous *adj* rigoureux; **~ly** *adv* rigoureusement.

rigour *n* rigueur *f*; sévérité *f*.

rim *n* bord *m*, monture *f*.

rind *n* peau, écorce *f*.

ring *n* anneau, cercle, rond *m*; bague *f*; tintement *m* de cloche; * *vt* sonner; * *vi* sonner, retentir; ~ **the bell** sonner.

ringer *n* carillonneur *m*.

ringleader *n* meneur *m*.

ringlet *n* anglaise *f*.

ringworm *n* (*med*) teigne *f*.

rink *n* (*also* **ice** ~) patinoire *f*.

rinse *vt* rincer.

riot *n* émeute *f*; * *vi* se livrer à une émeute.

rioter *n* émeutier *m*, -ière *f*.

riotous *adj* séditieux; dissolu; **~ly** *adv* de façon tapageuse.

rip *vt* déchirer, fendre.

ripe *adj* mûr.

ripen *vt vi* mûrir.

ripeness *n* maturité *f*.

rip-off *n* (*sl*): **it's a** ~! c'est du vol!

ripple *vt* rider; * *vi* se rider; * *n* ondulation *f*, ride *f*.

rise *vi* se lever; naître; se soulever; monter; provenir de; s'élever; croître; ressusciter; * *n* hausse *f*; augmentation *f*; montée *f*; lever *m*; source *f*.

rising *n* insurrection *f*; levée, clôture *f*.

risk *n* risque, danger *m*; * *vt* risquer.

risky *adj* risqué.

rissole *n* rissole *f*.

rite *n* rite *m*.

ritual *adj n* rituel *m*.

rival *adj* rival; * *n* rival *m* -e *f*; * *vt* rivaliser avec, concurrencer.

rivalry *n* rivalité *f*.

river *n* rivière *f*.

rivet *n* rivet *m*; * *vt* riveter, river.

rivulet *n* petit ruisseau *m*.

roach *n* blatte *f*.

road *n* route *f*.

roadsign *n* panneau de signalisation *m*.

roadstead *n* (*mar*) rade *f*.

roadworks *npl* travaux routiers *mpl*.

roam *vt* parcourir; errer dans; * *vi* errer.

roan *adj* rouan.

roar *vi* hurler, rugir; mugir; * *n* hurlement *m*; rugissement, mugissement *m*; grondement *m*.

roast *vt* rôtir; griller.

roast beef *n* rôti de bœuf *m*.

rob *vt* voler.

robber *n* voleur *m* -euse *f*.

robbery *n* vol *m*.

robe *n* robe (de cérémonie) *f*; peignoir de bain *m*; * *vt* revêtir d'une robe de cérémonie.

robin (redbreast) *n* rouge-gorge *m*.

robust *adj* robuste.

robustness *n* robustesse *f*.

rock *n* roche *f*; rocher *m*; roc *m*; * *vt* bercer; balancer; ébranler; * *vi* (se) balancer.

rock and roll *n* rock (and roll) *m*.

rock crystal *n* cristal de roche *m*.

rocket *n* fusée *f*.

rocking chair *n* fauteuil à bascule *m*.

rock salt *n* sel gemme *m*.

rocky *adj* rocheux.

rod *n* baguette, tringle, canne *f*.

rodent *n* rongeur *m*.

roe *n* chevreuil *m*; œufs *mpl* de poisson.

roebuck *n* chevreuil (mâle) *m*.

rogation *n* rogations *fpl*.

rogue *n* coquin, polisson *m*; gredin *m*.

roguish *adj* coquin.

roll *vt* rouler; étendre; enrouler; * *vi* (se) rouler; * *n* roulement *m*; rouleau *m*; liste *f*; catalogue *m*; liasse *f*; petit pain *m*.

roller *n* rouleau, cylindre *m*.

roller skates *npl* patins à roulettes *mpl*.

rolling pin *n* rouleau à pâtisserie *m*.

Roman Catholic *adj n* catholique *mf*.

romance *n* romance *f*; roman *m*; conte *m*; fable *f*.

romantic *adj* romantique.

romp *vi* jouer bruyamment.

roof *n* toit *m*; voûte *f*; * *vt* couvrir.

roofing *n* toiture *f*.

rook *n* freux *m*; tour *f* (*aux échecs*).

room *n* pièce, salle *f*; place *f*, espace *m*; chambre *f*.

roominess *n* grande envergure *f*.

rooming house *n* pension *f*.

roomy *adj* spacieux.

roost *n* perchoir *m*; * *vi* se percher.

root *n* racine *f*; origine *f*; * *vt vi* ~ **out** extirper; dénicher.

rooted *adj* enraciné; ancré.

rope *n* corde *f*; cordage *m*; * *vi* attacher.

ropemaker *n* cordier *m*.

rosary *n* rosaire *m*.

rose *n* rose *f*.

rosebed *n* massif de roses *m*.

rosebud *n* bouton de rose *m*.

rosebush *n* rosier *m*.

rosemary *n* (*bot*) romarin *m*.

rosette *n* rosette *f*.

rosé wine *n* (vin) rosé *m*.

rosewood *n* bois de rose *m*.

rosiness *n* couleur rosée *f*.

rosy *adj* rosé.

rot *vi* pourrir; * *n* pourriture *f*.

rotate *vt* faire tourner; * *vi* tourner.

rotation *n* rotation *f*.

rote *n*: **by** ~ par cœur.

rotten *adj* pourri; corrompu.

rottenness *n* pourriture *f*.

rotund *adj* rond, replet, arrondi.

rouble *n* rouble *m*.

rouge *n* rouge (à joues) *m*.

rough *adj* accidenté, inégal, rugueux; rude, brutal, brusque; houleux; ~**ly** *adv* rudement.

roughcast *n* crépi *m*.

roughen *vt* rendre rugueux.

roughness *n* rugosité *f*; rudesse, brusquerie *f*; agitation *f*.

round *adj* rond, circulaire; rondelet; franc; * *n* cercle *m*; rond *m*; tour *m*; tournée *f*; partie *f*; ronde *f*; canon *m*; série *f*; * *adv* autour de; environ; ~**ly** *adv* rondement; franchement; * *vt* contourner; arrondir.

roundabout *adj* détourné, indirect; * *n* rondpoint *m*.

roundness *n* rondeur *f*.

rouse *vt* réveiller; exciter.

rout *n* déroute, débâcle *f*; * *vt* mettre en déroute.

route *n* itinéraire *m*; route *f*.

routine *adj* habituel; * *n* routine *f*; numéro *m*.

rove *vi* vagabonder, errer.

rover *n* vagabond *m* -e *f*; pirate *m*.

row *n* querelle *f*; vacarme *m*.

row *n* rangée, file *f*; * *vt* (*mar*) ramer.

rowdy *n* hooligan, voyou *m*.

rower *n* rameur *m* -euse *f*.

royal *adj* royal; princier; ~**ly** *adv* royalement.

royalist *n* royaliste *mf*.

royalty *n* royauté *f*; droits d'auteur *mpl*; royalties *fpl*; redevance *f*; membres de la famille royale *mpl*.

rub *vt* frotter; irriter; * *n* frottement *m*; (*fig*) ennui *m*; difficulté *f*.

rubber *n* caoutchouc *m*, gomme *f*; préservatif *m*.

rubber band *n* élastique *m*.

rubbish *n* détritus *mpl*; ordures *fpl*; bêtises *fpl*; décombres *mpl*.

rubric *n* rubrique *f*.

ruby *n* rubis *m*.

rucksack *n* sac à dos *m*.

rudder *n* gouvernail *m*.

ruddiness *n* teint vif *m*, rougeur *f*.

ruddy *adj* coloré, rouge.

rude *adj* impoli, rude, brusque; grossier; primitif; ~**ly** *adv* impoliment, grossièrement.

rudeness *n* impolitesse *f*; rudesse, insolence *f*.

rudiment *n* rudiments *mpl*.

rue *vt* regretter amèrement; * *n* (*bot*) rue *f*.

rueful *adj* triste.

ruffian *n* voyou *m*, brute *f*; * *adj* brutal.

ruffle *vt* ébouriffer, déranger; rider.

rug *n* tapis *m*, carpette *f*.

rugged *adj* accidenté, déchiqueté; rude; robuste.

ruin *n* ruine *f*; perte *f*; ruines *fpl*; * *vt* ruiner; détruire.

ruinous *adj* ruineux.

rule *n* règle *f*; règlement *m*; pouvoir *m*; domination *f*; * *vt* gouverner, dominer; décider, régler, diriger.

ruler *n* dirigeant *m* -e *f*; règle *f*.
rum *n* rhum *m*.
rumble *vi* gronder, tonner.
ruminate *vt* ruminer.
rummage *vi* fouiller.
rumour *n* rumeur *f*; * *vt* faire courir le bruit.
rump *n* croupe *f*.
run *vt* diriger; organiser; faire couler; passer; ~ **the risk** courir le risque; * *vi* courir; fuir, se sauver; filer; fonctionner; aller; couler; concourir; * *n* course, compétition *f*; parcours *m*; cours *m*; série *f*; mode *f*; ruée *f*.
runaway *n* fugitif *m* -ive *f*, fuyard *m*.
rung *n* barreau, échelon *m*.
runner *n* coureur *m*; concurrent *m* -e *f*; messager *m*.
running *n* course *f*; direction *f*.
runway *n* piste de décollage *f*.

rupture *n* rupture *f*; hernie *f*; * *vt* rompre; * *vi* se rompre.
rural *adj* rural, champêtre.
ruse *n* ruse *f*, stratagème m.
rush *n* jonc *m*; ruée *f*; hâte *f*; * *vt* pousser vivement; * *vi* se précipiter, s'élancer.
rusk *n* biscotte *f*.
russet *adj* roux.
rust *n* rouille *f*; * *vi* se rouiller.
rustic *adj* rustique; * *n* paysan, rustaud *m*.
rustiness *n* rouille *f*.
rustle *vi* bruire; * *vt* faire bruire; froisser.
rustling *n* vol de bétail *m*; bruissement *m*.
rusty *adj* rouillé; roux.
rut *n* (*zool*) rut *m*; ornière *f*.
ruthless *adj* cruel, impitoyable; ~**ly** *adv* sans pitié.
rye *n* (*bot*) seigle *m*.

S

Sabbath *n* sabbat *m*; dimanche *m*.
sable *n* zibeline *f*.
sabotage *n* sabotage *m*.
sabre *n* sabre *m*.
saccharin *n* saccharine *f*.
sack *n* sac *m*; * *vt* mettre à sac; renvoyer.
sacrament *n* sacrement *m*; Eucharistie *f*.
sacramental *adj* sacramentel.
sacred *adj* saint, sacré; inviolable.
sacredness *n* (caractère) sacré *m*.
sacrifice *n* sacrifice *m*; * *vt* sacrifier.
sacrificial *adj* sacrificiel.
sacrilege *n* sacrilège *m*.
sacrilegious *adj* sacrilège.
sad *adj* triste, déprimé; attristant; regrettable; ~**ly** *adv* tristement.
sadden *vt* attrister.
saddle *n* selle *f*; col *m*; * *vt* seller.
saddlebag *n* sacoche de selle *f*.
saddler *n* sellier *m*.
sadness *n* tristesse *f*.
safe *adj* sûr; en sécurité; hors de danger; sans danger; ~**ly** *adv* sans accident; ~ **and sound** sain et sauf; * *n* coffre-fort *m*.
safe-conduct *n* sauf-conduit *m*.

safeguard *n* sauvegarde *f*; * *vt* sauvegarder, protéger.
safety *n* sécurité *f*; sûreté *f*.
safety belt *n* ceinture de sécurité *f*.
safety pin *n* épingle de nourrice *f*.
saffron *n* safran *m*.
sage *n* (*bot*) sauge *f*; sage *m*; * *adj* sage; ~**ly** *adv* avec sagesse.
Sagittarius *n* Sagittaire *m* (signe du zodiaque).
sago *n* (*bot*) sagou *m*.
sail *n* voile *f*; * *vt* piloter; * *vi* aller à la voile, naviguer.
sailing *n* navigation *f*.
sailor *n* marin *m*.
saint *n* saint *m* -e *f*.
sainted, saintly *adj* saint.
sake *n* bien *m*, égard *m*; **for God's** ~ pour l'amour de Dieu.
salad *n* salade *f*.
salad bowl *n* saladier *m*.
salad dressing *n* vinaigrette *f*.
salad oil *n* huile de table *f*.
salamander *n* salamandre *f*.
salary *n* salaire *m*.

sale *n* vente *f*; solde *m*.
saleable *adj* vendable.
salesman *n* vendeur *m*.
saleswoman *n* vendeuse *f*.
salient *adj* saillant.
saline *adj* salin.
saliva *n* salive *f*.
sallow *adj* jaunâtre, cireux.
sally *n* (*mil*) sortie, saillie *f*; * *vi* saillir.
salmon *n* saumon *m*.
salmon trout *n* truite saumonée *f*.
saloon *n* bar *m*.
salt *n* sel *m*; * *vt* saler.
salt cellar *n* salière *f*.
saltness *n* salinité *f*.
saltpetre *n* salpêtre *m*.
saltworks *npl* salines *fpl*.
salubrious *adj* salubre, sain.
salubrity *n* salubrité *f*.
salutary *adj* salutaire.
salutation *n* salutation(s) *f*(*pl*).
salute *vt* saluer; * *n* salut *m*.
salvage *n* (*mar*) droit de sauvetage *m*.
salvation *n* salut *m*.
salve *n* baume, onguent *m*.
salver *n* plateau *m*.
salvo *n* salve *f*.
same *adj* même, identique.
sameness *n* monotonie *f*.
sample *n* échantillon *m*; prélèvement *m*; * *vt* goûter.
sampler *n* échantillonneur *m* -euse *f*; modèle *m*.
sanatorium *n* sanatorium *m*.
sanctify *vt* sanctifier.
sanctimonious *adj* cagot.
sanction *n* sanction *f*; * *vt* sanctionner.
sanctity *n* sainteté *f*.
sanctuary *n* sanctuaire *m*; asile *m*.
sand *n* sable *m*; * *vt* sabler.
sandal *n* sandale *f*.
sandbag *n* (*mil*) sac *m* de sable.
sandpit *n* carrière de sable *f*.
sandstone *n* grès *m*.
sandy *adj* sablonneux, sableux.
sane *adj* sain.
sanguinary *adj* sanguinaire, sanglant.
sanguine *adj* sanguin.

sanitary towel *n* serviette *f* hygiénique.
sanity *n* santé mentale, raison *f*.
sap *n* sève *f*; * *vt* miner.
sapient *adj* sage, prudent.
sapling *n* jeune arbre *m*.
sapphire *n* saphir *m*.
sarcasm *n* sarcasme *m*.
sarcastic *adj* sarcastique, caustique; **~ally** *adv* d'une manière sarcastique.
sarcophagus *n* sarcophage *m*.
sardine *n* sardine *f*.
sash *n* écharpe *f*; ceinture *f*.
sash window *n* fenêtre à guillotine *f*.
sassy *adj* (US) insolent.
Satan *n* Satan *m*.
satanic(al) *adj* satanique.
satchel *n* cartable *m*.
satellite *n* satellite *m*.
satiate, sate *vt* rassasier, assouvir.
satin *n* satin *m*; * *adj* en *ou* de satin.
satire *n* satire *f*.
satirical *adj* satirique; **~ly** *adv* d'une manière satirique.
satirist *n* écrivain satirique *m*.
satirize *vt* faire la satire de.
satisfaction *n* satisfaction *f*.
satisfactorily *adv* d'une manière satisfaisante.
satisfactory *adj* satisfaisant.
satisfy *vt* satisfaire; convaincre.
saturate *vt* saturer.
Saturday *n* samedi *m*.
saturnine *adj* saturnien, sombre.
satyr *n* satyre *m*.
sauce *n* sauce *f*; assaisonnement *m*; * *vt* assaisonner.
saucepan *n* casserole *f*.
saucer *n* soucoupe *f*.
saucily *adv* avec impertinence.
sauciness *n* impertinence, insolence *f*.
saucy *adj* impertinent.
saunter *vi* flâner, se balader.
sausage *n* saucisse *f*.
savage *adj* sauvage, barbare; **~ly** *adv* sauvagement; * *n* sauvage *mf*.
savageness *n* sauvagerie *f*; barbarie *f*.
savagery *n* sauvagerie, barbarie *f*.
savannah *n* savane *f*.

save *vt* sauver; économiser; épargner; éviter; conserver; * *adv* sauf, à l'exception de; * *n* (*sport*) arrêt *m*.

saveloy *n* cervelas *m*.

saver *n* libérateur *m* -trice *f*; épargnant *m* -e *f*.

saving *adj* économique, économe; * *prep* sauf, à l'exception de; * *n* sauvetage *m*; ~s *pl* économies *fpl*, épargne *f*.

savings account *n* compte d'épargne *m*.

savings and loan association *n* (US) organisme *m* de crédit immobilier.

savings bank *n* caisse d'épargne *f*.

Saviour *n* Sauveur *m*.

savour *n* saveur *f*; goût *m*; * *vt* déguster, savourer.

savouriness *n* goût *m*; saveur *f*.

savoury *adj* savoureux.

saw *n* scie *f*; * *vt* scier.

sawdust *n* sciure *f*.

sawfish *n* poisson scie *m*.

sawmill *n* scierie *f*.

sawyer *n* scieur *m*.

saxophone *n* saxophone *m*.

say *vt* dire.

saying *n* dicton, proverbe *m*.

scab *n* gale *f*; croûte *f*.

scabbard *n* gaine *f*; fourreau *m*.

scabby *adj* galeux.

scaffold *n* échafaud *m*; échafaudage *m*.

scaffolding *n* échafaudage *m*.

scald *vt* échauder; * *n* brûlure *f*.

scale *n* balance *f*; échelle *f*; gamme *f*; écaille *f*; * *vt* escalader; écailler.

scallion *n* échalote *f*.

scallop *n* feston *m*; coquille *f* St Jacques; * *vt* festonner.

scalp *n* cuir chevelu *m*; * *vt* scalper.

scamp *n* coquin *m*.

scamper *vi* galoper.

scampi *npl* langoustines *fpl*.

scan *vt* scruter; explorer; scander.

scandal *n* scandale *m*; infamie *f*.

scandalize *vt* scandaliser.

scandalous *adj* scandaleux; ~ly *adv* scandaleusement.

scant, scanty *adj* rare, insuffisant.

scantily *adv* pauvrement, insuffisamment.

scantiness *n* insuffisance, pauvreté *f*.

scapegoat *n* bouc émissaire *m*.

scar *n* cicatrice *f*; * *vt* marquer d'une cicatrice.

scarce *adj* rare; ~ly *adv* à peine.

scarcity *n* rareté *f*; pénurie *f*.

scare *vt* effrayer; * *n* peur; panique *f*.

scarecrow *n* épouvantail *m*.

scarf *n* écharpe *f*.

scarlatina *n* scarlatine *f*.

scarlet *n* écarlate *f*; * *adj* écarlate.

scarp *n* escarpement *m*.

scat *interj* (*sl*) ouste!

scatter *vt* éparpiller; disperser.

scavenger *n* charognard *m*; éboueur *m*.

scenario *n* scénario *m*; (*also fig*).

scene *n* scène *f*; lieu *m*; spectacle *m*, vue *f*.

scenery *n* vue *f*; décor (de théâtre) *m*.

scenic *adj* scénique.

scent *n* parfum *m*, odeur *f*; odorat *m*; piste *f*; * *vt* parfumer.

scent bottle *n* flacon à parfum *m*.

scentless *adj* sans odeur, inodore.

sceptic *n* sceptique *mf*.

sceptic(al) *adj* sceptique.

scepticism *n* scepticisme *m*.

sceptre *n* sceptre *m*.

schedule *n* horaire *m*; programme *m*; liste *f*.

scheme *n* projet, plan *m*; schéma *m*; système *m*; machination *f*; * *vt* machiner; * *vi* intriguer.

schemer *n* conspirateur *m* -trice *f*, intrigant *m* -e *f*.

schism *n* schisme *m*.

schismatic *n* schismatique *mf*.

scholar *n* élève *mf*; érudit *m* -e *f*.

scholarship *n* savoir *m*, science *f*; bourse (d'études) *f*.

scholastic *adj* scolaire.

school *n* école *f*; * *vt* instruire.

schoolboy *n* écolier, élève *m*.

schoolgirl *n* écolière, élève *f*.

schooling *n* instruction, éducation *f*.

schoolmaster *n* instituteur, maître (d'école) *m*.

schoolmistress *n* institutrice, maîtresse (d'école) *f*.

schoolteacher *n* instituteur *m* -trice *f*; professeur *mf*.

schooner n (*mar*) goélette *f*.

sciatica n sciatique *f*.

science n science *f*.

scientific *adj* ~**ally** *adv* scientifique(ment).

scientist n scientifique *mf*.

scimitar n cimeterre *m*.

scintillate *vi* scintiller, étinceler.

scintillating *adj* brillant, scintillant.

scission n scission, division *f*.

scissors *npl* ciseaux *mpl*.

scoff *vi* se moquer.

scold *vt* réprimander; * *vi* grogner.

scoop n louche *f*; pelle *f*; exclusivité *f*; * *vt* évider; écoper.

scooter n scooter *m*; trottinette *f*.

scope n portée, envergure, étendue *f*; zone de compétence *f*; liberté d'action *f*.

scorch *vt* brûler; roussir, griller; * *vi* se brûler, roussir.

score n score *m*; marque *f*; entaille, rayure *f*; titre, égard *m*; compte *m*; (*mus*) partition *f*; vingtaine *f*; * *vt* marquer; souligner; * *vi* marquer un/des point(s).

scoreboard n tableau (d'affichage) *m*.

scorn *vt* mépriser; dédaigner; * *n* dédain, mépris *m*.

scornful *adj* dédaigneux; ~**ly** *adv* avec mépris.

Scorpio n Scorpion *m* (signe du zodiaque).

scorpion n scorpion *m*.

scotch *vt* contrecarrer.

Scotch n whisky *m*.

Scotch tape n scotch *m*.

scoundrel n vaurien *m*.

scour *vt* récurer, frotter; nettoyer; * *vi* battre la campagne.

scourge n fouet *m*; châtiment *m*; * *vt* fouetter; châtier.

scout n (*mil*) éclaireur *m* -euse *f*; guetteur *m*; reconnaissance *f*; * *vi* aller en reconnaissance.

scowl *vi* se renfrogner; * *n* mine renfrognée *f*.

scragginess n décharnement *m*, maigreur extrême *f*; rugosité *f*.

scraggy *adj* rugueux; famélique.

scramble *vi* avancer à quatre pattes; grimper; se battre, se disputer; * *n* bousculade, ruée *f*; ascension *f*.

scrap n bout *m*; restes *mpl*; petit morceau *m*; bagarre *f*; ferraille *f*.

scrape *vt* *vi* racler, gratter; * *vt* érafler; * *n* embarras *m*, ennui *m*.

scraper n racloir *m*.

scratch *vt* griffer, égratigner; gratter, griffonner; * *n* égratignure *f*.

scrawl *vt* *vi* gribouiller; * *n* griffonnage *m*.

scream, screech *vi* hurler, pousser des cris; * *n* cri perçant, hurlement *m*.

screen n écran *m*; paravent *m*; rideau *m*; écran de cheminée *m*; * *vt* abriter, cacher; projeter; passer au crible, sélectionner.

screenplay n scénario *m*.

screw n vis *f*; * *vt* visser; extorquer, soutirer.

screwdriver n tournevis *m*.

scribble *vt* gribouiller; * *n* gribouillage *m*.

scribe n scribe *m*.

scrimmage n mêlée *f*.

script n scénario *m*; script *m*.

scriptural *adj* biblique.

Scripture n Écriture *f* sainte.

scroll n rouleau (de papier *ou* parchemin) *m*.

scrub *vt* nettoyer à la brosse, récurer; annuler; * *n* broussailles *fpl*.

scruffy *adj* mal soigné.

scruple n scrupule *m*.

scrupulous *adj* scrupuleux; ~**ly** *adv* scrupuleusement.

scrutinize *vt* étudier minutieusement, examiner.

scrutiny n examen minutieux *m*.

scuffle n échauffourée, rixe *f*; * *vi* se bagarrer.

scull n aviron *m*.

scullery n arrière-cuisine *f*.

sculptor n sculpteur *m* -trice *f*.

sculpture n sculpture *f*; * *vt* sculpter.

scum n écume *f*; crasse *f*; rebut *m*.

scurrilous *adj* injurieux; vil, ignoble; ~**ly** *adv* injurieusement.

scurvy n scorbut *m*; * *adj* vil, mesquin.

scuttle n corbeille *f*; * *vi* courir précipitamment.

scythe n faux *f*.

sea n mer *f*; * *adj* marin; **heavy** ~ mer houleuse *f*.

sea breeze n brise de mer *f*.

sea coast *n* côte *f*.

sea fight *n* combat naval *m*.

seafood *n* fruits de mer *mpl*.

sea front *n* bord de mer *m*.

seagreen *adj* vert glauque.

seagull *n* mouette *f*.

sea horse *n* hippocampe *m*.

seal *n* sceau *m*; phoque *m*; * *vt* sceller.

sealing wax *n* cire à cacheter *f*.

seam *n* couture *f*; * *vt* faire une couture.

seaman *n* marin *m*.

seamanship *n* habileté à naviguer *f*.

seamstress *n* couturière *f*.

seamy *adj* sordide.

sea plane *n* hydravion *m*.

seaport *n* port de mer *m*.

sear *vt* cautériser.

search *vt* fouiller; inspecter; examiner; scruter, sonder; * *n* fouille *f*; recherche *f*; perquisition *f*.

searchlight *n* projecteur *m*.

seashore *n* rivage *m*, bord de mer *m*.

seasick *adj* sujet au mal de mer.

seasickness *n* mal de mer *m*.

seaside *n* bord de mer *m*.

season *n* saison *f*; moment opportun *m*; assaisonnement *m*; * *vt* assaisonner; dessécher.

seasonable *adj* opportun, à propos.

seasonably *adv* de façon opportune, à propos.

seasoning *n* assaisonnement *m*.

season ticket *n* carte d'abonnement *f*.

seat *n* siège *m*; place *f*; derrière *m*; fond *m*; * *vt* (faire) asseoir; placer.

seat belt *n* ceinture de sécurité *f*.

seaward *adj* du large; **~s** *adv* vers le large.

seaweed *n* algue *f*.

seaworthy *adj* en état de naviguer.

secede *vi* faire sécession, se séparer.

secession *n* sécession *f*; séparation *f*.

seclude *vt* éloigner, isoler.

seclusion *n* solitude *f*; isolement *m*.

second *adj* **~(ly)** *adv* deuxième(ment); * *n* second *m*; seconde *f*; (*mus*) seconde *f*; * *vt* aider; seconder.

secondary *adj* secondaire.

secondary school *n* collège d'enseignement secondaire *m*.

secondhand *adj* d'occasion.

secrecy *n* secret *m*; discrétion *f*.

secret *adj* *n* secret *m*; **~ly** *adv* secrètement.

secretary *n* secrétaire *mf*.

secrete *vt* cacher; (*med*) sécréter.

secretion *n* sécrétion *f*.

secretive *adj* secret, dissimulé.

sect *n* secte *f*.

sectarian *n* sectaire *mf*.

section *n* section *f*.

sector *n* secteur *m*.

secular *adj* séculaire.

secularize *vt* séculariser.

secure *adj* sûr; en sûreté; **~ly** *adv* en sécurité; * *vt* mettre en sûreté; assurer.

security *n* sécurité *f*; sûreté *f*; protection *f*; caution *f*.

sedan *n* (US) berline *f*.

sedan chair *n* chaise à porteurs *f*.

sedate *adj* **~ly** *adv* calme(ment), posé(ment).

sedateness *n* calme *m*.

sedative *n* sédatif *m*.

sedentary *adj* sédentaire.

sedge *n* (*bot*) carex *m*.

sediment *n* sédiment *m*; lie *f*; dépôt *m*.

sedition *n* sédition *f*.

seditious *adj* séditieux.

seduce *vt* séduire; corrompre.

seducer *n* séducteur *m* -trice *f*.

seduction *n* séduction *f*.

seductive *adj* séduisant.

sedulous *adj* assidu; **~ly** *adv* assidûment.

see *vt* voir, remarquer, découvrir; connaître; juger; comprendre; * *vi* voir; comprendre; **~!** regarde!; tu vois!

seed *n* graine, semence *f*; * *vi* monter en graine.

seedling *n* semis *m*.

seedsman *n* grainetier *m*.

seed time *n* (époque des) semailles *f(pl)*.

seedy *adj* minable.

seeing *conj*: **~ that** vu que.

seek *vt* chercher; demander.

seem *vi* paraître, sembler.

seeming *n* apparence *f*; **~ly** *adv* apparemment.

seemliness *n* bienséance *f*.

seemly *adj* convenable, bienséant.

seer *n* prophète *m*.

seesaw *n* bascule *f*; * *vi* osciller.
seethe *vi* bouillir, bouillonner.
segment *n* segment *m*.
seize *vt* saisir, attraper; opérer la saisie de.
seizure *n* capture *f*; saisie *f*.
seldom *adv* rarement, peu souvent.
select *vt* sélectionner, choisir; * *adj* choisi, sélectionné.
selection *n* sélection *f*.
self *n* soi-même; **the ~** le moi; * *pref* auto-.
self-command *n* maîtrise de soi *f*.
self-conceit *n* vanité *f*.
self-confident *adj* sûr de soi.
self-defence *n* autodéfense *f*.
self-denial *n* abnégation de soi *f*.
self-employed *adj* indépendant.
self-evident *adj* évident, qui va de soi.
self-governing *adj* autonome.
self-interest *n* intérêt personnel *m*.
selfish *adj* ~**ly** *adv* égoïste(ment).
selfishness *n* égoïsme *m*.
self-pity *n* apitoiement sur soi-même *m*.
self-portrait *n* autoportrait *m*.
self-possession *n* sang-froid *m*, assurance *f*.
self-reliant *adj* indépendant.
self-respect *n* respect de soi *m*.
selfsame *adj* exactement le même, identique.
self-satisfied *adj* suffisant.
self-seeking *adj* égoïste.
self-service *adj* libre-service.
self-styled *adj* autoproclamé.
self-sufficient *adj* autosuffisant.
self-taught *adj* autodidacte.
self-willed *adj* obstiné, volontaire.
sell *vt* vendre; attraper; * *vi* se vendre.
seller *n* vendeur *m* -euse *f*.
selling-off *n* liquidation *f*.
semblance *n* semblant *m*, apparence *f*.
semen *n* sperme *m*.
semester *n* semestre *m*.
semicircle *n* demi-cercle *m*.
semicircular *adj* semi-circulaire.
semicolon *n* point-virgule *m*.
semiconductor *n* semi-conducteur *m*.
seminary *n* séminaire *m*.
semitone *n* (*mus*) demi-ton *m*.
senate *n* sénat *m*.
senator *n* sénateur *m* -trice *f*.

senatorial *adj* sénatorial.
send *vt* envoyer, expédier, adresser; émettre; pousser.
sender *n* expéditeur *m* -trice *f*.
senile *adj* sénile.
senility *n* sénilité *f*.
senior *n* aîné *m* -e *f*; * *adj* aîné; supérieur.
seniority *n* ancienneté *f*.
senna *n* (*bot*) séné *m*.
sensation *n* sensation *f*.
sense *n* sens *m*; sensation *f*; raison *f*; bon sens *m*; sentiment *m*.
senseless *adj* insensé; sans connaissance; ~**ly** *adv* stupidement.
senselessness *n* manque de bon sens *m*; absurdité *f*.
sensibility *n* sensibilité *f*.
sensible *adj* sensé, raisonnable; sensible.
sensibly *adv* raisonnablement.
sensitive *adj* sensible.
sensual, sensuous *adj* ~**ly** *adv* sensuelle(-ment).
sensuality *n* sensualité *f*.
sentence *n* phrase *f*; condamnation *f*; * *vt* condamner, prononcer une sentence contre.
sententious *adj* sentencieux; ~**ly** *adv* sentencieusement.
sentient *adj* sensible.
sentiment *n* sentiment *m*; opinion *f*.
sentimental *adj* sentimental.
sentinel, sentry *n* sentinelle *f*.
sentry box *n* guérite *f*.
separable *adj* séparable.
separate *vt* séparer; * *vi* se séparer; * *adj* séparé; distinct; ~**ly** *adv* séparément.
separation *n* séparation *f*.
September *n* septembre *m*.
septennial *adj* septennal.
septuagenarian *n* septuagénaire *m*.
sepulchre *n* sépulcre *m*.
sequel *n* conséquence *f*; suite *f*.
sequence *n* ordre *m*, série *f*.
sequester, sequestrate *vt* séquestrer.
sequestration *n* séquestration *f*.
seraglio *n* sérail *m*.
seraph *n* séraphin *m*.
serenade *n* sérénade *f*; * *vt* jouer une sérénade pour.

serene *adj* serein; **~ly** *adv* sereinement.

serenity *n* sérénité *f*.

serf *n* serf *m*, serve *f*.

serge *n* serge *f*.

sergeant *n* sergent *m*; (US) caporal-chef *m*; brigadier *m*.

serial *adj* de/en série; * *n* feuilleton *m*; téléroman *m*.

series *n* série *f*.

serious *adj* sérieux, grave; **~ly** *adv* sérieusement.

sermon *n* sermon *m*.

serous *adj* séreux.

serpent *n* serpent *m*.

serpentine *adj* sinueux; * *n* (*chem*) serpentine *f*.

serrated *adj* en dents de scie.

serum *n* sérum *m*.

servant *n* domestique *mf*.

servant-girl *n* servante, bonne *f*.

serve *vt* servir; desservir; faire; accomplir; * *vi* servir; être utile; **~ a warrant** remettre un mandat.

service *n* service *m*; office *m*; entretien *m*; * *vt* entretenir; réviser.

serviceable *adj* utilisable; pratique.

service station *n* station-service *f*.

servile *adj* servile.

servitude *n* servitude *f*, esclavage *m*.

session *n* séance, session *f*; réunion *f*.

set *vt* mettre, poser, placer; fixer, déterminer; * *vi* se coucher (soleil); se figer; se mettre; * *n* jeu *m*; service *m*; ensemble *m*; (*cine*) plateau *m*; set *m*; groupe *m*, bande *f*; * *adj* fixe, figé; prêt; déterminé.

settee *n* canapé *m*.

setting *n* disposition *f*; cadre *m*; monture *f*; **~ of the sun** coucher du soleil *m*.

settle *vt* poser, installer, arranger; régler; calmer; * *vi* se poser; s'installer; se calmer.

settlement *n* règlement *m*; établissement *m*; accord *m*; résolution *f*; colonie *f*; colonisation *f*.

settler *n* colon *m*, colonisateur *m* -trice *f*.

set-to *n* lutte *f*; combat *m*.

seven *adj* *n* sept *m*.

seventeen *adj* *n* dix-sept *m*.

seventeenth *adj* *n* dix-septième *mf*.

seventh *adj* *n* septième *mf*.

seventieth *adj* *n* soixante-dixième *mf*.

seventy *adj* *n* soixante-dix *m*.

sever *vt* séparer.

several *adj* *pn* plusieurs.

severance *n* séparation *f*.

severe *adj* sévère, rigoureux, austère, dur; **~ly** *adv* sévèrement.

severity *n* sévérité *f*.

sew *vt* *vi* coudre.

sewer *n* égout *m*.

sewerage *n* (système d') égouts *mpl*; eaux d'égout *fpl*.

sewing machine *n* machine à coudre *f*.

sex *n* sexe *m*.

sexist *adj* *n* sexiste *mf*.

sextant *n* sextant *m*.

sexton *n* sacristain *m*.

sexual *adj* sexuel.

sexy *adj* sexy.

shabbily *adv* petitement, mesquinement.

shabbiness *n* aspect décrépit *ou* miteux *m*.

shabby *adj* miteux.

shackle *vt* enchaîner; **~s** *npl* chaînes *fpl*.

shade *n* ombre, obscurité *f*; nuance *f*; abat-jour *m*; * *vt* ombrager; abriter; atténuer.

shadiness *n* ombre *f*; ombrage *m*.

shadow *n* ombre *f*.

shadowy *adj* ombragé; sombre; indistinct.

shady *adj* ombreux, ombragé; sombre.

shaft *n* flèche *f*; fût *m*; puits *m*; (*tech*) arbre *m*; rayon *m*.

shag *n* tabac *m*; cormoran huppé *m*.

shaggy *adj* hirsute.

shake *vt* secouer; agiter; * *vi* trembler; chanceler; **~ hands** se serrer la main; * *n* secousse *f*; tremblement *m*.

shaking *adj* tremblant.

shaky *adj* tremblant.

shallow *adj* peu profond, superficiel; futile.

shallowness *n* manque de profondeur *m*; futilité *f*.

sham *vt* feindre; * *n* imitation *f*; imposture *f*; * *adj* feint, simulé.

shambles *npl* désordre *m*.

shame *n* honte *f*; * *vt* faire honte à, déshonorer.

shamefaced *adj* honteux, confus.

shameful *adj* honteux; scandaleux; ~**ly** *adv* honteusement.

shameless *adj* ~**ly** *adv* effronté(ment).

shamelessness *n* effronterie, impudeur *f*.

shammy *n* (peau de) chamois *m*.

shampoo *vt* faire un shampooing à; * *n* shampooing *m*.

shamrock *n* trèfle *m*.

shank *n* jambe *f*; hampe *f*; tuyau (de pipe) *m*; canon *m*.

shanty *n* baraque *f*.

shanty town *n* bidonville *m*.

shape *vt* former; façonner; modeler; * *vi* prendre forme; * *n* forme, figure *f*; modèle *m*.

shapeless *adj* informe.

shapely *adj* bien proportionné.

share *n* part, portion *f*; (*com*) action *f*; soc (de charrue) *m*; * *vt* partager; répartir; * *vi* partager.

sharer *n* participant *m*.

shark *n* requin *m*.

sharp *adj* aigu, acéré; malin; fin; pénétrant; âpre, mordant, cinglant; perçant; vif, violent; * *n* (*mus*) dièse *m*; * *adv* pile.

sharpen *vt* aiguiser, affûter.

sharply *adv* brusquement; sévèrement; vivement; nettement.

sharpness *n* tranchant *m*; finesse, acuité *f*; aigreur *f*.

shatter *vt* fracasser, détruire; * *vi* se fracasser.

shave *vt* raser, raboter; * *vi* se raser; *n* rasage *m*.

shaver *n* rasoir électrique *m*.

shaving *n* rasage *m*.

shaving brush *n* blaireau *m*.

shaving cream *n* crème à raser *f*.

shawl *n* châle *m*.

she *pn* elle.

sheaf *n* gerbe *f*; liasse *f*.

shear *vt* tondre; ~**s** *npl* cisailles *fpl*.

sheath *n* fourreau *m*.

shed *vt* verser, répandre; perdre; * *n* hangar *m*; cabane *f*.

sheen *n* lustre *m*.

sheep *n* mouton *m*.

sheepfold *n* parc à moutons *m*.

sheepish *adj* penaud; timide.

sheepishness *n* timidité *f*, air penaud *m*.

sheep-run *n* patûrage pour moutons *m*.

sheepskin *n* peau de mouton *f*.

sheer *adj* pur, absolu, véritable; abrupt; * *adv* abruptement.

sheet *n* drap *m*; plaque *f*; feuille (de papier) *f*; (*mar*) écoute *f*.

sheet anchor *n* ancre de veille *f*.

sheeting *n* toile pour draps *f*.

sheet iron *n* tôle *f*.

sheet lightning *n* éclairs en nappes *mpl*.

shelf *n* étagère *f*; (*mar*) écueil *m*; saillie *f*; **on the ~** au rancart.

shell *n* coquille *f*; carcasse *f*; écorce *f*; obus *m*; * *vt* écosser, décortiquer; bombarder; * *vi* se décortiquer.

shellfish *npl invar* crustacé *m*; fruits de mer *mpl*.

shelter *n* abri *m*; asile, refuge *m*; * *vt* abriter; protéger; * *vi* s'abriter.

shelve *vt* mettre au rancart.

shelving *n* rayonnage *m*.

shepherd *n* berger *m*.

shepherdess *n* bergère *f*.

sherbet *n* sorbet *m*.

sheriff *n* shérif *m*.

sherry *n* xérès *m*.

shield *n* bouclier *m*; écran protecteur *m*; * *vt* protéger.

shift *vi* changer; se déplacer; * *vt* changer, bouger; transférer; * *n* changement *m*; roulement *m*.

shinbone *n* tibia *m*.

shine *vi* briller, reluire, illuminer; * *vt* cirer; * *n* éclat *m*.

shingle *n* galets *mpl*; ~**s** *pl* (*med*) zona *m*.

shining *adj* resplendissant; * *n* éclat *m*.

shiny *adj* brillant, reluisant.

ship *n* bateau *m*; navire *m*; bâtiment *m*; * *vt* embarquer; transporter.

shipbuilding *n* construction navale *f*.

shipmate *n* (*mar*) camarade de bord *m*.

shipment *n* cargaison *f*.

shipowner *n* armateur *m*.

shipwreck *n* naufrage *m*.

shirt *n* chemise *f*.

shit *excl* (*sl*) merde!

shiver *vi* frissonner.

shoal *n* banc *m* (de poissons).

shock *n* choc *m*; décharge *f*; coup *m*; * *vt* bouleverser; choquer.

shock absorber *n* amortisseur *m*.

shoddy *adj* de mauvaise qualité.

shoe *n* chaussure *f*; fer (à cheval) *m*; * *vt* chausser; ferrer (un cheval.

shoeblack *n* cireur de chaussures *m*.

shoehorn *n* chausse-pied *m*.

shoelace *n* lacet de chaussure *m*.

shoemaker *n* cordonnier *m*.

shoestring *n* lacet de chaussure *m*.

shoot *vt* tirer, lancer, décocher; * *vi* pousser, bourgeonner; passer en flèche; s'élancer; * *n* pousse *f*.

shooter *n* tireur *m* -euse *f*.

shooting *n* fusillade *f*; tir *m*.

shop *n* magasin *m*; atelier *m*.

shopfront *n* devanture *f*.

shoplifter *n* voleur(-euse) à l'étalage *m(f)*.

shopper *n* acheteur *m* -euse *f*.

shopping *n* courses *fpl*.

shopping centre *n* centre commercial *m*.

shore *n* rivage, bord *m*, côte *f*.

short *adj* court, bref, succinct, concis; ~ly *adv* brièvement; rapidement.

shortcoming *n* insuffisance *f*; défaut *m*.

shorten *vt* raccourcir; abréger.

shortness *n* petitesse *f*; brièveté *f*.

short-sighted *adj* myope.

short-sightedness *n* myopie *f*.

shortwave *n* ondes courtes *fpl*.

shot *n* coup *m*; décharge *f*; plomb *m*; tentative *f*; prise *f*.

shotgun *n* fusil de chasse *m*.

shoulder *n* épaule *f*; accotement *m*; * *vt* charger sur son épaule.

shout *vi* crier; * *vt* crier; * *n* cri *m*, acclamation *f*.

shouting *n* cris *mpl*.

shove *vt vi* pousser; * *n* poussée *f*.

shovel *n* pelle *f*; * *vt* pelleter.

show *vt* montrer; faire voir, présenter; prouver; expliquer; * *vi* se voir; * *n* exposition *f*; spectacle *m*; manifestation *f*; salon *m*.

show business *n* monde du spectacle *m*.

shower *n* averse *f*; douche *f*; (*fig*) torrent *m*; * *vi* pleuvoir.

showery *adj* pluvieux.

showroom *n* salle d'exposition *f*.

showy *adj* voyant, ostentatoire.

shred *n* lambeau *m*, parcelle *f*; * *vt* mettre en lambeaux.

shrew *n* mégère *f*; musaraigne *f*.

shrewd *adj* astucieux; perspicace; ~ly *adv* astucieusement.

shrewdness *n* astuce *f*.

shriek *vt vi* hurler; * *n* hurlement *m*.

shrill *adj* aigu, strident.

shrillness *n* ton aigu *m*.

shrimp *n* crevette *f*; nabot *m* -e *f*, avorton *m*.

shrine *n* lieu saint *m*.

shrink *vi* rétrécir; se réduire, rapetisser.

shrivel *vi* se ratatiner, se flétrir; * *vt* ratatiner.

shroud *n* voile *m*; linceul *m*; * *vt* envelopper, voiler; ensevelir.

Shrove Tuesday *n* Mardi gras *m*.

shrub *n* arbuste *m*.

shrubbery *n* massif d'arbustes *m*.

shrug *vt* hausser les épaules; * *n* haussement d'épaules *m*.

shudder *vi* frissonner; * *n* frisson *m*.

shuffle *vt* mélanger; battre.

shun *vt* fuir, éviter.

shunt *vt* (*rail*) aiguiller.

shut *vt* fermer; *vi* (se) fermer.

shutter *n* volet *m*.

shuttle *n* navette *f*.

shuttlecock *n* volant *m*.

shy *adj* timide; réservé; embarrassé, gauche; ~ly *adv* timidement.

shyness *n* timidité *f*.

sibling *n*: ~s enfants de mêmes parents *mpl*.

sibyl *n* sibylle *f*.

sick *adj* malade; écœuré.

sicken *vt* rendre malade; * *vi* tomber malade.

sickle *n* faucille *f*.

sick leave *n* congé de maladie *m*.

sickliness *n* état maladif *m*.

sickly *adj* maladif.

sickness *n* maladie *f*.

sick pay *n* indemnité de maladie *f*.

side *n* côté *m*; flanc *m*; camp *m*; parti *m*; * *adj* latéral; secondaire; * *vi* se ranger du côté de.

sideboard *n* buffet *m*.

sidelight *n* veilleuse *f*.

sidelong *adj* oblique.

sideways *adv* de côté, obliquement.

siding *n* (*rail*) voie de garage *f*.

sidle *vi* avancer de côté; avancer furtivement.

siege *n* (*mil*) siège *m*.

sieve *n* tamis *m*; crible *m*; passoire *f*; * *vt* tamiser.

sift *vt* tamiser; passer au crible; dégager.

sigh *vi* soupirer, gémir; * *n* soupir *m*.

sight *n* vue *f*; mire *f*; spectacle *m*.

sightless *adj* aveugle.

sightly *adj* agréable à regarder; séduisant.

sightseeing *n* tourisme *m*.

sign *n* signe *m*, indication *f*; panneau *m*; geste *m*; trace *f*; * *vt* signer.

signal *n* signal *m*; * *adj* insigne, remarquable.

signalize *vt* signaler.

signal lamp *n* (*rail*) lampe de signalisation *f*.

signalman *n* (*rail*) aiguilleur *m*.

signature *n* signature *f*.

signet *n* sceau *m*.

significance *n* importance *f*.

significant *adj* considérable.

signify *vt* signifier.

signpost *n* poteau indicateur *m*.

silence *n* silence *m*; * *vt* imposer le silence à.

silent *adj* silencieux; ~ly *adv* silencieusement.

silex *n* silex *m*.

silicon chip *n* puce *f* électronique.

silk *n* soie *f*.

silken *adj* soyeux; satiné.

silkiness *n* soyeux *m*.

silkworm *n* ver à soie *m*.

silky *adj* soyeux; satiné.

sill *n* rebord *m*; seuil *m*.

silliness *n* stupidité, bêtise, niaiserie *f*.

silly *adj* bête, stupide.

silver *n* argent *m*; * *adj* en argent.

silversmith *n* orfèvre *m*.

silvery *adj* argenté.

similar *adj* semblable; similaire; ~ly *adv* de la même façon.

similarity *n* ressemblance *f*.

simile *n* comparaison *f*.

simmer *vi* cuire à feu doux, mijoter.

simony *n* simonie *f*.

simper *vi* minauder; * *n* sourire affecté *m*.

simple *adj* simple; naïf.

simpleton *n* nigaud *m* -e *f*.

simplicity *n* simplicité *f*; naïveté *f*.

simplification *n* simplification *f*.

simplify *vt* simplifier.

simply *adv* simplement; seulement.

simulate *vt* simuler, feindre.

simulation *n* simulation *f*.

simultaneous *adj* simultané.

sin *n* péché *m*; * *vi* pécher.

since *adv* depuis; * *prep* depuis; * *conj* depuis que; puisque.

sincere *adj* ~ly *adv* sincère(ment); **yours ~ly** veuillez agréer, Monsieur/Madame, l'expression de mes salutations distinguées.

sincerity *n* sincérité *f*.

sinecure *n* sinécure *f*.

sinew *n* tendon *m*.

sinewy *adj* musclé; tendineux.

sinful *adj* coupable, honteux; ~ly *adv* honteusement.

sinfulness *n* corruption *f*, péché *m*.

sing *vt vi* chanter; (*poet*) *vt* célébrer.

singe *vt* roussir.

singer *n* chanteur *m* -euse *f*.

singing *n* chant *m*.

single *adj* seul, unique, simple; célibataire; * *n* aller simple *m*; 45 tours *m*; * *vt* distinguer; séparer.

singly *adv* séparément.

singular *adj* singulier, rare; * *n* singulier *m*; ~ly *adv* singulièrement.

singularity *n* singularité *f*.

sinister *adj* sinistre; de mauvais augure, funeste.

sink *vi* couler; sombrer; s'affaisser; tomber très bas, baisser; * *vt* couler, faire sombrer; ruiner; * *n* évier *m*.

sinking fund *n* fonds d'amortissement *m*.

sinner *n* pécheur *m*; pécheresse *f*.

sinuosity *n* sinuosité *f*.

sinuous *adj* sinueux.

sinus *n* sinus *m*.

sip *vt* boire à petites gorgées; * *n* petite gorgée *f*.

siphon *n* siphon *m*.

sir *n* monsieur *m*.

sire *n* étalon *m*.

siren *n* sirène *f*.

sirloin *n* aloyau (de bœuf) *m*.

sister *n* sœur *f*.

sisterhood *n* solidarité féminine *f*.

sister-in-law *n* belle-sœur *f*.

sisterly *adj* de sœur.

sit *vi* s'asseoir; se trouver; * *vt* se présenter à.

site *n* emplacement *m*; site *m*.

sit-in *n* sit-in *m*, manifestation avec occupation de lieux publics *f*.

sitting *n* séance, réunion *f*; position assise *f*.

sitting room *n* salle de séjour *f*.

situated *adj* situé.

situation *n* situation *f*.

six *adj n* six *m*.

sixteen *adj n* seize *m*.

sixteenth *adj n* seizième *mf*.

sixth *adj n* sixième *mf*.

sixtieth *adj n* soixantième *mf*.

sixty *adj n* soixante *m*.

size *n* taille, grandeur *f*; volume *m*; dimension *f*; ampleur *f*; étendue *f*.

sizeable *adj* assez grand.

skate *n* patin *m*; * *vi* patiner.

skateboard *n* planche à roulettes *f*, skateboard *m*.

skating *n* patinage *m*.

skating rink *n* patinoire *f*.

skein *n* écheveau *m*.

skeleton *n* squelette *m*.

skeleton key *n* passe(-partout) *m*.

sketch *n* croquis *m*; esquisse *f*; * *vt* equisser, faire un croquis de.

skewer *n* broche *f*; brochette *f*; * *vt* embrocher.

ski *n* ski *m*; * *vi* skier.

ski boot *n* chaussure de ski *f*.

skid *n* dérapage *m*; * *vi* déraper.

skier *n* skieur *m* -euse *f*.

skiing *n* ski *m*.

skilful *adj* ~ly *adv* adroit(ement), habile(-ment).

skilfulness *n* habileté *f*.

skill *n* habileté, adresse, dextérité *f*.

skilled *adj* adroit; qualifié.

skim *vt* écrémer; effleurer.

skimmed milk *n* lait écrémé *m*.

skimmer *n* écumoire *f*.

skin *n* peau *f*; * *vt* écorcher.

skin diving *n* plongée sous-marine *f*.

skinned *adj* dépouillé.

skinny *adj* maigre, efflanqué.

skip *vi* sautiller, gambader; * *vt* sauter, passer; * *n* saut, bond *m*; benne *f*.

ski pants *npl* fuseau (de ski) *m*.

skipper *n* capitaine *m*.

skirmish *n* escarmouche *f*; * *vi* s'engager dans une escarmouche.

skirt *n* jupe *f*; bordure *f*; * *vt* contourner.

skit *n* parodie, satire *f*.

skittish *adj* espiègle, fantasque; coquet; inconstant; ~ly *adv* d'une manière espiègle.

skittle *n* quille *f*.

skulk *vi* se cacher, rôder furtivement.

skull *n* crâne *m*.

skullcap *n* calotte *f*.

sky *n* ciel *m*.

skylight *n* lucarne *f*.

skyrocket *n* fusée *f*.

skyscraper *n* gratte-ciel *m invar*.

slab *n* dalle *f*.

slack *adj* lâche, mou, indolent, négligent.

slack(en) *vt* relâcher; ralentir; diminuer; * *vi* se relâcher; ralentir.

slackness *n* manque d'énergie, ralentissement *m*; laisser-aller *m*.

slag *n* scories *fpl*.

slam *vt* claquer violemment; * *vi* se refermer en claquant.

slander *vt* calomnier, dire du mal de; * *n* calomnie *f*.

slanderer *n* calomniateur *m* -trice *f*.

slanderous *adj* calomnieux; ~ly *adv* calomnieusement.

slang *n* argot *m*.

slant *vi* pencher; être incliné; * *n* inclinaison *f*; point de vue *m*.

slanting *adj* en pente, incliné.

slap *n* claque *f*; (*on the face*) gifle *f*; * *adv* en plein; * *vt* donner une claque à, gifler.

slash *vt* entailler; * *n* entaille *f*.

slate *n* ardoise *f*.

slater *n* ardoisier *m*.

slating *n* recouvrement en ardoises *m*.

slaughter *n* carnage, massacre *m*; * *vt* abattre; massacrer.

slaughterer *n* tueur, meurtrier *m*.

slaughterhouse *n* abattoir *m*.

slave *n* esclave *mf*; * *vi* travailler comme un nègre.

slaver *n* bave *f*; * *vi* baver.

slavery *n* esclavage *m*.

slavish *adj* servile, d'esclave; **~ly** *adv* servilement.

slavishness *n* servilité *f*.

slay *vt* tuer.

slayer *n* tueur *m* -euse *f*.

sleazy *adj* louche, sordide.

sledge, sleigh *n* traîneau *m*.

sledgehammer *n* marteau de forgeron *m*.

sleek *adj* lisse et brillant, luisant.

sleep *vi* dormir; * *n* sommeil *m*.

sleeper *n* dormeur *m* -euse *f*.

sleepily *adv* d'un air endormi.

sleepiness *n* envie de dormir *f*.

sleeping bag *n* sac de couchage *m*.

sleeping pill *n* somnifère *m*.

sleepless *adj* sans sommeil.

sleepwalking *n* somnambulisme *m*.

sleepy *adj* qui a envie de dormir; endormi.

sleet *n* neige fondue *f*.

sleeve *n* manche *f*.

sleight *n*: **~ of hand** tour de passe-passe *m*.

slender *adj* svelte, mince, élancé; faible; **~ly** *adv* faiblement.

slenderness *n* sveltesse *f*, minceur *f*; faiblesse *f*.

slice *n* tranche *f*; spatule *f*; * *vt* couper (en tranches).

slide *vi* glisser; faire des glissades; * *n* glissade *f*; coulisse *f*; diapositive *f*; toboggan *m*.

sliding *adj* glissant; coulissant.

slight *adj* léger, mince, petit; * *n* affront *m*; * *vt* manquer d'égards pour.

slightly *adv* légèrement.

slightness *n* fragilité *f*; insignifiance *f*.

slim *adj* mince; * *vi* maigrir.

slime *n* vase *f*; dépôt visqueux *m*.

sliminess *n* viscosité *f*.

slimming *n* amaigrissement *m*.

slimy *adj* visqueux, gluant.

sling *n* fronde *f*; écharpe *f*; * *vt* lancer.

slink *vi* s'en aller furtivement; s'éclipser.

slip *vi* (se) glisser, se faufiler; * *vt* glisser; * *n* glissade *f*; faux pas *m*; oubli *m*; fiche *f*.

slipper *n* pantoufle *f*.

slippery *adj* glissant.

slipshod *adj* négligé.

slipway *n* (*mar*) cale *f*.

slit *vt* fendre, inciser; * *n* fente, incision *f*.

slobber *n* bave *f*.

sloe *n* (*bot*) prunelle *f*.

slogan *n* slogan *m*.

sloop *n* (*mar*) sloop *m*.

slop *n* fange *f*; bouillon *m*; **~s** *pl* eaux sales *fpl*.

slope *n* inclinaison *f*; pente *f*; déclivité *f*; versant *m*; * *vt* incliner.

sloping *adj* en pente; incliné.

sloppy *adj* négligé; peu soigné.

sloth *n* paresse *f*.

slouch *vi* manquer de tenue; se tenir d'une façon négligée.

slovenliness *n* négligence *f*; manque de soin *m*.

slovenly *adj* négligé, sale, débraillé.

slow *adj* lent; lourd; ennuyeux; **~ly** *adv* lentement.

slowness *n* lenteur, lourdeur *f*, manque d'intérêt *m*.

slow worm *n* orvet *m*.

slug *n* lingot *m*; limace *f*; jeton *m*; coup *m*.

sluggish *adj* paresseux; léthargique; **~ly** *adv* paresseusement.

sluggishness *n* paresse, mollesse *f*.

sluice *n* écluse *f*; * *vt* lâcher les vannes.

slum *n* taudis *m*; quartier pauvre *m*.

slumber *vi* dormir paisiblement; * *n* sommeil paisible *m*.

slump *n* effrondement *m*.

slur *vt* dénigrer; calomnier; mal articuler; * *n* calomnie *f*.

slush *n* neige fondante *f*.

slut *n* traînée *f*.

sly *adj* rusé; **~ly** *adv* de façon rusée.

slyness *n* ruse, finesse *f*.

smack *n* léger goût *m*; claque *f*; gros baiser retentissant *m*; * *vi* sentir; embrasser bruyamment; * *vt* donner une claque à.

small *adj* petit, menu.

smallish *adj* assez petit.

smallness *n* petitesse *f*.

smallpox *n* variole *f*.

smalltalk *n* conversation *f* banale.

smart *adj* élégant; rapide; astucieux; vif; * *vi* brûler.

smartly *adv* astucieusement, vivement; avec élégance; habilement.

smartness *n* astuce, vivacité, finesse *f*.

smash *vt* casser, briser; détruire; * *vi* se briser (en mille morceaux), se fracasser; * *n* fracas *m*; coup violent *m*.

smattering *n* connaissances superficielles *fpl*.

smear *n* (*med*) frottis *m*; * *vt* enduire; salir.

smell *vt vi* sentir; * *n* odorat *m*; odeur *f*; mauvaise odeur *f*.

smelly *adj* malodorant.

smelt *n* éperlan *m*; * *vt* fondre.

smelter *n* fondeur *m*.

smile *vi* sourire; * *n* sourire *m*.

smirk *vi* sourire d'un air affecté.

smite *vt* frapper.

smith *n* forgeron *m*.

smithy *n* forge *f*.

smock *n* blouse *f*.

smoke *n* fumée *f*; vapeur *f*; * *vt vi* fumer.

smokeless *adj* sans fumée.

smoker *n* fumeur *m* -euse *f*.

smoke shop *n* (US) bureau de tabac *m*.

smoking: 'no ~' 'interdiction de fumer'.

smoky *adj* enfumé; qui fume.

smooth *adj* lisse, uni, égal; doucereux, mielleux; * *vt* lisser; aplanir; adoucir.

smoothly *adv* facilement; doucement.

smoothness *n* douceur *f*; aspect lisse *m*; air doucereux *m*.

smother *vt* étouffer; réprimer.

smoulder *vi* couver, se consumer.

smudge *vt* étaler; * *n* tache *f*.

smug *adj* suffisant.

smuggle *vt* passer en contrebande.

smuggler *n* contrebandier *m* -ière *f*.

smuggling *n* contrebande *f*.

smut *n* saleté *f*; trace de suie *f*.

smuttiness *n* suie *f*; obscénité *f*.

smutty *adj* noirci; obscène.

snack *n* collation *f*.

snack bar *n* snack-bar *m*.

snag *n* obstacle *m*.

snail *n* escargot *m*.

snake *n* serpent *m*.

snaky *adj* sinueux.

snap *vt* casser net; * *vi* se casser net; claquer; mordre; parler sèchement; ~ **one's fingers** faire claquer ses doigts; * *n* claquement *m*; photographie *f*.

snapdragon *n* (*bot*) gueule-de-loup *f*.

snap fastener *n* bouton-pression *m*.

snare *n* piège *m*; collet *m*.

snarl *vi* gronder férocement.

snatch *vt* saisir; s'emparer de; * *n* geste vif *m*; vol *m*; fragment *m*.

sneak *vi* se glisser furtivement; * *n* faux-jeton *m*.

sneakers *npl* chaussures de basket *fpl*.

sneer *vi* parler d'un ton méprisant; ricaner.

sneeringly *adv* d'un ton méprisant.

sneeze *vi* éternuer.

sniff *vt* renifler; * *vi* renifler.

snigger *vi* ricaner.

snip *vt* donner de petits coups de ciseaux dans; * *n* petit coup de ciseaux *m*; petit bout *m*.

snipe *n* bécassine *f*.

sniper *n* franc-tireur *m*.

snivel *n* pleurnicherie *f*; * *vi* pleurnicher.

sniveller *n* pleurnicheur *m* -euse *f*.

snobbish *adj* snob.

snooze *n* petit somme *m*; * *vi* faire un somme.

snore *vi* ronfler.

snorkel *n* tube respiratoire *m*.

snort *vi* renifler fortement.

snout *n* museau *m*; groin *m*.

snow *n* neige *f*; * *vi* neiger.

snowball *n* boule de neige *f*.

snowdrop *n* (*bot*) perce-neige *m invar*.

snowman *n* bonhomme de neige *m*.

snowplough *n* chasse-neige *m invar*.

snowy *adj* neigeux; enneigé.

snub *vt* repousser, rejeter.

snub-nosed *adj* au nez retroussé.

snuff *n* tabac à priser *m*.

snuffbox *n* tabatière *f*.

snuffle *vi* parler d'une voix nasillarde, nasiller; renifler.

snug *adj* confortable, douillet; bien abrité.

so *adv* si, tellement, aussi; ainsi.

soak *vi* tremper; * *vt* faire tremper.

soap *n* savon *m*; * *vt* savonner.

soap bubble *n* bulle de savon *f*.

soap opera *n* feuilleton à l'eau de rose *m*.

soap powder *n* lessive *f*.

soapsuds *n* mousse de savon *f*.

soapy *adj* savonneux.

soar *vi* monter en flèche.

sob *n* sanglot *m*; * *vi* sangloter.

sober *adj* sobre; sérieux; ~**ly** *adv* sobrement; sérieusement.

sobriety *n* sobriété *f*; sérieux, calme *m*.

soccer *n* football *m*.

sociability *n* sociabilité *f*.

sociable *adj* sociable, liant.

sociably *adv* sociablement.

social *adj* social, sociable; ~**ly** *adv* socialement.

socialism *n* socialisme *m*.

socialist *n* socialiste *mf*.

social work *n* assistance sociale *f*.

social worker *n* assistant(e) social(e) *m(f)*.

society *n* société *f*; compagnie *f*.

sociologist *n* sociologue *mf*.

sociology *n* sociologie *f*.

sock *n* chaussette *f*.

socket *n* prise de courant *f*.

sod *n* gazon *m*.

soda *n* soude *f*; eau *f* de Seltz, soda *m*.

soft *adj* doux, moelleux; aimable, gentil; ~**ly** *adv* doucement; tendrement.

soften *vt* (r)amollir, adoucir; atténuer.

soft-hearted *adj* compatissant.

softness *n* douceur, mollesse *f*.

soft-spoken *adj* à la voix douce.

software *n* logiciel *m*.

soil *vt* salir, souiller; * *n* salissure, souillure *f*; sol *m*; terre *f*.

sojourn *vi* séjourner; * *n* séjour *m*.

solace *vt* consoler, soulager; * *n* consolation *f*.

solar *adj* solaire.

solder *vt* souder; * *n* soudure *f*.

soldier *n* soldat *m*.

soldierly *adj* militaire.

sole *n* plante du pied *f*; semelle (de chaussure) *f*; sole *f*; * *adj* seul, unique.

solecism *n* (*gr*) solécisme *m*.

solemn *adj* ~**ly** *adv* solennel(lement).

solemnity *n* solennité *f*.

solemnize *vt* solenniser.

solicit *vt* solliciter; quémander.

solicitation *n* sollicitation *f*.

solicitor *n* notaire *m*.

solicitous *adj* plein de sollicitude; ~**ly** *adv* avec sollicitude.

solicitude *n* sollicitude *f*.

solid *adj* solide, compact; * *n* solide *m*; ~**ly** *adv* solidement.

solidify *vt* solidifier.

solidity *n* solidité *f*.

soliloquy *n* soliloque *m*.

solitaire *n* solitaire *m* (jeu).

solitary *adj* solitaire, retiré; * *n* anachorète *m*.

solitude *n* solitude *f*.

solo *n* (*mus*) solo *m*.

solstice *n* solstice *m*.

soluble *adj* soluble.

solution *n* solution *f*.

solve *vt* résoudre.

solvency *n* solvabilité *f*.

solvent *adj* solvable; *n* (*chem*) solvant *m*.

some *adj* du, de la, de l', des; quelques; quelconque; certain(e)s; quelque.

somebody *pn* quelqu'un.

somehow *adv* d'une façon ou d'une autre.

someplace *adv* quelque part.

something *pn* quelque chose.

sometime *adv* au cours de, un jour ou l'autre.

sometimes *adv* quelquefois, parfois.

somewhat *adv* quelque peu.

somewhere *adv* quelque part.

somnambulism *n* somnambulisme *m*.

somnambulist *n* somnambule *mf*.

somnolence *n* somnolence *f*.

somnolent *adj* somnolent.

son *n* fils *m*.

sonata *n* (*mus*) sonate *f*.

song *n* chanson *f*.

son-in-law *n* gendre *m*.

sonnet *n* sonnet *m*.

sonorous *adj* sonore.

soon *adv* bientôt; **as ~ as** dès que.

sooner *adv* plus tôt; plutôt.

soot *n* suie *f*.

soothe *vt* calmer, apaiser; flatter.

soothsayer *n* devin *m*.

sop *n* pain trempé *m*.

sophism *n* sophisme *m*.

sophist *n* sophiste *mf*.

sophistical *adj* sophistiqué.

sophisticate *vt* falsifier; sophistiquer.

sophisticated *adj* sophistiqué.

sophistry *n* sophistique *f*.

sophomore *n* (US) étudiant(e) *m(f)* de seconde année.

soporific *adj* soporifique.

sorcerer *n* sorcier *m*.

sorceress *n* sorcière *f*.

sorcery *n* sorcellerie *f*.

sordid *adj* sordide, sale.

sordidness *n* bassesse *f*, saleté *f*.

sore *n* plaie, blessure *f*; * *adj* douloureux, sensible; contrarié; ~**ly** *adv* fortement.

sorrel *n* (*bot*) oseille *f*; * *adj* alezan, roux.

sorrow *n* peine *f*; chagrin *m*; * *vi* se lamenter.

sorrowful *adj* triste, affligé; ~**ly** *adv* tristement.

sorry *adj* désolé, navré; déplorable; **I am** ~ je suis désolé.

sort *n* sorte *f*; genre *m*; espèce *f*; race *f*; manière *f*; * *vt* classer; trier.

soul *n* âme *f*; essence *f*; personne *f*.

sound *adj* sain; solide; valide; ~**ly** *adv* sainement, solidement; * *n* son *m*; bruit *m*; * *vt* sonner (de); * *vi* sonner, retentir; ressembler; sembler.

sound effects *npl* bruitage *m*.

sounding board *n* table d'harmonie *f*; abat-voix *m*.

soundings *npl* (*mar*) sondages *mpl*; (*mar*) fonds *mpl*.

soundness *n* santé *f*; solidité *f*.

soundtrack *n* bande sonore *f*.

soup *n* soupe *f*.

sour *adj* aigre, acide; acerbe; revêche; ~**ly** *adv* aigrement; * *vt* aigrir, faire tourner; * *vi* s'aigrir; tourner.

source *n* source *f*; origine *f*.

sourness *n* acidité, aigreur *f*; acrimonie *f*.

souse *n* (*sl*) soûlard *m* -e *f*; * *vt* mariner; faire tremper.

south *n* sud *m*; * *adj* sud, du sud, au sud; * *adv* au sud; vers le sud.

southerly, southern *adj* du sud, sud, méridional.

southward(s) *adv* vers le sud.

southwester *n* (*mar*) vent du sud-ouest *m*; suroît *m*.

sovereign *adj n* souverain *m* -e *f*.

sovereignty *n* souveraineté *f*.

sow *n* truie *f*.

sow *vt* semer; disperser.

sowing time *n* époque des semailles *f*.

soy *n* soja *m*.

space *n* espace *m*; intervalle *m*; * *vt* espacer.

spacecraft *n* vaisseau spatial *m*.

spaceman/woman *n* astronaute *mf*.

spacious *adj* spacieux, ample; ~**ly** *adv* spacieusement.

spaciousness *n* dimensions spacieuses *fpl*; espace *m*.

spade *n* bêche *f*; pique *m* (carte).

span *n* envergure *f*; * *vt* enjamber; embrasser.

spangle *n* paillette *f*; * *vt* orner de paillettes.

spaniel *n* épagneul *m*.

Spanish *adj* espagnol; * *n* espagnol *m*; Espagnol *m* -e *f*.

spar *n* (*mar*) espar *m*; * *vi* s'entraîner.

spare *vt vi* épargner; ménager; éviter; se passer de; * *adj* de trop; de réserve.

sparing *adj* limité, modéré, économe; ~**ly** *adv* frugalement, avec modération.

spark *n* étincelle *f*.

sparkle *n* scintillement *m*, étincelle *f*; * *vi* étinceler; briller.

spark plug *n* bougie *f*.

sparrow *n* moineau *m*.

sparrowhawk *n* épervier *m*.

sparse *adj* clairsemé; épars; ~**ly** *adv* faiblement.

spasm *n* spasme *m*.

spasmodic *adj* spasmodique.

spatter *vt* éclabousser; * *vi* gicler.

spatula *n* spatule *f*.

spawn *n* frai *m*; * *vt* pondre; engendrer.

spawning *n* frai *m*.

speak *vt* parler; dire; * *vi* parler, s'entretenir; prendre la parole.

speaker *n* haut-parleur *m*; interlocuteur *m* -trice *f*; orateur *m*.

spear *n* lance *f*; harpon *m*; * *vt* transpercer d'un coup de lance.

special *adj* spécial, particulier; ~**ly** *adv* spécialement.

speciality *n* spécialité *f*.

species *n* espèce *f*.

specific *adj* spécifique; * *n* remède spécifique *m*.

specifically *adv* spécifiquement; explicitement.

specification *n* spécification *f*.

specify *vt* spécifier.

specimen *n* spécimen *m*; exemple *m*.

specious *adj* spécieux.

speck(le) *n* grain, tache *f*; * *vt* tacheter, moucheter.

spectacle *n* spectacle *m*.

spectator *n* spectateur *m* -trice *f*.

spectral *adj* spectral; ~ **analysis** *n* analyse spectrale *f*.

spectre *n* spectre *m*.

speculate *vi* spéculer; méditer.

speculation *n* spéculation *f*; conjecture *f*; méditation *f*.

speculative *adj* spéculatif, méditatif.

speculum *n* spéculum *m*.

speech *n* parole *f*; discours *m*; langage *m*; élocution *f*.

speechify *vi* discourir, pérorer.

speechless *adj* muet.

speed *n* vitesse *f*; rapidité *f*; * *vt* presser; accélérer; * *vi* se presser.

speedboat *n* vedette *f*.

speedily *adv* rapidement, vite.

speediness *n* rapidité, promptitude, célérité *f*.

speed limit *n* limitation de vitesse *f*.

speedometer *n* compteur de vitesse *m*.

speedway *n* piste de course *f*.

speedy *adj* rapide, prompt.

spell *n* charme, sortilège *m*; période *f*; * *vt* écrire; épeler; ensorceler, envoûter; * s'écrire; s'épeler.

spelling *n* orthographe *f*.

spend *vt* dépenser; passer; épuiser; gaspiller.

spendthrift *n* dépensier *m* -ière *f*.

spent *adj* épuisé.

sperm *n* sperme *m*.

spermaceti *n* spermaceti *m*.

spew *vi* (*sl*) vomir.

sphere *n* sphère *f*.

spherical *adj* sphérique; ~**ly** *adv* de forme sphérique.

spice *n* épice *f*; * *vt* épicer.

spick-and-span *adj* impeccable; tiré à quatre épingles.

spicy *adj* épicé.

spider *n* araignée *f*.

spigot *n* clef de robinet *f*.

spike *n* pointe *f*; clou *m*; * *vt* clouter.

spill *vt* renverser, répandre; * *vi* se répandre.

spin *vt* filer; inventer, fabriquer; faire tourner; * *vi* tourner; * *n* tournoiement *m*; tour (en voiture) *m*.

spinach *n* épinard *m*.

spinal *adj* spinal.

spindle *n* fuseau *m*; broche *f*.

spine *n* colonne vertébrale, épine dorsale *f*.

spinet *n* (*mus*) épinette *f*.

spinner *n* fileur *m*; fileuse *f*.

spinning wheel *n* rouet *m*.

spin-off *n* sous-produit *m*.

spinster *n* célibataire *f*.

spiral *adj* ~**ly** *adv* en spirale.

spire *n* flèche *f*; aiguille *f*; tige *f*.

spirit *n* esprit *m*; âme *f*; caractère *m*, disposition *f*; courage *m*; humeur *f*; * *vt* encourager; animer; ~ **away** faire disparaître comme par enchantement.

spirited *adj* vif, fougueux; ~**ly** *adv* fougueusement.

spirit lamp *n* lampe à alcool *f*.

spiritless *adj* sans entrain, abattu.

spiritual *adj* ~**ly** *adv* spirituel(lement).

spiritualist *n* spiritualiste *mf*.

spirituality *n* spiritualité *f*.

spit *n* crachat *m*; salive *f*; * *vt vi* cracher; crépiter.

spite *n* dépit *m*, rancune *f*; **in** ~ **of** en dépit de, malgré; * *vt* vexer.

spiteful *adj* rancunier, malveillant; ~**ly** *adv* par méchanceté, par rancune.

spitefulness *n* méchanceté *f*; rancune *f*.

spittle *n* salive *f*; crachat *m*.

splash *vt* éclabousser, faire gicler; * *vi* barboter; * *n* éclaboussure *f*; tache *f*.

spleen *n* rate *f*; spleen *m*.

splendid *adj* splendide, magnifique; ~**ly** *adv* splendidement.

splendour *n* splendeur *f*; magnificence *f*.

splice *vt* (*mar*) épisser, abouter.

splint *n* éclisse *f*.

splinter n éclat m; esquille f; écharde f; * vt (vi) (se) fendre en éclats.

split n fente f; rupture f; * vt fendre, diviser; * vi se fendre.

spoil vt abîmer; gâter; gâcher.

spoiled adj abîmé; gâté.

spoke n rayon (de roue) m.

spokesman/woman n porte-parole mf.

sponge n éponge f; * vt éponger; * vi être un parasite.

sponger n parasite m.

sponginess n spongiosité f.

spongy adj spongieux.

sponsor n caution m; parrain m; marraine f.

sponsorship n parrainage m.

spontaneity n spontanéité f.

spontaneous adj ~ly adv spontané(ment).

spool n bobine f; rouleau m.

spoon n cuiller f.

spoonful n cuillerée f.

sporadic(al) adj sporadique.

sport n sport m; jeu m; divertissement, amusement m.

sports car n voiture de sport f.

sports jacket n veste sport f.

sportsman/woman n sportif m -ive f.

sportswear n vêtements de sport mpl.

spot n tache f; point m; endroit m; pois m; * vt apercevoir; tacher.

spotless adj impeccable, immaculé.

spotlight n feu de projecteur m.

spotted, spotty adj tacheté; à pois.

spouse n époux m, épouse f.

spout vi jaillir; gicler; déblatérer; * vt faire jaillir; * n bec m; gargouille f; jet m.

sprain vt fouler; * n entorse f.

sprawl vi s'étaler.

spray n spray m; pulvérisation f; embruns mpl.

spread vt étendre, étaler; répandre, propager; * vi s'étendre, se répandre; * n propagation, diffusion f.

spree n fête f.

sprig n brin m.

sprightliness n vivacité f, entrain m.

sprightly adj alerte, vif, fringant.

spring vi bondir, sauter; provenir, découler; émaner, naître; * n printemps m; élasticité f; ressort m; saut m; source f.

springiness n élasticité f.

springtime n printemps m.

springwater n eau de source f.

springy adj élastique.

sprinkle vt arroser.

sprinkling n arrosage m.

sprout n pousse f, germe m; ~s npl choux de Bruxelles mpl; * vi germer.

spruce adj net, impeccable; ~ly adv tiré à quatre épingles; * vi se mettre sur son trente-et-un.

spruceness n élégance f.

spur n éperon m; ergot (coq) m; stimulant m; * vt éperonner; stimuler.

spurious adj faux, feint; falsifié, de contrefaçon.

spurn vt repousser avec mépris.

sputter vi postillonner; bredouiller; bafouiller.

spy n espion m -ne f; * vt apercevoir; espionner; vi espionner.

squabble vi se disputer, se quereller; * n querelle, dispute f.

squad n escouade f; brigade f; équipe f.

squadron n (mil) escadron m.

squalid adj misérable, sordide.

squall n rafale f; bourrasque f; * vi brailler.

squally adj qui souffle en rafales.

squalor n saleté f; misère f.

squander vt gaspiller, dilapider.

square adj carré; catégorique; honnête; * n carré m; place f; équerre f; * vt cadrer; mettre en ordre, régler; * vi cadrer.

squareness n forme carrée f.

squash vt écraser; * n squash m.

squat vi s'accroupir; * adj accroupi; trapu, courtaud.

squaw n squaw, femme peau-rouge f.

squeak vi grincer, crier; * n cri, couinement m.

squeal vi pousser un cri aigu, couiner.

squeamish adj impressionable; délicat.

squeeze vt presser, tordre; comprimer; * n pression f; serrement de main m; cohue f.

squid n calmar m.

squint adj atteint de strabisme; * vi loucher; * n strabisme.

squirrel n écureuil m.

squirt *vt* faire gicler; * *n* giclée *f*; jet *m*.

stab *vt* poignarder; * *n* coup de couteau *m*.

stability *n* stabilité, solidité *f*.

stable *n* écurie *f*; * *vt* mettre à l'écurie; * *adj* stable.

stack *n* pile *f*; * *vt* empiler.

staff *n* personnel *m*; bâton *m*; soutien *m*.

stag *n* cerf *m*.

stage *n* étape *f*; scène *f*; échafaudage *m*; théâtre *m*; stade *m*; estrade *f*.

stagger *vi* vaciller, tituber; hésiter; * *vt* stupéfier; échelonner.

stagnation *n* stagnation *f*.

stagnant *adj* stagnant.

stagnate *vi* stagner.

staid *adj* posé, sérieux, guindé.

stain *vt* tacher; ternir; * *n* tache *f*.

stainless *adj* sans tache; immaculé.

stair *n* marche *f*; **~s** *pl* escalier *m*.

staircase *n* escalier *m*.

stake *n* pieu *m*; enjeu *m*; * *vt* marquer; délimiter.

stale *adj* rassis, rance.

staleness *n* manque de fraîcheur *m*; rance *m*.

stalk *vi* avancer d'un air majestueux; * *n* tige, queue *f*, trognon *m*.

stall *n* stalle *f*; stand, étalage *m*; (fauteuil d') orchestre *m*; emplacement *m*; * *vt* caler; * *vi* caler; atermoyer.

stallion *n* étalon *m*.

stalwart *n* partisan fidèle *m*.

stamen *n* étamine *f*.

stamina *n* résistance *f*.

stammer *vi* bégayer; * *n* bégaiement *m*.

stamp *vt* trépigner; timbrer, affranchir; tamponner; * *vi* trépigner; * *n* timbre *m*; cachet *m*; tampon *m*; empreinte *f*; estampille *f*.

stampede *n* débandade *f*.

stand *vi* être debout, se tenir; se maintenir; résister; être situé, se trouver; rester, durer; s'arrêter, faire halte; * *vt* poser; résister; soutenir, supporter; * *n* position, prise de position *f*; pied, support *m*; étalage *m*; état *m*; tribune *f*; stand *m*.

standard *n* étendard *m*; modèle *m*; étalon *m*; norme *f*; * *adj* normal.

standing *adj* permanent, fixe, établi; en pied; * *n* durée *f*; importance *f*; rang *m*.

standstill *n* arrêt *m*; immobilisation *f*.

staple *n* agrafe *f*; * *adj* principal, de base; * *vt* agrafer.

star *n* étoile *f*; astérisque *m*.

starboard *n* tribord *m*.

starch *n* amidon *m*; * *vt* amidonner.

stare *vi*: **to ~ at** regarder fixement; * *n* regard fixe *m*.

stark *adj* raide, rigide; cru; * *adv* complètement.

starling *n* étourneau *m*.

starry *adj* étoilé.

start *vi* commencer, débuter; sursauter, tressaillir; démarrer, se mettre en route; * *vt* commencer; amorcer; lancer; mettre en marche; * *n* début *m*; ouverture *f*; sursaut *m*; départ *m*; avance *f*.

starter *n* starter, démarreur *m*.

starting point *n* point de départ *m*.

startle *vt* faire sursauter.

startling *adj* surprenant, alarmant.

starvation *n* inanition, faim *f*.

starve *vi* mourir de faim.

state *n* état *m*; condition *f*; pompe *f*, apparat *m*; **the S~s** les Etats-Unis *mpl*; * *vt* déclarer; exposer.

stateliness *n* majesté, grandeur *f*.

stately *adj* majestueux, imposant.

statement *n* déclaration, affirmation *f*.

statesman *n* homme d'État *m*.

statesmanship *n* qualité d'homme politique *f*.

static *adj* statique; * *n* parasites *mpl*.

station *n* station *f*; place, position *f*; condition *f*, rang *m*; situation *f*; condition *f*; (*rail*) gare *f*; * *vt* placer.

stationary *adj* stationnaire, immobile.

stationer *n* papetier *m* -ière *f*.

stationery *n* papeterie *f*.

station wagon *n* (US) break *m*.

statistical *adj* statistique.

statistics *npl* statistiques *fpl*.

statuary *n* statuaire *f*.

statue *n* statue *f*.

stature *n* stature, taille *f*.

statute *n* statut *m*; loi *f*.

stay *n* séjour *m*; **~s** *npl* corset *m*; * *vi* rester, demeurer; tenir; loger; **~ in** rester à la maison; **~ on** rester encore quelque temps; **~ up** ne pas se coucher.

stead *n* place *f*, lieu *m*.

steadfast *adj* ferme, résolu, inébranlable; **~ly** *adv* fermement, résolument.

steadily *adv* fermement; régulièrement.

steadiness *n* fermeté, stabilité *f*.

steady *adj* stable, solide; * *vt* affermir.

steak *n* bifteck *m*; steak *m*.

steal *vt vi* voler.

stealth *n* discrétion *f*; **by ~** à la dérobée.

stealthily *adv* furtivement.

stealthy *adj* furtif.

steam *n* vapeur *f*; buée *f*; * *vt* cuire à la vapeur; * *vi* fumer.

steam engine *n* locomotive à vapeur *f*.

steamer, steamboat *n* (bateau à) vapeur, paquebot *m*.

steel *n* acier *m*; * *adj* d'acier.

steelyard *n* balance romaine *f*.

steep *adj* abrupt; excessif; * *vt* tremper.

steeple *n* clocher *m*; flèche *f*.

steeplechase *n* steeple (course) *m*.

steepness *n* raideur *f*; escarpement *m*.

steer *n* bouvillon *m*; * *vt* conduire; diriger; gouverner; * *vi* tenir le gouvernail.

steering *n* direction *f*.

steering wheel *n* volant *m*.

stellar *adj* stellaire.

stem *n* tige *f*, tronc *m*; souche *f*; pied *m*; tuyau *m*; * *vt* endiguer.

stench *n* odeur fétide *f*.

stencil *n* stencil *m*, pochoir *m*.

stenographer *n* sténographe *mf*.

stenography *n* sténographie *f*.

step *n* pas *m*, marche *f*; trace *f*; * *vi* faire un pas; marcher.

stepbrother *n* demi-frère *m*.

stepdaughter *n* belle-fille *f*.

stepfather *n* beau-père *m*.

stepmother *n* belle-mère *f*.

stepping stone *n* pierre de gué *f*.

stepsister *n* demi-sœur *f*.

stepson *n* beau-fils *m*.

stereo *n* stéréo *f*.

stereotype *n* stéréotype *m*; * *vt* stéréotyper.

sterile *adj* stérile.

sterility *n* stérilité *f*.

sterling *adj* de bon aloi, vrai, véritable; * *n* livres sterling *fpl*.

stern *adj* sévère, rigide, strict; * *n* (*mar*) poupe *f*; **~ly** *adv* sévèrement.

stethoscope *n* (*med*) stéthoscope *m*.

stevedore *n* (*mar*) docker *m*.

stew *vt* faire cuire à l'étouffée; * *n* ragoût *m*.

steward *n* intendant *m*; (*mar*) steward *m*.

stewardess *n* hôtesse de l'air *f*.

stewardship *n* intendance *f*.

stick *n* bâton *m*; canne *f*; baguette *f*; * *vt* coller; piquer; planter; supporter; * *vi* tenir; se planter; rester fidèle.

stickiness *n* viscosité *f*.

stick-up *n* braquage *m*, hold-up *m*.

sticky *adj* collant, poisseux.

stiff *adj* raide, rigide; inflexible; dur; entêté; **~ly** *adv* raidement; obstinément.

stiffen *vt* raidir, renforcer; * *vi* se raidir.

stiff neck *n* torticolis *m*.

stiffness *n* raideur, rigidité *f*; opiniâtreté *f*.

stifle *vt* étouffer.

stifling *adj* suffocant.

stigma *n* stigmate *m*.

stigmatize *vt* stigmatiser.

stile *n* tourniquet *m*.

stiletto *n* stylet *m*; talon aiguille *m*.

still *vt* calmer, apaiser; faire taire; * *adj* silencieux, calme; * *n* alambic *m*; * *adv* encore; toujours; quand même, tout de même.

stillborn *adj* mort-né.

stillness *n* calme *m*, tranquillité *f*.

stilts *npl* échasses *fpl*.

stimulant *n* stimulant *m*.

stimulate *vt* stimuler.

stimulation *n* stimulant *m*; stimulation *f*.

stimulus *n* stimulant *m*.

sting *vt* piquer; * *vi* brûler; * *n* dard *m*; piqûre *f*; aiguillon *m*.

stingily *adv* avec avarice.

stinginess *n* mesquinerie, avarice *f*.

stingy *adj* mesquin, avare, pingre.

stink *vi* puer; * *n* puanteur *f*.

stint *n* tâche assignée *f*.

stipulate *vt* stipuler.

stipulation *n* stipulation *f*.

stir *vt* remuer; agiter; exciter; * *vi* remuer, bouger; * *n* agitation *f*; émoi *m*.

stirrup *n* étrier *m*.

stitch *vt* coudre; * *n* point *m*; point de suture *m*.

stoat *n* hermine *f*.

stock *n* réserve *f*; provision *f*; bouillon *m*; souche *f*; lignée *f*; capital *m*; fonds *mpl*; **~s** *pl* valeurs mobilières *fpl*; * *vt* approvisionner, stocker.

stockade *n* prison militaire *f*.

stockbroker *n* agent de change *m*.

stock exchange *n* Bourse *f*.

stockholder *n* actionnaire *mf*.

stocking *n* bas *m*.

stock market *n* Bourse *f*.

stoic *n* stoïque *mf*.

stoical *adj* **~ly** *adv* stoïque(ment).

stoicism *n* stoïcisme *m*.

stole *n* étole *f*.

stomach *n* estomac *m*; ventre *m*; * *vt* digérer; endurer.

stone *n* pierre *f*; caillou *m*; noyau *m*; * *adj* de pierre; * *vt* lancer des pierres sur; dénoyauter; empierrer.

stone deaf *adj* sourd comme un pot.

stoning *n* empierrement *m*.

stony *adj* pierreux, rocailleux; dur.

stool *n* tabouret *m*; rebord, appui *m*.

stoop *vi* se baisser, se pencher; * *n* inclination en avant *f*.

stop *vt* arrêter, interrompre; boucher; * *vi* s'arrêter, cesser; * *n* arrêt *m*; halte *f*; pause *f*; point *m*.

stopover *n* escale; étape *f*.

stoppage, stopping *n* obstruction *f*; engorgement *m*; (*rail*) suppression *f*.

stopwatch *n* chronomètre *m*.

storage *n* emmagasinage *m*; entreposage *m*.

store *n* provision *f*; réserve *f*; entrepôt *m*, magasin *m*; * *vt* mettre en réserve, accumuler, emmagasiner.

storekeeper *n* marchand *m* -e *f*.

storey *n* (UK) étage *m*.

stork *n* cigogne *f*.

storm *n* tempête *f*, orage *m*; assaut *m*; * *vt* prendre d'assaut; * *vi* faire rage.

stormily *adv* violemment.

stormy *adj* orageux; houleux.

story *n* histoire *f*; récit *m*; (US) étage *m*.

stout *adj* corpulent, robuste, vigoureux; solide; **~ly** *adv* solidement; vaillamment; résolument.

stoutness *n* vigueur *f*; puissance *f*; corpulence *f*.

stove *n* poêle *m*; cuisinière *f*.

stow *vt* ranger, mettre en place; (*mar*) arrimer.

straggle *vi* être disséminé.

straggler *n* traînard *m* -e *f*.

straight *adj* droit; direct; franc; * *adv* droit; directement.

straightaway *adv* immédiatement, tout de suite.

straighten *vt* redresser.

straightforward *adj* honnête; franc; direct.

straightforwardness *n* honnêteté *f*.

strain *vt* tendre; fouler; forcer; mettre à l'épreuve; * *vi* peiner; * *n* tension *f*; effort *m*; entorse *f*; contrainte *f*; lignée *f*; accent *m*; ton *m*.

strainer *n* passoire *f*.

strait *n* détroit *m*; embarras *m*; situation critique *f*.

strait-jacket *n* camisole de force *f*.

strand *n* brin *m*; rivage *m*, rive *f*.

strange *adj* inconnu; étrange; **~ly** *adv* étrangement, curieusement.

strangeness *n* étrangeté *f*; nouveauté *f*.

stranger *n* inconnu(e) *m*(*f*), étranger *m* -ère *f*.

strangle *vt* étrangler.

strangulation *n* strangulation *f*.

strap *n* lanière, sangle *f*; courroie *f*; * *vt* attacher avec une courroie.

strapping *adj* robuste, charpenté.

stratagem *n* stratagème *m*.

strategic *adj* stratégique *m*.

strategy *n* stratégie *f*.

stratum *n* strate *f*.

straw *n* paille *f*.

strawberry *n* fraise *f*.

stray *vi* s'égarer; vagabonder; * *adj* perdu; errant.

streak *n* raie, bande *f*; filet *m*; * *vt* strier.

stream *n* ruisseau *m*, rivière *f*; torrent *m*; * *vi* ruisseler.

streamer *n* serpentin *m*.

street *n* rue *f*.

streetcar *n* tramway *m*.

strength *n* force, puissance *f*; vigueur *f*; robustesse *f*.

strengthen *vt* fortifier; confirmer, renforcer.

strenuous *adj* ardu; vigoureux.

stress *n* pression *f*; stress *m*; tension *f*; contrainte *f*; importance *f*; accent *m*; * *vt* souligner; accentuer.

stretch *vt* étendre, étirer; élargir; forcer; * *vi* s'étendre, s'étirer; * *n* extension *f*; étendue *f*; période *f*.

stretcher *n* brancard *m*.

strew *vt* éparpiller; semer.

strict *adj* strict, sévère; exact, rigoureux, précis; **~ly** *adv* strictement, sévèrement.

strictness *n* sévérité *f*; rigueur *f*.

stride *n* grand pas *m*; * *vi* marcher à grandes enjambées.

strife *n* conflit *m*, lutte *f*.

strike *vt* frapper; heurter; attaquer; rayer; * *vi* frapper; se mettre en grève; sonner; * *n* coup *m*; grève *f*; découverte *f*.

striker *n* gréviste *mf*.

striking *adj* frappant; saisissant; **~ly** *adv* remarquablement.

string *n* ficelle *f*; corde *f*; cordon *m*; rang *m*; fibre *f*; * *vt* munir d'une corde; enfiler; suspendre.

stringent *adj* rigoureux.

stringy *adj* filandreux.

strip *vt* déshabiller, dévêtir; * *vi* se déshabiller; * *n* bande *f*; langue *f*; bandelette *f*.

stripe *n* raie, rayure *f*; coup de fouet *m*; * *vt* rayer.

strive *vi* s'efforcer; s'évertuer; lutter, se battre.

stroke *n* coup *m*; trait *m*; course *f*; caresse *f*; apoplexie *f*; * *vt* caresser.

stroll *n* petit tour; * *vi* flâner.

strong *adj* fort, vigoureux, robuste; puissant; intense; **~ly** *adv* fortement, énergiquement.

strongbox *n* coffre-fort *m*.

stronghold *n* forteresse *f*.

strophe *n* strophe *f*.

structure *n* structure *f*; construction *f*.

struggle *vi* lutter; se battre; se démener; * *n* lutte *f*.

strum *vt* (*mus*) tapoter de.

strut *vi* se pavaner; * *n* démarche affectée *f*.

stub *n* souche *f*; bout *m*; talon *m*.

stubble *n* chaume *m*; barbe de plusieurs jours *f*.

stubborn *adj* entêté, obstiné; **~ly** *adv* obstinément.

stubbornness *n* entêtement *m*, obstination *f*.

stucco *n* stuc *m*.

stud *n* clou *m*; crampon *m*; écurie *f*.

student *n*, *adj* étudiant *m* -e *f*.

stud horse *n* étalon *m*.

studio *n* studio, atelier *m*.

studio apartment *n* studio *m*.

studious *adj* studieux; sérieux; **~ly** *adv* studieusement, sérieusement.

study *n* étude *f*; études *fpl*; méditation *f*; * *vt* étudier; observer; * *vi* étudier; faire des études.

stuff *n* matière *f*; matériaux *mpl*; étoffe *f*; * *vt* (rem)bourrer, remplir; empailler.

stuffing *n* rembourrage *m*.

stuffy *adj* mal aéré; collet monté.

stumble *vi* trébucher; * *n* faux pas, trébuchement *m*.

stumbling block *n* hésitation *f*; pierre d'achoppement *f*.

stump *n* souche *f*; moignon *m*; bout *m*.

stun *vt* étourdir; stupéfier.

stunner *n* personne *ou* chose extraordinaire *f*.

stunt *n* cascade *f*; coup de publicité *m*; * *vt* empêcher de croître.

stuntman *n* cascadeur *m*.

stupefy *vt* hébéter; stupéfier.

stupendous *adj* prodigieux, remarquable.

stupid *adj* **~ly** *adv* stupide(ment).

stupidity *n* stupidité *f*.

stupor *n* stupeur *f*.

sturdily *adv* fortement.

sturdiness *n* force, robustesse *f*; résolution *f*.

sturdy *adj* vigoureux, robuste, fort; hardi, résolu.

sturgeon *n* esturgeon *m*.

stutter *vi* bégayer.

sty *n* porcherie *f*; taudis *m*.

stye *n* orgelet *m*.

style *n* style *m*; mode *f*; * *vt* appeler, dénommer; créer, dessiner.

stylish *adj* élégant, qui a du chic.

suave *adj* suave.

subdivide *vt* subdiviser.

subdivision *n* subdivision *f*.

subdue *vt* subjuguer, assujettir; contenir, réfréner; adoucir.

subject *adj* soumis; sujet à; * *n* sujet *m*; thème *m*; * *vt* soumettre; exposer.

subjection *n* sujétion *f*.

subjugate *vt* subjuguer, assujettir.

subjugation *n* subjugation *f*.

subjunctive *n* subjonctif *m*.

sublet *vt* sous-louer.

sublimate *vt* sublimer.

sublime *adj* sublime, suprême; **~ly** *adv* sublimement; * *n* sublime *m*.

sublimity *n* sublimité *f*.

submachine gun *n* mitraillette *f*.

submarine *adj n* sous-marin *m*.

submerge *vt* submerger.

submersion *n* submersion *f*.

submission *n* soumission *f*.

submissive *adj* soumis, docile; **~ly** *adv* avec soumission.

submissiveness *n* docilité *f*; soumission *f*.

submit *vt* soumettre; * *vi* se soumettre.

subordinate *adj* subalterne, inférieur; * *vt* subordonner.

subordination *n* subordination *f*.

subpoena *n* assignation *f* à comparaître; * *vt* assigner.

subscribe *vi* souscrire; * *vt* apposer; signer.

subscriber *n* souscripteur *m* -trice *f*.

subscription *n* souscription *f*.

subsequent *adj* **~ly** *adv* ultérieur(ement).

subservient *adj* subordonné; utile.

subside *vi* s'affaisser, baisser.

subsidence *n* affaissement *m*.

subsidiary *adj* subsidiaire.

subsidize *vt* subventionner, fournir des subsides à.

subsidy *n* subvention *f*; subside *m*.

subsist *vi* subsister; exister.

subsistence *n* existence *f*; subsistance *f*.

substance *n* substance *f*; fond *m*; essentiel *m*.

substantial *adj* considérable; réel, substantiel; solide; **~ly** *adv* considérablement.

substantiate *vt* justifier.

substantive *n* substantif *m*.

substitute *vt* substituer; * *n* remplaçant *m* -e *f*.

substitution *n* substitution *f*.

substratum *n* substrat *m*.

subterfuge *n* subterfuge *m*; faux-fuyant *m*.

subterranean *adj* souterrain.

subtitle *n* sous-titre *m*.

subtle *adj* subtile.

subtlety *n* subtilité *f*.

subtly *adv* subtilement.

subtract *vt* (*math*) soustraire.

suburb *n* banlieue *f*.

suburban *adj* de banlieue.

subversion *n* subversion *f*.

subversive *adj* subversif.

subvert *vt* subvertir, renverser.

subway *n* (US) métro *m*.

succeed *vi* réussir; succéder; avoir du succès; * *vt* succéder à, suivre.

success *n* succès *m*.

successful *adj* couronné de succès, qui réussit; **~ly** *adv* avec succès.

succession *n* succession *f*.

successive *adj* successif; **~ly** *adv* successivement.

successor *n* successeur *m*.

succinct *adj* succinct, concis; **~ly** *adv* succinctement.

succulent *adj* succulent.

succumb *vi* succomber.

such *adj* tel, pareil; **~ as** tel que.

suck *vt vi* sucer; *vi* téter.

suckle *vt* allaiter.

suckling *n* nourrisson *m*.

suction *n* succion *f*.

sudden *adj* **~ly** *adv* soudain(ement), subit(ement).

suddenness *n* soudaineté *f*.

suds *npl* mousse de savon *f*.

sue *vt* poursuivre en justice; supplier.

suede *n* daim *m*.

suet *n* graisse de rognon *f* de bœuf.

suffer *vt* souffrir, subir; tolérer, endurer; * *vi* souffrir.

suffering *n* souffrance *f*; douleur *f*.

suffice *vi* suffire, être suffisant.

sufficiency *n* quantité suffisante *f*; aisance *f*.

sufficient *adj* suffisant; **~ly** *adv* suffisamment.

suffocate *vt vi* étouffer.

suffocation *n* suffocation *f*.

suffrage *n* suffrage, vote *m*.

suffuse *vt* baigner, se répandre sur.

sugar *n* sucre *m*; * *vt* sucrer.

sugar beet *n* betterave à sucre *f*.

sugar cane *n* canne à sucre *f*.

sugar loaf *n* pain de sucre *m*.

sugar plum *n* bonbon *m*.

sugary *adj* sucré.

suggest *vt* suggérer.

suggestion *n* suggestion *f*.

suicidal *adj* suicidaire.

suicide *n* suicide *m*; suicidé *m* -e *f*.

suit *n* procès *m*; pétition *f*; costume *m*; tailleur *m*; requête *f*; * *vt* convenir à; aller à; arranger, adapter.

suitable *adj* qui convient, approprié.

suitably *adv* convenablement.

suitcase *n* valise *f*.

suite *n* suite *f*; escorte *f*; mobilier *m*; cortège *m*.

suitor *n* plaideur *m*; prétendant *m*.

sulkiness *n* bouderie *f*.

sulky *adj* boudeur, maussade.

sullen *adj* maussade; sombre; ~ly *adv* d'un air maussade; de mauvaise grâce.

sullenness *n* maussaderie *f*; silence *m*.

sulphur *n* soufre *m*.

sulphurous *adj* sulfureux.

sultan *n* sultan *m*.

sultana *n* sultane *f*; raisin sec *m*.

sultry *adj* étouffant; chaud.

sum *n* somme *f*; total *m*; ~ **up** *vt* résumer; récapituler; * *vi* résumer.

summarily *adv* sommairement.

summary *adj n* résumé *m*.

summer *n* été *m*.

summerhouse *n* gloriette *f*, pavillon de jardin *m*.

summit *n* sommet *m*; cime *f*.

summon *vt* convoquer, citer à comparaître; sommer; (*mil*) sommer de se rendre.

summons *n* convocation *f*; sommation *f*.

sumptuous *adj* somptueux, ~ly *adv* somptueusement.

sun *n* soleil *m*.

sunbathe *vi* prendre un bain de soleil, se faire bronzer.

sunburnt *adj* bronzé, hâlé.

Sunday *n* dimanche *m*.

sundial *n* cadran solaire *m*.

sundry *adj* divers, différent.

sunflower *n* tournesol *m*.

sunglasses *npl* lunettes de soleil *fpl*.

sunless *adj* sans soleil.

sunlight *n* lumière du soleil *f*.

sunny *adj* ensoleillé; radieux.

sunrise *n* lever de soleil *m*.

sun roof *n* toit ouvrant *m*.

sunset *n* coucher de soleil *m*.

sunshade *n* parasol *m*.

sunshine *n* (lumière du) soleil *m*; ensoleillement *m*.

sunstroke *n* insolation *f*.

suntan *n* bronzage *m*.

suntan oil *n* huile solaire *f*.

super *adj* (*fam*) sensationnel.

superannuated *adj* en retraite.

superannuation *n* retraite, pension de retraite *f*.

superb *adj* ~ly *adv* superbe(ment).

supercargo *n* (*mar*) subrécargue *m*.

supercilious *adj* hautain, dédaigneux; ~ly *adv* avec dédain.

superficial *adj* ~ly *adv* superficiel(lement).

superfluity *n* surabondance, superfluité *f*.

superfluous *adj* superflu.

superhuman *adj* surhumain.

superintendent *n* directeur *m* -trice *f*.

superior *adj n* supérieur *m* -e *f*.

superiority *n* supériorité *f*.

superlative *adj n* superlatif *m*; ~ly *adv* extrêmement, au suprême degré.

supermarket *n* supermarché *m*.

supernatural *n* surnaturel.

supernumerary *adj* surnuméraire.

superpower *n* superpuissance *f*.

supersede *vt* remplacer; supplanter.

supersonic *adj* supersonique.

superstition *n* superstition *f*.

superstitious *adj* superstitieux; ~ly *adv* superstitieusement.

superstructure *n* superstructure *f*.

supertanker *n* gros pétrolier, supertanker *m*.

supervene *vi* survenir.

supervise *vt* surveiller, superviser.

supervision *n* surveillance *f*.
supervisor *n* surveillant *m* -e *f*.
supine *adj* couché, étendu sur le dos; indolent.
supper *n* dîner *m*.
supplant *vt* supplanter.
supple *adj* souple, flexible; obséquieux.
supplement *n* supplément *m*.
supplementary *adj* supplémentaire.
suppleness *n* souplesse *f*.
suppli(c)ant *n* suppliant *m* -e *f*.
supplicate *vt* supplier.
supplication *n* supplique, supplication *f*.
supplier *n* fournisseur *m*.
supply *vt* fournir, approvisionner; suppléer à, remédier à; * *n* approvisionnement *m*; provision *f*.
support *vt* soutenir; supporter, appuyer; * *n* appui *m*.
supportable *adj* supportable.
supporter *n* partisan *m*; supporter *m*, adepte *mf*.
suppose *vt vi* supposer.
supposition *n* supposition *f*.
suppress *vt* supprimer.
suppression *n* suppression *f*.
supremacy *n* suprématie *f*.
supreme *adj* ~**ly** *adv* suprême(ment).
surcharge *vt* surcharger; * *n* surtaxe *f*.
sure *adj* sûr, certain; infaillible; **to be** ~ certainement; ~**ly** *adv* sûrement, certainement, sans doute.
sureness *n* certitude, sûreté *f*.
surety *n* certitude *f*; caution *f*.
surf *n* (*mar*) ressac *m*.
surface *n* surface *f*; * *vt* revêtir; * *vi* remonter à la surface.
surfboard *n* planche (de surf) *f*.
surfeit *n* excès *m*.
surge *n* vague, montée *f*; * *vi* déferler.
surgeon *n* chirurgien *m*.
surgery *n* chirurgie *m*.
surgical *adj* chirurgical.
surliness *n* air revêche, bourru *m*.
surly *adj* revêche, bourru.
surmise *vt* conjecturer; * *n* conjecture *f*.
surmount *vt* surmonter.
surmountable *adj* surmontable.

surname *n* nom de famille *m*.
surpass *vt* surpasser, dépasser.
surpassing *adj* sans pareil, incomparable.
surplice *n* surplis *m*.
surplus *n* excédent *m*; surplus *m*; * *adj* en surplus.
surprise *vt* surprendre; * *n* surprise *f*.
surprising *adj* surprenant.
surrender *vt* rendre; céder; * *vi* se rendre; * *n* reddition *f*.
surreptitious *adj* ~**ly** *adv* subreptice(ment).
surrogate *vt* remplacer; * *n* substitut *m*.
surrogate mother *n* mère porteuse *f*.
surround *vt* entourer, cerner, encercler.
survey *vt* examiner, inspecter; faire le relevé de; * *n* enquête *f*; relevé (des plans) *m*.
survive *vi* survivre; * *vt* survivre à.
survivor *n* survivant *m* -e *f*.
susceptibility *n* sensibilité *f*.
susceptible *adj* sensible.
suspect *vt* soupçonner; * *n* suspect *m* -e *f*.
suspend *vt* suspendre.
suspense *n* incertitude *f*; suspense *m*.
suspension *n* suspension *f*.
suspension bridge *n* pont suspendu *m*.
suspicion *n* soupçon *m*.
suspicious *adj* soupçonneux; ~**ly** *adv* soupçonneusement.
suspiciousness *n* caractère soupçonneux *m*.
sustain *vt* soutenir, supporter, maintenir; subir.
sustenance *n* (moyens de) subsistance *f*.
suture *n* suture *f*.
swab *n* tampon *m*; prélèvement *m*.
swaddle *vt* emmailloter.
swaddling clothes *npl* langes *mpl*.
swagger *vi* plastronner.
swallow *n* hirondelle *f*; * *vt* avaler.
swamp *n* marais *m*.
swampy *adj* marécageux.
swan *n* cygne *m*.
swap *vt* échanger; * *n* échange *m*.
swarm *n* essaim *m*; grouillement *m*; nuée *f*; * *vi* fourmiller; grouiller de monde; pulluler.
swarthy *adj* basané.
swarthiness *n* teint basané *m*.
swashbuckling *adj* fanfaron.

swath *n* andain *m*.

swathe *vt* emmailloter; * *n* bande *f*.

sway *vt* balancer; * *vi* se balancer, osciller; * *n* balancement *m*; emprise, domination, puissance *f*.

swear *vt* jurer; faire prêter serment; * *vi* jurer.

sweat *n* sueur *f*; * *vi* suer, transpirer.

sweater, sweatshirt *n* pullover *m*.

sweep *vt* balayer; ramoner; * *vi* s'étendre; avancer rapidement, majestueusement; * *n* coup de balai *m*; grand geste *m*; champ *m*.

sweeping *adj* rapide; ~s *pl* balayures *fpl*.

sweepstake *n* sweepstake *m*.

sweet *adj* sucré, doux, agréable; suave; gentil; mélodieux; adorable; * *adv* doux; sucré; * *n* bonbon *m*.

sweetbread *n* ris de veau *m*.

sweeten *vt* sucrer; adoucir; assainir; purifier.

sweetener *n* édulcorant *m*.

sweetheart *n* petit(e) ami(e) *m(f)*; chéri *m* -e *f*.

sweetmeats *npl* sucreries *fpl*.

sweetness *n* goût sucré *m*, douceur *f*.

swell *vi* gonfler; enfler; augmenter; * *vt* gonfler, enfler, grossir; * *n* houle *f*; * *adj* (*fam*) génial, épatant.

swelling *n* gonflement *m*; boursouflure, tuméfaction *f*.

swelter *vi* étouffer de chaleur.

swerve *vi* faire un écart; * *vt* dévier.

swift *adj* rapide, prompt, vif; * *n* martinet *m*.

swiftly *adv* rapidement.

swiftness *n* rapidité, promptitude *f*.

swill *vt* boire avidemment; * *n* pâtée *f*.

swim *vi* nager; * *vt* traverser à la nage; * *n* baignade *f*.

swimming *n* natation *f*, nage *f*; vertige *m*.

swimming pool *n* piscine *f*.

swimsuit *n* maillot de bain *m*.

swindle *vt* escroquer.

swindler *n* escroc *m*.

swine *n* pourceau, porc *m*.

swing *vi* se balancer, osciller; virer; * *vt* balancer; faire tourner; influencer; * *n* balancement *m*; rythme *m*.

swinging *adj* (*fam*) rythmé.

swinging door *n* porte battante *f*.

swirl *n* tourbillon.

switch *n* baguette *f*; interrupteur *m*; (*rail*) aiguille *f*; * *vt* changer de; ~ **off** éteindre; ~ **on** allumer.

switchboard *n* standard (téléphonique) *m*.

swivel *vt* faire pivoter.

swoon *vi* s'évanouir; * *n* évanouissement *m*, défaillance *f*.

swoop *vi* fondre sur; * *n* descente en piqué *f*; descente, rafle *f*; **in one** ~ d'un seul coup.

sword *n* épée *f*.

swordfish *n* espadon *m*.

swordsman *n* tireur d'épée *m*.

sycamore *n* sycomore *m*.

sycophant *n* sycophante *mf*.

syllabic *adj* syllabique.

syllable *n* syllabe *f*.

syllabus *n* programme *m* (d'un cours).

syllogism *n* syllogisme *m*.

sylph *n* sylphe *m*; sylphide *f*.

symbol *n* symbole *m*.

symbolic(al) *adj* symbolique.

symbolize *vt* symboliser.

symmetrical *adj* ~**ly** *adv* symétrique(ment).

symmetry *n* symétrie *f*.

sympathetic *adj* compatissant; ~**ally** *adv* avec compassion.

sympathize *vi* compatir.

sympathy *n* compassion *f*.

symphony *n* symphonie *f*.

symptom *n* symptôme *m*.

synagogue *n* synagogue *f*.

synchronism *n* synchronisme *m*.

syndicate *n* syndicat *m*.

syndrome *n* syndrome *m*.

synod *n* synode *m*.

synonym *n* synonyme *m*.

synonymous *adj* synonyme; ~**ly** *adv* de façon synonyme.

synopsis *n* synopsis *f*; résumé *m*.

synoptical *adj* synoptique.

syntax *n* syntaxe *f*.

synthesis *n* synthèse *f*.

syringe *n* seringue *f*; * *vt* seringuer.

system *n* système *m*.

systematic *adj* ~**ally** *adv* systématique(ment).

systems analyst *n* analyste de systèmes *mf*.

T

tab *n* patte *f*; étiquette *f*.

tabernacle *n* tabernacle *m*.

table *n* table *f*; * *vt* mettre en forme de tableau; ajourner; ~ **d'hôte** repas à prix fixe *m*.

tablecloth *n* nappe *f*.

tablespoon *n* grande cuiller *f*.

tablet *n* tablette *f*; comprimé *m*.

table tennis *n* ping-pong *m*.

taboo *adj n* tabou *m*; * *vt* proscrire.

tabular *adj* tabulaire.

tacit *adj* ~**ly** *adv* tacite(ment).

taciturn *adj* taciturne.

tack *n* broquette *f*; bordée *f*; * *vt* clouer; * *vi* tirer des bordées.

tackle *n* attirail, équipement, matériel *m*; plaquage *m*; (*mar*) appareil de levage *m*, apparaux *mpl*.

tactician *n* tacticien *m*.

tactics *npl* tactique *f*.

tadpole *n* têtard *m*.

taffeta *n* taffetas *m*.

tag *n* ferret *m*; étiquette *f*; * *vt* ferrer.

tail *n* queue *f*; basque *f*; * *vt* suivre, filer.

tailgate *n* hayon arrière *m*.

tailor *n* tailleur *m*.

tailoring *n* métier de tailleur *m*.

tailor-made *adj* fait sur mesure.

tailwind *n* vent arrière *m*.

taint *vt* infecter, polluer; vicier; * *n* tache, souillure *f*.

tainted *adj* infecté; souillé.

take *vt* prendre, saisir; apporter, emporter; conduire; enlever, retirer; passer; * *vi* prendre; ~ **away** *vt* enlever; emporter; ~ **back** *vt* reprendre; raccompagner; ~ **down** *vt* descendre; prendre (notes); ~ **in** *vt* saisir, comprendre; recevoir; ~ **off** *vi* décoller; *vt* enlever; imiter; ~ **on** *vt* accepter; engager; s'attaquer à; ~ **out** *vt* sortir; enlever; ~ **to** *vt* se prendre d'amitié pour; ~ **up** *vt* monter; occuper; se mettre à; * *n* prise *f*.

takeoff *n* décollage *m*.

takeover *n* prise *f* de contrôle.

takings *npl* recette *f*.

talent *n* talent *m*; don *m*.

talented *adj* talentueux.

talisman *n* talisman *m*.

talk *vi* parler, bavarder; causer; * *n* conversation *f*; discussion *f*; entretien *m*.

talkative *adj* loquace.

talk show *n* débat télévisé *m*.

tall *adj* grand, élevé; incroyable.

tally *vi* correspondre.

talon *n* serre *f*.

tambourine *n* tambourin *m*.

tame *adj* apprivoisé, domestiqué; ~**ly** *adv* docilement; fadement; * *vt* apprivoiser, domestiquer.

tameness *n* nature apprivoisée *f*; soumission *f*.

tamper *vi* tripoter.

tampon *n* tampon *m*.

tan *vt vi* bronzer; * *n* bronzage *m*.

tang *n* saveur forte *f*.

tangent *n* tangente *f*.

tangerine *n* mandarine *f*.

tangible *adj* tangible.

tangle *vt* enchevêtrer, embrouiller.

tank *n* réservoir *m*; citerne *f*.

tanker *n* pétrolier *m*; camion-citerne *m*.

tanned *adj* bronzé.

tantalizing *adj* tentant.

tantamount *adj* équivalent (à).

tantrum *n* accès de colère *m*.

tap *vt* taper doucement; exploiter; inciser; * *n* petite tape *f*; robinet *m*.

tape *n* ruban *m*; * *vt* enregistrer.

tape measure *n* mètre à ruban *m*.

taper *n* cierge *m*.

tape recorder *n* magnétophone *m*.

tapestry *n* tapisserie *f*.

tar *n* goudron *m*.

target *n* cible *f*.

tariff *n* tarif *m*.

tarmac *n* piste *f* (d'aéroport).

tarnish *vt* ternir.

tarpaulin *n* bâche (goudronnée) *f*.

tarragon *n* (*bot*) estragon *m*.

tart *adj* acidulé; * *n* tarte, tartelette *f*.

tartar *n* tartre *m*.

task *n* tâche *f*.

tassel *n* gland *m* (décoration).

taste *n* goût *m*; saveur *f*; pincée *f*; penchant *m*; * *vt* sentir le goût de; goûter à; déguster; savourer; * *vi* avoir du goût.

tasteful *adj* de bon goût; **~ly** *adv* avec goût.

tasteless *adj* insipide, sans goût.

tasty *adj* savoureux.

tattoo *n* tatouage *m*; * *vt* tatouer.

taunt *vt* railler; accabler de sarcasmes; * *n* raillerie *f*, sarcasme *m*.

Taurus *n* Taureau *m* (signe du zodiaque).

taut *adj* tendu.

tautological *adj* tautologique.

tautology *n* tautologie *f*.

tawdry *adj* tapageur, voyant, clinquant.

tax *n* impôt *m*; contribution *f*; * *vt* imposer; mettre à l'épreuve.

taxable *adj* imposable.

taxation *n* imposition *f*.

tax collector *n* percepteur *m*.

tax-free *adj* exonéré d'impôts.

taxi *n* taxi *m*; * *vi* rouler sur la piste.

taxi driver *n* chauffeur de taxi *m*.

taxi stand *n* station de taxis *f*.

tax payer *n* contribuable *mf*.

tax relief *n* dégrèvement fiscal *m*.

tax return *n* déclaration d'impôts *f*.

tea *n* thé *m*.

teach *vt* enseigner, apprendre; * *vi* enseigner.

teacher *n* professeur *m*; instituteur *m* -trice *f*.

teaching *n* enseignement *m*.

teacup *n* tasse à thé *f*.

teak *n* teck *m*.

team *n* équipe *f*.

teamster *n* (US) routier *m*.

teamwork *n* travail d'équipe *m*.

teapot *n* théière *f*.

tear *vt* déchirer; **~ up** mettre en morceaux.

tear *n* larme *f*.

tearful *adj* larmoyant; **~ly** *adv* en pleurant.

tear gas *n* gaz lacrymogène *m*.

tease *vt* taquiner.

tea-service, tea-set *n* service à thé *m*.

teaspoon *n* petite cuiller *f*.

teat *n* tétine *f*, mamelon *m*.

technical *adj* technique.

technicality *n* technicité *f*.

technician *n* technicien *m* -ne *f*.

technique *n* technique *f*.

technological *adj* technologique.

technology *n* technologie *f*.

teddy (bear) *n* ours en peluche *m*.

tedious *adj* ennuyeux, fastidieux; **~ly** *adv* fastidieusement.

tedium *n* ennui, manque d'intérêt *m*.

teem *vi* grouiller (de).

teenage *adj* adolescent; **~r** *n* adolescent(e) *m(f)*.

teens *npl* adolescence (de 13 à 20 ans) *f*.

tee-shirt *n* T-shirt *m*.

teeth *npl* de **tooth**.

teethe *vi* faire ses premières dents.

teetotal *adj* antialcoolique, qui ne boit jamais d'alcool.

teetotaller *n* personne qui ne boit jamais d'alcool *f*.

telegram *n* télégramme *m*.

telegraph *n* télégraphe *m*.

telegraphic *adj* télégraphique.

telegraphy *n* télégraphie *f*.

telepathy *n* télépathie *f*.

telephone *n* téléphone *m*.

telephone booth *n* cabine téléphonique *f*.

telephone call *n* appel téléphonique *m*.

telephone directory *n* annuaire *m*.

telephone number *n* numéro de téléphone *m*.

telescope *n* télescope *m*.

telescopic *adj* télescopique.

televise *vt* téléviser.

television *n* télévision *f*.

television set *n* téléviseur, poste de télévision *m*.

telex *n* télex *m*; *vt* envoyer par télex.

tell *vt* dire; raconter.

teller *n* (banque) caissier *m* -ière *f*.

telling *adj* révélateur.

telltale *adj* dénonciateur.

temper *vt* tempérer, modérer; * *n* colère *f*.

temperament *n* tempérament *m*.

temperance *n* tempérance, modération *f*.

temperate *adj* tempéré, modéré, mesuré.

temperature *n* température *f*.

tempest *n* tempête *f*.

tempestuous *adj* de tempête.

template *n* gabarit *m*.

temple *n* temple *m*; tempe *f*.

temporarily *adv* temporairement.

temporary *adj* temporaire.

tempt *vt* tenter.

temptation *n* tentation *f*.

tempting *adj* tentant.

ten *adj n* dix *m*.

tenable *adj* défendable.

tenacious *adj* tenace, **~ly** *adv* avec ténacité.

tenacity *n* ténacité *f*.

tenancy *n* location *f*.

tenant *n* locataire *mf*.

tend *vt* garder, surveiller; * *vi* avoir tendance (à).

tendency *n* tendance *f*.

tender *adj* tendre, délicat; sensible; **~ly** *adv* tendrement; * *n* offre *f*; * *vt* offrir.

tenderness *n* tendresse *f*.

tendon *n* tendon *m*.

tenement *n* appartement *m*.

tenet *n* doctrine *f*; principe *m*.

tennis court *n* court *ou* terrain de tennis *m*.

tennis player *n* joueur(-euse) de tennis *m(f)*.

tennis racket *n* raquette de tennis *f*.

tennis shoes *npl* chaussures de tennis *fpl*.

tenor *n* (*mus*) ténor *m*; sens *m*; substance *f*.

tense *adj* tendu; * *n* (*gr*) temps *m*.

tension *n* tension *f*.

tent *n* tente *f*.

tentacle *n* tentacule *m*.

tentative *adj* timide, hésitant; **~ly** *adv* à titre d'essai.

tenth *adj n* dixième *mf*.

tenuous *adj* ténu.

tenure *n* titularisation *f*.

tepid *adj* tiède.

term *n* terme *m*; trimestre *m*; mot *m*; condition, clause *f*; * *vt* appeler, nommer.

terminal *adj* terminal; * *n* aérogare *f*; terminal *m*.

terminate *vt* terminer.

termination *n* fin, conclusion *f*.

terrace *n* terrace *f*.

terrain *n* (*mil*) terrain *m*.

terrestrial *adj* terrestre.

terrible *adj* terrible.

terribly *adv* terriblement.

terrier *n* terrier *m* (chien).

terrific *adj* terrifiant; fantastique.

terrify *vt* terrifier, épouvanter.

territorial *adj* territorial.

territory *n* territoire *m*.

terror *n* terreur *f*.

terrorism *n* terrorisme *m*.

terrorist *n* terroriste *mf*.

terrorize *vt* terroriser.

terse *adj* concis, net.

test *n* essai *m*; épreuve *f*; * *vt* essayer; examiner.

testament *n* testament *m*.

tester *n* contrôleur *m* -euse *f*.

testicles *npl* testicules *mpl*.

testify *vt* témoigner, déclarer sous serment.

testimonial *n* certificat *m*.

testimony *n* témoignage *m*.

test pilot *n* pilote d'essai *m*.

test tube *n* éprouvette *f*.

testy *adj* irritable.

tetanus *n* tétanos *m*.

tether *vt* attacher.

text *n* texte *m*.

textbook *n* manuel *m*.

textiles *npl* textile *m*.

textual *adj* textuel.

texture *n* texture *f*; (*med*) tissu *m*.

than *adv* que; de.

thank *vt* remercier, dire merci à.

thankful *adj* reconnaissant; **~ly** *adv* avec reconnaissance.

thankfulness *n* reconnaissance *f*.

thankless *adj* ingrat.

thanks *npl* remerciement(s) *m(pl)*.

thanksgiving *n* action de grâce *f*.

that *pn* cela, ça, ce; qui, que; celui-là; * *conj* que; afin que; **so ~** pour que.

thatch *n* chaume *m*; * *vt* couvrir de chaume.

thaw *n* dégel *m*; * *vi* fondre, dégeler.

the *art* le, la, l', les.

theatre *n* théâtre *m*.

theatre-goer *n* habitué(e) du théâtre *m(f)*.

theatrical *adj* théâtral.

theft *n* vol *m*.

their *pn* leur(s); **~s** le leur; la leur; les leurs; à elles; à eux.

them *pn* les; leur.

theme *n* thème *m.*

themselves *pn pl* eux-mêmes *mpl,* elles-mêmes *fpl;* se.

then *adv* alors, à cette époque-là; ensuite; en ce cas; * *conj* donc; en ce cas; * *adj* d'alors; **now and ~** de temps en temps.

theological *adj* théologique.

theologian *n* théologien *m* -ne *f.*

theology *n* théologie *f.*

theorem *n* théorème *m.*

theoretical *adj* **~ly** *adv* théorique(ment).

theorize *vt* théoriser.

theorist *n* théoricien *m* -ne *f.*

theory *n* théorie *f.*

therapeutics *n* thérapeutique *f.*

therapist *n* thérapeute *mf.*

therapy *n* thérapie *f.*

there *adv* y, là.

thereabout(s) *adv* par là, près de là.

thereafter *adv* par la suite; après.

thereby *adv* de cette façon.

therefore *adv* donc, par conséquent.

thermal *adj* thermal.

thermal printer *n* imprimante thermique *f.*

thermometer *n* thermomètre *m.*

thermostat *n* thermostat *m.*

thesaurus *n* trésor *m;* dictionnaire de synonymes *m.*

these *pn pl* ceux-ci, celles-ci.

thesis *n* thèse *f.*

they *pn pl* ils, elles.

thick *adj* épais, gros; dense; obtus.

thicken *vi* (s')épaissir, grossir.

thicket *n* fourré *m.*

thickness *n* épaisseur *f.*

thickset *adj* trapu; râblé.

thick-skinned *adj* endurci, blindé.

thief *n* voleur *m* -euse *f.*

thigh *n* cuisse *f.*

thimble *n* dé (à coudre) *m.*

thin *adj* mince, fin, maigre; clair; * *vt* amincir; délayer; éclaircir.

thing *n* chose *f;* objet *m;* truc *m.*

think *vi* penser, réfléchir, imaginer; * *vt* penser, croire, juger; **~ over** *vt* réfléchir à; **~ up** *vt* imaginer.

thinker *n* penseur *m* -euse *f.*

thinking *n* pensée *f;* réflexion *f;* opinion *f.*

third *adj* troisième; * *n* troisième *mf;* tiers *m;* **~ly** *adv* troisièmement.

third rate *adj* médiocre, de mauvaise qualité.

thirst *n* soif *f.*

thirsty *adj* assoiffé.

thirteen *adj n* treize *m.*

thirteenth *adj n* treizième *mf.*

thirtieth *adj n* trentième *mf.*

thirty *adj n* trente *m.*

this *adj* ce, cet, cette, ces; * *pn* ceci, ce.

thistle *n* chardon *m.*

thorn *n* épine *f;* aubépine *f.*

thorny *adj* épineux.

thorough *adj* consciencieux, approfondi; **~ly** *adv* minutieusement, à fond.

thoroughbred *adj* pur-sang, de race.

thoroughfare *n* rue, artère *f.*

those *pn pl* ceux-là, celles-la; * *adj* ces, ces… là.

though *conj* bien que, malgré le fait que; * *adv* pourtant.

thought *n* pensée, réflexion *f;* opinion *f;* intention *f.*

thoughtful *adj* pensif.

thoughtless *adj* étourdi; irréfléchi; **~ly** *adv* étourdiment, à la légère.

thousand *adj n* mille *m.*

thousandth *adj n* millième *mf.*

thrash *vt* battre; rouer de coups.

thread *n* fil *m;* filetage *m;* * *vt* enfiler.

threadbare *adj* râpé, élimé.

threat *n* menace *f.*

threaten *vt* menacer.

three *adj n* trois *m.*

three-dimensional *adj* à trois dimensions, tridimensionnel.

three-ply *adj* à trois fils *ou* épaisseurs.

threshold *n* seuil *m.*

thrifty *adj* économe.

thrill *vt* faire frissonner; * *n* frisson *m.*

thriller *n* film *ou* roman à suspense *m.*

thrive *vi* prospérer; bien se développer.

throat *n* gorge *f.*

throb *vi* palpiter; vibrer; lanciner.

throne *n* trône *m.*

throng *n* foule *f;* * *vi* affluer.

throttle *n* accélérateur *m;* * *vt* étrangler.

through *prep* à travers; pendant; par, grâce à; * *adj* direct; * *adv* complètement.

throughout *prep* partout dans; * *adv* partout.

throw *vt* jeter, lancer, projeter; * *n* jet *m*; lancement *m*; ~ **away** *vt* jeter; ~ **off** *vt* rejeter; ~ **out** *vt* jeter dehors; ~ **up** *vt* *vi* vomir.

throwaway *adj* jetable.

thru (US) = **through.**

thrush *n* grive *f*.

thrust *vt* pousser violemment; enfoncer; * *n* poussée *f*.

thud *n* bruit sourd *m*.

thug *n* voyou *m*.

thumb *n* pouce *m*.

thumbtack *n* punaise *f*.

thump *n* coup de poing *m*; * *vi* frapper, cogner; * *vt* cogner à.

thunder *n* tonnerre *m*; * *vi* tonner.

thunderbolt *n* foudre *f*.

thunderclap *n* coup de tonnerre *m*.

thunderstorm *n* orage *m*.

thundery *adj* orageux.

Thursday *n* jeudi *m*.

thus *adv* ainsi, de cette manière.

thwart *vt* contrecarrer.

thyme *n* (*bot*) thym *m*.

thyroid *n* thyroïde *f*.

tiara *n* tiare *f*.

tic *n* tic *m*.

tick *n* tic-tac *m*; instant *m*; * *vt* cocher; ~ **over** *vi* tourner au ralenti; aller doucement.

ticket *n* billet, ticket *m*; étiquette *f*; carte *f*.

ticket collector *n* (*rail*) contrôleur *m* -euse *f*.

ticket office *n* guichet *m*.

tickle *vt* chatouiller.

ticklish *adj* chatouilleux.

tidal *adj* (*mar*) de la marée.

tidal wave *n* raz-de-marée *m*.

tide *n* marée *f*; (*fig*) afflux *m*, cours *m*.

tidy *adj* rangé, en ordre; ordonné; soigné.

tie *vt* attacher, nouer; * *vi* se nouer; ~ **up** *vt* ficeler; attacher; amarrer; conclure; * *n* attache *f*; lacet *m*; égalité *f*.

tier *n* gradin *m*; étage *m*.

tiger *n* tigre *m*.

tight *adj* raide, tendu; serré; hermétique; * *adv* très fort.

tighten *vt* (re)serrer, tendre.

tightfisted *adj* avare.

tightly *adv* très fort.

tightrope *n* corde raide *f*.

tigress *n* tigresse *f*.

tile *n* tuile *f*; carreau *m*; * *vt* couvrir de tuiles.

tiled *adj* en tuiles, carrelé.

till *n* caisse *f*; * *vt* labourer, cultiver.

tiller *n* barre du gouvernail *f*.

tilt *vt* pencher; * *vi* s'incliner.

timber *n* bois de construction *m*; arbres *mpl*.

time *n* temps *m*; période *f*; heure *f*; moment *m*; (*mus*) mesure *f*; **in** ~ à temps; **from** ~ **to** ~ de temps en temps; * *vt* fixer; chronométrer.

time bomb *n* bombe à retardement *f*.

time lag *n* décalage *m*.

timeless *adj* éternel.

timely *adj* opportun.

time off *n* temps libre *m*.

timer *n* sablier *m*; minuteur *m*.

time scale *n* durée *f*.

time zone *n* fuseau horaire *m*.

timid *adj* timide, timoré; ~**ly** *adv* timidement.

timidity *n* timidité *f*.

timing *n* chronométrage *m*.

tin *n* étain *m*; boîte (de conserve) *f*.

tinfoil *n* papier d'aluminium *m*.

tinge *n* teinte *f*.

tingle *vi* picoter; vibrer, frissonner.

tingling *n* picotement *m*; frisson *m*.

tinker *n* rétameur *m*.

tinkle *vi* tinter.

tinplate *n* fer-blanc *m*.

tinsel *n* guirlande *f*.

tint *n* teinte *f*; * *vt* teinter.

tinted *adj* teinté; fumé.

tiny *adj* minuscule, tout petit.

tip *n* pointe *f*, bout *m*; pourboire *m*; conseil, tuyau *m*; * *vt* donner un pourboire à; pencher; effleurer.

tip-off *n* avertissement *m*.

tipsy *adj* gai, éméché.

tiptop *adj* excellent, de premier ordre.

tirade *n* diatribe *f*.

tire *n* (US) pneu *m*; * *vt* fatiguer; * *vi* se fatiguer; se lasser.

tireless *adj* infatigable.

tire pressure *n* (US) pression *f* des pneux.

tiresome *adj* ennuyeux, fatigant.

tiring *adj* fatigant.

tissue *n* (US) tissu *m*(*bot*); mouchoir *m* en papier.

tissue paper *n* papier *m* de soie.

titbit *n* friandise *f*; bon morceau *m*.

titillate *vt* titiller.

title *n* titre *m*.

title deed *n* titre de propriété *m*.

title page *n* page de titre *f*.

titter *vi* rire sottement; * *n* petit rire sot *m*.

titular *adj* titulaire.

to *prep* à; vers; en; chez; moins; de.

toad *n* crapaud *m*.

toadstool *n* (*bot*) champignon vénéneux *m*.

toast *vt* (faire) griller; porter un toast à la santé de; * *n* toast *m*.

toaster *n* grille-pain *m invar*.

tobacco *n* tabac *m*.

tobacconist *n* marchand(e) de tabac *m*(*f*).

tobacco pouch *n* blague à tabac *f*.

tobacco shop *n* bureau de tabac *m*.

toboggan *n* toboggan *m*, luge *f*.

today *adv* aujourd'hui.

toddler *n* enfant qui commence à marcher *m*.

toddy *n* grog *m*.

toe *n* orteil *m*; pointe *f*.

together *adv* ensemble; en même temps.

toil *vi* travailler dur, peiner; se donner du mal; * *n* dur travail *m*; labeur *m*; peine *f*.

toilet *n* toilette *f*; toilettes *fpl*; * *adj* de toilette.

toilet bag *n* trousse de toilette *f*.

toilet bowl *n* cuvette des toilettes *f*.

toilet paper *n* papier hygiénique *m*.

toiletries *npl* articles de toilette *mpl*.

token *n* signe *m*; marque *f*; souvenir *m*; bon *m*; jeton *m*.

tolerable *adj* tolérable; passable.

tolerance *n* tolérance *f*.

tolerant *adj* tolérant.

tolerate *vt* tolérer.

toll *n* péage *m*; nombre de victimes *m*; * *vi* sonner le glas.

tomato *n* tomate *f*.

tomb *n* tombeau *m*; tombe *f*.

tomboy *n* garçon manqué *m*.

tombstone *n* pierre tombale *f*.

tomcat *n* matou *m*.

tomorrow *adv*, *n* demain *m*.

ton *n* tonne *f*.

tone *n* ton *m*; tonalité *f*; * *vi* s'harmoniser; ~ **down** *vt* adoucir.

tone-deaf *adj* qui n'a pas l'oreille musicale.

tongs *npl* pinces *fpl*.

tongue *n* langue *f*.

tongue-tied *adj* muet.

tongue-twister *n* phrase difficile à prononcer *f*.

tonic *n* (*med*) tonique *m*.

tonight *adv*, *n* ce soir (*m*).

tonnage *n* tonnage *m*.

tonsil *n* amygdale *f*.

tonsure *n* tonsure *f*.

too *adv* aussi; trop.

tool *n* outil *m*; ustensile *m*.

tool box *n* caisse à outils *f*.

toot *vi* klaxonner.

tooth *n* dent *f*.

toothache *n* rage de dents *f*.

toothbrush *n* brosse à dents *f*.

toothless *adj* édenté.

toothpaste *n* dentifrice *m*.

toothpick *n* cure-dent *m*.

top *n* sommet *m*, cime *f*; haut *m*; tête *f*; dessus *m*; couvercle *m*; étage supérieur *m*; * *adj* du haut; premier; * *vt* dépasser; être au sommet de; ~ **off** couronner.

topaz *n* topaze *f*.

top floor *n* dernier étage *m*.

top-heavy *adj* instable, déséquilibré.

topic *n* sujet *m*; ~**al** *adj* d'actualité.

topless *adj* torse nu, aux seins nus.

top-level *adj* au plus haut niveau.

topmost *adj* le plus haut.

topographic(al) *adj* topographique.

topography *n* topographie *f*.

topple *vt* renverser; * *vi* basculer.

top-secret *adj* ultra-secret.

topsy-turvy *adv* sens dessus dessous.

torch *n* torche *f*.

torment *vt* tourmenter; * *n* tourment *m*.

tornado *n* tornade *f*.

torrent *n* torrent *m*.

torrid *adj* torride.

tortoise *n* tortue *f*.

tortoiseshell *adj* en écaille de tortue.

tortuous *adj* tortueux, sinueux.

torture *n* torture *f*; * *vt* torturer.

toss *vt* lancer, jeter; agiter, secouer.

total *adj* total, global; **~ly** *adv* totalement.

totalitarian *adj* totalitaire.

totality *n* totalité *f*.

totter *vi* chanceler.

touch *vt* toucher; **~ on** effleurer; **~ up** retoucher; * *n* toucher *m*; contact *m*; touche *f*.

touch-and-go *adj* incertain, précaire.

touchdown *n* atterrissage *m*; but *m*.

touched *adj* touché; timbré.

touching *adj* touchant, attendrissant.

touchstone *n* pierre de touche *f*.

touchwood *n* amadou *m*.

touchy *adj* susceptible.

tough *adj* dur; pénible; résistant; fort; * *n* dur *m*.

toughen *vt* durcir.

toupee *n* postiche *m*.

tour *n* voyage *m*; visite *f*; * *vt* visiter.

touring *n* tourisme *m*.

tourism *n* tourisme *m*.

tourist *n* touriste *mf*.

tourist office *n* office de tourisme *m*.

tournament *n* tournoi *m*.

tow *n* remorquage *m*; * *vt* remorquer.

toward(s) *prep* vers, dans la direction de; envers, à l'égard de.

towel *n* serviette *f*.

towelling *n* tissu éponge *m*.

towel rack *n* porte-serviette *m invar*.

tower *n* tour *f*.

towering *adj* imposant.

town *n* ville *f*.

town clerk *n* secrétaire de mairie *mf*.

town hall *n* mairie *f*.

towrope *n* câble de remorquage *m*.

toy *n* jouet *m*.

toyshop *n* magasin de jouets *m*.

trace *n* trace, piste *f*; * *vt* tracer, esquisser; retrouver.

track *n* trace *f*; empreinte *f*; chemin *m*; voie *f*; piste *f*; * *vt* suivre à la trace.

tracksuit *n* survêtement *m*.

tract *n* étendue *f*, région *f*; brochure *f*.

traction *n* traction *f*.

trade *n* commerce *m*, affaires *fpl*; échange *m*;

métier *m*; * *vi* faire le commerce (de), commercer.

trade fair *n* foire commerciale *f*.

trademark *n* marque de fabrique *f*.

trade name *n* raison commerciale *f*.

trader *n* négociant *m* -e *f*.

tradesman *n* fournisseur, commerçant *m*.

trade(s) union *n* syndicat *m*.

trade unionist *n* syndicaliste *mf*.

trading *n* commerce *m*; * *adj* commercial.

tradition *n* tradition *f*

traditional *adj* traditionnel.

traffic *n* circulation *f*; négoce *m*; * *vi* faire le commerce (de).

traffic circle *n* (US) rond-point *m*.

traffic jam *n* embouteillage *m*.

trafficker *n* trafiquant *m* -e *f*.

traffic lights *npl* feux de signalisation *mpl*.

tragedy *n* tragédie *f*.

tragic *adj* **~ally** *adv* tragique(ment).

tragicomedy *n* tragi-comédie *f*.

trail *vt* suivre la piste de; traîner; *vi* traîner; * *n* traînée *f*; trace *f*; queue *f*.

trailer *n* remorque *f*; caravane *f*; bande-annonce *f*.

train *vt* entraîner; former; * *n* train *m*; traîne *f*; file *f*.

trained *adj* qualifié; diplômé.

trainee *n* stagiaire *mf*.

trainer *n* entraîneur *m*.

training *n* formation *f*; entraînement *m*.

trait *n* trait *m*.

traitor *n* traître *m*.

tramp *n* clochard *m* -e *f*; (*sl*) putain *f*; * *vi* marcher d'un pas lourd; * *vt* piétiner.

trample *vt* piétiner.

trampoline *n* trampoline *m*.

trance *n* transe *f*; extase *f*.

tranquil *adj* tranquille.

tranquillize *vt* tranquilliser.

tranquillizer *n* tranquillisant *m*.

transact *vt* traiter.

transaction *n* transaction *f*; opération *f*.

transatlantic *adj* transatlantique.

transcend *vt* transcender, dépasser; surpasser.

transcription *n* transcription *f*; copie *f*.

transfer *vt* transférer, déplacer; * *n* transfert *m*; mutation *f*; décalcomanie *f*.

transform *vt* transformer.
transformation *n* transformation *f.*
transfusion *n* transfusion *f.*
transient *adj* transitoire, passager.
transit *n* transit *m.*
transition *n* transition *f;* passage *m.*
transitional *adj* de transition.
transitive *adj* transitif.
translate *vt* traduire.
translation *n* traduction *f.*
translator *n* traducteur *m* -trice *f.*
transmission *n* transmision *f.*
transmit *vt* transmettre.
transmitter *n* transmetteur *m;* émetteur *m.*
transparency *n* transparence *f;* diapositive *f.*
transparent *adj* transparent.
transpire *vi* transpirer; arriver.
transplant *vt* transplanter; * *n* transplantation *f.*
transport *vt* transporter; * *n* transport *m.*
transportation *n* moyen de transport *m.*
trap *n* piège *m;* * *vt* prendre au piège; bloquer.
trap door *n* trappe *f.*
trapeze *n* trapèze *m.*
trappings *npl* ornements *mpl.*
trash *n* camelote *f;* inepties *fpl.*
trash can *n* poubelle *f.*
trashy *adj* sans valeur, de mauvaise qualité.
travel *vi* voyager; * *vt* parcourir; * *n* voyage *m.*
travel agency *n* agence de voyages *f.*
travel agent *n* agent de voyages *m.*
traveller *n* voyageur *m* -euse *f.*
traveller's cheque *n* chèque de voyage *m.*
travelling *n* voyages *mpl.*
travel sickness *n* mal de mer/de l'air *m.*
travesty *n* parodie *f.*
trawler *n* chalutier *m.*
tray *n* plateau *m;* tiroir *m.*
treacherous *adj* traître, perfide.
treachery *n* traîtrise *f.*
tread *vi* marcher; écraser; * *n* pas *m;* bruit de pas *m;* bande de roulement *f.*
treason *n* trahison *f;* **high** ~ haute trahison *f.*
treasure *n* trésor *m;* * *vt* conserver précieusement.
treasurer *n* trésorier *m* -ière *f.*
treat *vt* traiter; offrir; * *n* cadeau *m;* plaisir *m.*

treatise *n* traité *m.*
treatment *n* traitement *m.*
treaty *n* traité *m.*
treble *adj* triple; * *vt vi* tripler; * *n (mus)* soprano *m.*
treble clef *n* clef de sol *f.*
tree *n* arbre *m.*
trek *n* randonnée *f.*
trellis *n* treillis *m.*
tremble *vi* trembler.
trembling *n* tremblement *m;* frisson *m.*
tremendous *adj* terrible; énorme; formidable.
tremor *n* tremblement *m.*
trench *n* fossé *m; (mil)* tranchée *f.*
trend *n* tendance *f;* direction *f;* mode *f.*
trendy *adj* dernier cri.
trepidation *n* vive inquiétude *f.*
trespass *vt* transgresser, violer.
tress *n* boucle de cheveu *f;* **~es** chevelure *f.*
trestle *n* tréteau, chevalet *m.*
trial *n* procès *m;* épreuve *f;* essai *m;* peine *f.*
triangle *n* triangle *m.*
triangular *adj* triangulaire.
tribal *adj* tribal.
tribe *n* tribu *f.*
tribulation *n* tribulation *f.*
tribunal *n* tribunal *m.*
tributary *adj n* tributaire *m.*
tribute *n* tribut *m.*
trice *n* instant *m.*
trick *n* ruse, astuce *f;* tour *m;* blague *f;* pli *m;* * *vt* attraper.
trickery *n* supercherie *f.*
trickle *vi* couler goutte à goutte; * *n* filet *m.*
tricky *adj* délicat; difficile.
tricycle *n* tricycle *m.*
trifle *n* bagatelle, vétille *f;* * *vi* jouer; badiner.
trifling *adj* futile, insignifiant.
trigger *n* gâchette *f;* **~ off** *vt* déclencher.
trigonometry *n* trigonométrie *f.*
trill *n* trille *f;* * *vi* triller.
trim *adj* net, soigné; bien tenu; en parfait état; * *vt* arranger; tailler; orner.
trimmings *npl* ornements *mpl.*
Trinity *n* Trinité *f.*
trinket *n* bibelot *m,* babiole *f;* colifichet *m.*
trio *n (mus)* trio *m.*
trip *vt* faire trébucher; * *vi* trébucher; faire un

faux pas; **~ up** *vi* trébucher; *vt* faire trébucher; * *n* faux pas *m*; voyage *m*.

tripe *n* tripes *fpl*; bêtises *fpl*.

triple *adj* triple; * *vt vi* tripler.

triplets *npl* triplés *mpl*.

triplicate *n* copie en trois exemplaires *f*.

tripod *n* trépied *m*.

trite *adj* banal; usé.

triumph *n* triomphe *m*; * *vi* triompher.

triumphal *adj* triomphal.

triumphant *adj* triomphant; victorieux; **~ly** *adv* triomphalement.

trivia *npl* futilités *fpl*.

trivial *adj* insignifiant, sans importance; **~ly** *adv* banalement.

triviality *n* banalité *f*.

trolley *n* chariot *m*.

trombone *n* trombone *m*.

troop *n* bande *f*; **~s** *npl* troupes *fpl*.

trooper *n* soldat de cavalerie *m*.

trophy *n* trophée *m*.

tropical *adj* tropical.

trot *n* trot *m*; * *vi* trotter.

trouble *vt* affliger; tourmenter; * *n* problème *m*; ennui *m*; difficulté *f*; affliction, peine *f*.

troubled *adj* inquiet; agité.

troublemaker *n* agitateur *m* -trice *f*.

troubleshooter *n* médiateur *m*.

troublesome *adj* pénible.

trough *n* abreuvoir *m*; auge *f*.

troupe *n* troupe *f*.

trousers *npl* pantalon *m*.

trout *n* truite *f*.

trowel *n* truelle *f*.

truce *n* trêve *f*.

truck *n* camion *m*; wagon *m*.

truck driver *n* routier *m*.

truck farm *n* jardin maraîcher *m*.

truculent *adj* brutal, agressif.

trudge *vi* marcher lourdement.

true *adj* vrai, véritable; sincère; exact.

truelove *n* bien-aimé *m* -e *f*.

truffle *n* truffe *f*.

truly *adv* vraiment; sincèrement.

trump *n* atout *m*.

trumpet *n* trompette *f*.

trunk *n* malle *f*, coffre *m*; trompe *f*.

truss *n* botte *f*; * *vt* botteler; trousser.

trust *n* confiance *f*; trust *m*; fidéicommis *m*; * *vt* avoir confiance en; confier à.

trusted *adj* de confiance.

trustee *n* fidéicommissaire *m*, curateur *m* -trice *f*.

trustful *adj* confiant.

trustily *adv* fidèlement.

trusting *adj* confiant.

trustworthy *adj* digne de confiance.

trusty *adj* fidèle, loyal; sûr.

truth *n* vérité *f*; **in ~** en vérité.

truthful *adj* véridique; qui dit la vérité.

truthfulness *n* véracité *f*.

try *vt* essayer, tâcher, chercher à; expérimenter; mettre à l'épreuve; tenter; juger; * *vi* essayer; **~ on** *vt* essayer; **~ out** *vt* essayer; * *n* tentative *f*; essai *m*.

trying *adj* pénible; fatigant.

tub *n* cuve *f*, bac *m*; baignoire *f*.

tuba *n* tuba *m*.

tube *n* tube *m*; métro *m*.

tuberculosis *n* tuberculose *f*.

tubing *n* tuyaux *mpl*.

tuck *n* pli *m*; * *vt* mettre.

tucker *vt* (US) fatiguer.

Tuesday *n* mardi *m*.

tuft *n* touffe *f*; houppe *f*.

tug *vt* remorquer; * *n* remorqueur *m*.

tuition *n* cours, enseignement *m*.

tulip *n* tulipe *f*.

tumble *vi* tomber, faire une chute; se jeter; * *vt* renverser; culbuter; * *n* chute *f*; culbute *f*.

tumbledown *adj* délabré.

tumbler *n* verre *m*.

tummy *n* ventre *m*.

tumour *n* tumeur *f*.

tumultuous *adj* tumultueux.

tuna *n* thon *m*.

tune *n* air *m*; accord *m*; harmonie *f*; * *vt* accorder; syntoniser.

tuneful *adj* mélodieux, harmonieux.

tuner *n* syntoniseur *m*.

tunic *n* tunique *f*.

tuning fork *n* (*mus*) diapason *m*.

tunnel *n* tunnel *m*; * *vt* creuser un tunnel dans.

turban *n* turban *m*.

turbine *n* turbine *f*.

turbulence *n* turbulence, agitation *f*.

turbulent *adj* turbulent, agité.

tureen *n* soupière *f*.

turf *n* gazon *m*; * *vt* gazonner.

turgid *adj* gonflé.

turkey *n* dinde *f*.

turmoil *n* agitation *f*; trouble *m*.

turn *vi* (se) tourner; devenir; changer; se retourner; se changer, se transformer; ~ **around** se retourner; tourner; ~ **back** revenir; ~ **down** *vt* rejeter; rabattre; ~ **in** aller se coucher; ~ **off** *vi* tourner; *vt* éteindre; fermer; ~ **on** *vt* allumer; ouvrir; ~ **out** s'avérer; ~ **over** *vi* se retourner; *vt* tourner; ~ **up** *vi* arriver; se présenter; *vt* monter; * *n* tour *m*; tournure *f*; virage *m*; tendance *f*.

turncoat *n* renégat *m*.

turning *n* embranchement *m*.

turnip *n* navet *m*.

turn-off *n* sortie (d'autoroute) *f*; embranchement *m*.

turnout *n* production *f*.

turnover *n* chiffre d'affaires *m*.

turnpike *n* barrière *f* de péage.

turnstile *n* tourniquet *m*.

turntable *n* platine *f*.

turpentine *n* (essence de) térébenthine *f*.

turquoise *n* turquoise *f*.

turret *n* tourelle *f*.

turtle *n* tortue marine *f*.

turtledove *n* tourterelle *f*.

tusk *n* défense *f*.

tussle *n* lutte *f*.

tutor *n* professeur particulier *m*; directeur d'études *m*; * *vt* enseigner, donner des cours particuliers à.

tuxedo *n* smoking *m*.

twang *n* vibration *f*; ton nasillard *m*.

tweezers *npl* pince à épiler *f*.

twelfth *adj* n douzième *mf*.

twelve *adj* n douze *m*.

twentieth *adj* n vingtième *mf*.

twenty *adj* n vingt *m*.

twice *adv* deux fois.

twig *n* brindille *f*; * *vi* piger.

twilight *n* crépuscule *m*.

twin *n* jumeau *m* -elle *f*.

twine *vi* s'enrouler; serpenter; * *n* ficelle *f*.

twinge *vt* élancer; * *n* élancement *m*; remords *m*.

twinkle *vi* scintiller; clignoter.

twirl *vt* faire tournoyer; * *vi* tournoyer; * *n* tournoiement *m*.

twist *vt* tordre, tortiller; entortiller; * *vi* serpenter; * *n* torsion *f*; tournant *m*; rouleau *m*.

twit *n* (*sl*) crétin *m* -e *f*.

twitch *vi* avoir un mouvement nerveux; * *n* tic *m*.

twitter *vi* gazouiller; * *n* gazouillis *m*.

two *adj* n deux *m*.

two-door *adj* à deux portes.

two-faced *adj* hypocrite.

twofold *adj* double; * *adv* au double.

two-seater *n* voiture/avion à deux places *f*/*m*.

twosome *n* paire *f*; couple *m*.

tycoon *n* magnat *m*.

type *n* type *m*; caractère *m*; exemple *m*; * *vi* taper à la machine.

typecast *adj* enfermé dans un rôle.

typeface *n* police *f* de caractère.

typescript *n* texte dactylographié *m*.

typewriter *n* machine à écrire *f*.

typewritten *adj* dactylographié.

typical *adj* typique.

tyrannical *adj* tyrannique.

tyranny *n* tyrannie *f*.

tyrant *n* tyran *m*.

tyre *n* pneu *m*.

tyre pressure *n* pression *f* des pneus.

U

ubiquitous *adj* doué d'ubiquité.

udder *n* pis *m*.

ugh *excl* pouah!, berk!

ugliness *n* laideur *f*.

ugly *adj* laid; inquiétant.

ulcer *n* ulcère *m*.

ulterior *adj* ultérieur.

ultimate *adj* final; ~**ly** *adv* finalement; à la fin.

ultimatum *n* ultimatum *m*.

ultramarine *n, adj* outremer *m.*
ultrasound *n* ultrason *m.*
umbilical cord *n* cordon ombilical *m.*
umbrella *n* parapluie *m.*
umpire *n* arbitre *m.*
umpteen *adj* un très grand nombre de, beaucoup de.
unable *adj* incapable.
unaccompanied *adj* non accompagné, seul.
unaccomplished *adj* inaccompli, inachevé.
unaccountable *adj* inexplicable.
unaccountably *adv* inexplicablement.
unaccustomed *adj* inaccoutumé, inhabituel.
unacknowledged *adj* non reconnu; (resté) sans réponse.
unacquainted *adj* qui ignore, qui n'a pas connaissance de.
unadorned *adj* sans ornement.
unadulterated *adj* pur; sans mélange.
unaffected *adj* sincère; non affecté.
unaided *adj* sans aide.
unaltered *adj* inchangé.
unambitious *adj* sans ambition.
unanimity *n* unanimité *f.*
unanimous *adj* ~**ly** *adv* unanime(ment).
unanswerable *adj* incontestable.
unanswered *adj* sans réponse.
unapproachable *adj* inaccessible.
unarmed *adj* non armé, désarmé.
unassuming *adj* sans prétention, modeste.
unattached *adj* indépendant; libre.
unattainable *adj* inaccessible.
unattended *adj* sans surveillance.
unauthorized *adj* sans autorisation.
unavoidable *adj* inévitable.
unavoidably *adv* inévitablement.
unaware *adj* ignorant; inconscient.
unawares *adv* à l'improviste; par mégarde.
unbalanced *adj* déséquilibré; non soldé.
unbearable *adj* insupportable.
unbecoming *adj* malséant, déplacé, peu seyant.
unbelievable *adj* incroyable.
unbend *vi* se détendre; * *vt* redresser.
unbiased *adj* impartial.
unblemished *adj* sans tache, sans défaut.
unborn *adj* à naître, pas encore né.
unbreakable *adj* incassable.

unbroken *adj* non brisé; intact; ininterrompu; indompté.
unbutton *vt* déboutonner.
uncalled-for *adj* injustifié.
uncanny *adj* mystérieux.
unceasing *adj* incessant, continu.
unceremonious *adj* brusque.
uncertain *adj* incertain, douteux.
uncertainty *n* incertitude *f.*
unchangeable *adj* immuable.
unchanged *adj* inchangé.
unchanging *adj* invariable, immuable.
uncharitable *adj* peu charitable.
unchecked *adj* non maîtrisé.
unchristian *adj* peu chrétien.
uncivil *adj* impoli, grossier.
uncivilized *adj* barbare, non civilisé.
uncle *n* oncle *m.*
uncomfortable *adj* inconfortable; incommode; désagréable.
uncomfortably *adv* inconfortablement; mal; désagréablement.
uncommon *adj* rare, extraordinaire.
uncompromising *adj* intransigeant.
unconcerned *adj* indifférent.
unconditional *adj* inconditionnel, absolu.
unconfined *adj* illimité, sans bornes.
unconfirmed *adj* non confirmé.
unconnected *adj* sans rapport.
unconquerable *adj* invincible, insurmontable.
unconscious *adj* inconscient; ~**ly** *adv* inconsciemment, sans s'en rendre compte.
unconstrained *adj* non contraint, libre.
uncontrollable *adj* irrésistible; qui ne peut être maîtrisé.
unconventional *adj* peu conventionnel.
unconvincing *adj* peu convaincant.
uncork *vt* déboucher.
uncorrected *adj* non corrigé.
uncouth *adj* grossier.
uncover *vt* découvrir.
uncultivated *adj* inculte.
uncut *adj* non taillé, intégral.
undamaged *adj* non endommagé, indemne.
undaunted *adj* intrépide.
undecided *adj* indécis.
undefiled *adj* pur, immaculé.

undeniable *adj* indéniable, incontestable; **~bly** *adv* incontestablement.

under *prep* sous; dessous; moins de; selon; * *adv* au-dessous, en-dessous.

under-age *adj* mineur.

undercharge *vt* ne pas faire payer assez.

underclothing *n* sous-vêtements *mpl*.

undercoat *n* première couche *f*.

undercover *adj* secret, clandestin.

undercurrent *n* courant sous-marin *m*.

undercut *vt* vendre moins cher que.

underdeveloped *adj* sous-développé, insuffisamment développé.

underdog *n* opprimé *m* -e *f*.

underdone *adj* pas assez cuit.

underestimate *vt* sous-estimer.

undergo *vt* subir; supporter.

undergraduate *n* étudiant(e) en licence *m(f)*.

underground *n* mouvement clandestin *m*.

undergrowth *n* broussailles *fpl*, sous-bois *m*.

underhand *adv* en cachette; * *adj* secret, clandestin.

underlie *vi* être à la base de.

underline *vt* souligner.

undermine *vt* saper.

underneath *adv* (en) dessous; * *prep* sous, au-dessous de.

underpaid *adj* sous-payé.

underprivileged *adj* défavorisé.

underrate *vt* sous-estimer.

undersecretary *n* sous-secrétaire *mf*.

undershirt *n* (US) maillot de corps *m*.

undershorts *npl* (US) caleçon *m*.

underside *n* dessous *m*.

understand *vt* comprendre.

understandable *adj* compréhensible.

understanding *n* compréhension *f*; intelligence *f*; entendement *m*; accord *m*; * *adj* compréhensif.

understatement *n* affirmation en dessous de la vérité *f*.

undertake *vt* entreprendre.

undertaking *n* entreprise *f*; engagement *m*.

undervalue *vt* sous-estimer.

underwater *adj* sous-marin; * *adv* sous l'eau.

underwear *n* sous-vêtements *mpl*, dessous *mpl*.

underworld *n* pègre *f*.

underwrite *vt* souscrire à; assurer contre.

underwriter *n* assureur *m*.

undeserved *adj* immérité; **~ly** *adv* à tort, indûment.

undeserving *adj* peu méritant.

undesirable *adj* peu souhaitable.

undetermined *adj* indéterminé; indécis.

undigested *adj* non digéré.

undiminished *adj* non diminué.

undisciplined *adj* indiscipliné.

undisguised *adj* non déguisé.

undismayed *adj* non découragé.

undisputed *adj* incontesté.

undisturbed *adj* non dérangé, paisible.

undivided *adj* indivisé, entier.

undo *vt* défaire; détruire.

undoing *n* ruine *f*.

undoubted *adj* **~ly** *adv* indubitable(ment).

undress *vi* se déshabiller.

undue *adj* excessif; injuste.

undulating *adj* ondulant.

unduly *adv* trop, excessivement.

undying *adj* éternel.

unearth *vt* déterrer.

unearthly *adj* surnaturel.

uneasy *adj* inquiet; troublé, gêné.

uneducated *adj* sans instruction.

unemployed *adj* au chômage.

unemployment *n* chômage *m*.

unending *adj* interminable.

unenlightened *adj* peu éclairé.

unenviable *adj* peu enviable.

unequal *adj* **~ly** *adv* inégal(ement).

unequalled *adj* inégalé.

unerring *adj* **~ly** *adv* infaillible(ment).

uneven *adj* inégal; impair; **~ly** *adv* inégalement.

unexpected *adj* inattendu; inopiné; **~ly** *adv* de manière inattendue; inopinément.

unexplored *adj* inexploré.

unfailing *adj* infaillible, certain.

unfair *adj* injuste; inéquitable; **~ly** *adv* injustement.

unfaithful *adj* infidèle.

unfaithfulness *n* infidélité *f*.

unfaltering *adj* ferme, assuré.

unfamiliar *adj* peu familier, peu connu.

unfashionable *adj* démodé; **~bly** *adv* sans se préoccuper de la mode.

unfasten *vt* détacher, défaire.
unfathomable *adj* insondable, impénétrable.
unfavourable *adj* défavorable.
unfeeling *adj* insensible, impitoyable.
unfinished *adj* inachevé, incomplet.
unfit *adj* inapte; impropre.
unfold *vt* déplier; révéler; * *vi* s'ouvrir.
unforeseen *adj* imprévu.
unforgettable *adj* inoubliable.
unforgivable *adj* impardonnable.
unforgiving *adj* implacable.
unfortunate *adj* malheureux, malchanceux; ~ly *adv* malheureusement, par malheur.
unfounded *adj* sans fondement.
unfriendly *adj* inamical.
unfruitful *adj* stérile; infructueux.
unfurnished *adj* non meublé.
ungainly *adj* gauche.
ungentlemanly *adj* peu galant.
ungovernable *adj* ingouvernable, indomptable.
ungrateful *adj* ingrat; peu reconnaissant; ~ly *adv* avec ingratitude.
ungrounded *adj* infondé.
unhappily *adv* malheureusemnt.
unhappiness *n* tristesse *f*.
unhappy *adj* malheureux.
unharmed *adj* indemne, sain et sauf.
unhealthy *adj* malsain; maladif.
unheard-of *adj* inédit, sans précédent.
unheeding *adj* insouciant; distrait.
unhook *vt* décrocher; dégrafer.
unhoped(-for) *adj* inespéré.
unhurt *adj* indemne.
unicorn *n* licorne *f*.
uniform *adj* uniforme; ~ly *adv* uniformément; * *n* uniforme *m*.
uniformity *n* uniformité *f*.
unify *vt* unifier.
unimaginable *adj* inimaginable.
unimpaired *adj* non diminué, intact.
unimportant *adj* sans importance.
uninformed *adj* mal informé.
uninhabitable *adj* inhabitable.
uninhabited *adj* inhabité, désert.
uninjured *adj* indemne, sain et sauf.
unintelligible *adj* inintelligible.
unintelligibly *adv* inintelligiblement.

unintentional *adj* involontaire.
uninterested *adj* indifférent.
uninteresting *adj* inintéressant.
uninterrupted *adj* ininterrompu, continu.
uninvited *adj* sans être invité.
union *n* union *f*; syndicat *m*.
unionist *n* syndicaliste *mf*.
unique *adj* unique, exceptionnel.
unison *n* unisson *m*.
unit *n* unité *f*.
unitarian *n* unitarien *m* -ne *f*.
unite *vt* unir; * *vi* s'unir.
unitedly *adv* conjointement, ensemble.
United States (of America) *npl* États-Unis *mpl*.
unity *n* unité, harmonie *f*, accord *m*.
universal *adj* ~ly *adv* universel(lement).
universe *n* univers *m*.
university *n* université *f*.
unjust *adj* ~ly *adv* injuste(ment).
unkempt *adj* négligé; débraillé.
unkind *adj* peu aimable; méchant.
unknowingly *adv* inconsciemment.
unknown *adj* inconnu.
unlawful *adj* illégal, illicite; ~ly *adv* illégalement.
unlawfulness *n* illégalité *f*.
unleash *vt* lâcher, déchaîner.
unless *conj* à moins que/de, sauf.
unlicensed *adj* illicite.
unlike *adj* différent, dissemblable.
unlikelihood *n* improbabilité *f*.
unlikely *adj* improbable; invraisemblable; *adv* improbablement.
unlimited *adj* illimité.
unlisted *adj* ne figurant pas sur une liste/sur l'annuaire.
unload *vt* décharger.
unlock *vt* ouvrir, déverrouiller.
unluckily *adv* malheureusement.
unlucky *adj* malchanceux.
unmanageable *adj* difficile, peu maniable, impossible.
unmannered *adj* mal élevé, impoli.
unmannerly *adj* rustre.
unmarried *adj* célibataire, qui n'est pas marié.
unmask *vt* démasquer.

unmentionable *adj* qu'il ne faut pas mentionner.

unmerited *adj* immérité.

unmindful *adj* oublieux, indifférent.

unmistakable *adj* indubitable; ~**ly** *adv* sans aucun doute.

unmitigated *adj* absolu.

unmoved *adj* insensible, impassible.

unnatural *adj* non naturel; pervers; affecté.

unnecessary *adj* inutile, superflu.

unneighbourly *adj* peu aimable avec ses voisins, peu sociable.

unnoticed *adj* inaperçu.

unnumbered *adj* innombrable.

unobserved *adj* inaperçu.

unobtainable *adj* impossible à obtenir; introuvable.

unobtrusive *adj* discret.

unoccupied *adj* inoccupé.

unoffending *adj* inoffensif, innocent.

unofficial *adj* non officiel.

unorthodox *adj* hétérodoxe; peu orthodoxe.

unpack *vt* défaire; déballer.

unpaid *adj* non payé.

unpalatable *adj* désagréable au goût.

unparalleled *adj* incomparable; sans pareil.

unpleasant *adj* ~**ly** *adv* désagréable(ment).

unpleasantness *n* caractère désagréable *m*.

unplug *vt* débrancher.

unpolished *adj* non ciré; fruste, rude.

unpopular *adj* impopulaire.

unpractised *adj* inexpérimenté, inexercé.

unprecedented *adj* sans précédent.

unpredictable *adj* imprévisible.

unprejudiced *adj* impartial.

unprepared *adj* qui n'est pas préparé.

unprofitable *adj* inutile; peu rentable.

unprotected *adj* sans protection; exposé.

unpublished *adj* inédit.

unpunished *adj* impuni.

unqualified *adj* non qualifié; inconditionnel.

unquestionable *adj* incontestable, indiscutable; ~**ly** *adv* indiscutablement, sans conteste.

unquestioned *adj* incontesté, indiscuté.

unravel *vt* débrouiller.

unread *adj* qui n'a pas été lu; inculte.

unreal *adj* irréel.

unrealistic *adj* irréaliste.

unreasonable *adj* déraisonnable.

unreasonably *adv* déraisonnablement.

unregarded *adj* négligé; dont on fait peu de cas.

unrelated *adj* sans rapport; sans lien de parenté.

unrelenting *adj* implacable.

unreliable *adj* peu fiable.

unremitting *adj* inlassable, constant.

unrepentant *adj* impénitent.

unreserved *adj* sans réserve; franc; ~**ly** *adv* sans réserve.

unrest *n* agitation *f*; troubles *mpl*.

unrestrained *adj* non contenu; non réprimé.

unripe *adj* vert, pas mûr.

unrivalled *adj* sans égal, sans pareil.

unroll *vt* dérouler.

unruliness *n* indiscipline *f*; turbulence *f*.

unruly *adj* indiscipliné.

unsafe *adj* dangereux, peu sûr.

unsatisfactory *adj* peu satisfaisant.

unsavoury *adj* désagréable, insipide.

unscathed *adj* indemne.

unscrew *vt* dévisser.

unscrupulous *adj* sans scrupules.

unseasonable *adj* hors de saison, inopportun.

unseemly *adj* inconvenant.

unseen *adj* invisible; inaperçu.

unselfish *adj* généreux.

unsettle *vt* perturber.

unsettled *adj* perturbé; instable; variable.

unshaken *adj* inébranlable, ferme.

unshaven *adj* non rasé.

unsightly *adj* disgracieux, laid.

unskilful *adj* maladroit, malhabile.

unskilled *adj* inexpérimenté.

unsociable *adj* insociable, sauvage.

unspeakable *adj* ineffable, indicible.

unstable *adj* instable.

unsteadily *adv* d'un pas chancelant; d'une manière mal assurée.

unsteady *adj* instable.

unstudied *adj* naturel; spontané.

unsuccessful *adj* infructueux, vain; ~**ly** *adv* sans succès.

unsuitable *adj* peu approprié; inopportun.

unsure *adj* peu sûr.

unsympathetic *adj* peu compatissant.

untamed *adj* sauvage.

untapped *adj* non exploité.

untenable *adj* insoutenable.

unthinkable *adj* inconcevable.

unthinking *adj* irréfléchi, étourdi.

untidiness *n* désordre *m*.

untidy *adj* en désordre; peu soigné.

untie *vt* dénouer, défaire.

until *prep* jusqu'à; * *conj* jusqu'à ce que.

untimely *adj* intempestif.

untiring *adj* infatigable.

untold *adj* jamais révélé; indicible; incalculable.

untouched *adj* intact.

untoward *adj* fâcheux; inconvenant.

untried *adj* qui n'a pas été essayé *ou* mis à l'épreuve.

untroubled *adj* tranquille, paisible.

untrue *adj* faux.

untrustworthy *adj* indigne de confiance.

untruth *n* mensonge *m*, fausseté *f*.

unused *adj* neuf, inutilisé.

unusual *adj* inhabituel, exceptionnel; ~**ly** *adv* exceptionnellement, rarement.

unveil *vt* dévoiler.

unwavering *adj* inébranlable.

unwelcome *adj* importun.

unwell *adj* indisposé, souffrant.

unwieldy *adj* peu maniable.

unwilling *adj* peu disposé; ~**ly** *adv* de mauvaise grâce.

unwillingness *n* mauvaise grâce, mauvaise volonté *f*.

unwind *vt* dérouler; * *vi* se détendre.

unwise *adj* imprudent.

unwitting *adj* involontaire.

unworkable *adj* impraticable.

unworthy *adj* indigne.

unwrap *vt* défaire.

unwritten *adj* non écrit.

up *adv* en haut, en l'air; levé; * *prep* au haut de; plus loin.

upbringing *n* éducation *f*.

update *vt* mettre à jour.

upheaval *n* bouleversement *m*.

uphill *adj* difficile, pénible; * *adv* en montant.

uphold *vt* soutenir.

upholstery *n* tapisserie *f*.

upkeep *n* entretien *m*.

uplift *vt* élever.

upon *prep* sur.

upper *adj* supérieur; (plus) élevé.

upper-class *adj* aristocratique.

upper-hand *n* (*fig*) dessus *m*.

uppermost *adj* le plus haut, le plus élevé; **to be ~** prédominer.

upright *adj* droit, vertical; droit, honnête.

uprising *n* soulèvement *m*.

uproar *n* tumulte, vacarme *m*.

uproot *vt* déraciner.

upset *vt* renverser; déranger, bouleverser; * *n* désordre *m*; bouleversement *m*; * *adj* vexé; bouleversé.

upshot *n* résultat *m*; aboutissement *m*; conclusion *f*.

upside-down *adv* sens dessus dessous.

upstairs *adv* en haut (d'un escalier).

upstart *n* parvenu *m* -e *f*.

uptight *adj* très tendu.

up-to-date *adj* à jour.

upturn *n* amélioration *f*.

upward *adj* ascendant; ~**s** *adv* vers le haut; en montant.

urban *adj* urbain.

urbane *adj* courtois.

urchin *n* gamin *m*; **sea ~** oursin *m*.

urge *vt* pousser; * *n* impulsion *f*; désir ardent *m*.

urgency *n* urgence *f*.

urgent *adj* urgent.

urinal *n* urinoir *m*.

urinate *vi* uriner.

urine *n* urine *f*.

urn *n* urne *f*.

us *pn* nous.

usage *n* utilisation *f*; usage *m*.

use *n* usage *m*; utilisation *f*, emploi *m*; * *vt* se servir de, utiliser.

used *adj* usagé.

useful *adj* ~**ly** *adv* utile(ment).

usefulness *n* utilité *f*.

useless *adj* ~**ly** *adv* inutile(ment).

uselessness *n* inutilité *f*.

user-friendly *adj* facile à utiliser.

usher *n* huissier *m*; placeur *m*.

usherette *n* ouvreuse *f*.
usual *adj* habituel, courant; **~ly** *adv* habituellement.
usurer *n* usurier *m* -ière *f*.
usurp *vt* usurper.
usury *n* usure *f*.
utensil *n* ustensile *m*.
uterus *n* utérus *m*.

utility *n* utilité *f*.
utilize *vt* utiliser.
utmost *adj* extrême, le plus grand; dernier.
utter *adj* complet; absolu; total; * *vt* prononcer; proférer; émettre.
utterance *n* expression *f*.
utterly *adv* complètement, tout à fait.

V

vacancy *n* chambre libre *f*.
vacant *adj* vacant; inoccupé; libre.
vacant lot *n* (US) terrain vague *m*.
vacate *vt* quitter; démissionner.
vacation *n* vacances *fpl*.
vacationer *n* vacancier *m* -ière *f*.
vaccinate *vt* vacciner.
vaccination *n* vaccination *f*.
vaccine *n* vaccin *f*.
vacuous *adj* vide.
vacuum *n* vide *m*.
vacuum bottle *n* thermos *m*.
vagina *n* vagin *m*.
vagrant *n* vagabond *m* -e *f*.
vague *adj* **~ly** *adv* vague(ment).
vain *adj* vain, inutile; vaniteux.
valet *n* valet de chambre *m*.
valiant *adj* courageux, brave.
valid *adj* valide, valable.
valley *n* vallée *f*.
valour *n* courage *m*, bravoure *f*.
valuable *adj* précieux, de valeur; **~s** *npl* objets de valeur *mpl*.
valuation *n* évaluation, estimation *f*.
value *n* valeur *f*; * *vt* évaluer; tenir à, apprécier.
valued *adj* précieux, estimé.
valve *n* soupape *f*.
vampire *n* vampire *m*.
van *n* camionnette *f*.
vandal *n* vandale *mf*.
vandalism *n* vandalisme *m*.
vandalize *vt* saccager.
vanguard *n* avant-garde *f*.
vanilla *n* vanille *f*.
vanish *vi* disparaître, se dissiper.

vanity *n* vanité *f*.
vanity case *n* vanity-case *m*.
vanquish *vt* vaincre.
vantage point *n* position avantageuse *f*.
vapour *n* vapeur *f*.
variable *adj* variable; changeant.
variance *n* désaccord, différend *m*.
variation *n* variation *f*.
varicose vein *n* varice *f*.
varied *adj* varié.
variety *n* variété *f*.
variety show *n* spectacle de variétés *m*.
various *adj* divers, différent.
varnish *n* vernis *m*; * *vt* vernir.
vary *vt* *vi* varier; *vi* changer.
vase *n* vase *m*.
vast *adj* vaste; immense.
vat *n* cuve *f*.
vault *n* voûte *f*; cave *f*, caveau *m*; saut *m*; * *vi* sauter.
veal *n* veau *m*.
veer *vi* (*mar*) virer.
vegetable *adj* végétal; * *n* végétal *m*; **~s** *pl* légumes *mpl*.
vegetable garden *n* (jardin) potager *m*.
vegetarian *n* végétarien *m* -ne *f*.
vegetate *vi* végéter.
vegetation *n* végétation *f*.
vehemence *n* véhémence, fougue *f*.
vehement *adj* véhément, violent; **~ly** *adv* avec véhémence.
vehicle *n* véhicule *m*.
veil *n* voile *m*; * *vt* voiler, dissimuler.
vein *n* veine *f*; nervure *f*; disposition *f*.
velocity *n* vitesse *f*.
velvet *n* velours *m*.

vending machine *n* distributeur automatique *m*.

vendor *n* vendeur *m*.

veneer *n* placage *m*; vernis *m*.

venerable *adj* vénérable.

venerate *vt* vénérer.

veneration *n* vénération *f*.

venereal *adj* vénérien.

vengeance *n* vengeance *f*.

venial *adj* véniel.

venison *n* venaison *f*.

venom *n* venin *m*.

venomous *adj* vénéneux; ~**ly** *adv* avec animosité.

vent *n* orifice *m*; conduit *m*; * *vt* (*fig*) décharger.

ventilate *vt* aérer.

ventilation *n* ventilation, aération *f*.

ventilator *n* ventilateur *m*.

ventriloquist *n* ventriloque *mf*.

venture *n* entreprise *f*; * *vi* s'aventurer; * *vt* risquer, hasarder.

venue *n* lieu *m* (de réunion).

veranda(h) *n* véranda *f*.

verb *n* (*gr*) verbe *m*.

verbal *adj* verbal, oral; ~**ly** *adv* verbalement.

verbatim *adv* textuellement, mot pour mot.

verbose *adj* verbeux.

verdant *adj* verdoyant.

verdict *n* (*law*) verdict *m*; jugement *m*.

verification *n* vérification *f*.

verify *vt* vérifier.

veritable *adj* véritable.

vermin *n* vermine *f*.

vermouth *n* vermouth(h) *m*.

versatile *adj* doué de talents multiples; versatile.

verse *n* vers *m*; verset *m*.

versed *adj* versé.

version *n* version *f*.

versus *prep* contre.

vertebra *n* vertèbre *f*.

vertebral *adj* vertébral.

vertebrate *adj n* vertébré *m*.

vertex *n* sommet *m*.

vertical *adj* ~**ly** *adv* vertical(ement).

vertigo *n* vertige *m*.

verve *n* verve *f*, brio *m*.

very *adj* vrai, véritable; exactement, même; * *adv* très, fort, bien.

vessel *n* récipient *m*; vase *m*; navire *m*.

vest *n* gilet *m*.

vestibule *n* vestibule *m*.

vestige *n* vestige *m*.

vestment *n* vêtement de cérémonie *m*; chasuble *f*.

vestry *n* sacristie *f*.

veteran *adj n* vétéran *m*.

veterinarian *n* vétérinaire *mf*.

veterinary *adj* vétérinaire.

veto *n* véto *m*; * *vt* opposer son véto à.

vex *vt* contrarier.

vexed *adj* contrarié.

via *prep* via, par.

viaduct *n* viaduc *m*.

vial *n* fiole, ampoule *f*.

vibrate *vi* vibrer.

vibration *n* vibration *f*.

vicarious *adj* par personne interposée.

vice *n* vice *m*; défaut *m*; étau *m*.

vice-chairman *n* vice-président *m*.

vice versa *adv* vice versa.

vicinity *n* voisinage *m*, proximité *f*.

vicious *adj* méchant; ~**ly** *adv* méchamment.

victim *n* victime *f*.

victimize *vt* prendre pour victime.

victor *n* vainqueur *m*.

victorious *adj* victorieux.

victory *n* victoire *f*.

video *n* vidéo *f*; vidéocassette *f*; magnétoscope *m*.

video tape *n* bande vidéo *f*.

viewer *n* téléspectateur *m* -trice *f*.

vie *vi* rivaliser.

view *n* vue *f*; perspective *f*; opinion *f*; panorama *m*; * *vt* voir; examiner.

viewfinder *n* viseur *m*.

viewpoint *n* point de vue *m*.

vigil *n* veille *f*; vigile *f*.

vigilance *n* vigilance *f*.

vigilant *adj* vigilant, attentif.

vigorous *adj* vigoureux; ~**ly** *adv* vigoureusement.

vigour *n* vigueur *f*; énergie *f*.

vile *adj* vil, infâme; exécrable.

vilify *vt* diffamer.

villa *n* pavillon *m*; maison de campagne *f*.
village *n* village *m*.
villager *n* villageois *m* -e *f*.
villain *n* scélérat *m*.
vindicate *vt* venger, défendre.
vindication *n* défense *f*; justification *f*.
vindictive *adj* vindicatif.
vine *n* vigne *f*.
vinegar *n* vinaigre *m*.
vineyard *n* vignoble *m*.
vintage *n* millésime *m*; époque *f*.
vinyl *n* vinyle *m*.
viola *n* (*mus*) viole *f*.
violate *vt* violer.
violation *n* violation *f*.
violence *n* violence *f*.
violent *adj* violent; ~**ly** *adv* violemment.
violet *n* (*bot*) violette *f*.
violin *n* (*mus*) violon *m*.
violinist *n* violiniste *mf*.
violoncello *n* (*mus*) violoncelle *m*.
viper *n* vipère *f*.
virgin *n*, *adj* vierge *f*.
virginity *n* virginité *f*.
Virgo *n* Vierge *f* (signe du zodiaque).
virile *adj* viril.
virility *n* virilité *f*.
virtual *adj* virtuel; quasiment; ~**ly** *adv* de fait, pratiquement.
virtue *n* vertu *f*.
virtuous *adj* virtueux.
virulent *adj* virulent.
virus *n* virus *m*.
vis-à-vis *prep* vis-à-vis.
viscous *adj* visqueux, gluant.
visibility *n* visibilité *f*.
visible *adj* visible.
visibly *adv* visiblement.
vision *n* vision *f*; vue *f*.
visit *vt* visiter; * *n* visite *f*.
visitation *n* visite *f*.
visiting hours *npl* heures *fpl* de visite.
visitor *n* visiteur *m* -euse *f*; touriste *mf*.
visor *n* visière *f*.
vista *n* vue, perspective *f*.
visual *adj* visuel.
visual aid *n* support visuel *m*.
visualize *vt* s'imaginer.

vital *adj* vital; essentiel; indispensable; ~**ly** *adv* vitalement; ~**s** *npl* organes vitaux *mpl*.
vitality *n* vitalité *f*.
vital statistics *npl* statistiques démographiques *fpl*.
vitamin *n* vitamine *f*.
vitiate *vt* vicier.
vivacious *adj* vif.
vivid *adj* vif; vivant; frappant; ~**ly** *adv* de façon éclatante; de façon frappante.
vivisection *n* vivisection *f*.
vocabulary *n* vocabulaire *m*.
vocal *adj* vocal.
vocation *n* vocation *f*; profession *f*, métier *m*; ~**al** *adj* professionnel.
vocative *n* vocatif *m*.
vociferous *adj* bruyant.
vogue *n* vogue *f*; mode *f*.
voice *n* voix *f*; * *vt* exprimer.
void *adj* vide; * *n* vide *m*.
volatile *adj* volatile; versatile.
volcanic *adj* volcanique.
volcano *n* volcan *m*.
volition *n* volonté *f*.
volley *n* volée *f*; salve *f*; grêle *f*.
volleyball *n* volley-ball *m*.
voltage *n* voltage *m*.
voluble *adj* volubile, loquace.
volume *n* volume *m*.
voluntarily *adv* volontairement.
voluntary *adj* volontaire.
volunteer *n* volontaire *mf*; * *vi* se porter volontaire.
voluptuous *adj* voluptueux.
vomit *vt vi* vomir; * *n* vomissement *m*.
voracious *adj* ~**ly** *adv* vorace(ment).
vortex *n* tourbillon *m*.
vote *n* vote, suffrage *m*; voix *f*; * *vt* voter.
voter *n* électeur *m* -trice *f*.
voting *n* vote *m*.
voucher *n* bon *m*.
vow *n* vœu *m*; * *vt* jurer.
vowel *n* voyelle *f*.
voyage *n* voyage par mer *m*; traversée *f*.
vulgar *adj* vulgaire; grossier.
vulgarity *n* grossièreté *f*; vulgarité *m*.
vulnerable *adj* vulnérable.
vulture *n* vautour *m*.

W

wad *n* tampon *m*; bouchon *m*, liasse *f*.

waddle *vi* se dandiner.

wade *vi* patauger.

wading pool *n* petit bassin (pour enfants) *m*.

wafer *n* gaufrette *f*; plaque *f*.

waffle *n* gaufre *f*.

waft *vt* porter, apporter; * *vi* flotter.

wag *vt vi* remuer.

wage *n* salaire *m*.

wage earner *n* salarié *m* -e *f*.

wager *n* pari *m*; * *vt* parier.

wages *npl* salaire *m*.

waggle *vt* remuer.

waggon *n* chariot *m*; (*rail*) wagon *m*.

wail *n* gémissement *m*, plainte *f*; * *vi* gémir.

waist *n* taille *f*.

waistline *n* taille *f*.

wait *vi* attendre; * *n* attente *f*; arrêt *m*.

waiter *n* serveur *m*.

waiting list *n* liste d'attente *f*.

waiting room *n* salle d'attente *f*.

waive *vt* renoncer à.

wake *vi* se réveiller; * *vt* réveiller; * *n* veillée *f*; (*mar*) sillage *m*.

waken *vt* réveiller; * *vi* se réveiller.

walk *vi* marcher, aller à pied; * *vt* parcourir; * *n* promenade *f*; marche *f*.

walker *n* marcheur *m* -euse *f*.

walkie-talkie *n* talkie-walkie *m*.

walking *n* marche à pied *f*.

walking stick *n* canne *f*.

walkout *n* grève *f* surprise.

walkover *n* (*sl*) victoire facile *f*, gâteau *m*.

walkway *n* passage pour piétons *m*.

wall *n* mur *m*; muraille *f*; paroi *f*.

walled *adj* muré.

wallet *n* portefeuille *m*.

wallflower *n* (*bot*) giroflée *f*.

wallow *vi* se vautrer.

wallpaper *n* papier peint *m*.

walnut *n* noix *f*; noyer *m*.

walrus *n* morse *m*.

waltz *n* valse *f*.

wan *adj* pâle.

wand *n* baguette (magique) *f*.

wander *vi* errer; aller sans but.

wane *vi* décroître.

want *vt* vouloir; demander; * *vi* manquer; * *n* besoin *m*; manque *m*.

wanting *adj* manquant, qui manque, qui fait défaut.

wanton *adj* lascif; capricieux.

war *n* guerre *f*.

ward *n* salle *f*; pupille *mf*.

wardrobe *n* garde-robe *f*, penderie *f*.

warehouse *n* entrepôt *m*.

warfare *n* guerre *f*.

warhead *n* ogive *f*.

warily *adv* avec circonspection.

wariness *n* circonspection, prudence *f*.

warm *adj* chaud; chaleureux; * *vt* réchauffer; ~ up *vi* se réchauffer; s'échauffer; s'animer; *vt* réchauffer.

warm-hearted *adj* affectueux.

warmly *adv* chaudement, chaleureusement.

warmth *n* chaleur *f*.

warn *vt* prévenir; avertir.

warning *n* avertissement *m*.

warning light *n* voyant lumineux *m*.

warp *vi* se voiler; * *vt* voiler; fausser.

warrant *n* garantie *f*; mandat *m*.

warranty *n* garantie *f*.

warren *n* terrier *m*.

warrior *n* guerrier *m* -ière *f*.

warship *n* navire de guerre *m*.

wart *n* verrue *f*.

wary *adj* prudent, circonspect.

wash *vt* laver; * *vi* se laver; * *n* lavage *m*; lessive *f*.

washable *adj* lavable.

washbowl *n* lavabo *m*.

washcloth *n* gant de toilette *m*.

washer *n* rondelle *f*.

washing *n* linge à laver *m*; lessive *f*.

washing machine *n* machine à laver *f*.

washing-up *n* vaisselle *f*.

wash-out *n* (*sl*) fiasco *m*.

washroom *n* toilettes *fpl*.

wasp *n* guêpe *f*.

wastage *n* gaspillage *m*; perte *f*.

waste *vt* gaspiller; dévaster, saccager; perdre; * *vi* se perdre; * *n* gaspillage *m*; détérioration *f*; terre inculte *f*; déchets *mpl*.

wasteful *adj* gaspilleur; prodigue; ~ly *adv* avec prodigalité.

waste paper *n* vieux papiers *mpl*.

waste pipe *n* tuyau d'échappement *m*.

watch *n* montre *f*; surveillance *f*; garde *f*; * *vt* regarder; observer; surveiller; faire attention à; * *vi* regarder; monter la garde.

watchdog *n* chien de garde *m*.

watchful *adj* vigilant; ~ly *adv* avec vigilance.

watchmaker *n* horloger *m*.

watchman *n* veilleur de nuit *m*; gardien *m*.

watchtower *n* tour de guet *f*.

watchword *n* mot de passe *m*; mot d'ordre *m*.

water *n* eau *f*; * *vt* arroser, mouiller; * *vi* pleurer, larmoyer.

water closet *n* W.C. *mpl*.

watercolour *n* aquarelle *f*.

waterfall *n* cascade *f*.

water heater *n* chauffe-eau *m invar*.

watering-can *n* arrosoir *m*.

water level *n* niveau de l'eau *m*.

waterlily *n* nénuphar *m*.

water line *n* ligne de flottaison *f*.

waterlogged *adj* imprégné d'eau.

water main *n* conduite principale d'eau *f*.

watermark *n* filigrane *m*.

watermelon *n* pastèque *f*.

watershed *n* (*fig*) moment *m* critique.

watertight *adj* étanche.

waterworks *npl* usine hydraulique *f*.

watery *adj* aqueux; détrempé; délavé.

wave *n* vague *f*; lame *f*; onde *f*; * *vi* faire signe de la main; onduler; * *vt* agiter.

wavelength *n* longueur d'ondes *f*.

waver *vi* vaciller, osciller.

wavering *adj* hésitant.

wavy *adj* ondulé.

wax *n* cire *f*; * *vt* cirer; * *vi* croître.

wax paper *n* papier paraffiné *m*.

waxworks *n* musée de cire *m*.

way *n* chemin *m*; voie *f*; route *f*; manière *f*; direction *f*; **to give** ~ céder.

waylay *vt* attaquer, arrêter au passage.

wayward *adj* capricieux.

we *pn* nous.

weak *adj* ~ly *adv* faible(ment).

weaken *vt* affaiblir.

weakling *n* personne faible *f*.

weak-minded *adj* faible d'esprit.

weakness *n* faiblesse *f*; point faible *m*.

wealth *n* richesse *f*; abondance *f*.

wealthy *adj* riche.

wean *vt* sevrer.

weapon *n* arme *f*.

wear *vt* porter; user; * *vi* s'user; ~ **away** *vt* user; *vi* s'user; ~ **down** *vt* user; épuiser; ~ **off** *vi* s'effacer; ~ **out** *vi* s'user; s'épuiser; *vt* user; * *n* usage *m*; usure *f*.

weariness *n* lassitude *f*; fatigue *f*; ennui *m*.

wearisome *adj* fatigant.

weary *adj* las, fatigué; ennuyeux.

weasel *n* belette *f*.

weather *n* temps *m*; * *vt* surmonter.

weather-beaten *adj* ayant souffert des intempéries.

weathercock *n* girouette *f*.

weather forecast *n* prévisions météorologiques *fpl*.

weave *vt* tisser; entrelacer.

weaving *n* tissage *m*.

web *n* tissu *m*; toile *f* d'araignée; palmure *f*.

wed *vt* épouser; * *vi* se marier.

wedding *n* mariage *m*; noces *fpl*.

wedding day *n* jour du mariage *m*.

wedding dress *n* robe de mariée *f*.

wedding present *n* cadeau de mariage *m*.

wedding ring *n* alliance *f*.

wedge *n* cale *f*; * *vt* caler; enfoncer.

wedlock *n* mariage *m*.

Wednesday *n* mercredi *m*.

wee *adj* petit.

weed *n* mauvaise herbe *f*; * *vt* désherber.

weedkiller *n* désherbant *m*.

weedy *adj* envahi par les mauvaises herbes.

week *n* semaine *f*; **tomorrow** ~ demain en huit; **yesterday** ~ il y a eu une semaine hier.

weekday *n* jour de semaine, jour ouvrable *m*.

weekend *n* week-end *m*, fin de semaine *f*.

weekly *adj* de la semaine, hebdomadaire; * *adv* chaque semaine, par semaine.

weep *vt vi* pleurer.

weeping willow n saule pleureur m.
weigh vt vi peser.
weight n poids m.
weightily adv pesamment.
weightlifter n haltérophile m.
weighty adj lourd; important.
welcome adj opportun; ~! bienvenue !; * n accueil m; * vt accueillir.
weld vt souder; * n soudure f.
welfare n bien-être m; assistance sociale f.
welfare state n État-providence m.
well n source f; fontaine f; puits m; * adj bien, bon; * adv bien; **as ~ as** aussi bien que, en plus de, comme.
well-behaved adj bien élevé, sage.
well-being n bien-être m.
well-bred adj bien élevé.
well-built adj bien bâti, solide.
well-deserved adj bien mérité.
well-dressed adj bien habillé.
well-known adj connu, célèbre.
well-mannered adj poli, bien élevé.
well-meaning adj bien intentionné.
well-off adj aisé, dans l'aisance.
well-to-do adj aisé, riche.
well-wisher n admirateur m -trice f.
wench n jeune fille, jeune femme f.
west n ouest, Occident m; * adj ouest, de/à l'ouest; * adv vers/à l'ouest.
westerly, western adj (d')ouest.
westward adv vers l'ouest.
wet adj mouillé, humide; * n humidité f; * vt mouiller.
wetnurse n nourrice f.
wet suit n combinaison de plongée f.
whack vt donner un grand coup à; * n grand coup m.
whale n baleine f.
wharf n quai m.
what pn qu'est-ce qui,(qu'est-ce) que, quoi; que, qui; ce qui, ce que; quel(le), que; * adj quel(s), quelle(s); * excl quoi! comment!.
whatever pn quoi que; tout; n'importe quoi.
wheat n blé m.
wheedle vt cajoler, câliner.
wheel n roue f; volant m; gouvernail m; * vt tourner; pousser, rouler; * vi tourner en rond, tournoyer.

wheelbarrow n brouette f.
wheelchair n fauteuil roulant m.
wheelclamp n sabot m.
wheeze vi respirer bruyamment.
when adv, conj quand.
whenever adv quand; chaque fois que.
where adv où; * conj où; **any~** n'importe où; **every~** partout.
whereabout(s) adv où.
whereas conj tandis que; attendu que.
whereby pn par lequel (laquelle), au moyen duquel (de laquelle).
wherever adv où que.
whereupon conj sur quoi; après quoi.
wherewithal npl ressources fpl.
whet vt aiguiser.
whether conj si.
which pn lequel, laquelle; celui/celle(s)/ceux que, celui/celle(s)/ceux qui; ce qui, ce que; quoi, ce dont * adj quel(s), quelle(s).
whiff n bouffée, odeur f.
while n moment m; **a ~** quelque temps; * conj pendant que; alors que; quoique.
whim n caprice m.
whimper vi gémir, pleurnicher.
whimsical adj capricieux, fantasque.
whine vi gémir, se plaindre; * n gémissement m, plainte f.
whinny vi hennir.
whip n fouet m; cravache f; * vt fouetter; battre.
whipped cream n crème fouettée f.
whirl vi tourbillonner, tournoyer; aller à toute allure; * vt faire tourbillonner, faire tournoyer.
whirlpool n tourbillon m.
whirlwind n tornade f.
whisper vi chuchoter; murmurer.
whispering n chuchotement m; murmure m.
whistle vi siffler; * n sifflement m.
white adj blanc; pâle; * n blanc m; blanc d'œuf m.
white elephant n bibelot m.
white-hot adj chauffé à blanc.
white lie n petit mensonge, mensonge innocent m.
whiten vt vi blanchir.
whiteness n blancheur f; pâleur f.

whitewash *n* blanc de chaux *m*; * *vt* blanchir à la chaux; disculper.

whiting *n* merlan *m*.

whitish *adj* blanchâtre.

who *pn* qui.

whoever *pn* quiconque, qui que ce soit, quel(le) que soit.

whole *adj* tout, entier; intact, complet; sain; * *n* tout *m*; ensemble *m*.

wholehearted *adj* sincère.

wholemeal *adj* complet.

wholesale *n* vente en gros *f*.

wholesome *adj* sain, salubre.

wholewheat *adj* complet.

wholly *adv* complètement.

whom *pn* qui; que.

whooping cough *n* coqueluche *f*.

whore *n* putain *f*.

why *n* pourquoi *m*; * *conj* pourquoi; * *excl* eh bien!, tiens!

wick *n* mèche *f*.

wicked *adj* méchant, mauvais; ~**ly** *adv* méchamment.

wickedness *n* méchanceté, perversité *f*.

wicker *n* osier *m*; * *adj* en osier.

wide *adj* large, ample; grand; ~**ly** *adv* partout; **far and** ~ de tous côtés.

wide-awake *adj* bien réveillé.

widen *vt* élargir, agrandir.

wide open *adj* grand ouvert.

widespread *adj* très répandu.

widow *n* veuve *f*.

widower *n* veuf *m*.

width *n* largeur *f*.

wield *vt* manier, brandir.

wife *n* femme *f*; épouse *f*.

wig *n* perruque *f*.

wiggle *vt* agiter; * *vi* s'agiter.

wild *adj* sauvage, féroce; désert; fou; furieux; ~**ly** *adv* violemment; furieusement; follement.

wilderness *n* étendue déserte *f*.

wild life *n* faune *f*.

wilful *adj* délibéré; entêté.

wilfulness *n* obstination *f*.

wiliness *n* ruse, astuce *f*.

will *n* volonté *f*; testament *m*; * *vt* vouloir.

willing *adj* prêt, disposé; ~**ly** *adv* volontiers, de bon cœur.

willingness *n* bonne volonté *f*, empressement *m*.

willow *n* saule *m*.

willpower *n* volonté *f*.

wilt *vi* se fâner.

wily *adj* astucieux.

win *vt* gagner, conquérir; remporter.

wince *vi* tressaillir.

winch *n* treuil *m*.

wind *n* vent *m*; souffle *m*; gaz *mpl*.

wind *vt* enrouler; envelopper; donner un tour de; * *vi* serpenter.

windfall *n* fruit abattu par le vent *m*; (*fig*) aubaine *f*.

winding *adj* tortueux.

windmill *n* moulin à vent *m*.

window *n* fenêtre *f*.

window box *n* jardinière *f*.

window cleaner *n* laveur(-euse) *m(f)* de carreaux.

window ledge *n* appui *m* de fenêtre.

window pane *n* carreau *m*.

window sill *n* rebord *m* de fenêtre.

windpipe *n* trachée *f* artère.

windscreen *n* pare-brise *m invar*.

windscreen washer *n* lave-glace *m invar*.

windscreen wiper *n* essuie-glace *m invar*.

windy *adj* venteux.

wine *n* vin *m*.

wine cellar *n* cave (à vin) *f*.

wine glass *n* verre à vin *m*.

wine list *n* carte des vins *f*.

wine merchant *n* négociant en vins *m*.

wine tasting *n* dégustation de vins *f*.

wing *n* aile *f*.

winged *adj* ailé.

winger *n* ailier *m*.

wink *vi* faire un clin d'œil; * *n* clin d'œil *m*; clignement *m*.

winner *n* gagnant *m* -e *f*; vainqueur *m*.

winning post *n* poteau d'arrivée *m*.

winter *n* hiver *m*; * *vi* hiverner.

winter sports *npl* sports d'hiver *mpl*.

wintry *adj* d'hiver, hivernal.

wipe *vt* essuyer; effacer.

wire *n* fil *m*; télégramme *m*; * *vt* installer des fils électriques à; télégraphier.

wiring *n* installation électrique *f*.

wiry *adj* effilé et nerveux.

wisdom *n* sagesse, prudence *f*.

wisdom teeth *npl* dents de sagesse *fpl*.

wise *adj* sage, avisé, judicieux, prudent.

wisecrack *n* bon mot *m*, plaisanterie *f*.

wish *vt* souhaiter, désirer; * *n* souhait, désir *m*.

wishful *adj* désireux.

wisp *n* brin *m*; mince volute *f*.

wistful *adj* nostalgique, rêveur.

wit *n* esprit *m*, intelligence *f*.

witch *n* sorcière *f*.

witchcraft *n* sorcellerie *f*.

with *prep* avec; à; de; contre.

withdraw *vt* retirer; rappeler; annuler; * *vi* se retirer.

withdrawal *n* retrait *m*.

withdrawn *adj* réservé.

wither *vi* se flétrir, se faner.

withhold *vt* détenir, retenir, empêcher.

within *prep* à l'intérieur de; * *adv* dedans; à l'intérieur.

without *prep* sans.

withstand *vt* résister à.

witless *adj* sot, stupide.

witness *n* témoin *m*; témoignage *m*; * *vt* être témoin de; attester.

witness stand *n* barre des témoins *f*.

witticism *n* mot d'esprit *m*.

wittily *adv* spirituellement.

wittingly *adv* sciemment, à dessein.

witty *adj* spirituel, plein d'esprit.

wizard *n* sorcier, magicien *m*.

wobble *vi* trembler.

woe *n* malheur *m*; affliction *f*.

woeful *adj* triste, malheureux; ~**ly** *adv* tristement.

wolf *n* loup *m*; **she** ~ louve *f*.

woman *n* femme *f*.

womanish *adj* de femme.

womanly *adj* féminin, de femme.

womb *n* utérus *m*.

women's lib *n* mouvement de libération de la femme *m*.

wonder *n* merveille *f*; miracle *m*; émerveillement *m*; * *vi* s'émerveiller.

wonderful *adj* merveilleux; ~**ly** *adv* merveilleusement.

wondrous *adj* merveilleux.

won't *abrev* de **will not**.

wont *n* coutume *f*.

woo *vt* faire la cour à.

wood *n* bois *m*.

wood alcohol *n* alcool méthylique *m*.

wood carving *n* sculpture sur bois *f*.

woodcut *n* gravure sur bois *f*.

woodcutter *n* bûcheron *m*.

wooded *adj* boisé.

wooden *adj* de bois, en bois.

woodland *n* région boisée *f*.

woodlouse *n* cloporte *m*.

woodman *n* forestier *m*; garde-forestier *m*.

woodpecker *n* pic *m*.

woodwind *n* (*mus*) bois *mpl*.

woodwork *n* menuiserie *f*.

woodworm *n* ver du bois *m*.

wool *n* laine *f*.

woollen *adj* de laine.

woollens *npl* lainages *mpl*.

woolly *adj* laineux, de laine.

word *n* mot *m*; parole *f*; * *vt* exprimer; rédiger.

wordiness *n* verbosité *f*.

wording *n* formulation *f*.

word processing *n* traitement *m* de texte.

word processor *n* machine *f* à traitement de texte.

wordy *adj* verbeux.

work *vi* travailler; opérer; fonctionner; fermenter; * *vt* (faire) travailler, faire fonctionner; façonner; * ~ **out** *vi* marcher; * *vt* résoudre; * *n* travail *m*; œuvre *f*; ouvrage *m*; emploi *m*.

workable *adj* exploitable.

workaholic *n* drogué du travail *m*.

worker *n* travailleur *m* -euse *f*; ouvrier *m* -ère *f*.

workforce *n* main-d'œuvre *f*.

working-class *adj* ouvrier.

workman *n* ouvrier, artisan *m*.

workmanship *n* exécution *f*; qualité du travail *f*.

workmate *n* camarade de travail *mf*.

workshop *n* atelier *m*.

world *n* monde *m*; * *adj* du monde; mondial.

worldliness *n* mondanité *f*; attachement aux choses matrielles *m*.

worldly *adj* mondain; terrestre.

worldwide *adj* mondial.

worm *n* ver *m*.

worn-out *adj* épuisé; usé.

worried *adj* inquiet.

worry *vt* inquiéter; *n* souci *m*.

worrying *adj* inquiétant.

worse *adj adv* pire; * *n* le pire.

worship *n* culte *m*; adoration *f*; **your ~** Monsieur le Maire, Monsieur le Juge; * *vt* adorer, vénérer.

worst *adj* le pire; * *adv* le plus mal; * *n* le pire *m*.

worth *n* valeur *f*, prix *m*; mérite *m*.

worthily *adv* dignement, à juste titre.

worthless *adj* sans valeur; inutile.

worthwhile *adj* qui vaut la peine; louable.

worthy *adj* digne; louable.

would-be *adj* soi-disant.

wound *n* blessure *f*; * *vt* blesser.

wrangle *vi* se disputer; * *n* dispute *f*.

wrap *vt* envelopper.

wrath *n* colère *f*.

wreath *n* couronne, guirlande *f*.

wreck *n* naufrage *m*; ruines *fpl*; destruction *f*; épave *f*; * *vt* causer le naufrage de; démolir.

wreckage *n* naufrage *m*; épave *f*, débris *mpl*.

wren *n* roitelet *m*.

wrench *vt* tordre; forcer; tourner violemment; * *n* clé *f*; torsion violente *f*.

wrest *vt* arracher.

wrestle *vi* lutter.

wrestling *n* lutte *f*.

wretched *adj* malheureux, misérable.

wriggle *vi* remuer, se tortiller.

wring *vt* tordre; essorer; arracher.

wrinkle *n* ride *f*; * *vt* rider; * *vi* se rider.

wrist *n* poignet *m*.

wristband *n* manchette de chemise *f*.

wristwatch *n* montre-bracelet *f*.

writ *n* écriture *f*; assignation *f*; acte judiciaire *m*.

write *vt* écrire; composer; **~ down** consigner par écrit; **~ off** annuler; réduire; **~ up** rédiger.

write-off *n* perte *f*.

writer *n* écrivain *m*; auteur *m*.

writhe *vi* se tordre.

writing *n* écriture *f*; œuvres *fpl*; écrit *m*.

writing desk *n* bureau *m*.

writing paper *n* papier à lettres *m*.

wrong *n* mal *m*; injustice *f*; tort *m*; injure *f*; * *adj* mauvais, mal; injuste; inopportun; faux, erroné; * *adv* mal, inexactement; * *vt* faire du tort à, léser.

wrongful *adj* injuste.

wrongly *adv* injustement.

wry *adj* ironique, narquois.

XYZ

xenon *n* xénon *m*.

xenophobe *n* xénophobe *mf*.

xenophobia *n* xénophobie *f*.

xenophobic *adj* xénophobique.

Xmas *abbr* Noël *m*.

X-ray *n* rayon X *m*.

xylophone *n* xylophone *m*.

yacht *n* yacht *m*.

yachting *n* navigation de plaisance *f*.

Yankee *n* yankee *m*.

yard *n* yard (0.914 m) *m*; cour *f*.

yardstick *n* critère d'évaluation *m*.

yarn *n* longue histoire *f*; fil *m*.

yawn *vi* bâiller; * *n* bâillement *m*.

yawning *adj* béant.

yeah *adv* (*fam*) oui, ouais.

year *n* année *f*.

yearbook *n* annuaire *m*.

yearling *n* animal âgé d'un an *m*.

yearly *adj adv* annuel(lement).

yearn *vi* languir.

yearning *n* désir ardent *m*.

yeast *n* levure *f*.

yell *vi* hurler; * *n* hurlement *m*.

yellow *adj n* jaune *m*.

yellowish *adj* jaunâtre.

yelp *vi* japper, glapir; * *n* jappement *m*.

yes *adv*, *n* oui *m*.

yesterday *adv, n* hier (*m*).

yet *conj* pourtant; cependant; * *adv* encore.

yew *n* if *m*.

yield *vt* donner, produire; rapporter; * *vi* se rendre; céder; * *n* production *f*; récolte *f*; rendement *m*.

yoga *n* yoga *m*.

yog(h)urt *n* yaourt *m*.

yoke *n* joug *m*.

yolk *n* jaune d'œuf *m*.

yonder *adv* là-bas.

you *pn* vous; tu; te; toi.

young *adj* jeune; **~er** *adj* plus jeune.

youngster *n* jeune *mf*.

your(s) *pn* ton, ta, tes; votre, vos; le tien, la tienne, les tiens, les tiennes; le/la vôtre, les vôtres; **sincerely ~s** je vous prie d'agréer, Monsieur/Madame, l'expression de mes sentiments les meilleurs.

yourself *pn* toi-même; vous-même(s).

youth *n* jeunesse, adolescence *f*; jeune homme *m*.

youthful *adj* jeune.

youthfulness *n* jeunesse *f*.

yuppie (*adj*) *n* (de) jeune cadre dynamique *m*.

zany *adj* farfelu.

zap *vt* flinguer.

zeal *n* zèle *m*; ardeur *f*.

zealous *adj* zélé.

zebra *n* zèbre *m*.

zenith *n* zénith *m*.

zero *n* zéro *m*.

zest *n* enthousiasme *m*.

zigzag *n* zigzag *m*.

zinc *n* zinc *m*.

zip, zipper *n* fermeture éclair *f*.

zip code *n* code postal *m*.

zodiac *n* zodiaque *m*.

zone *n* zone *f*; secteur *m*.

zoo *n* zoo *m*.

zoological *adj* zoologique.

zoologist *n* zoologiste *mf*.

zoology *n* zoologie *f*.

zoom *vi* vrombir.

zoom lens *n* zoom *m*.

Verbes Irréguliers en Anglais

Verbe	Prétérit	Participe passé	Verbe	Prétérit	Participe passé
arise	arose	arisen	eat	ate	eaten
awake	awoke	awaked, awoke	fall	fell	fallen
be	[I am, you/we/they are, he/she/it is, *gérondif* being]		feed	fed	fed
			feel	felt	felt
	was, were	been	fight	fought	fought
bear	bore	borne	find	found	found
beat	beat	beaten	flee	fled	fled
become	became	become	fling	flung	flung
begin	began	begun	fly	[he/she/it flies]	
behold	beheld	beheld		flew	flown
bend	bent	bent	forbid	forbade	forbidden
beseech	besought, beseeched	besought, beseeched	forecast	forecast	forecast
			forget	forgot	forgotten
beset	beset	beset	forgive	forgave	forgiven
bet	bet, betted	bet, betted	forsake	forsook	forsaken
bid	bade, bid	bid, bidden	forsee	foresaw	foreseen
bite	bit	bitten	freeze	froze	frozen
bleed	bled	bled	get	got	got, (US) gotten
bless	blessed, blest	blessed, blest			
blow	blew	blown	give	gave	given
break	broke	broken	go	[he/she/it goes]	
breed	bred	bred		went	gone
bring	brought	brought	grind	ground	ground
build	built	built	grow	grew	grown
burn	burnt, burned	burnt, burned	hang	hung, hanged	hung, hanged
burst	burst	burst	have	[I/you/we/they have, he/she/it has, *gérondif* having]	
buy	bought	bought			
can	could	(been able)		had	had
cast	cast	cast	hear	heard	heard
catch	caught	caught	hide	hid	hidden
choose	chose	chosen	hit	hit	hit
cling	clung	clung	hold	held	held
come	came	come	hurt	hurt	hurt
cost	cost	cost	keep	kept	kept
creep	crept	crept	kneel	knelt	knelt
cut	cut	cut	know	knew	known
deal	dealt	dealt	lay	laid	laid
dig	dug	dug	lead	led	led
do	[he/she/it does]		lean	leant, leaned	leant, leaned
	did	done	leap	leapt, leaped	leapt, leaped
draw	drew	drawn	learn	learnt, learned	learnt, learned
dream	dreamed, dreamt	dreamed, dreamt	leave	left	left
			lend	lent	lent
drink	drank	drunk	let	let	let
drive	drove	driven	lie	[*gérondif* lying]	
dwell	dwelt, dwelled	dwelt, dwelled		lay	lain

372

Verbe	Prétérit	Participe passé	Verbe	Prétérit	Participe passé
light	lighted, lit	lighted, lit	speed	sped, speeded	sped, speeded
lose	lost	lost	spell	spelt, spelled	spelt, spelled
make	made	made	spend	spent	spent
may	might	—	spill	spilt, spilled	spilt, spilled
mean	meant	meant	spin	spun	spun
meet	met	met	spit	spat	spat
mistake	mistook	mistaken	split	split	split
mow	mowed	mowed, mown	spoil	spoilt	spoilt
must	(had to)	(had to)	spread	spread	spread
overcome	overcame	overcome	spring	sprang	sprung
pay	paid	paid	stand	stood	stood
put	put	put	steal	stole	stolen
quit	quit, quitted	quit, quitted	stick	stuck	stuck
read	read	read	sting	stung	stung
rid	rid	rid	stink	stank	stunk
ride	rode	ridden	stride	strode	stridden
ring	rang	rung	strike	struck	struck
rise	rose	risen	strive	strove	striven
run	ran	run	swear	swore	sworn
saw	sawed	sawn, sawed	sweep	swept	swept
say	said	said	swell	swelled	swelled, swollen
see	saw	seen	swim	swam	swum
seek	sought	sought	swing	swung	swung
sell	sold	sold	take	took	taken
send	sent	sent	teach	taught	taught
set	set	set	tear	tore	torn
sew	sewed	sewn, sewed	tell	told	told
shake	shook	shaken	think	thought	thought
shall	should	—	throw	threw	thrown
shear	sheared	sheared, shorn	thrust	thrust	thrust
shed	shed	shed	tread	trod	trodden, trod
shine	shone	shone	understand	understood	understood
shoot	shot	shot	upset	upset	upset
show	showd	shown, showed	wake	woke	woken
shrink	shrank	shrunk	wear	wore	worn
shut	shut	shut	weave	wove,	wove, woven
sing	sang	sung	wed	wedded	wed, wedded
sink	sank	sunk	weep	wept	wept
sit	sat	sat	win	won	won
slay	slew	slain	wind	wound	wound
sleep	slept	slept	withdraw	withdrew	withdrawn
slide	slid	slid	withhold	withheld	withheld
sling	slung	slung	withstand	withstood	withstood
smell	smelt, smelled	smelt, smelled	wring	wrung	wrung
sow	sowed	sown, sowed	write	wrote	written
speak	spoke	spoken			

French Verbs

Regular Verbs

infinitive	**donner**	**finir**	**vendre**
	to give	to finish	to sell
present participle	donnant	finissant	vendant
past participle	donné	fini	vendu
present	je donne	je finis	je vends
	tu donnes	tu finis	tu vends
	il donne	il finit	il vend
	nous donnons	nous finissons	nous vendons
	vous donnez	vous finissez	vous vendez
	ils donnent	ils finissent	ils vendent
imperfect	je donnais	je finissais	je vendais
	tu donnais	tu finissais	tu vendais
	il donnait	il finissait	il vendait
	nous donnions	nous finissions	nous vendions
	vous donniez	vous finissiez	vous vendiez
	ils donnaient	ils finissaient	ils vendaient
future	je donnerai	je finirai	je vendrai
	tu donneras	tu finiras	tu vendras
	il donnera	il finira	il vendra
	nous donnerons	nous finirons	nous vendrons
	vous donnerez	vous finirez	vous vendrez
	ils donneront	ils finiront	ils vendront
conditional	je donnerais	je finirais	je vendrais
	tu donnerais	tu finirais	tu vendrais
	il donnerait	il finirait	il vendrait
	nous donnerions	nous finirions	nous vendrions
	vous donneriez	vous finiriez	vous vendriez
	ils donneraient	ils finiraient	ils vendraient
past historic	je donnai	je finis	je vendis
	tu donnas	tu finis	tu vendis
	il donna	il finit	il vendit
	nous donnâmes	nous finîmes	nous vendîmes
	vous donnâtes	vous finîtes	vous vendîtes
	ils donnèrent	ils finirent	ils vendirent
present subjunctive	je donne	je finisse	je vende
	tu donnes	tu finisses	tu vendes
	il donne	il finisse	il vende
	nous donnions	nous finissions	nous vendions
	vous donniez	vous finissiez	vous vendiez
	ils donnent	ils finissent	ils vendent
imperfect subjunctive	je donnasse	je finisse	je vendisse
	tu donnasses	tu finisses	tu vendisses
	il donnât	il finît	il vendît
	nous donnassions	nous finissions	nous vendissions
	vous donnassiez	vous finissiez	vous vendissiez
	ils donnassent	ils finissent	ils vendissent

Auxiliary Verbs

infinitive	**être**	**avoir**	conditional	je serais	je aurais
	to be	to have		tu serais	tu aurais
present				il serait	il aurait
participle	étant	ayant		nous serions	nous aurions
past				vous seriez	vous auriez
participle	été	eu		ils seraient	ils auraient
present	je suis	j'ai	past historic	je fus	j'eus
	tu es	tu as		tu fus	tu eus
	il est	il a		il fut	il eut
	nous sommes	nous avons		nous fûmes	nous eûmes
	vous êtes	vous avez		vous fûtes	vous eûtes
	ils sont	ils ont		ils furent	ils eurent
imperfect	j'étais	j'avais	present	je sois	j'aie
	tu étais	tu avais	subjunctive	tu sois	tu aies
	il était	il avait		il soit	il ait
	nous étions	nous avions		nous soyons	nous ayons
	vous étiez	vous aviez		vous soyez	vous ayez
	ils étaient	ils avaient		ils soient	ils aient
future	je serai	j' aurai	imperfect	je fusse	j'eusse
	tu seras	tu auras	subjunctive	tu fusses	tu eusses
	il sera	il aura		il fût	il eût
	nous serons	nous aurons		nous fussions	nous eussions
	vous serez	vous aurez		vous fussiez	vous eussiez
	ils seront	ils auront		ils fussent	ils eussent

Irregular Verbs

	acheter	**acquérir**	**aller**	**appeler**
	to buy	to acquire	to go	to call
present	achète	acquiers	vais	appelle
	achètes	acquiers	vas	appelles
	achète	acquiert	va	appelle
	achetons	acquérons	allons	appelons
	achetez	acquérez	allez	appelez
	achètent	acquièrent	vont	appellent
imperfect	achetais	acquérais	allais	appelais
	achetais	acquérais	allais	appelais
	achetait	acquérait	allait	appelait
	achetions	acquérions	allions	appelions
	achetiez	acquériez	alliez	appeliez
	achetaient	acquéraient	allaient	appelaient
future	achèterai	acquerrai	irai	appellerai
	achèteras	acquerras	iras	appelleras
	achètera	acquerra	ira	appellera
	achèterons	acquerrons	irons	appellerons
	achèterez	acquerrez	irez	appellerez
	achèteront	acquerront	iront	appelleront
conditional	achèterais	acquerrais	irais	appellerais
	achèterais	acquerrais	irais	appellerais
	achèterait	acquerrait	irait	appellerait

	achèterions	acquerrions	irions	appellerions
	achèteriez	acquerriez	iriez	appelleriez
	achèteraient	acquerraient	iraient	appelleraient
past historic	achetai	acquis	allai	appelai
	achetas	acquis	allas	appelas
	acheta	acquit	alla	appela
	achetâmes	acquîmes	allâmes	appelâmes
	achetâtes	acquîtes	allâtes	appelâtes
	achetèrent	acquirent	allèrent	appelèrent
present subjunctive	achète	acquière	aille	appelle
	achètes	acquières	ailles	appelles
	achète	acquière	aille	appelle
	achetions	acquérions	allions	appelions
	achetiez	acquériez	alliez	appeliez
	achètent	acquièrent	aillent	appellent
imperfect subjunctive	achetasse	acquisse	allasse	appelasse
	achetasses	acquisses	allasses	appelasses
	achetât	acquît	allât	appelât
	achetassions	acquissions	allassions	appelassions
	achetassiez	acquissiez	allassiez	appelassiez
	achetassent	acquissent	allassent	appelassent

	appuyer	**s'asseoir**	**battre**	**boire**
	to lean	*to sit down*	*to hit*	*to drink*
present	appuie	m'assieds	bats	bois
	appuies	t'assieds	bats	bois
	appuie	s'assied	bat	boit
	appuyons	nous asseyons	battons	buvons
	appuyez	vous asseyez	battez	buvez
	appuient	s'asseyent	battent	boivent
imperfect	appuyais	m'asseyais	battais	buvais
	appuyais	t'asseyais	battais	buvais
	appuyait	s'asseyait	battait	buvait
	appuyions	nous asseyions	battions	buvions
	appuyiez	vous asseyiez	battiez	buviez
	appuyient	s'asseyaient	battaient	buvaient
future	appuierai	m'assiérai	battrai	boirai
	appuieras	t'assiéras	battras	boiras
	appuiera	s'assiéra	battra	boira
	appuierons	nous assiérons	battrons	boirons
	appuierez	vous assiérez	battrez	boirez
	appuieront	s'assiéront	battront	boiront
conditional	appuierais	m'assiérais	battrais	boirais
	appuierais	t'assiérais	battrais	boirais
	appuierait	s'assiérait	battrait	boirait
	appuierions	nous assiérions	battrions	boirions
	appuieriez	vous assiériez	battriez	boiriez
	appuieraient	s'assiéraient	battraient	boiraient
past historic	appuyai	m'assis	battis	bus
	appuyas	t'assis	battis	bus
	appuya	s'assit	battit	but
	appuyâmes	nous assîmes	battîmes	bûmes
	appuyâtes	vous assîtes	battîtes	bûtes
	appuyèrent	s'assirent	battirent	burent

present subjunctive	appuie	m'asseye	batte	boive
	appuies	t'asseyes	battes	boives
	appuie	s'asseye	batte	boive
	appuyions	nous asseyions	battions	buvions
	appuyiez	vous asseyiez	battiez	buviez
	appuient	s'asseyent	battent	boivent
imperfect subjunctive	appuyasse	m'assisse	battisse	busse
	appuyasses	t'assisses	battisses	busses
	appuyât	s'assît	battît	bût
	appuyassions	nous assissions	battissions	bussions
	appuyassiez	vous assissiez	battissiez	bussiez
	appuyassent	s'assissent	battissent	bussent
	commencer	**conduire**	**connaître**	**courir**
	to begin	*to drive*	*to know*	*to run*
present	commence	conduis	connais	cours
	commences	conduis	connais	cours
	commence	conduit	connaît	court
	commençons	conduisons	connaissons	courons
	commencez	conduisez	connaissez	courez
	commencent	conduisent	connaissent	courent
imperfect	commençais	conduisais	connaissais	courais
	commençais	conduisais	connaissais	courais
	commençait	conduisait	connaissait	courait
	commencions	conduisions	connaissions	courions
	commenciez	conduisiez	connaissiez	couriez
	commençaient	conduisaient	connaissaient	couraient
future	commencerai	conduirai	connaîtrai	courrai
	commenceras	conduiras	connaîtras	courras
	commencera	conduira	connaîtra	courra
	commencerons	conduirons	connaîtrons	courrons
	commencerez	conduirez	connaîtrez	courrez
	commenceront	conduiront	connaîtront	courront
conditional	commencerais	conduirais	connaîtrais	courrais
	commencerais	conduirais	connaîtrais	courrais
	commencerait	conduirait	connaîtrait	courrait
	commencerions	conduiirions	connaîtrions	courrions
	commenceriez	conduiriez	connaîtriez	courriez
	commenceraient	conduiraient	connaîtraient	courraient
past historic	commençai	conduisis	connus	courus
	commenças	conduisis	connus	courus
	commença	conduisit	connut	courut
	commençâmes	conduisîmes	connûmes	courûmes
	commençâtes	conduisîtes	connûtes	courûtes
	commencèrent	conduisirent	connurent	coururent
present subjunctive	commence	conduise	connaisse	coure
	commences	conduises	connaisses	coures
	commence	conduise	connaisse	coure
	commencions	conduisions	connaissions	courions
	commenciez	conduisiez	connaissiez	couriez
	commencent	conduisent	connaissent	courent
imperfect subjunctive	commençasse	conduisisse	connusse	courusse
	commençasses	conduisisses	connusses	courusses
	commençât	conduisît	connût	courût

	commençassions	conduisissions	connussions	courussions
	commençassiez	conduisissiez	connussiez	courussiez
	commençassent	conduisissent	connussent	courussent

	couvrir	**craindre**	**croire**	**devoir**
	to cover	*to fear*	*to believe*	*to owe, to have to*
present	couvre	crains	crois	dois
	couvres	crains	crois	dois
	couvre	craint	croit	doit
	couvrons	craignons	croyons	devons
	couvrez	craignez	croyez	devez
	couvrent	craignent	croient	doivent
imperfect	couvrais	craignais	croyais	devais
	couvrais	craignais	croyais	devais
	couvrait	craignait	croyait	devait
	couvrions	craignions	croyions	devions
	couvriez	craigniez	croyiez	deviez
	couvraient	craignaient	croyaient	devaient
future	couvrirai	craindrai	croirai	devrai
	couvriras	craindras	croiras	devras
	couvrira	craindra	croira	devra
	couvrirons	craindrons	croirons	devrons
	couvrirez	craindrez	croirez	devrez
	couvriront	craindront	croiront	devront
conditional	couvrirais	craindrais	croirais	devrais
	couvrirais	craindrais	croirais	devrais
	couvrirait	craindrait	croirait	devrait
	couvririons	craindrions	croirions	devrions
	couvririez	craindriez	croiriez	devriez
	couvriraient	craindraient	croiraient	devraient
past historic	couvris	craignis	crus	dus
	couvris	craignis	crus	dus
	couvrit	craignit	crut	dut
	couvrîmes	craignîmes	crûmes	dûmes
	couvrîtes	craignîtes	crûtes	dûtes
	couvrirent	craignirent	crurent	durent
present subjunctive	couvre	craigne	croie	doive
	couvres	craignes	croies	doives
	couvre	craigne	croie	doive
	couvrions	craignions	croyions	devions
	couvriez	craigniez	croyiez	deviez
	couvrent	craignent	croient	doivent
imperfect subjunctive	couvrisse	craignisse	crusse	dusse
	couvrisses	craignisses	crusses	dusses
	couvrît	craignît	crût	dût
	couvrissions	craignissions	crussions	dussions
	couvrissiez	craignissiez	crussiez	dussiez
	couvrissent	craignissent	crussent	dussent

	dire	**écrire**	**envoyer**	**faire**
	to say	*to write*	*to send*	*to do; to make*
present	dis	écris	envoie	fais
	dis	écris	envoies	fais
	dit	écrit	envoie	fait

	disons	écrivons	envoyons	faisons
	dites	écrivez	envoyez	faites
	disent	écrivent	envoient	font
imperfect	disais	écrivais	envoyais	faisais
	disais	écrivais	envoyais	faisais
	disait	écrivait	envoyait	faisait
	disions	écrivions	envoyions	faisions
	disiez	écriviez	envoyiez	faisiez
	disaient	écrivaient	envoyaient	faisaient
future	dirai	écrirai	enverrai	ferai
	diras	écriras	enverras	feras
	dira	écrira	enverra	fera
	dirons	écrirons	enverrons	ferons
	direz	écrirez	enverrez	ferez
	diront	écriront	enverront	feront
conditional	dirais	écrirais	enverrais	ferais
	dirais	écrirais	enverrais	ferais
	dirait	écrirait	enverrait	ferait
	dirions	écririons	enverrions	ferions
	diriez	écririez	enverriez	feriez
	diraient	écriraient	enverraient	feraient
past historic	dis	écrivis	envoyai	fis
	dis	écrivis	envoyas	fis
	dit	écrivit	envoya	fit
	dîmes	écrivîmes	envoyâmes	fîmes
	dîtes	écrivîtes	envoyâtes	fîtes
	dirent	écrivirent	envoyèrent	firent
present subjunctive	dise	écrive	envoie	fasse
	dises	écrives	envoies	fasses
	dise	écrive	envoie	fasse
	disions	écrivions	envoyions	fassions
	disiez	écriviez	envoyiez	fassiez
	disent	écrivent	envoient	fassent
imperfect subjunctive	disse	écrivisse	envoyasse	fisse
	disses	écrivisses	envoyasses	fisses
	dît	écrivît	envoyât	fît
	dissions	écrivissions	envoyassions	fissions
	dissiez	écrivissiez	envoyassiez	fissiez
	dissent	écrivissent	envoyassent	fissent

	fuir	**haïr**	**jeter**	**lire**
	to flee	to hate	to throw	to read
present	fuis	hais	jette	lis
	fuis	hais	jettes	lis
	fuit	hait	jette	lit
	fuyons	haïssons	jetons	lisons
	fuyez	haïssez	jetez	lisez
	fuient	haïssent	jettent	lisent
imperfect	fuyais	haïssais	jetais	lisais
	fuyais	haïssais	jetais	lisais
	fuyait	haïssait	jetait	lisait
	fuyions	haïssions	jetions	lisions
	fuyiez	haïssiez	jetiez	lisiez
	fuiront	haïssaient	jetaient	lisaient

verbs

future	fuirai	haïrai	jetterai	lirai
	fuiras	haïras	jetteras	liras
	fuira	haïra	jettera	lira
	fuirons	haïrons	jetterons	lirons
	fuirez	haïrez	jetterez	lirez
	fuiront	haïront	jetteront	liront
conditional	fuirais	haïrais	jetterais	lirais
	fuirais	haïrais	jetterais	lirais
	fuirait	haïrait	jetterait	lirait
	fuirions	haïrions	jetterions	lirions
	fuiriez	haïriez	jetteriez	liriez
	fuiraient	haïraient	jetteraient	liraient
past historic	fuis	haïs	jetai	lus
	fuis	haïs	jetas	lus
	fuit	haït	jeta	lut
	fuîmes	haïmes	jetâmes	lûmes
	fuîtes	haïtes	jetâtes	lûtes
	fuirent	haïrent	jetèrent	lurent
present subjunctive	fuie	haïsse	jette	lise
	fuies	haïsses	jettes	lises
	fuie	haïsse	jette	lise
	fuyions	haïssions	jetions	lisions
	fuyiez	haïssiez	jetiez	lisiez
	fuient	haïssent	jettent	lisent
imperfect subjunctive	fuisse	haïsse	jetasse	lusse
	fuisses	haïsses	jetasses	lusses
	fuît	haït	jetât	lût
	fuissions	haïssions	jetassions	lussions
	fuissiez	haïssiez	jetassiez	lussiez
	fuissent	haïssent	jetassent	lussent

	manger	**mettre**	**mourir**	**mouvoir**
	to eat	*to put*	*to die*	*to drive, to move*
present	mange	mets	meurs	meus
	manges	mets	meurs	meus
	mange	met	meurt	meut
	mangeons	mettons	mourons	mouvons
	mangez	mettez	mourez	mouvez
	mangent	mettent	meurent	meuvent
imperfect	mangeais	mettais	mourais	mouvais
	mangeais	mettais	mourais	mouvais
	mangeait	mettait	mourait	mouvait
	mangions	mettions	mourions	mouvions
	mangiez	mettiez	mouriez	mouviez
	mangeaient	mettaient	mouraient	mouvaient
future	mangerai	mettrai	mourrai	mouvrai
	mangeras	mettras	mourras	mouvras
	mangera	mettra	mourra	mouvra
	mangerons	mettrons	mourrons	mouvrons
	mangerez	mettrez	mourrez	mouvrez
	mangeront	mettront	mourront	mouvront
conditional	mangerais	mettrais	mourrais	mouvrais
	mangerais	mettrais	mourrais	mouvrais
	mangerait	mettrait	mourrait	mouvrait

	mangerions	mettrions	mourrions	mouvrions
	mangeriez	mettriez	mourriez	mouvriez
	mangeraient	mettraient	mourraient	mouvraient
past historic	mangeai	mis	mourus	mus
	mangeas	mis	mourus	mus
	mangea	mit	mourut	mut
	mangeâmes	mîmes	mourûmes	mûmes
	mangeâtes	mîtes	mourûtes	mûtes
	mangèrent	mirent	moururent	murent
present subjunctive	mange	mette	meure	meuve
	manges	mettes	meures	meuves
	mange	mette	meure	meuve
	mangions	mettions	mourions	mouvions
	mangiez	mettiez	mouriez	mouviez
	mangent	mettent	meurent	meuvent
imperfect subjunctive	mangeasse	misse	mourusse	musse
	mangeasses	misses	mourusses	musses
	mangeât	mît	mourût	mût
	mangeassions	missions	mourussions	mussions
	mangeassiez	missiez	mourussiez	mussiez
	mangeassent	missent	mourussent	mussent

	naître	**partir**	**plaire**	**pouvoir**
	to be born	*to leave*	*to please*	*to be able; can*
present	nais	pars	plais	peux
	nais	pars	plais	peux
	naît	part	plaît	peut
	naissons	partons	plaisons	pouvons
	naissez	partez	plaisez	pouvez
	naissent	partent	plaisent	peuvent
imperfect	naissais	partais	plaisais	pouvais
	naissais	partais	plaisais	pouvais
	naissait	partait	plaisait	pouvait
	naissions	partions	plaisions	pouvions
	naissiez	partiez	plaisiez	pouviez
	naissaient	partaient	plaisaient	pouvaient
future	naîtrai	partirai	plairai	pourrai
	naîtras	partiras	plairas	pourras
	naîtra	partira	plaira	pourra
	naîtrons	partirons	plairons	pourrons
	naîtrez	partirez	plairez	pourrez
	naîtront	partiront	plairont	pourront
conditional	naîtrais	partirais	plairais	pourrais
	naîtrais	partirais	plairais	pourrais
	naîtrait	partirait	plairait	pourrait
	naîtrions	partirions	plairions	pourrions
	naîtriez	partiriez	plairiez	pourriez
	naîtraient	partiraient	plairaient	pourraient
past historic	naquis	partis	plus	pus
	naquis	partis	plus	pus
	naquit	partit	plut	put
	naquîmes	partîmes	plûmes	pûmes
	naquîtes	partîtes	plûtes	pûtes
	naquirent	partirent	plurent	purent

present subjunctive	naisse	parte	plaise	puisse
	naisses	partes	plaises	puisses
	naisse	parte	plaise	puisse
	naissions	partions	plaisions	puissions
	naissiez	partiez	plaisiez	puissiez
	naissent	partent	plaisent	puissent
imperfect subjunctive	naquisse	partisse	plusse	pusse
	naquisses	partisses	plusses	pusses
	naquît	partît	plût	pût
	naquissions	partissions	plussions	pussions
	naquissiez	partissiez	plussiez	pussiez
	naquissent	partissent	plussent	pussent
	préférer	**prendre**	**recevoir**	**rire**
	to prefer	*to take*	*to receive*	*to laugh*
present	préfère	prends	reçois	ris
	préfères	prends	reçois	ris
	préfère	prend	reçoit	rit
	préférons	prenons	recevons	rions
	préférez	prenez	recevez	riez
	préfèrent	prennent	reçoivent	rient
imperfect	préférais	prenais	recevais	riais
	préférais	prenais	recevais	riais
	préférait	prenait	recevait	riait
	préférions	prenions	recevions	riions
	préfériez	preniez	receviez	riiez
	préféraient	prenaient	recevaient	riaient
future	préférerai	prendrai	recevrai	rirai
	préféreras	prendras	recevras	riras
	préférera	prendra	recevra	rira
	préférerons	prendrons	recevrons	rirons
	préférerez	prendrez	recevrez	rirez
	préféreront	prendront	recevront	riront
conditional	préférerais	prendrais	recevrais	rirais
	préférerais	prendrais	recevrais	rirais
	préférerait	prendrait	recevrait	rirait
	préférerions	prendrions	recevrions	ririons
	préféreriez	prendriez	recevriez	ririez
	préféreraient	prendraient	recevraient	riraient
past historic	préférai	pris	reçus	ris
	préféras	pris	reçus	ris
	préféra	prit	reçut	rit
	préférâmes	prîmes	reçûmes	rîmes
	préférâtes	prîtes	reçûtes	rîtes
	préférèrent	prirent	reçurent	rirent
present subjunctive	préfère	prenne	reçoive	rie
	préfères	prennes	reçoives	ries
	préfère	prenne	reçoive	rie
	préférions	prenions	recevions	riions
	préfériez	preniez	receviez	riiez
	préfèrent	prennent	reçoivent	rient
imperfect subjunctive	préférasse	prisse	reçusse	risse
	préférasses	prisses	reçusses	risses
	préférât	prît	reçût	rît

	préférassions	prissions	reçussions	rissions
	préférassiez	prissiez	reçussiez	rissiez
	préférassent	prissent	reçussent	rissent

	savoir	**suffire**	**suivre**	**tenir**
	to know	*to be enough*	*to follow*	*to hold*
present	sais	suffis	suis	tiens
	sais	suffis	suis	tiens
	sait	suffit	suit	tient
	savons	suffisons	suivons	tenons
	savez	suffisez	suivez	tenez
	savent	suffisent	suivent	tiennent
imperfect	savais	suffisais	suivais	tenais
	savais	suffisais	suivais	tenais
	savait	suffisait	suivait	tenait
	savions	suffisions	suivions	tenions
	saviez	suffisiez	suiviez	teniez
	savaient	suffisaient	suivaient	tenaient
future	saurai	suffirai	suivrai	tiendrai
	sauras	suffiras	suivras	tiendras
	saura	suffira	suivra	tiendra
	saurons	suffirons	suivrons	tiendrons
	saurez	suffirez	suivrez	tiendrez
	sauront	suffiront	suivront	tiendront
conditional	saurais	suffirais	suivrais	tiendrais
	saurais	suffirais	suivrais	tiendrais
	saurait	suffirait	suivrait	tiendrait
	saurions	suffirions	suivrions	tiendrions
	sauriez	suffiriez	suivriez	tiendriez
	sauraient	suffiraient	suivraient	tiendraient
past historic	sus	suffis	suivis	tins
	sus	suffis	suivis	tins
	sut	suffit	suivit	tint
	sûmes	suffîmes	suivîmes	tînmes
	sûtes	suffîtes	suivîtes	tîntes
	surent	suffirent	suivirent	tinrent
present subjunctive	sache	suffise	suive	tienne
	saches	suffises	suives	tiennes
	sache	suffise	suive	tienne
	sachions	suffisions	suivions	tenions
	sachiez	suffisiez	suiviez	teniez
	sachent	suffisent	suivent	tiennent
imperfect subjunctive	susse	suffisse	suivisse	tinsse
	susses	suffisses	suivisse	tinsses
	sût	suffît	suivît	tînt
	sussions	suffissions	suivissions	tinssions
	sussiez	suffissiez	suivissiez	tinssiez
	sussent	suffissent	suivissent	tinssent

	valoir	**venir**	**vivre**	**voir**
	to be worth	*to come*	*to live*	*to see*
present	vaux	viens	vis	vois
	vaux	viens	vis	vois
	vaut	vient	vit	voit

	valons	venons	vivons	voyons
	valez	venez	vivez	voyez
	valent	viennent	vivent	voient
imperfect	valais	venais	vivais	voyais
	valais	venais	vivais	voyais
	valait	venait	vivait	voyait
	valions	venions	vivions	voyions
	valiez	veniez	viviez	voyiez
	valaient	venaient	vivaient	voyaient
future	vaudrai	viendrai	vivrai	verrai
	vaudras	viendras	vivras	verras
	vaudra	viendra	vivra	verra
	vaudrons	viendrons	vivrons	verrons
	vaudrez	viendrez	vivrez	verrez
	vaudront	viendront	vivront	verront
conditional	vaudrais	viendrais	vivrais	verrais
	vaudrais	viendrais	vivrais	verrais
	vaudrait	viendrait	vivrait	verrait
	vaudrions	viendrions	vivrions	verrions
	vaudriez	viendriez	vivriez	verriez
	vaudraient	viendraient	vivraient	verraient
past historic	valus	vins	vécus	vis
	valus	vins	vécus	vis
	valut	vint	vécut	vit
	valûmes	vînmes	vécûmes	vîmes
	valûtes	vîntes	vécûtes	vîtes
	valurent	vinrent	vécurent	virent
present subjunctive	vaille	vienne	vive	voie
	vailles	viennes	vives	voies
	vaille	vienne	vive	voie
	valions	venions	vivions	voyions
	valiez	veniez	viviez	voyiez
	vaillent	viennent	vivent	voient
imperfect subjunctive	valusse	vinsse	vécusse	visse
	valusses	vinsses	vécusses	visses
	valût	vînt	vécût	vît
	valussions	vinssions	vécussions	vissions
	valussiez	vinssiez	vécussiez	vissiez
	valussent	vinssent	vécussent	vissent